BUDDHIST SPIRITUALITY
Later China, Korea, Japan, and the Modern World

D0931909

World Spirituality

An Encyclopedic History of the Religious Quest

1. Asian Archaic Spirituality
2. European Archaic Spirituality
3. African and Oceanic Spirituality
4. South and Meso-American Native Spirituality
5. North American Indian Spirituality
6. Hindu Spirituality: Vedas through Vedanta
7. Hindu Spirituality: Postclassical and Modern
8. Buddhist Spirituality: Indian, Southeast Asian, Tibetan, and Early Chinese
9. Buddhist Spirituality: Later China, Korea, Japan, and the Modern World
10. Taoist Spirituality
11. Confucian Spirituality
12. Ancient Near Eastern Spirituality: Zoroastrian, Sumerian, Assyro-Babylonian, Hittite
13. Jewish Spirituality: From the Bible to the Middle Ages
14. Jewish Spirituality: From the Sixteenth-Century Revival to the Present
15. Classical Mediterranean Spirituality: Egyptian, Greek, Roman
16. Christian Spirituality: Origins to the Twelfth Century
17. Christian Spirituality: High Middle Ages and Reformation
18. Christian Spirituality: Post-Reformation and Modern
19. Islamic Spirituality: Foundations
20. Islamic Spirituality: Manifestations
21. Modern Esoteric Spirituality
22. Spirituality and the Secular Quest
23. Encounter of Spiritualities: Past to Present
24. Encounter of Spiritualities: Present to Future
25. Dictionary of World Spirituality

Board of Editors and Advisors

Ewert Cousins, *General Editor*

Volume 9 of
World Spirituality:
An Encyclopedic History
of the Religious Quest

BUDDHIST SPIRITUALITY

LATER CHINA, KOREA, JAPAN, AND THE MODERN WORLD

Edited by
Takeuchi Yoshinori
in association with
James W. Heisig, Paul L. Swanson,
and Joseph S. O'Leary

A Herder & Herder Book
The Crossroad Publishing Company
New York

The Crossroad Publishing Company
370 Lexington Avenue, New York, NY 10017

World Spirituality, Volume 9

Printed in the United States of America

Library of Congress Cataloging-in-Publication Data

Buddhist spirituality : later China, Korea, Japan, and the modern world / edited
    by Takeuchi Yoshinori in association with James W. Heisig, Paul L. Swanson,
    and Joseph S. O'Leary.
       p. cm. — (World spirituality ; v. 9)
       Includes bibliographical references and index.
       ISBN 0-8245-1595-1 (hc). — ISBN 0-8245-1596-X (pbk)
         1. Buddhism—East Asia—History. 2. Buddhism—History—20th cen-
tury. I. Takeuchi, Yoshinori, 1913– .   II. Series.
BQ614.B83 1996
294.3'095—DC21   98-43116

1 2 3 4 5 6 7 8 9 10   04 03 02 01 00 99

Contents

PREFACE TO THE SERIES   xi

INTRODUCTION
The Staff of the Nanzan Institute   xiii

Part Three: Later China

15 Ch'an
    I. A Historical Sketch
       Philip Yampolsky   3
    II. Ch'an Spirituality
       Thomas P. Kasulis   24
    III. Four Ch'an Masters
       Dale S. Wright   33
    IV. The Encounter of Ch'an with Confucianism
       Julia Ching   44

Part Four: Korea

16 Silla Buddhist Spirituality
    Sung Bae Park   57

17 The Koryŏ Period
    Robert E. Buswell, Jr.   79

18 Buddhist Spirituality in Premodern and Modern Korea
    Henrik H. Sørensen   109

Part Five: Japan

19 Foundations
   I. The Birth of Japanese Buddhism
     Hanayama Shinshō and Hanayama Shōyū   137
   II. The Impact of Buddhism in the Nara Period
     Thomas P. Kasulis   144
   III. The Japanese Transformation of Buddhism
     Royall Tyler   156

20 Heian Period
   I. Saichō
     Umehara Takeshi   164
   II. Kūkai
     Paul B. Watt   174
   III. Heian Foundation of Kamakura Buddhism
     David Lion Gardiner   186

21 Pure Land
   I. Early Pure Land Leaders
     Tamaru Noriyoshi   201
   II. Hōnen's Spiritual Legacy
     Fujimoto Kiyohiko   213
   III. Shinran's Way
     Alfred Bloom   222

22 The Spirituality of Nichiren
     Laurel Rasplica Rodd   239

23 Zen
   I. A Historical Sketch
     Philip Yampolsky   256
   II. Dōgen
     Tsuchida Tomoaki   274
   III. Three Zen Thinkers
     Minamoto Ryōen   291
   IV. Hakuin
     Michel Mohr   307

24 Tokugawa Period
    I. Buddhist Responses to Confucianism
       Minamoto Ryōen   329
    II. The Buddhist Element in Shingaku
       Paul B. Watt   337
    III. Jiun Sonja
       Paul B. Watt   348

25 Kiyozawa Manshi's "Spiritualism"
    Gilbert Johnston and Wakimoto Tsuneya   359

26 Philosophy as Spirituality: The Way of the Kyoto School
    James W. Heisig   367

Part Six: Art, Society, and New Directions

27 Buddha's Bodies and the Iconographical Turn
    Mimi Hall Yiengpruksawan   391

28 Buddhist Spirituality in Modern Taiwan
    Heng-Ching Shih   417

29 Sōka Gakkai and the Modern Reformation of Buddhism
    Shimazono Susumu   435

30 Contemporary Buddhist Spirituality and Social Activism
    Sallie King   455

31 Theravāda Spirituality in the West
    Egil Fronsdal   482

32 Zen and the West
    Franz Aubrey Metcalf   496

GLOSSARY OF TECHNICAL TERMS   511

CONTRIBUTORS   523

PHOTOGRAPHIC CREDITS   526

NAME INDEX   527

SUBJECT INDEX   539

Preface to the Series

THE PRESENT VOLUME is part of a series entitled World Spirituality: An Encyclopedic History of the Religious Quest, which seeks to present the spiritual wisdom of the human race in its historical unfolding. Although each of the volumes can be read on its own terms, taken together they provide a comprehensive picture of the spiritual strivings of the human community as a whole—from prehistoric times, through the great religions, to the meeting of traditions at the present.

Drawing upon the highest level of scholarship around the world, the series gathers together and presents in a single collection the richness of the spiritual heritage of the human race. It is designed to reflect the autonomy of each tradition in its historical development, but at the same time to present the entire story of the human spiritual quest. The first five volumes deal with the spiritualities of archaic peoples in Asia, Europe, Africa, Oceania, and North and South America. Most of these have ceased to exist as living traditions, although some perdure among tribal peoples throughout the world. However, the archaic level of spirituality survives within the later traditions as a foundational stratum, preserved in ritual and myth. Individual volumes or combinations of volumes are devoted to the major traditions: Hindu, Buddhist, Taoist, Confucian, Jewish, Christian, and Islamic. Included within the series are the Jain, Sikh, and Zoroastrain traditions. In order to complete the story, the series includes traditions that have not survived but have exercised important influence on living traditions—such as Egyptian, Sumerian, classical Greek and Roman. A volume is devoted to modern esoteric movements and another to modern secular movements.

Having presented the history of the various traditions, the series devotes two volumes to the meeting of spiritualities The first surveys the meeting of spiritualities from the past to the present, exploring common themes that

A longer version of this preface may be found in Christian Spirituality: Origins to the Twelfth Century, *the first published volume in the series.*

can provide the basis for a positive encounter, for example, symbols, rituals, techniques. The second deals with the meeting of spiritualities in the present and future. Finally, the series closes with a dictionary of world spirituality.

Each volume is edited by a specialist or a team of specialists who have gathered a number of contributors to write articles in their fields of specialization. As in this volume, the articles are not brief entries but substantial studies of an area of spirituality within a given tradition. An effort has been made to choose editors and contributors who have a cultural and religious grounding within the tradition studied and at the same time possess the scholarly objectivity to present the material to a larger forum of readers. For several years some five hundred scholars around the world have been working on the project.

In the planning of the project, no attempt was made to arrive at a common definition of spirituality that would be accepted by all in precisely the same way. The term "spirituality," or an equivalent, is not found in a number of the traditions. Yet from the outset, there was a consensus among the editors about what was in general intended by the term. It was left to each tradition to clarify its own understanding of this meaning and to the editors to express this in the introduction to their volumes. As a working hypothesis, the following description was used to launch the project:

> The series focuses on that inner dimension of the person called by certain traditions "the spirit." This spiritual core is the deepest center of the person. It is here that the person is open to the transcendent dimension; it is here that the person experiences ultimate reality. The series explores the discovery of this core, the dynamics of its development, and its journey to the ultimate goal. It deals with prayer, spiritual direction, the various maps of the spiritual journey, and the methods of advancement in the spiritual ascent.

By presenting the ancient spiritual wisdom in an academic perspective, the series can fulfill a number of needs. It can provide readers with a spiritual inventory of the richness of their own traditions, informing them at the same time of the richness of other traditions. It can give structure and order, meaning and direction to the vast amount of information with which we are often overwhelmed in the computer age. By drawing the material into the focus of world spirituality, it can provide a perspective for understanding one's place in the larger process. For it may well be that the meeting of spiritual paths–the assimilation not only of one's own spiritual heritage but of that of the human community as a whole–is the distinctive spiritual journey of our time.

EWERT COUSINS

Introduction

CHINESE BUDDHISM had come to full maturity, as we saw in volume 1, in the great speculative systems of its San-lun, T'ien-t'ai, Hua-yen, and Yogācāra schools, and in the rich array of meditative practices systematized especially by Chih-i (538–597). Translations of a wide range of Mahāyāna sūtras, as well as a substantial assortment of materials from the Tripiṭaka collections of the Sarvāstivāda, Dharmaguptaka, and other Indian schools, along with a host of apocryphal sūtras composed by the Chinese themselves, had provided Chinese Buddhism with scriptural foundations sufficient to sustain it in the new directions it was giving to the already rich inheritance it had received from the Indian subcontinent and Central Asia.

China's transformation of what was already one of the leading religions of the world, shaped for close on a millennium in India, was an inculturation even more thorough than the Hellenization and Romanization of Jewish traditions in Christianity. Two characteristic inflections it brought to the tradition can be identified as an emphasis on this-worldliness and a preoccupation with methods of attaining enlightenment, particularly through the idea of Buddha-nature. We shall find them recurring at every stage in the unfolding of East Asian Buddhism.

The first of our two volumes on Buddhism was dominated by the speculative and analytical spirit of India, and its methodical ascetic quest for a definitive liberation (*mokṣa*, nirvāṇa), a clinically pure emptying out of all illusion. The present volume, in contrast, is pervaded by the Chinese realization of enlightenment here and now, and by the practical, down-to-earth, this-worldly terms in which the enlightened vision was expressed and enacted. Of course Buddhism has never known the dualism of profane and sacred, sense and spirit; enlightenment has always meant to perceive reality just as it is; and a major emphasis in Mahāyāna Buddhism is the teaching that nirvāṇa is nothing other than samsāra perceived in its emptiness. Nonetheless, the ancient Indian ideology of release from the cycle of birth and death, and the vastitudes of Indian cosmology, give to Indian Buddhism a grandiose aura that was not assimilated in China, with its more positivist culture and its more concrete, unspeculative set of words and concepts.

If meditation and emptiness were the regulating themes of the first volume, an emphasis on sudden or immediate enlightenment and its accompanying doctrine of immanent Buddha-nature come to the foreground in the present one. Indian Buddhism emerges against the background of Brahmanism, with its long tradition of ascetic cultivation, and Yoga, which provides Buddhism with its basic repertory of meditative techniques. Chinese Buddhism flowers in a quite different soil and against the broad horizons of Confucianism, with its long tradition of cultivating the virtues requisite for the life of family and state, and Taoism, with its ideal of the enlightened sage roaming freely through life, unimpeded by barriers of social convention, and—to borrow a phrase from Hölderlin—"dwelling poetically on the earth."

The Birth of Ch'an

Kumārajīva (343–413) had bridged Indian and Chinese culture, bringing the first stage of adaptation, the "matching words" period, to its culmination. But a century later a transmission of a very different sort occurred when the Indian monk Bodhidharma (active c. 480–520) embodied the Buddhist path in his intensive focus on the practice of meditation. The Ch'an tradition stemming from this relatively obscure figure did not attempt to reconstruct Buddhism on the basis of immense philological labors. It reenacted the Buddha's own quest for enlightenment, and developed fresh ways of thinking and speaking within the context of this praxis. Its "words" no longer "matched" Indian ones, but pointed directly to what was being lived in the here and now.

Here China's reshaping of Buddhism becomes truly radical and original, so much so that along with the emergence of Mahāyāna and the Diamond Vehicle, the formation of Ch'an must count as one of the major historical turnings of the wheel of the Dharma. Just as the authoritative insight of Śākyamuni provided an opportunity to break through deeply encrusted layers of ritual, myth, and speculation in ancient India, so it was with Ch'an. This "separate tradition outside the scriptures" rose up amid the prodigious speculative and myth-making creativity of Mahāyāna Buddhism, already no less developed in China than in its Indian birthplace, and boldly turned a new page. The legendary silent smile of Mahākāśyapa, who alone among the disciples understood the Buddha's turning a flower in his hand, meant more to the practitioners of Ch'an than the profuse elaborations of sūtra and śāstra. They claimed that a direct transmission of insight from mind to mind could cut through all words to the enlightened awareness of reality.

The resounding laugh of the Zen monks has few prececents in India, with the special exception of the *Vimalakīrti Sūtra* (very popular in China). Rather, the laughter sends us back to the subversive humor of Chuang-tzu, whose dazzling use of anecdote and paradox prefigure the Zen kōans. Listen to him advocate the life of the Tao as the highest ideal by means of a fictional dialogue between Confucius and his favorite disciple, Yen Hui:

> Another day, the two met again and Yen Hui said, "I'm improving!"
> "What do you mean by that?"
> "I can sit down and forget everything!"
> Confucius looked very startled and said, "What do you mean, sit down and forget everything?"
> Yen Hui said, "I smash up my limbs and body, drive out perception and intellect, cast off form, do away with understanding, and make myself identical with the Great Thoroughfare. That is what I mean by sitting down and forgetting everything."[1]

"Sit down and forget everything"—the expression is echoed in East Asian Buddhist meditation from Bodhidharma's legendary wall-gazing down to Dōgen's "just sitting." The image of smashing the limbs and driving out perception anticipates a central teaching that Dōgen was to learn from his Chinese Zen master Ju-ching: "to drop off body and mind." The elimination of the discursive also prefigures the Ch'an ideal of mind: "no thoughts, no images."

When Chuang-tzu speaks of "some wordless teaching, some formless way of bringing the mind to completion," one is irresistibly reminded of the Zen proclamation of a special transmission not based on words or letters, directly pointing to the mind. Again, the emphasis Zen put on the ideas of emptiness and no-self is foreshadowed in another of his dialogues:

> Confucius said, "Make your will one! Don't listen with your ears, listen with your mind. No, don't listen with your mind, but listen with your spirit. Listening stops with the ears, the mind stops with recognition, but spirit is empty and waits on all things. The Way gathers in emptiness alone. Emptiness is the fasting of the mind."
> Yen Hui said, "Before I heard this, I was certain that I was Hui. But now that I have heard it, there is no more Hui. Can this be called emptiness?"[2]

The Taoist mentality is a major matrix of Zen wisdom not only in terms of its critique of reason but also in its absolute affirmation of the way of nature. The transition from a spirituality of release from the world to an awakening to the world in its naturalness entails a conviction that salvation is not something deferred to a dauntingly remote future, but a reality to be apprehended here and now. Ch'an's delight in "emptiness" is more than a metaphysic; it is first and foremost a reverence for the fullness of things as they are, without the clutter of discursive reasoning.

This volume opens with an authoritative survey of the history of Ch'an in China by the late Philip Yampolsky, one of the pioneers in the revision of Zen history inspired by the discovery of the Tun-huang documents. He shows how Ch'an created for itself a lineage going back to the Buddha and specified procedures for orthodox transmission from master to disciple. Institutionalization is said to have made the Ch'an of the capital cities rather formal and overly concerned for scriptural warrants. It was in the freedom of the countryside that Ch'an really came into its own, in the colloquial jests, the shouts and blows, the mind-teasing kōans and dharma battles of Ma-tsu, Huang-po, and Lin-chi. Thomas Kasulis and Dale Wright fill out the picture by taking a closer look at these figures, showing how their disorienting teaching techniques fit into a comprehensive system whereby the burgeoning Ch'an movement was skillfully managed. The intricacies of this completely Sinicized Ch'an culture—its original linguistic conventions and literary genres, its reshaping of the monastic lifestyle, and its complex philosophical classifications—show how spiritual insight, when it is fresh, recreates its entire environment. None of this was very pleasing to the bearers of the indigenous Confucian tradition; Buddhism flourished in time of trouble or under nonethnic Chinese rulers, and Confucianism regained strength with renewed social and political order, as in the Sung period (960–1279). But from Julia Ching's article we see that even as it challenged Buddhism to be alert to social and political realities, Sung period Confucianism developed its own brand of enlightenment, in creative rivalry with Ch'an.

Korea

Korean Buddhism, still greatly underexplored in Western scholarship, has a vigor in thought and practice that gives it a quite distinctive place. Here the adjustment of Buddhism to worldly realities is shown in its syncretization with a shamanized Taoism and in the constructive harmonizing spirit with which the Dharma unfolded in the Land of Morning Calm, where the cultivation of unity and harmony was also highly prized on the political front. The Korean inculturation of Buddhism was also marked by bold speculative breakthroughs, catalyzed by this quest for total integration, as can be seen in the monumental achievement of Wŏnhyo, described in Sung Bae Park's study. Hua-yen thought provided a capacious and integrated philosophical framework, within which this-worldly phenomena could be prized as manifesting the ultimate.

The integration of scriptural study and Sŏn meditation was perhaps the deepest challenge in this quest for harmony. Robert Buswell shows how the well-known topics and controversies of Chinese Zen are approached in original style within the Hua-yen/Zen dialogue in which the central figure is Chinul, a name that is now becoming known in the West as one of the greatest in the Zen tradition. The degree to which Buddhism had become the very pulse of national life is shown in the stirring tale, with which Buswell closes, of how the Koreans carved on woodblocks a superb critical edition of the entire Tripiṭaka, undiscouraged by the wanton destruction of an earlier set by Mongol invaders.

Confucian elements had been fused with Buddhist ones in the code of the *hwarang* knights of the Silla period and in the "ten injunctions" of the Koryŏ dynasty founder Wang Kŏn (r. 918–943). With the foundation of the Chosŏn dynasty (1392–1910) by Neo-Confucian leaders, Buddhism knew leaner years, as Henrik Sørensen relates. Though Neo-Confucianists had learned much from the Buddhist cultivation of the interior life, they strongly resisted Buddhism, seeing it as losing awareness of the external world. Natural integration now gave way to a bureaucratic unification of all sects into two major groupings, Kyo and Sŏn, in 1424. Buddhism, though the largest religion in the country, and despite the outstanding contribution of Sŏsan Hyŭjŏng (1520–1604), seems to have played little part in the sometimes bloody ideological debates of these centuries.

Sŏn emerged with new vibrancy in the twentieth century, responding to Japanese influence. But it resisted the modernization undergone in Japanese Zen and instead remained close to the traditional medieval form, tinged with Confucian influence. At present, the old-style monastic culture is evolving into a broader, more popular Sŏn centered on meditation courses for the general public. The lay-oriented Wŏn Buddhism, a "new" religious movement, has gone much farther in the direction of a completely this-worldly interpretation of Buddhism, centered on the family. Between the extremes of traditionalism and secularization, Korean Buddhism struggles to find a creative modern equivalent of the middle path.

Japan

Six essays guide us through the haunting world of the earliest Japanese Buddhism up to the end of the Heian period. The late Hanayama Shinshō and his son Hanayama Shōyū discuss the earliest Japanese Buddhism, which bore a strong Korean stamp. Great temples, scriptural commentaries, and a political vision inspired by Buddhist principles give luster to the name of Prince Shōtoku, a fine addition to the list of Buddhist rulers. Six different Buddhist traditions had their headquarters in Nara when it was the capital, and Japan tasted for the first time the pleasures of a thriving scholasticism. Thomas Kasulis and Royall Tyler focus on the interplay of city and country, monastic scholasticism and mountain asceticism, Korean and Chinese imports and indigenous Shintō and folk traditions, to reveal the rich and tension-ridden texture of Nara Buddhism. The this-worldly character of Buddhism was accentuated as a missionary technique of inculturation, and the message was often linked to the strengthening of the state and the acquisition of worldly benefits. A masterstroke in this cultural adjustment was the *honji suijaku* system of identifying the indigenous gods with Buddhist bodhisattvas. Buddhism in Japan retained a link with ancient and vital folk traditions above all through the unregulated ascetic movements flourishing in the countryside and in mountain retreats—and still surviving in the *shugendō* or *yamabushi* tradition.

The full, mature inculturation of Buddhism in Japan is the work of two figures who had much in common—both combining the treasures of Chinese learning with the intrepid spirit of mountain asceticism—but who were estranged by radical differences in personality and ideology: Saichō and Kūkai, presented by Umehara Takeshi and Paul Watt. Thanks to Saichō, the capacious T'ien-t'ai (Tendai) doctrine, taught at the monastery-cum-university on Mount Hiei, acquired the most commanding position among the Japanese schools, comparable to that of Hua-yen in Korea. The *Lotus Sūtra*, the "Bible of East Asia," gave the school a breadth of vision and an ideal of bodhisattva compassion and zeal that made it a fertile seedbed for later developments.

The headquarters of Kūkai's Shingon school, on remote Mount Kōya, drew on equally potent sources, centering its cult on the cosmic Buddha Dainichi (Mahāvairocana), source of all other Buddhas. Kūkai's tantric methods promised Buddhahood in this very life, inheriting the power of Indian Tantrism as an immediate practical force. Kūkai was also a master of secular arts and education, a calligrapher, and conceivably Japan's first philosopher. Like many Japanese religious leaders he is also a cultural hero, just as, conversely, many Japanese poets, playwrights, and painters reflect and communicate Buddhist wisdom—a topic beyond the scope of this volume.

The wealth of Heian Buddhism was fully revealed in the line of masters who emerged from it in the Kamakura period. These founders of new schools concentrated the universal potential of the *Lotus Sūtra*'s "one vehicle" Buddhism in select single practices to which ordinary people could dedicate themselves wholeheartedly. Their critical relationship to the Tendai doctrine that all sentient beings possess original enlightenment (*hongaku*) is revealed in David Gardiner's essay as part of a multi-faceted problematic that gives medieval Japanese Buddhism its distinctive identity. *Hongaku* theory allowed the Japanese to unite their cult of the sacred landscape of Japan with the quest of enlightenment and buddhahood. Whether this entailed spiritual complacency and national chauvinism, as modern critics urge, is a question to be faced only when we have fully appreciated the power of the idea and the ramifications of its influence in the culture.

Descending from Mount Hiei, the Kamakura-period Buddhist founders brought the Dharma to the world, not in the sense of the politicking and militarization that had corrupted the Tendai establishment, but in a bodhisattva spirit of service. Hōnen and Shinran preached Pure Land as an "easy way" of faith and repentance. This contradicted Kūkai's "become a Buddha in this very life," but it affirmed that in this very life we are embraced by the infinite compassion of Amida Buddha, which assures rebirth in the Pure Land in our next life, and thereafter enlightenment. Nichiren concentrated Buddhist practice in the recitation of the title of the *Lotus Sūtra*, rechanneling the lofty T'ien-t'ai tradition into the form of a zealous and patriotic religion, and Dōgen identified enlightenment with everyday life to an unprecedented degree, assuring the followers of Sōtō Zen that to sit in quiet meditation was already to be in the enlightened state, reconceived as an ongoing process rather than a sudden disruptive event.

The Kamakura shogunate were strong rulers and warriors, and the Buddhist founders of the time show a comparable heroism and determination on the plane of the spirit. Even the gentle Hōnen, portrayed by Tamaru Noriyoshi and Fujimoto Kiyohiko, pursued his course with a quiet determination and single-mindedness, willing to face persecution if his patient attempts at persuasion and appeasement failed. His Pure Land gospel of salvation through trust in Amida Buddha was dramatically radicalized by Shinran, who even more than his master brought Buddhism close to the hearts and minds of the ordinary Japanese people, as Alfred Bloom shows. Nichiren, as portrayed by Laurel Rasplica Rodd, is an even more awesome figure. He called for a step back to T'ien-t'ai orthodoxy based on the *Lotus*

Sūtra, yet his interpretation of Buddhism turns out to be the most idiosyn-cratic produced in Japan—tinged with fanaticism, perhaps, but supremely effective in energizing the masses of the faithful.

It was only at this time, in the thirteenth century, that Zen became a major element in Japanese Buddhism. As in the early Heian days, sojourns in China, this time by Eisai and Dōgen, were the occasion for the trans-mission of a new and vibrant style of Buddhist practice and thought. Yam-polsky once again provides the historical framework, which is filled out by Tsuchida Tomoaki's study of Dōgen, Minamoto Ryōen's presentation of three outstanding seventeenth-century figures, and Michel Mohr's detailed examination of Hakuin, who is surprisingly neglected in the scholarly literature.

The Confucian polemic against Buddhism as other-worldly, escapist, and nihilistic continued down to the nineteenth century, as did the Buddhist counterclaims that the level of enlightenment reached by Confucian sages was limited. Buddhism in East Asia was never allowed to rest on its medi-tative laurels, but had always to exhibit an active social conscience. Though Japan was a closed country during the Tokugawa period (17th–19th c.), one senses a certain modernity in the Buddhist thinkers of that period, notably in their dialogue with Confucianism, recounted by Minamoto, which may recall debates between religion and rationalism in the West. The new representations of enlightenment that emerged at this time, accompa-nied by new styles of missionizing activity, as in Takuan's or Bankei's preaching or Ishida Baigan's "philosophy of the heart," may remind one of spiritual revivals in early modern Europe—Fox, Wesley, or the Pietists. Meanwhile, a faint echo of the European Enlightenment may be sensed in Jiun Sonja's scholarly pursuits, as described by Watt.

With the Meiji period a flood of Western philosophical culture over-whelmed Buddhist thinkers. What they made of it can be sampled in the study of Kiyozawa Manshi by Gilbert Johnston and Wakimoto Tsuneya and in James Heisig's account of the Kyoto School. Buddhism, as these accounts make clear, more than held its own, and indeed presented themes and per-spectives that are altering the Western philosophical landscape in our time, beginning with Heidegger's response to his Japanese interlocutors.

Buddhist Self-Understanding in Today's World

The matters discussed in this book might have been considered mere anti-quarianism just a few decades ago. Yet read amid the current resurgence of Buddhist practice, philosophy, and scholarship in the Western world, there is hardly one of the figures discussed here who does not seem to step out of the pages with a startling contemporaneity. We are living at the time of a new turning of the wheel of the Dharma, as countless Westerners seek a more enlightened style of life and perception through adopting and adapting Theravāda, Tibetan, and Zen practices. Egil Fronsdal and Franz Aubrey Metcalf assess the relationship of these developments to classical tradition and note how the perpetual tension between spiritual freedom and institutional forms is being negotiated afresh in the West.

This Western Buddhism is firmly oriented to the needs of society. But as Sallie King and Heng-Ching Shih show, Buddhism in Asia has also become engaged with these needs to an unprecedented degree. The new prominence of women in Buddhism should further help reground the tradition in real life experience. The search for a Buddhist response to contemporary problems has called into being new Buddhist movements, of which the most powerful, the Sōka Gakkai, draws its inspiration from the life and teachings of Nichiren. Shimazono Susumu's essay focuses on a phase in the development of this religion when it had to meet the distress of postwar Japanese people, and shows how it combined Nichiren's doctrine with modern Western philosophical or psychological ideas.

In Buddhism, doctrine has always been subject to experiential verification. Today, the experience of socially engaged Buddhists is not merely the gung-ho application of ethical principles, but an enactment and verification of Buddhist insight. The paths of Buddhist liberation are clarified not only in the quiet of the meditation hall but also in their efficacy in situations of injustice, violence, and environmental depredation. But human suffering is of different orders, and so is human growth. To feed the hungry may be the supreme expression of bodhisattva compassion in one situation; to address the spiritual malaise of people whose lives have lost meaning may be what is required in another. The distinctive contribution of Buddhism is a vision and a wisdom that can transform the unsatisfying conditions of samsaric existence into a path of daily growth, both for the individual and for communities. Socially engaged Buddhists seek to enlarge the space of recollection and concentration, of mental cleansing and healing, which the monastery provides. Not urgent necessities, but the spirit in which actions are carried out is what is paramount. In its style of praxis Buddhism strives to counter the noise and acrimony that arise from "attachment to views." It calls all ideologies back to the reality of the situations to which they claim to refer, and cultivates an integral vision of the suffering of sentient beings and their potential for full liberation. In short, this-worldly engagement in a distinctively Buddhist style is inseparable from the quest for enlightenment. There is the danger, of course, that "returning to the world" will result in a loss of insight. A bodhisattva who comes down the mountain to serve the people and in the process ceases to be a "being of enlightenment" will fail to communicate the heart of the bodhisattva path. And yet, a failure to "return to the world" is a betrayal of the bodhisattva spirit.

Buddhist tradition has been marked by a proliferation of sectarian divisions, from the twenty or so schools of early Buddhism, through the divergences of Mādhyamika and Yogācāra, and of the meditation, tantric, Pure Land, and scholastic currents. Ecumenical symbiosis has prevailed within some cultural spheres: the T'ien-t'ai (Tendai) synthesis played an integrating role in China and Japan, as did union of Kyo and Sŏn in Korea, and the joint practice of Zen and Pure Land meditation in China, Korea, and the Ōbaku school of Japanese Zen. Japan has perhaps shown a more marked tendency to split into separate sects. The rivalry between the Nara schools and the new Heian movements, the tension between Saichō and Kūkai, the unease generated by the Kamakura founders, the quarrels about orthodoxy between Jōdoshū and Jōdo Shinshū, and within the latter the long division between Higashi Hongan-ji and Nishi Hongan-ji—mild enough when compared with the fierce mutual anathematizing in other religions—suggest a deficiency of broad, integrating ecumenical vision in this island country that received all the Buddhist traditions at the latest stage of their development.

In its transition from India to Tibet, through central Asia to China, and from there to Korea and Japan, Buddhism underwent constant transformation. As it integrated into each new land and culture, transforming native religiosity even as it was being transformed, it looked continually to its past for guidance, but did not return to the countries and cultures where that past was still alive to insinuate its own innovations there. Like a stream that cannot flow backwards, the current grows stronger but the distance of the present from the past grows ever wider. In the spread of Buddhism during the present century to the lands of Europe and the Americas, the same pattern holds. Efforts by these new Buddhists to introduce Western ideas of morality, human rights, democracy, and so forth to southeast Asian lands have had some effect, but alteration in Buddhist practice and doctrine is still resisted. The one apparent exception are the so-called New Religions of Korea, Japan, and Taiwan, which have turned back to the neighboring lands of Asia to seek converts for their new version of the Buddhist tradition. But here again, their conversions have tended to draw individual people away from their native Buddhism, rather than to engage in critical dialogue with the native Buddhist religiosity of these cultures in the way that their own culture was first proselytized.

In a globalized world, communication between Buddhists of every cultural background is quickening rapidly, and a new and powerful understanding of the sense of the entire tradition is emerging. What unites all Buddhists is not the complex heritage of doctrines but the challenge of the Buddhist path. Perhaps the concrete character of this path is most persuasively expressed in the visual symbols in which the tradition is so rich.

It might be thought that artistic representations of buddhas or bodhisattvas would have a merely esthetic interest, their study a mere appendage, or perhaps a chance to relax in the silent presence of these lofty figures after the exhausting reel of names, dates, and titles unavoidable in an "Encyclopedic History." Mimi Hall Yiengpruksawan's study of Buddhist iconography reveals, however, that Buddhism is as subtle and as eloquent in its images as in its verbal teachings. Here we are given a glimpse of another complex, many-sided history. But again, what is offered is not a mere survey but a probing reflection on the significance of Buddhist images within the development of Buddhist doctrine and spirituality. Images bring the saving figures of Buddhism, and their teaching, immediately close to us in the here and now. This immense history, and these serene and beautiful images, suggest that the Buddhist tradition stands poised on the threshold of new ventures as the world comes to know and appreciate more and more "the Middle Course awakened to by the Tathāgata, making for vision, making for knowledge, and conducing to calm, super-knowledge, self-awakening, and liberation," a teaching that is "lovely at the beginning, lovely in the middle, and lovely at the ending" (*Mahāvagga* I 6. 17; VI 34.11).

The Staff of the Nanzan Institute for Religion and Culture
Nagoya, Japan

Notes

1. Burton Watson, trans., *The Complete Works of Chuang Tzu* (New York: Columbia University Press, 1968), 90.

2. *The Complete Works of Chuang Tzu*, 57–58.

Part Three

LATER CHINA

Ch'an

I. *A Historical Sketch*

PHILIP YAMPOLSKY

CH'AN (ZEN)—as we understand it today—is a form of Buddhism that emphasizes enlightenment obtained through a process of intensive meditation. This enlightenment is achieved through a transmission from master to disciple, a transmission that is made from one mind to another, usually without the use of words or letters. Tradition has it that Ch'an was brought to China by a monk, Bodhidharma, the third son of a prince of Southern India, who is honored as the first Ch'an Patriarch in China, and the twenty-eighth in an unbroken line from the historical Buddha. Bodhidharma transmitted the teaching to a Chinese disciple, Hui-k'o, who in turn transmitted it to the Third Patriarch, Seng-ts'an. The Fourth Patriarch was Tao-hsin (580–651) and the Fifth, Hung-jen (601–674), who in turn handed on the teaching to Hui-neng (638–713), celebrated as the Sixth Patriarch, to whom all present-day Zen traces its ancestry.

Meditation has always played a major role in all forms of Buddhism. As Buddhism developed in Northern China, many individual practitioners came to emphasize meditation techniques. At the same time great importance was attached to the development of meditation theory and practice within the established schools of Buddhism, particularly the T'ien-t'ai school. Eventually practitioners from both groups, who devoted themselves exclusively to meditation, came together to form communities. By the mid-seventh century a prominent center for Ch'an meditation had developed on Mt. Shuang-feng in Hupei under the Fifth Patriarch, Hung-jen. Hung-jen, whose teaching is known as the East Mountain school, had eleven principal disciples who spread the teaching throughout China, three of whom founded major schools of Ch'an: Shen-hsiu (606?–706), Chih-hsien (609–702), and Hui-neng (638–713). If we examine only the standard Ch'an historical tradition, we learn that Hui-neng had two important heirs—Nan-yüeh Huai-jang (677–744) and Ch'ing-yüan Hsing-ssu (d. 740), and that it was from these two masters that all of later Ch'an descended. Virtually nothing is known of these two figures; biographical sources that describe their activities appear only very long after their deaths. They are unmentioned in the few contemporary literary sources that remain. However, traditional Ch'an records the names of their descendants as well as those of all the Ch'an patriarchs and masters who followed. Their names and lineages are also recorded in later Ch'an histories in both China and Japan.

Tun-huang

If we had to depend on traditional Ch'an sources we would have a very inaccurate picture of the history of Ch'an Buddhism. Fortunately, in 1900, a great hoard of documents was recovered from a walled-up cave at Tun-huang, a desert oasis in Kansu in the northwesternmost part of China. This cave had been sealed to protect its contents from invading barbarians in the early eleventh century and it contained documents that can be dated between 406 and 996.

A large proportion of the manuscripts, some twenty thousand or more, are Chinese Buddhist texts. Other materials include literary works, poems, many documents related to finances and law, dictionaries and works related to education, Confucianist writings, and texts in Tibetan, Uighur, and other Central Asian languages. Occasionally the recto of some document has a Buddhist text and the verso a secular record. Taoism is represented by a fair number of texts, some of which had been lost and were not included in the Taoist canon. Almost ninety per cent of the Buddhist materials are routine copies of standard scriptural texts, all readily available elsewhere in printed form in various editions of the Tripiṭaka. They are of interest mainly to linguists and students of calligraphy. There are also Buddhist texts in Tibetan and Sanskrit; several of the Tibetan works are translations of Chinese texts that are no longer extant in China.

The Tun-huang documents are a major source for our knowledge of the history, literature, language, religion—in fact all aspects—of the Sui and T'ang periods. Of immediate concern are the Ch'an materials found at Tun-huang. If it were not for these fragments, our knowledge of the history and development of Ch'an Buddhism would certainly be fragmentary, if not largely erroneous. Schools that have not persisted, monks whose fame has

1. Bodhidharma, from a late 15th-century drawing by Soga Dasaku.

faded with the passage of time, and works otherwise lost have become known to us through these manuscripts.

The documents include early examples of literary forms that later became standard in Ch'an literature, notably the *t'eng-shih* (transmission of the lamp): histories of Ch'an told in the form of biographies of the patriarchs and the Ch'an masters who followed them over the centuries. They take their form from the *Kao-seng chuan* (Biographies of eminent monks, 519) and its sequel the *Hsü kao-seng chuan* (645). These famous biographies were non-sectarian. The Ch'an biographical works, however, aimed to establish Ch'an as a legitimate school of Buddhism traceable to its Indian origins, and at the same time championed a particular form of Ch'an. Historical accuracy was of little concern to the compilers; old legends were repeated, new stories

三十三祖慧能大師

2. Hui-neng (638–713).

were invented and reiterated until they too became legends.

The first work to establish a Ch'an lineage, in other words a succession of Ch'an patriarchs, was the *Ch'uan fa-pao chi* (Records of the transmission of the Dharma-treasure), compiled about 710. It draws on the *Hsü kao-seng chuan* for the biographies of the five Chinese patriarchs but recasts them as a sequence from patriarch to heir. This line of succession—Bodhidharma, Hui-k'o, Seng-ts'an, Tao-hsin, and Hung-jen—is standard in all later Ch'an works. The position of Sixth Patriarch (in later works the most important one) is here, and here only, ascribed to Fa-ju (637–689). He is followed by Shen-hsiu (606?–706), revered at this time as the leading Ch'an master, but destined, as we shall see, for ill-treatment by posterity. On the basis of quotations in the *Ch'uan fa-pao chi* we know that it represented a school that based its teachings on the *Laṅkāvatāra Sūtra*.

The documents include another more detailed work of a similar nature: the *Leng-ch'ieh shih-tzu chi* (Record of the transmission of the *Laṅkāvatāra*), which was probably compiled between 713 and 716. This work, as the title indicates, champions the transmission of the *Laṅkāvatāra Sūtra*. It and it alone makes Guṇabhadra, the translator of the *Laṅkāvatāra Sūtra*, the first patriarch in China, followed by the usual five patriarchs, with Shen-hsiu numbered as the seventh and his disciple P'u-chi (651–739) as the eighth. The place given to Shen-hsiu here is characteristic of the school that would later be referred to as Northern Ch'an.

Shen-hsiu and Shen-hui

Northern Ch'an, like most other schools, derived from Hung-jen and his East Mountain School. It also based its authority on the teaching of Shen-hsiu, who had attracted many students to his temple at Mount Yü-ch'üan in Hupei from 674 to the turn of the century and was at this stage of Ch'an history by far the most important of Hung-jen's eleven disciples. Although later to be virtually forgotten, the school he established was, at least in the first three decades of the eighth century, the most prominent school of Ch'an. In 701 or 702 Shen-hsiu was summoned to court by Empress Wu, who greatly revered Buddhism, but also managed to make use of it skillfully to increase her power. The court received his preaching with the utmost veneration, and he taught in the capital cities (Lo-yang and Ch'ang-an) until his death in 706. His funeral, infinitely elaborate, was attended by the highest officials.

Shen-hsiu's success in propagating his teachings at court contributed greatly to the spread of Ch'an. His work was continued by priests who had been his fellow students under the Fifth Patriarch, and by his own disciples, several of whom were famous in their own right. I-fu (658–736) continued to serve the religious needs of the Imperial Court, but he appears to have had no heirs. P'u-chi was by far the most renowned teacher of Northern Ch'an in the middle years of the eighth century. His activities centered on the capital of Lo-yang. It is said that during his lifetime as many as ten thousand students came to study under him, of whom some forty became significant teachers in their own right. However, with the gradual decline in power of the T'ang court and the central government in the mid-eighth century the Northern School began to lose its importance. Although remnants of the Northern School can be traced in the late ninth century, it was no longer of much significance.

The term "Northern School" was applied to the teachings of Shen-hsiu by a priest of the name of Shen-hui, who claimed to teach the Ch'an of the Southern School (Nan-tsung), a term that used to refer to Southern India and was then applied to the Laṅkāvatāra school, which based itself on Bodhidharma's teachings (later known as the Northern School!). Determined to establish a new school of his own, Shen-hui, then still unknown, attacked the Ch'an of Shen-hsiu and his descendants. Born in 670 or 672 in Hsiang-yang in Hupei, he was drawn at first to Taoism and Confucianism, but heard later of Buddhist teachings and, abandoning an official career, became a monk under Shen-hsiu at the Yü-ch'üan temple. When Shen-hsiu was called to court, Shen-hui turned south to Ts'ao-ch'i, near Canton, to study with Hui-neng, staying with him for several years; later he traveled about China visiting famous teachers. After receiving full ordination as a monk he returned to Hui-neng, with whom he stayed until the latter's death in 713. Little is known of his activities for the next fifteen years, but apparently he lived quietly in Nan-yang in Honan. In 730 he moved to the Ho-tse temple in Lo-yang. In 732 on the fifteenth day of the first month he mounted a platform at the Ta-yün Temple in Hua-t'ai (also in Honan) and launched a grand attack on the teachings of Shen-hsiu's school. Details of his attack are to be found in a group of Tun-huang documents, including the *Platform Sutra* and the *Determination of the Truth of the Southern Teachings*. These works are early examples of a form of Ch'an literature known as *yu-lu* (recorded sayings). Compiled by the master's disciples, they contain biographical information, stories of encounters with other monks, brief sermons, and verse. Works of this sort in later years became a distinct form of Ch'an literature, characterized for a while by the use of colloquial language instead of a formal literary style.

Shen-hui made a large variety of pronouncements and accusations. His polemics against Northern Ch'an were frequently inaccurate and unjust. His major allegation was that Shen-hsiu of the Northern School had no right to claim to be the Sixth Patriarch. He claims that Bodhidharma's robe, the symbol of the transmission, had been handed down from patriarch to patriarch for six generations; it was now housed at the temple of Hui-neng, his own teacher; Hui-neng, not Shen-hsiu, was the Sixth Patriarch; indeed Shen-hsui himself had never dared claim that title. "But now P'u-chi calls himself the Seventh Patriarch and falsely states that his teacher was the Sixth. This must not be permitted." He accuses P'u-chi of sending people to cut the head from Hui-neng's mummified body and to replace the inscription on Hui-neng's stele with one calling Shen-hsiu the Sixth Patriarch. He denounces P'u-chi's attempts to destroy the Southern School. "When Shen-hsiu was alive, all students referred to these two great masters, saying: In the South, Hui-neng, in the North, Shen-hsiu..., therefore we have the two schools Southern and Northern.... P'u-chi now recklessly calls his teaching the Southern Sect. This is not to be permitted."

This attack created the image of two competing factions, Northern and Southern, that has persisted to this day, and also established a stark contrast between them: the Northern teaching was gradual, a slow step-by-step approach to enlightenment, while the Southern School adopted a sudden method. (In reality the Northern School also advocated a sudden approach after an initial mastery of meditation techniques.) Northern Ch'an had emphasized, at least in its early history, the *Laṅkāvatāra Sūtra*. Shen-hui quite arbitrarily claimed that the Fifth Patriarch, Hung-jen, had transmitted the *Diamond Sūtra* to Hui-neng and that this sūtra formed the basis of the teaching. This Northern/Southern dichotomy has persisted in China in fields quite unrelated to Ch'an. In painting there are Northern and Southern Schools, connected somehow to gradual and sudden approaches, though this analogy was not created until the seventeenth century, when it also became fashionable to discuss poetry in terms of the sudden and the gradual. When we come to the Sung dynasty, Ch'an is again referred to by some in terms of the two schools that Shen-hui fabricated in his drive for recognition.

We know very little of Shen-hui's activities between the years 732, when he launched his masterful attack on P'u-chi and Northern Ch'an, and 745. He appears to have continued his preaching, to have made many converts and to have traveled widely, associating with high officials. In 745 he was invited to take up residence in the Ho-tse temple in Lo-yang, where his teaching and his continued attacks on Northern Ch'an attracted a large audience. In 753 he fell foul of the censor Lu I, allegedly a proponent of Northern Ch'an, and was banished from the capital. He went first to Ch'ang-an, where he was interviewed by Emperor Hsuan-tsung and then sent into exile, an exile that was perhaps not particularly severe since it included a stay in his home village. During his exile the country was shattered by the rebellion of An Lu-shan, a general of Sogdian and Turkish ancestry, whose forces swept over Lo-yang and Ch'ang-an and drove the Imperial Court into exile in 756. The Emperor fled, leaving affairs in the hands of the heir apparent, who rallied the government forces and succeeded in suppressing the revolt. The T'ang dynasty lasted for more than another century and a half, but the central government gradually lost control of the outlying areas. In its efforts to suppress the revolt the government found itself in severe financial difficulties. One money-raising method was to establish ordination platforms in each prefecture for the investiture of monks and the selling of certificates. Shen-hui was called to Lo-yang to assist in these efforts. He enjoyed exceptional success and contributed substantial aid to the beleagured government. A new temple was built for him in the ruined city. He passed away in 762.

Shen-hui was responsible for the establishment of the so-called Southern School of Ch'an in the capital cities. He succeeded in ensuring Hui-neng's position as the Sixth Patriarch, a status that has been accepted without question from Shen-hui's time on. Northern Ch'an did not simply vanish; there is evidence that it continued for several generations after P'u-chi's death. Shen-hui's own school seems to have suffered a fate similar to that of Northern Ch'an. He did have one famous descendant in a later generation, the scholar priest Tsung-mi (780–841), but his school seems to have died out with the persecution of 845, when Buddhism, particularly that in the capital cities, suffered a setback from which it never recovered.

Hui-neng, the Sixth Patriarch (born 638 near Canton; died 713), is venerated as one of the greatest figures in the history of Ch'an. An elaborate biography has grown up about him, much of it legendary in nature. The

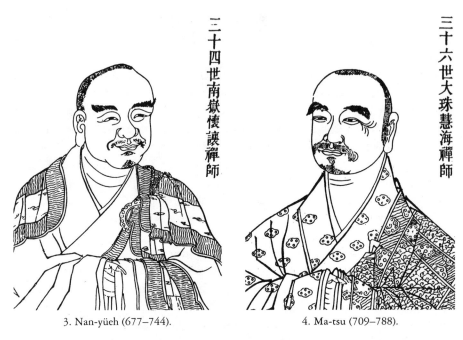

3. Nan-yüeh (677–744).   4. Ma-tsu (709–788).

Liu-tsu t'an-ching (Platform Sūtra of the Sixth Patriarch) purports to convey his teachings. An edition of this work was found at Tun-huang and later versions, many of them greatly enlarged, appeared over the centuries. The legend has it that Hui-neng, an illiterate peasant, joined the assembly of the Fifth Patriarch, where the priest Shen-hsiu was a leading disciple. There he displayed his innate understanding and was secretly designated as the Sixth Patriarch. He instructed a large number of disciples at his temple at Ts'ao-ch'i. Some sources state that when Shen-hsiu was invited to the Imperial Court by the Empress Wu, Hui-neng and other famous Ch'an masters were called at the same time. Hui-neng is said to have declined the invitation. Scholars are divided on the question of how much fabrication the stories of Hui-neng contain. Yanagida Seizan has argued rather persuasively that the *Platform Sūtra* was the product of an entirely different and unrelated school of Ch'an, namely the Niu-t'ou (Oxhead) School, which claimed a succession from Fourth Patriarch Tao-hsin through Fa-jung (594–667) and Chih-yen (577–654).

The Rise of Rural Ch'an

By the middle of the eighth century the T'ang dynasty was collapsing, and the Ch'an of the capital cities began to lose its status. Northern Ch'an and the Ch'an of Shen-hui still persisted, but other schools were arising in out-lying areas controlled by local warlords. These are the forerunners of the Ch'an we know today. Their origins are obscure; the power of Shen-hui's preaching is shown by the fact that they all trace themselves to Hui-neng. The Szechwan School established by Chih-hsien (609–702), a disciple of the Fifth Patriarch, also flourished at this time. A Tun-huang document, the *Li-tai fa-pao chi* (Historical record of the Dharma-treasure), composed around 780, details its history and teachings. It contains an exposition of the teach-ings of Wu-chu (714–774), fourth in the lineage of this school. It does not take sides in the conflict between Northern and Southern Ch'an, no longer a live issue. It acknowledges Hui-neng as the Sixth Patriarch, but makes the obviously spurious claim that Bodhidharma's robe, handed down to Hui-neng and symbol of the transmission within Ch'an, had been given by Hui-neng to the Empress Wu, who in turn presented it to Chih-hsien.

Symbols of the transmission played an important role in early Ch'an. Shen-hui had claimed that Bodhidharma's robe was handed down within the school until it reached Hui-neng, at which time it was no longer trans-ferred to the succeeding heir. The *Platform Sūtra* indicates that a copy of the sūtra itself serves as a symbol of transmission. The principal symbol of transmission, however, was the transmission verse *(ch'uan fa chieh)*. In Ch'an these verses were used to epitomize the teachings or to reveal the degree of the writer's enlightenment. With the later emphasis on "a separate trans-mission outside of the teaching, not dependent on words and phrases," these verses played a significant role in the teaching. Transmission verses attributed to the first six patriarchs are found in the *Platform Sūtra* and also in the *Pao-lin chuan*, a Ch'an biographical compilation dating to around 800 that is not included among the works found at Tun-huang. From this time on, it became customary for Ch'an masters to compose such verses when they were about to die, and thus to transmit the essence of their teaching.

The Tun-huang documents include many apocryphal sūtras and works of dubious origin that were attributed to the early patriarchs, particularly Bodhidharma. Quite soon after the introduction of Buddhism into China these works began to appear. A catalogue dating to 730 lists some 403 spu-rious sūtras. Perhaps as many as a thousand were composed. The Chinese compilers of the canonical collections made great efforts to exclude them from the Tripiṭaka. Many have been lost; many are known by name alone, others by fragmentary quotations. Some of these apocryphal works were of high literary value and of great use to Buddhists, and they played a significant role in early Ch'an. Typical among these was the *Chin-kang san-mei ching* (Diamond Samādhi Sūtra) composed perhaps by 680. Scholars hold that this work links the thought of Bodhidharma with that of the East Mountain School of the Fifth Patriarch.

By the ninth century Ch'an had shed many of the characteristics derived from India and had acquired a more practical Chinese character, merging into the everyday life of the people. A new school developed in Chiang-hsi and Hunan, and its leaders were two men whom we have not mentioned up to now, Ma-tsu Tao-i (709–788) and Shih-t'ou Hsi-ch'ien (700–790), disciples of the two putative heirs of the Sixth Patriarch, Nan-yüeh Huai-jang and Ch'ing-yüan Hsing-ssu. Neither Nan-yüeh nor Ch'ing-yüan are among the ten major disciples of Hui-neng listed in the Tun-huang edition of the *Platform Sūtra*, but standard Ch'an tradition lists them as disciples: further evidence that by this time it was necessary for all Ch'an schools to claim a lineage traceable to Hui-neng, the Sixth Patriarch.

Chiang-hsi and Hunan were rich, fertile regions, controlled by local governors who were becoming more and more independent of the central government. Ma-tsu and Shih-t'ou made converts of the local landowners and warlords and became famous as the two great Masters of these areas. Their Ch'an differed from that of the capital cities. It was rural, rustic, popular; and it sought lay support. Priests wandered among the common people while engaging in their ascetic practices. From mid-T'ang on, this Ch'an rejected the formal trappings of Buddhism, the "union of meditation and wisdom," and the intellectualism of the Ch'an of the capital cities. It did not reject meditation as such, but sought enlightenment within the activities of everyday life, and spoke of Buddhism in terms of such daily activities as drawing water and chopping wood.

Ma-tsu came from Szechwan, where he first studied under a master of the Szechwan school. Later he came to Nan-yüeh and became an heir in the line of the Sixth Patriarch. His teaching is referred to as Hung-chou Ch'an, taking its name from the area of Chiang-hsi where he taught. Described as a huge man of imposing presence, he was an original and independent priest, proud of his rural origins. Throughout his life he retained his family name Ma, and the stories in which he figures make frequent mention of animals, tools, and other artifacts of his rural background.

Shortly after his death the first *yu-lu* (recorded sayings) appeared, representing a new departure in Chinese Buddhism. No longer was there concern for doctrinal matters; the text dealt with problems of spiritual progress in dialogues between master and disciple, sermons, lectures and verses, written in colloquial language and filled with slang and everyday sayings. Such expressions as "everyday mind is the way" and "this very mind is Buddha" reflect Ma-tsu's emphasis on the present; everyday life was the activity of the Buddha-nature. He held that all striving, all practice with the aim of gaining awakening, all distinctions of good and bad, were the activities of a mind concerned with birth and death. He held that everyone is potentially a Buddha, but that one does not become a Buddha merely by sitting in meditation.

Ma-tsu is said to have had a large number of disciples, of various types: the number varies from eighty to eight hundred. Although Ma-tsu himself had no contact with the Buddhism of the capital cities, his teachings gradually became known toward the end of his life and after he had passed away. Several of his students preached in Ch'ang-an and lectured to the Imperial Court. Some had been scholars of Buddhism; others retreated into isolation in the mountains and were not heard from again; others were well-known laymen.

The *Pao-lin chuan* (Transmission of the Pao-Lin Temple) is a history of this new Zen. Written in 800, it records the lineage of the Ch'an school from India through the Sixth Patriarch. The work was never incorporated into the Tripiṭaka, although at one time it must have been fairly widely used. It is a ten-volume work, several volumes of which are missing. One volume was discovered in the 1930s in a Kyoto temple, indicating that copies had come to Japan. According to the T'ien-t'ai lineage, the transmission had been cut off in India with the Twenty-fourth Patriarch. Ch'an, in order to establish a continuity, maintained that there were in fact twenty-eight Indian Patriarchs, leading to Bodhidharma. The *Pao-lin chuan* covers them all, followed by the Chinese Patriarchs down to Hui-neng. Although the chapter on Hui-neng is missing, a verse contained in the biography of Prajñātāra, the Twenty-seventh Patriarch, predicts the coming of Nan-yüeh and Ma-tsu—evidently a piece of propaganda for the new Ch'an. The *Platform Sūtra* had given transmission verses for the six Chinese Patriarchs; the *Pao-lin chuan* gives them for all the Indian Patriarchs as well, establishing a precedent followed in all later histories. The *Pao-lin chuan* was a compilation of major importance, designed to proclaim the start of Hung-chou Ch'an. Incidentally, it is not found among the Tun-huang documents, which make no reference to this new school of Ch'an.

The independent Ch'an movement begun by Ma-tsu soon developed into organized groups of considerable size. Once established, these organizations had to provide shelter, food, and clothing for those who stayed at the temple. The regulations of Indian Buddhism forbade productive work. In India the monks depended entirely on lay support. In China these regulations were not feasible, especially among groups in isolated areas that did not enjoy government protection or the support of wealthy parishioners. Ma-tsu's disciple Pai-chang Huai-hai (720–814) composed new regulations in the *Pai-chang ch'ing-kuei* (Pure regulations of Pai-chang), which is no longer extant, although a Yüan dynasty version exists.

The first extant code is the *Ch'an-men kuei-shih* (Ch'an regulations) appended to the biography of Huai-hai in the *Ch'ing-te ch'uan-teng-lu* of 1004. This brief work proclaims the need for independent Ch'an regulations, describes the monks' hall where a communal meditative life is to be led, and states that a monk's position within the hall should be based on the length of time spent in the monastery, not on social status. It calls for meditation platforms to be erected along the walls of the monks' hall and provides for stands and shelves for storage of the monks' belongings. It sets up rules for assemblies in the Dharma hall to hear the Master's lectures and to question or discuss Ch'an matters with him. It prescribes work periods for all members of the community and establishes procedures for expelling offenders who breach the regulations.

But this code reveals only a small part of the regulations that existed prior to the year 1000. The first work of a comprehensive character was the *Ch'an-yüan ch'ing-kuei* (Pure regulations of the garden of Zen) of 1103. Used widely during the Sung dynasty, this served as a model for later codes in both China and Japan. It gives detailed regulations for (1) the proper use and observance of Hīnayāna and Mahāyāna precepts, (2) clothing, equipment and documentation, including procedures for requesting overnight lodging or entrance into a monastery, (3) etiquette at meals, (4) meeting with the abbot for guidance and instruction, (5) the conduct of regular monastery activities, (6) the appointment of temple officers, (7) sūtra recitation, and official letters, (8) hygiene, and treatment of ill monks, and (9) procedures to be followed when a monk dies, and for the installation of new abbots.

While Huai-hai was formulating rules for the monastic community, other Ch'an practitioners engaged in solitary practice in isolated areas or chose to travel about the country, having little if anything to do with Ch'an communities. This tendency was more prevalent in the school that developed under Shih-t'ou Hsi-ch'ien (700–790) than among the disciples of his contemporary Ma-tsu. Shih-t'ou preferred a life of mountain solitude to community living. He left behind poems widely used in Ch'an circles, *Ts'an-t'ung chi* (In praise of identity) and *Ts'ao-an ko* (Song of the grass hut). His followers appear to have emulated him in seeking seclusion in the mountains, and they too were frequently moved to express themselves in verse.

While this new Ch'an was developing in Chiang-hsi and Hunan, the intellectual Ch'an of the capital cities was represented by such figures as the scholar and philosopher Kuei-feng Tsung-mi (780–841), whose temple was located close to Ch'ang-an. Originally from Szechwan, where he studied under a priest of the Szechwan school named Shen-hui, for some reason he later claimed to be a fifth-generation descendant of the famous Shen-hui (the champion of Hui-neng), whose name is written with the same characters. In his youth Tsung-mi read works of the First Patriarch of Hua-yen Buddhism as well as the apocryphal but important *Yüan-chüeh ching* (Sūtra of Perfect Enlightenment). He studied under the Hua-yen master Ch'eng-kuan (738–838), receiving his sanction, and became the Fifth Patriarch of the Hua-yen Sect. At the same time he was the fifth and last Patriarch in the succession of the Ho-tse Sect, as Shen-hui's school was called. Tsung-mi was greatly honored. He obtained the conversion of the prime minister, P'ei Hsiu (797–870), and was called on to lecture at court. He was a prolific writer, compiling the hundred-volume *Ch'an-yüan chu-ch'üan* (Compendium of interpretations of the fundamentals of Ch'an), of which only the preface, itself a substantial work, remains, as well as an extensive commentary on the *Yüan-chüeh ching*, in which he attempted to reconcile an academic approach to Buddhism with Ch'an. These writings had considerable influence on later Neo-Confucianists.

Tsung-mi died in 841, a few years before the great persecution of Buddhism by the Emperor Wu-tsung in 845–846. On the surface this event represented a confrontation between Taoism and Buddhism, but in actuality it was a desperate attempt on the part of the hard-pressed central government, which had been in disarray since the An Lu-shan rebellion of 756, to gain some measure of political, economic, and military relief by preying on the Buddhist temples with their immense wealth and extensive lands. Buddhist statues of bronze, iron, gold, and silver were ordered to be turned over to the government. Efforts were made to eliminate the great number of tax-exempt individuals, chiefly monks and nuns and slaves who worked in the temples. According to the *Ch'iu T'ang-shu* (Old T'ang history), some 4,600 temples were destroyed, over 40,000 smaller temples removed; 260,500 monks and nuns returned to lay life, vast land holdings were confiscated, and 150,000 slaves belonging to the temples were made subject to a double tax. Metropolitan Buddhism was delivered a blow from which it never recovered, but Ch'an practitioners in outlying areas were little affected, and the descendants of Ma-tsu and Shih-t'ou used the occasion to propagate their style of Ch'an, which from late T'ang on dominated Chinese Buddhism.

The Five Houses

Various schools prospered for a while only to die out, others prospered and continue to this day. They are generally referred to as the Five Houses and Seven Schools of Ch'an. The first of these Houses was that of Kuei-yang, one of two lines that descended from Ma-tsu. Its founders were Ling-yu (771–853), who resided at Kuei-shan in Hunan, and his disciple Hui-chi (807–883), who taught at Yang-shan in Chiang-hsi. The name Kuei-yang represents a combination of these two place-names. Although not located in the capital, this new Ch'an gained the patronage of high officials in the central government, including Prime Minister P'ei Hsiu.

Emperor Wu-tsung died in 846, and Hsuan-tsung, who succeeded him, immediately called off the anti-Buddhist movement and eased to a certain degree the strict restrictions that had been placed on Buddhism. The Five Houses did not exist in isolation; there was a certain interaction among them in the period following the Buddhist suppression. Stories in the histories and *yu-lu* indicate that the various masters and their disciples visited one another, tested one another, respected and at times disdained one another. Each master had his distinctive style of teaching. Some used the shout, some the stick, some more gentle methods of guiding their students toward enlightenment.

The second of the Five Houses was that of Lin-chi I-hsüan (d. 866), known in Japan as the Rinzai Sect. Lin-chi derives its name from the small temple in Hopei in which I-hsüan lived. After the persecutions had ended, Lin-chi, who had the support of Prime Minister P'ei Hsiu, received the teachings of his master, Huang-po Hsi-yüan (d. 850?). Lin-chi was originally from Tsao-chou in present-day Shantung. He had a literary Buddhist background, having studied the Yogācāra, Vijñaptimātra, and other doctrines. At the age of twenty-five he abandoned his scholarly pursuits to study with Hsi-yüan at Mt. Huang-po, becoming his heir after many years of study. Lin-chi's temple was located in Chen-chou in Hopei, an area which had long been a bastion against attacks from barbarians to the north, and the warlords who controlled the area were virtually beyond the control of the central government. Thus the anti-Buddhist regulations were largely ignored here. Lin-chi stressed a form of Buddhism compatible with the thinking of the powerful lords, who had little sympathy for the Han cultural sphere south of the Yangtze. He is famous for the use of the shout and the stick. His preaching reflected a thoroughgoing criticism of established values and a complete rejection of formalized sitting. To engage in long-standing Buddhist practices was described as creating the karma leading to hell. He called for true understanding on the part of the practitioners and ascribed its absence to a lack of faith. Faith in oneself means to live fully in the present, to activate in oneself an unconditioned ability not to discriminate. Inability to accomplish this is due to incompetent teachers and long-standing traditions, to delusions created by man.

The third of the Five Houses, Ts'ao-tung (in Japan, Sōtō), was established by Tung-shan Liang-chieh (807–869). He studied under several well-known masters, including Kuei-shan Ling-yu (771–853). Kuei-shan sent him to study with Yün-yen T'an-sheng (780–841), whose heir he became. Tung-shan wandered widely, meeting with his fellow masters, and many of these encounters are recorded in his *yu-lu*. He studied, practiced, and taught in the relatively peaceful Chiang-hsi area, under conditions quite the opposite of those under which Lin-chi worked. His association with Ch'an masters of varied backgrounds gave him a comparatively broad view of the Ch'an of his time. His teacher, Yün-yen, was the author of a poetical work, the *Pao-ching san-mei*, which is highly valued in the Ts'ao-tung sect and recited daily in its services. It is a rather abstruse work that sets forth the concept of the five ranks, or steps through which this doctrine is to be comprehended. Tung-shan had two major disciples, Ts'ao-shan Pen-chi (840–901) and Yün-chü Tao-ying (d. 902), from whose line all current Ts'ao-tung school masters descend. The Ts'ao-tung School derives its name from a combination of Ts'ao-shan and Tung-shan, the names of the mountains on which these masters lived.

Ch'an flourished also in southern and western China. In South China in the area of present-day Canton the Yün-men school, the fourth of the Five Houses, flourished, and the Fa-yen, the Fifth House, developed somewhat later in the Fukien and Honan areas. The area around Fu-chow was fertile and economically stable and had been the home of several of the priests famous in the late T'ang. Here a noted master, Hsüeh-feng I-ts'un (822–908), taught, and under him came Yün-men Wen-yen (862/4–949) and later Fa-yen Wen-i (885–958). The Houses they founded produced several masters during the Sung period who were celebrated for their literary accomplishments.

Of the Five Houses of Ch'an, Kuei-yang lasted almost one hundred and fifty years and eventually merged with the Lin-chi school; Yün-men flourished among the upper classes of society during the Sung, but gradually declined during the Southern Sung and died out in the Yüan. Fa-yen similarly flourished in early Sung and died out in the Southern Sung. Only Lin-chi and Ts'ao-tung continued as schools of Ch'an, Lin-chi being by far the larger and more active. As for the Seven Schools, they refer to the Five Houses plus the two branches of Lin-chi that stem from Shih-shuang Ch'u-yüan

(986–1039), the Yang-ch'i founded by Yang-ch'i Fang-hui (992–1049), and the Huang-lung founded by Huang-lung Hui-nan (1002–1069). The Huang-lung never prospered greatly, although some famous Sung figures such as the poet Su Tung-p'o (1036–1101), the statesman Wang An-shih (1021–1086), and the minister Chang Shang-ying (1043–1121) were associated with it. The Yang-ch'i school developed somewhat later and attracted a large number of the literati, members of the upper bureaucracy, all of whom were staunch Neo-Confucianists, yet linked themselves with Ch'an temples.

The development of this vibrant Ch'an culture was chronicled in numerous historical records. Some are lost, and only fragments or their names alone remain; others have been preserved and incorporated into Tripiṭika collections. An early work was the *Tsu-t'ang chi,* compiled in 952 by two Korean monks of whom nothing is known. It records the biographies of some two hundred and forty-six Ch'an patriarchs from the fabulous Seven Buddhas of the Past to Hsueh-feng I-t'sun, providing records of their teachings and of question-and-answer sessions in which they took part, miscellaneous writings, and transmission verses. The work was published at Haein-ssu in Korea in 1245, but was not included in the Tripiṭaka, for which blocks were being cut at the time. It lay unused until discovered by Japanese scholars in 1900. The book is important for the information it contains that is not found elsewhere, and for the light it sheds on T'ang colloquial language. What connection, if any, this work had with the most famous of Ch'an histories, the *Ching-te chuan-teng lu* (Record of the transmission of the lamp), is not known. The latter was completed in 1004 and presented to the throne in 1011. It contains thirty volumes of the records, biographies, sayings, conversations of Ch'an monks up to shortly before its compilation. Traditionally the work is said to contain the biographies of 1,701 monks; in actuality there are biographies of 960. The names of the remaining monks are simply listed. This work set the precedent for numerous works of the same genre, published over the centuries.

Later History of Ch'an

Buddhism in the Sung period is usually described as in a state of decline. The Sung government, hard-pressed for funds, began to sell monks certificates instead of granting them to those who had passed examinations on the scriptures. The holders were entitled to exemption from taxation and labor service.

The development of printing greatly influenced Buddhism and the whole of Chinese culture in the Sung. Tripiṭaka collections and individual works were printed and received wide distribution. Thus works of the T'ang and Five Dynasties periods were made readily available for the first time. Frequently they were edited to eliminate some of the colloquialisms and to couch them in more elegant literary language. Neo-Confucian tracts were also produced in abundance, and anti-Buddhist polemics gained a wider circulation. In late T'ang Chinese scholars had begun to concern themselves once again with the Chinese cultural heritage, and in early Sung they turned to the Confucian classics as a source for a system of ethics, and developed a metaphysics that served to refute Buddhist practices and doctrines. They attacked the doctrine of *śūnyatā*, emptiness, which they ascribed to Ch'an Buddhists despite the latter's lack of interest in doctrinal analysis. Actually, these new Confucianists, while attacking Ch'an, adopted many of its practices, such as meditative sitting.

Another factor that led to the decline of Ch'an was the expansion of the civil service examination system. Begun in the Han, it had developed during the T'ang and reached a highly elaborate form in the Sung. These examinations were held every three years for scholars who sought positions in the imperial bureaucracy, and those who passed were assured positions of power and prestige. Since the examinations were based mainly on the Confucian Classics, all candidates had to memorize these works and to be capable of writing essays in a specified and appropriate style. References to Buddhism were excluded. In fact, four times during the Sung edicts were issued forbidding the quotation of Ch'an works in the examinations, which indicates both the continued popularity of Ch'an and the zeal of the Neo-Confucians in trying to root it out.

During the early Sung, the publication of Ch'an works increased greatly, especially in the areas of Chekiang and Fukien that had largely escaped the disturbances of the late T'ang and Five Dynasties periods. The *Ch'ing-te ch'uan-teng lu*, a Fa-yen work, brought a new dimension to Ch'an, for its stories form the basis of the kōan collections so prominent in the Ch'an of the Sung period. The Yün-men School also produced several priests of literary distinction, notably Fo-jih Ch'i-sung (1007–1072), who sought in his writings to effect a rapprochement between Ch'an and Neo-Confucianism. As biographical compilations and the *yu-lu* of individual masters became more readily available, the encounter stories, the question-and-answer dialogues between Ch'an masters and their disciples, were avidly studied, and used in practice. In time these kōans began to lose their freshness and degenerated into intellectual constructions. The masters of the Yün-men and Fa-yen Houses had established a custom of providing their own comments on old stories or kōan, adding verses or giving alternative answers to some dialogues. Early in the Sung period Hsüeh-tou Ch'ung-hsien (980–1052) produced a compilation of verses commenting on kōan stories, entitled *Pai-tse sung-ku* (One hundred kōans with comments in verse), which represented a further step toward the literary approach to Ch'an through works suitable for study, memorization, and discussion, and away from the free and spontaneous Ch'an of the T'ang. Later, Yüan-wu K'o-ch'in (1063–1135) of the Yang-ch'i line of the Lin-chi school made comments on the hundred kōans that Hsüeh-tou had collected, and added his own verse and commentary. This was the most famous of kōan collections, the *Pi-yen lu*, or *Blue Cliff Records*.

When the Sung court, under barbarian pressure, was forced to abandon its capital at K'ai-feng and move to the south in 1126, it established itself in Ling-an, south of the Yangtze, an area in which Buddhism had long flourished. The principal figures of the Yang-ch'i school of Lin-chi, who had the support of officials at the highest level of government, moved with them. The Sung government, in order to maintain control over Buddhism, instituted a large number of regulations and an elaborate administrative organization to carry them out. Chief among them was the Five Mountains and Ten Temple system, a form of temple ranking that was later introduced into Japan. Five principal mountains, or important temples, together with ten temples of lesser rank, were designated as official government temples. These temples were located chiefly in the areas of present-day Chekiang, Anhui, and Fukien provinces. Abbots were appointed by the Court, and one of their principal functions was to offer prayers and services for the emperor and the nation. This system further contributed to the formalization of temple activities and the stabilization of temple life. Since these designated temples were generally in the area south of the Yangtze, many famous temples were never included in the classification.

By far the most eminent Sung priest was Ta-hui Tsung-kao (1089–1163), whose successors played a prominent role in this Five Mountains system. He is most noted for organizing the kōans into a system, making Ch'an more accessible to monks and laymen alike. By this time the *Pi-yen lu* had gained immense popularity, and students read the work eagerly, memorizing passages, and seeking for answers to Ch'an within this book rather than attending to their own practice. Ta-hui, distressed by the situation, had the woodblocks of the book burned and any copies at hand destroyed, so great a hindrance to Ch'an practice did he find this work that had been compiled by his own teacher, Yüan-wu K'o-ch'in.

Ta-hui was himself a prominent literary figure, and several works, including a collection of letters to prominent government officials, are associated with his name. Ch'an was moving more and more towards expression in literary terms. Despite his literary leanings, Ta-hui sought to return to the original form of the kōan as a device for probing and illumining the depths of the mind. He advocated a form of meditation in which the whole body and mind was concentrated in an ardent search for enlightenment, always under the guidance of a teacher. He attacked the kind of Ch'an known as silent illumination *(mo-chao)* Ch'an, which failed, he felt, to instill the "great doubt," so essential to awakening, and advocated instead "introspecting the kōan" *(k'an-hua)* Ch'an. Silent illumination or quiet sitting had, of course, long been subject to critical attack. Shen-hui accused Northern Ch'an of a meditation that consisted of examining the mind and examining purity. In the Sung "silent illumination" was associated with the Ts'ao-tung school, whose leading practitioner was Hung-chih Cheng-chüeh (1091–1157). Despite spirited controversy, Hung-chih and Ta-hui were friends; indeed, Hung-chih requested that Ta-hui attend to his affairs after his death. Their disagreement has been seen as one between the Lin-chi and Ts'ao-tung schools; between the use of the kōan and the reliance on meditation alone. During the Sung, however, the Ts'ao-tung school used the kōan extensively. Hung-chih himself compiled a collection of a hundred kōans to which he attached verses. Later Wan-sung Hsing-hsiu (1166–1246) lectured twice on the collection and used it as the basis of his *Ts'ung-jung lu* (Record of the Ts'ung-jung hermitage) published in 1224. This work occupied roughly the same position in the Ts'ao-tung School as did the *Pi-yen lu* in the Lin-chi, although the latter is far better known. The organized kōan system was the hallmark of Sung Ch'an. This Ch'an was exported to Japan by Chinese priests going to that country or through Japanese priests coming to the mainland for study. Virtually all extant Chinese texts made their way to Japan. One of the later works, of much greater importance in Japan than in China, was the *Wu-men kuan*, the Gateless Barrier (1229), compiled by Wu-men Hui-k'ai (1183–1260), a collection of forty-eight selected kōan to which commentaries and verses were added. In form it is similar to the *Pi-yen lu*; however, emphasis is placed on the celebrated *wu* (J. *mu*) kōan, to which Ta-hui Ch'an attached great importance, and which to this day is often the first kōan assigned to the beginning student.

In 1279 the Sung surrendered to the Mongol invaders and the Yüan dynasty was established. The Mongols embraced an uncomplicated folk religion, as well as Lamaism; they were, however, sympathetic to existing Ch'an temples, protected them, and gave them support. Many Japanese came to China for study during this period, and the records show that a large number of Chinese priests flourished at this time. Of particular importance was the priest Chung-feng Ming-pen (1263–1323), who taught a form of Buddhism that combined Pure Land and Ch'an teachings. He had several Japanese disciples who were instrumental in establishing a school known as the Genju-ha, after the name of Chung-feng's hermitage, and he was for a while a dominant force in Rinzai Zen in Japan. This association of Ch'an and Pure Land was not a new phenomenon. Already in the T'ang dynasty we hear of Ch'an priests, especially in the Fa-yen line, who advocated the calling of the Buddha's name (nien-fo). Yung-ming Yen-shou (904–975), a second-generation Fa-yen monk, was an early supporter of this practice. He is famous as the compiler of the monumental Tsung-ching lu (Mirror of the teaching) of 951, a work of 100 volumes that contains quotations from some sixty canonical works, selected passages from three hundred Indian and Chinese worthies, selections from yu-lu, and excerpts from the works of other schools of Buddhism. The work was designed as a means of bringing together Ch'an and the other schools of Buddhism.

When the Yüan dynasty was succeeded by the native Chinese Ming dynasty (1368–1644), Ch'an had changed completely, although the traditional transmission of the lineage from master to disciple was maintained. The kōan Ch'an of the Sung that had developed from the great masters of the late T'ang and Five Dynasties periods was no longer practiced. Neo-Confucianism continued to dominate in government and literati circles and Ch'an and Pure Land doctrines were taught side by side. Buddhism, part popular, part scholarly, continued to exist, but played an insignificant role in the intellectual scene. Celebrated Ch'an practitioners of the period include Yun-ch'i Chu-hung (1535–1615), a prolific writer whose Ch'an-kuan ts'e-chin (Progress in the path of Ch'an) was widely used in both China and Japan, and Ou-i Chih-hsu (1599–1655), who emphasized a highly syncretic form of Buddhism that attempted to combine Ch'an with the teaching schools of Buddhism.

Bibliography

Abe Chōichi. Zen no sekai: kōan. Tokyo: Chikuma Shobō, 1966.

Buswell, Robert. E. The Formation of Ch'an Ideology in China and Korea: The Vajrasamādhi-Sūtra, a Buddhist Apocryphon. Princeton: Princeton University Press, 1989.

Dumoulin, Heinrich. Zen Buddhism: A History. 2 vols. New York: Macmillan, 1988, 1990.

Gimello, Robert M., and Peter N. Gregory, eds. Studies in Ch'an and Hua-yen. Honolulu: University of Hawai'i Press, 1983.

Gregory, Peter N. Tsung-mi and the Sinification of Buddhism. Princeton: Princeton University Press, 1991.

Hu Shih. "Ch'an (Zen) Buddhism in China, its History and Method." *Philosophy East and West* 3:1 (April 1953).

――――. "The Development of Zen Buddhism in China." *The Chinese Social and Political Science Review* 15:4 (January 1932).

Lai, Whalen and Lewis Lancaster, eds. *Early Ch'an in China and Tibet*. Berkeley Buddhist Studies 5. Berkeley: Asian Humanities Press, 1983.

McRae, John R. *The Northern School and the Formation of Early Ch'an Buddhism*. Honolulu: University of Hawai'i Press, 1986.

Tanaka Ryōshō and Shinohara Hisao, eds. *Tonkō butten to zen*. Kōza Tonkō, vol. 8. Tokyo: Daitō Shuppansha.

Tanaka Ryōshō. *Tonkō zenshū bunken no kenkyū*. Tokyo: Daitō Shuppansha, 1983.

Yampolsky, Philip. *The Platform Sutra of the Sixth Patriarch*. New York: Columbia University Press, 1967.

Yanagida Seizan. *Shoki zenshū shisho no kenkyū*. Kyoto: Zen Bunka Kenkyūjo, 1967.

――――. "Chūgoku zenshū shi." In *Kōza zen*, vol. 3. Tokyo: Chikuma Shobō, 1967.

II. *Ch'an Spirituality*

THOMAS P. KASULIS

Accounting to tradition, Ch'an Buddhism began with a smile, a knowing smile. The story is that the Buddha Śākyamuni was sitting with his disciples to give a lecture when, instead of speaking, he held up a flower, twirled it, and winked. Only one monk, Mahākāśyapa, understood and smiled. That, according to the legend, was the birth of Ch'an. But what did Mahākāśyapa know and how did he come to know it?

The word *ch'an* ultimately derives from the Sanskrit term *dhyāna*, a high-level meditative state that achieves insight by quieting the passions. But how is this *dhyāna* achieved and what is its function? Through *dhyāna* what can one know? Ch'an's very survival depended on its ability to answer these questions in a manner appropriate to its Chinese context in different historical periods.

From Bodhidharma through Seng-ts'an, the first through the third patriarchs, Ch'an meditation was primarily solitary and consisted exclusively of sitting contemplation. Though meditation is important to virtually all Buddhist schools, in Bodhidharma's case, even in the earliest legendary accounts of his life, meditation is given a unique prominence. On arriving at the Shao-lin temple, it is said, Bodhidharma sat for nine years "wall-gazing" (*pi-kuan*). We do not know exactly what this practice entailed, but obviously, given the story's emphasis, the early Chinese Buddhist historians were struck by Bodhidharma's single-minded focus on meditation instead of chanting, reading sūtras, preaching, or writing commentaries. Furthermore, this practice was meant to gain insight, not to develop magical powers, a goal to which meditation had often been subordinated in traditions of that time, Taoist as well as Buddhist. Apparently, Bodhidharma did not even want disciples, and Hui-k'o, the eventual Second Patriarch, had to cut off his own arm before Bodhidharma would be moved by his earnestness and allow him to sit with him.

What was the purpose of this wall-gazing? Again, there is no reliable documentation, but the traditional story is suggestive: Bodhidharma handed Hui-k'o a copy of the *Laṅkāvatāra Sūtra* as a sign of the Ch'an transmission.

This emphasis on the *Laṅkāvatāra Sūtra* continued for the next few generations, early records often referring to Ch'an as a "Laṅkāvatāra school." So, the sūtra must give at least a clue about the purpose of Bodhidharma's sitting.

The *Laṅkāvatāra Sūtra*, especially the sections translated into Chinese by Bodhidharma's time, is an abstruse text so full of Indian Buddhist jargon that one wonders how well the early Ch'an Buddhists could have understood it. Two aspects stand out, however, as themes important throughout Ch'an history. First, as primarily an idealist text loosely associated with the Yogācāra tradition, the *Laṅkāvatāra Sūtra* makes mind the basis for experience. We know not the world itself, but the world as it appears in our minds. If the mind is pure, it reflects reality; if tainted, it distorts. Fortunately, according to the Sūtra, purity is attainable. Within each of us is the originally pure store-consciousness *(ālaya-vijñāna),* or alternatively, the Buddha-womb or Buddha-embryo *(tathāgatagarbha)*. By shutting down the functions of the egocentric passions in meditation, we can manifest this inherent enlightenment.

The second emphasis in the *Laṅkāvatāra Sūtra* important to our purposes is ineffability. The sūtra is conscious of its own limitations: words can only suggest or point; ultimately, the pure mind must be experienced through meditation to be understood. Like the emphasis on mind, the idea of the limitations of doctrine and the importance of experiential verification runs throughout the Ch'an tradition. It becomes increasingly important for Ch'an Buddhists to insist that their school is not based in any text (it is *not* a "Laṅkāvatāra school"). Rather, Ch'an's basis is the direct transmission of mind from master to disciple.

Three elements in the early Ch'an tradition ran counter to general Chinese spiritual tendencies. First, there was the emphasis on practicing alone or with just one's master. China is a community-oriented society that frowns upon overly individualistic behavior. Although Taoism did have a tradition of the hermit recluse, the Confucian intellectuals increasingly criticized that lifestyle as antisocial, and hence not fully human. Whereas Indian mythology celebrated the superhuman realm of devas, buddhas, and bodhisattvas, the indigenous Chinese mythology sang the praises of *human* perfection, the sage-king. So for Ch'an to take root in China it had to mute its Indian transcendental tendencies and show an interest in societal life within this world.

It is not surprising, therefore, that the fourth Ch'an patriarch, Tao-hsin (580–651), established the idea of a Ch'an monastic community in which monks cultivated fields as well as the mind. These communities could, therefore, be self-sufficient, not depending on begging. Begging remained a spiritual exercise, but unlike Buddhist communities in India, the Ch'an Buddhists did not need the charity of others for survival. Although often secluded in mountains far from the secular society of the lowlands and cities, the Ch'an communities still developed social, as well as individual, character. This made them more acceptable to those holding traditional Chinese values.

A second, closely associated, non-Chinese element in early Ch'an was its tendency toward escapism. To gaze at a wall for nine years is not only anti-social; it is also a rejection of the phenomena in everyday life. Even the Taoist hermits, upon leaving the secular world, communed with nature in the mountains. They at least were seeking at least a natural, if not social, harmony. Wall-gazing, on the other hand, seemed so introspective as to be solipsistic. To be accepted as a Chinese spiritual tradition, Ch'an had to integrate its introspective tendencies with the search for naturalness. The need for such integration is found in the story of the meeting between Tao-hsin and Niu-t'ou Fa-jung (594–657).

According to the legend, Tao-hsin, the strong advocate of meditation, work, and communal spirituality, went to visit the renowned Ch'an mountain recluse, Fa-jung. Fa-jung lived alone in the mountains among the wild beasts, emphasizing naturalness rather than communal meditation, hoping in this way to be a spontaneous manifestation of the buddha-activity. In this respect, Fa-jung acted much like a Taoist. When talking quietly with Fa-jung, Tao-hsin heard a tiger's roar close by and was visibly shaken (or pretended to be). Fa-jung snorted, "There is still this in you." When Fa-jung went away for a moment, Tao-hsin painted the character for "Buddha" on the rock Fa-jung used for a seat. When Fa-jung returned to sit down, he saw the character and hesitated. Tao-hsin retorted, "There is still this in you." The tradition says that Fa-jung then became Tao-hsin's student.

In this story we see an emphasis on the need for integrating social and natural harmony. One should be at home and at peace with both nature and other people. One should also recognize that the Buddha-nature is omnipresent and that to retreat from society to find the Buddha is not to see what is right under you.

In short, in the early seventh century, Ch'an developed two ideals that would remain central themes in its spirituality: monastic community and harmony with nature. Also, around this time there were the first indications of a subtle shift in emphasis from the *Laṅkāvatāra Sūtra* to the *Diamond Sūtra*, a text in the perfection of wisdom (*prajñāpāramitā*) tradition. Fa-jung's own teachings, for example, interpreted enlightenment in terms of

5. Lin-chi (d.866), from a late 15th-century drawing by Soga Dasaku

emptiness *(śūnyatā)* as much as mind. This shift in terminology would ultimately be an element in the schism between the northern and southern
branches of Ch'an.

Although both the *Laṅkāvatāra* and the *Diamond* sūtras maintained the
ineffability of enlightenment, the former's emphasis on the purity of mind
seemed more positive in formulation than the latter's focus on emptiness.
This difference is relevant to practice as well as theory. If *dhyāna*'s focus is
the purification of mind, there can be gradations of purity and one may

need to practice continuously to maintain that purity. Such an interpretation was associated with the northern branch established by Shen-hsiu
(605–706) and rooted in the *Laṅkāvatāra* tradition. Emptiness, on the other
hand, must be realized totally or not at all. So the southern branch associated with Hui-neng (638–713) and the *Diamond Sūtra* emphasized the sud-
denness of realization. Shen-hui (670–762) provoked the conflict between
the southern and northern schools after the deaths of both Shen-hsiu and
Hui-neng. His apologetics claimed that only his master, Hui-neng,
deserved the title of sixth patriarch, so Shen-hsiu's tradition was unauthentic.

Viewed from our historical distance, the philosophical difference was simply a matter of emphasis. Even the "gradual enlightenment" masters in the
north recognized the importance of conversion, the sudden turning point in
one's spiritual development. And the "sudden enlightenment" practitioners
of the south admitted that insight had to be continuously integrated into
everyday life. The Niu-t'ou (Oxhead) school, among others, managed not
to ally itself with either faction, seeing itself as consistent with the thrust of
both traditions. Why, then, did the difference between north and south
result in schism instead of synthesis? A major factor was political.

Through Empress Wu's patronage of Shen-hsiu, the northern branch of
Ch'an became urbanized, attaining the status of a state religion. In
attempting to undermine the northern branch's political base by calling
into question the legitimacy of its lineage, Shen-hui cast the two branches
as adversaries, and what were once differences in nuance became hard and
fast positions. Then, as the political stability of the court declined, the
northern school lost its base of support. So, too, did Shen-hui's urban oriented lineage of the southern school. The more distant, rural, and less literate centers of the southern branch were not seriously affected, however.
The northern branch gradually died out and the southern branch endured,
at least insofar as all future Ch'an patriarchs would trace their lineage
through Hui-neng, not Shen-hsiu. Accompanying this development was
the shift from the literary study of Ch'an in the cities to the practice of
Ch'an amidst the everyday activities of the country.

The next phase in the development of Ch'an spirituality resulted from the
repercussions of the schism. In particular, as the *Laṅkāvatāra Sūtra* was deemphasized, along with the associated ideal of mind-cultivation, the role of
meditation also underwent reevaluation. Rather than using constant sitting
to purify the mind, the masters developed new techniques to trigger the
sudden manifestation of no-mind. Enlightenment was no longer cultivated
in the meditation hall, but manifested suddenly in otherwise ordinary activities: washing the bowls, hearing the bamboo strike a stone, seeing the

plum blossoms. Ma-tsu (709–788)—and such famous dharma descendants of his as Nan-ch'uan (748–835), Chao-chou (778–897), Huang-po (?–850?), and Lin-chi (?–866?)—developed shock techniques such as shouting, beating, and using irrational retorts to startle their students into realization. Their preliminary aim was to frustrate their disciples, bringing them to the brink of the breakdown known as the Great Doubt. Only then could they spur them to break through that crisis, to transcend all delusive egocentricity and to realize the way things really are.

Such radical, disorienting techniques worked best within a larger, stable context of training. The rules of Pai-chang Huai-hai (720–814) established a comprehensive system to regulate all monastic affairs, at least those outside the direct interaction between master and disciple. So the seemingly irrational, even bizarre, behavior of the masters was within a highly structured environment. This was the strength of the enduring Lin-chi (Japanese Rinzai) lineage.

The other major line continuing into the present is the Ts'ao-tung (Japanese Sōtō). This tradition placed less emphasis on the shock techniques of the Lin-chi line and more on meditation itself. Two founding patriarchs, Tung-shan (807–869) and Ts'ao-shan (840–901), were famous for developing the five ranks theory. This doctrine articulated in detail the fivefold relations between the universal and particular or the absolute and relative (*cheng* and *p'ien*). The theory outlined the various states of integration between the two, the enlightened state representing complete unity. Ts'ao-shan wrote extensive commentaries on the theory, using terminology borrowed from the *I Ching*, Confucianism, and other Chinese Buddhist philosophies.

The systemization represented by the five ranks theory was by no means limited to the Ts'ao-tung school, however. The eighth century was a time in which various sets of categories and systems developed within all the Ch'an traditions. This interest in classification was partly a response to the comprehensive philosophical systems Hua-yen and T'ien-t'ai Buddhism had conceived in the preceding century and a half. These Chinese Buddhist schools had, for the first time, gone beyond the ideas of their Indian predecessors and developed distinctively Chinese Buddhist interpretations of reality. Their hallmark was an interest in explaining the complete integration and harmony of all things.

Given the unsatisfactory attempts to explain Ch'an doctrine using the Indian *Laṅkāvatāra* or *Diamond* sūtras, it was natural for the Ch'an Buddhists to be interested in Buddhist ideas developed in their own country, especially insofar as they could help articulate the meaning of harmony experienced through Ch'an practice. So even Lin-chi, for example, showed a propensity for classification not found in Ma-tsu or Huang-po, using such schemata as the fourfold relation between guest and host, the three mysteries, and the four classifications (relating to subject and object). Early commentators as well as modern scholars have pointed out the Hua-yen influence in these categories. Indeed, Tsung-mi (780–841), a master in the Ho-tse line, so integrated Hua-yen and Ch'an philosophies that he became a patriarch in both traditions.

This tendency to look for indigenous rather than foreign roots for its tradition also affected Ch'an's view of its texts. The Indian sūtras were deemphasized and a new form of textual tradition developed through the compilations of records or sayings (yu-lu) of the Ch'an masters. Although the masters did not generally write themselves, their students recorded their sayings for them, writing them posthumously and handing them down to future generations of Ch'an students.

In the recorded sayings, we find the culmination of a process going back to the early days of Ch'an. The essence of enlightenment came to be identified with the interaction between masters and students. Whatever insight dhyāna might bring, its verification was always interpersonal. In effect, enlightenment came to be understood not so much as an insight, but as a way of acting in the world with other people. It is significant, for example, that Lin-chi shifted his focus from the terminology of the "pure mind" to an emphasis on the "true person without status." In this respect, Ch'an spirituality had become completely Sinicized.

As the records of Ch'an masters accumulated and the Lin-chi as well as Ts'ao-tung schools put increasing emphasis on kōan study, snippets of the records were collected separately in kōan anthologies. So the key points in previous Ch'an encounters between masters and students became the vehicle for later interactions. Masters would assign students specific kōans to ponder and break through, just as the original students in the Ch'an records had achieved insight when the kōan had been first uttered.

The Lin-chi and Ts'ao-tung schools ultimately diverged over how much emphasis should be given to such kōan practice. In the twelfth century, Hung-chih (1091–1157) of the Ts'ao-tung school argued for a return to the "silent illumination" of meditation, whereas his Lin-chi rival Ta-hui (1089–1163) criticized this view as an inauthentic divergence from understanding enlightenment to be activity, not quiescence. Since the two masters remained on good terms personally throughout their lives, the difference was probably again a matter of degree. Hung-chih worried about an overuse of the kōan practice that would reduce it to mere wordplay and verbal gymnastics, whereas Ta-hui wanted to prevent meditation from degenerating into escapism. In any case, the descendants of these masters were not always so generous in their estimation of the other position and the debate was even rekindled in Japan half a millennium later.

A final stage in the development of Ch'an spirituality was its synthesis with Pure Land teachings during the Ming dynasty. The Pure Land tradition focused on A-mi-t'o (J. Amida) Buddha as a salvational figure who would help those who expressed faith in him. By expressing trust in A-mi-t'o through visualizing his glorious form or voicing his name, the devout Pure Land Buddhist obtained the assurance of birth in the Pure Land. In the early days of Ch'an, there were some meditative Pure Land practices such as contemplating the image of A-mi-t'o, but these died out with the dominance of the southern Ch'an.

By the tenth century, however, Pure Land Buddhism had become a significant spiritual force in China, and various Pure Land practices found their way into Ch'an communities. Sometimes these practices were considered equivalents of Ch'an practice, sometimes supplements for those who could not succeed in the more rigorous Ch'an discipline, and sometimes anathema. Where they were accepted, a common interpretation was that the Buddha A-mi-t'o was not a transcendent saving deity on whom one had to depend, but a symbol for the buddhahood inherent in each person's mind. In any case, by the end of the fourteenth century Pure Land practices were accepted in almost all Ch'an temples.

Reviewing this rich history, it is easy to miss the forest for the trees. One can focus too much on the differences among the schools and miss their common core. Indeed, at their worst moments even the Ch'an Buddhists themselves engaged in divisive apologetics. But if we go back to Mahākāśyapa's smile, we can more clearly see what characterized the distinctiveness of Ch'an spirituality in all its historical manifestations.

Ch'an was founded not on a text or doctrine, not even on an explicitly defined practice. It originated in a gesture and a response—Śākyamuni's twirling the flower and Mahākāśyapa's smile. The essence of Ch'an is in that singular moment of personal encounter wherein a master's insight touches the student's inherent purity of being. The student is forever changed by seeing self and world from a new perspective. Whether the smile is the capstone of years of sitting in meditation or a sudden reversal in the direction one has been going, whether it is the complete expression of enlightenment or only its emergence, and whether it represents the purity of mind or an immersion into emptiness are all secondary considerations. The interaction itself and the insight it triggers are the essence of Ch'an. On this point there is no disagreement.

Bibliography

Aitken, Robert, trans. *The Gateless Barrier: The Wu-men Kuan (Mumonkan)*. San Francisco: North Point Press, 1990.

Dumoulin, Heinrich. *Zen Buddhism: A History*. 2 vols. New York: Macmillan, 1988, 1990.

Foster, Nelson, and Jack Shoemaker, eds. *The Roaring Stream: A New Zen Reader*. Hopewell, NJ: Ecco Press, 1996.

Hoover, Thomas. *The Zen Experience*. New York: New American Library, 1980.

Kasulis, Thomas P. *Zen Action, Zen Person*. Honolulu: University of Hawai'i Press, 1981.

Miura, Isshū, and Ruth Fuller Sasaki. *Zen Dust: The History of the Koan and Koan Study in Rinzai (Lin-chi) Zen*. New York: Harcourt, Brace, and World, 1966.

Morinaga, Soko, trans. *A Treatise on the Ceasing of Notions*. London: Zen Center, 1988.

Nan Huai-Chin. *The Story of Chinese Zen*. Boston-Tokyo: Tuttle, 1995.

Pine, Red, trans. *The Zen Teaching of Bodhidharma*. New York-Tokyo: Weatherhill, 1992.

Powell, William F., trans. *The Record of Tung-shan*. Honolulu: University of Hawai'i Press, 1986.

Sekida Katsuki, trans. *Two Zen Classics:* Mumonkan *and* Hekiganroku. New York-Tokyo: Weatherhill, 1977.

Sheng-yen, Ch'an Master, trans. *Complete Enlightenment: Translation and Commentary on The Sutra of Complete Enlightenment*. Elmhurst, NY: Dharma Drum Publications, 1997.

Shibayama Zenkei. *Zen Comments on the* Mumonkan. New York: Harper and Row, 1974.

Wu, John C. H. *The Golden Age of Zen*. New York: Doubleday, 1996.

III. *Four Ch'an Masters*

DALE WRIGHT

W HEN, IN 833, the great Chinese Buddhist scholar, Kuei-feng Tsung-mi (780-841), completed his detailed description and evaluation of Ch'an Buddhism in his era, one kind of Ch'an that he paid particular attention to, especially by way of criticism, was what he called the "Hung-chou" school (see *Zen no goroku* 8, 156). This title referred to a new style of Ch'an spirituality that originated in the Hung-chou region of south-central China (now northern Chiang-si province) and that was by 833 being rapidly disseminated throughout southern China. According to the leading historian of this religious movement, Yanagida Seizan, what Tsung-mi feared—the dominance of this seemingly crude, rural form of spirituality—was already a foregone conclusion. Indeed, retrospectively, we can see that all versions of Ch'an/Zen that exist today and that have been so influential in East Asian cultural history since the tenth century trace their emergence and lineage in some way to this Hung-chou Ch'an.

Historical origins are often obscure, and this is especially so in this case. How Hung-chou religious practices and concerns emerged out of and are related to the early Ch'an of the "East Mountain" monastery, or of Shen-hsiu and Shen-hui, or the voluminous Ch'an documents found at Tun-huang, is a puzzling issue. Nevertheless, it is clear that the teaching practice of one monk, the renowned Ma-tsu Tao-i (709-788), is what brought Hung-chou Ch'an to the forefront of T'ang dynasty religious concern. Originally a monk from Szechwan, Ma-tsu settled in the Hung-chou region of Chiang-si, where he developed a unique style of Ch'an practice and teaching. Drawing upon the strength of his rural background, he rejected the practice in earlier Ch'an—indeed in Chinese Buddhism generally—of a cloistered life of study, ritual, and meditation in favor of an active life of involvement in and among the people of this region. Traveling from town to town and temple to temple, lecturing publicly and to the local elite, and presenting an unschooled but powerful presence, Ma-tsu converted the people of this region to a dynamic new form of spirituality.

Records claim that Ma-tsu taught well over a hundred monks who, spreading out into adjacent areas, became the next generation of teachers propagating the Hung-chou style of Ch'an.

By the early ninth century, during the time of the second and third generation of monks following Ma-tsu, it appears that Hung-chou Ch'an had organized itself into clearly defined monastic communities supported by, in addition to their own labor, the increasingly prosperous villages and cities that spread out over the Chiang-si farmlands. These monasteries, only traces of which remain today, were typically located in mountain valleys often ten miles or so apart with supporting temples in the towns and cities. The most famous of these institutions at times housed up to a thousand practitioners, although generally they were smaller. Tradition tells us the Pai-chang Huai-hai (720-814), perhaps Ma-tsu's most important student, was the first to construct a new set of monastic regulations to suit this new kind of Buddhist practice. A slightly later textual version of this code published in 1004, the *Ch'an-men-kuei-shih* in the *Transmission of the Lamp* (T 51.250-1), is the oldest available to us. It describes the monastery layout with its focus on the monks' hall where all practitioners meditate, eat, and sleep. It discusses hierarchy and organization, and stipulates rules of conduct for all participants. This and other documents also allude to kinds of spiritual practice characteristic of the community, on which we now focus our attention.

The word Ch'an means meditation, and that was no doubt the primary practice as well as descriptive characteristic of early Ch'an. Meditation had from the beginning been one dimension of Buddhist practice, at least in principle if not in actuality, but the early Ch'an monks were the first in China to accord it a central place. Without discarding meditation altogether, Hung-chou Ch'an seems to have once again shifted the focus of concern away from this contemplative practice. Without question, meditation continued to have a role in their practice. But more often than recommending it, the literature of Hung-chou Ch'an criticizes the practice of meditation, or more precisely, it criticizes the attitude or understanding in terms of which meditation was being practiced.

A famous story in one biography of Ma-tsu's teacher, Nan-yüeh Huai-jang, in the *Transmission of the Lamp*, has traditionally been taken as the most powerful expression of this point. Ma-tsu, a student eager for spiritual progress, sat long hours in meditation. Observing his absorption one day, his teacher asked the obvious question, "What is the great virtue of sitting in meditation?" Ma-tsu replied, "Accomplishing Buddhahood!" The teacher then picked up a tile and began to rub it on a stone. Ma-tsu asked,

"What are you doing?" "Making a mirror." Ma-tsu asked again, "How is it possible to obtain a mirror by rubbing a tile?" The story ends with Huai-jang's rhetorical question, "How is it possible to obtain Buddhahood by sitting in meditation?" (T 51.240c).

That it would indeed bring about that goal was an assumption of early Ch'an. But at least by Ma-tsu's time some teachers began to conclude that the understanding supporting this practice had the effect of precluding the very realization to which it was directed. What practice aimed at a goal of attainment presupposes is that human beings lack something fundamental, that there is something that is attainable from someplace else. But this is just what the Hung-chou masters denied: "Since you are already fundamentally complete, don't add on spurious practices" (Ch'uan-hsin fa-yao, T 48.379c).

One of the most common Hung-chou sayings provides the rationale for this shift of understanding concerning the practice of meditation or any other practice: "This very mind is Buddha!" What Ma-tsu and others communicated through this saying is that what seems to be the most remote, transcendental goal is, paradoxically, nearest to us. Hung-chou monks, like other Buddhists before them, spoke of enlightenment as a "return," a return to and encounter with one's own deepest nature. This "original nature," a spontaneous attunement to the world, is what is most easily overlooked in the act of striving for a remote goal. Therefore, Huang-po (d. 850), Pai-chang's most celebrated student, responds to the question—How does one bring about enlightened mind?—in the following way:

> "Enlightenment is not something to be attained. If right now you bring forth this 'non-attaining' mind, steadfastly not obtaining anything, then this *is* enlightened mind. Enlightenment is not a place to reside. For this reason there is nothing attainable. Therefore, [the Buddha] said: 'When I was still in the realm of Dīpaṃkara Buddha, there was not the slightest thing attainable'." (Wan Ling-lu, T 48.385c; Blofeld, 83)

The act of striving is itself what creates the distance or separation that striving seeks to overcome. A "dualism" separating the practitioner from the goal of practice was the presupposed background that had supported not only the practice of meditation but also the entirety of Buddhist practice. Yet even striving could not be rejected in a dualistic way; somehow the appropriate posture was beyond both extremes, striving and its negation. Thus, *The Extensive Record of Pai-chang (Pai-chang kuang-lu)* claims:

> A Buddha is a person who does not seek. If you seek this you spoil it. The principle is one of non-seeking. Seek it and it is lost. If one holds onto non-seeking, this is still the same as seeking. (411)

The admonition not to seek, difficult indeed in an institution centered on spiritual quest, functioned to direct the practitioner to what is already here, that is, to the "ordinary" that one previously hoped to transcend. This redirection of attention to the "ordinary" and the "everyday" is perhaps the most characteristic theme of Hung-chou Ch'an. For them, "Everyday mind is the Way." Meditation, therefore, need not be a special activity requiring its own time, setting, and posture. Every moment of life, "sitting, standing, or lying down," ought to be seen as a primordial manifestation of Buddha-nature. This reorientation to the ordinary enabled a dramatic transformation of Ch'an practice—anything could be considered a "practice" if by practice one means, not one activity among others that one does toward a pregiven goal, but just what one does. According to Tsung-mi's more traditional point of view this went too far, even to the point of regarding "the moving of a muscle or the blinking of an eye" as a sign of Buddha-nature. A sanctification of the ordinary meant that, to be a Buddhist, one need not speak in a classical language; ordinary, colloquial language was even closer to the fundamental attunement within which one dwells by birthright anyway. The manual labor that at least partially supported the Hung-chou monasteries could likewise be taken, not as something menial and base, but as a practice expressing one's deepest nature. "Chopping wood and carrying water," the most ordinary of T'ang dynasty tasks, were to be seen as the extraordinary Way itself. Given this reversal of Buddhist priorities, the presumptuous young monk, Lin-chi, could say that what his teacher, Huang-po, had to transmit to him was "not much" (T 47.504c; Sasaki, 51).

That the extra-ordinary was to be found nowhere except within the ordinary was perhaps the most important principle in T'ang dynasty Buddhist thought generally, and had therefore been formulated in various theoretical ways before Ma-tsu's time. What the Hung-chou masters contributed to this principle was twofold: first, a realization that the principle had the effect of undermining the theoretical (and dualistic) formalism within which it was established, and second, a way of integrating the principle into authentic daily life.

Integrating Ch'an thought and realization into daily life required not only a new way of acting, but also a new way of speaking. No practice so distinctly characterizes Hung-chou Ch'an as its discursive practice. In examining the kinds of rhetoric found in the literary traditions of Hung-chou Ch'an, we need to reflect briefly on our sources. There are numerous texts that transmit this kind of Ch'an to us. They consist not in the writings of Hung-chou masters but in collections of "sayings" remembered, recorded, and circulated among monks and laypeople of the area.

These include segments of lectures, question and answer sessions, uncon-textualized sayings, and descriptions of actions—especially encounters between Ch'an masters—all of which circulated in manuscript form until they were collected, edited, and printed in later centuries. What this means is that our sources for and access to Hung-chou Ch'an, like any other great epoch of spirituality, are historically mediated. We understand Hung-chou Ch'an today via the intense religious interests and needs of later monks (in the early Sung dynasty and beyond) reflected in their projects of collecting, editing, and publishing texts.

The Hung-chou masters did not write for ideological reasons—they rejected the kinds of formal study that characterized Buddhist practice up until their time. Following Bodhidharma's criticism of "dependence on words and letters," they sought a mode of being free from the kinds of clo-sure and rigidity that language and texts suggested to them. They tended to stress their difference from earlier traditions in order to set out a new identity for practicing monks. In retrospect, we can see that these differ-ences, while real, were not as great as Hung-chou rhetoric claimed. The language of Pai-chang and Huang-po, for instance, is laced with references to Buddhist sūtras; clearly, they were accustomed to closing an argument with a sūtra quotation, thereby substantiating the point, as was the prac-tice in Buddhist discourse. Sometimes, sayings recorded as the language of the master were actually segments from sūtras or other texts. Nevertheless, a movement away from dependence on sūtras began to take place in Hung-chou Ch'an. The colloquial language of these monks was also a significant departure from the formal language of the earlier tradition. Many of their contemporary critics, including Tsung-mi, took this deviation from tradition to be a sign of "ignorance" rather than realization.

Though a great deal of Hung-chou rhetoric is anti-study, anti-text, and anti-language, it would be a mistake on our part to read this "language" literal-ly, without recognizing the fundamental role that study, text, and language did in fact play in Hung-chou Ch'an. Reading, for example, continued to be an important practice, although what Hung-chou monks read and how they read underwent transformation. The way of reading shifted from focus on the objective content of sūtras to personal, experiential appropriation by the reader, while what they read gradually shifted from sūtras to accounts of words and actions of Ch'an masters. There was also a greater emphasis on spoken discourse, on lectures, question and answer sessions, and what came to be known as encounter dialogues. But whenever spoken discourse seems important, it inevitably gets written down, especially in a society as thoroughly literate as China had become. On this basis a new genre of

6. Huang-po (d.849?).　　　　7. Pai-chang (749–814).

Buddhist literature emerged in Hung-chou Ch'an, the *yu-lu* or "Discourse Record" texts. So eager were these monks to appropriate the language of their masters and other renowned teachers of Ch'an that they kept personal notebooks recording significant sayings and events. These eventually circulated, first among copractitioners and then more broadly, becoming in effect the new sūtras.

Although these monks typically spoke and wrote of overcoming emphasis on language, none of the foregoing would indicate that this was in fact what they did. Quite to the contrary, focus on language was heightened. Although monks reduced the volume and scope of their reading, they practiced "close reading" to the extreme, attempting to realize and then to embody the depth indicated in the words. By the late ninth century it seems to have been widely understood that, given proper focus and meditation on them, certain words could evoke a sudden breakthrough and turn in awareness. In Lin-chi's recorded sayings, examples of this enabling language are called "turning words" (T 47.503a; Sasaki, 40). Many *yu-lu* texts record accounts of these events, for example: "*At these words* [Pai-chang] experienced realization" (*Pai-chang yu-lu*, 409; my emphasis).

This shift of focus, from knowledge of sūtra or treatise content to in-depth appropriation of the sayings, is significant. It parallels a shift from argument—or "proof"—oriented discourse to rhetoric that demonstrates or reveals. Many Hung-chou texts contain both styles, interconnected in interesting ways, but the historical drift was clearly toward the latter. According to the *Pai-chang yu-lu* (409; Cleary, 19), when Huang-po came in search of Hung-chou wisdom, the first thing he asked was not what sūtra did the great Ma-tsu study (which in earlier times would have been the fundamental question), but what were his sayings—what, from all his study and practice, did he appropriate and realize as his own.

These "sayings," however, like the words of sūtras, were thought to be hindrances to spirituality if they were taken as objects of knowledge, or as somehow sufficient in themselves. Sayings indicated, hinted at, or evoked, elicited, something beyond themselves, which was clearly unattainable through direct reference. They referred to no spiritual object at all but rather, indirectly, to a disclosure of something that was prior to all conceptualization. In this context, language and its set of conceptual categories seemed to run aground. What they sought to encounter was beyond all categories, and even beyond their negation; it always stood in the background of focal awareness even when the spiritually adept sought to grasp it. This realization brought the Hung-chou masters to deny their own religious categories—Buddha, Mind, and so on—and then, even further, to deny that negation. Thus, Pai-chang claims: "The "nature" of fundamental existence cannot be specified in language. Originally it is neither ordinary nor sacred. Nor is it defiled or pure. And it is neither empty nor existent, neither good nor evil" (411). Regarding references to *what* is revealed in spiritual awareness as dangerous or at least misleading, more often than not texts show greater concern with the stance or posture required for the disclosure to occur than they do with its "source" or referent. "When affirmation and negation, like and dislike, the principled and unprincipled, and all knowing and feeling are exhausted, unable to entangle you, then there is free spontaneity in all situations" (411).

The detachment called for in this passage is perhaps the primary element in Hung-chou spirituality or, at least, a prerequisite to other elements. Letting go of habitual categories and forms of awareness was essential to the process of opening up a dimension within which deeper awareness might be disclosed. What obstructs this "deeper awareness" or "original nature" is the search for security through fixation and enclosure. Seeking to effect release and freedom by calling attention to forms of human bondage, Hung-chou rhetoric employs the following verbal metaphors: holding on, grasping, fixating, obstructing, losing and seeking, separating, differentiating, blocking and screening ourselves off from more extensive attunement.

Detachment requires a "letting go" and "release," not of things so much as of the kind of self-understanding that holds and grasps at things, unaware of the more primordial background within which both self and things have their existence. Thus, after establishing "detachment as the fundamental principle" (T 48.381c), Huang-po claims that one who is "free" is not "separate from all affairs" (384a). That freedom is not an escape from things or affairs takes us back to the Hung-chou concern for the "ordinary." Freedom, Buddhahood, is available nowhere else but here, within the "everyday." Thus it is not so much a matter of release from our current situation as it is an awakening to that situation, as well as a deep sense of *being* situated or contextualized within a larger, encompassing whole.

Although reflexivity (reflecting back on oneself) is sometimes an element in this reorientation, Hung-chou spirituality does not consist in focus on the self, or subjectivity, but instead seeks to discover a ground of experience and action more primordial than subjectivity. On this point Hung-chou Ch'an can be seen to be in continuity with the basic Buddhist concept of "no-self." Although the precise sense in which there is "no-self" can, and indeed did, change, these monks and masters understood themselves to stand in a tradition of spirituality that called them into a dimension that is "presubjective"—prior to and deeper than the separation of self and world, subject and object. Thus in continuity with the world, yet without losing uniqueness and individuality (indeed enhancing it), the practice of Hung-chou Ch'an was thought to enable an open involvement in and responsiveness to the world. The character of this responsiveness was thus seen in radical opposition to the narrow and enclosed disposition that accompanies self-centeredness.

Polarization of self and world gives way to a reciprocity between them, or, in Huang-po's words, a "mutual correspondence" (*hsiang-ying*; T 48.383b). Living within such correspondence meant that the motivation for action derived from a source beyond the willfulness of personal subjectivity. Freedom of movement, therefore, meant something quite different from the liberty to move as one desires. On the contrary, it meant a freedom from the tyranny of those desires such that one could move in accordance with, and thus be moved by, the world around one. This freedom and spontaneity of speech and action became the hallmark of Hung-chou spirituality.

Is there a sense in which something like "faith" was required in this fundamental shift of understanding and experience? Certainly, and Hung-chou masters occasionally alluded to it. This is not, however, a faith of required belief in a set of basic propositions. It has more the character of a trust that supports and makes possible a willingness to let go of conventional self-understanding. Although the extensive practice of critical discourse—

a self-negating rhetoric—ruled out the possibility and need of a strong doctrinal basis for spirituality, nevertheless, certain doctrines, even if subject to denial, were clearly maintained in the experiential form of trust: trust, for example, that submitting oneself to these practices did indeed open toward more authentic experience rather than its opposite. This Hung-chou style of faith is expressed in a variety of ways, from Ma-tsu's call to affirm that "this mind is Buddha" to Lin-chi's accusation of faithlessness. Perhaps Huang-po's rhetoric of faith is the most radical. His "Discourse Record" develops the imagery of one suspended over the abyss (T 48.380a), of letting go with both hands (383b), and of a sudden "leap" (383c) out of the false security of conceptual self-enclosure.

That enlightenment occurs suddenly as an event of release and disclosure was by this time the prevailing understanding within Chinese Buddhism. Without needing to argue for that understanding of it, Hung-chou masters developed practical techniques for the evocation of "sudden awakening." As we have seen, many of these techniques were linguistic, consisting, among other things, in an evolving and extensive imagery of enlightenment. In Huang-po's *Ch'uan-hsin fa-yao*, for instance, at least forty different terms or images associated with the event of enlightenment can be found. When one of these or some other fragment of language evoked a "sudden awakening," it came to be known as a "turning word"—a word or phrase by means of which a sudden and radical transformation of experience is effected. The truth of these phrases, therefore, was taken to be a function of their power to elicit such a disclosure or to bring about a fundamental "turn," rather than being a matter of measuring their correspondence to a standard available by some other means. No such alternative standard was thought to be available.

Stories about enlightening events, although all appear in linguistic form, did not always tell about what the master *said*. Some stories emphasize what the master *did*. These stories set up actions or events in such a way that they "speak" for themselves. A sudden shout, a slap, the kicking of an object, or an unexpected gesture, all were thought to be capable of transmitting the point of Hung-chou Ch'an. Extending the realm of significance from written to spoken language, and then to the "language" of action, monks began to be aware of all dimensions of a teacher's life. Famous teachers were thought to embody the truth of Ch'an experience. Every move, every act, therefore, could be seen as an expression of the Buddha-nature. More than ever before in the history of Chinese Buddhism, teachers came to be exemplars or models of what they taught. Monks sought to learn the language of their teacher, including the language of movement, facial expression, and gesture, and modeled themselves in accordance with it.

More than in other contexts it became clear that the way a teacher taught was actually an important dimension of what was being taught. The language "used" in communicating was part of the content communicated. In virtually every sense, the Ch'an master stood as a concrete image of what the quest was all about. But since the monks' goal was "freedom," merely following the script provided by the teacher would not do. Monks who slavishly replicated the master's style were ridiculed. Somehow, by repeating the teacher's practice and by taking him as a concrete model, the monk sought an original experience, one that was truly free in being one's own.

The issue of how "transmission" from teacher to student and from generation to generation could take place was very important in Hung-chou Ch'an. Their conclusion, that transmission took place directly "from mind to mind," is the best-known doctrine of this school. Before this time "transmission" usually meant teaching the words and content of a given sūtra to the next generation. Lines of descent, or lineages, were therefore identifiable in terms of the sūtra's language and doctrinal content. Given the Hung-chou critique of language and concept, and the fact that enlightenment was understood in terms of freedom, no such transmission was possible. Instead, in the course of years of training and the development of receptivity, the character of the teacher's mind was itself to be transmitted directly to the student.

The "transmission of mind" was thus creative participation in a line or stream moving from past to future through a "lineage" of Ch'an masters. Since this *is* the experience of enlightenment, no grasping for transmission of mind could be successful. One joins in to this "One Mind," but never grasps, encompasses, or stands above it. Again, this event was taken to involve both passivity and activity or, better, to have gotten beyond that opposition. The monk receives and performs the teacher's words and practices until they become his own. Yet since the essence of transmission was freedom and spontaneity, merely repeating the master's words and acts fell short of receiving his transmission. The goal was to speak and to act in his spirit or "mind" but on one's own, freely and spontaneously. Those who could do so were considered to be spiritual successors, and then they sought to transmit that capacity on to a further generation.

The *Pai-chang yu-lu* (409; Cleary, 19-20) tells us that, at least by the early Sung dynasty, transmission required "going beyond" the teacher:

> The master [Pai-chang] said, "Will you not go on to succeed Ma-tsu?" Huang-po replied, "Not so. By means of your disclosure today I have received an image of the functioning of Ma-tsu's great power. Never-

theless, I do not know Ma-tsu. If I were to succeed Ma-tsu, I would thereupon lose my descendents." The master said: "So it is, so it is. When one's vision is the same as the teacher's, one's power is decreased to half of the teacher's. When one's vision goes beyond the teacher's, then one is fit for transmission. You clearly have a vision that surpasses the teacher's."

Where freedom is the point, mere replication is inadequate. If Huang-po simply did "what was done" in Ma-tsu's lineage, failing to take the teaching up into a new appropriation, he would have missed the transmission and proved himself unable to be an inheritor of Ma-tsu's "mind." This recognition and sanctification of change in Hung-chou Ch'an enabled the movement to retain its lively, spontaneous character through many generations. But it also set the historical stage for changes leading beyond Hung-chou Ch'an to other historical forms. How Hung-chou was "transmitted" throughout East Asia in later epochs, and how it was transformed in the process, becoming in effect the entire Ch'an/Zen tradition as we know it today, is a matter well worth further inquiry.

Bibliography

Pai-chang yu-lu and *Pai-chang kuang-lu*, in *Ssu-chia yu-lu, Dai Nihon zokuzōkyō*.

Blofeld, John. *The Zen Teaching of Huang Po*. New York: Grove Press, 1958.

Chang Chung-yuan. *Original Teachings of Ch'an Buddhism*. New York: Vintage Books, 1971.

Cleary, Thomas. *Sayings and Doings of Pai-chang*. Los Angeles: Center Publications, 1978.

Sasaki, Ruth F. *The Record of Lin-chi*. Kyoto: The Institute for Zen Studies, 1975.

IV. *The Encounter of Ch'an with Confucianism*

JULIA CHING

THE HISTORY OF the interaction between Buddhism and Confucianism in China is a protracted one. Confucianism was the prevalent native cultural tradition; Buddhism came as an intruder, and seemed to focus on rather different concerns. Buddhism taught the way of deliverance from suffering, emphasizing the monastic orientation away from this world, toward the absolute goal of *nirvāṇa*, whereas Confucianism emphasized the family, social concerns and political responsibilities, and aimed to build a better human world here and now. Their encounter was marked by sometimes acrimonious controversy, for national and cultural pride made it hard for Confucians to accept a foreign religion, while on the more ideological level, the Buddhists criticized the Confucians for being too attached to this world and its impermanent relationships, and the Confucians attacked what they called Buddhist escapism and pessimism.

In the course of their disputes, Buddhism and Confucianism learned and borrowed from each other. Mahāyāna Buddhism was especially successful in China. Its central insight, that *nirvāṇa* is to be found in *saṃsāra*, in this life and this world, made it more acceptable than Theravāda Buddhism. With time, Buddhism underwent a transformation in East Asia, adopting some of the values it found in that vast region.

Rapprochement within Buddhism

Chinese Ch'an, especially as represented by the school of Hui-neng (638–713), is known for its preference for freedom of expression and respect for the natural, both of which entail some disrespect for the sūtras and the traditions of the past. Such attitudes helped to unleash a certain creative genius in discussions of spirituality and mysticism as well as in art and culture. But many were disturbed by the iconoclastic and anti-intellectual cynicism accompanying these attitudes. This explains the opposition of mainline Buddhists to the Ch'an movement. On the other hand, efforts were made to reconcile the Ch'an movement with the rest of Mahāyāna Buddhism, especially through the "union between the Buddhism of meditation and the Buddhism of the sūtras" *(Ch'an-chiao yi-chih)*. This was the rallying call of Tsung-mi (780–841), the T'ang monk who first studied Ch'an and later became a Hua-yen patriarch. His *Ch'an-yüan chu-ch'üan chi-tu hsü* (T 48, No. 2015) aimed to reconcile Ch'an teachings with those of other Buddhist schools, especially Hua-yen.[1]

The anti-Buddhist persecutions, especially that of 845, nearly wiped out the Buddhist religion, and rendered even more urgent the task of intra-Buddhist reconciliation. During the Sung period, a time of cultural renaissance, Buddhism recovered from some of the political reverses it had suffered previously. With state encouragement, it enjoyed a minirevival of its own, with the restoration of temples, the printing of the Buddhist Canon, the reemergence of the T'ien-t'ai and Hua-yen schools, and the continued prosperity of Ch'an and Pure Land.[2] In the T'ang period Buddhism had shone in the realm of advanced metaphysical speculation; in the Sung period its strongest achievements were in the development of practical spirituality. Ch'an and Pure Land shared a somewhat antitheoretical, even anti-intellectual reputation. They were now brought further together by a syncretist movement advocating "dual cultivation of Ch'an (meditation) and of *nien-fo* (J. *nembutsu*) (recitation of the Buddha's name)."

It was Yung-ming Yen-shou (904–975), author of *Tsung-ching lu* (The mirror's record), who sought hardest to harmonize the doctrines of T'ien-t'ai, Hua-yen, and Wei-shih (Yogācāra) with those of Ch'an and Pure Land. He was also the first to advocate "dual cultivation." In this joint practice *nien-fo* invocation was seen as another form of meditation, involving visualization of the Buddha Amitābha, and combining self-reliance *(tzǔ-li*; J. *jiriki)* with reliance on Other-Power *(t'a-li*; J. *tariki)*. The argument was that since *nien-fo* could terminate discursive thought, it could lead as well to enlightenment, a Ch'an goal.[3] To consider *nien-fo* as a form of meditation was not original with Yung-ming Yen-shou. Other Pure Land Buddhists had done so, but unlike him they had not made efforts to promote it among their followers, nor had they pursued this meditation with the conscious goal of enlightenment, now given more importance even than rebirth in the Pure Land. The dual practice was especially encouraged by some members of the Ch'an school who preferred Pure Land to Ch'an. It served to integrate Ch'an followers into the Pure Land movement of devotional Buddhism. Such a process of amalgamation on the popular level was probably responsible for the eventual disappearance of distinctively Ch'an teachings after the thirteenth century.[4]

Debates within Buddhism

Apart from this Ch'an/Pure Land syncretism, the Sung period was marked by vigorous debates within Ch'an, which, as the strongest Buddhist school, was itself divided into schools or lineages.[5] With the focus on practical matters of spirituality, the Lin-chi and the Ts'ao-tung schools both prospered, and their rival teachings on enlightenment and how it might be attained drew considerable attention. Ts'ao-tung emphasized silent enlightenment (*mo-chao*; J. *mokusho*, a reference to the "silently shining" inner light) and the importance of sitting in meditation (*tso-ch'an*; J. *zazen*) as a discipline that can lead to mystical enlightenment through the gradual transformation of life and character. The Lin-chi school, in contrast, aimed at sudden enlightenment (J. *satori*) through the use of shouting, beating, and riddles called *kung-an* (J. *kōan*), considered as aids in provoking mystical experience, for which no slow preparation is necessary or possible. And while the differences led to polemics, such leading masters as Ta-hui Tsung-kao (1089–1163) on the Lin-chi side and Hung-chih Cheng-chüeh (1091–1157) on the Ts'ao-tung side continued to respect each other profoundly.[6]

The differences between Lin-chi and Ts'ao-tung are sometimes represented by the words *mo-chao* and *k'an-hua*. *Mo-chao* (silent illumination) points to the centrality of meditation as a spiritual exercise. The Ts'ao-tung adherents were eager to point out that it did not imply inactivity or passivity. Rather, the silence in question is the primal stillness of the ultimate ground of the enlightened mind, which is naturally radiant and "shining." They considered silent meditation and the quiet deeds of ordinary living to be preferable to constant dwelling upon the kōan, itself an irrational and pointless riddle. Hung-chih compares quiet meditation to the effort of "the bird hatching the egg" and describes the inner light as "a ray penetrating past and present" (T 48.72). But far from being entirely opposed to kōans, he even composed some himself.

K'an-hua (observing the kōan) is a colloquial expression used by the Lin-chi school to describe the effort of attention required in kōan practice. By posing a problem that cannot be solved by the rational intellect, the kōan is supposed to lead to the dissolution of the boundary between the conscious and the unconscious in the human psyche, and bring about a sudden experience, described metaphorically as the blossoming of a lotus, or the sun emerging from behind the clouds. Ta-hui urges the practitioner to maintain an alert spiritual awareness, whether in sitting, moving, or reposing. "When an illusory thought arises, you do not need to ward it off with energy; you only have to raise the 'No' of Chao-chou [778–897]" (T 51. 899). This refers to the monk Chao-chou's famous reply to the question,

"Has a dog the Buddha-nature?" Though Ch'an philosophy holds that the Buddha-nature is present in all creatures, this "No" *(wu;* J. *mu)* is seen as pointing to ultimate truth.[7] But Ta-hui equally deprecates excessive reliance on kōans:

> There are two mistakes among the seekers of the Tao today.... The one is to learn too many words and sentences, and seek to make something unusual with them.... The other is... to abandon all words and sentences, and always keep the eyes closed, as though dead, and call it quiet-sitting, contemplating the mind, and silently reflecting the light *(mo-chao)*. (T 47. 895)

Generally, Lin-chi followers accused Ts'ao-tung of a passivity in meditation that could only enervate the mind, while Ts'ao-tung adherents accused the Rinzai of playing dangerous games, not only with the psyche but also with the entire tradition of Buddhist spirituality, by allowing possibly illusory experiences to be mistaken for enlightenment. This is not to say that the Ts'ao-tung Buddhists ignored kōans altogether, or that Lin-chi Buddhists did not engage in meditation. The difference was much more of nuances of emphasis than of practice. But the nuances were important enough. Meanwhile, a steady exchange of Chinese and Japanese monks, from the middle of the twelfth century on, brought also to Japan these two Zen Buddhist schools (Rinzai and Sōtō), which are still active there today.

The vigorous growth of Ch'an Buddhism during the Sung dynasty is reflected in a prolific literature, including such famous collections as the *Pi-yen lu* (Blue cliff records) (1125), and the *Wu-men kuan* (J. *Mumonkan;* The gateless barrier) (1228). The controversy between Ch'an and T'ien-t'ai inspired great historical labors. While Ch'an Buddhists attached scant importance to the study of the sūtras, they sought to discard any appearance of heterodoxy and to prove themselves the legitimate heirs of the historical Buddha. They outlined the transmission of Ch'an insights through allegedly correct lineages, in such works as Tao-yüan's *Ch'ing-te ch'uan-teng lu* (The transmission of the lamp, 1011) and Ch'i-sung's *Ch'uan-fa cheng-tsung chi* (The transmission of the Dharma in the true school, 1061).

Though it had fewer followers than Ch'an, T'ien-t'ai regarded itself as representing orthodox Buddhism, and responded with Tsung-chien's *Shih-men cheng-t'ung* (The orthodox lineage in Buddhism) and Chih-p'an's *Fo-tsu t'ung-chi* (The record of the Buddhist patriarchs) (1270).[8] The proliferation of Ch'an writings was in direct contradiction to original Ch'an principles of not establishing written directives and of seeking a direct intuition into the mind without the assistance of other agents. Despite its usefulness for later generations, some have seen in this proliferation the beginning of the decline of the true Ch'an spirit.

Rapprochement between Ch'an and Confucianism

Confucianism also underwent a renewal as it sought to respond to the threat posed by Buddhism and Taoism to its survival. The earlier Confucian classical texts, including the *Book of Changes,* the *Book of Poetry*, the *Book of History*, the *Book of Rites*, and the *Spring-Autumn Annals* were still studied, but the movement was away from philology, toward a deeper interest in philosophical questions as well as in spiritual cultivation. More and more Confucian scholars chose to focus on the Four Books—the *Analects* (conversations between Confucius and his disciples), the *Book of Mencius* (conversations between Mencius and his disciples), the *Great Learning,* and the *Doctrine of the Mean* (originally two chapters from the *Book of Rites*, the former making moral and spiritual cultivation the beginning of good rulership, and the latter concentrating on inner equilibrium and harmony).[9] In English, the new movement is sometimes called Neo-Confucianism.

The rapprochement between Buddhism and Confucianism was prepared by people on both sides. Even when they criticized Buddhism, Confucian scholars continued to associate, if only occasionally, with talented Buddhist monks. Indeed, they were especially open to those monks who made genuine intellectual efforts to rebuff Confucian attacks on their religion. In this respect, Tsung-mi's essay, *Yüan-jen lun* (On the original man), a defence of Buddhist teachings against Han Yü's (768–824) well-known criticisms, also paved the way for an understanding with Confucianism.[10] His own insights into the origin of humankind and of things, and especially his assertion that "even the primal *ch'i* is conditioned by the transformations of the mind" (T 45.708–10), became the starting points for philosophical elaboration, to be undertaken by some of the greatest Confucian (or Neo-Confucian) thinkers of the Sung and Ming dynasties.[11]

The Northern Sung monk Ming-chiao Chi-sung (d. 1071) was tireless in defending the claims of Ch'an Buddhism, in particular of his own Yün-men sect, against other Buddhist schools, especially T'ien-t'ai. But in other ways he was a worthy successor to Tsung-mi. In defending Buddhism against Confucian attacks, he sought to blend Confucian family and social values with Buddhist spirituality and doctrine. He taught that "Buddhism and Confucianism are basically one," that the five precepts of Buddhism (against violence, theft, adultery, dishonesty, and drinking alcohol), when properly understood, are just other names for the five constant virtues of Confucianism (benevolence or humanity, righteousness, propriety, wisdom and faithfulness).[12]

Entering a monastery, for example, became a way of practicing filial piety, either by obeying parental wishes and/or by freeing oneself to gain merit for one's family, especially its deceased members. Ming-chiao expresses it this way:

> The Buddhist follows a monastic rule and cultivates his mind and heart…
> achieving a high degree of virtue. He also extends his way (Tao) to others,
> wanting to do good to all with no distinction of things.… Although he
> does not marry, he serves his parents with his virtue. Although he destroys
> his appearance [through shaving his head], he serves his kin with his Tao.
> (T 52.651)

Debates within Neo-Confucianism

Neo-Confucian thinkers were struck by the parallels between their own disputes and the intra-Buddhist controversy between Lin-chi and Ts'ao-tung spiritualities. Chu Hsi (1130–1200) and Lu Chiu-yüan (1139–1193) were younger contemporaries of Ta-hui and Hung-chih, and their disagreements and arguments reveal the continuity of certain spiritual concerns. Chu Hsi, the great Neo-Confucian philosopher and scholar, is reported to have carried with him only one book—the recorded dialogues of Ta-hui, when he went to the capital to take his civil service examinations.[13] But in later life Chu moved to a position much closer to the Ts'ao-tung school. Besides criticizing Buddhism generally for its allegedly antisocial stance, Chu Hsi attacked the use of kōans as playing games with the mind until it became "anesthetized" and could no longer function properly. Chu's rival, Lu Chiu-yüan, is said to have associated with Ta-hui's disciple Fo-chao Te-kuang. He was a less vocal critic of Buddhism than Chu, and he showed in his teachings a closer affinity with the Lin-chi position.[14]

The controversy between the two thinkers often recalls the Buddhist arguments over gradual or sudden enlightenment. Here, the goal is the achievement of sagehood, a goal neglected over many centuries, which both Chu and Lu agreed was important, though they differed on the method of achieving it. Chu insists on interpreting the words of the *Great Learning*, "investigating things" *(ko-wu),* as meaning "pursuing exhaustively the *li* or essences of things," by the assiduous study of the classics and of the external world, as well as by silent meditation. Lu Chiu-yüan regards this method as fragmented, since it assumes that sagehood is associated with the information acquired through learning. In a language with Buddhist resonances, he speaks about "recovering the original mind." According to him, neither learning nor meditation is absolutely essential in this quest. What counts is single-mindedness, the untiring quest for wisdom. And wisdom, of course, is immanent in the quest itself—in a virtuous, sagely life.[15]

Both Buddhist and Taoist influences can be clearly discerned in Sung Neo-Confucianism. The association of Neo-Confucian thinkers with learned Buddhist monks is well documented, and Buddhist influence on Neo-Confucian philosophy is too pervasive to be fully discussed here. The Neo-Confucian preference for discussing matters of mind (hsin) and nature (hsing) is itself suggestive of Buddhist stimulus. The Neo-Confucian philosophy of human nature appears to owe much to Tsung-mi. In spirituality, the importance attached to "tranquility" and meditation is another sign of Buddhist influence. It is very marked in the lives and philosophies of Chou Tun-yi (1017–1073), Ch'eng Yi (1033–1107, though he was an articulate critic of Buddhism), and Chu Hsi.

Nevertheless, Neo-Confucianism is not Buddhism in disguise, as it is sometimes said to be. In the case of Chu Hsi, the most important of the Sung thinkers, we may discern both the extent and the limitations of Buddhist influences. Chu acknowledged a youthful interest in Ch'an—but as one of many concerns for a person of immense intellectual curiosity. He was personally acquainted with the famous Ch'an monk Ta-hui Tsung-kao, knew well Ta-hui's recorded dialogues, corresponded with Ta-hui's lineal disciple Tao-ch'ien, and seems to have known a number of Buddhist works, including the Ch'uan-teng lu.[16]

According to his own account, his serious conversion away from Ch'an Buddhism dates to his meeting with Li T'ung (1153), who advised him to put aside an abstract quest. Chu then immersed himself in reading Confucian works, until he discovered more and more "lacunae and inconsistencies" in the Buddhist writings to which he had previously been attracted. He would criticize Ch'an Buddhism, for "idly guarding [the mind]," for offering riddles, frequently in coarse and uncouth language, and for its neglect of real learning and social morality.

While Chu Hsi practiced sitting in meditation, he was opposed to a complete emptying of the mind. He sought, rather, the emptying from the mind of perverse thoughts, and the practice of a disposition of reverence (ching) in and out of meditation. Chu Hsi teaches a philosophy of essences or "principles" (li). The word li is also a key word in Hua-yen Buddhism, where it refers to the noumenon as opposed to the phenomenon. But it acquires an added, moral connotation in Neo-Confucianism. Chu distinguishes the Neo-Confucian ethical quest from the Ch'an quest for enlightenment:

> Generally the learning of the sages is based on the mind's quest for principles (li), and the response to things and affairs according to these principles.... But the Buddhists seek the mind with the mind... as though the mouth should bite itself, and the eye should eye itself.[17]

A question that arises in discussions of spiritualities is that of mysticism. Buddhism in general, and Ch'an Buddhism in particular, can without doubt be called a mystical religion. Even if not every Buddhist need be or become a mystic, the religion itself represents a quest for mystical enlightenment. Confucianism, in contrast, defines itself principally in moral terms. Although the Neo-Confucian scholars and thinkers did highlight the spiritual quest and pursued certain spiritual exercises, including meditation, they never made mystical enlightenment the ultimate goal of striving. Confucian meditation developed under Buddhist influence, but its orientation was always toward the whole of life, including its social responsibilities. Confucians emphasized the knowledge of the moral self—of one's own strengths and weaknesses—in view of achieving self-improvement. They focused on realizing the principle of Heaven *(t'ien-li)* within, and of removing passions or "human desires" *(jen-yü)*.

True, Confucian meditation is not just an examination of conscience. It is oriented to a higher consciousness, through emptying of the self and its desires, and this is where it resembles Buddhist meditation. To put it paradoxically, Confucian meditation, referred to sometimes as "quiet-sitting," lies somewhere between two other forms: the intellectual concentration of discursive thought and the spiritual concentration that assures that there is no thought. Confucian meditation seeks peace without doing violence to human nature. It does not require the attainment of a state of intellectual and emotional impassivity, and it does not rely as much as Buddhist or Taoist meditation on the use of various techniques. There were Neo-Confucian mystics; usually, these had been influenced by Buddhism, as in the case of Wang Yang-ming (1472–1529). In the last analysis, however, even he was much more a man of the world, a philosopher, statesman, and soldier, than a monk with a mystical doctrine.

Moral and spiritual cultivation had always been valued in Confucianism; mystical enlightenment gained importance much later, through the penetration of Taoist and Buddhist influence in Neo-Confucianism. Superficially, the tension between "cultivation" and "enlightenment" may appear to resemble that between asceticism and mysticism, self-reliance and surrender to a higher power. But the cultivation-enlightenment polarity represents also an inner tension in the mystical quest itself. The way of cultivation can be rooted in a basic attitude of trust and readiness to wait for light—even of finding light in darkness and waiting—and this entails some form of subconscious reliance upon a higher power. Conversely, the way of enlightenment may require the inducement of a sudden, psychic experience, through one's own efforts. Underlying these polarities is a problem of "attachment" or "detachment" posed by the subtlety of the spiritual experience. When experience is sought after for itself, it may become emptied of real content. Attachment to enlightenment can fetter the spirit, so that self-preoccupation replaces any possible self-forgetfulness. For this reason, the great Buddhist and Confucian masters described authentic self-cultivation as being akin to "non-cultivation"—implying a necessary attitude of detachment from one's own deepest desires.

Neo-Confucian discussions and debates did not simply repeat Ch'an Buddhist ones. Neo-Confucian philosophers were committed to meeting the intellectual, social, and political needs of their times, and they tended to regard as individualistic the Ch'an Buddhist preoccupation with finding or recovering the Buddha-nature. Neo-Confucians were concerned with the building or rebuilding of a *Weltanschauung*, which would include spirituality but extend beyond it into cosmology, metaphysics, philosophy of human nature, and also political ethics.

Actually, the Neo-Confucian debates and discussions on moral and spiritual cultivation became better known than the Buddhist debates regarding "silent illumination" or the use of kōans. The rise of Neo-Confucianism manifested the acceptance, by Confucianism, of certain Buddhist—especially Ch'an Buddhist—teachings. It also signaled, by the same token, the decline, one might even say demise, of Ch'an. In China, the Ch'an rapprochement with Pure Land on the one side and with Confucianism on the other would eventually dissolve the identity of Ch'an Buddhism itself.

In conclusion, let us note that the great mystics of all religions share a common experience of the mystical quest itself—the waiting, the frustration, the joy. They find a common meeting ground in this experience, even if they differ as to its precise theological interpretation. All mystics refer to a point of centripetal recollection and concentration, where immanence is experienced and transcendence is perceived. It is here that the person meets that which is greater than himself or herself, greater than his or her heart, and yet is within the mind and heart. The Buddhists may call it Buddha-nature, the Confucians the principle of Heaven (*t'ien-li*) or Great Ultimate (*t'ai-chi*), and the Christians God.

Both Confucian and Buddhist spiritualities have much to teach the modern world, so united technologically, fragmented politically, and aimless spiritually. Both have something to say also to those believers of Western religions, including Christianity, who regard the place of spirituality to be at the center, rather than on the periphery, of religion.[18]

Notes

1. Takeuchi Yoshio, *Takeuchi Yoshio zenshū* 8 (Tokyo: Kadokawa Shoten, 1985) 162–63.

2. Kusumoto Bun'yū, *Sōdai jugaku no Zen shisō kenkyū* (The study of Zen thought in Sung Confucianism), (Nagoya: Nisseido, 1985) 12–22.

3. Yung-ming Yen-shou, *Wan-shan t'ung-kuei chi*, T 48.960–61. Yung-ming Yen-shou started training in a T'ien-t'ai monastery, and is considered both a Ch'an master of the Fa-yen lineage and a Pure Land patriarch.

4. Chang Chung-yuan, trans., *Original Teachings of Ch'an Buddhism* (New York: Grove Press, 1969) vi.

5. See Heinrich Dumoulin, *Zen Buddhism: A History I: India and China* (New York: Macmillan, 1988) 243–64.

6. See their biographies in the *Hsü ch'uan-teng lu* (Supplement to the Transmission of the Lamp), T 51.649–54, and 579.

7. See Ta-hui's recorded dialogue, T 51.1998a.

8. See Kamata Shigeo, *Chūgoku bukkyō shi* (Tokyo: Iwanami, 1978); Jan Yün-hua, "Buddhist Historiography in Sung China," *Zeitschrift der Deutschen Morgenländischen Gesellschaft* 114 (1964) 260–381.

9. See Peter N. Gregory, *Inquiry into the Origin of Humanity: An Annotated Translation of Tsung-mi's Yüan jen lun with a Modern Commentary* (University of Hawai'i Press, 1995).

10. Together with the commentaries supplied by Ch'eng Yi (1033–1107) and Chu Hsi (1120–1200), these were made the official curriculum for the civil service examinations in 1313.

11. See Fung Yu-lan, *Chung-kuo che-hsueh shih* (A history of Chinese philosophy), (Shanghai: Commercial Press, 1935) 796–99 (not included in the English translation by Derk Bodde).

12. See his essay, *Yüan-tao* (On the original Tao), T 522.649–51; also in *Zen no goroku* 14 (Tokyo: Chikuma Shobō, 1981) 17–22.

13. Tokiwa Daijo, *Shina ni okeru bukkyō to jukyō dōkyō* (Buddhism, Confucianism, and Taoism in China), (Tokyo, 1930) 379. See E. Sargent, *Tchou Hi contre le Bouddhisme*, Mélanges publiés par l'Institut des Hautes Études Chinoises (Paris: Presses universitaires de France, 1957).

14. On the entire subject of Sung Confucianism and its relation to Buddhism, see especially Takeuchi Yoshio, *Takeuchi Yoshio zenshū* 4 (Tokyo: Kadokawa, 1979) 266–309; Kusumoto Bun'yū, op. cit., 42–55, 403–27.

15. Julia Ching, "The Goose Lake Monastery Debate (1175)," *Journal of Chinese Philosophy* (1974) 161–78, for the differences between Chu and Lu on this matter of spiritual methodology.

16. Ch'ing Chia-yi [Julia Ching], "Zhu Xi yu Fojiao," (Chu Hsi and Buddhism) in Zhu Ruikai, ed., *Song Ming sixiang he Zhonghua wenming* (Sung-Ming Thought and Chinese Culture), (Shanghai, Xuelin Press, 1995), 346–61.

17. "Kuan-hsin shuo" (On observing the mind), in *Hui-an Chu Wen-kung wen-chi* (Collected writings of Chu Hsi), (Taipei: Chung-wen, 1972) vol. 17, ch. 67.21b.

18. See Julia Ching, *Confucianism and Christianity* (Tokyo: Kodansha International, 1977) 166–68.

Part Four

KOREA

16

Silla Buddhist Spirituality

S U N G B A E P A R K

THROUGHOUT ITS long history, Korean Buddhism has always been concerned with issues of syncretism. On one level, this syncretic tendency has involved interchange with other philosophical and spiritual systems, in particular Confucianism, Taoism, and indigenous Korean shamanism. On another level, the syncretic process has been internal, involving the reconciliation of conflicting schools of Buddhist thought in an effort to create a single harmonious whole. Borrowing the terminology traditional to Korean Buddhism itself, we can say that the history of Korean Buddhism has been focused on the effort to create an all-inclusive Buddhist doctrine, or *t'ong pulgyo* (Buddhism of total interpenetration).

When we consider the development of *t'ong pulgyo* during the Silla Period, it is inevitable that we focus on the Korean monk Wŏnhyo (617–686 CE), one of the most important figures in the history of Korean Buddhism, and a significant influence on the course of East Asian Buddhism in general. Through his application of the principle of *hwajaeng* (harmonization of all disputes) to the central Buddhological issues of his day, Wŏnhyo created the conceptual framework in which all subsequent discussion of *t'ong pulgyo* has taken place, up to and including the present.

Historical Background

The Three Kingdoms Period (37 B.C.E.–668 C.E.)

Up to the seventh century CE, the Korean peninsula was divided into three separate kingdoms: Koguryŏ (37 B.C.E.–668 CE), Paekche (18 B.C.E.–660 C.E.), and Silla (57 B.C.E.–668 C.E.). Of these three, Buddhism took hold in Koguryŏ first. Introduced by Chinese monks late in the fourth century, it was quickly adopted by the country's aristocracy, receiving extensive government support.[1] Koguryŏ's ruling class was attracted to Buddhism in part because of the supernatural powers attributed to it, as a means of strengthening the kingdom against attack—the strength of neighboring China being considered a prime illustration of its magical efficacy. But Buddhism also offered Koguryŏ's nobility an entire system of advanced culture, bringing with it an exalted philosophical vision of reality, as well as magnificent art, architecture, music, and literature.

By this time, two other powerful religio-philosophical systems had already entered the Korean Peninsula from China. The first of these, Confucianism, was too closely associated with the Chinese-style bureaucratic examination system to appeal to the aristocratic governments of the Korean kingdoms, all three of which determined leadership through family lineage.[2] The second, Taoism, was more successful. A religion emphasizing quiescence, magic, inner alchemy, and a naturalistic philosophy, its pantheon of spirits and gods was soon grafted onto the archaic religious complex of Korean shamanism, forming what may be termed a shamanistic Taoism. For a period, this hybrid creation overshadowed both Buddhism and Confucianism on the peninsula, becoming the basic religion of the people, especially the common folk of the countryside. The introduction of Buddhism into Korea must therefore ultimately be understood in the context of its syncretic harmonization with the shamanistic Taoism already present in the Three Kingdoms of early Korea.

Paekche followed close behind Koguryŏ in its adoption of Buddhism,[3] but developments in Silla took longer because of its geographical isolation and the resistance of its aristocracy, which was strongly committed to the indigenous shamanism.[4] At first Buddhism spread only in rural areas among the common folk and did not reach the ruling class, but eventually Silla followed Koguryŏ and Paekche in extending state support to the new religion.

The political function that Buddhism took on in all three of the Korean kingdoms can be seen in its gradual absorption of Confucian influences. For example, the Korean Buddhist monk Wŏn'gwang (531–630) expounded the Five Secular Admonishments, an ethical code that was adopted by the elite military youth corps of Silla known as the Hwarangdo (Flower Path): (1) Serve your king with loyalty; (2) Tend your parents with filial piety; (3) Treat your friends with sincerity; (4) Be brave in battle; and (5) Be discriminating in taking life. It is remarkable to find a monk of Wŏn'gwang's stature formulating such essentially Confucian tenets. We see here the characteristic Korean tendency toward syncretic harmonization.

The Hwarangdo was itself an important expression of the religio-philosophical syncretism of Korea during this period. Somewhat analogous to the legendary knights of King Arthur's court, this elite society of aristo-

8. Maitreya, Three Kingdoms Period.

cratic warriors was trained in a rigorous system of ethical chivalry based on Confucian precepts, but also influenced by a Taoist discipline of patience, solitude, simplicity, contentment, and harmony, along with the Buddhist ethic of compassion. Members were also initiated into highly secretive Buddhist religious mysteries and were devoted to the cult of Maitreya, the future incarnation of Buddha. Yet for all that, the Hwarangdo was actually profoundly shamanistic in character. The earliest symbol of the Hwarangdo was the emblem of two beautiful maidens, thought to represent *Mudangs*, or female shamans. Furthermore, members of the Hwarangdo were regularly called upon to help in cases of illness or demon-possession, which they would solve through singing, dancing, and shamanistic rituals. Thus we find in the Hwarangdo a striking syncretic harmonization of shamanism, Confucianism, Taoism, and Buddhism, all interfused in a single system of internal discipline and social praxis.

In general, the kingdom of Silla was characterized by its synthesis of indigenous shamanism and the newly imported Buddhist religion into a Buddho-shamanistic culture. One could indeed call the Koreanization of Chinese Mahāyāna Buddhism the shamanization of Buddhism. Unless one grasps the syncretic harmonization of shamanism with Buddhism effected in early Silla, it is impossible to comprehend the general character of Buddhism in Korea. Even today, most Korean Buddhist temples contain a small shamanistic shrine dedicated to the local mountain spirit *(sanshin),* usually portrayed on the altar by a painting or statue of an old man sitting with a tiger, which is itself an ancient Taoist symbol, again indicating the early Korean fusion of Buddhism with shamanistic Taoism.

The Unified Silla Dynasty (668–935 CE)

By 668 Silla had managed to conquer both Paekche and Koguryŏ, its rivals on the peninsula. Subsequently it turned its attention to organizing the Three Kingdoms into a single state, Unified Silla. This drive toward political unification created a concomitant desire for unification and synthesis in other parts of the national life, including the religious and philosophical. During this period, the major Chinese sects of Buddhism began their influx into Korea, including the San-lun (K. Samnon), or Three Treatises, school (Mādhyamika in India); Fa-hsiang (K. Yushik), or Dharma Mark, school (Yogācāra); Ching-tu (K. Chongt'o) or Pure Land; Ch'an (K. Sŏn); Hua-yen (K. Hwaŏm); and the esoteric Mi-chiao (K. Shinin/Chin'on) school (Tantra in India). The cultural atmosphere in early Unified Silla did not allow these schools to maintain their separate sectarian identities, however, as the drive toward political unification created a concomitant desire for unification and synthesis in other parts of the national life, including the religious and philosophical. Over time, the various Buddhist sects were fused together into a single, unified tradition against the background of shamanistic Taoism, a tradition that came to be characterized by the name *t'ong pulgyo*, the Buddhism of total interpenetration.

Given the syncretic tendencies of Unified Silla culture, it was perhaps inevitable that the Hwaŏm school, with its all-embracing, systematic metaphysics, would become the preeminent influence on Korean Buddhist thought, providing the theoretical framework for the development of a completely syncretic Buddhism. Based upon the *Avataṃsaka Sūtra*, first translated into Chinese in 418, Hwaŏm was established as a school in Korea during the early period of Unified Silla by the Korean monk Uisang (605-672), a contemporary of Wŏnhyo, who also played a crucial role in spreading the Hwaŏm teachings. It was primarily due to Wŏnhyo that Hwaŏm eventually became the predominant mode of philosophical discourse in the Kyo (scriptural studies) tradition of Korean Buddhism.

Theory of Harmonization

Most scholars of Korean Buddhist philosophy agree that Wŏnhyo's lifelong goal was the establishment of a doctrinal foundation for *t'ong pulgyo* by means of the principle of *hwajaeng*, harmonization of all disputes. Through *hwajaeng*, Wŏnhyo attempted to reconcile the various doctrinal disputes, thus unifying conflicting sectarian perspectives into a single, comprehensive Dharma, or teaching. In order to understand the highly syncretic character of Korean Buddhist thinking, one must therefore first grasp the importance

9. Buddha statue at the ruins of Pori Temple. Early Unified Silla Period.

of Wŏnhyo's fundamental principle of *hwajaeng*. This principle underlies his entire system and is most explicitly set forth in his *Simmun hwajaeng non* (Treatise on the harmonization of all disputes), usually regarded as the most original of his philosophical writings.

The earliest extant record of the principle of *hwajaeng* appearing in Wŏnhyo's philosophy is found in an inscription at Koson Monastery, which reads in part:

> When Wŏnhyo was staying at a small shrine in the suburbs to the north west of the King's castle, he read secular books such as *The Book of Predictions*... and non-Buddhist books that had been rejected by the Buddhist world for a long time.
>
> Finally he wrote the *Simmun hwajaeng non*, a part of which states: "When the Tathāgata was in the world, everybody relied on his perfect teaching. After the Buddha's death, however, people's opinions were like rain and pointless theories like rising clouds. Some said, 'I am right, others are wrong.' Some argued, 'Mine is like this but others' is not like this.' Finally, theories and opinions became a flood... The attitude of wanting to stay in a deep valley and avoid great mountains, or of loving emptiness while hating existence, is just like the attitude of wanting to go into a forest and avoid trees. One should be aware of the fact that green and blue are identical in essence, and ice and water are identical in origin; a mirror reflects myriad forms, and parted waters will perfectly intermingle once they are reunited." Therefore, Wŏnhyo wrote the *Simmun hwajaeng non*, which everybody accepts. Everyone says it is excellent.[5]

While the author of this inscription refers to the motives behind, and the impact of, Wŏnhyo's *Simmun hwajaeng non*, he does not discuss the theory contained in it. However, two aspects of this inscription are worth noting. First, of Wŏnhyo's many works, only the *Simmun hwajaeng non* is mentioned. This would indicate that the idea of harmonization was generally recognized as central to Wŏnhyo's thought. Second, and more important, are the five similes referring to the harmonization of doctrinal disputes, all of which graphically express Wŏnhyo's belief in the underlying unity of Buddhist thought. The first of these is the simile of the forest and the trees, referring to the ignorance of people who know names but fail to see what the names really mean. The second and third are about the relationship between green and blue, ice and water, implying that the appearances of things may vary, but their essences remain the same. The fourth simile, of the mirror in which myriad forms are reflected, refers to the relationship between an essence and its variant forms. The fifth simile, of water for which no real division is possible, refers to the possibility of harmonizing all disputes.

The next record of Wŏnhyo's ideas concerning the principle of *hwajaeng* is found in the *Che Punhwangsa Hyosong Mun* (Funeral odes for Wŏnhyo of

Punhwang Monastery) composed by the Koryŏ dynasty scholar-monk Ŭich'ŏn. Ŭich'ŏn's remarks are more general than those of the Koson monastery inscription:

> Wŏnhyo harmonized the disputes of all people by penetratingly clarifying the relationship between essence and marks and by comprehensively embracing the past and the present. He harmonized all disputes so that he established an extremely impartial theory for that time.... I have examined all philosophers of the past, but there are none like Wŏnhyo. (HPC 4.555a)

Though Ŭich'ŏn is considered by later scholars to be the first person to have fully appreciated Wŏnhyo's significance in the development of Korean Buddhism, it was not until the twentieth century, when Cho Myŏng-gi's *Wŏnhyo taesa chonjip* (Collected works of the Great Master Wŏnhyo) was published, that comprehensive research on Wŏnhyo began. However, nearly all research on Wŏnhyo up to the present day has been biographical in content, or has only addressed very specialized topics, and very few scholars have devoted themselves to Wŏnhyo's central philosophy of harmonization. Park Chong-hong's article on Wŏnhyo's philosophical thought, which became available in 1966, was the first scholarly discussion of Wŏnhyo's theory of harmonization from a philosophical perspective.[6]

In this article, Park attempted to demonstrate that Wŏnhyo had accomplished a reconciliation of the long-standing Mādhyamika/Yogācāra conflict by synthesizing the two seemingly contradictory ideologies. Moreover, Park made a lasting contribution by elucidating the logic operating throughout Wŏnhyo's doctrine of harmonization. According to Park, the principle of *hwajaeng* functions to establish interpenetration between the many and the one, on the basis of the doctrines of Hwaŏm Buddhism. Park elaborates on Wŏnhyo's logic of interpenetrating opposites in terms of the relationship between "doctrine" (*chong*) and "essence" (*yo*), and by means of the concepts of "opening" (*kae*) and "sealing" (*hap*) the truth. Here, "doctrine" refers to the development of the one into the many, while "essence" refers to the unification of the many into the one. When the truth is "opened," it is called doctrine; when it is "sealed," it is called essence. The opening of the truth is also called the "arising aspect of dharmas," while the sealing of the truth is also called the "ceasing aspect of dharmas." Furthermore, the arising aspect is sometimes referred to as "the accomplishment of myriad virtues," while the ceasing aspect is sometimes referred to as "the return to One Mind." In Wŏnhyo's view, although these two aspects seem to be contradictory, they freely interpenetrate each other without any obstruction.

Essentials of the *Nirvāṇa Sūtra*

In order to make the principle of *hwajaeng* clearer, it is necessary to analyze the manner in which Wŏnhyo attempts to harmonize specific sectarian disputes by reconciling seemingly conflicting perspectives. In a section of his *Simmon hwajaeng non*, for example, Wŏnhyo attempts to synthesize contradictory theories concerning the indwelling Buddha-nature, an issue central to both Wŏnhyo's own writing and the literature of East Asian Mahāyāna Buddhism in general. The locus classicus of the Buddha-nature theory is the *Mahāparinirvāṇa Sūtra*, upon which the Chinese Nirvāṇa school is based. Because of ambiguities in this sūtra, many debates arose concerning such issues as exactly what Buddha-nature is, where it is located, how it functions, whether it is already actualized or merely potential, whether it is activated gradually or suddenly, and whether it is inherent in all sentient beings to the same degree.

Wŏnhyo composed two commentaries on the *Mahāparinirvāṇa Sūtra*, namely, the *Yŏlban chong'yo* (Essentials of the *Nirvāṇa Sūtra*), which is still extant, and the *Yŏlban gyŏng so* (Commentary on the *Nirvāṇa Sūtra*), which is lost. In the *Yŏlban chong'yo* he classified the different perspectives on Buddha-nature within the Nirvāṇa school into six categories, then attempted to synthesize these categories into a single comprehensive doctrine on the basis of a Mind-only framework:

> All of the above views are both correct and incorrect. Why is that so? Because Buddha-nature is neither "thus" nor "not-thus." From the standpoint of "thus," all six positions are correct, while from the standpoint of "not-thus," all are incorrect. What does this mean? This means that the viewpoints of the six masters can actually be subsumed under just two categories. The first master points to the effect as a future potentiality of inherent Buddha-nature, while the other five masters refer to the cause as a present actuality (of inherent Buddha-nature). Among these five masters there are also two kinds of inversions. The last master follows the ultimate truth (*paramārthasatya*), whereas the preceding four masters follow the conventional truth (*samvṛtisatya*). These four are not outside of either the subjective self or the objective dharma. The first master in this group upholds the subjective self, whereas the last three base themselves on the objective dharmas. These three are nothing but "up" or "down." The last of the three focuses on the seed [consciousness], while the other two focus on the present consciousness, upon which there are many different opinions according to one's perspective. (HPC 1.538b)

Wŏnhyo then stated that One Mind has two aspects. It is "not defiled, yet works as if defiled," and it is "defiled, without being defiled." Hence, One Mind is immaculate, though it participates in the six levels of defilement because of permeation by *vāsanās* inherited through karmic causation. It is both defiled and pure at the same time. According to his analysis, the sixth master comprehends this idea of "Suchness-Buddha-nature" as being "defiled yet pure," but the other five only describe it in terms of degrees of defilement. Even when One Mind participates in *saṃsāra* because of its permeation by negative *vāsanās* (i.e., defilements), it is still capable of realizing its original purity because of its "internal permeation" by positive *vāsanās*, which effect a return to the immaculate state of *nirvāṇa*. Wŏnhyo continues:

> The sixth master says that the Buddha-nature of Suchness is not tainted even if it is amid impurity; why then did the mind following the impurity not keep the one nature? Contacting conditions and expecting their results, there must be a birth. The nature of the birth is not made by the external permeations. Hence, the seed by nature. This reflects the fifth position. Furthermore, when such a mind follows impurity and creates phenomenal arising and ceasing, it stays in the position of consciousness, yet it does not lose the nature of divine understanding. Since it does not lose this nature, ultimately it returns to the origin of the mind. This constitutes the fourth view. Now, if the mind of arising and ceasing follows impurity and, because of its internal permeation power, creates two kinds of karma, such as the dislike of suffering and the desire for pleasure, which are causes of those activities, this becomes the origin that should reach the ultimate end. This is the view of the third master. Thus when One Mind works with impurity, whenever it does so, it perfectly governs all the dharmas. As a result, it is embodied every moment. Hence, the embodiment. This corresponds to the view of the second master. Thus when the Original Enlightenment of sentient beings works, it naturally and necessarily reaches the end of Great Enlightenment. Hence the future Enlightenment. This is the view of the first master. (HPC 1.538c–539a)

Wŏnhyo concludes his analysis by asserting that in the end all six masters fail to fully comprehend Buddha-nature, articulating only a partial description of it from a particular perspective. He compares the attempts of these masters to describe Buddha-nature to the group of blind men trying to describe an elephant on the basis of touch alone, each man limited to the part of the elephant nearest his reach. They cannot know what the elephant as a whole is really like, and yet their partial description of it do not describe something other than the elephant. In the same way, insofar as One Mind is like the elephant—from the standpoint of its phenomenal aspects—each of the above six doctrines accurately describes a particular stage in the tainting of One Mind through its *vāsanās* or permeation. Insofar as One Mind is not like the elephant, still—from the standpoint of its absolute aspect—all six descriptions are incomplete, since One Mind is the Buddha's

10. Buddha images at the ruins of Ch'ilbul Hermitage, early Unified Silla period.

reality of non-discrimination. Hence, the six perspectives on inherent Buddha-nature are each partially valid on the *samvṛti* (conventional) level, but are ultimately incorrect on the *paramārtha* level. On the *paramārtha* level, the reality of One Mind is completely devoid of self-nature, even though it inexhaustibly follows conditions and is free from all extremes.

Buddhism of Total Interpenetration

Of great importance to Wŏnhyo's efforts at doctrinal harmonization is his *p'an-chiao* system, or classification of the various Buddhist teachings. The earliest reference to this aspect of his thought appears in Fa-tsang's (643–712) well-known *Hua-yen t'an hsüan chi*. Subsequent works of Hua-yen scholarship, including Li T'ung-hsüan's *Hsin hua-yen lun*, Hui-yüan's *Kan-ting chi*, and Ch'eng-kuan's *Hua-yen ching su*, have all quoted this passage from Fa-tsang, which is based on Wŏnhyo's no longer extant commentary on the *Hwaŏmgyŏng (Hua-yen Sūtra)*. In Fa-tsang's text, we read:

> Dharma-master Wŏnhyo of the Silla Dynasty wrote a commentary on the *Hua-yen sūtra*, in which he also established a *p'an-chiao* system of Four Doctrines as follows: first, the Particular Teachings of the Three Vehicles, such as the Teaching of Four Noble Truths and the *Dependant Origination Sūtra*; second,

the Comprehensive Teaching of Three Vehicles, such as the teachings of the prajñā texts and the *Sandhinirmocana Sūtra*; third, the particular teachings of One Vehicle, such as the *Sūtra of Brahmā's Net*, etc.; fourth, the Complete Teachings of One Vehicle, namely the *Hua-yen sūtra*, a teaching of Samantabhadra Bodhisattva.

Although Wŏnhyo's fourfold *p'an-chiao* system deviates from the fivefold *p'an-chiao* systems of Chih-yen and Fa-tsang, important theoreticians of the Chinese Hua-yen school, he clearly proclaims the Hwaŏm school to have the most comprehensive Buddhist doctrinal teachings. However, despite the superiority he attributes to the Hwaŏm school, it is clear that he wants his *p'an-chiao* system understood as a purely philosophical concept, rather than as a vehicle of sectarian propaganda. This can be seen in the concluding sentence of his *Commentary on the Nirvāṇa Sūtra*: "If someone tries to read the intention of the Buddha manifested in the sūtras by means of a sectarian *p'an-chiao* system, it is a serious mistake." And in the preface to his *Hwaŏmgyŏng so* he adds:

> The teaching of the dharma-field of non-hindrance is originally neither dharma nor non-dharma, neither vast nor small, neither one nor many. Since it is not vast, it collapses into a small particle of dust but remains nothing; since it is not small, it becomes an expansive space but still leaves more; since it is not short, it is able to contain the kalpic waves of the three worlds; since it is not long, it enters into one moment with its entirety; since it is neither dynamic nor static, *saṃsāra* becomes *nirvāṇa* and *nirvāṇa* becomes *saṃsāra*; since it is neither one nor many, one dharma is all dharmas and all dharmas are one dharma. Thus, the dharma of non-hindrance creates the dharma-gate to the dharma realm, and that is where all bodhisattvas enter and all Buddhas of the three worlds exist.... If someone is able to grasp the essence of the dharma-gate, they are immediately able to manifest throughout the three boundless worlds before a single thought-instant has lapsed. Furthermore, they will place all worlds of the ten directions into a single particle of dust.

In this passage Wŏnhyo presents his basic interpretation of the structure of the *Hwaŏmgyŏng* and the essential method of his own Hwaŏm thought-system, a dialectical logic that reconciles contradictions and the interpenetration of opposites in terms of the relation between doctrine *(chong)* and essence *(yo),* and the opening *(kae)* and sealing *(hap)* of truth.

As explained earlier, "doctrine" here refers to the unfolding of the one into the many, and "essence" refers to the unification of the many back into the one. When the truth is opened, it is called doctrine; when it is sealed, it is called essence. Consequently, when Wŏnhyo says, "Since [the teaching of the dharma-field] is not vast, it collapses into a small particle of dust but remains nothing," he is referring to the sealing of the truth into its essence through the unification of the many into one. Conversely, when he says, "Since it is not small, it becomes an expansive space but still leaves more," he is referring to the opening of the essence of the truth into doctrine, or the unfolding of the one into the many. Also, when he says, "Since it is not short, it is able to contain the kalpic waves of the three worlds," he is referring to the opening of the essence of the truth into doctrine; whereas, when he says, "Since it is not long, it enters into one moment with its entirety," he is referring to the sealing of the truth into its essence.

Thus, when Wŏnhyo writes, "Since it is neither dynamic nor static, *saṃsāra* becomes *nirvāṇa* and *nirvāṇa* becomes *saṃsāra*; since it is neither one nor many, one dharma is all dharmas and all dharmas are one dharma," he is summarizing the dialectical interplay between essence and doctrine by means of the sealing and opening of truth. It is this dialectic of interpenetration that provides the theoretical infrastructure for Wŏnhyo's *t'ong pulgyo*, or Buddhism of total interpenetration.

The Treatise on the Awakening of Mahāyāna Faith

Long treasured as the foremost synthesis of all major Mahāyāna Buddhist doctrines, the *Treatise on the Awakening of Mahāyāna Faith* (a sixth-century Chinese apocryphon attributed to Aśvaghoṣa) is the seminal text of East Asian Mahāyāna Buddhism.[7] It is also the subject of Wŏnhyo's most important work, the *Kisillon so* (Commentary on the Treatise on the Awakening of Mahāyāna Faith), also known as the *Haedong so* (C. Hai-dong shu, or The Korean commentary). Though traditionally considered to be one of the three most authoritative commentaries on the *Awakening of Faith*, Wŏnhyo's commentary is still not widely known, having been overshadowed by Fa-tsang's work on the same subject. Yet Fa-tsang himself made great use of many of Wŏnhyo's basic philosophical writings, including the *Kisillon so*.

In his commentary, Wŏnhyo argues that the *Awakening of Faith* was originally a nonsectarian text revealing a key hermeneutical principle through which *hwajaeng* and *t'ong pulgyo* can be achieved. This principle is contained in the Chinese *ti-yung* (K. *ch'e-yong*), or essence-function, formula. According to Wŏnhyo, by using the essence-function (or substance-operation) formula, all dialectical contradictions and polarized opposites (e.g., the One and the many, subject and object, *nirvāṇa* and *saṃsāra*) can be perfectly harmonized, just as it is argued in Hwaŏm Buddhism. *Ch'e* signifies the internal, universal, and invisible dimensions of reality, whereas *yong* signifies its external, particular, and visible dimensions. *Ch'e* can likewise refer to the static and unmoving aspect of reality while *yong* can refer to its dynamic aspect, which continually responds to causal conditions.

The purpose of using the *ch'e-yong* formula is to show the inseparability or non-duality of two apparently contradictory concepts. This Mahāyāna Buddhist formulation contrasts with the dualistic *neng-so* (K. *nung-so*), or subject-object formulation that fits the ordinary discriminating mind of sentient beings. The *Platform Sūtra*, another major text of East Asian Buddhism, contains a famous analysis using the essence-function construction to illustrate the inseparability of meditation *(samādhi)* and wisdom *(prajñā)*. While according to the *neng-so* construction meditation must "precede" the attainment of wisdom, making enlightenment the "object" of practice, through the *ch'e-yong* construction of Mahāyāna Buddhism, meditation and wisdom, or practice and enlightenment, are simultaneous and inseparable aspects of the Buddha's mind of non-discrimination.

Here is how the *ch'e-yong* formulation of the relationship between practice and enlightenment is expressed by the Ch'an patriarch Hui-neng in the *Platform Sūtra*:

> Good friends, my teaching of the Dharma takes meditation *(ting)* and wisdom *(hui)* as its basis. Never under any circumstances say mistakenly that meditation and wisdom are different; they are a unity, not two things. Meditation itself is the substance of wisdom, wisdom itself is the function of meditation. At the very moment when there is wisdom, then meditation exists in wisdom. At the very moment when there is meditation, then wisdom exists in meditation. Good friends, this means that meditation and wisdom are alike. Students, be careful not to say that meditation gives rise to wisdom, or that wisdom gives rise to meditation, or that meditation and wisdom are different from each other.

Hui-neng then goes on to develop the simile of the lamp (representing *ch'e*) and its light (representing *yong*):

> Good friends, how then are meditation and wisdom alike? They are like the lamp and the light it gives forth. If there is a lamp there is light; if there is no lamp there is no light. The lamp is the substance of light; the light is the function of the lamp. Thus, although they have two names, in substance they are not two. Meditation and wisdom are also like this.[8]

Wŏnhyo's interpretation of the *Awakening of Faith* also depends on the use of the *ch'e-yong* hermeneutic device, as can be seen from the very first paragraph of his commentary:

> The essence of Mahāyāna is generally described as being completely empty and very mysterious. However, no matter how mysterious it may be, can it exist anywhere but in the world of myriad phenomena? No matter how

empty it may be, it is still present in the conversations of the people. Although it exists nowhere except in the world of phenomena, none of the five eyes can see its form. Although it is always present in discourse, none of the four unlimited explanatory attributes can describe its shape. One may desire to call it "vast," but it enters into the interiorless and nothing remains. One may want to call it "infinitesimal," but it envelops the exteriorless without exhausting itself. One might say it is "something," yet because of it, every thing is empty. One might say it is "nothing," yet through it all the myriad things arise. I do not know its name, but if forced to name it, I will call it "Mahāyāna." (T 44.202a-b)

The *ch'e-yong* construction clearly complements Wŏnhyo's Hwaŏm-based dialectic of opening *(kae)* and sealing *(hap)*. For example, when Wŏnhyo states, "One wants to call it [Mahāyāna] great, but it enters the interiorless and nothing remains," he is describing the process of sealing the truth *(ch'e);* whereas when he states, "but it envelops the exteriorless without exhausting itself," he is describing the process of opening the truth *(yong)*. Again, the phrase "everything is empty because of it" represents sealing, while the phrase "yet myriad things arise through it" represents opening.

Wŏnhyo goes on to analyze directly the *ch'e-yong* structure of the *Awakening of Faith* in terms of this opening-sealing, doctrine-essence dialectic:

Because this is the intent of the treatise, when it is unfolded, immeasurable and limitless meanings are found in its doctrine. Conversely, when it is sealed, the principle of the two aspects of One Mind is found to be its essence. Within the two aspects, myriad meanings are included without confusion. These limitless meanings are identical to One Mind and are completely amalgamated with it. Therefore, it unfolds and seals freely and it establishes and refutes without restrictions. Unfolding without complicating, sealing without narrowing, establishing without gaining, refuting without losing—this is Aśvaghoṣa's wonderful skill and the essence of the *Awakening of Faith*. (202b)

Ch'e, representing the universal essence of One Mind, seals without diminishing, while *yong*, representing the external function, opens into myriad phenomena without exhausting itself. These two aspects of essence and function, or sealing and opening, are both identical to One Mind and therefore freely interpenetrate without obstruction.

Wŏnhyo systematically applies the essence-function soteriological formula, now understood in terms of the dialectical logic of sealing and opening, to nearly every problem raised by the *Awakening of Faith*. At the beginning of the third section of his commentary, he interprets the first line of the invocation of the treatise and divides the Buddha-treasure *(buddharatna)* into two elements: (1) the merit of Buddha's mind; and (2) the merit of Buddha's body. He then subdivides each element into its essence and function. Using the essence/function formula, he analyzes the text referring to the merit of Buddha's mind as follows:

> In praising the excellence of Buddha's mind, [one] is praising both its function and its essence. The words, "whose acts are most excellent, who pervades all the ten directions," praise the function of the Buddha's acts.... The words "he is omniscient" praise the essence of Buddha's wisdom. The function of the Buddha's acts pervades all the ten directions because there is nowhere that the essence of Buddha's wisdom does not penetrate. The essence of Buddha's wisdom penetrates everywhere, hence it is "omniscient."

In this analysis, Wŏnhyo utilizes the essence-function formula to portray the inseparability of the acts and wisdom of the Buddha. Here, enlightened wisdom, which comprehends emptiness (śūnyatā), is the Buddha's internal essence, and the compassionate acts, which liberate all sentient beings, are the Buddha's external function. He goes on to apply the essence-function formula to the account of the Buddha's body:

> The praise of the excellence of the Buddha's form is twofold: (1) the words "who has form but is unimpeded" refer to the marvelousness of the essence of Buddha's form; (2) the word "omnipotent" refers to the excellence of the function of Buddha's form.

Here, in agreement with Hwaŏm teaching, Wŏnhyo identifies the internal essence of the Buddha's body with unimpededness or non-obstruction and its external function with complete freedom. In contrast, the Chinese commentaries on the *Awakening of Faith*, written by T'an-yen and Hui-yüan prior to Wŏnhyo's, did not use the essence-function formula in analyzing these important passages. T'an-yen held that the phrase "whose acts are most excellent and omniscient" refers to the truth-body (*dharmakāya*), and the phrase "whose body is unimpeded and completely free" refers to the reward-body (*saṃbhogakāya*). Hui-yüan, in contrast, claims that the "acts" and "omniscience" in this phrase refer to the notion of the "marks of good fortune," and to the wisdom of the incarnate Buddha. While both of these interpretations analyze the virtues of the *Buddha-ratna* using different aspects of other well-known Buddhist doctrines, such as *trikāya*, or three-body theory, Wŏnhyo illustrates the inseparability of the two seemingly different virtues through the *ch'e-yong* hermeneutic device.

The ingenuity of Wŏnhyo's analysis of the *Awakening of Faith* is evinced in his application of essence-function construction to the Mahāyāna Buddhist notion of faith (C. *hsin*), the concept at the core of the treatise. At one point, Wŏnhyo uses *ch'e-yong* construction as a hermeneutic device to interpret the meaning of the text's title, *Ta-ch'eng ch'i-hsin lun*. If the Chinese title is translated into English as the "Treatise on the Awakening of Faith in Mahāyāna" (as has been done by virtually all translators), the word Mahāyāna *(ta-ch'eng)*—a Sanskrit term meaning "Great Vehicle"—becomes the object of "awakening faith" *(ch'i-hsin)*, thereby establishing a dualistic subject-object structure wholly alien to the text and to Mahāyāna Buddhism in general. Wŏnhyo is careful to point out that *ta-ch'eng* is not the object of *ch'i-hsin* but that "Mahāyāna" represents an internal essence—One Mind, or the Mind of Sentient Beings—while "faith" represents its external function. In Wŏnhyo's own words:

> In conclusion, "Mahāyāna" is the essence of the doctrine of this treatise; and "awakening faith" is its efficacious operation. Thus, the title is composed to show the unity of essence and function. Hence the words, "Treatise on the Awakening of Mahāyāna Faith." (T 44.203b)

Thus, Wŏnhyo dispenses with the dualistic subject-object or "faith-in" construction, predominant in theistic religions, and replaces it with the *ch'e-yong* formulation of faith, or "faith-of." According to Wŏnhyo, faith is simply the external function of One Mind, and the phrase *ta-ch'eng* in the title simply means: "the naturally functioning mind," "the properly operating mind," or "the mind of faith."

An even more direct reading of the text's title is achieved by simply following the natural order of the Chinese characters *(ta ch'eng ch'i-hsin)*, which means "Mahāyāna arouses faith," or "Mind arouses faith." This rendering is in agreement with one of the first sentences of the treatise, which reads: "There is a principle that can arouse the root of Mahāyāna faith." As the treatise then goes on to specify, the term "principle" here refers to One Mind, which is the Buddha's enlightened Mind of non-discrimination, and the above sentence actually means: "There is a Mind that can arouse the root of Mahāyāna faith." In this sentence, "Mind" is the *ch'e*, and "faith" is the *yong*, so that One Mind and faith cannot be separated.

In his *Kisillon so,* Wŏnhyo elaborates on this statement in the following terms:

> The words "there is a Dharma" refer to the principle of One Mind. If people are able to understand this Dharma, they are bound to arouse the broad and great root of faith, hence, the words "that can arouse the root of Mahāyāna Faith." The marks of "the root of Mahāyāna faith" are analogous to the description of faith given in the section on the explanation of the title. Once the root of faith is established, one immediately enters the Buddha's way. Having entered the Buddha's way, one obtains inexhaustible treasures.

Wŏnhyo's analysis of Mahāyāna Buddhist faith in terms of the essence-function formula, where One Mind is the essence and faith is the function, can be regarded as one of his most valuable contributions to Buddhist studies. In this analysis he demonstrates that faith does not actually require an external object, as is assumed by the "faith-in" construction of dualistic thinking. Instead, from the perspective of essence-function construction, an act of faith can be seen as a form of return to one's own true mind (One Mind). The contrast between the essence-function and subject-object structures of faith thus takes on crucial soteriological implications. While the subject-object construction of faith posits that faith is merely a condition preliminary to enlightenment, the *ch'e-yong* view, in which faith is perceived as the external operation of one's own mind, envisions faith and enlightenment as simultaneous and inseparable. This implies that as soon as a resolute faith is awakened, the One Mind of Buddha is instantly realized. This is the conceptual leap that provides both the theoretical and practical basis for the doctrine of sudden enlightenment developed later, for example, in Chinul's syncretic harmonization of Hwaŏm and Sŏn Buddhism.

Wŏnhyo then goes on to describe the characteristics of Mahāyāna faith using the essence-attributes-function *(ch'e-sang-yong)* formulation that appears in the *Awakening of Faith*, essentially a variation on the basic essence-function construction described earlier. The treatise posits One Mind and then divides it into, first, the absolute dimension of One Mind, and second, the phenomenal dimension of One Mind. Then it explains these two dimensions of One Mind in terms of the Three Greatnesses *(ch'e, sang, and yong)*. Here, *ch'e* signifies the absolute dimension of One Mind, while *sang* and *yong* denote different aspects of the phenomenal dimension. Using this essence-attributes-functions formula to distinguish between the three components of Mahāyāna faith, Wŏnhyo writes:

> This treatise causes the faith of people to be awakened, hence the words [in its title], "Awakening [of] Faith." Faith is a term that indicates certainty. Here, faith refers to certainty that the Truth really exists, that practice can get results, and that when practice does get results, there will be boundless merit. Faith that the Truth really exists is faith in the greatness of the essence [of Suchness]. Since we believe that all dharmas are unobtainable, we also believe that there really is a Dharma-world of equality. Faith that practice can get results is faith in the greatness of the attributes [of Suchness]. Since [we believe that the attributes of Suchness] possess the merit that belongs to the essence [but] permeate sentient beings, [we] also believe that [we] surely return to the Source by being permeated by the attributes [of Suchness]. Faith in the operation of boundless merit is faith in the greatness of the operation [of Suchness], because there is nothing that Suchness does not do. If one can awaken these three faiths, one can enter the world of the Buddha's

Dharma, produce all merits, be free from all demonic states, and attain the Peerless Way.

In this analysis, Wŏnhyo defines faith as "a term that indicates being certain." Moreover, it is being certain of the following three truths: (1) One Mind exists; (2) practice gets results; and (3) when practice gets results, there will be boundless merits. Faith as a form of certainty means the removal of all doubts and wrong attachments. In Wŏnhyo's own words:

> Sentient beings fall into the sea of life and death and do not hasten to the shore of *nirvāṇa* for so long because of doubts and wrong attachments. Therefore, what is meant by "saving sentient beings" is to help them to eliminate their doubts and forsake their wrong attachments.... Specifically, two things are doubted by those seeking Mahāyāna. The first is the Dharma. Doubting this prevents the determination to practice. The second is the method. Doubting this prevents practice itself.

According to Wŏnhyo, doubt of the Dharma is eradicated by establishing the principle of One Mind; whereas doubt about method is eradicated by establishing the efficacy of practice. Through the elimination of doubt and the attainment of certainty, one acquires the resolute confidence of "non-backsliding" or "non-retrogressive" faith, which means reaching the level of *aniyata rāśi*, or the "determined class," the standard for the "perfection of faith" established by *The Awakening of Faith*. The first part of the treatise explains the principles of non-backsliding faith in terms of One Mind, its two dimensions, and the Three Greatnesses, for the benefit of those who have not attained the level of *niyata rāśi* or the determined class. Later, the treatise explains the principles of the second, lower level of faith, or the "faith of those who have not yet returned to One Mind." This concept of a second level of faith, or a backsliding faith belonging to those who are still at the level of *aniyata rāśi*, or the undetermined class, originates in the theory of four faiths and five practices found in Chapter Four of the treatise, "On Faith and Practice." The beginning of Chapter Four reads: "We will now present a discussion of faith and practice. This discussion is intended for those who have not yet joined the *niyata rāśi*, or the determined class." Thus, we know this second kind of faith refers to those who are still in a retrogressive state and can "fall back" at any time. Concerning those in this state, the treatise asks: "What kind of faith (should they have), and how should they practice it?" The response follows:

> Briefly speaking, there are four faiths. What are they? The first is to believe in the Ultimate Source, or to be mindful, with the utmost willingness, of the principle of Suchness. The second is to believe that the Buddha has innu-

merable excellent virtues, or to think always of being close to Buddha, to make offerings to him, and to respect him. Furthermore, it means to awaken the capacity for goodness, which means wishing to have the omniscience that the Buddha has. The third is to believe that the Dharma is the source of great benefits, or to always think of practicing all of the perfections. The fourth is to believe that the saṅgha is able to correctly practice the Mahāyāna ideal of benefiting both oneself and others, or to rejoice always in being close to the assembly of bodhisattvas and to pursue genuine practice as it does.

Thus, the "four faiths" described by the treatise consist of faith in Suchness, followed by faith in the Three Jewels, namely, the Buddha, the Dharma, and the Saṅgha. Traditionally, it has been believed that establishing a deep faith in the Three Jewels is the very foundation of Buddhist religious life, but this treatise is unique in that it adds another aspect of faith, namely, a deep faith in the principle of Suchness.

One of the great contributions Wŏnhyo's commentary on the treatise makes is the clarification that this secondary mode of faith—the affirmation of both Suchness and the Three Jewels—is itself only an externalized and symbolic form of the primary mode of faith—the affirmation of One Mind and the Three Greatnesses. Rhi Ki-yong, a scholar of Wŏnhyo's philosophy and the author of a book entitled *Wŏnhyo sasang* (Wŏnhyo's thought), provides a valuable synopsis of Wŏnhyo's doctrine of returning to the Three Jewels *(triratna),* and the central role it plays in his system of thought.

At the crux of Buddhism is the "three surrenders to the Three Jewels *(triratna)."* The shortest path to Wŏnhyo's Buddhist thought is to delve into his conception of *triratna:*

> The Buddha, the Dharma, and the saṅgha. The invocation in the *Taesung kisillon so* offers the following characteristics of his thought: (1) Buddhism consists of returning to the *triratna* and depending on them; (2) The Three Jewels are nothing but the external expression of *ilsim* (One Mind); (3) The object of what Wŏnhyo thought of as religion is One Mind, the external expression of which is the *triratna....* Wŏnyho is particularly emphatic on this point. His profound understanding of the essential nature of the *triratna* is explicit in the explanation of the *trisarana* (three returnings) he gives in his first invocation of the *Taesung kisillon*: "that which the One Mind returns to is but the *triratna.*" This is an important contribution to the Mahāyānist understanding of *triratna.*[9]

Rhi adds that Wŏnhyo's doctrine of returning to the *triratna* is an example of his principle of *hwajaeng,* because it reconciles the Hīnayānist view of the Three Jewels, which considers them to be real objects of faith, with the Mahāyānist view, which emphasizes the interiority or symbolic quality of the *triratna.*

According to Wŏnhyo, those at the level of *aniyata rāśi*, who have a back-sliding faith, are attached to the dualistic *neng-so* (faith-in) framework, con-sequently, they mistakenly externalize the *triratna* as "objects" of faith. However, those at the level of *niyata rāśi*, who have a non-backsliding faith, are governed by the non-dualistic *ch'e-yong* ("faith-of") construction, according to which faith does not require an object but is instead the natu-ral operation of one's own mind. At this level, the secondary faith directed outward to Suchness and the Three Jewels is recognized as an externalized objectification of primary faith, which is directed inward to One Mind and the Three Greatnesses. In Wŏnhyo's view, Buddha represents *ch'e* (essence) at the absolute level of One Mind, while Dharma is *sang* (attribute), and sangha is *yong* (function) at the phenomenal level of One Mind. Thus, according to Wŏnhyo's principle of *hwajaeng*, the Greatnesses (essence, attributes, and functions), and the Jewels (Buddha, Dharma, and sangha), signify the inner and outer dimensions of One Mind, and ultimately are identical in both structure and content.

Wŏnhyo's Legacy

We have looked at Wŏnhyo's efforts at reconciling the various doctrinal disputes of the Unified Silla period in an attempt to create a fully compre-hensive, all-inclusive Buddhism—*t'ong pulgyo*. As stated earlier, Wŏnhyo's syncretic outlook was very much in keeping with the overall cultural cli-mate of Silla, an atmosphere that favored synthesis in all fields of intellec-tual and artistic endeavor. But even after the fall of Silla, syncretism con-tinued as the fundamental, driving force in Korean Buddhism, and the search for *t'ong pulgyo* still occupied Buddhist thinkers of the succeeding Koryŏ dynasty, as well as those coming after. In this light, Wŏnhyo's con-tribution is obvious: by combining the dialectical device of essence-function with that of opening-sealing, he created a powerful interpretive tool for the examination of Buddhist texts, one that allowed him to apply the principle of *hwajaeng*, or harmonization, to a wide variety of theoretical conflicts. In so doing, he established the basic conceptual structure within which all sub-sequent discussion of *t'ong pulgyo* would take place.

But it would be a mistake to see Wŏnhyo as concerned primarily with the reconciliation of sectarian differences. His interest in harmonization goes much farther, for he was one of the first thinkers directly to confront the latent tension within Buddhism between scriptural theory and meditative experience—that is, between the intellectual, language-based study of scripture, and direct experiential learning, or meditation. As can be seen in his discussion of the idea of faith in his commentary on the *Awakening of Faith*, Wŏnhyo tries to strike a delicate and subtle balance between a series of interconnected opposites: between scriptural study and meditation, language and direct experience, intellect and intuition. Using the principle of *hwajaeng*, he shows how both sides of the equation are ultimately subsumed within the larger, all-inclusive entity of Mahāyāna faith, coexisting separately and yet completely interpenetrative. In the final analysis, we can see that this is where Wŏnhyo's true value lies, for the opposition between theory and praxis cuts across simple school divisions, and it eventually became the focus of all later attempts at the development of *t'ong pulgyo*.

Notes

1. In 372, Shun-tao, a Chinese monk, traveled to Koguryŏ at the invitation of King Sosurim (r. 371–383), bringing sacred images and scriptures. In 375 a second Chinese Buddhist priest, A-tao, came to Koguryŏ, and the government built the first two Buddhist temples in Korea for these priests, the Songmunsa and the Ibullansa. Buddhism flourished, and within twenty years there were nine Buddhist temples in the capital city alone. In 393 King Sosurim converted to Buddhism. This established a deep, unifying bond between Buddhism and the state, which was thereafter a principal characteristic of Buddhism in Korea.

2. Confucianism, the profound tradition of social rectification based on the teachings of Confucius (551 B.C.E.–479 B.C.E.), entered Korea most likely in the early period of the Koguryŏ dynasty. We know from the *Samkuk Saki* (Chronicles of the Three Kingdoms) that in 372 C.E., the second year of King Sosurim's reign, a national university dedicated to Confucian studies was established in Koguryŏ. But it was not until the Yi dynasty (1393–1910) that the Confucian sociopolitical system rose to a position of great power.

3. In 385, thirteen years after Buddhism was introduced to Koguryŏ, an Indian monk named Mananata came to Paekche from China and was openly welcomed by the Paekche king, Chinmyu. Within a year a temple was erected, and soon thereafter Buddhism became the state religion.

4. Korean tradition has it that the Chinese missionary priest A-tao, who introduced Buddhism into Koguryŏ, later brought Buddhism to Silla during the reign of King Nulji (417–457). However, A-tao's Buddhism spread only among the common people, and did not reach the ruling class. The second Chinese monk to enter Silla was Yüan-piao, an envoy from the Liang dynasty in China. Despite continual resistance from Silla's aristocracy, Yüan-piao's Buddhism was welcomed by the royal court, since it was institutionalized, universalized, and scripturalized, all of which could help in governing the nation.

5. Pulgyohak T'ongin Hoe, ed. *Wŏnhyo chonjip* (Seoul: Dongguk Yokkyong Won, 1973) 383–84.

6. Park Chong-hong, "Wŏnhyo ui chŏrhak sasang," in *Han'guk sasang sa* (A history of Korean thought), edited by Han'guk Sasang Yon'guhoe (The Association for the Study of Korean Thought) (Seoul: Ilshinsa, 1976), 59–88.

7. See Yoshito S. Hakeda, *The Awakening of Faith, attributed to Aśvaghoṣa* (New York: Columbia University Press, 1969).

8. Philip Yampolsky, trans. *The Platform Sūtra of the Sixth Patriarch* (New York: Columbia University Press, 1967) 135–37.

9. Rhi Ki-yong, *Wŏnhyo sasang* (Wŏnhyo's thought) (Seoul: Hongbŏpwon, 1978).

Bibliography

HPC = *Han'guk pulgyo chonso* (The collected works of Korean Buddhism). Seoul: Dongguk University Press, 1979.

Taegak kuksa munjip (The collected writings of Ŭich'ŏn). HPC 4.528–567.

Wŏnhyo's works:

Hwaŏmgyŏng so (Commentary on the *Avataṃsaka Sūtra*). One roll [i.e., preface and fascicle three only]. HPC 1.495–497.

Kisillon so (Commentary on *The Treatise on the Awakening of Mahāyāna Faith*). T 44 No. 1844 202a–226a.

Yŏlban chong'yo (Essentials of the *Nirvāṇa Sūtra*). HPC 1.524–47.

Studies

Kim, Young-tae. "Buddhism in the Three Kingdoms." In *The History and Culture of Buddhism*, edited by The Korean Buddhist Research Institute, 35–74. Seoul: Dongguk University Press, 1993.

———. *Introduction to the Buddhist History of Korea*. Seoul: Kyongsowon, 1986.

Lancaster, Lewis R. and Chai-shin Yu, eds. *Introduction of Buddhism to Korea: New Cultural Patterns*. Berkeley: Asian Humanities Press, 1989.

———. *Assimilation of Buddhism in Korea: Religious Maturity and Innovation in the Silla Dynasty*. Berkeley: Asian Humanities Press, 1991.

Lee, Ki-Baik. *A New History of Korea*. Trans. Edward W. Wagner. Cambridge: Harvard University Press, 1984.

Lee, Peter H., ed. *Sourcebook of Korean Civilization. Vol. 1, From Early Times to the Sixteenth Century*. New York: Columbia University Press, 1993.

Park, Sung Bae. *Buddhist Faith and Sudden Enlightenment*. Albany: State University of New York Press, 1983.

Yu, Dong-shik. *Shamanism in Korea*. Seoul: Yonse University Press, 1975.

17

The Koryŏ Period

ROBERT E. BUSWELL, JR.

T HE TRANSFER OF political power from Unified Silla to the Koryŏ dynasty in 937 initially had little effect on the then firmly entrenched Buddhist schools of the peninsula. The early Koryŏ rulers inherited from their Silla predecessors a confidence in the ability of Buddhism to guarantee the safety of the nation. In order to ensure the efficacy of that protection, the court ordered the general worship of the Buddha, sponsored numerous temple-construction projects, and lent lavish support to the Buddhist ecclesia both economically and politically. Buddhist monks were accorded a semi-aristocratic status, and gained thereby an opportunity for secular advancement while remaining within the ecclesiastical ranks. A monastic examination system, modeled after the civil-service examinations, allowed students in both the meditative (Sŏn) and doctrinal (Kyo) schools to rise to the top of the church hierarchy, and thus gain access to the sources of secular power as well. While this system boosted the educational level of the saṅgha and fostered considerable social mobility for a semi-feudal state, it ultimately enervated the spiritual aspirations of Buddhism by encouraging interest in secular pursuits. The exemption of monks from corvée labor and the military draft filled the monasteries with people seeking either personal aggrandizement or an escape from the hardships of military and agricultural service.

Another symptom of crisis was the increasing stridency of the debates between the Sŏn and Kyo schools, which had begun during the Silla. The resolution of these intersectarian tensions would occupy the greatest representatives of both traditions, including Ŭich'ŏn (1055–1101), the putative founder of the Korean branch of the T'ien-t'ai (K. Ch'ŏnt'ae) school, and Chinul (1158–1210), the preeminent Sŏn exegete, whose contributions to the evolution of Koryŏ Buddhism far outweigh those of his contemporaries. Chinul's thought, in particular, informs so profoundly all subsequent developments during the Koryŏ period that it perforce will be the focus of attention in this section. The search for an "ecumenical Buddhism" (t'ong pulgyo), which was the goal of the Koryŏ Buddhists, informed much of the subsequent evolution of the tradition, and produced a unique form of Buddhism in the Chogye-chong, which thenceforth was the dominant school in Korean Buddhism. This school merged Sŏn practice with the scholastic philosophy of the Kyo schools, especially that of Hwaŏm (C. Hua-yen).

Synthetic Approaches

Ŭich'ŏn and Chinul represent two diametrically opposed perspectives from which the reconciliation between the Sŏn and Kyo schools could be pursued. Whereas Ŭich'ŏn, steeped in Hwaŏm and Ch'ŏnt'ae thought, tried to incorporate Sŏn into Kyo, Chinul was a fervent champion of the Sŏn approach, and sought to merge Kyo with Sŏn. Each in his own way sought to restore what they perceived to be the fundamental harmony between doctrinal exegesis and meditative development. Chinul's successor, Chin'-gak Hyesim (1178–1234), subsequently broached the possibility that this syncretic tendency could be expanded to embrace the "Three Religions" of Buddhism, Confucianism, and Taoism, thus anticipating the rapprochement that would be so prominent in Chosŏn dynasty religion.

The principal concern of this syncretism was to find a common ground underlying contrasting approaches to Buddhist religious endeavor. Both Sŏn and Kyo philosophers accepted that there was an essential unity, variously called the one mind, the Buddha-nature (S. *buddhadhātu*), the numinous awareness *(yongji)*, or the realm of reality (Skt. *dharma-dhātu*), that harmonized the diversity of religious views. Each of these different approaches could be seen as a unique expression of the same whole. As Chinul often notes in his treatises, citing the Silla Hwaŏm exegete, Ŭisang (625–668), "Within the one there is everything, and within the many is the one. The one is precisely everything; the many are precisely the one" (KZ 216, quoting Ŭisang). East Asians in general, and the Koreans in particular, conceived of Buddhist doctrine as a mass of often disparate teachings, adapted to different needs, capacities, and temperaments. Dissension between rival schools was seen as the result of grasping at any one of these particular interpretations of the Dharma as being absolute truth and rejecting the validity of all other approaches. The Buddha had warned that intellectual positions based on speculative opinion inevitably occasioned conflict, clinging, and pride, thus impeding the apprehension of the ultimate Dharma that transcends all limiting views. The Buddha claimed that he held no views of his own: it was the world that conflicted with him, he says, not he with the world.[1] The Dharma was a raft that could ferry one across the river of birth and death to the "other shore" of nirvāṇa; but after this raft had served its purpose, it was wrong to be so attached to it that one would pick it up and carry it on one's back.[2] Using the Dharma to vanquish one's religious rivals ran counter to its specific salvific purpose, and was more perilous to such disputants than complete ignorance of the Dharma would have been. Eschewing controversy based on speculative views was essential to the success of one's spiritual vocation.

The harmonization of conflicting accounts of Buddhist doctrine and practice could enhance the prospects of spiritual advancement, showing that it

11. Chinul (1158–1210).

was only because people had not penetrated to the source of their own being that sectarian contention occurred. Thus Ŭich'ŏn writes:

> The doctrine established by the saints valued the practice of meditation. [That doctrine] is not something which is to be merely proclaimed by the mouth but ought, in fact, to be practiced by the body. How can [practice] be considered something as useless as a bitter gourd that is hung to one side [and never eaten]?[3]

Chinul confirms this diagnosis:

> What the World Honored One [the Buddha] spoke with his lips is Kyo; what the Patriarchs [of Sŏn] transmitted with their minds is Sŏn. The mind and words of the Buddha and patriarchs cannot be contradictory. How is it that you fail to penetrate to the source, and instead, self-satisfied in your habits, wrongly foment contention and pass the entire day in a futile way?[4]

The rapprochement between meditation and doctrine worked out by Ŭich'ŏn and Chinul was an attempt to restore a proper attitude toward the Dharma. Both strove to resolve the conflict plaguing the Koryŏ church by countering the rival positions of Sŏn and Kyo: on the one hand, that doctrinal understanding served no purpose whatsoever in effecting spiritual liberation, as the most radical factions within Sŏn insisted; and on the other, that a firm foundation in scriptural learning was essential if meditation was to be efficacious, as Kyo contended.

Ŭich'ŏn's approach to Buddhist syncretism was based upon the symbiosis he envisaged between doctrinal study and formal meditation practice. To perfect the student's understanding of Buddhism, he developed a stringent curriculum that led the student through a series of texts drawn from the Hīnayāna, Yogācāra, Tathāgatagarbha, and Hua-yen traditions. By demonstrating the affinities between these different strata of Buddhist philosophical literature, he was able to reconcile the variant accounts of Buddhist doctrine and thereby mitigate sectarian conflicts between the Kyo schools. The motivation for the study of Buddhism was, however, as important as its content. To study merely in order to build one's knowledge or to dispute with rivals emasculated the true purpose of the Dharma as an aid to liberation: "I observe that the present generation of theological students studies the whole day through without knowing why it is studying. Some are lost in biased heterodoxies; others are lost in the pursuit of fame and fortune; some are prideful; others are slothful; some are ambivalent [about their study]. Hence, even by the end of their lives, they will be unable to find the path [leading to enlightenment]."[5] It is only when study is coupled with personal commitment to the quest for enlightenment that its justification is apparent. Ŭich'ŏn was attempting to guarantee a role for formal meditation practice within Koryŏ scholasticism, knowing that it was only through personal meditative experience that the rapprochement he sought between Kyo and Sŏn would be effected.

But meditation would not be efficacious unless it was based on profound doctrinal knowledge. This was the principal qualm that Ŭich'ŏn felt concerning the Sŏn school, with its near-exclusive stress on meditation. As an avid bibliophile, who had collected thousands of volumes by East Asian exegetes, Ŭich'ŏn was repelled by Sŏn's vociferous claims that scriptural knowledge had no role at all in spiritual cultivation, and rejected them as inauthentic: "What was called Sŏn in the past was an approach that matured one's meditation while relying on

12. Śākyamuni Buddha. Kŏryŏ Period.

Kyo. What is called Sŏn nowadays is to talk about Sŏn while abandoning Kyo. To speak about Sŏn nowadays is to grasp at the name but to forget the theme; to practice Sŏn [correctly] is to base oneself on the scriptural explanations and realize their meaning [through meditation practice]."[6] Ŭich'ŏn consistently supported the Kyo schools, to the detriment of Sŏn, giving Kyo its last chance to restore itself to the prominence it enjoyed during the Unified Silla period. After his premature death at the age of forty-seven, however, Kyo succumbed to the inevitable. Unable to counter the rise to primacy of the Sŏn school, Kyo retained only a subsidiary role in Koryŏ Buddhism after Chinul's time.

As a Sŏn meditator who nevertheless retained a strong interest in the scriptural teachings of Kyo, Chinul began his reconciliation of the two branches of Buddhism by attempting to authenticate the Sŏn approach in the sūtras. In the preface to his *Excerpts from the Exposition of the Avataṃsaka*

Sūtra, he tells of the events that led to his syncretic vision. He had long had deep faith in the Sŏn approach, and had been practicing under the assumption made by Sŏn that one could achieve Buddhahood simply by deepening one's introspection until the noumenal nature of the mind was perceived. But when he asked some Hwaŏm scholars about their contemplative system, he was told that the Hwaŏm adept was to meditate on the multivalent state of interaction obtaining between all the phenomenal objects in the universe—the state that Hwaŏm called the "unimpeded interpenetration between all phenomena" *(sasa muae;* C. *shih-shih wu-ai).* Chinul felt that such an externally oriented approach would disturb one's concentration of mind. But if through introspection one could control the mind's tendency to view things always in terms of oneself—if one could remove the subjective tendency to inject the ego into the perceptual process—then those phenomena would naturally be seen to be in interaction with one another, and the state of infinite interfusion described by Hwaŏm would be accomplished effortlessly. Unable to resolve his doubts on the matter through discussions with established teachers, Chinul reviewed the Buddhist scriptures, searching for a passage that might substantiate the Sŏn claim that enlightenment could be achieved through introspection. It was in the *Avataṃsaka Sūtra,* the principal text of the Hwaŏm school itself, that such verification was found: "The wisdom of the Tathāgata is just the same. It is complete in the bodies of all sentient beings. It is merely that deluded ordinary persons are unaware of it."[7] From then on he was convinced of the affinities between the scriptural teachings of Buddhism—particularly the Hwaŏm interpretations of those teachings—and the practices of Sŏn. A subsequent reading of Li T'ung-hsüan's (635–730) commentary on the *Avataṃsaka Sūtra* revealed a method by which ordinary persons could awaken to their innate Buddhahood at the inception of practice. This proved to Chinul that statements made by Sŏn masters, which were informed by their enlightenment experiences, could be confirmed in the sūtras, which were ostensibly spoken by the Buddha himself. In this way, the esoteric, mind-to-mind transmission of Sŏn was shown to have the same authority as any of the scriptures of Buddhism. Since the words of the Buddha and the mind-transmission of the patriarchs could not be contradictory, the steps of practice outlined in the Sŏn and Kyo schools differed only because they were designed for people at different stages of spiritual development.

Chinul was fundamentally a Sŏn master who upheld the authenticity of the esoteric transmission of that school. But he could draw on Hwaŏm philosophy to explain the content of the Sŏn enlightenment experience and defend it against charges of heterodoxy. His reading of the scriptures suggested to

13. Block-print of the *Avataṃsaka Sūtra*, Koryŏ Period.

Chinul that the experience engendered by Sŏn meditation was actually identical with the sudden realization of the realm of reality (*dharma-dhātu*) as taught in Hwaŏm. To counter charges that Sŏn introspection was nothing more than a glorified aphasia, Chinul stresses in *Complete and Sudden Attainment of Buddhahood* (KZ 200–266) that Buddhahood as it is interpreted in Sŏn does not mean the mere passive vision of the self-nature; it is rather the dynamic application of all the qualities brought to light in that vision. This realization of the fundamental, non-dual nature that is identical in both ignorant sentient beings and enlightened Buddhas brings to light two aspects of that nature: the phenomenal function (*yong*), which manifests objects in the sensory realms in all of their diversity, and the noumenal essence (*ch'e*), which is the perfect, bright, and autonomous foundation of the *dharma-dhātu*. It is through these two aspects that the nature exhibits itself amid all plurality and thus accomplishes the unimpeded interpenetration of all phenomena. Since the functioning of that self-nature is unimpeded in all affairs, and since its functioning in the phenomenal sphere is never separate from its noumenal essence, if someone will look back on the radiance emanating from the enlightened nature, falsity will be extinguished, the mind's activities will be purified, and the myriad phenomena will be shown to exist in a state of perfect harmony. Consequently, the perfect interfusion of all phenomena as taught by Hwaŏm is not distinct from the fundamental nature of sentient beings; and if that nature is realized through Sŏn practice, the Hwaŏm vision of enlightenment will be spontaneously realized as well.

Conversely, Chinul also tried to counter the notion prevalent among Sŏn adepts that the scholastic schools, and especially Hwaŏm, were simply engaged in speculative philosophy, and had no interest in meditation practice. Sŏn valued a minimum of words, and tried to keep the presentation of its teachings as simple and unpretentious as possible. Many Sŏn students assumed that because this terse style was antithetical to the prolix conceptual descriptions prevalent in the scholastic schools, its rhetoric was closer to non-conceptual reality. Speculative philosophy, as a product of the conceptualizing processes of thought, only sustained the tendency toward discrimination, which was regarded as the force that prevented beings from realizing the undifferentiated, enlightened nature. Chinul, however, cautioned Sŏn adepts that the conceptual descriptions used in the scholastic teachings were actually intended to incite the student toward the attainment of Buddhahood, the same goal as that sought in Sŏn practice. Doctrinal descriptions were aimed at sentient beings of lesser capacity, who were not yet capable of engendering the radical non-attachment from even thought itself that Sŏn demanded. Hence, such descriptions could instill proper understanding of the path and the results anticipated from following it, and encourage students to have confidence in their ability to apply themselves in their practice. Eventually, such conventional descriptions would have to be abandoned in order to gain direct access to non-conceptual truth. Chinul himself did not hesitate to use Hwaŏm thought as a heuristic tool in explaining his own school. Always stressing the utilitarian function of Hwaŏm theory, however, he never advocated the classic contemplations of the orthodox Hwaŏm school, but instead encouraged introspection on the fundamental essence of the *dharma-dhātu* itself.

Introspection and Buddha-Nature

Chinul's syncretic outlook was based on his equation of the Hwaŏm teaching that Buddhahood may be achieved at the very inception of practice with the Sŏn tenet that Buddhahood could be accomplished instantly merely by seeing one's own original nature. As a corollary to this, Chinul saw a correspondence between, on the one hand, Li T'ung-hsüan's premise that the discriminative minds of sentient beings are originally identical to the fundamental wisdom of Buddhahood, and, on the other, the Sŏn claim that "mind is Buddha." The essential unity of Kyo and Sŏn will be recognized when the unmoving wisdom of universal brightness—the quality of sentience that is most fundamental to all "sentient" beings—is perceived. Such insight is achieved through the faculty of introspection or "counter-illumination" *(panjo):* looking back on the mind itself and verifying thereby the truth of one's innate Buddhahood. Thus the sectarian rapprochement forged by Chinul was based on direct experience of the mind-nature, not simply on hypothesis or logical proof. The vision of an undiscriminated reality that is no longer bound by the limitations inherent in conceptualization reconciles all rival standpoints, and consummates ecumenism.

Analytical treatments of truth are generally eschewed in Sŏn. Although Sŏn masters, Chinul included, often use doctrinal concepts in order to explain Buddhism in such a way that people of lesser capacity will be able to grasp it for themselves, this is done with the sole purpose of prompting the student to put that theory into practice by introspection into the mind itself, and not to promulgate still more theoretical positions. Descriptions that are intended to provide a logically consistent, theoretical perspective, which delimits and separates the true from the false, are inherently incapable of expressing a comprehensive position that could embrace all possible viewpoints. The narrowness of any such perspective, and the clinging to

that perspective that ignorance engenders, will inevitably entangle the proponent in argumentation and contention instead of leading to that truth
itself. As Chinul says, "When those of lesser spiritual faculties grasp at
words, everything becomes different. When those who are accomplished
understand properly, everything becomes the same" (KZ 218). Hence, one
of the primary results of speculative views is that the person is forced into
conflict with those who hold different views.

It is through introspection—"tracing back the radiance of the mind" or
"tracing the radiance emanating from the mind back to its source"—that
limited conceptual understanding is overcome and one is able to have a
direct vision of the unimpeded interpenetration of all phenomena. "If you
can suddenly forget the differences in the theoretical interpretations of the
established verbal teachings and, while sitting quietly in a private room,
empty your heart and cleanse your thoughts, trace back the radiance of
your own mind, and return to its source, then you can consider the pure
nature of the sublime mind which appears in that immediate thought-
moment to be the original enlightenment that is involved in defilement,
the original enlightenment of the nature's purity, the unimpeded *dharma-
dhātu*, the Buddha of Unmoving Wisdom, or Vairocana Buddha. Where
noumenon and phenomena and self and other are identical, any of these
alternatives is justified" (KZ 217). Rather than advocate another conceptual
position from which to confront the pluralism of religious views, Chinul
proposed raising the debate to an entirely different level. His focus on the
"pure nature of the mind" was an entirely new criterion for the assessment
of theological positions, which demanded direct, empirical confirmation of
its validity, not mere speculative support.

Introspection was a technique that turned the usual propulsion of the
mind out into the world of the senses back in upon the mind itself, until the
fundamental source of the mind, the wisdom of universal brightness, was
discovered. To trace the inherent radiance of the mind back to its source
meant to realize instantaneously that one had oneself always been completely enlightened, and that it was only one's mistaken belief that one was
not enlightened that impeded this realization. If adepts

> can trace back the light and look back on the mind, the defilements that
> have abided on the ground of ignorance for vast eons of time become the wis-
> dom of universal brightness of all the Buddhas.... These are all entirely their
> own essence and not external things. (KZ 218)

Introspection is the means of showing the essential oneness of all external
phenomena, and the fusion that exists between the noumenon and all par-

ticularities. It engenders an all-encompassing outlook that, by absorbing all differences, can resolve all conflicts and tensions both within oneself and in one's interactions with the external environment. The direct realization of one's innate enlightenment, which is achieved through introspection, is therefore the experience that reveals the commonality of concern between the meditative and scholastic enterprises within Buddhism.

The central role of introspection in Korean Sŏn testifies to the durability of the Tathāgatagarbha tradition in East Asian Buddhism. The utility of this technique demands the presence of an innate enlightened nature, i.e., Buddhahood, within each individual, which merely needs to be restored to its original primacy. Rather than seek to remove unwholesome or create wholesome tendencies of mind, introspection merely "looks back" on this deeply recessed, yet ever-present reality, allowing it to reassert itself. As the enlightened nature resurfaces, all problems in the phenomenal sphere that were caused by the estrangement from this reality are resolved, and the full potential force inherent in that nature is again able to express itself freely. On the basis this ontology of mind, Chinul developed the first of three principal approaches to Buddhist spiritual praxis: a proleptic faith in and understanding of the truth of one's inherent Buddhahood, which was based on Li T'ung-hsüan's (635-730) unique interpretation of Chinese Hua-yen thought. The Korean Sŏn school asserts that Buddhahood is immanent at all times, in all beings; a student need only allow it to manifest itself freely. There is no need to look outside oneself for Buddhahood, for Buddhahood is nothing more than one's own mind: "The Buddha-nature exists at present right within yourself; why do you vainly seek for it outside?" (KZ 141). Consequently, "If you want to know the source of all the Buddhas, awaken to the fact that your own ignorance originally is Buddha" (KZ 207, quoting Li T'ung-hsüan). This conviction of one's own inherent enlightenment provides a vital motivation for practice. The ultimate destiny of all sentient beings—their achievement of enlightenment, of Buddhahood—is staring them in the face at every moment they are sentient. It only remains for one to turn away from the deluded pursuits that continue to entangle one in the never-ending cycle of birth and death, and look back into oneself in faith, for that destiny to be fulfilled.

Sudden Awakening/Gradual Cultivation

The Koryŏ Sŏn church derived from this view of the innateness of Buddhahood a special soteriological stratagem: "sudden awakening/gradual cultivation." This approach had its roots in the long controversy within East

Asian Buddhism as to whether enlightenment was achieved instantaneously or by a gradual process of development. The Koreans accepted the sudden awakening/gradual cultivation approach as being the most appropriate for the majority of people, because it provided the most comprehensive and utilitarian account of the processes governing praxis and gnosis. While the rectitude of other approaches was not at issue, their viability as a means of practice was questionable. The view that the initial sudden awakening had to be followed by gradual cultivation was first promulgated in Korea by Chinul, who adopted it from the writings of the Chinese exegete, Tsung-mi (780–841), regarded as the Fourth Patriarch of both the Hua-yen scholastic school and the Ho-tse school of Ch'an. Awakening and cultivation were further subdivided: the understanding and realization awakenings are distinguished, as are the absolute cultivation of no-thought and the provisional cultivation that deals with all matters. For heuristic purposes, we may treat awakening and cultivation separately; however, in practice they would have had to function symbiotically.

The approach of the Ho-tse school, as formalized by Tsung-mi, involved an initial understanding-awakening, which produced correct comprehension of both the nature and characteristics of dharmas as well as of the conventional and absolute aspects of phenomena. This awakening, which occurs instantaneously, allows the student to know that he is in fact innately enlightened and is identical in principle with all of the Buddhas.

> Just what is sudden awakening? Due to beginningless delusion, you consider materiality to be the body, deluded thoughts to be the mind, and these together to be the self. But if you come across a spiritual advisor who explains the significance of such concepts as the immutability and adaptability of the mind, you can abruptly awaken to the fact that your own true mind is originally calm and devoid of all dualities; it is the *dharmakāya* itself. This nonduality of body and mind is the true I; there is not the slightest difference between it and all the Buddhas. Consequently, it is said that awakening is sudden. (KZ 278, quoting Tsung-mi)

The illusion of bondage and the achievement of sudden awakening is compared to a free man dreaming that he is incarcerated, who, by simply waking from his nightmare, would see that he in fact has always been free. In this scheme, the initial understanding-awakening allows the comprehension of the true nature of the mind and one's innate potential for enlightenment. This understanding is, however, fully authenticated only after the realization-awakening, the culmination of one's vocation, when one experiences full enlightenment for oneself. At that point, the passive knowledge of one's potential enlightenment is transformed into a dynamic capacity to draw on that enlightenment in guiding other beings toward liberation as well.

It is through the process of gradual cultivation that the understanding achieved through one's initial awakening is allowed to permeate all of one's being, leading ultimately to the realization-awakening. The habitual patterns of thought and action developed during innumerable previous lifetimes are so thoroughly engrained that there is little hope of their being brought to an abrupt end. To change their inertial force requires a long process of gradual cultivation, which may begin only after one has the understanding gained through initial awakening. Gradual cultivation is described as follows:

> Even though you suddenly awaken to the fact that your true mind is exactly the same as all the buddhas, for many eons you have mistakenly grasped at materiality as being the self. Since your habits have become second nature it is extremely difficult to abandon them suddenly. For this reason, while relying on your awakening you must cultivate gradually. Once there are no more defilements remaining to eliminate, you will have achieved Buddhahood. However, there is no Buddhahood that can be achieved outside this true mind. Hence, even though you must cultivate gradually, you have previously awakened to the fact that the defilements are originally void and the nature of the mind originally pure. While eliminating the unwholesome, you therefore eliminate without eliminating anything; while cultivating the wholesome, you cultivate without cultivating anything. (KZ 280, quoting Tsung-mi)

Only cultivation that follows awakening will be efficacious, however, because one will have already recognized through the initial awakening that cultivation is not a necessary precondition of the achievement of enlightenment, as had been mistakenly claimed by the so-called gradualistic schools of Buddhism, which Korean Sŏn invariably condemned. Since the understanding-awakening has revealed at the very inception of practice that the mind is innately pure and free of all defilements, one eliminates such defilements while knowing that there is really nothing there that needs to be eliminated. Similarly, one also develops wholesome qualities of mind while realizing that there is nothing that needs to be developed. This interpretation of cultivation is analogous to the gradual calming of waves (the defilements) after the wind that whipped them up (the fundamental ignorance of one's innate Buddhahood) has stopped: one is simply allowing a natural process to complete itself.

Since this gradual cultivation is conducted while remaining aware of the undifferentiated nature of the mind, cultivation is thus able to include two distinct yet complementary types of practice. These are the cultivation of no-thought, which accords with the non-conceptual, noumenal nature of the mind, and the cultivation that deals with all matters, which allows one to develop the infinite wholesome qualities inherent in that nature in order to aid other beings. Because the adept knows that enlightenment is not a product of cultivation, practice can mean maintaining a passive state of no-thought, in which the individual is simply to keep the mind in an undifferentiated, non-conceptual state. No-thought compels the adept to develop a radical detachment from the process of conceptualization and the limiting view that process creates concerning the nature of one's world. The cultivation that deals with all matters is the dynamic aspect of practice, in which the power inherent in that noumenal nature is used to rectify one's ways of interacting with the world and to enhance one's ability to edify one's fellow beings. But because it is simply the application of the noumenal nature, this approach need not involve the discriminative processes of thought, as would the gradualistic schools' interpretation of this sort of practice. In this wise, the gradual cultivation that follows awakening allows a place in praxis for the active development of all the positive qualities of the bodhisattva and the effacement of negative traits, while still keeping the mind in an undifferentiated, spontaneous state.

This relationship between more passive and dynamic forms of cultivation is possible because of the teaching mentioned above concerning the essence (ch'e) and function (yong) of the unitary mind-nature. Using this distinction, no-thought could be viewed as the essence of the cultivation that deals with all matters, while the cultivation that deals with all matters would be the function of no-thought. While their operation may differ, because one has understood at the first moment of awakening that they are both based upon the undifferentiated nature of the mind, one can engage in both types of cultivation while never wavering from that essential unity.

Simultaneous Cultivation of Concentration and Wisdom

The symbiosis between passive and dynamic approaches to practice led in turn to the second of the three major approaches to meditation taught in Koryŏ Sŏn, namely, the dual cultivation of concentration (samādhi) and wisdom (prajñā). Samādhi and prajñā (along with śīla, or morality) were the principal constituents of spiritual development taught in the scriptures of Buddhism. One was to begin practice by learning to delimit the range of one's response to external stimuli through moral restraint (śīla). Subsequently, the meditator was to start controlling the volition that prompted action by concentrating the mind (samādhi). The power of mind engendered through *samādhi* was finally to be applied to investigate oneself, one's world, and the interrelationships that obtained between the two, with wisdom *(prajñā)*. By learning about the processes governing life, one could use *prajñā* to see things as they truly were, rather than from one's biased, subjective viewpoint, and thereby cut the bonds (especially craving) that bind one to the continued round of *saṃsāra*. This was enlightenment and liberation. Because this scriptural outline of *samādhi* and *prajñā* regarded enlightenment as the final product of a long process of development, the Korean Sŏn Buddhists, like their Chinese counterparts, regarded it as an inferior, gradualistic approach, which could not be correct cultivation because it was not informed by initial sudden awakening.

In their attempts to find a role in Sŏn practice for this traditional account of *samādhi* and *prajñā*, the Koreans described a relative form of both these faculties that could be used during the gradual cultivation that followed awakening. In this interpretation, *samādhi* and *prajñā* were to be used in counteracting variant forms of the defilements. *Samādhi* could control errant thoughts, creating a stability of mind that would allow *prajñā* to penetrate the veil of ignorance and expose the true nature of phenomena. *Prajñā* could rouse the mind from lethargy, and help the meditator remain attentive to his practice. There was, however, a still more sophisticated interpretation of *samādhi* and *prajñā*, taken from the *Platform Sūtra* attributed to the sixth Ch'an patriarch, Hui-neng (638–713), that constituted what the Korean Sŏn school termed an absolute form of *samādhi* and *prajñā*, now identified with the essence and function of the self-nature of the mind itself. *Samādhi* and *prajñā* were viewed as innate qualities of mind, discovered through the initial sudden awakening to one's non-dual, enlightened nature. *Samādhi* came to mean the essence of the mind, and was characterized by calmness and tranquility. *Prajñā* meant the functioning of the mind, and was characterized by alertness. But because the essence and function of the mind were not to be differentiated, *samādhi* was in fact the essence of *prajñā*: thus the mind could be calm and yet simultaneously alert. By the same token, *prajñā* was the functioning of *samādhi*: thus the mind could be alert and yet ever calm.

As inherent properties of the mind, not qualities to be perfected, *samādhi* and *prajñā* were operative at all levels of practice. At the inception of practice, at the time of the arousal of the thought of enlightenment *(bodhicittotpāda)*, these faculties were termed calmness *(śamatha)* and insight *(vipaśyanā)* respectively; when the practice continued naturally in all situations, they were called *samādhi* and *prajñā*; and upon the attainment of Buddhahood, they were called nirvāṇa and *bodhi*. "From the initial activation of the *bodhicitta* [the aspiration to enlightenment] until the attainment of Buddhahood, there is only calmness [=*samādhi*] and only awareness [=*prajñā*], unchanging and uninterrupted. It is only according to the respective position [on the path of practice] that their designations and attributes differ slightly" (KZ 111, following Tsung-mi).

Since advanced meditators could remain centered in the self-nature, and thus come effortlessly into communion with that nature's essence *(samādhi)* and function *(prajñā)*, they could remain simultaneously active and passive amidst all activities. When activity and tranquility were thus equated, any efforts to deal with the defilements as being ultimately real were rendered unnecessary. By the same token, when all the differentiations of thought naturally returned to their undifferentiated source, and when all thoughts were in conformity with the path, the student, even though faced with the effects of past actions, would then be cultivating *samādhi* and *prajñā* as a pair. The *samādhi* and *prajñā* of the self-nature required no effort to maintain, for, once they had achieved equilibrium, they operated automatically and effortlessly. It is this interpretation of these faculties that Sŏn termed the simultaneity of *samādhi* and *prajñā*, and constituted what Sŏn more commonly described as "seeing the nature" *(kyonsŏng*; C. *chien-hsing*; J. *kenshō)* (see KZ 152).

Hwadu

We have seen the important influence exerted in the development of Koryŏ Buddhism by exegetes like Li T'ung-hsüan and Tsung-mi, who had close ties with the doctrinal schools of Buddhism. In the eventual synthesis of Kyo and Sŏn forged during the Koryŏ period, however, there was another element that derived from explicitly Ch'an sources: the investigation of the "critical phrase" *(hwadu*; C. *hua-t'ou)*. This was a new, uniquely Ch'an form of meditation, which was developed within the Chinese Lin-chi lineage by such teachers as Yüan-wu K'o-ch'in (1063–1135) and Ta-hui Tsung-kao (1089–1163). Ta-hui's systematization of *hwadu* practice strongly influenced Chinul's later works. Chinul, who was only one generation removed from Ta-hui, was the first Sŏn adept to teach the formal *hwadu* technique on the peninsula. Chinul's successors pushed *hwadu* investigation to the forefront of Korean Buddhist praxis, and today virtually all Sŏn practitioners in Korea still practice *hwadu* meditation.

Chinul's earlier works did not deal with the *hwadu* technique, and it is given a prominent place only in his magnum opus, *Excerpts from the Dharma Collection and Special Practice Record*, published in 1209, just one year before his death. Even in that text he hesitates to prescribe the *hwadu* to any but the most exceptional of meditators. Although the gifted student might gain an apparent awakening through investigating the *hwadu*, Chinul feared that that awakening would be of value only while he was totally absorbed in his meditation. As soon as the meditator withdrew from his absorption and began to engage in action again, his lack of previous under-standing about the nature and characteristics of the mind would prompt him mistakenly to view the defilements as being real. Hence, even for one who had started *hwadu* practice, Chinul still recommended use of more tra-ditional Buddhist techniques, such as the relative form of *samādhi* and *prajñā*, whenever defiled tendencies of mind arose. The *hwadu* was thus brought within the schema of sudden awakening/gradual cultivation.

In Chinul's *Resolving Doubts about Observing the Hwadu*, published posthu-mously, a crystallization of his views on this Lin-chi technique seems to have occurred. No longer do we find the liberal attitude toward the scholastic schools and the restrained discussion of the Sŏn teachings that characterized his earlier work. No longer does Chinul act as the Sŏn apologist, attempting to vin-dicate the outlook of Sŏn by ferreting out scriptural parallels. In this work, Chinul fully accepts Ta-hui's interpretation of Ch'an, and seeks to prove that, in terms of technique, efficiency, and Buddhist orthodoxy, the *hwadu* approach is superior to all other forms of Buddhist meditation. Chinul's change of attitude augurs the eventual eclipse of Tsung-mi's influence on the Korean tradition, and the resulting preeminence of the Lin-chi methods.

Hwadu literally means the "head *(tu)* of speech *(hwa)*," and refers to the topic, principal theme, or critical phrase appearing in a *kongan* (J. *kōan*). Thus, in the popular *kongan* in which Chao-chou Ts'ung-shen (778–897), in reply to the question "Does a dog have Buddha-nature or not?" answers "No! *(mu)*," the critical phrase, or *hwadu*, would be just the word *mu*. In *hwadu* investigation the student is taught to focus solely on the word *mu*, and thereby bring an end to the incessant process of conceptualization. As the "head of speech," the *hwadu* could be taken metaphorically as leading to the "apex of speech" or "the point at which speech exhausts itself." Since speech was always regarded by the Buddhists as simply the verbalization of the internal processes of thought and imagination, investigating the *hwadu* leads to the very limits of thought itself, and acts as a cure to the inveter-ate tendency toward conceptualization. Investigating the *hwadu* thus instantly perfects the cultivation of no-thought, which leads to the realization-awakening in Tsung-mi's soteriological schema, but without demanding that that cultivation be continued during a period of gradual cultivation. *Hwadu* thus provided a shortcut to enlightenment.

Hwadu serves to catalyze a radical renunciation of the conceptualizing tendencies of mind. Most forms of Buddhist meditation demand as much, but *hwadu* is unusual in making this the cardinal feature of its practice. *Hwadu* seeks to repudiate all the hopes and desires that the dualistic mind has ever cherished, and, hence, is a device designed to remove the subtlest of defilements, even those that may arise from a desire to understand Buddhism or to achieve enlightenment. One is simply to keep the *hwadu* before oneself at all times and during all activities until it is finally penetrated and the unconditioned realm discovered. As Chinul says:

> If you want to understand the principle of the shortcut, you must suddenly break through the one thought [of the *hwadu*]—then and only then will you comprehend birth and death. This is called the access of awakening. You should not retain any thought that waits for that breakthrough to occur, however. If you retain a thought that simply waits for a breakthrough, then you will never break through for an eternity of eons. You need only lay down, all at once, the mind full of deluded thoughts and inverted thinking, the mind of logical discrimination, the mind that loves life and hates death, the mind of knowledge and views, interpretation and comprehension, and the mind that rejoices in stillness and turns from disturbance. Only when you have laid down everything will you be really looking into the *hwadu*. (KZ 337-38, citing Ta-hui)

Chinul distinguished two types of *hwadu* examination: investigation of the meaning of the *hwadu* and investigation of just the word itself. Taking the *mu hwadu* as an example once again, a student investigating the meaning might consider the question, "With what intent in mind did Chao-chou say a dog does not have the Buddha-nature? Don't the scriptures, after all, proclaim unequivocally that all sentient beings are innately enlightened?" Because this type of investigation is intellectually more palatable (lit. has "taste"), it is easier for the beginner to undertake. While this type of examination is not explicitly described by Ta-hui, even he notes that when reading the sūtras or the stories about the enlightenment experiences of Ch'an masters, one might not "understand them clearly" (KZ 336), suggesting that he too recognized some form of investigation of the meaning. In any case, because this type of examination would not bring a final end to the conceptual processes of thought, and thus would not allow thought to return to its preconceptual source, it had to be abandoned eventually in favor of investigating the word. In this more advanced approach, the student is to remain unconcerned with Chao-chou's motives in saying "no," and focus just on the word itself. Because that approach does not lead the student into a train of thought concerning the *hwadu*, it can produce the experience of no-thought, which initiates the realization-awakening and full enlightenment.

These types of investigation correspond to a distinction drawn in Ch'an between "dead words" and "live words." The meaning of the *hwadu* would be the dead word, because it does not lead the student to abandon conceptual understanding: that is, the ordinary, discriminative processes of thought. Despite its provisional value in intensifying the inquiry into the *hwadu*, focusing on the dead word allows the "obstacle of understanding" to remain, and thus leaves the student subject to the ten defects of *hwadu* investigation, listed by Ta-hui and adapted by Chinul. Given with reference to the *mu hwadu*, various of these hindrances to practice apply to every *hwadu*. (1) Do not understand *mu* ("no") to mean either "yes" or "no." (2) Do not consider it in relation to doctrinal theory: e.g., perhaps the dog does not have a Buddha-nature because his mind is overcome by ignorance. (3) Do not ponder over its meaning logically. (4) Do not try to infer the meaning of the *hwadu* from gestures a master might make, such as raising the eyebrows or twinkling the eyes. (5) Do not use ratiocination to think up ready answers to the *hwadu*. (6) Do not busy oneself inside the tent of unconcern, as did followers of the so-called "silent illumination" or Ts'ao-tung school. (7) Do not consider the *hwadu* at the place where it is raised to attention, by wondering how the mind itself works. (8) Do not look for evidence about the answer to the *hwadu* by examining the wording. (9) Do not take mu to mean "nothing" or "non-existence." (10) Do not linger in a deluded state of mind, passively waiting for enlightenment to come (see KZ 338, 244-45). If any of these defects occur, they are to be discarded immediately, but without assuming that something real has arisen that needs to be discarded. Such an assumption would allow further discrimination to creep into one's practice, thus aggravating the defects. Most of the defects involve attempts to come up with an answer to the *hwadu* through ratiocination. The Koreans were not looking for answers to the *kongans*, nor did they require that the student master a whole series of *kongans* before enlightenment could be achieved. Any *kongan* was as good as any other, because all led back to the source of thought itself. Thus there was no need for the meditator to change *hwadu* in the course of his meditation, as in the Japanese Rinzai schools, but one should rather go deeper and deeper into a single *hwadu* until full realization was achieved. The *hwadu* served merely as a tool to bring an end to conceptualization.

Only when the student's investigation changed to the "live word," the investigation of the word, could the above defects be skirted and true *hwadu* practice begun. This live word is described as the weapon that smashes theoretical knowledge and limiting conceptualization: Chinul's disciple, Hyesim, explained that the *hwadu* destroys the fundamental activating consciousness (C. *yeh-shih*), which creates the bifurcation between subject and object, and leads the hapless individual toward delusion and craving. It is only when the activating consciousness is brought to an end through non-conceptualization that the breakthrough into enlightenment can be won. The force that impels the mind toward this breakthrough is the perplexity or sense of wonder—in Ch'an terminology, the "sensation of doubt"—that results from the inquiry into the *hwadu*. It was expected that after reflecting again and again, "Why did Chao-chou say no?" the student would finally become frustrated at his inability to find a solution, and accept that all possibilities of understanding the question through rational means were utterly exhausted. At that point only the sense of doubt would remain. Thus doubt is the ultimate expression of spiritual honesty, causing one to surrender one's ignorance and to accept that one simply does not have the capacity to grasp the true significance of the *hwadu*. Only such surrender brings the radical detachment from even one's own patterns of thought that allows awakening to occur.

Doubt could also arise as a natural outgrowth of a deep inquiry into the meaning of difficult passages from the talks of a Sŏn master or from the scriptures:

> When you are reading the sūtras or the stories about the enlightenment [lit. the entrance to the path] of ancient masters and you do not understand them clearly, your mind will become puzzled, frustrated, and "tasteless"—just as if you were gnawing on an iron rod. When this occurs you should put forth all your energy. First, do not let go of your perplexity, for that is where the intellect cannot operate and thought cannot reach; it is the road through which discrimination is cut and theorizing ended. (KZ 336, quoting Ta-hui)

The intensity of one's doubt is a function of whether one is investigating the meaning or the word. Doubt developing from the investigation of the meaning leads only to the understanding awakening, for it does not free the mind from intellectual comprehension. Doubt produced through investigation of the word, however, leads to the realization awakening, and thus full enlightenment. As that doubt intensifies, the "normal" processes of mind are no longer able to operate and conceptualization is brought to an end. The strain on the intellect created by the doubt finally forces thought to implode in on itself, producing an internal pressure so intense that it causes the "mass of doubt" to "explode." This explosion brings an end to the ordinary processes of conceptualization, which are all dependent on a limiting point of view—the sense of ego. The artificial distinctions one has created between self and other disintegrate and one becomes aware of the many levels of symbiotic interrelationship that pertain between oneself and all other things in the universe. Just this vision of universal interconnectedness is enlightenment in the Korean view. Thus the Koryŏ Buddhists could claim that the enlightenment experience engendered through Sŏn practice had its precise analogue in the Hwaŏm teaching of "unimpeded penetration between all phenomena" *(sasa muae)* and provided a basis for uniting the two systems at a gnoseological level.

In line with Chinul's attempts to reconcile variant trends within the Buddhism of his age, Koryŏ Buddhists sought to make the *hwadu* a comprehensive meditative tool that could be used by students at all levels of spiritual advancement. Though Chinul himself was interested in Ta-hui's shortcut approach to Ch'an practice, in the end he seems to have despaired of the ability of the great majority of meditators to investigate the word and not the meaning of the *hwadu*. Even in *Resolving Doubts about Observing the Hwadu*, his strongest statement in support of Ta-hui's approach, Chinul laments: "Those who have manifested such realization-wisdom [achieved through the investigation of the word] are seldom seen and seldom heard of nowadays. Consequently, these days we should value the approach that investigates the meaning of the *hwadu* and thereby produce right knowledge and vision" (KZ 253). Thus, while the interest of the Koryŏ Buddhists turned increasingly to *hwadu* practice, it never completely supplanted the sudden awakening/gradual cultivation soteriology of Tsung-mi, which sought to produce "right knowledge and vision."

The teaching of the Three Mysterious Gates, a nascent hermeneutical principle adapted from Lin-chi I-hsüan (d. 866), was employed both to distinguish the various levels of Sŏn discourse and to differentiate Sŏn rhetoric from that used in the Kyo schools. The first of these levels was the "mystery in the essence," in which Sŏn exegetes might use rhetoric reminiscent of the scholastic schools to describe the religious goal of Buddhism and the process leading to it. Thus both Ta-hui and Chinul could offer the following description of enlightenment: "Throughout boundless world systems, oneself and others are not separated by as much as the tip of a hair; the ten time periods, from beginning to end, are not separate from the present thought-moment" (KZ 240).[8] Because such an explanation would be more accessible to the average student, it was an expedient way in which to initiate a person into Sŏn practice. The majority of meditators required the mediation of concepts if they were to make progress, for without it they simply "sit around dozing with their minds in a haze, their labors all in vain, or else they lose their presence of mind in agitation and confusion during their practice of meditation" (KZ 264). The novice must come to realize that his fundamental misperception that he and his world are polluted by the defilements stems from his own ignorance. But this ignorance is itself based on the pure nature of the mind, on the essential suchness out of which all plurality develops—hence the term "mystery of the essence." The student realizes then that only a readjustment of his mistaken perception is required for this inherent nature of suchness to remanifest itself. With this understanding, one can embark on one's training convinced of one's capacity to succeed.

The first mysterious gate is an expedient means designed to instill correct views in beginners, giving them faith in their vocation and in their ability to fulfill it. As the student's understanding matures, however, another step must be taken, to ensure that such understanding does not become an obstacle to the direct realization of truth. The compulsion to conceptualize all of one's experiences is one of the most deep-seated tendencies of mind; it vitiates the person's capacity to experience phenomena in their uniqueness, rather than in terms of one's preconceptions.

The second mysterious gate, the "mystery of the word," aims to restore the direct level of cognition. "Word" here means the *hwadu*, which is of course still a word, and thus involves at least a modicum of conceptualization. But because the *hwadu* is much "terser" than the often periphrastic descriptions used in the first mysterious gate, and thus less reliant on concepts to convey its meaning, it is much closer to replicating the non-conceptual experience of the unconditioned realm. That is why later Ch'an writers describe the *hwadu* as a homeopathic device, which uses a small dose of poison (the "word" or "concept" that was the *hwadu*) in order to cure a virulent disease ("conceptualization"). The *hwadu* thus produces a "cleansing knowledge and vision" that loosens the attachment of the mind to the conceptual descriptions promulgated on the first gate.

Continued investigation of the *hwadu* helps to accustom the mind to the experience of the nonconceptual, and to free it from its need to rely on concepts. Nevertheless, the mere fact of investigating the *hwadu* can still leave the mistaken impression that one's striving is creating the causes that will lead to enlightenment, that is, that there are specific conditions that produce the realization of the unconditioned. This dependence on one's own efforts is the subtlest of the attachments that keep the student from experiencing the unconditioned, and generates the mistaken idea that truth is somehow external to oneself, something to be achieved rather than simply accepted. Chinul laments:

> It is tragic. People have been deluded for so long. They do not recognize that their own minds are the true Buddhas. They do not recognize that their own natures are the true dharma. They want to search for the dharma, yet they

still look far away for the holy ones. They want to search for the Buddha, yet they will not observe their own minds. If they aspire to the path of Buddha-hood while obstinately holding to their feeling that the Buddha is outside the mind or the dharma is outside the nature, then, even though they pass through eons as numerous as dust motes… it will only add to their tribula-tion…. Consequently, you should know that outside this mind there is no Buddhahood that can be attained. (KZ 141)

One final catalyst is necessary to prompt recognition of the fallacy of "trying," of believing that one is going to make oneself enlightened, and to inspire the courage to drop everything—including any pretension in regard to one's practice or whatever higher states of consciousness one may have achieved through this practice—and "take a step off the hundred-foot pole" into the realization of the unconditioned. The third mysterious gate, the "mystery in the mystery," is this catalyst. This gate includes pauses, silence, and other nonverbal expressions of the translinguistic functioning of the enlightened mind, all of which Sŏn masters would use in order to shock the student out of the complacency fostered by the "normal" conceptual oper-ation of the mind. Hence, finally even the "cleansing knowledge and vision" of the hwadu must be abandoned if true realization is to occur. Often this catalyst may be nothing more than a shock that results from an environ-mental stimulus, such as a sudden sound. Or it may be the intentional beat-ings and beratings administered by Sŏn masters to goad the student to let go of attachment even to the self. The direct, intuitive experience of the unconditioned realm to which this gate gives access induces a sudden real-ization of the dharma-dhātu and confers on the student the ability to engage in practice unhindered and unswayed by defilements or misconceptions of any sort. Because this third mystery abandons the conceptual understand-ing sanctioned on the two earlier gates, it comes as close as is possible in conventional terms to describing the unconditioned realm that lies beyond concepts.

Sŏn rhetoric thus progressed from kataphatic descriptions of the innate purity of the mind in the first mysterious gate, through the more apophat-ic descriptions of the second, to the radically nonconceptual formulations of the third, whose experientially based kataphasis sanctions the conceptually based kataphasis of the first gate. It was through these three gates that the kanhwa Sŏn (the "Sŏn of observing the hwadu") of the Lin-chi school could be incorporated into Tsung-mi's soteriological approach of sudden awaken-ing/gradual cultivation, and this new synthesis then combined with the scholastic teachings of Hwaŏm. This synthesis was the hallmark of Korean Buddhism from the Koryŏ period on.

Koryŏ Buddhism after Chinul exhibits an increasingly prominent focus on *kanhwa* Sŏn, the style of practice emblematic of the Chinese Lin-chi school since the time of Ta-hui. Ties between Korean Sŏn and the Chinese Lin-chi school were fostered not simply because of their natural contemplative affinities but also because of political exigencies, for Korea had come under the suzerainty of the Mongolian Yüan dynasty after the mid-thirteenth century.

Two representative Korean Sŏn teachers of the late-Koryŏ period, T'aego Pou (1301–1382) and Naong Hyegŭn (1320–1376), both traveled to China to seek transmission from Yüan-dynasty Lin-chi masters, but, interestingly enough, after already achieving enlightenment in Korea. Hence, such pilgrimages need not suggest inadequacies in the indigenous Korean tradition, nor were they intended to promote any formal consolidation between the Korean Chogye-chong and the Chinese Lin-chi school, as some scholars have alleged. Instead, they were attempts to authenticate the indigenous tradition of Buddhism in the eyes of Korean government bureaucrats dominated by the Yüan. By receiving sanction from an orthodox Chinese school, late-Koryŏ Sŏn masters gained the legitimacy that allowed them to proceed with their efforts to rejuvenate Sŏn teachings and practices.

Despite these close genealogical ties between the Chinese Lin-chi school and late-Koryŏ Sŏn, the Sŏn teachings of the period are clearly beholden most to Chinul. The writings of both Pou and Hyegŭn emphasize repeatedly the "interfusion *(wŏnyung)* of Sŏn and Kyo," a telling parallel to the synthesis between Sŏn and Hwaŏm forged by Chinul. This syncretic focus of Koryŏ Buddhism appears even at the institutional level, in the 1356 establishment of the Wŏnyung-pu ("Interfusion Office") as an official government vehicle for merging the remnants of the Nine Mountains Sŏn school with the Chogye-chong.

In marked contrast with the Chinese Lin-chi school, however, which putatively follows a sudden awakening/sudden cultivation soteriological approach, the main *mārga* schema of late-Koryŏ Son masters remains unabashedly Chinul's sudden awakening/gradual cultivation. Perhaps the major difference between Korean Sŏn in the mid and late Koryŏ was the overriding stress on *hwadu* meditation in the latter period, to the detriment of the other types of Sŏn practice also taught by Chinul. But this emphasis was in fact already emerging in Chinul's later works, and is clearly present in the writings of Chinul's successor, Hyesim. So even the focus on *kanhwa* Sŏn in the late-Koryŏ period owes as much to Chinul and the Korean Chogye school as it does to Yüan-dynasty Lin-chi masters. Hence, there clearly is a continuity of approach within the Korean Chogye school of Sŏn, most of which derives ultimately from Chinul, and which sets it apart from all other East Asian Buddhist schools.

The Koryŏ Buddhist Canons

It was during the Koryŏ dynasty that Korean Buddhism accomplished one of its greatest cultural feats: the compilation and publication of two separate editions of the Buddhist scriptural canon, the *P'alman taejangyong*. Indian Buddhists are said to have orally redacted the canon immediately following the Buddha's *parinirvāṇa*, and the Chinese, with their love of written literature, compiled their own manuscript canons early in the history of their own tradition. It was such a Ch'en-dynasty Tripiṭaka that, in 565, was the first complete canonical collection to be introduced into Korea. Catalogues of such early manuscript canons show that they included translations of Indian and Central Asian sūtras, doctrinal treatises, and disciplinary books. Xylographic printing technologies that evolved from the seventh century onward eventually culminated in the first woodblock carving of the Buddhist Tripiṭaka: the Northern Sung K'ai-pao edition, commonly known as the Shu-pen (Szechwan edition), which was completed in 983. This edition was sent to Koryŏ in 991, and served as the basis for the first carving of a Koryŏ canon, which was started in 1011.

The direct catalyst for the production of that Tripiṭaka was the 1010 invasion of Koryŏ by the forces of the Khitan Liao. King Hyŏnjong (r. 1009–1031), who was compelled to flee from the capital of Kaesŏng, vowed that if the invading army were repulsed, he would have the entire Buddhist canon carved on woodblocks. Ten days later, it is said, the Khitan forces voluntarily withdrew. In fulfillment of his vow, Hyŏnjong initiated this massive project, which culminated some forty years later in the publication of the first Koryŏ edition of the canon. Thus it was the canon's presumed talismanic value in warding off external threats to the nation that gave the impetus to its compilation. Because the "word of the Buddha" (*buddhavacana*) was considered to be the expression of the forces of right in the world (*dharmatā*), the preservation and dissemination of all those words in a canon carried tremendous power that, it was felt, could vanquish all aggressors. This attitude of the Koreans toward their canon is a continuation of the national-protection ideology (*hoguk sasang*) that was such an important aspect of Unified Silla Buddhism.

The Buddhist canons of China and Korea were open canons, which permitted dramatic expansions in the scope of coverage as compared with the

Indian Tripiṭakas. Any material that represented the "word of the Buddha" was deemed appropriate for inclusion. But the East Asians regarded as the Buddha's words not only the restatements of those teachings by other enlightened individuals, but even their own personal insights. Thus, there was justification for the continual insertion of new material. A particularly liberal policy was followed by Ŭich'ŏn. Earlier Chinese Buddhist cataloguers, who were charged with determining textual authenticity, had limited canonicity primarily to Indian materials. The principal criterion for authenticity was proof of a text's foreign origins, either by providing evidence of the existence of a Sanskrit or Middle-Indic archetype, or clear stylistic or linguistic evidence that its translation had been made from such an archetype. Ŭich'ŏn, however, felt that indigenous East Asian exegetes and authors had made seminal contributions to Buddhist thought on a par with their counterparts in India, which warranted the inclusion of their writings in the canon as well. Unless the canon was opened to accommodate such works, they were doomed, Ŭich'ŏn feared, eventually to drop from circulation and be lost to posterity. To prevent such a fate, Ŭich'ŏn sent agents throughout East Asia to procure Buddhist texts, and he himself returned from a fourteen-month sojourn in Sung China with some three thousand fascicles of texts. In 1090 he published his catalogue of this collection, entitled *Sinp'yŏn chejong kyojang ch'ongnok* (A comprehensive catalogue of the scriptural repositories of all the schools), which listed some 1,010 titles in 4,740 fascicles. In the preface to his catalogue, Ŭich'ŏn clarifies the reasons behind its compilation:

> While [earlier catalogues] include scriptures and treatises [translated from Indian languages], as they omit some of the tracts and commentaries [of East Asian authors, I was concerned lest these] have no chance of circulating. Hence,... I have considered it my personal duty to track down the traces of the teachings. For almost twenty years now, I have been diligent about [this quest] and have never abandoned it.[9]

Xylographs for each of these texts were carved, and Ŭich'ŏn termed his collection a *Supplement to the Canon (Sokchanggyŏng)*. The blocks of both the Koryŏ Tripiṭaka and its *Supplement* were stored at Puin Monastery, near present-day T'aegu.

Whatever protection may have been provided by the first Koryŏ canon was, unfortunately, short-lived. In 1231 the Mongols invaded the peninsula, forcing the royal family to flee into exile on Kanghwa Island. Meeting little resistance, the Mongols ravaged the peninsula, and in the course of the pillage, burned all of the xylographs of the canon and its *Supplement*, a deed intended both to demoralize their Korean victims and to annul any residual apotropaic efficacy of the xylographs. The Mongols withdrew only after assuring their domination of peninsular politics.

Thoroughly humiliated, and determined never to let their homeland be desolated again, the Koreans decided once more to compile a Tripiṭaka. Yi Kyu-bo (1168–1241), noted statesman and supporter of Buddhism, offered an invocation during a ceremony commencing the second project, in which he indicates that the canon was to serve as a focus of national protection, empowered through faith with the ability to ward off future invaders. But his prayer also reveals how profoundly Buddhism had entered the national psyche in its account of the remarkably equanimous sense of mission with which the Koreans set about the Herculean task of recarving the canon:

> The golden mouth and jade sayings [of the Buddha] are originally free from production or destruction. That which has been devastated is the receptacle, and nothing more. The production and destruction of a receptacle is but a natural event. Destroyed, it must be made anew: this also is appropriate. How much more so is this the case for a kingdom and households that honor and worship the Buddha-dharma![10]

Editorial control of the project was charged to Sugi (fl. mid-thirteenth century), a monk about whom little else is known. Sugi drew upon three principal canons in editing the new Koryŏ Tripiṭaka: the first Koryŏ edition, printed copies of which were still extant; the Sung K'ai-pao Tripiṭaka, which had been the basis of the earlier Koryŏ edition; and the Khitan Liao canon, which was published ca. 1031–1055 and brought to Korea in 1083. In style and format the second Koryŏ canon followed the K'ai-pao and first Koryŏ canons. The new canon included some 1,512 titles in 6,791 fascicles; but because of a different editorial policy, the texts Ŭich'ŏn had included in his *Supplement* were not reprinted, and, as he had feared, many were lost to history. Each individual block was made from specially cured hardwood to guard against warpage, and was two feet three inches long, ten inches wide, and one inch thick, with text carved on both sides. The 81,258 xylographs of this second Koryŏ Tripiṭaka are still preserved today at Haein Monastery, in a hall specially designed to assure even air circulation and humidity.

Despite the similarity in format with its national predecessor, the readings of the second Koryŏ canon most closely paralleled those of the Khitan canon, which, in its selection of texts and editorial accuracy, was renowned throughout the region as the preeminent Tripiṭaka of its day. The attempt of Sugi and his associates to produce a canon that was impeccable critically and indicative of the highest aspirations of the Korean intellectual elite suggests that the Koryŏ leadership was hoping to restore national pride by producing a canon that would surpass even that apex of East Asian Tripiṭakas.

Given the indigenous scholarly climate in Korea at the time, it was inevitable that Koryŏ would undertake the compilation of its own Tripiṭaka. Koryŏ-dynasty Koreans were the heirs to a flourishing Buddhist intellectual tradition, and their scholarship sought to provide the grounding for an informed Buddhist faith. To preserve the full efficacy inherent in the Buddha-word, it was necessary, they believed, that the canon as a precise record of that sacred speech not be sullied by textual interpolations or scribal errors, spurious materials, or other misrepresentations of content, authorship, or provenance.

The care with which Sugi and his associates approached their duty is documented in a thirty-fascicle record of the editorial procedures used in compiling the canon, the *Koryŏ-kuk sinjo taejang kyojŏng pyŏllok* (Collation notes to the new carving of the great canon of the Koryŏ kingdom).[11] Sugi's precise accounts of the major variant readings for each scripture provide invaluable documentation for xylographic recensions of the canon that are no longer extant. Sugi's descriptions of the methodology he followed in preparing his editions reveal him to be a competent and intelligent editor, who avoided many of the mistakes of Western textual critics in the incipient stages of their art. Sugi was far more facile and astute in establishing his text than, for example, was Erasmus (1466–1536), the father of Western textual criticism, in editing the New Testament. Sugi rejected the Erasmian policy of following the majority of manuscripts, as well as other discredited techniques, such as adhering uncritically to the presumedly "best" or "oldest" manuscript.

Of all the Western canons of textual criticism, Sugi most consistently follows those of intrinsic probability (i.e., accepting the reading that seems to fit the context best) and *brevior lectio praeferenda verbosiori* ("the shorter reading is to be preferred to the longer one"). Indeed, the Koryŏ canon's reputation for scholarly accuracy is so secure that its scriptural editions were adopted verbatim in the modern Japanese edition of the Tripiṭaka, *Taishō shinshū daizōkyō* (T), compiled in Japan between 1922 and 1934, which relegated all alternative readings from other canons to the footnotes. Hence, it is hardly an exaggeration to regard Sugi, who lived some two centuries before Erasmus, to be the earliest religious who practiced the formal art of textual criticism. All modern buddhological research using East Asian materials is fundamentally beholden to the care with which Sugi and his editorial team established the Korean Tripiṭaka, the lasting legacy of the Koryŏ period to Buddhist culture.

Notes

1. *Sutta-nipāta* xxii, 94.
2. I. B. Horner, trans., *The Middle Length Sayings* I (Pali Text Society, 1976) 173–74.
3. *Si sinch'am hakto Ch'isu*, in *Taegak kuksa munjip* (Seoul: Kon'guk University, 1974), *kwon* 16; the simile is an allusion to *Analects* xvii, 17.
4. Preface to *Hwaŏn-ron chŏryo*, ed. by Kim Chigyŏn (Tokyo: Seifu Gakuen, 1968) 2–3, 16.
5. *Si sinch'am hakto Ch'isu, kwon* 16.
6. Postface to *Pieh-ch'uan-hsin fa i*, HTC no. 949.101.323.
7. *Ta-fang-kuang fo hua-yen ching*, T 10.272c (no. 279).
8. This account of enlightenment has its precise parallel in Hua-yen's "unimpeded penetration of all phenomena" teaching and is in fact taken verbatim from Li T'ung-hsüan, the Hua-yen exegete so important for Chinul's syncretism. See its use by Ta-hui at KZ 213.
9. *Sinp'yŏn chejong kyojang ch'ongnok so*, T 55.1165c21–24 (no. 2184).
10. Yi Kyu-bo, "Taejang kakp'an kunsin kigo-mun," in *Tongguk Yi sangguk chip* (Seoul, 1958), k. 25, 19a7–10.
11. *Koryŏ-kuk sinjo taejang kyojŏng pyŏllok, Koryŏ taejanggyŏng* (Seoul: Tongguk University, 1976), vol. 38, 512a–725a (no. 1402).

Bibliography

Sources

KZ = Buswell, Robert E., Jr.. *The Korean Approach to Zen: The Collected Works of Chinul*. Honolulu: University of Hawai'i Press, 1983. Abridged as *Tracing Back the Radiance: Chinul's Korean Way of Zen*. Honolulu: University of Hawai'i Press, 1991.
Lee, Peter H., ed. *Sourcebook of Korean Civilization*. Vol. 1, *From Early Times to the Sixteenth Century*. New York: Columbia University Press, 1993.

Studies

Buswell, Robert E., Jr. "Ch'an Hermeneutics: A Korean View." In *Buddhist Hermeneutics*, ed.. Donald S. Lopez, Jr. Honolulu: University of Hawai'i Press, 1988, 231–56.
———. "Chinul's Systematization of Chinese Meditative Techniques in Korean Sŏn Buddhism." In *Traditions of Meditation in Chinese Buddhism*, ed. Peter N. Gregory. Honolulu: University of Hawai'i Press, 1986, 199–242.
Hŏ Hŭngsik. *Koryŏ pulgyosa yŏn'gu*. Seoul: Ilch'ogak, 1986.
Keel, Hee-sung. *Chinul: The Founder of the Korean Sŏn Tradition*. Berkeley: Berkeley Buddhist Studies Series, 1984.
Lancaster, Lewis R. and Sung-bae Park, eds. *The Korean Buddhist Canon: A Descriptive Catalogue*. Berkeley and Los Angeles: University of California Press, 1979.
Lancaster, Lewis R., Suh Kikun, and Yu Chai-shin, eds. *Buddhism in Koryŏ: A Royal Religion*. Berkeley: Institute of East Asian Studies, 1996.

Park, Sung Bae. *Buddhist Faith and Sudden Enlightenment*. Albany: State University of New York Press, 1983.

Yi Chongik. *Kankoku bukkyō no kenkyū: Kōrai Fujō kokushi o chūshin to shite*. Tokyo: Kokusho Kankōkai, 1980. The most extensive study of Chinul in an Asian language.

18

Buddhist Spirituality in Premodern and Modern Korea

HENRIK H. SØRENSEN

BUDDHISM, HAVING dominated the spiritual life of the Korean throughout the Koryŏ dynasty (935–1392), fell from grace with the rise of the Chosŏn dynasty (1392–1912), which was controlled by the educated class of Confucian literati. From the start of the dynasty the Confucians monopolized the political and economic control of the country, and initiated a suppression of Buddhism. Although not directly persecuted or forbidden, Buddhism was severely weakened. As temple land was confiscated, and the temples nationwide became subject to taxation, the Buddhist saṅgha faced severe economic hardship. The monks were furthermore called upon to perform corvée labor, and in certain cases temples were forced to contribute various kinds of goods to local strongmen. Even then Buddhism continued as the largest active religion in the country up to the turn of the present century.[1]

After 1875 Korea came to the attention of the colonial powers, including Japan, which was the first foreign country to gain a foothold on the Peninsula. Being Buddhists themselves, the Japanese used the religion as a spearhead for their political designs on Korea. Through various missionary efforts and political pressures they succeeded in repealing the anti-Buddhist measures implemented by the Confucians in 1895.[2] In 1910 Japan annexed Korea and with it Buddhism came under the political control of the colonial government.

The Buddhist revival that began to take form at the close of the last century, although not caused by the Japanese influence alone, certainly owed much to it. It is an undeniable fact that Japanese Buddhism did much to foster a growing confidence and self-esteem among Korean Buddhists, and despite the fact that not all the efforts of the missionaries and their sympathizers met with equal enthusiasm from the Korean saṅgha, there was a general feeling of good-will and collaboration. On the negative side, the massive Japanese influence on, and incessant attempts at controlling, Korean Buddhism, resulted in the bifurcation and division of the latter. The Temple Ordinance (*sach'al yŏng;* J. *jisetsu rei*) of 1911, imposed by the Japanese on the Korean Buddhist community, was designed to place all control over the temples directly in the hands of the Japanese governor-general. Needless to say, this ordinance caused major problems for the Korean saṅgha.[3]

After the liberation from Japan in 1945, and in particular after the end of the Korean War in 1951, Korean Buddhism entered a period of growth. This expressed itself in a proliferation of Buddhist schools and sects, of which there are at present over twenty officially registered denominations with their own headquarters and subtemples. The Chogye Order (Chogye Chonglim) is the largest denomination among the Buddhist schools in contemporary Korea. It was officially founded in 1962 by the traditionalist monks, who regained their power from the old pro-Japanese faction during the reign of Syngman Rhee (1948–1960), the first president of the Republic of Korea.[4] The Chogye Order is sometimes considered to have originated in the mid-Koryŏ as a result of a misunderstanding caused by its name, which it shares with traditional Korean Sŏn Buddhism, but it is in fact primarily a political and sectarian amalgamation of several collateral lines of transmission that made up the Sŏn Buddhist tradition prevalent during the latter half of the Chosŏn dynasty. Today the Chogye Order, with its headquarters in the Chogye Temple in Seoul, controls the vast majority of the Buddhist temples in Korea, including most of the important historical monuments, and also accounts for the greatest activity among the laity, including missionary work abroad. The order is economically rather strong, although its infrastructure and executive power are often weakened by the diverse and contradictory interests of the various lineages and temple families of which it is made up.

Korean Buddhism under the Chosŏn

During the Chosŏn a number of important Buddhist monks arose who in various ways contributed to the preservation and continuation of the tradition. Among these were Hŏung Pou (1510?–1566),[5] who during his youth had received a traditional Confucian education. He rose to prominence during the reign of Queen Munjŏng (?–1565), a period when Buddhism was actively supported by the court.[6] Pou was in many ways a man of his day, and the type of Buddhism he promoted reflected the increasing harmonization and rapprochement between the meditation (Sŏn) and doctrinal (Kyo) branches into which Korean Buddhism was then divided.[7]

Hŏung Pou also showed a deep interest in esoteric Buddhist practices, in Korea known as *milgyo*, discussing them in his important work the *Suwŏl toryang konghwa pulsa yŏhwan binju mongchung mundap* (Dream questions and answers between guest and host about the imaginary water-moon Bodhimanda and illusory Buddhist affairs).[8] This work, in the form of a dialogue between the author and an imaginary interlocutor, is basically a discussion of the true meaning and value of Buddhist rituals. In a significant passage Pou discusses the compatibility between *milgyo* and Sŏn as follows:

> Now, as regards the One Mind *(ilsim)*, it is the wondrous essence of the ten thousand phenomena. The ten thousand phenomena are the spiritual activity of the One Mind. Outside the mind there are no phenomena, and outside phenomena there is no mind. Hence mind is phenomena, and phenomena are mind. Essence and function are completely fused. Since the Mind Mirror is without obstruction, the spiritual activity of the three wisdoms *(samban)* accords with the complete vision of the One Mind. (HPC 7.596c)

Here Pou discusses the Buddha-nature *(pulsŏng)*, or Buddha mind, as the origin and foundation of all phenomena. In accordance with traditional Sŏn/Hwaŏm doctrine, the mutual unobstructedness of the twofold aspect

14. Samjang painting in Yonju Temple. Chosŏn Period.

of this mind, namely, its essence *(ch'e)* and function *(yŏng)*, constitutes the underlying logic of his statements. In effect this means that physical appearances are actually made of "mind-stuff," that is, they are non-substantial. This seems to take the basic Yogācāra tenet of "mind-only" to its logical extreme, no doubt stretching it a little beyond its original meaning. However, to a Korean Buddhist of the sixteenth century it was precisely such a doctrinal reduction that made possible an identification between the mind cultivation of Sŏn and ritual practices:

> The mind-*dharma* is non-dual, wondrously transforming and eternal, and therefore it cannot be grasped by the intellect. Then one-pointedly hold and intone the *dhāraṇī* called "Limitless majestic virtue Suchness, brilliance, victorious wonder, and strength," which our Buddha taught.[9] What are the three virtues that this one food-transforming mantra commands? "Limitless majestic virtue Suchness" is the liberating virtue; "brilliance" is the virtue of *prajñā*; and "victorious wonder" is the virtue of the Dharmakāya. As regards "strength," it is the strength and function of these three virtues. *Dhāraṇī* means to control and hold *(ch'ongji)*. The controlling and holding of the three virtues simply rests in the One Mind. The three virtues of the One Mind, the *dharma*, and the Complete Wonder *(wŏnmyŏ)* do not have a different essence. (HPC 7.598a–599b)

This passage states how it is that the practitioner's undivided mind and the mantras he intones are not two: they are unified not only as sharing the same essence, but as being one and the same thing. The common reality underlying both Sŏn and *milgyo* is the One Mind. Thus Pou established a doctrinal common ground whereby he could justify the combined practice of the two types of Buddhism.

The greatest and most influential Buddhist monk of the Chosŏn period was undoubtedly Hyŭjŏng (1520–1604), also known as Sŏsan Taesa.[10] Not a great thinker or in any sense an innovator, he should rather be seen as an important paragon of the Korean Buddhist tradition. Though normally considered to belong to the Imje (Rinzai) line of Korean Sŏn, Hyŭjŏng did not teach a "pure" form of Patriarch Sŏn *(chosa sŏn)* in accord with Imje tradition. Like Hŏung before him, he advocated the combination of Sŏn meditation and doctrinal studies. Notwithstanding his reputation as a master of Sŏn, he can also be called a literary monk, in view of his prolific output of religious essays, injunctions, inscriptions, liturgy, and poetry of many kinds. With regard to the kind of Sŏn he represents, there is a clear indication that his method of instruction accommodated Chinul's model of sudden awakening followed by gradual cultivation. A passage in the popular Sŏn manual he authored, the *Sŏnga kugam* (The tortoise mirror of the Sŏn family; HPC 7.634c-647b), reads:

Those who study the Way should first, through the true words of Kyo, be clear about the two meanings, permanence and impermanence, which are the nature and characteristics of one's own mind. Then they should understand the two gates of sudden enlightenment followed by gradual cultivation, which are the beginning and end of one's practice respectively. Following this they may lay down the doctrinal meanings, and take hold of the one thought appearing before their minds. Only then will they be capable of investigating Sŏn with care and obtaining the results. (HPC 7.636b)

Here Hyujŏng states that any practitioner of Sŏn should acquire familiarity with the doctrinal aspects of Buddhism before embarking on *kongan* meditation. The positive appraisal of "sudden enlightenment followed by gradual cultivation" *(tonŏ chŏmsu)* shows him to be an heir of Chinul. He clearly does not reject doctrinal Buddhism but sees it as a temporary means or preparatory stage that can help one advance in one's practice.

Hyujŏng's writings also show the influence of Chinul on his view of Sŏn and Kyo, though he rarely quotes him directly. In the *Sŏnga kugam* we read:

The Buddha's transmission of the Mind in the Three Locations has Sŏn as its purport.[11] What he spoke throughout his whole life constitutes the gate of Kyo. Therefore it is said that Sŏn is the Mind of the Buddha whereas Kyo is his speech. (HPC 7.635b)

Here Hyujŏng shows himself a wholehearted advocate of both scriptural study and the practice of Sŏn meditation. It is interesting to see that several of the final sections of the *Sŏnga kugam* are devoted to a criticism of the adherents of both Sŏn and Kyo who stubbornly maintain that only their way is the right one. Hyujŏng points out the defects found in monks of both denominations. Despite this, because he considered Sŏn superior to Kyo (as did Chinul), he was later credited with advocating "rejection of Kyo and entry into Sŏn" *(sagyo ipsŏn).*[12] In light of the sources, this superficial label does justice neither to Hyujŏng nor to his Sŏn teaching, which was essentially ecumenical and accommodated both Sŏn and Kyo.

From the extant sources we know that, in addition to Sŏn, Hyujŏng taught Pure Land invocation *(nyŏmbul)* as well as the use of mantras *(chinon)* according to esoteric Buddhist practices. That he considered the Pure Land practices aiming at rebirth in Sukhāvatī very highly is evident in several of his writings, but perhaps nowhere is its value more clearly spelled out than in the *Sŏnga kugam:*

Someone has said: "Your own mind is the Pure Land, hence there is no point in seeking to be reborn in the Pure Land! Your own nature is Amitābha, so there is no reason for wanting to see him!" These words seem true, but are not so! That Buddha [Amitābha] has no desire and no hatred; we [ordinary beings], however, have both. The Buddha transforms the hells into a lotus flower simply by turning his hand, but we, because of the force of karma, always worry that we may fall into the hells, far from being able to turn them into a lotus flower! The Buddha is able to behold numberless world systems as if they were in front of his eyes, but we are not even able to see things on the other side of a wall, not to speak of seeing the worlds of the ten directions as if they were in front of our eyes! Therefore, although everybody's nature is [in reality] the Buddha, in practice, we are just sentient beings. Hence, theory and its practical application are as far apart as the distance between heaven and earth. (HPC 7.640c–641a)

Clearly Hyŭjŏng was fully aware of the differences separating the practice of Sŏn and nyŏmbul, but as a master of both traditions he also knew their respective weaknesses and strengths. His Sŏn teachings express "sudden enlightenment," and he insists on the importance of the Pure Land invocation as "gradual cultivation." This again accords with Chinul's approach. His high praise of Pure Land Buddhism in the Sŏnga kugam shows that he considered it indispensable to spiritual cultivation alongside the practice of Sŏn.

Hyŭjŏng's advocacy of esoteric Buddhism is most pronounced in his liturgical compositions, but it may also be found in the Sŏnga kugam:

Concerning the practice of reciting mantras, it is done because former karma is difficult to cut off, while present karma may be regulated through self-cultivation. For this reason it is necessary to avail oneself of their spiritual power. (HPC 7.640a-b)

His understanding and evaluation of the esoteric practices are much like his attitude to Pure Land Buddhism. The mantras help the practitioner to deal with karma accumulated in past lives. Unlike Pou before him Hyŭjŏng did not develop any method or special philosophy whereby to integrate Sŏn with the esoteric practices. In fact, he took the esoteric practices more or less for granted, and throughout his works he can be seen to employ them relatively frequently.[13]

During the seventeenth and eighteenth centuries practices relating to Pure Land Buddhism, as part of the Kyo tradition, became increasingly popular, to such an extent that they tended to overshadow the otherwise dominant Sŏn tradition. This development was a natural consequence of the teachings expounded by Hyŭjŏng and his numerous disciples, many of whom were themselves practitioners of nyŏmbul. Even some of the time-honored bastions of Sŏn, such as Chinul's Suson sa, known during the Chosŏn as Songgwang Temple in South Chŏlla Province, and the Ssangye Temple on Mt. Chiri, came under the sway of Pure Land practices. It was less a case of Sŏn practice being supplanted by nyŏmbul, than of a combined practice of both methods, as was also the norm in Chinese Buddhism of that time. This development can readily be seen in the works of Sŏngch'ŏng (1631–1700), a master in the line of transmission from Hyūjŏng. In his *Chŏngt'o posŏ* (Precious Writings on the Pure Land; HPC 8.485a–511a) the following can be found:

> Those who practice Sŏn attain Great Awakening, whereupon they are released from the turning wheel of *saṃsāra*. This is decidedly the highest [way]! However, those who are able to reach this, do not even constitute two or three out of a hundred [practitioners]. If they cultivate the Western Direction (the Pure Land practices), then they will escape the turning wheel of *saṃsāra*, just like the others, but by a shortcut just like the others. And out of ten thousand there will not be a single one who will not succeed. If practitioners do not cultivate the karma leading to [rebirth in] the Western Pure Land, they cannot avoid being carried along by karmic conditions. Even if they are master of the *Vinaya* and Sŏn, living in a hut thatched with green grass, and are well-versed in suchness, all of them will rise and fall in the turning wheel. This is certainly to be feared! (HPC 8.486a-b)

While it is clear that Sŏngch'ŏng was basically following the teachings on Sŏn and Pure Land Buddhism as laid down by Hyūjŏng, he went one step further in regard to which is superior. Though accepting Sŏn in theory as the highest approach to liberation, he obviously did not credit it with much practical value. As he saw it, the burden of past karma was too heavy a load even for the most sincere practitioner of Sŏn, and hence his chances of escaping the wheel of transmigration were simply too slim. To Sŏngch'ŏng and to many other Buddhists of the seventeenth and eighteenth centuries, of the two ways, faith in Amitābha Buddha's Pure Land held the greater promise of spiritual salvation.

During the last century of the Chosŏn period Sŏn Buddhism gradually rose to prominence again, thanks in part to the fairly positive attitude towards Buddhism in general on the part of King Chŏngjo (1776–1800), but chiefly thanks to a resurgence of Sŏn Buddhist scholarship accompanied by a growing relationship between Confucian intellectuals and Buddhist monks. A central event in this development was the controversy sparked off by a publication of Paekp'a Kungsŏn (1767–1852), the *Sŏnmun sugyŏng* (Hand-mirror of the Sŏn tradition; HPC 10.514c–527c). Aiming to set up a new Sŏn ideology, this work proposed an original interpretation of the famous Three Phrases (C. *san-chü*),[14] and Three Subtleties (C. *san-hsüan*)[15] ascribed to Lin-chi I-hsüan (d. 867). Paekp'a subsumed all Sŏn doctrine and practice under the Three Phrases. He clarified his thought in a graphic representation known as the *Samju to* (Three Phrases Chart; HPC 10.517–519). Here the first phrase is identified with the so-called Patriarch

Sŏn (K. *chosŏn*), the highest expression of Sŏn, in which the Mind Seal is handed down from master to master within the tradition. It is identical with the absolute beyond words, also known as true emptiness *(chingong)*. The second phrase Paekp'a interpreted as indicating Tathāgata Sŏn *(yoraesŏn)*, the kind of Sŏn taught in the sūtras. The third phrase he saw as representing Rational Sŏn *(ŭiri sŏn)*—a term of his own invention. In explaining this threefold division of Sŏn he states:

> As concerns the first phrase it is suited for those who are worthy of taking the Buddhas and Patriarchs as their masters (Patriarch Sŏn).... As concerns the second phrase it is suited for those who are worthy of taking men and gods as their masters (Tathāgata Sŏn).... As concerns the third phrase, it is suited for those who while seeking themselves are not able to realize it (Rational Sŏn). (HPC 10.514c–515b)

The introduction of the concept of Rational Sŏn of course contravenes the teachings of traditional Sŏn, and Paekp'a was probably well aware that he was challenging the establishment. In any case his novel interpretation of the Three Phrases of Lin-chi resulted in a curious blending of Sŏn and Kyo. The "transmission of the mind in three locations" was classified under the second phrase; thus the Buddha's "holding of the flower" and "forty-nine years of teaching without uttering a word" were identified with Tathāgata Sŏn. Paekp'a placed the *kongan* "What is the meaning of Bodhidharma's coming from the West?" under Rational Sŏn.

Paekp'a's assertions provoked a number of contemporary Sŏn masters, and a counterattack was first formulated by Chŏŭi Ŭisun (1786–1866) in his *Sŏnmun sabyon mano* (Four arguments of the Sŏn tradition against overflowing words; HPC 10.820b–830b).[16] He deals as follows with the central issue of the three kinds of Sŏn:

> The men of old only had extraordinary words, they did not have the name "extraordinary Sŏn." They had just the word "rational" *(ŭiri)*, but not the name "Rational Sŏn." The old masters of our [Sŏn] family who wished to enlighten their students would first speak of this, and tell them that they should not follow the verbalized teaching, after which they transmitted mind with the mind. This is what we mean by Patriarch Sŏn, and this is how they taught it.... Ordinary persons [first] hear the words, and then talk about the meaning. Relying on words they understand the principle *(ri)*. This is what we mean by Tathāgata Sŏn. It consists in following the meaning and principle of the verbalized teaching and then entering enlightenment, and should be called Sŏn of Meaning and Principle. These two—the Sŏn beyond [the established teaching] and the Rational Sŏn—are as the names they were first given indicate; therefore people have called them Tathāgata Sŏn and Patriarch Sŏn respectively. After their methods they have been named Sŏn of Meaning and Principle and Sŏn beyond [the established teaching]. This is

how it has universally been explained in the old monastic transmission. (HPC 10.827c–828a)

In line with tradition Choŭi accepted the division of Patriarch Sŏn and Tathāgata Sŏn as a matter of course, but opposed Paekp'a's idea of Rational Sŏn as an additional level of conceptualized Sŏn. As he saw it, this third type of Sŏn had never been taught in the Sŏn tradition previously, and hence it was essentially heterodox. Since Tathāgata Sŏn already included the intellectual and conceptual approaches, to add Rational Sŏn to the original system would disturb its inherent logic and make necessary the formulation of a new set of values. To Choŭi, Paekp'a's way of combining Lin-chi's Three Phrases with three kinds of Sŏn was wrong in principle, since it not only contravened the orthodox hermeneutics of Korean Imje Sŏn, but also set up a new system that did not have a proper foundation. Following the publication of the *Sŏnmun sabyŏn mano* a virtual "battle of books" ensued in which followers of Paekp'a and Choŭi attacked one another. In the long run the traditionalists prevailed, and the scheme of the three types of Sŏn was discarded.

During the closing years of the Chosŏn a charismatic Buddhist leader, the Sŏn master Kyŏnghŏ (1849–1912), arose from the ranks of the traditionalists.[17] He began his Buddhist career as a popular lecturer, but eventually abandoned scriptural studies for intensive meditation. After several months in solitary confinement he experienced a great awakening and composed the following *Odo ka* (Song of Awakening):

> The beauty of the mountain is Mañjuśrī's eye,
> And the sound of water is Avalokiteśvara's ear.
> When I hear the bellowing of the ox and the neighing of the horse,
> Then I hear the speech of Samantabhadra.
> All the Changs and Yis are fundamentally Vairocana,
> Buddhas and Patriarchs, Sŏn and Ky —
> How can they differ but through the discrimination of men?
> The stone man plays the flute,
> And the wooden horse nods in time.
> Ordinary men do not know their own nature, but merely say:
> "The highest plane is not my lot."[18]

Here is described a non-dual state in which the practitioner experiences the unfolding of the *dharma-dhātu*, the realm of reality. Although using a pure Sŏn vocabulary, the song freely draws on the *Avataṃsaka Sūtra* for its underlying ideas.

Following his awakening Kyŏnghŏ traveled throughout the country reestablishing and rebuilding the old training centers as well as organizing

15. Sŏn master Kyŏnghŏ (1849–1912).

retreats. He worked tirelessly to infuse the Sŏn tradition with new strength
and presided over numerous assemblies. He also corresponded extensively
with his followers, and in a letter to a monk gave the following instruction
on how to meditate with a *hwadu*:[19]

> Sometimes when one is investigating the *hwadu* it is like going against a cur-
> rent under full sail. At times the *hwadu* seems distant and tasteless; some-
> times the mind is hot and sluggish. But then on the other hand, this is not
> really anybody else's affair. There is nothing to do but take a firm grip on the
> *hwadu* and do the extraordinary. The correct thing to do is to collect one's

energy, neither too quickly nor too slowly. Be alert and tranquil, firm and continuous. Your breathing must be regular, and you must neither be hungry nor satiated. Keep your nose level and the eyes [half closed]. Be in a harmonious frame of mind and keep your back straight; then no obstructions can arise.[20]

This instruction is characteristic of the way Kyŏnghŏ taught: simply and directly, with a stress on practical application.

What is perhaps of greatest import is his special dedication to the laity. In the course of his career he established several Buddhist societies that included lay people along with monks and nuns. In a public address he stated:

For men of common views and abilities, it is not a question of whether a person is a monk or a layman, male or female, old or young, wise or stupid, noble or mean, and it is also not a question of whether he is intimate or rejected, distant or near, separated from or together with, first or last—all are eligible to enter [into the practice of Sŏn]. This is because all people have a limitless treasure-house that is no different from that of the Buddha. It is only those who in successive *kalpas* have not met with the advice of good friends *(kalyānamitras)* who must crawl through the Threefold Worlds, careering through the four modes of rebirth.[21]

In this talk meant for the average Buddhist he stresses the doctrine of the Buddha-nature present in all sentient beings as the fountainhead of all practice, then points out the importance of having a good teacher to show the way. While there was nothing really new in Kyŏnghŏ's brand of Sŏn, through his ceaseless work he came to exert a tremendous influence on the revival of traditional Korean Buddhism that began after the removal of the anti-Buddhist decree in 1895.

Korean Buddhism under the Japanese Occupation (1910–1945)

One of the important developments within Korean Buddhism during the early years of the Japanese occupation of the Peninsula was the rise of a reform movement that sought to modernize Korean Buddhism along Japanese lines, so that the religion might cope more efficiently with the problems of modern life. This intellectual and scholarly renaissance in Korean Buddhism, which got underway immediately after the Japanese annexation, was headed by men like Yi Nŭnghwa (1869–1943) and Han Yŏngun (1879–1944).[22] It was in fact directly stimulated by an intimate contact with Japanese intellectuals and institutions of higher learning.[23]

One of the important issues was the modernization of the traditional Buddhist saṅgha system, which was considered outmoded and incapable of

renewing the role of Buddhism in Korean society. In order to achieve a lasting reform of traditional Buddhism Han Yŏngun proposed a thorough revision of nearly all facets of the religion, including the understanding of the
purpose and duty of Korean Buddhism, the education of the members of
the saṅgha, the practice of meditation, doctrinal learning, recitation, ritual, monastic organization, ethics, the question of celibacy, economy, and
temple management. To create better understanding of his ideas, he wrote
extensively on the modernization of Korean Buddhism, an issue treated in
considerable detail in his major work, the *Chosŏn pulgyo yusin non* (Essays on
the reformation of Korean Buddhism).[24] In the *Non sŭngnyŏ chi kyoyuk*
(Essay on the Education of Monks) we read:

> For people who wish to be able to choose by themselves, it is necessary that
> they first educate themselves. Civilization is born from education. Education
> is the flower of civilization, and civilization is the fruit of education.... Con-
> sider the essentials of study: one should make wisdom the foundation, self-
> liberation of one's thought the universal rule, and the principle of truth the
> object of study. If any of these three aspects is missing [in one's study], there
> will be no wisdom and no principle of truth, and it will all amount to just so
> many words![25]

According to Han's vision the reform of Korean Buddhism could be realized
by infusing the traditional teachings with a new meaning. He saw Buddhism
as consisting of two basic types of teaching: *P'yŏngdŭng chuwi* (the doctrine
of equality), and *Kuse chŭwi* (the doctrine of universal salvation). Following
the first of these, reform could build on the idea that all sentient beings are
equally endowed with the same enlightened nature. A modern utilization
of the second would instill more social consciousness in regard to the people making up Korean society. Han saw the first of the two doctrines as providing the basis of a Buddhist form of democracy, that is, a philosophy of
equality, while the second would represent the practical implementation of
this ideal. For this to be achieved the community of monks and nuns would
have to abandon their cherished abodes in the remote mountains, and enter
the cities in order to perform their religious duty to the general public.
Only by becoming a truly popular religion, on a par with Christianity,
would Buddhism be able to face the challenges of the modern world.[26]

Though Han Yŏngun was an outspoken advocate of the secularization of
Buddhism, he nevertheless maintained a fairly strict attitude to traditional
Sŏn practice. This was no doubt due to his association with such respected
Sŏn masters as Kyŏnghŏ and his disciple Mangong (1872–1946). Howev-
er, he was highly critical of the static and formal way Sŏn was practiced in
many temples at that time, and he addressed this problem as follows:

How different is the way people of today practice Sŏn! While the people of old kept their minds tranquil, those of today only care for a tranquil abode. While people of old kept their minds unmoving, those of today only keep their bodies so. If one cares only for a tranquil dwelling-place, this merely amounts to a rejection of the world; and if one only keeps one's body still, one is merely self-complacent. Buddhism is a teaching meant for the world, a religion devoted to the liberation of sentient beings! If this is so, should self-complacency and the rejection of the world not be shunned by followers of the Buddha?[27]

There is a thinly veiled criticism here of the traditional monks, who cherished an ascetic life deep in the mountains far from the towns and villages. Han openly takes them to task for being attached to their style of life, and for not caring to enter the towns and cities to instruct the common people in Buddhism. The essential platform for his attack is an appeal to the bodhisattva ideal in its active aspect.

Among Han Yŏngun's many proposals for reform, the one that caused the greatest friction and resentment within the traditional Korean Buddhist community was his insistence that the celibate saṅgha be replaced by a new institution based on a married priesthood. It might appear that this rather outrageous suggestion followed as a natural consequence from his views on the need to make Buddhism more available to ordinary Koreans. However, it is clear that Han had borrowed the idea from the Buddhist "parish priest" system that had developed in Japan under the Meiji Restoration, and which had been largely responsible for the secularization and loss of independence of the Japanese Buddhist saṅgha.[28]

Han Yŏngun's campaign for a modernization of Korean Buddhism eventually foundered. Although the Japanese government in Korea supported his ideas concerning a married priesthood, and had them implemented as well, the traditionalist faction of Korean monks, which was still fairly strong, rejected not only his "saṅgha reform" but most of his other ideas as well. To them Han was basically a corrupt, collaborating monk, who sought merely his own aggrandizement through the launching of a dubious and unsavory reform program with an unmistakably Japanese orientation that in their eyes could only undermine the integrity of Korean Buddhism. However, the traditionalist faction within the saṅgha was quite unable to invigorate Korean Buddhism, and with the exception of structural and administrative changes within the temple administration, as well as sectarian developments of the 1930s, no dramatic changes took place within the spiritual framework of the religion.

Later, as the editor of the reform Buddhist magazine *Pulgyo* (Buddhism), Han Yŏngun, now more moderate and less openly pro-Japanese in his approach, continued to market his ideas for a reformation of Korean Buddhism in the editorials of this publication. With the exception of a group of young Buddhists, his influence in Korea's Buddhist community was no longer strong, and by the time of his death in 1944 his attempts at a Buddhist reform were all but forgotten.[29]

However, the rise of a new spiritual movement outside the orthodox tradition would eventually see the unfolding of Han's ideas. Wŏn Buddhism, which is variously considered a type of modernized Korean Buddhism or simply a new religious movement, was founded by the highly charismatic Pak Chŏngbin (1891–1943) during the latter half of the Japanese occupation of Korea.[30] Pak, who is known under his Buddhist name So T'aesan, founded his new order as a Buddhist reform movement. A cursory glance at his teachings reveals his great indebtedness to the reform program formulated by Han Yŏngun. Like Han, he actively promoted the secularization of Buddhism and saw the laity as the basis of his order. It is beyond the scope of this presentation to discuss the details of So T'aesan's reform of Buddhist doctrines and practice, which is much more systematized and syncretic than what Han Yŏngun had suggested.[31]

The practical consequence of So T'aesan's reform was the complete secularization of Buddhism. He focused on the family as the center of practice. Hence, social morals and family ethics with a clear Confucian inspiration play a dominant role in his system:

> The Great Master said, "A home is like a nation in reduced size, and a nation is a gathering of homes. A home is like a small nation and at the same time is a basic unit of a large country. Therefore one who is able to manage a home perfectly may rule over a society or a nation well. Furthermore, if each member of a family can manage a home well, a nation will naturally be governed in an orderly manner. Therefore, the head of a home should recognize that one's role or obligation as the head is an important and great one."[32]

In another clear-cut example of the presence of Confucian family ethics we find So T'aesan praising the principle of filial piety as a cardinal virtue:

> The Great Master said, "One who offers filial piety to one's parents and loves one's brothers in one's home rarely acts wickedly toward other people. But one who never offers filial piety and causes trouble and hatred between one's brothers and sisters cannot do good for other people. Therefore, in Confucianism it is said that 'filial piety is the basic conduct among all conducts,' and 'a loyal subject is sure to be found in a home which is well-known for a son upholding filial piety.' This is surely a well-spoken truth."[33]

The main religious functionaries in the order are the clergy, that is, married priests, and celibate lay-sisters. However, it is obvious that it is the lay believer who constitutes the foundation and backbone of Wŏn Buddhism. This can be seen from the ethical code of the order, which incorporates only a rather modified version of the traditional ten basic Buddhist precepts, over which a superstructure consisting of adapted Confucian moral concepts is placed. In his early writings So T'aesan advocated celibate life for his followers. Over time, however, there has been an increasing tendency towards married priesthood in the order. Today it is rare to find any celibate male practitioners in Wŏn Buddhism, but they do exist.

In principle there is equality between the two sexes in Wŏn Buddhism. This is stated repeatedly in the injunctions of So T'aesan, especially in his teaching on the Four Essentials (sayo).[34] For example, in his discussion of the third essential one reads:

> After marriage one's financial life should be managed independently; husband and wife should not indulge in love only, but should also make it their principal goal to fulfill their duties and obligations.
> All other affairs should be managed in accordance with the cases involved and the doctrine (pŏp). Men and women should not be discriminated between, as in the past, but they should be treated well in accordance with what they do.[35]

Further on he prescribes:

> Women, like men, should be educated sufficiently so that they can work in society.
> Men and women should work diligently at their occupations so that they may live comfortably. They must be equal in the performance of their duties and obligations to their families and their nation.[36]

On the surface these injunctions of equality between men and women appear rather impressive, taking the time and place into account. Unfortunately, they are so only in theory. The role of women in Wŏn Buddhism is still inferior to that of men, and as such reflects the current norm in Korean society at large. Basically there are two ideals pertaining to women in the order. The first is that of the mother, which in effect is no different from the time-honored Confucian ideal of the loving and self-sacrificing wife and mother, whose highest purpose in life is dedication to her husband and her children and submission to her in-laws. The other, is that of the lay-sister, essentially a female religious functionary of the Wŏn Buddhist order, much like the nursing sisters in Christianity. However, they are not allowed to marry, but ideally live their whole lives in complete dedication to the order. They are in fact celibate nuns, but with emphasis on practical social activities, such as teaching and social work, rather than on meditative practices and doctrinal learning as carried on in the traditional Buddhist nunneries throughout the country.

It can be argued that Wŏn Buddhism has succeeded in realizing a reformation of traditional Korean Buddhism, at least as regards the social dimension. It has established a well-functioning, and by Korean standards, modern university, hospitals, schools, kindergartens, nurseries, training centers, and churches, all the time upholding the Buddhist ideals of self-cultivation as laid down by So T'aesan. Thus, many of the proposals marketed by Han Yŏngun have become reality for the followers of Wŏn Buddhism, and it cannot be denied that what we have today is a thoroughly lay-oriented movement, with its norms and values firmly based in the life of the traditional Korean family unit.

On the practical level there are many aspects of Wŏn Buddhism that have been taken over from Christianity. These include the institution of married priests, liturgy, charity organizations, and a somewhat puritanical view of human behavior. It is noteworthy that the movement was the first Korean Buddhist organization to establish hospitals and public schools as charity institutions mainly staffed with a personnel consisting of lay-sisters. In this way the Wŏn Buddhists carried out the ideal of the self-sacrificing bodhisattva on a wholly social basis, while at the same time they endeavored to modernize Korean society.

Wŏn Buddhism emerged after 1945 as a relatively strong and close-knit movement, and it has continued to expand ever since. However, the patriarchs succeeding So T'aesan have done little to change the spiritual inheritance received from the founder, and the doctrines of Wŏn Buddhism have not developed much. This has become one of the main obstacles to the further development of the movement, since what claims to be a modern form of Buddhism chiefly rests on a system that has remained basically unchanged since the 1930s.

Korean Buddhism since 1945

As Sŏn Buddhism is still the most dominant expression of Buddhism in Korea, meditation has remained at the heart of the monastic training throughout most of the present century, although it no longer enjoys the same popularity among the members of the saṅgha.

In the past, nearly all the great Buddhist masters won their status by personifying the traditional ideal of the ascetic, spending decades of their lives in rigorous training, including many years in intensive meditation. Although this ideal is rarely emulated today, both the Chogye Order

16. Sŏn master Kusan Suryŏng (1908–1983).

and the T'aego School officially promote it as the most direct way to spiritual attainment. At the beginner's level Sŏn meditation is undertaken in a special hall—the *Sŏnbang*—that is set aside for this purpose. Here, twenty to fifty monks live, meditating in the cross-legged posture for up to twelve hours every day during the three-month-long meditation seasons *(kyŏlche)* held twice annually, in summer and winter. Having trained in the *Sŏnbang* for several years, the serious adept normally spends a further five to ten years in a small hermitage, where he perfects his meditation and is meant to attain some form of spiritual awakening.

The goal of Sŏn training is, of course, to attain enlightenment and to become a leader of the Buddhist community so as to secure the continuation of the tradition. While the requirements for attaining the rank of Sŏn master were still very strict twenty years ago, today it is rare to find monks who have undergone the entire program of Sŏn training, including basic monastic training under a qualified master, prolonged meditation in solitary seclusion, spiritual awakening *(kansŏng,* "seeing the nature"), and official sanction from a recognized master. In spite of this the lore surrounding Sŏn is still dominated by the traditional medieval vision. Today the title Master of Meditation *(sŏnsa)* is frequently given by a teacher to a trusted disciple, or a senior monk, regardless of the degree of their spiritual insight. This devaluation of the title has inevitably led to a decline in the quality of the so-called Sŏn masters, many of whom flaunt their lack of insight in published tracts and public lectures.

Although Buddhism in Korea has an old account to settle with Confucianism for the suppression it suffered during the Chosŏn dynasty, there is remarkably little antagonism to be discerned between the two traditions today. This is no doubt due to the general Confucianization of Korean society, which has also affected the structure of the Buddhist saṅgha. The

Confucian influence on Buddhism is not obvious at first glance, but gradually becomes apparent the longer one deals with Korean Buddhism. The seniority system in the temples automatically makes an old monk venerable just because he is old—in contrast to Chinese Buddhism, where seriousness of religious commitment takes precedence. This is only one aspect of the Confucian influence. Indeed, the whole monastic code of behavior has much more to do with Confucian ethics than with the Buddhist *Vinaya*. This may indirectly explain why the attitude to the traditional Buddhist precepts is generally not very serious in the Korean saṅgha. Probably the low position of women within Korean Buddhism should also be seen as reflecting Confucian norms. In any case, as regards the equality of the sexes, it appears that the Mahāyāna philosophy of emptiness and universal interrelation is being grossly neglected.[37]

Since Sŏn dominates the landscape of contemporary Korean Buddhism, it is its practices and associated doctrines that remain the spiritual core of the tradition. Although one might expect the practice of Korean Sŏn to have undergone considerable modification similar to that which Japanese Zen Buddhism has known within the past century, it has somehow been able to maintain itself surprisingly close to the classical ideal derived from the Koryŏ period, whereas the highly diverse and syncretic type of Sŏn that was current during the Chosŏn dynasty can no longer be seen. Of course, contemporary Sŏn practice is a restoration of the "pure Sŏn," centered on meditation with a *kongan* or *hwadu* according to the orthodox Lin-chi (K. Imje) School introduced from Yüan China (1279–1368) towards the end of the Koryŏ period. Despite the fact that there are two contending streams of Sŏn in Korean Buddhism today—the "Sudden-sudden brand" advocated by the late Sŏngch'ol and his adherents based in Haein Temple, and the "Sudden-gradual brand" advocated by those following the teachings of Chinul—in actual practice they all use the *kongan* system that originated with the important Chinese Ch'an master Ta-hui Tsung-kao (1088–1163). Hence, the differences between the two brands of Sŏn are mainly questions of doctrines and of lineage.

On the basic *hwadu* practice, Kusan Suryŏng (1908–1983), an important Sŏn master, has this to say:

> In Sŏn meditation, the key factor is to maintain a constant sense of questioning. So, once you have taken hold of the *hwadu* "What is this?", try to always sustain the questioning: "What is seeing?" "What is hearing?" "What is moving these hands and feet?" and so on. Before the initial sense of questioning fades, it is important to give rise to the question again. In this way, the process of questioning can continue uninterrupted, with each new ques-

tion overlapping the previous one. In addition you should try to make this overlapping smooth and regular. But this does not mean that you should just mechanically repeat the question as though it were a mantra. It is useless to just say to yourself day and night, "What is this?" "What is this?" The key is to sustain the sense of questioning, not the repetition of the words. Once this inquiry gets underway there will be no room for boredom. If the mind remains quiet, the *hwadu* will not be forgotten, and the sense of questioning will continue unbroken. In this way, awakening will be easy.[38]

Every fortnight during the three-month-long meditation retreats *(kyŏlche)* it is customary for the Sŏn master of a given training-temple to give formal instructions to the assembly of practicing monks. These addresses serve two purposes: first, they are inspirational pep talks, stimulating the monks to work harder at their spiritual cultivation, and secondly, they are meant to give advanced practitioners a chance to formally engage the master in a so-called "dharma-combat" *(mundap)*, in which they test their insight against his. On one such occasion the Sŏn master Hyŏbong (1888–1966), having ascended the high seat, hit it thrice with his staff, and addressed the assembly with these words:

> "This year is a new year, this month is a new month, and this day is a new day! Is there anyone in the great assembly who can speak a new word?" The great assembly remained silent. After some time had passed the Master said: "With the Wisdom Eye you can see that it is unreal and not of the world! With the Dharma Eye you can see that it is unworldly and not real! With the Buddha Eye you can see the two levels of real and unreal. When all living and dead come into contact with the three eyes, they cannot remain [i.e., their actual nature will be revealed]. Does anybody have an idea about this?" The great assembly remained silent. After some time the Master said: "Somebody has said: 'Śākyamuni entered *nirvāṇa*, and Maitreya has entered his coffin!'" [i.e., there is nobody enlightened around]. Thereupon he descended the high seat.[39]

This highly abstruse form of address is typical of the kind of talk a Sŏn master gives. It is designed to cut off discursive thinking, and to introduce the listeners directly to the realm of enlightenment. The master's questions to the assembly are meant to provoke a reaction in the individual practitioners whereby they may open up their minds to the reality beyond words, the inherent Buddha-nature *(pulsŏng)*.

Otherwise traditional Buddhist lore and belief are still very much intact in contemporary Sŏn Buddhism, and issues such as karma, rebirth, ethics, and virtually any topic belonging to the unseen realm of the spirits, are often presented straight out of the context of medieval Korean culture. In the following passage we are provided with a fine example of how the doctrine

of rebirth was taught by Sŏngch'ol in a Dharma-lecture given at Haein
Temple in 1981:

> Western psychology, on the basis of Freud's work, divides the human mind
> into three levels: the conscious, the latent or pre-conscious, and the sub- or
> unconscious. Freud of course pioneered theories on the unconscious, but it
> was Sir Alexander Cannon who really did extensive work on the subject. He
> was knighted in England and he was an outstanding lecturer at institutes in
> five European nations. Perhaps his greatest contributions were in the inves-
> tigation of former lives. Initially, as a scientist, he had denied the validity of
> both the spirit and reincarnation. But using hypnosis as an investigative
> method, he consistently came across accounts of previous lives through his
> hypnotic regression process. He brought some people even as far back as the
> Roman Empire, and much of what he recorded was proven through histori-
> cal evidence. On the basis of what he collected from a total of 1,382 patients,
> he published a book, *The Power Within*, in 1952.[40]

Sŏngch'ol presents a wholly tradition-based Buddhist view on rebirth,
and attempts to reinforce the credibility of his view by a wholly pseudosci-
entific appeal to the evidence of hypnosis. Later he even goes as far as to
draw on the American medium Edgar Cayce:

> Cayce had a lot to say about cause-and-effect in relation to former lives. One
> case study was about a couple who had a very unhappy marriage, and upon
> hypnotic regression, Cayce discovered that in a former life they had been
> enemies. In some instances, happily married couples were revealed to have
> had parent-child relationships in former lives. We find this hard to believe,
> but this is how cause-and-effect can work.[41]

Despite this appeal to the Western occult tradition, the main line of the
master's argument is strictly in accord with medieval Korean Buddhism.
Bluntly presented without the slightest degree of sophistication, it is devoid
of the usual ambiguity or ironic distance that characterizes the Sŏn Buddhist attitude to dogmatic belief.

However, we also find the question of rebirth treated in a somewhat more
subtle fashion, as in the following explanation provided by Kusan:

> When the body grows old it dies, and one gets another body. It is just like
> changing one's old clothes. The same good feeling one has when one changes
> one's old clothes and takes on new ones is also there, when the old body is
> exchanged with a new one. If you understand and realize the Mind you will
> get rid of all the sufferings connected with birth and death. The buddha of
> the past has already gone, the buddha of the future has not come yet. The
> buddha of the present is right there where you attain enlightenment, and
> this world is no longer *saṃsāra*, but the Pure Land itself.

We see here the issue of rebirth given a more absolutist twist. The central theme is no longer whether rebirth takes place or not, but who it is that is reborn. In the following, the Buddha Mind as the underlying quality beyond rebirth is explained:

> This body is subject to birth and death; however, the Mind is not born with the body, nor does it die with it. As the work on the *hwadu* is seeking to realize the Mind, it does not follow that the body has to die in order to attain its realization. It is possible to realize the Mind while still alive. To realize the Mind is identical with the realization of *nirvāṇa*, and for this reason there is no need to worry about life and death.[42]

This account of the absolute aspect of the human mind, that is, the Buddha-nature, which is unborn and therefore unaffected by rebirth, shows a tendency inherent in Sŏn to emphasize realization over belief, thus making the spiritual quest a more intimate part of the everyday experience of the practitioner.

Concluding Remarks

Korean Buddhism is the largest religion in Korea, and despite the fact that its monastic communities have degenerated considerably within the past two decades, it still commands a very active lay following. However, the increasingly rapid transformations of modern society have also affected the practice of Buddhism. Monastic communities living in isolation deep in the mountains are a thing of the past. Buddhism has not come down from the mountains and into the cities as Han Yŏngun wished; instead, the cities have come to the mountains.

Most of the great monasteries and temples in Korea have undergone modernization in various ways, including the acquisition of motorized transport, telephone, television, video, laundry machines. Many monks now own their own cars, and even private hermitages are now commonly found. The Buddhist laity and tourists in general visit the Buddhist temples in ever increasing numbers, which has forced many temples to function as hotels and render other services that have little to do with Buddhism. The growing importance of lay Buddhist associations has also opened many monasteries and temples to organized meditation courses for the general public. While it is obvious that the monastic way of life is declining, lay Buddhism is clearly growing in size and dedication, which would seem to indicate a general, and more popular, shift in the expression of Korean Buddhist spirituality.

Notes

1. For a general presentation of Korean Buddhism under the Chosŏn, see Takahashi Tōru, *Richō bukkyō*.

2. See Henrik H. Sørensen, "Japanese Buddhist Missionaries and Their Impact on the Revival of Korean Buddhism at the Close of the Chosŏn Dynasty," 46–62.

3. The full text of the ordinance is reproduced in U Chŏngsang and Kim Yŏngt'ae, *Hanguk pulgyo sa* (Seoul: Chinsu Tang, 1968) 175–89.

4. For a discussion of this, see Robert E. Buswell, *The Zen Monastic Experience: Buddhist Practice in Contemporary Korea* (Princeton University Press, 1992) 30–33.

5. For a survey of his life and teaching, see Nukariya Kaiten, *Chosŏn sŏngyo sa* (Seoul: Poryŏn Kak, 1978) 466–74.

6. Pou's merits as a Buddhist master became known to the Dowager Queen in 1548, and shortly thereafter they met. Pou mentions this in a poem found in *Hŏung tang chip* (HPC 7.548a).

7. A brief survey of his extant works reveals a comprehensive understanding of the teachings and literature of both denominations. The high esteem in which he held the *Avataṃsaka Sūtra* can be seen in his *Hwaŏm kyŏng huba*. See *Nanam chapchŏ*, HPC 7.579b–580a.

8. For a brief discussion of this text, see Henrik H. Sørensen, "A Bibliographical Survey of Buddhist Ritual Texts from Korea," CEA 6 (1991–1992) 159–200 (entry no. 56).

9. This *dhāraṇi* is taught by Śākyamuni Buddha to Ānanda in the important *Chiu pa yen k'ou e kuei t' o lo ni ching* (T 21.464c).

10. For a study of Hyūjŏng's disciples and their teachings, see Yi Yŏngcha, "Chosŏn chung hugi ŭi sŏnp'ung," in *Hanguk sŏn sasang yŏngu* (hereafter HSSY), ed. Pulgyo munhwa yŏnguwŏn (Seoul: Tongguk Taekakkyŏ ch'ulp'an pu, 1984) 339-410.

11. According to traditional Korean Sŏn Śākyamuni taught the non-verbalized *dharma* that constitutes the foundation for the claim to be a "special transmission outside the established teaching," i.e., doctrinal Buddhism. Śākyamuni's non-verbalized teaching is said to have been given on three different occasions throughout his career. According to the Sŏn master Pyŏksong Chiŏm (1464– 1534) they are: 1) the appearance of the Precious Stūpa in the *Saddharmapuṇḍarika Sūtra*, 2) Śākyamuni holding the lotus flower on the Vulture Peak, and 3) his entry into nirvāṇa (see HPC 7.387c).

12. See, for example, Shin Pŏpin, "Hyūjŏg ŭi sagyo ipsŏn kwan," *Hanguk pulgyo hak* 7 (1982) 123–42.

13. See his *Unsu tan,* HPC 7.743c–752a, and the *Sŏn sŏrwi*, HPC 7. 737a–743b.

14. The origin of the Three Phrases is found in the celebrated T'ang compilation *Lin-chi lu* (The record of Lin-chi) (T. 47, No. 1585), in which the following account appears:

> While [the Master taught] in the hall a monk asked: "What is the first phrase?" The Master said: "When the Seal of the Three Essentials is lifted the vermilion mark stands clear, not permitting the deliberation that separates host and guest." The other asked: "What is the second phrase?" The Master said: "How could the wonderful meaning allow Asaṅga to question it? How could the bubbles fight against and obstruct the current's movement?" The other

asked: "What is the third phrase?" The Master said: "Look at the figures in the puppet show, their movements all come from the man behind!" (T 47.497a)

15. According to Lin-chi the Three Subtleties are as follows: "The words of each [of the Three] Phrases has Three Subtle Entrances; each Subtle Entrance has Three Essentials as well as expedients and functioning. All you fellows here, how do you understand this?" (T. 47.497a).

16. For a discussion of the essential points of the debate, see Han Kidu, "Chosŏn malgi ŭi sŏn non," HSSY, 339–481.

17. For a study of this monk and his teaching, see Henrik H. Sørensen, "The Life and Thought of the Korean Sŏn Master Kyŏnghŏ." For his collected writings, see *Kyŏnghŏ pŏbŏ* (Recorded sayings of Kyŏnghŏ) (Seoul: Kyŏnghŏ Sŏn'u Sŏnsa pŏbŏ chip kanhaeng hoe, 1981).

18. *Kyŏnghŏ pŏbŏ*, 48–49.

19. A *hwadu* is the focal point of a *kongan,* i.e., the topic on which the meditator exerts himself.

20. *Kyŏnghŏ pŏbŏ*, 129.

21. *Kyŏnghŏ pŏbŏ*, 219–20.

22. For two brief studies of this important figure in premodern Korean Buddhism, see An Pyŏng-jik, "Han Yong-un's Liberalism: An Analysis of the *Reformation of Korean Buddhism," Korea Journal* 19:12 (1979) 13–18, and Kim Uchang, "Han Yong-un and Buddhism," *Korea Journal* 19:12 (1979) 19–27.

23. See Henrik H. Sørensen, "Korean Buddhist Journals during the Early Japanese Colonial Rule," *Korea Journal* 30:1 (1990) 17–27.

24. Published by Pulgyo sŏgwan, Keijŏ, 1913.

25. Han Yŏngun, *Chosŏn pulgyo yusin non,* 17–18.

26. *Chosŏn pulgyo yusin non*, 12–15.

27. *Chosŏn pulgyo yusin non*, 26.

28. *Chosŏn pulgyo yusin non*, 58–63.

29. Ironically, Han Yŏngun is hailed in modern Korea as a great patriot and "freedom fighter" for his involvement in the March 1st Independence Movement against the Japanese in 1919, and also for highly sentimental poetry. His more controversial role as an exponent of a Japanized form of Korean Buddhism has generally been ignored.

30. For a useful introduction to the history of Wŏn Buddhism, see Mark Cozin, "Wŏn Buddhism: Origin and Growth of a New Korean Religion," in *Religion and Ritual in Korean Society*, ed. Laurel Kendall and Griffin Dix, Korea Research Monograph 12 (UC Berkeley), (Berkeley, 1987) 171–84.

31. For a very useful comparative study of the thought of these two men, see Han Kidu, "*Pulgyo yusin non* kwa *Pulgyo shinnon*," 233–57.

32. *The Scripture of Wŏn Buddhism*, 198 (section 42).

33. *The Scripture of Wŏn Buddhism*, 181 (section 11).

34. The Four Essentials are: 1) Attaining to Self-reliance, 2) Setting up the Sage as the Foundation, 3) Educating the Sons and Daughters of Others, and 4) Paying Respect to Those [performing] Public Welfare. See *Chŏnsŏ,* 39–46.

35. Scripture, p. 22. *Chŏnsŏ*, 40–41.

36. *Chŏnsŏ*, 22, 41.

37. For a highly informative study of temple life in a contemporary Korean Sŏn Buddhist temple, see Buswell, *The Zen Monastic Experience.*

38. See Kusan Sunim, *The Way of Korean Zen*, 61.
39. *Hyŏbong ŏrok* (Recorded sayings of Hyŏbong), ed. Hyŏbong mundo hoe (Songgwang sa, 1975) 19-20.
40. See Ven. Sŏng-chol, *Echoes from Mt. Kaya*, 69.
41. *Echoes from Mt. Kaya*, 71.
42. From a series of talks given in Copenhagen in July 1982.

Bibliography

An Pyŏng-jik. "Han Yong-un's Liberalism: An Analysis of the *Reformation of Korean Buddhism*." *Korea Journal* 19:12 (1979) 13–18.

Buswell, Robert E. *The Zen Monastic Experience: Buddhist Practice in Contemporary Korea*. Princeton University Press, 1992.

Cozin, Mark. "Wŏn Buddhism: Origin and Growth of a New Korean Religion." In *Religion and Ritual in Korean Society*, ed. Laurel Kendall and Griffin Dix. Korea Research Monograph (UC Berkeley)12 (1987) 171–84.

Dumoulin, Heinrich. "Contemporary Buddhism in Korea." In *Buddhism in the Modern World,* ed. H. Dumoulin and John C. Maraldo. New York: Collier Macmillan, 1976, 202–14.

Han Kidu. *"Pulgyo yusin non* kwa *Pulgyo shinnon."* In *Ch'angchak kwa ch'ŭp'yŏng*. Seoul: Ch'angchak kwa ch'ŭp'yŏng sa, 1976, 233–57.

———. "Chosŏn malgi ŭi sŏn non." In *Hanguk sŏn sasang yŏngu*, ed. Pulgyo munhwa yŏnguwŏn. Seoul: Tongguk Taehakkyo ch'ulp'an pu, 1984, 411–81.

HPC = *Hanguk pulgyo chŏnsŏ* vols. 7–11. Seoul: Tongguk Taekakkyŏ ch'ulp'an sa, 1986–1993.

Hyŏbong mundo ho, ed. *Hyŏbong ŏrok*. Songgwang sa, 1975.

Kim Uchang. "Han Yong-un and Buddhism." *Korea Journal* 19:12 (1979) 19–27.

Kusan Sunim. *The Way of Korean Zen*. Trans. Martine Fages. Tokyo: Weatherhill, 1985.

Lee Young Ho. "The Ideal Mirror of the Three Religions: The *Samga kwigam* of Hyŭjŏng." *Korea Journal* 33:3 (1993) 56–66.

Mok Jeong-bae. "Buddhism in Modern Korea." *Korea Journal* 33:3 (1993) 23–49.

Nukariya Kaiten. *Chosŏn sŏngyo sa*. Trans. Chŏng Hogyŏng. Seoul: Poryŏn Kak, 1978.

Shim Jae-ryong. "Buddhist Responses to Modern Transformation of Society in Korea." *Korea Journal* 33:3 (1993) 50–55.

Shin Pŏpin, "Hyŭjŏng ŭi sagyo ipsŏn kwan." *Hanguk pulgyo hak* 7 (1982) 123–42.

Song-chol. *Echoes from Mt. Kaya*. Ed. Won-tek and trans. Brian Barry. Seoul: Lotus Lantern International Buddhist Center, 1988.

Sørensen, Henrik H. "The Life and Thought of the Korean Sŏn Master Kyŏnghŏ." *Korean Studies* 7 (1983) 9–33.

———. "Korean Buddhist Journals during the Early Japanese Colonial Rule." *Korea Journal* 30:1 (1990) 17–27.

———. "Japanese Buddhist Missionaries and Their Impact on the Revival of Korean Buddhism at the Close of the Chosŏn Dynasty." In *Perspectives on Japan and Korea,* ed. Arne Kalland and Henrik H. Sørensen. *Nordic Proceedings in Asian Studies* No. 1. Copenhagen, 1991, 46–62.

————. "A Bibliographical Survey of Buddhist Ritual Texts from Korea," *Cahiers d'Extrême Asie* 6 (1991–92) 159–200.

Takahashi Tōru. *Richō bukkyō*. Tokyo: Kōyōsha, 1929.

The Scripture of Won Buddhism (Wŏn Pulgyo Kyojon) 2nd edition. Trans. Pal Khn Chon. Iri: Won Kwang Publishing, 1988.

U Chŏngsang and Kim Yŏngt'ae. *Hanguk pulgyo sa*. Seoul: Chinsu Tang, 1968.

Wŏn pulgyo chŏnghwa sa, ed. *Wŏn pulgyo chŏnsŏ*. Iri: Wŏn pulgyo ch'ulp'an sa, 1992.

Yi Yŏngcha, "Chosŏn chung hugi ŭi sŏnp'ung." In *Hanguk sŏn sasang yŏngu,* ed. Pulgyo munhwa yŏnguwŏn. Seoul: Tongguk Taehakkyo ch'ulp'an pu, 1984, 339–410.

Part Five

JAPAN

19

Foundations

I. *The Birth of Japanese Buddhism*

HANAYAMA SHINSHŌ AND HANAYAMA SHŌYŪ

UDDHISM WAS propagated among the Japanese people by Korean and Chinese immigrants early in the sixth century. Imperial recognition of the new religion begins with the famous story in the Japanese chronicle *Nihonshoki:* in 552 (more probably 538) Sŏng-myŏng, the king of Paekche, anxious to strengthen his alliance with Japan against the neighboring Korean states of Silla and Koguryŏ, presented Emperor Kinmei (r. 531–571) with a gold-plated bronze image of Śākyamuni Buddha, some ritual pennants, and some Buddhist scriptures, accompanied by a letter in which he urged the propagation of Buddhism:

> This teaching is the very best of all existing doctrines. Nevertheless it is hard to explain or understand. Neither the Duke of Chou nor Confucius could comprehend it. This teaching is capable of producing happiness and reward in unlimited quantities and without boundaries. It leads indeed to distinguishing the sublime *bodhi.*[1]

The Emperor was overjoyed and exclaimed: "Never have I heard of such an exquisite teaching.... Never have I seen anything so radiant and beautiful as this Buddha image." The Emperor consulted his vassals, however, as to whether or not he should accept this new religion from the continent. There was a heated argument on the question among the clans. The Soga clan, who had been in charge of military and foreign affairs, advocated acceptance of the new faith, while the Mononobe and Nakatomi clans, who had been in charge of Shintō rituals, opposed it, claiming that the acceptance of a foreign religion would offend the indigenous Shintō *kami* or deities who had protected the country for so long. The upshot of this debate was that the Emperor gave official permission to the Soga clan to adopt Buddhism.

137

Despite the fact that the Japanese had followed and preserved Shintō tradition as the only state religion for a long period of time, Buddhism quickly flourished, and it replaced Shintō as the state religion within the short space of fifty years. This success was due more to political and cultural factors than to those virtues of Buddhism which won it popularity in later periods: its tolerance, rationality, and philosophical depth; these did not attract attention at this early stage. The new religion enjoyed the patronage of the Imperial Household and was actually practiced by some of the emperors, beginning with Emperor Yōmei (r. 585–587). Since it became a political tool in the strife between the progressive Sogas and the conservative Mononobes, it shared in the triumph of the Sogas.

At the popular level it offered a more secure refuge amid frequent plagues and famines than the indigenous *kami* could provide, and was believed to have magical efficacy in warding off misfortunes and disasters, curing illness, and bringing security and prosperity to the nation and individuals. Japanese culture at that time was still in an undeveloped state, and the splendor of Buddhist art held a great attraction for the members of the Japanese court. The Japanese admired Buddhism as an aspect of the higher civilization of the continent.

Emperor Yōmei's son, Shōtoku (574–622), enjoys legendary status as the founding father of Japanese Buddhism. At the age of nineteen he became Prince Regent for the Empress Suiko (r. 593–628). In 594 he promulgated an Imperial Decree urging people to accept and cherish the Three Treasures of Buddhism. This is the first time that any religion was recommended under the Emperor's name in the history of Japan. In 604 he promulgated the Constitution in Seventeen Articles, a set of moral injunctions for government officials, based on Buddhist and Confucian teaching as well as indigenous belief in the emperor's divine origins. In this document the Buddhist ideals of equality and harmony are applied to state administration. It expresses the attitudes of a Buddhist *dharma rājā* (dharma monarch):

Article I

Harmony is to be valued, and an avoidance of wanton opposition to be honored. All men are influenced by partisanship, and there are few who are intelligent. Hence there are some who disobey their lords and fathers, or who maintain feuds with the neighboring villages. But when those above are harmonious and those below are friendly, and there is concord in the discussion of business, right views of things spontaneously gain acceptance. Then what is there which cannot be accomplished?

Article II

Sincerely reverence the three treasures. The three treasures, viz., Buddha, the Law, and the monastic orders, are the final refuge of the four generated beings, and are the supreme objects of faith in all countries. Few men are utterly bad. They may be taught to follow it. But if they do not betake them to the three treasures, wherewithal shall their crookedness be made straight?

Article IX

Good faith is the foundation of right. In everything let there be good faith, for in it there surely consist the good and the bad, success and failure. If the lord and vassal observe good faith one with another, what is there that cannot be accomplished? If the lord and the vassal do not observe good faith towards one another, everything without exception ends in failure.

Article X

Let us cease from wrath, and refrain from angry looks. Nor let us be resentful when others differ from us. For all men have hearts, and each heart has its own leanings. Their right is our wrong, and our right is their wrong. We are not unquestionably sages, nor are they unquestionably fools. Both of us are simply ordinary men. How can any one lay down a rule by which to distinguish right from wrong? For we are all, one with another, wise and foolish, like a ring that has no end. Therefore, although others give way to anger, let us on the contrary dread our own faults, and though we alone may be in the right, let us follow the multitude and act like them.

Article XVII

Decisions on important matters should not be made by one person alone. They should be discussed with many. But small matters are of less consequence. It is unnecessary to consult a number of people. It is only in the case of the discussion of weighty affairs, when there is a suspicion that they may miscarry, that one should arrange matters in concert with others, so as to arrive at the right conclusion.[2]

Shōtoku also patronized the foundation of seven ancient temples, including Shitennō-ji (in present-day Osaka) in 593, which became the center of social welfare activities in Japan, and Hōryū-ji (in Nara) in 607, which became the headquarters of Buddhist study.

Shōtoku has also been celebrated as a profound student of Buddhist philosophy and the author of eight volumes of commentaries on the *Lotus,* the *Vimalakīrti,* and the *Śrīmālādevī* sūtras, known as the *Sangyō-gisho* (Commentaries on the Three Scriptures). These commentaries, like the Constitution, reflect characteristic emphases of Japanese Buddhism and have strongly influenced its development, notably through their reception in Saichō's Tendai school. The choice of these three scriptures from the many Chinese versions of the Mahāyāna scriptures which were brought to Japan is significant in itself. In the *Śrīmālādevī Sūtra* (J. *Shōmangyō*), Queen Śrīmālā discourses on the fundamental truths and practices of one-vehicle or Ekayāna Buddhism in the presence of Śākyamuni Buddha, who approves of each of her utterances. The choice of this sūtra may have been intended to honor Empress Suiko, for it reveals the exemplary personality of a devout Buddhist Queen. The *Vimalakīrti Sūtra* (J. *Yuimagyō*) was popular among the lay devotees of Mahāyāna Buddhism and establishes norms for lay Buddhists such as Prince Shōtoku himself was. The *Lotus Sūtra* (J. *Hokkekyō*) lucidly expounds the Ekayāna philosophy and has always been regarded as one of the most important sūtras in Japan, especially in the Tendai and Nichiren schools. The preface to the *Hokkegisho* presents this philosophy:

> Śākyamuni appeared in this world in order to expound the teaching of this *Lotus Sūtra*, so that all sentient beings, without any discrimination, might be able eventually to attain true and excellent enlightenment by practicing the primary disciplines for it. Yet sentient beings, because of the scarcity of good merits accumulated in their past lives and because of their ignorant nature by birth—and moreover because of various factors such as time and environment preventing them from acknowledging Mahāyāna teachings—were not readily able to embrace the excellent teaching expounding the causes and the conditions of the Ekayāna.
>
> In view of this, as an expedient, Śākyamuni Buddha preached the Three Vehicles (of *śrāvakas*, *pratyekabuddhas*, and *bodhisattvas*), enabling people to attain enlightenment according to their respective conditions. Thereafter, he preached the doctrine of *śūnyatā*, or non-substantiality that transcends all forms, and recommended people to study and practice it; later he preached the doctrine of the middle path and clarified the merits and demerits of

17. Painting of Shōtoku Taishi, 14th century.

Hīnayāna and Mahāyāna. Sentient beings were gradually enabled to understand the teaching more deeply by listening to and practicing it after a long period of time. Finally he preached the One Great Vehicle, presenting the ultimate truth from the standpoint of Dharmakāya, the True Body of the Buddha endowed with every kind of virtue. Thus he led all sentient beings equally to the one great enlightenment.[3]

Ekayāna teaches that enlightenment can be attained universally and equally by all sentient beings, with no distinctions between many and one, lay and priest, man and woman, or even between humankind and other sentient beings. It teaches that all good deeds are of equal virtue, and that all sentient beings finally attain the absolute enlightenment or buddhahood. This absolute buddhahood is nothing other than Dharmakāya, the manifestation of truth itself, possessing supreme wisdom and eternal life. Dharmakāya transcends time and space and is free from all changes and from birth and death.

Although these commentaries rely on Chinese models, there are frequent original strokes. For instance, the thirteenth chapter of the *Lotus Sūtra* lists various objects that a bodhisattva ought not to seek out—kings, heretics, sportsmen, slaughterers, monks, nuns, laypeople, women—and urges instead concentration of mind in a calm place. In the commentary, however, even this meditation is counted among the things not to be sought after.[4] In order to propagate Ekayāna Buddhism one must resist the lure of solitude. The anchorite's life should not be adopted by any who wish to share the destiny of the actual nation and to lead the people in daily life. To think that meditation in a secluded place is the only way to real enlightenment is a false view, which fails to recognize that there is no contradiction between being and non-being, real and unreal, becoming and non-becoming, or good and evil, holy and ignorant, in the life of practice according to the *Lotus Sūtra*. This non-duality is to be found in the worldly life as much as in the life of seclusion, and Hīnayāna's narrow concern with the latter should be rejected by aspirants to the way of the Buddha. Similar emphases are found in the *Vimalakīrti Sūtra*, which teaches that there is no absolute reality apart from phenomena and holds up the practical life of the lay bodhisattva as its ideal. The *Śrīmālādevī Sūtra*, too, teaches that the nature of sentient beings is intrinsically pure and that they can, without distinction, become the Buddha; it stresses that women can become the Buddha as well as men.

We may conclude by listing the distinctive characteristics of Japanese Buddhism anticipated in the writings attributed to Prince Shōtoku.

First, Ekayāna thought is based on the idea that all beings are endowed with Buddha-nature or the potential to be enlightened. Although some

Mahāyāna schools advocated the Three Vehicle teaching, corresponding to three levels of human capacity for enlightenment, only those that had accepted the Ekayāna standpoint flourished in Japan. Japanese Buddhism thus stressed that the road to Buddhahood was open to all, and that it cannot be confined to those who observe monastic discipline.

Second, Mahāyāna Buddhism was always concerned with the meaning and spirit of the teachings rather than with strict adherence to formal precepts and traditional doctrine. The Japanese interpreted all the teachings and disciplines of Buddhism spiritually and based their practice on this understanding. Thus no Japanese denomination at present actually follows the teachings and disciplines of original Buddhism, and no Japanese denomination has ever imposed disciplines as strict as those observed by Theravāda monks in Southeast Asia. Because of this, Japanese Buddhism has often been criticized as a degenerate type of Buddhism.

Third, within the tolerant framework of Japanese Buddhism, the distinctions between priests and laity, and male and female, gradually disappeared in the course of history. The aim of religious practices for both priests and laity was the life of a bodhisattva whose love and compassion towards fellow beings is unlimited, except that the priests were also expected to play a role as religious leaders in society.

Fourth, in Theravāda Buddhism, the process of becoming a Buddha originally required almost superhuman effort during an immeasurably long period of accumulating virtues and merits through countless transmigrations. In Japanese Buddhism, on the contrary, it was believed that this highest goal could be attained either in the present life or in the next. Even though the way to Buddhahood differs in each type of Japanese Buddhism, most denominations stress that deliverance from the cycle of birth and death can be attained during a single lifetime, and that it is not necessary to wait for limitless cycles of births and deaths, or to practice rigorous austerities.

Fifth and finally, until the end of the Muromachi Period (1338–1573) Buddhism in Japan was identified with the welfare of the nation. Buddhist worship and practice were seen as the basis for prosperity and peace. Annual national events and the everyday life of the people became closely interwoven with Buddhist teachings. Buddhist priests were invited to conduct religious rites and prayers for the welfare of the nation, and many prominent priests acted as government consultants. The close religious, economic, and political relationships between Buddhism and the State resulted in the amalgamation of the imported religion with native Shintō, and during the Heian Period (794–1192) there emerged a unique type of Buddhism using both Shintō and Buddhist types of worship.

The first four of these traits still characterize Japanese Buddhism, but the close association between Buddhism and the State came to an end with the Meiji Restoration of 1868.

Notes

1. For another translation, see W. G. Aston, *Nihongi: Chronicles of Japan from the Earliest Times to A.D. 697.* T.P.J.S., Suppl. I (London: 1896), vol. 2, 66, reproduced in Wm. Theodore de Bary et al., eds., *Sources of Japanese Tradition* (New York: Columbia University Press, 1958) vol. 1, 91.

2. Adapted from Aston, *Nihongi*, vol. 2, 128–33, in de Bary, *Sources*, vol. 1, 48–51.

3. *Shōtoku Taishi: Hokkegisho*, ed. Hanayama Shinshō (Tokyo: Iwanami, 1975), vol. 1, 9–12. For a modern translation, see Nakamura Hajime, ed., *Shōtoku Taishi* (Tokyo: Chūō Kōronsha, 1970), 311–32.

4. *Hokkegisho*, vol. 2, 178–208.

Bibliography

Durt, Hubert. "Clichés canoniques bouddhiques dans les légendes sur les débuts du bouddhisme au Japon." *Cahiers d'Extrême-Asie* 1 (1985) 11–20.

Kamstra, J. H. *Encounter or Syncretism?: The Initial Growth of Japanese Buddhism.* Leiden: Brill, 1967.

Tamura Enchō. "The Influence of Silla Buddhism on Japan during the Asuka-Hakuhō Period." In *Buddhist Culture in Korea*, ed. Chun Shin-yong, 55–79. Seoul: International Cultural Foundation, 1974.

Visser, M. V. de. *Ancient Buddhism in Japan.* Leiden: Brill, 1935.

II. *The Impact of Buddhism in the Nara Period*

THOMAS P. KASULIS

I N DEPICTING Japanese spirituality during the Nara period (710–794), we will focus on how Buddhism influenced social institutions, intellectual life, and religious practice. We will attempt to show how these three cultural spheres interacted, providing the foundation for the future development of Japanese religion.

The Institutionalization of Buddhism in Nara Society

To appreciate the dynamics of Nara Japan, we must consider the fragility of the culture at the time. First, Japan was just emerging from its preliterate stage. The writing system had been introduced from the mainland only about three centuries earlier. Because of the syntactical differences between Chinese and Japanese, the Chinese script was not really adequate for rendering Japanese, and throughout the Nara period, the style of writing the native language (in so-called *man'yōgana*) was still somewhat in flux. Hence, most Japanese intellectuals simply found it easier to write in Chinese. Since Chinese and Japanese have radically different linguistic structures, the Nara intellectuals were actually expressing their thoughts and feelings in a language totally foreign to the vernacular. This situation exemplifies a serious dualism in Nara culture: the tension between the Chinese and the indigenous.

Another example of this dualism is that when the Nara court decided to chronicle the country's history, two different texts were written, the *Kojiki* and the *Nihonshoki* (or *Nihongi*), the former in Japanese and the latter in Chinese. Similarly, there were two imperially sponsored compilations of Japanese poetry, one in Chinese (the *Kaifūsō*) and one in the native language (the *Man'yōshū*). Even when it came to justifying the authority of the emperor, there were two quite independent theories. One theory can be found, for example, in the Seventeen Article Constitution dating from the early seventh century. It gives a basically Confucian account of a political hierarchy ultimately grounded in the emperor as the agent of heaven. The *Kojiki,* on the other hand, emphasized the authority of the imperial family as deriving from their sacred lineage, their direct descent from Amaterasu, the *kami* of the sun.

The children of the aristocrats learned their Chinese by laboriously memorizing and copying various texts: some poetry, but primarily histories and the early Confucian classics, especially those advocating such virtues as filial piety and loyalty to the emperor. Thus Confucianism was a major vehicle for the aristocrats' sense of morality, sociopolitical order, and literary style. It was not, however, viewed as a religious tradition with a spiritual practice, but only as a rationale for social harmony. Through its influence, the idea of a centralized state blossomed in the Japanese mind. The seventh century witnessed Japan's first constitution as well as a series of land reforms intended to take the financial and political power away from the clans and to bring taxation and the military under the aegis of the court. These reforms were not entirely successful, but the plan to centralize authority under the emperor did make significant progress. The establishment of Nara as a permanent capital was another phase in this process.

Previous to the Nara period, the court established new quarters with the ascension of each new emperor. The general assumption today is that this practice was the result of a purification ritual, that the death of the emperor was a defilement of the old palace and a new one had to be built. Yet the idea of a permanent state required a permanent center. Thus, Nara was chosen to be the home of the Japanese government and the city was modeled on the plan of the Chinese capital of the time, Ch'ang-an. Nara was to serve as the heart of the emergent Japanese state. It was to be a grand city laid out in a carefully designed grid pattern. Construction of the capital was never completed, however, because the capital was again transferred by the end of the eighth century to Kyoto.

The plan for Nara included the construction of Buddhist temples at several strategic points—a telling sign of the status the religion had acquired. The official story of the introduction of Buddhism into Japan focuses on a Buddhist artwork, the bronze Buddha presented to the Emperor by a Korean ruler. In the indigenous Japanese religion, which may be considered a proto-Shintō tradition, there were no images for the sacred beings, the *kami*. Thus, the idea of a religious aesthetic was strikingly new to the Japanese, and Buddhism has from that time been closely associated with Japanese art. If Confucianism served as a vehicle for literary and moral development, it was Buddhism that caused the Japanese to develop a deep appreciation for music, dance, painting, architecture, and sculpture. Buddhism, like Confucianism, was associated with the high culture of China. This in itself would be a reason for its prominence in the city plan of Nara.

Yet there was another reason for its prominence, perhaps one even more revealing of the nature of Nara spirituality: Buddhism's connection with magic, or what is better termed thaumaturgy (wonder-working). From the scanty early records we have of ancient Chinese visits to the Japanese archipelago, it seems that preliterate Japan was shamanistic and oracular, the chief priestess or priest serving as both a political and religious ruler. The ancient term *matsurigoto* referred to both ritual and governance. The sacred images, incantations, and rituals of the new religion appealed as much to the thaumaturgical as to the aesthetic side of the Japanese. It supplied the court with a battery of rituals for the prosperity and preservation of the country, thus playing as important a role as Confucianism and proto-Shintō in the emergent Japanese state. Confucianism supplied the moral and political rationale, Shintō the theological or mythological justification, and Buddhism the thaumaturgical power to protect and sustain. This tripodal support of the state continued until modern times, although at any given time the three traditions were not necessarily equal in their supportive functions.

To specify more precisely the institutional role of Buddhism in Nara affairs, we can consider the case of the Emperor Shōmu. In 741 he decreed that each province establish its own national temple *(kokubunji)* and he instituted a hierarchical system of intertemple relationships that culminated in the focal point of Nara Buddhism, the temple called Tōdai-ji, the "Great Eastern Temple" of the new capital. To create a centerpiece for this imperially supported system of Buddhist temples, Shōmu arranged for a 450-ton bronze statue of the Buddha Birushana (S. Vairocana) to be cast for Tōdai-ji. For the dedication ceremony in 757, he invited Buddhists from all over the known world. He himself underwent a layperson's initiation in which he formally declared himself a "servant of the three treasures of Buddhism." This was an unprecedented imperial act. However, in taking the initiation name of Roshana, another variant of "Vairocana," Shōmu may have wished to associate himself and his power with that of the great Buddha cast in bronze. Vairocana was the central light of the whole universe, a Buddha whose radiance shone everywhere. By establishing an official Buddhist temple in every corner of the empire and by making himself the chief Buddhist in Japan, Shōmu was reinforcing his political position. The institutionalization of Buddhism was proceeding hand in hand with the institutionalization of the Japanese state.

All of these factors led to the urbanization and politicization of Nara Buddhism. It became increasingly difficult for politics to be free of Buddhist influence. Buddhist scholars and monks assumed ever more powerful positions as advisors to the throne. For example, Shōmu's daughter, the Empress Kōken (718–770), became enamored of the thaumaturgy displayed by a Rasputin-like monk named Dōkyō, and she almost turned over her throne to him. Because of such incidents, the political potential of Buddhism was well understood, and it became such an entrenched part of Nara intrigue that the only way for the court to escape its influence was to move the capital—first to Nagaoka and then permanently to Heiankyō (Kyōto)—and start over again. When Emperor Kanmu established the new capital, he did not permit the Nara Buddhist schools to relocate. This strategy was quite successful, at least temporarily. Eventually, however, the new Heian schools would become once again involved in the political scene.

The Intellectual Contribution of the Nara Schools

Some of the most lasting Buddhist influences on Japan have been of a more strictly intellectual order. In fact, at least up to the Tokugawa period (1615–1867), it could be said that Japanese philosophical history has been dominated by Buddhist thought. This dominance has its roots in the Nara period. Nara Buddhism was formally divided into six sects or schools (*shū*). To merit the official designation of *shū* a Buddhist group needed the permission of the government. Not surprisingly, therefore, much of what was spiritually important in Nara Buddhism occurred outside the sphere of these six schools. Each school was more a philosophical orientation within the Buddhhist tradition than a comprehensive sect involving a system of doctrine, a correlated set of practices, and a group of devout adherents. It was not unusual for a given monk to be recognized as a leader in more than one sect at a time. This tolerance across doctrinal lines was reinforced by the early acceptance of the *Lotus Sūtra*, which teaches that all Buddhist paths are ultimately one. The six schools are the Ritsu, Kusha, Jōjitsu, Sanron, Hossō, and Kegon. Each had a complex set of doctrines and theories, imported wholesale from China, and destined to have little permanent influence on Japanese spirituality. Nevertheless, in the array of doctrines we can find certain Buddhist themes that have served as important focal points for Japanese religious thought both in the Nara period and much later.

The Ritsu school is really more liturgical than philosophical. It is based on the Chinese translation of the *Vinaya*. As Buddhism took root in Japan and people converted to the new religion, questions arose about the proper form of initiation, dietary restrictions, moral precepts, monastic life, and so forth. Since no one in Japan could answer these questions with any authority, liturgical experts from the mainland were brought into the country and the Vinaya (Ritsu) school was established. Philosophically, the school has little to say except that the structure of religious and moral practice is critical: one must adhere strictly to the rites and precepts. To maintain some control over the burgeoning new religion, the government accepted this point and insisted that all monks be ordained by a Ritsu master at a governmentally appointed "precept platform" *(kaidan)*. In all of Japan, there were only three such *kaidan* and all were affiliated with Tōdai-ji. Thus, to have official status, the members of the other five Nara schools had to be ordained under the auspices of a Ritsu master at a governmentally sponsored site. This is yet another way in which Buddhism was institutionalized in Japan.

The Kusha school is also based on the Chinese translation of an Indian text, the *Abhidharma-kośa* by Vasubandhu. *Kusha* is, in fact, the Japanese rendering of *kośa*. The text is associated with the Sarvāstivāda and Sautrāntika schools of the southern ("Hīnayāna") Buddhist tradition, especially with Sarvāstivāda. The Jōjitsu school is based on the Chinese translation of Harivarman's *Satyasiddhi Śāstra*, a representative text of the Sautrāntika viewpoint. Hence, these two schools have a common ethos and set of philosophical concerns. Of special importance are their respective interpretations of dharmas or phenomena. Like all Buddhists, the Kusha and Jōjitsu schools maintain that existence is characterized by impermanence *(mujō)*. From an analytic standpoint, however, the problem is how to explain the nature of things or dharmas. If things are always in flux, is their appearance illusory or real? The Kusha school maintains that the dharmas actually exist, but their duration is instantaneous. For the briefest moment, they come into being and pass away. Throughout that moment, but only for that moment, they endure by virtue of their "own nature" *(jishō)*. This "own nature" is the basis of their reality and the foundation for our experience of things. Against this Sarvāstivāda emphasis, the Jōjitsu school takes a Sautrāntika line: it rejects the notion of "own nature" and claims that the affirmation of even such a momentary substantiality runs counter to the Buddhist idea of impermanence. This radical position leads to the teaching that the dharmas are "empty" *(kū)*, not real. Why then do we experience a world of things and not merely a void? The Jōjitsu response is that there are two levels of truth, the absolute and the conventional. If we are grounded in the realization that all dharmas are ultimately empty, we can still treat them as having conventional significance. In fact, the Jōjitsu school analyzes eighty-four kinds of dharma. Ironically, the Kusha school, which maintains the reality of dharmas, lists only seventy-five.

The other three Nara schools are offshoots of the Mahāyāna. Sanron evolved from what was originally the Indian Mādhyamika tradition, Hossō from the Indian Yogācāra, and Kegon from the Chinese Hua-yen. As Mahāyāna schools, they all maintain, for example, the ideal of the bodhisattva vow and the doctrine of the three embodiments of the Buddha. The bodhisattva ideal emphasizes universal, rather than individual, enlightenment. That is, the accomplished person holds back in the final stage of one's own enlightenment process so as to help others, vowing not to enter nirvāṇa until all sentient beings can be enlightened together. This collective image of enlightenment appealed to the Japanese, so much so, in fact, that the Hossō school was criticized for believing that there were a very few individuals who were so intrinsically corrupt that enlightenment was impossible for them.

The doctrine of the three embodiments of the Buddha maintains that the Buddha functions in three different capacities or dimensions: as a historical person who teaches in this world; as a sublime being in a heavenly realm who transfers his own merit in order to help others; and as a universal principle whose spiritual presence pervades the whole universe. The historical Buddha who lived in India two and a half millennia ago was a manifestation of the first sort; the marvelous buddhas and bodhisattvas such as Amida, Yakushi, and Kannon, who are so often the objects of devotion and the theme of artistic expression, are usually considered to be manifestations of the second sort; the third manifestation is usually considered impersonal and formless, but it serves as the metaphysical ground that makes possible all spirituality.

On the basis of the bodhisattva ideal and the triple embodiment theory, it is not surprising that the Mahāyāna forms of Buddhism ultimately dominated in Japan. Mahāyāna appealed more directly to the Japanese understanding of Buddhism as a binding social force, as a source of thaumaturgical power, and as a vehicle for aesthetic expression. Of course, despite the common ground, the Mahāyāna schools of Nara Japan have their sharply defined philosophical differences. We can again express the gist of these differences by referring to their distinctive views on the nature of dharmas.

The Sanron ("Three Treatise") school, which is based on three Mādhyamika texts, sees the distinctions among dharmas as based in linguistic and conceptual discrimination, not in the things themselves. A corollary is that any expressible viewpoint is relative, conventional, and unsatisfactory as a philosophical statement on reality. Every concept is said to be ultimately "empty" (kū) and useful only by convention as a practical device. Like the Jōjitsu school, therefore, the Sanron perspective leads to a dualism between the relative and absolute, although the dualism is somewhat differently defined. For Sanron the dualism derives from the difference in perspective between the conceptual grasp of dharmas and the direct intuition of reality through wisdom or *prajñā* (in Japanese, *e* or *hannya*). Jōjitsu, on the other hand, stresses the ontological difference between the two realms. Sanron's position is primarily epistemological whereas Jōjitsu's is more metaphysical. Because of the Japanese preference for the Mahāyāna tradition and because of the general similarity between Jōjitsu and Sanron on the idea of emptiness, the Jōjitsu school was eventually absorbed into Sanron. Through its dialectical logic, its emphasis on emptiness, and its concern for the limits and possibilities of language, the Sanron perspective has played a major role in the development of Japanese philosophy, even though it never had a large number of adherents as a religious group.

As a development of the Yogācāra tradition, the Hossō ("dharma aspect") school emphasizes the mental or phenomenal side of dharmas. Thus, rather than simply accepting or rejecting the reality of dharmas, it affirms their *ideational* reality. This contrasts with the emphasis on emptiness found in the Jōjitsu and Sanron schools, and an affinity between Kusha and Hossō was assumed. In fact, by the end of the Nara period, Kusha was formally absorbed by its Mahāyānistic partner. Following Dharmapāla's line of Yogācāra, Hossō recognizes eight levels of consciousness: the five extrospective and one introspective sensory forms of awareness, a delusionary egocentric consciousness that must ultimately be disengaged, and a transpersonal "store" consciousness that serves as the ground of all experience. If the tainting action of the seventh consciousness can be eliminated, the eighth consciousness will be purified and enlightenment attained. Hossō enjoyed somewhat more success than Sanron as a religious sect and it continues today with about fifty thousand Japanese followers. Like Sanron, however, Hossō's primary impact has been philosophical. The analysis of experience or consciousness as well as the assumption of a pure ground to the mind or heart have continued as major themes in the history of Japanese thought.

The sixth of the formally recognized Nara schools is Kegon, a school derived from the Chinese Hua-yen school. The central scripture of the tradition is the Chinese translation of the *Avataṃsaka Sūtra*. Kegon is marked by its intricate and comprehensive systems of classification analyzing the four different realms of the dharma, the ten kinds of relationships, the five divisions of the Buddhist teachings, the ten stages leading to enlightenment, and so forth. Despite this complexity, the central teaching of the school with relation to dharmas is simple and striking. Kegon maintains a harmonious view of the totality of existence in which each dharma has its own individual place, yet is also an inseparable part of the whole. A favored metaphor is that of Indra's net. The universe is compared to a vast net and

18. Miroku Bosatsu, Nara Period.

each dharma is a gem at the intersection of the ropes. Though each dharma is an individual, it has an infinite number of facets, each reflecting one of the other jewels or dharmas. Hence, the image suggests all-in-one and one-in-all. This is the realm of the deepest insight: the interpenetration of thing with thing (*jiji-muge*). It is noteworthy that Kegon considers this view more profound than that of the interpenetration of principle (or substratum) with thing (*riji-muge*). This means that Kegon ultimately rejects any ontological or epistemological transcendence; the world of things, just as it is, is the realm of enlightenment. Though Kegon has always been deeply respected by the Japanese as one of the pinnacles of East Asian thought, it did not win a popular following in Japan, probably because its teachings were so complex and its religious practices not as distinctive and original as its philosophy. Kegon still exists today as a religious sect, but it is only slightly larger than Hossō.

The six Nara schools played a critical role in introducing Japan to Buddhist theories about such topics as impermanence, the nature of conceptualization, the analysis of the mind, and the harmony of concrete things. To the people of Nara Japan itself, the effect of Buddhist thought was perhaps less dramatic than were the effects of Buddhist art, thaumaturgy, and institutionalization. Yet, from our distant vantage point, we can see in Nara Buddhism the roots of ideas that would later dominate Japanese thought. Going beyond the myths of proto-Shintō and the social mores of Confucianism, the ancient Japanese found in Buddhism a concern for the analysis of reality, whether that reality be ultimately grounded in metaphysical principles or in the mind, whether it be transcendent or immanent. In this respect, Nara Buddhist philosophy familiarized the Japanese with a new vocabulary and introduced a new critical methodology for understanding themselves and their world.

The Impact of Buddhism on Religious Practice

In examining the institutional and philosophical features of Nara Buddhism, our focus was primarily on developments within the capital. That is, we have considered Buddhism thus far as primarily an urban development. In the mountains, however, Buddhism had a quite different significance, and we cannot fully understand the spirituality of the Nara period without considering the religious traditions that were thriving there.

We have already mentioned that the ancient Japanese were interested in thaumaturgical powers. To them, the mountains were a place of ascetic training and magico-religious practices, as well as the home of various forest spirits and powerful *kami*. Thus, it is not surprising that while Buddhist philosophy made its way to the city, Buddhist asceticism moved into the mountains. In the Nara period, there were the predecessors of what would eventually be known as the *yamabushi* (mountain ascetics) and the practitioners of *shugendō* (a form of Buddhist-Shintō syncretism combined with mountain asceticism that exists even today).

An important center for such practices was the area of Yoshinō, a mountainous region adjoining the Yamato plain in which Nara is located. Located in Yoshinō was Hisosan-ji, a central temple for the influential Jinenchi ("natural wisdom") school. This was not one of the six formally recognized schools of Nara, but neither was it viewed as heretical. Hisosan-ji was in fact used as a retreat center by some of the major leaders of the six Nara schools. Gomyō (749–834) of the Hossō school, Tao-hsüan (699–757) of the Ritsu and Kegon, and Dōji (674–744) of the Sanron were regular visitors. Masters of thaumaturgy, probably including the Dōkyō who so entranced Empress Kōken, used to go on retreat in the mountains periodically in order to renew their powers. This phenomenon can be correlated with the fact that the six Nara schools themselves seemed to be mainly centers of scholarship rather than religious practice. That is, even the prominent leaders of the six established schools looked to the mountain traditions for much of their religious discipline. This leads us to interpret Nara spirituality as having two separate, but interrelated, foci of religious activity: the institutional, philosophical schools of the capital and the ascetic, thaumaturgical, shamanistic cults of the mountains. This latter focus merits our further consideration.

The early mountain cults are generally called today either "miscellaneous esotericism" (*zōmitsu*) or "ancient esotericism" (*komitsu*). This terminology serves to distinguish them from the highly systematic "esoteric teaching" (*mikkyō*) starting in the Heian period, but at the same time recognizes the two to be phases of a single tradition. Precisely because of their esoteric nature, many of the practices of these ancient mountain religions were transmitted orally and scholars have to rely on scattered documentation. Yet a few general features of the tradition are clear. The basic tenet of the Jinenchi group, for example, seems to have been that the mind has innate, generally unrealized, capacities which can be developed through special meditations, visualization practices, and incantations. Through such techniques, the mind is supposed to be opened to deeper possibilities, that is, the latent wisdom can naturally manifest itself. Kūkai (774–835), founder of the esoteric Shingon school, undertook the practice of these techniques just after the end of the Nara period. By his own account, he retreated into the mountains of Yoshino to chant a sacred incantation (*dhāraṇī*) one million times. As the result of such a practice, he expected to be able to memorize and interpret any passage from any Buddhist scripture. This example shows to what extent even intellectual growth was attached to thaumaturgical practice.

The mountains were the home of *kami* and the locale for various purification rites. According to the proto-Shintō myths recorded in the *Kojiki*, rocks, rivers, and trees had genealogies and they were once able to speak and move about. Given this context, it is not surprising that a romanticized view of nature appears in the poetry of the Nara period. In the *Man'yōshū*, for instance, the poems often assume a sentimental, even spiritual, bond between the human and natural worlds. It is likely, therefore, that from the earliest years after the appearance of Buddhism in Japan, Buddhist spiritual training was practiced in the mountains alongside ancient indigenous practices. Taoist prognostication and alchemical rites were undoubtedly practiced as well. There was very little philosophical systemization among these mountain religions, but they did coalesce around a series of common assumptions. The mountain practitioners generally agreed that insight derives mainly from a self-imposed religious discipline rather than from philosophical study. Second, they assumed that living in proximity to the primitive, natural world yielded spiritual benefits that could not be found in sophisticated city life. Third, they believed there was an awesome spiritual power latent in the mind and in the physical forces of nature.

This last point brings us back to the issue of thaumaturgy as constituting part of the rationale for institutionalizing Buddhism in the capital. As we now see, the thaumaturgy so admired in the court was cultivated in, and derived from, the mountain traditions of such places as Yoshinō. Thus we cannot, in the final analysis, separate our consideration of the institutional-ization of Buddhism in the city from the development of ascetic cults in the mountains. In this respect, we need a more holistic view of Nara spiritual-ity, which can grasp how the single phenomenon of Buddhism simultane-ously affected three dimensions of the culture: its institutions, its philoso-phy, and its religious practice. The key to Nara Japan's response to Bud-dhism lies in the fact that the culture was still in a formative stage. The ten-uous sovereignty of the emperor faced the internal peril of unreliable, pow-erful clans, and the external threat of the military power of T'ang China. To minimize the awareness of its fragility, it was in the interest of the court to present the image of a burgeoning, prosperous, and stable society. The national temple system, the forging of the great Buddha, the writing of his-torical chronicles; the anthologization of poetry, and even the very layout of a grand, permanent capital were all part of a (perhaps only semiconscious) public relations program.

The imperial support of the scholarly, literate, philosophical schools of Nara also fits into this scheme. It may have been that the abstruse doctrines were only fully understood by the foreign specialists and a few gifted Japanese scholars, but the very fact that Japan could recognize and accept such a high level of foreign thought was a cultural accomplishment earning international prestige. This is not to say that Nara culture was a sham, a superficial attempt to cloak a primitive society in the trappings of high civ-ilization. Yet much of Nara Japan's cultural accomplishment was admit-tedly imitative rather than autochthonous, a public posturing rather than a creative form of self-expression. The court accepted Buddhism as part of its image of refinement. As a sign of its wealth and power, it invested its resources in Buddhist artifacts: sculpture, architecture, painting, music, and ritual. For the more profound marks of Japanese spirituality, we must look up from the city into the mountains.

In the mountains, far away from the public relations image of the Nara court, a distinctive form of Japanese religious consciousness could flourish. There the various traditions of spiritual discipline, whether native or for-eign, could meet on common ground outside the realm of governmental regulation, with no need for official ordination platforms or formal recog-nition of schools. Undoubtedly, these mountain groups included many of the misfits from the city: those who could not live in a lawful society, those who were mad or obsessed with the black arts, and those who simply want-ed to run away. But they also included genuine spiritual aspirants who wished to leave the regulations of Nara society, in order to impose on themselves a more demanding regimen, those whose desire for spiritual cultivation could not be fulfilled in the climate of political intrigue and urban distraction, and those who retreated into the mountains so that they could confront themselves. Such were the true spiritual Buddhists of the time, and to its credit, the Nara court recognized their charisma, even if only in the form of thaumaturgy.

Technically speaking, these mountain groups were not identifiably Buddhist at all. The practices were often followed without any clear commitment to Buddhist doctrine and there were many syncretistic practices whose origins cannot be definitively traced. Herein we find another dualism of the Nara period: the city had the Buddhist doctrines without any clearly defined practice, while the mountains had the practices without any clearly defined doctrine. Obviously, what was needed was a merging of the mountain spirituality with the city's philosophy. The practices could then be framed in Buddhist terms and the doctrines could be given a practice through which they might be directly experienced and lived. Without this synthesis, Japanese Buddhism would always be divided. As long as the mountain practices lacked a systematic philosophy, the urbanites would see them as nothing more than thaumaturgy. As long as the Nara schools lacked a commitment to spiritual practice, the mountain ascetics would see them as merely academic enterprises.

During the Nara period, the great synthesis never occurred, but at the end of the era, Saichō was living in a hermitage on Mount Hiei and Kūkai was living in the mountains of Yoshino. These two were to become respectively the founder of Japanese Tendai Buddhism and the founder of Japanese Shingon Buddhism, the two great religious developments of the ensuing Heian era. It is an important fact that both acquired their initial spiritual insight during mountain retreats. Next they went to China to study doctrine. Upon returning to Japan, they critically evaluated the systems of thought and practice for all the known schools of Buddhism, and eventually institutionalized their schools in comprehensive mountain monasteries where doctrine and practice were intimately related. Furthermore, both Tendai and Shingon developed their own esoteric teachings (*mikkyō*) into consistent systems. In so doing, they fulfilled the promise of Nara spirituality not only by correlating Buddhist practice and thought, but also by integrating thaumaturgy into religion, thereby giving wonder-working a legitimate place within Japanese Buddhism. Thus, Heian Buddhism, indeed later Japanese Buddhism in general, developed out of a synthesis of Nara elements.

III. *The Japanese Transformation of Buddhism*

ROYALL TYLER

LTHOUGH BUDDHISM entered Japan long ago, its foreignness has often been an issue. At times in Japanese history, Buddhism has been accused outright of being alien; while at others, devout Buddhists have lamented the gap that separated them from the Buddha's land and time. Thus the "Japanization" of Buddhism has been a perennial concern.

Of course Japanese Buddhism, like Japanese baseball, inevitably acquired a flavor of its own. But what does "Japanization" really refer to? The matter can be approached in various ways. One may ask what Buddhism the Japanese received, and what this same Buddhism would have become elsewhere. Unfortunately such questions are exceedingly difficult to answer. By the time Buddhism reached Japan in the mid-sixth century C.E. it was roughly a thousand years old, had permeated most of Asia, and was thoroughly diverse. Moreover, having lived long and traveled far, it had learned to address the varied religious needs of whole peoples: for example, the need for answers to ultimate questions, the need for appealing objects of faith, and the need for protection from misfortune. Many styles and levels of Buddhism entered Japan even in early times.

Another approach, adopted by some influential Japanese scholars, is to celebrate the profundity of Buddhist philosophical texts and the deep spiritual impulses that must have prompted their composition. Such scholars then go on to observe early Buddhist Japan, and to draw from what they find pessimistic conclusions about the Japanese national character. One reads pained references to "this-worldly benefits" or to "magic and incantation." Yet considering what practical religion has generally been around the world, this criticism may be unfair. Surely Japanization is not really synonymous with degradation.

Another school of thought applauds subsequent developments as welcome expressions of the native genius. The Heian period (794–1185) witnessed the achievements of such great monks as Kūkai (774–835), the Shingon founder, and Saichō (767–822), the founder of Japanese Tendai. Writers may evoke these in terms of the rise of a properly Japanese Buddhism. Then in the Kamakura period (1185–1333) there arose the Buddhist schools which are still so prominent in modern Japan: the exclusive Pure Land teaching of Hōnen (1133–1212) and Shinran (1173–1262); Zen; and the often intransigent Buddhism of Nichiren (1222–1282). It is not surprising that certain aspects of these have been called not only unique, but also uniquely Japanese, yet this Japaneseness, however intensely felt, is hard to prove. The terms of the argument elude satisfactory definition.

The approach I shall take to the theme of Japanization here is a straightforward one. Like other peoples absorbed in an originally foreign religion, the Japanese naturally incorporated Buddhism into their own world. Japanization in this sense corresponds to the process which, elsewhere, made a pilgrimage center out of Le Puy or Santiago de Compostela, or set a painted nativity scene in a medieval French landscape. That is to say, its motive is universal, although its precise forms depend inevitably on accidents of history and geography.

The Early Period

Buddhism officially reached the Japanese court from Korea in either 538 or 552 C.E. Though it encountered some initial resistance, by the early seventh century it seems to have been firmly established. Backed by all the weight of continental civilization, Buddhism enjoyed a prestige which is nowhere more visible than in the famous dedication of the Great Buddha of Tōdai-ji in 752. Emperor Shōmu's vision of a nationwide network of temples, centered on Tōdai-ji, was significant both politically and religiously. It certainly represented a major effort to incorporate Buddhism into the fabric of Japanese life.

Meanwhile, monks like the charismatic preacher Gyōki (668–749) were spreading Buddhist faith among the people. Since Gyōki taught without official approval, his activities remained illegal until he became simply too famous for the government to condemn. This gives added significance to his enthusiasm, and that of others like him. The lives of such men show that already by the eighth century Buddhism had become a powerful force at all levels, official or unofficial, of Japanese civilization. Moreover, in those days, monks who were active among the people did not spread only religion. They built roads, bridges or reservoirs, and they brought to the provinces knowledge of such fields as architecture and medicine. Buddhism was then as modern as the ideas of Voltaire and Diderot in eighteenth-century Europe.

And what of the native Japanese deities, known as *kami?* In these early centuries, they too were understood to be awed (like the humans) by the excellence of the Buddhist teaching, and moreover appalled by the baseness of their own condition. A late eighth-century document relates how a monk erected a large buddha-image at a certain *kami*'s shrine. The *kami* then spoke through a medium and said, "For countless kalpas I committed grave sins, and so was rewarded by birth into the *kami*-realm. Now I wish to take refuge in the Three Treasures, in order to rid myself of my *kami*-body." This *kami*, and other similar ones, felt himself to be miserably unenlightened. No doubt his attitude was continuous with that of many forward-looking humans of the time—people who, in the presence of the Buddhist teaching and all it represented, felt their land to be hopelessly backward and provincial. *Kami* like this would ask to be helped along the path by such typically Buddhist gestures of devotion as the copying of sūtras, the making of buddha-images, and the building of temples. In this spirit began the symbiosis of Buddhism and Shintō which remained characteristic of Japanese religion until the modern era.

Already in this early period, the Japanization of Buddhism can be seen also in a growing tendency to "buddhicize" the Japanese landscape. Certain monks from the great, government-sponsored institutions spent time on retreat at smaller temples in the mountains, where they did practices and encountered divine manifestations not necessarily to be found in the best canonical texts. Their experiences helped to deepen the roots of Buddhism in Japan. Other monks, roaming the land, "opened" countless sacred mountains to Buddhist influence: first by climbing them, then by erecting temples on them. Each such "opener of the mountain" obtained the permission and the support of the local mountain *kami*. An outstanding example is En no Gyōja (d. 700?), who subjugated the aboriginal powers of the Ōmine mountains, established there instead an obviously tantric-style deity peculiar to the place, and so "opened" this important range to centuries of ascetic practice deeply colored by Buddhism.

Exoteric-Esoteric Buddhism

As the centuries passed, Japanese Buddhists naturally gathered confidence in their collective mastery of the tradition. At first a text or a practice was valued to the extent that it was approved by the best continental teachers to whom the Japanese had access. In time, however, the Japanese built up their own body of writings, which came to stand as an intermediate authority between Japanese Buddhism and its ultimately continental sources. Hossō scholars, for example, might cite the works of Zenju (723–797) or Gomyō (750–834); Tendai scholars those of Saichō or Annen (841–ca. 890).

19. Eleven-faced Kannon, Kamakura Period, Japan.

This growing body of Japanese Buddhist writings is an aspect of Japanization. So are the lengthening lines of succession to the major Buddhist establishments in Japan; and the development of subsects ("streams") within the main Buddhist schools, each with its own Japanese founder and its own history on Japanese soil.

Another important facet of Japanization was the rise of "exoteric-esoteric Buddhism" *(kenmitsu bukkyō)*, a style of Buddhism that no doubt owed more to historical circumstance than to the Japanese national character. This term, useful now to describe the phenomenon, was never official. People then spoke of the different schools then current in Japan (Shingon, Tendai, Hossō, etc.); or, more typically, of the traditions of different temples (Mt. Kōya, Mt. Hiei, Kōfuku-ji, etc.). In truth, however, most Buddhist institutions in the Heian period, whatever their announced "school," practiced a form of *kenmitsu bukkyō*. This "exoteric-esoteric Buddhism" was a combination of esoteric Buddhism *(mikkyō)* and one form or another of "exoteric" Buddhism, such as the *Lotus Sūtra* tradition of Tendai (Mt. Hiei) or the Yogācāra tradition of Hossō (Kōfuku-ji). Esoteric-exoteric fusion no doubt began in the Nara period, when esoteric texts and practices first entered Japan. However, it really blossomed in Heian times, after Kūkai and Saichō, when esotericism penetrated Japanese Buddhism. Nevertheless, esoteric and exoteric Buddhism do not fit together very well. Perhaps not only historical precedent but also the sheer incompatibility of the two made it urgent constantly to affirm their unity *(dōitsu)*—a unity impossible to grasp in terms of logic. At any rate, their paradoxical relationship is perhaps related to that fostered in *kenmitsu bukkyō* between the buddhas and the native *kami*.

Shintō-Buddhist Syncretism

The *kami*, who were once suffering sentient beings hungry for enlightenment, rose during the Heian period to be representatives of enlightenment itself. This evolution parallels the rising self-confidence of Japan as a Buddhist country. In the process the *kami* were assisted by their devotees, who showered them with Buddhist attentions. Hachiman, a supremely important deity who, among other things, protected Tōdai-ji, claimed in 783 the title of bodhisattva. Other major deities later did the same. There also grew up an understanding that such *kami* were *gongen* ("provisional manifestations" or "avatars") of the great Buddhist deities. For example an inscription dated 1011 identifies the Ōmine mountain deity as a *gongen* of Śākyamuni.

The concept of *gongen* is closely related to that of a *kami* as the *suijaku* ("trace manifested below") of a particular buddha or bodhisattva. The Buddhist deity in question is then called the *honji* ("original ground" or "source") of that *kami*. The terms *honji* and *suijaku* come from Tendai commentaries on the *Lotus Sūtra*, but this meaning of them is special to Japan. It is hard to tell when the *honji-suijaku* interpretation of the relation between buddhas and *kami* began. The evidence of art (primarily Buddhist images connected with shrines) suggests a much earlier period than can be proven from written records. However, it is clear that *honji-suijaku* links became common after about 1100. By the thirteenth century they were routine. All *kami* of any importance were understood to manifest on this earth the enlightenment of a certain buddha or bodhisattva. Not that *kami* and buddhas were ever confused with each other. The two were served in separate establishments and their fundamental rituals were quite different. However, the intimate relationship between them was plainly visible not only in the Buddhist rites performed expressly for the *kami*, but also in the Buddhist temples associated with all important shrines. In many cases the temple wholly dominated the shrine and its staff of specialized priests. Under such circumstances both "Shintō" and "Buddhism" become somewhat unsatisfactory terms. Certain Buddhist images, iconographically quite normal, can be identified thanks to inscriptions or other evidence as being actually the portraits of specific *kami*.

A key issue in this syncretistic mode of faith was to determine authoritatively the *honji* counterpart of a *kami;* for then the *kami*'s "true nature" could be correctly grasped. Where did such knowledge come from? Most commonly, apparently, from divinely inspired dreams. Thus, for instance, Nichizō, a tenth-century monk, visited a certain shrine with the purpose of discovering the *honji* of the *kami*. The account states:

> There was a violent thunderstorm and darkness fell. Then a voice from inside the sanctuary said, "The Buddha Bibashi." The awed Nichizō went forward and came before an ancient man who had the face of a child.

The Bibashi (S. Vipaśyin) of this fairly early example never had widespread appeal. Nor did Fukūkenjaku (S. Amoghapāśa), identified until the twelfth century as the *honji* of another important *kami*. In time, such early *honji* became obsolete and were replaced as appropriate by currently major Buddhist deities. In the late twelfth century, for example, an inspired monk heard a voice from the sky proclaim that Śākyamuni, not Fukūkenjaku, was the *honji* of the *kami* just mentioned. Other popular *honji* were Amida (S. Amitābha), Dainichi (S. Mahāvairocana), or various forms of Kannon (S. Avalokiteśvara).

The significance of such *kami*-buddha links was that the *kami* made enlightenment accessible to ordinary beings in Japan—beings to whom the unmediated Buddhist deities might seem too awesome or remote. Not that the Buddhist deities had no direct cult of their own. Thousands of temples were dedicated to them, and some among these temples were the object of popular pilgrimages. Pious people, or people in distress, turned as a matter of course to Amida, for example, or to the various forms of Kannon. In fact the implantation of Kannon in the Japanese landscape, often on mountains, is itself an aspect of the Japanization of Buddhist faith. But it is particularly with reference to the *kami* that one reads in countless writings how the eternal Buddha "tempers his light" and "mingles with the dust" in order to let sentient beings conceive the aspiration to enlightenment. Thus the compassionate Buddhist deities were universally understood to infuse with the purest truth, through the *kami*, the nobler features of the otherwise benighted Japanese world.

This world was benighted particularly because Japan was so far from the place where the living Buddha taught, and so far from the Buddha's time. Japanese Buddhists never forgot this distance, and the thought of it inspired two opposing attitudes: despair over the gulf between Japan and the source of the Buddhist teaching, and confidence that the true teaching shone abundantly in Japan itself. Both attitudes found vivid expression in the works of a scholar-monk famous for his defense of *kenmitsu bukkyō* against the exclusive Pure Land pietism that first emerged during his lifetime. This was Jōkei (Gedatsu Shōnin, 1155–1213), of Kōfuku-ji in Nara. Jōkei wrote:

> Persons like myself, in a small land and in the latter age [of the Law], are not born so as to meet the living [Shaka, i.e. Śākyamuni]; nor do we go to see his holy places. For us, the Teaching of Lord Shaka is as though delivered in vain.

Yet Jōkei found consolation in his own "small land," precisely thanks to the Kasuga *kami* who protected Kōfuku-ji. Jōkei was deeply devoted to this *kami*, whose sacred hill is near the temple, and wrote movingly of his trust in the *kami*'s living power. Acknowledging the *kami*'s standing as a bodhisattva (claimed by the *kami* in an oracle of 937), Jōkei exclaimed, "Shall I then—low, evil and ignorant as I am—declare him an unworthy guide?" He next invoked a still higher inspiration: this complex *kami*'s five *honji:* "Yet how much more worthy," he wrote, "are his inwardly realized sources Shaka, Yakushi, Jizō, Kannon, and Monju!" In fact, for Jōkei and for others of his time, the Kasuga *kami*'s sacred hill was a multiple paradise, where the paradises of Śākyamuni, Miroku (S. Maitreya), Kannon, Monju

(S. Mañjuśrī), and others could be found, as it were superimposed on one another. In this the hill was not at all unique, for many others in Japan were understood likewise to be paradises, thanks to their own, local *kami*. Thus Jōkei could look forward to being welcomed at last into this paradise which was at once peculiar to the Kasuga *kami*, and as universal as the Buddhist teaching itself. He wrote:

> When the moment [of my death] comes, [the *kami*] will appear in my room, filling me, body and mind, with his deep peace.... The relics I have will then reveal anew their wonders, and the True Teaching in which I take refuge will confer on me its power. Already Śākyamuni ... and Miroku... appear in welcome before my eyes.

Such words convey vividly how urgent it was to affirm Japan, too, as a land sanctified by the Buddha's full manifestation; for the alternative was to dwell on Japan's insignificance and spiritual poverty. Of course, not all monks felt the dilemma so keenly. Jōkei was far from alone, however, and it may be said that his faith sums up perfectly the spirit of Shintō-Buddhist syncretism. This syncretism remained integral to the common fund of Japanese Buddhist lore, at the most popular level, until the absolute separation of Shintō and Buddhism were decreed by the Meiji government in the early 1870s.

Meanwhile, in Jōkei's own time and shortly after, there arose the three new types of Buddhism already mentioned: Zen, exclusive Pure Land faith, and the teachings of the fiery Nichiren. None of the three were much concerned with the *kami*. The first two certainly had a Japanese coloring, but in claiming universal validity they refused to attach any importance to the tension that monks like Jōkei had felt so keenly. On the other hand, Nichiren, acutely aware of the dilemma, was inspired to declare Buddhism dead in India, and to affirm Japan as the new center of living Buddhism. In fact, toward the end of his life he declared himself the one true voice of the eternal Śākyamuni. In this he gave the theme of Japan as an enlightened land perhaps its most extreme expression.

20

Heian Period

I. *Saichō*

UMEHARA TAKESHI

THOSE FIGURES IN the history of Japanese Buddhism who exerted a great influence on posterity through the new sects they founded are chiefly grouped in the ninth and in the twelfth to thirteenth centuries, which are the major turning points in Japanese Buddhist history. Named after the political centers of their times, the new Buddhism that replaced Nara Buddhism in the ninth century is called Heian Buddhism, and the movements that emerged in the twelfth century are called Kamakura Buddhism. Saichō (767–822), posthumously known as Dengyō Daishi, along with Kūkai (Kōbō Daishi, 774–835), is one of the founders of Heian Buddhism, which differs from the old Nara schools in two respects.

First, Nara Buddhism was an urban religion, based almost exclusively in the capital. In opposition to this model, Heian Buddhism chose the mountain retreat as its headquarters. Saichō made Mount Hiei his base for Buddhist practice. This was quite a remote place at the time, as the capital was still located in Nara. Kūkai, for his part, chose the distant Mount Kōya as his headquarters, even though he approached the emperors and propagated his teaching in Kyoto, the new capital. The mountain retreat had a double significance for Japan's Buddhists. On the one hand it was seen as a place of purity far from the corruption of human society, and one who had not practiced asceticism for a long time in such a place of purity could not become a real Buddhist. But there was another reason for their choice: to the Japanese, from of old the mountain forest had been the abode of the spirits of the dead, a sacred place.

The second difference between Heian and Nara Buddhism is that, while the Nara schools relied on the śāstras, the commentaries on Buddhist teaching composed by Nāgārjuna, Vasubandhu, and other Indian patriarchs, Heian Buddhism made the sūtras themselves the core of its teaching, the *Lotus Sūtra* in Saichō's case and the *Mahāvairocana Sūtra (Dainichikyō)* in Kūkai's. This shift from śāstra Buddhism to sūtra Buddhism spelled a real transformation of the religion.

20. Sūtra scroll container, Heian period.

Saichō is said to have been born in a village of the Shiga district at the foot of Mount Hiei in 767 and to have belonged to the Mitsu-no-obito clan, of Chinese immigrant origin. His personal name was Hirono. He left home at fourteen, and in 785, aged seventeen, he received initial ordination as a *shami*. In 787 he received full formal ordination, the license to act as a Buddhist priest, but he soon withdrew alone to Mount Hiei, to enter on a life entirely consecrated to asceticism and contemplation. In the written vows he composed on this occasion Saichō describes himself as the most foolish among the foolish, the maddest among the mad. Here and now, he vows to make every effort to realize five wishes aroused in him by his faith, and to extend the merit for this to all people:

1. As long as I am unable to raise the six internal bases *(indriya)* of sight, hearing, smell, taste, touch, and thought to a state of purity like the Buddha's, I shall perform no good deeds on behalf of other people.

2. As long as I am unable to obtain a mind radiant with truth, I shall practice no skill or art.

3. As long as I do not perfectly put into practice the pure life according to the precepts, I shall not take part in any of the functions of a temple officiant.

4. As long as I have not attained a mind full of wisdom, I shall not become involved in any worldly relationship; however, after coming to a state resembling purity of the six bases, these restrictions on my activity will be ended.

5. The merits I gather by ascetic practice in this world will not be for my own benefit only, but will be extended to all, so that absolutely everyone may attain to highest enlightenment.[1]

The young Saichō's earnestness in seeking the path is apparent throughout this document, written at a time when Nara Buddhism had reached an

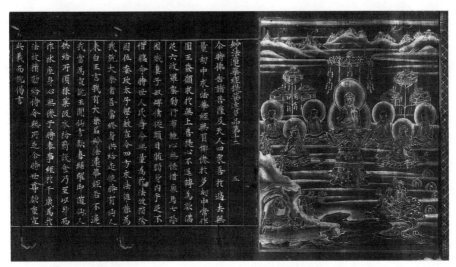

21. Chapter 5 of the *Lotus Sūtra*, late Heian Period.

extreme pitch of corruption. The reliance of successive emperors on Buddhism produced many corrupt priests, who sought their own interests and cultivated their connections with power. Dōkyō, in particular, won the favor of Empress Kōken (r. 749–758 and 764–770) and the title of Imperial Priest. He seized both secular and religious authority to himself, and exerted it in a tyrannical way. With the death of the Empress, Dōkyō lost his position, but Nara Buddhism was not in a condition to recover quickly from the shock he had inflicted on it.

Though ordained in Nara's Tōdai-ji temple, the young Saichō had retired from the world to Mount Hiei, fleeing the degenerate Buddhism of the capital in order to erect a new, purified, and rigorous Buddhism. However, by an ironic twist of fate, this young anchorite was soon to leap into eminence as the man of his times. Emperor Kanmu (r. 781-806) felt that to save politics from the stranglehold of a corrupt Buddhism it was necessary to move the capital from Nara. In 784, the third year of his reign, he moved the capital to Nagaoka, and when this proved to be unsuccessful he finally moved the capital to the site of present-day Kyoto in 794. Saichō is reported to have met Emperor Kanmu for the first time in the year of this second moving of the capital. The Emperor seems to have been deeply impressed by this young priest who had shown his uprightness and seriousness of purpose by choosing headquarters as far as possible from the corruption of Nara Buddhism—on Mount Hiei, just to the east of the new capital. In 797 the Emperor made Saichō one of the *Naigubusō*, or court priests, and in the following year Saichō is said to have given ten lectures on the *Lotus Sūtra*, to which many scholar priests were summoned from Nara. Thus through the unexpected patronage of the Emperor, the unknown young monk had suddenly become famous.[2]

In 804 Saichō traveled to T'ang China as an official visiting student, and stayed at the headquarters of T'ien-t'ai Buddhism on Mount T'ien-t'ai. Here he was initiated into the T'ien-t'ai school by Hsing-man, a disciple of the sixth (or ninth) T'ien-t'ai patriarch, Chan-jan (711–782), who had restored the tradition. Kūkai was another member of that year's party of legates to China, but his status differed from Saichō's. One might say that Saichō was regarded as a professor, whose speedy return was required, whereas Kūkai was treated as a brilliant research student; his instructions were to study in China for twenty years. In sharp contrast to Saichō's devotion to T'ien-t'ai, a school that had old-fashioned associations with the Sui period (581–618), Kūkai headed immediately for the capital, Ch'ang-an, and plunged into study of the most up-to-the-minute fashion in Buddhism at that time, the esoteric Shingon tradition.

Saichō returned to Japan in 805. The death of his patron, Emperor Kanmu, in 806 brought a sudden change for the worse in Saichō's circumstances. Nara Buddhism had until now been under strong pressure from Saichō and his imperial patron, but now it was in a position to launch a counterattack. Kūkai returned from China two years after Saichō, and his presence in the capital from 809 further complicated Saichō's position. Saichō considered the T'ien-t'ai (Tendai) system of Chih-i (538–597) to be the ideal form of Buddhism, yet he saw difficulties in the exclusive propagation of this doctrinally superior and morally rigorous creed. After Emperor Kanmu's death the succession was eventually transferred from his son, Emperor Heizei (r. 806–809), to the younger brother Emperor Saga (r. 809–823), in circumstances that gave rise to conflict among the leading figures. In this period of unrest, doctrine had little appeal to the minds of the aristocrats; they wanted instead a practical religion, which would bring prosperity and security to their families and defeat to their enemies.

Saichō realized that the esoteric school was well suited to meet this demand, and he had heard that Kūkai had brought many Tantric sūtras back from China. He borrowed some of these texts from Kūkai, and in 813 he went to Takaosan-ji to receive the Matrix Kanjō (esoteric baptism) at Kūkai's hands. This brought Kūkai immediate fame. A rivalry soon developed between the two men, the inevitable result of their differences in doctrine and personality. Kūkai placed Saichō's Tendai school on a lower rung than esoteric Buddhism, and even beneath the Kegon school. Their names, which in all probability they chose themselves, reveal the diametrical opposition of their personalities: Saichō means "most pure" and reflects his ideal of attaining the purest inward state; Kūkai means "sky and sea" and suggests an infinitely capacious expanse of these elements, which could tolerate the admixture of some impurities. When Saichō's dearest pupil, Taihan, went to visit Kūkai and never returned, and when Kūkai repeatedly refused to lend Tantric texts for consultation, relations between the two were broken off.

Just before Emperor Kanmu's death, Saichō had obtained a subsidy from the imperial palace to keep two priests every year as official annual students of the Tendai Lotus school. To become priests, they had to receive ordination either at Tōdai-ji or at the Yakushi temple in Shimotsuke. The Nara priests were naturally reluctant to grant priestly qualifications to disciples of Saichō, whom they saw as infringing on their vested privileges. Thus, after years of study and ascetic discipline under his intimate guidance, many of Saichō's disciples were obliged to leave him and to submit to the Nara priests, in order to acquire their formal qualifications. Clearly, if the Tendai school were ever to match Nara Buddhism in strength, an independent *kaidan* (platform for the transmission of the precepts, place of ordination) was required. Appealing for the establishment of such a platform of strict Mahāyāna observance, Saichō composed three treatises, the *Sange gakushō shiki*, in six, eight, and four parts, respectively. These were sets of regulations for the Tendai sect and its students. Most controversial was the treatise in four parts, in which, in arguing for the establishment of a platform at Mount Hiei's Enryaku-ji which could grant qualifications for priesthood equivalent to those of the Tōdai-ji and the Yakushi-ji, Saichō underlined the difference between Hīnayāna and Mahāyāna precepts, and claimed that the platforms at the Nara temples were Hīnayāna platforms that could not transmit the precepts needed by Mahāyānists. The Mahāyāna schools of Nara were still using the unchanged Hīnayāna rules. The anomaly created by the defectiveness of the Nara platforms could be amended by a Mahāyāna platform that would transmit not only the Hīnayāna rules, 250 precepts full of purity bestowed by ten men of great virtue as the essential commandments, but also the precepts proper to Mahāyāna, namely, the ten heavy and forty-eight light precepts granted as the essential ones by such figures as the Buddha and Bodhisattva Mañjuśrī rather than by mere human beings.

Indeed, Saichō claimed, the 250 precepts, which regulated the details of daily life, were virtually meaningless outside their original Indian context, and had now become unnecessarily troublesome. He raised questions about the actual practice of the priests who had received these numerous detailed precepts, for despite their severity the present state of Buddhism was distinguished by an abundance of lax and corrupt priests. This situation called for a drastic simplification of the precepts. The "ten commandments" of Buddhism, binding on priests and laity alike, forbade killing, stealing, fornication, lying, consumption of alcohol, use of cosmetics, attendance at stage spectacles, sleeping in big beds, eating outside mealtimes, and wearing gold, silver, or jewels. Saichō replaced the last five, which he saw as prescribing external virtue in an Indian context, with precepts directed against universal vices and aiming to shape an interior ethic: (1) not to speak about the sins of four kinds of living beings; (2) not to praise oneself and slander others; (3) not to nurse resentment or malice; (4) not to allow anger to lead to hatred; (5) not to despise the Three Jewels. The upshot of this revision is to direct one back to one's true inner nature, the pure mind within the mind, to which merely external precepts can never bring one. It is imperative constantly to subject oneself to severe self-examination, practicing conversion of heart, until through this repentance one has returned to the pure mind that is one's true nature. The reformative aspirations Saichō expresses here are reminiscent of those of Luther or Calvin.

Apparently Saichō was claiming that none of the Buddhist clergy, least of all those at Nara, were qualified to confer precepts, and that he alone was so qualified. The issue was not simply a doctrinal one. The establishment of a platform on Mount Hiei in accordance with Saichō's claims would be a body blow to the privileged position of Nara and to the survival of many of the temples of Nara allegiance. Led by Gomyō (749–834), the supporters of Nara devoted all their energy to the task of refuting Saichō. Their chief argument was that Saichō could not substantiate his claim that pure observance Mahāyāna platforms existed in India, China, and ancient Japan; no sūtras provided evidence of their existence. In reply, Saichō argued from various sūtras and from his own experience in China, but it must be admitted that his opponents had the stronger case, for Indian and Chinese sources provide not the slightest documentary evidence for his claim, and his appeal to the state of things in Chinese temples seems to be based on misunderstandings.

Moreover, the temples built in Japan by Shōtoku Taishi, Gyōki (668–749), and others before the arrival of the Chien-chen (J. Ganjin, 688–763), founder of Tōshōdai-ji in Nara, could not have been strict-observance Mahāyāna temples, as Saichō claimed, for the Mahāyāna precepts had not yet been formally introduced into the country. Nevertheless, the emergence of a claim of this kind within Mahāyāna Buddhism is of profound interest. As the entry of Christianity into the Germanic world brought a deepening of the interior dimension, culminating in the religious movement called Protestantism, so Buddhism, in coming to Japan, shed its preoccupation with external laws and became a religion of interior self-purification through conversion of heart.

The controversy with Nara occupied most of Saichō's energies in his later years, giving rise to such works as the *Shugo kokkai shō* (Defense of the fatherland) and *Kenkairon* (Clarification of the precepts). In controversy he had a remarkable lucidity and an ability to marshal evidence from numerous sūtras, quite crushing his opponents. The Japanese do not enjoy controversy, and pitched battles between opposing viewpoints are rare in their history. Saichō's thorough and uncompromising refutations are an exception which one might explain by the gravity of the issues at stake; yet Hōnen, in the comparable conditions of Kamakura Buddhism, refrained from such exhaustive refutation. Saichō continued to address frequent requests for the independent platform to the Imperial Court. Permission for its establishment did not come until a little after his death. The result of this elevation of Tendai Buddhism to parity with the Nara schools was exactly what the Nara Buddhists had feared: Tendai Buddhism from its basis in a mountain retreat in close proximity to the capital, together with Kūkai's Shingon school, completely overcame the old Buddhism, now consigned to irremediable decline.

Saichō, like most Buddhist thinkers, had no intention to establish a new doctrine. His only aim was to build a stronghold of the Tendai teaching systematized by Chih-i, which he saw as the most orthodox form of Buddhism.

Central to Tendai are two doctrines. First is the theory of the Five Periods and Eight Teachings. This attempted to iron out the inconsistencies between the innumerable sūtras that had been attributed to the Buddha over the centuries. It did so by ascribing them to different periods between the Buddha's attainment of enlightenment and first teaching at the age of thirty-eight and his entry into final nirvāṇa at age eighty. The theory could then determine which sūtra enjoys primacy over the others and conveys the Buddha's essential message. Moved by the natural desire to clear up the confusion generated by the translation and importation into China of so many Hīnayāna and Mahāyāna sūtras, Chih-i studied many of these, and after deep reflection divided them into five groups: the Kegon group, the Agon (*āgama*) group, the expanded scriptures (*vaipulya*) group, the Perfection of Wisdom group, and the Lotus group. All of these were authentic collections of the Buddha's teachings, but the last was the one in which he expounded his teaching directly and fully, and so it enjoyed a superior authority.

Second is the doctrine that "one thought is three thousand worlds." The ten realms which make up this world, namely, hell, *preta*, animal, *asura*, human, *deva*, *śrāvaka*, *pratyekabuddha*, *bodhisattva*, and buddha, are seen as each containing within themselves all ten realms, making up one hundred worlds. Each of these worlds in turn possesses the ten aspects of external appearance, internal characteristics, total body, inherent power, function, origin, conditions, resultant actuality, manifestation thereof, and interrelatedness of the previous nine aspects. To the thousand worlds thus produced is added the theory of the threefold division of the universe into the world of the five psychophysical constituents *(skandhas)*, subjective entity (the human world), and the container world (the earthly habitation of humanity). Thus in a fraction of a second three thousand worlds are thought to be contained within the mind simultaneously. This theory, which reminds one of Leibniz's monadology, acknowledges human free will and gives human beings the possibility of going either to hell or to the Buddha, while also supplying a practical imperative aiding them to turn in the latter direction.

Saichō's Tendai ideology shows clear affinities with the commentaries attributed to Prince Shōtoku, which accorded primacy to the *Lotus* and *Śrīmālādevī* sūtras, the only sūtras in which the theory of a single vehicle *(ekayāna)* is expounded. Though Buddhism begins with the direct disciples, the *śrāvakas*, who attained enlightenment after hearing the voice of the Buddha himself, and the *pratyekabuddhas*, who after the Buddha's extinction attained enlightenment under his influence, the Mahāyāna tradition saw the teaching of these disciples as excessively negative. These disciples had seen the human world as suffering, and desire as the root of suffering, and they had sought to extinguish this desire by a secluded life devoted to the precepts, meditation, and the cultivation of wisdom. In doing so, they had found only the standpoint of the "little vehicle." Followers of the "great vehicle," or Mahāyāna, adopted the standpoint of the bodhisattva, who comes back into the midst of suffering humanity. Bodhisattvas are not captive to desire, but neither do they fall captive to the rejection of desire. They perpetually live in the freedom of emptiness.

When Mahāyāna became the dominant form of Buddhism in China, it saw the tradition from its viewpoint as falling into three forms, the Buddhism of *śrāvaka, pratyekabuddha*, and *bodhisattva*, respectively. The latter was superior to the other two. But the *Lotus Sūtra* shows that a movement was already afoot to reunite these three into a single-vehicle Buddhism, no longer disqualifying followers of the two lesser paths as objects of salvation, but giving them a place within the general one-vehicle economy. This movement was inspired by a concern with unity and equality. It refused to leave Buddhism in its divided state, and sought to make salvation equally available to all human beings.

Saichō was not exclusively concerned with Tendai; he also made Mount Hiei a center for "combined study of the four learnings," the other three being Tantrism, Zen, and Vinaya. Indeed, he succeeded in making Mount Hiei a kind of university. Whereas, unlike Kūkai, he authored no works of systematic doctrine, many later doctrines had their origin on Mount Hiei and within the Tendai school. Most central among these was the incomparable doctrine that the Buddha-nature is within all living things; the Tendai esoteric doctrine of Ennin (794–864) and Enchin (814–891), which differs from Shingon esotericism; the Pure Land Nenbutsu thinking developed by Genshin and later by Hōnen and Shinran; and the Zen philosophies of Eisai and Dōgen. Paradoxically, these fruits of Saichō's educational enterprise overshadowed the Tendai school itself and led to its decline. Nichiren angrily rejected these flourishing sects and called for a return to the original teaching of Śākyamuni Buddha and the orthodox form of Japanese Buddhism, based on the *Lotus Sūtra*.

Saichō's choice of the mountain retreat as Buddhist headquarters produced a fusion between Buddhism and traditional Japanese religious sensibility, for which these sacred abodes of spirits were so important; this fusion gave rise to the Shugendō movement. The success of Pure Land Buddhism since the tenth century can also be attributed to the association of the mountain abode of departed spirits with the paradise to which people would go after death. It is clear that, irrespective of the degree to which he himself was an original thinker, Saichō was the Buddhist who exerted the greatest influence on posterity. Applying to him what Windelband says of Kant, we may say that all previous Japanese Buddhism is summarized in him and that all that followed comes from him.

Notes

1. Kiuchi Gyōō, *Saichō to tendai kyōdan* (Tokyo: Kyōikusha, 1978) 59.
2. On the institution of *Lotus Sūtra* lectures, see Willa Jane Tanabe, "The Lotus Lectures: *Hokke hakkō* in the Heian Period," *Monumenta Nipponica* 39 (1984) 393–407.

Bibliography

De Bary, William Theodore, et al., eds. *Sources of Japanese Tradition*. New York: Columbia University Press, 1958.
Groner, Paul. *Saichō: The Establishment of the Japanese Tendai School*. Berkeley Buddhist Studies Series 7. Seoul: Po Chin Chai, 1984.

Matsunaga, Daigan and Alicia Matsunaga. *Foundation of Japanese Buddhism* I. Los Angeles-Tokyo: Buddhist Books International, 1974.

Petzold, Bruno. *Tendai Buddhism*. Yokohama: International Buddhist Exchange Center, 1979.

Robert, Jean-Noël. *Les doctrines de l'école japonaise Tendai: Gishin et le Hokke-shū gi shū*. Paris: Maisonneuve et Larose, 1990.

Swanson, Paul L., ed. "Tendai Buddhism in Japan." *Japanese Journal of Religious Studies* 14:2–3 (June–September 1987).

Tamura Yoshirō, "Tendaishū." *The Encyclopedia of Religion* 14.396–401.

Ui Hakuju. "A Study of Japanese Tendai Buddhism." *Philosophical Studies of Japan* 1 (1959) 33–74.

Weinstein, Stanley. "The Beginnings of Esoteric Buddhism in Japan: The Neglected Tendai Tradition." *Journal of Asian Studies* 34 (1974) 177–91.

{*translated by Joseph S. O'Leary*}

II. *Kūkai*

PAUL B. WATT

ŪKAI, OR Kōbō Daishi (Great Teacher Who Spread the Dharma)
as he is also known, occupies a unique place in Japanese history. Revered as the founder of the Shingon sect, he is also one of
Japan's greatest cultural leaders.[1] His activities spanned such
varied fields as calligraphy, architecture, social welfare, public education,
lexicography, literature and literary theory. In less than a century after his
death, the belief began to spread that this great man had not passed away
but lives on in a state of unceasing meditation, watching over those who
put their faith in him and awaiting the coming of the future Buddha,
Maitreya. From the Kamakura period (1185–1333) on, legends about him
were transmitted throughout the country, and so thoroughly did Kūkai
capture the hearts of millions of Japanese over the centuries that, although
the title of Great Teacher has been granted to many Buddhist masters by
the Japanese court, it has come to refer first and foremost to him.

Biography

Kūkai was born on the island of Shikoku in Sanuki Province at present-day
Zentsūji City.[2] The traditionally accepted year of his birth is 774, but there
are documents that support a 773 date as well.[3] His father was Saeki Tagimi; his mother came out of the Atō family. Both the Saeki and the Atō
were prominent in the region and played important roles in the political
and cultural life of the nation. At the age of fifteen (788), Kūkai went to
the capital with his maternal uncle, Atō Ōtari, and received instruction
from him in the Chinese classics. Ōtari was a distinguished scholar and
served as a tutor to Prince Iyo, a son of Emperor Kanmu. At eighteen,
Kūkai entered the state university where he continued his study of the Confucian classics, especially the *Book of Poetry*, the *Book of History*, and the
Spring and Autumn Annals. Since Kanmu had decided to move the capital
from Nara to Nagaoka in 784 (before settling finally in Kyoto in 794), it is
usually assumed that Kūkai was in Nagaoka during this period.[4]

Just when Kūkai became seriously interested in Buddhism is uncertain, but in his *Indications of the Goals of the Three Teachings*, completed when he was twenty-four, he states that after he entered the university, he met "a certain Buddhist monk" who showed him a scripture called the *Kokūzō gumonji no hō*.[5] The text contains a *dhāraṇī,* or incantation, of the same name, which if recited a million times endows the practitioner with miraculous powers of memory and understanding. Kūkai had apparently become dissatisfied with his Confucian studies and, according to the *Indications*, had concluded that Taoism, too, taught little that was of lasting significance. The encounter with the monk thus provided him with the stimulus he needed to withdraw from the university, which he did against the wishes of his family. Thereafter, he left the capital and, as a lay Buddhist ascetic, engaged in the practice of the *gumonji no hō* in remote areas of the countryside. In taking up the life of a wandering ascetic, Kūkai joined a tradition of so-called *shidosō*, or privately ordained monks, that stood outside of the official ecclesiastical structure and that for decades the government had been attempting to bring under its control. The later success of Shingon, and also Tendai, was in part due to their incorporation of this strain of popular Buddhism.

There is little information on Kūkai's activities from the time of his writing of the *Indications* to his departure for China, at thirty-one. It appears that he continued to live as a Buddhist ascetic and that he spent time in the mountains of Yoshino and the Kii peninsula, south of the capital. He must also have read widely in Buddhist materials during these years. The *Indications* alone reveal his acquaintance with twenty-six Buddhist texts, including such major Mahāyāna scriptures as the *Lotus* and *Avataṃsaka* sūtras,[6] and the learning he displayed in China and in the following years confirms that he continued these studies.

In this period Kūkai also encountered the Tantric or Esoteric text, the *Mahāvairocana Sūtra* (J. *Dainichikyō*). This sixth- or seventh-century Indian work was translated into Chinese in 725, and by 736 a copy had made its way to Japan. In contrast to the Tantric material that had earlier been brought to Japan, which stressed techniques for acquiring magical powers, the *Mahāvairocana Sūtra* was based upon the mature philosophy of Mahāyāna Buddhism and taught a method for the sudden attainment of Buddhahood. However, the type of meditation it advocated required the mastery of numerous *mudrās*, or hand gestures, and *dhāraṇīs* (or *mantras*), and involved the use of a *maṇḍala*, or sacred diagram. Although Kūkai sensed that this scripture represented the culmination of Buddhist teachings, there was much that he could not understand. He therefore set his mind on traveling to China in the hope of finding a teacher who could answer his questions. By 803 he had officially become a Buddhist monk, and in 804, in spite of the fact that he was still a relatively unknown figure, he managed to have himself appointed to the government mission that was about to leave for China.[7] His intention was to remain there for twenty years.

Of the four ships that set sail in 804, only ships one and two survived the dangerous journey. Kūkai[8] was on the first, which carried the head of the mission, as well as Tachibana Hayanari, who was later remembered, along with Kūkai and Emperor Saga, as one of the three great calligraphers of Japan. Saichō (767–822), the founder of Tendai Buddhism, was on the second vessel. Thrown off course by a storm, the ambassador's ship landed in the southern province of Fukien in the eighth month of 804. Unaccustomed to dealing with foreign envoys, the local authorities refused the embassy permission to land. It was not until Kūkai wrote the governor of the province on behalf of the mission that they were treated as official representatives of the Japanese government and permitted to travel to Ch'ang-an, which they reached near the end of the twelfth month. The city that they found was one of the great urban centers of the world, attracting people from all across the Asian continent.

By the early ninth century in China, Esoteric Buddhism had already won a large following that included emperors and high officials. Its systematic introduction had taken place nearly a century earlier. In 716 the Indian master Śubhākarasiṃha (637–735) arrived in Ch'ang-an, and with the aid of his Chinese disciple I-hsing (683–727) translated the *Mahāvairocana Sūtra*. A second esoteric teacher, Vajrabodhi (671–741), reached Ch'ang-an in 719, and he and his disciple, Amoghavajra (705–774), made partial translations of the *Vajraśekhara Sūtra* (J. *Kongōchōkyō*)—more accurately referred to as the *Tattvasaṃgraha Sūtra*. These two sūtras later provided the scriptural foundation of the Shingon sect in Japan. Although these texts and the meditative practices associated with them are believed to have been transmitted separately in India, in China, at least by the time of Amoghavajra's disciples, a few individuals appeared who had received both transmissions, the most notable of whom was Hui-kuo (746–805) of Ch'ing-ling-ssu, who was to become Kūkai's teacher. The Shingon sect in Japan recognizes two lineages of patriarchs, one associated with the *Vajraśekhara Sūtra*, the other with the *Mahāvairocana Sūtra*. In both lineages Hui-kuo is regarded as the Seventh Patriarch and Kūkai as the Eighth.

In Ch'ang-an, Kūkai remained with the embassy until it left for Japan in the second month of 805.[8] Saichō returned at that time, but Kūkai stayed on, taking up residence at Hsi-ming-ssu, a temple where Japanese students had lodged in the past. It may have been around this time that Kūkai met Prajñā and Muniśri, two Indian monks with whom he studied Sanskrit and Indian religion. Prajñā also gave him both Sanskrit and translated texts, which Kūkai subsequently brought back to Japan.

It was late in the fifth month of 805 or early in the sixth that Kūkai finally met Hui-kuo, who immediately accepted him as a disciple, and— concerned over his own poor health and the fact that he had not yet designated an heir—at once began Kūkai's instruction. In the sixth month, Kūkai received the *abhiṣeka,* or ritual initiation, into the meditative techniques associated with the *Mahāvairocana Sūtra;* in the seventh, he was initiated into those related to the *Vajraśekhara;* and in the eighth month, he received ordination as an Esoteric Buddhist master. Hui-kuo also had *maṇḍalas* prepared, scriptures copied, and ritual implements cast, which he passed on to Kūkai. Noting that his disciple I-ming would carry on the tradition in China, he ordered Kūkai to return to Japan to transmit the teaching there. Hui-kuo died shortly thereafter in the twelfth month of 805. Early in 806 Kūkai was selected to compose the epitaph for Hui-kuo's grave, an honor that indicates the high position he held among his teacher's followers. After collecting further materials, Kūkai, taking his dead master's words to heart, set sail for Japan in the eighth month of 806, with the embassy of Takashina Tōnari, which had arrived in Ch'ang-an several months earlier.

Kūkai arrived in Kyūshū in the tenth month of 806. There he composed the *Shōrai mokuroku,* in which he gave a brief account of his activities in China, described the chief characteristics of the Esoteric Buddhism he now desired to teach, and listed the sūtras and other items he had collected. He entrusted this document to Takashina as his report to the court, but he received no response for three years. In the interim he was obliged to remain in Kyūshū. Although Kūkai himself seems to have been concerned about the court's attitude toward a monk who returned eighteen years ahead of schedule, it appears that political unrest in the capital and the great popularity Saichō then enjoyed were factors in the delay. In 809, Emperor Heizei (r. 806–809), a supporter of Saichō, retired and the new Emperor Saga ordered Kūkai to move to Takaosan-ji, a temple located in the northern suburbs of Kyoto. At the time, Takaosan-ji, later known as Jingo-ji, was the center of the Kyoto Buddhist world. From 809 to 823 it was the main temple with which Kūkai was affiliated.

Once back in the capital, Kūkai commenced a vigorous and sustained effort to propagate Esoteric Buddhism. He quickly forged a close relationship with Emperor Saga, presenting him with examples of his calligraphy and performing Esoteric Buddhist rituals for the protection of the state. Indicative of the esteem in which Kūkai rapidly came to be held, not only at court but also in the Nara Buddhist community, was his appointment in 810 as *bettō*, or administrative head, of the great Nara temple Tōdai-ji. Such appointments were made by the government in consultation with leaders of the Buddhist community. (In 811 Kūkai was appointed *bettō* of Otoku-ni-dera, located on the southern outskirts of the capital, and in 829, of Daian-ji in Nara.)

Early in his Takaosan-ji period Kūkai benefited from Saichō's support as well. Saichō, too, had studied Esoteric Buddhism in China along with other Buddhist teachings, and before Kūkai's return he was regarded as an authority on it. However, Saichō recognized Kūkai's superior knowledge and requested the loan of Esoteric texts and further initiations into the tradition. That such an eminent monk would turn to Kūkai for instruction must have contributed dramatically to the latter's rise. But there were limits to the extent Kūkai felt he could meet Saichō's appeals, and by 816 their relationship had collapsed. Perhaps it is not a coincidence that, in the same year, Kūkai petitioned the court for land on Mount Kōya, a spot he had visited in his youth, as a place where he might establish his own center for the practice of Esoteric Buddhist meditation. The petition was granted, and while other responsibilities prevented Kūkai from staying long on the mountain, his disciples carried on the planned construction. (During these years, Kūkai also served as an advisor to the Emperor and as supervisor of repairs to the dam of Mannō no Ike, a reservoir in his home province.)

As another means of advancing the cause of Esoteric Buddhism, Kūkai also wrote in this period the first works in which he systematically argued for its superiority. The *Benkenmitsu nikyōron* (The difference between exoteric and esoteric Buddhism), probably completed in 815, is the only piece that can be dated with any certainty, but his *Sokushin jōbutsu gi* (Attaining enlightenment in this very body), *Shōji jissō gi* (The meanings of sound, word, and reality), and *Unji gi* (The meanings of the word *Hūṃ*) are also considered products of these years.[9]

After Saichō's death in 822, Kūkai was unrivaled in the Japanese Buddhist community. In 823 Emperor Saga placed him in charge of Tō-ji, an official temple located at the southern entrance to the capital. Kūkai immediately took measures to make it another Esoteric Buddhist training ground. In 823 he compiled the *Sangakuroku*, a curriculum of Esoteric Buddhist studies for monks who would reside at the temple. For the first time, the words "Shingon sect" appear in this document, and indeed in its original title, *Shingonshū shogaku kyūritsuron mokuroku*.[10] The new emperor,

Junna (r. 823–833), approved the curriculum and granted Kūkai fifty students who were to follow this course of study. To further increase Tō-ji's prestige, Kūkai gathered there many of the items he had brought back from China. Much of this material can be seen there today, along with religious artwork attributed to Kūkai or completed under his direction during this period.

Kūkai engaged in a wide variety of activities while at Tō-ji. He was responsible for directing construction there and on Mount Kōya; in 824 and 827 he reportedly brought rain to the capital through the performance of Esoteric rituals; and in 828 he established the Shugeishuchi-in or School for Arts and Sciences, the first educational institution in Japan open to students without regard to social or economic status. It is thought that the dictionary he compiled, the *Tenrei banshō myōgi*, which is the oldest extant dictionary in Japan, may have been used at this school. His most important achievement in this period, however, was his authorship of the *Jūjū shinron* (Ten stages of the development of mind). Written in response to an imperial command that all sects submit a statement of their teachings, the work stands as the final summation of his thought; in it he traces the growth of religious consciousness from its lowest level to its full flowering in the mind of the Shingon practitioner. He also compiled an abridged edition of this work under the title *Hizō hōyaku* (Precious key to the secret treasury).[11]

In 831 Kūkai's health began to fail and by 832 he had withdrawn to Mount Kōya. His request that a Shingon chapel be provided at the palace was granted, and in 835 the court gave permission for three monks to be ordained annually on Mount Kōya. Kūkai died in that year and, instead of being cremated, was interred on the mountain, clad in his robes.

Thought and Practice

From his youth Kūkai appears to have been engaged in a search for religious truth. As he pursued that goal, his thought eventually took shape on a scale seldom seen in Japanese Buddhist history. The first stage of its unfolding is represented by the *Indications of the Goals of the Three Teachings*; the second, by the *Benkenmitsu nikyōron* and other writings of the Takaosan-ji period; and the third, by the *Jūjū shinron*. In the *Indications*, a work that at many points more closely resembles dramatic than philosophic literature, the young Kūkai weighed the respective claims of Confucianism, Taoism, and Buddhism and settled upon the last as the most profound teaching. This was not a repudiation of Confucianism and Taoism, for they too are "the teachings of the Sages"; but only Buddhism, he concluded, takes into account the utter transiency of life and offers a path to release from suffering that encompasses all sentient beings.

Having cast his lot with Buddhism, Kūkai was confronted with a variety of Buddhist teachings from which to choose. He confesses that as he studied its diverse forms, he "cried many a time standing at the crossroad,"[12] but his search came to an end when he encountered Esoteric Buddhism. Although a lack of material makes it difficult to determine the degree to which his thought is indebted to Hui-kuo, it is generally agreed that the system Kūkai articulated in the works of the Takaosan-ji period is uniquely his own. In distinguishing Esoteric from exoteric Buddhism (i.e., all earlier forms of the religion), he stresses, first, that while exoteric Buddhism was taught by the historical Buddha and was adjusted to the capacity of the listener, Esoteric Buddhism was taught by the ultimate Buddha "body" or Dharmakāya, Mahāvairocana, and constitutes the final truth; and second, that while exoteric Buddhism held that the attainment of enlightenment takes an indefinite period of time, Esoteric Buddhism teaches a practice that leads to "the attainment of enlightenment in this very body" (sokushin jōbutsu).

Behind Kūkai's first assertion lies the traditional Mahāyāna doctrine of the three bodies (trikāya) of the Buddha. Early in its history, Mahāyāna Buddhism had developed the view that the historical Buddha was a kind of "apparition body," or nirmāṇakāya, whose role was to spread Buddhist teachings in the temporal world. All sūtras were attributed to him. Mahāyāna Buddhism further recognized the existence of certain other buddhas, the so-called "bodies of bliss" or saṃbhogakāyas, who disclosed a fuller version of this message to the bodhisattvas, beings of advanced spiritual accomplishment. As regards the source of both of these types of Buddhas, the Dharmakāya or Dharma body—another name for Suchness or absolute truth itself—the common Mahāyāna position was that it did not preach and that nothing could be predicated about it. In contrast to this view, Kūkai identified the Buddha Mahāvairocana, the central Buddha in the Esoteric tradition he had inherited, with the Dharmakāya and argued that he in fact does preach. In the narrowest sense this preaching took the form of the dhāraṇis and mantras of the Esoteric Buddhist scriptures, but Kūkai also pointed out that, since Mahāvairocana is nothing other than the body, speech, and mind of the universe itself, to the enlightened, the entire cosmos is continually preaching the ultimate truth. Kūkai expressed this conception of the universe in the doctrine of the Six Great Elements (roku-dai)—earth, water, fire, wind, space, and consciousness—which constitute all buddhas, sentient beings, and material worlds, and which also constitute

22. Scroll painting of Kōbō Daishi, 14th century.

23. Modern-day statue of Kōbō Daishi's legendary forgiveness of the rich miser who had insulted him, Emon Saburō.

the body and mind of Mahāvairocana and exist in a state of eternal harmony.[13] Mahāvairocana's speech originates from the "vibrations" of the first five of these elements.[14] Thus the universe is ultimately seen as Mahāvairocana engaged in a continuous process of self-manifestation. The purpose of that process is understood as twofold: Mahāvairocana's own enjoyment and the edification of all sentient beings. From the perspective of these two purposes, Mahāvairocana is conceived as existing in four forms: (1) as the Dharmakāya in the Absolute State *(jishō hosshin);* (2) as the Dharmakāya in Bliss and Participation *(juyō hosshin),* i.e., as it exists for its own enjoyment and, in the form of various buddhas, for the guidance of the bodhisattvas; (3) as the Dharmakāya in Transformation *(henge hosshin),* i.e., as it exists for the guidance of ordinary people in the form of the historical Buddha; and (4) as the Dharmakāya in Emanation *(tōru hosshin),* i.e., as it exists for the guidance of dwellers in hells and nonhuman beings.[15]

In defense of exoteric Buddhism, it has been pointed out that the doctrines of the T'ien-t'ai and Hua-yen sects imply a similar view of the universe as a cosmic Buddha-body and that these sects also teach that it is possible to attain enlightenment in this life.[16] Kūkai contended, however, that while their teachings are profound these sects are deficient in the area of practice. What Shingon offers is not merely a vision for our contemplation, but a type of meditation that permits direct participation in the "innermost spiritual experience" of the Dharmakāya, and with that, "the attainment of enlightenment in this very body." The resultant transformation of the individual encompasses not only the mind, which the exoteric schools emphasized, but the body as well.

The aim of Shingon meditation is the realization of a preexistent union between Mahāvairocana's body, speech, and mind—spoken of as his Three Mysteries *(sanmitsu)* because they are subtle and difficult to comprehend—and the body, speech, and mind of the practitioner. Each of these points of correspondence is represented symbolically in Shingon meditation. The *mudrās,* which the practitioner forms with his hands, symbolize the element of the body; the *dhāranīs* and *mantras,* which he recites, stand for the element of Mahāvairocana's speech; and the *mandalas* from which the objects of concentration are selected, represent the various forms and attendant states of mind in which Mahāvairocana manifests himself. These manifestations are most commonly portrayed as Buddhas and bodhisattvas.

Although a variety of *mandalas* are used in Shingon meditation, unquestionably the two most important are the Womb or Matrix *(taizō),* Mandala, based on the *Mahāvairocana Sūtra;* and the Diamond *(kongōkai)* Mandala, derived from the *Vajraśekhara Sūtra.* In Kūkai's interpretation, these *maṇḍalas* together represent two inseparable aspects of Mahāvairocana. The Matrix Maṇḍala, whose chief symbol is the Lotus, signifies his Body of Principle *(rishin)*, or "that which is to be realized." The Diamond Maṇḍala, symbolized by the *vajra* or thunderbolt, represents his Wisdom Body *(chishin)*, or "that which realizes." These two aspects of Mahāvairocana are distinguished as a conceptual expedient for the practitioner—for whom they also represent the practitioner's own true nature and powers of insight—but Kūkai repeatedly asserted that fundamentally they are nondual *(richi funi)*. The Shingon student is guided in his meditation by an Esoteric Buddhist Master, who alone has the authority to transmit these intricate and potent meditative techniques. However, even if the student is successful in gaining an experience of union with Mahāvairocana within the meditative context, he has not reached the final goal of his training. Kūkai conceived of yet another form of "practice," within the context of ordinary life, in which the ideal was conformity to Mahāvairocana's Three Mysteries in every act of body, speech, and mind.[17]

Five years before his death, Kūkai wrote the *Jūjū shinron* and its summary, the *Hizō hōyaku*. Inasmuch as these works also assert the superiority of Esoteric Buddhism, they share a common ground with the writings of the Takaosan-ji years. But the *Jūjū shinron* is best understood as a last and all-encompassing synthesis of this thought. In describing the development of religious consciousness in these works, Kūkai begins with three non-Buddhist states of mind. In the first, the human being is ruled entirely by his basest desires; in the second, a sense of morality appears; and in the third, the individual cherishes the hope of rebirth in a heavenly existence. Kūkai associates the second stage with Confucianism, and the third primarily with Taoism and various forms of Hinduism.

In stages four through nine, Kūkai takes up the exoteric Buddhist schools. The fourth and fifth are the stages of Hīnayāna Buddhism, in which the individual realizes, on the one hand, that there is no permanent ego and, on the other, that rebirth is due to the working of karma. The sixth through ninth stages cover the major Mahāyāna schools (Yogācāra, Mādhyamika, T'ien-t'ai, and Hua-yen). Kūkai points out that, when one has progressed this far, "the stains covering the mind have been completely removed,"[18] but it is in Shingon Buddhism, at the tenth stage, that we are able "to open the inner treasury and to receive the treasures therein."[19] While Shingon is ranked above all other teachings, the emphasis in this work is on the value of all prior stages of religious consciousness as points of departure for full enlightenment. Even the lowest stage is seen as carrying the seeds of Buddhahood within it. This line of argument appears in earlier works, but never as prominently as in these final master-pieces.

The religion that Kūkai taught had a powerful impact on the Japan of his day. Attracted by the beauty of its artwork, the air of mystery sur-rounding its rituals, and the efficacy of its magic, the aristocrats of the cap-ital gave Esoteric Buddhism a warm reception. Indeed, Shingon Buddhism was so popular among them that Saichō's successors, in order to compete, hastened to push the Esoteric elements in Tendai to the fore. In the end, the Tendai center on Mount Hiei surpassed Mount Kōya in its influence as a vehicle for the dissemination of Esoteric Buddhism. Nevertheless, in the generations after Kūkai, the Shingon sect established temples throughout the country and gathered large numbers of adherents from among the gen-eral population as well as the aristocracy. This success was in part due to the appeal of the syncretism of Buddhism and Shinto which it developed. In *Ryōbu*, or Dual, Shinto, as it was known, the gods of Japan were identified as manifestations of the buddhas and bodhisattvas of the Matrix and Dia-mond Maṇḍalas.

Notes

1. The name Shingon, literally meaning "True Word," refers to the incantations *(dhāraṇīs* or *mantras)* used in Tantric meditation and ritual.

2. Our knowledge of Kūkai's life is hampered by significant gaps in the primary sources. Among Kūkai's own writings, the most important biographical sources are the *Sangō shiiki* (Indications of the goals of the three teachings) and *Shōrai mokuroku* (Memorial presenting a list of newly imported sūtras and other items), both translated in Hakeda, *Major Works;* and the *Seireishū* (Collected works of prose and poetry) in *Kōbō Daishi zenshū* III, 385–560. Other early texts common-ly consulted are the *Nijū gokajō goyuigō* (Twentyifive article will), attributed to Kūkai, and the *Kūkai Sōzu den* (Biography of Kūkai Sōzu), attributed to his disci-ple Shinzei (780–860).

3. For a discussion of these documents, see Miyasaka Yūshō, "Kōbō Daishi no shōgai," in *Kūkai no jinsei to shisō* (Kōza Mikkyō 3) (Tokyo: Shunjūsha, 1976) 81–82.

4. Watanabe Shōkō and Miyasaka Yūshō have argued, however, that he may well have been in Nara, at least during his university years. In support of this view, they note that it is uncertain whether the university ever moved to Nagaoka and that the shift of Kūkai's attention to Buddhism that took place around this time is more easily imagined as having occurred in Nara, where Buddhist influence was strong. See their *Shamon Kūkai* (Tokyo: Chikuma Shobō, 1967) 32.

5. Hakeda, *Major Works*, 102. This work had been translated into Chinese by the Tantric master Śubhākarasiṃha in 717 and was brought to Japan in the fol-lowing year.

6. Hakeda, *Major Works*, 23.

7. The precise date of Kūkai's entry into the clergy is unknown, but it is likely that he took this step in 803 just before leaving for China; see Miyasaka, "Kūkai no shōgai," 93–94.

8. Hakeda dates the departure of the embassy and Kūkai's move to Hsi-ming-ssu to the third month of 805 (*Major Works*, 31), but Kūkai himself states in the *Shōrai mokuroku* that these events took place in the second month (*Kōbō Daishi zenshū* I, 69, 98).

9. Translations of all these works can be found in Hakeda, *Major Works*. Kūkai also complete his *Bunpitsu ganshin shō* (The essentials of poetry and prose) and a draft of the *Bunkyō hifun ron* (The secret treasure-house of the mirrors of poetry) around this time.

10. Text in *Kōbō Daishi zenshū* I, 105–22.

11. The full title of the unabridged version is *Himitsu mandara jūjū shinron* (text in *Kōbō Daishi zenshū* I, 125–414). A translation of the *Precious Key* is contained in Hakeda, *Major Works*.

12. Hakeda, *Major Works*, 27.

13. Hakeda, *Major Works*, 229–30

14. Hakeda, *Major Works*, 240.

15. See Hakeda, *Major Works*, 83.

16. See for example, de Bary et al., eds., *Sources of Japanese Tradition* I, 137, and Miyasaka Yūshō and Umehara Takeshi, *Bukkyō no shisō 9: Seimei no umi (Kūkai)*, (Tokyo: Kadokawa Shoten, 1968) 55–56.

17. See his *Dainichikyō kaidai*, in *Kōbō Daishi zenshū* I, 659, and the discussion of this passage by Takagami Kakushō, *Mikkyō gairon* (Tokyo: Daiichi Shobō, 1937) 100.

18. Hakeda, *Major Works*, 160.

19. Hakeda, *Major Works*, 161.

Bibliography

De Bary, Wm. Theodore, et al., eds. *Sources of Japanese Tradition*, vol. 1, 13–51. New York: Columbia University Press, 1958.

Hakeda, Yoshito S. *Kūkai: Major Works, Translated, with an Account of His Life and a Study of His Thought*. New York: Columbia University Press, 1972.

———. *Shingon himitsu yuga*. Gendai Mikkyō Kōza. Tokyo: Daitō Shuppansha, 1975.

Katsumata Shunkyō. *Mikkyō no Nihonteki tenkai*. Tokyo: Shunjūsha, 1970.

———. *Kōbō Daishi no shisō to sono genryū*. Tokyo: Sankibō, 1981.

Kitagawa, Joseph. "Master and Savior." In *Studies of Esoteric Buddhism and Tantrism*. Kōyasan: Kōyasan University, 1965. 1–26.

Kōbō Daishi zenshū, 8 vols. Kōyasan: Kōyasan University, 1965.

Miyasaka Yūshō, Umehara Takeshi, and Kanaoka Shūyū, eds. *Kūkai no jinsei to shisō*. Tokyo: Shunjūsha, 1976.

Miyasaka Yūshō et al., eds. *Kōbō Daishi Kūkai zenshū*, I–IV, VI–VII. Tokyo: Chikuma Shobō, 1983.

Watanabe Shōkō and Miyasaka Yūshō. *Shamon Kūkai*. Tokyo: Chikuma Shobō, 1967.

III. *Heian Foundations of Kamakura Buddhism*

DAVID LION GARDINER

AMONG THE PARADIGM shifts emphasized in the traditional historical narratives of Japanese Buddhism, the most prominent is the emergence of the so-called "new" Buddhism of the Kamakura period (1185–1333). While many scholars now question whether it is right to call this shift a "reformation," few will deny that the Pure Land, Zen, and Nichiren schools, which have been the main forms of sectarian Buddhist faith from this period until today, rely heavily, in their doctrinal foundations, on reformist rhetoric. But the image of a reformation can lead one to overlook continuities between Heian and Kamakura Buddhism, missing the presence in the new schools of powerful resonances from the past.

Scholarly investigation of the period faces a challenging problem: it must use the invaluable research done by Japanese scholars, most of whom have been ordained in one of these sects, while at the same time resisting the distortions introduced by the special slant that a given school is likely to have on its own history. A frequently-noted distortion introduced by the rhetoric of reformation is that it highlights the teachings of a handful of "founders" who are not adequately representative of the great diversity of the time. Without passing judgment on this issue, I shall try to focus on some doctrinal matters of particular spiritual import that may serve to illuminate any discussions of this period. My presentation will, however, lean in favor of recognizing continuities throughout medieval Japanese Buddhism.[1]

Each of the major figures commonly held up as representative of new Buddhism in Kamakura—Hōnen, Shinran, Nichiren, Dōgen—was originally ordained on Mt. Hiei as a monk of the Tendai school. They formulated their new doctrines and practices in response to problems they had come to identify as central to Buddhist theory and practice as found on Mt. Hiei. The Tendai school is often referred to as the "birthing ground" of Kamakura Buddhism. The variety of texts and practices available by the late Heian period to monks of this eclectic school was so extensive that its capacity to spawn the diverse forms that appeared during the Kamakura period comes as no surprise. The eclecticism goes back to the Tendai founder, Saichō (767–822), who promoted the study of the Chinese T'ien-t'ai, Preceptual (Ritsu), Ch'an, and esoteric traditions.

Equally unsurprising is the emergence within Tendai of great differences over matters of doctrine and practice. The founders of the new schools broke with past tradition in very different ways, yet they shared a preoccupation with aspects of Tendai teaching that are associated with the idea of original enlightenment *(hongaku)*. Though none of them framed his teaching in explicit contradistinction to original enlightenment theories, the influence of these theories can be detected in each case.

Hōchibō Shōshin, a Barometer of the Times

One Tendai monk of the early Kamakura period, who was not a founder of a major new school, was forthright in condemning the *hongaku* theories. His name was Hōchibō Shōshin (active 1165–1207) and his writings provide a template for grasping some of the key issues of his day.[2] Shōshin was also a reformer of sorts, but, in contrast to the founders named above, his ambition seems to have been to revive traditional forms of scholasticism on Mt. Hiei. He was known as a dedicated student of scripture, so much so that all biographies of him tell how, immersed in reading, he was oblivious to the Genpei War that raged through Kyoto from 1180 to 1185. His overriding concern, it appears, was the character and quality of monastic study and practice. One of his writings in particular, *Commentary on the Profound Meaning of the Lotus Sūtra* (*Hokke gengi shiki*, a commentary on the *Fa-hua hsüan-i* by the Chinese founder of the T'ien-t'ai school, Chih-i), mounts a critique of the premises of *hongaku* theories and argues that these theories undermine traditional forms of Buddhist practice.

Shōshin condemns what he sees as doctrinal jargon about the supposed immanence of buddhahood, taking as his target the phrase "original and naturally enlightened Buddha" *(honrai jikaku butsu)*. This phrase includes the two Chinese glyphs that make up the term "original enlightenment" (*hon* means "original" and *gaku* means "enlightenment"), and can be understood as an elaboration of its meaning. Shōshin attacks the phrase on both philosophical and scriptural grounds, but the heart of his critique is that the proponents of *hongaku* thought deny the essential truth that Buddhist enlightenment depends on particular effort and insights, in other words on *practice.*

One of the key scriptural sources he cites is the *Awakening of Faith*, which gives a classic and influential statement of the distinction between original enlightenment *(hongaku)* and incipient enlightenment *(shikaku)*. Shōshin points out that the text treats original enlightenment as a principle *(ri)* residing within the bonds of ignorance that characterize *saṃsāra*, the cycle of death and rebirth. It is a potential that can be activated, and when it is activated through spiritual practice (an activation known as "incipient enlightenment") it can manifest as complete enlightenment *(kukyō kaku)*, which is no longer just a principle but is *actual (ji)* enlightenment. This distinction between principle *(ri)* and actuality *(ji)* is central to Shōshin's critique. He sees the proponents of original enlightenment doctrines as confusing the two, by mistaking what is merely a potential for buddhahood for the real thing. He argues at length that original enlightenment cannot denote an actual Buddha who exists apart from the bonds of ignorance *(hi betsu-u butsu)*. He counters the *hongaku* terms one by one, pitting actuality *(ji)* against principle *(ri)*, cultivated *(shu)* against natural *(ji*, also read *mizukara)*, and manifest *(gen)* against original *(honrai)*.

24. Temple precincts of Mt. Hiei.

Another scripture he draws on is the *Lotus Sūtra*. To show that buddhahood is an actual attainment that results from the deliberate cultivation of specific practices, he quotes the Buddha in that sūtra as saying: "O good men, since I actually achieved Buddhahood it has been incalculable, limitless... kalpas." Elsewhere the Buddha explains that his long lifespan is something that he "gained after cultivation of long practice."[3] The phrases *actually achieved (jitsu jō)* and *gained after cultivation of long practice (kushu shotoku)* show that Buddhahood is not a universal and timeless principle that one can bandy about. Rather, it is a personal and temporally grounded state of being, resulting from traditional contemplation methods that transform a deluded person into an enlightened one.

Shōshin disdains what he sees as an ill-conceived total affirmation of the relative world that undermines any rationale for the conventions of religious practice and the ethical principles upon which such practice ought to be based. While he may exaggerate the extent to which *hongaku* doctrine led in fact to antinomianism, other thinkers of the Kamakura period shared his dissatisfaction, if not his impatience, with certain elements of this doctrine. In stark contrast to the tendency of *hongaku* thought to depreciate religious practice, in the complacent assurance that the goal of buddhahood is already immanent, the Pure Land thinkers Hōnen and Shinran declared the impossibility of attaining the goal even when one did rely on conventional practices. The powerlessness of the individual left no alternative but to depend on the Other-Power of the vow of Amida Buddha. Shōshin's recognition of the reality of *saṃsāra* and ignorance, and of the need to engage in some particular method for liberation, is close to Hōnen's attitude. It is known, in fact, that he attended one of Hōnen's early gatherings in Ōhara and later engaged in the Pure Land *nenbutsu* practice of reciting the name of Amida.

Hongaku and Practice in Saichō and Kūkai

Shōshin's critique of facile claims of immanent buddhahood by some proponents of *hongaku* thought was aimed at what he saw as an overestimation of the proximity of the goal. His approach to Buddhist soteriology falls into a category known in the Tendai school as "upwardly turning" *(jōten),* which means it lays stress on the imperative of carefully attending to the actualities of the practices (causes) leading to Buddhahood. In this regard, Shōshin is a good representative of classical Tendai thought and, for that matter, of the thinking of the two "founders" of Heian Buddhism, Saichō and Kūkai.

Although both of these figures stood firmly on the doctrine of the inherent Buddha-nature, they nevertheless demonstrated a high regard for the careful cultivation of specific practices. In fact the monastic compounds established by each man, Saichō's Mt. Hiei in Kyoto and Kūkai's Mt. Kōya to the south in the hills of Wakayama Prefecture, were portrayed by their respective founders as providing much-needed contemplative training grounds for practitioners of the Mahāyāna path. Both men wrote of the lack of sincere Buddhist practice at the established temples of the old capital of Nara, and expressed their preference for training monks in the relative calm of a mountain environment. Both of them were also desirous of promoting the practice of esoteric Buddhism, although not for entirely the same reasons, and by the late Heian period it was the theory and practice of Taimitsu (Tendai esotericism) and Tōmitsu (Shingon esotericism) that probably best characterized the spirit of Heian Buddhism.[4]

Significantly, Shōshin's critique of *hongaku* thought was explicitly directed to practitioners of *shingon*. This term should not be understood as designating members of Kūkai's Shingon school alone, but rather as referring to a particular group of those practitioners of esoteric Buddhism (or of *mantra*, which is the original meaning of *shingon*) in both schools who manifested the antinomian, immanentist tendencies he so sharply disparaged. It seems as though the careful balance between theory and practice favored by Saichō and Kūkai, or for that matter by most of the scholastic Buddhist masters in China of the Sung and T'ang periods, such as Chih-i and Fa-tsang (whose works, as well as those of their disciples, were read by Saichō and Kūkai), had collapsed within some of the ranks of the subsequent generations of both schools. The central paradigm of the esoteric traditions was the practice of the Three Mysteries (*sanmitsu*) of body, speech, and mind in ritual use of *mudrā* (bodily gestures), *mantra* (the utterance of sacred formulae), and *maṇḍala* (the cosmic diagrams depicting deities), with the aim of embodying the very essence and power of the Buddha's mysteries in one's own being. In both the Tendai and Shingon schools, the practice of the Three Mysteries involved complex ritual procedures and an array of liturgical implements. Esoteric practice entailed a disciplined enactment of what were seen as "acts" of the Buddha, with the purpose of manifesting the practitioner's inherent Buddha qualities. Because the practice is modeled after the imagined qualities of the exalted state of Buddhahood itself, it is referred to as a "sudden" method. It would have been primarily in an environment characterized by this avowedly "sudden" practice that the *hongaku* proponents targeted by Shōshin were nourished. According to Shōshin, for them the most sudden practice would be no practice at all. Shōshin was naturally concerned that such a radical affirmation of the world as being already perfected would result in spiritual inertia.

As for Saichō's Tendai school, his commitment to the ideals of the Mahāyāna path of the bodhisattva, the Buddhist practitioner who vows to seek enlightenment for the sake of aiding other beings, is evidenced in his *Regulations for Students of the Mountain School (Sange gakushō shiki),* written in 818, in which he expresses the wish that the Enryaku-ji temple complex on Mt. Hiei should produce monks who will be servants, teachers, and treasures of the nation. In this text he lays out his plan for all Tendai monks to train on the mountain for twelve years while engaged in constant textual and ritual study. Saichō insisted that the 250 traditional precepts of monks be maintained, while adding to them ten precepts derived from a Mahāyāna scripture, which were more spiritual than practical in nature and set forth the compassionate duties of bodhisattva practice.

Later he proposed that Tendai monks bypass the standard ordination ceremony in which the 250 precepts were conferred, arguing that the ten bodhisattva precepts were sufficient to guarantee the purity of their religious practice. His motivation for this has frequently been misunderstood. The problem was that the ordinations were administered at the main government-sponsored temple of Tōdai-ji. He wanted to gain administrative independence from the government bureau that controlled them. He was not dismissing as useless the millennia-old Buddhist preceptual tradition. Although his disregard for the Tōdai-ji ordination platform may have contributed indirectly to a relaxation of attitudes toward the formal ethical commitments embodied in the precepts, his personal and institutional ethical principles were traditional and conservative to the core.

While Saichō's program was explicitly eclectic, incorporating formally two branches of practice—*shikan-gyō* (concentration and insight meditation, based on a system designed by the T'ien-t'ai founder Chih-i) and *shana-gyō* (based on the esoteric teachings of the *Dainichikyō*)—Kūkai's program for Shingon monks was more exclusive and focused entirely on esoteric Buddhist practices.

Like Saichō, however, Kūkai allowed his students to receive the basic monastic precepts conferred at ordination at Tōdai-ji, and again like Saichō he supplemented these, with special esoteric precepts known as *sanmayakai*. Although Kūkai encouraged his monks in the Shingon to limit themselves to texts and contemplations peculiar to the esoteric tradition, his school is often considered to have a relatively catholic approach to Buddhism, since he affirmed the inherent value of all other Buddhist schools of study and practice, a position most clearly expressed in his famous *Treatise on the Ten Stages of the Mind (Jūjū shinron)*. In this treatise, Kūkai emphasized the important contributions made to humankind's advancement toward enlightenment not only by the various Buddhist teachings but by non-Buddhist doctrines as well. Though he was later criticized by adherents of other schools for making Shingon the final stage in an individual's spiritual development, his systematization expresses nonetheless a remarkably comprehensive religious vision.

Saichō and Kūkai accepted the doctrine of inherent enlightenment (which is akin to that of the universal presence of the Buddha-nature) and built their systems of practice upon this theory. It is evident in the lengthy debates on the issue of the Buddha-nature carried on via treatises between Saichō and the monk Tokuitsu of the Hossō school that not everyone in their day supported this view. For Kūkai, the issue was not as central as it was for Saichō, but his presentation of esoteric Buddhist theory was unmistakably

clear in its attribution of an "originally existent" *(honnu)* status to the Three
Mysteries of the Buddha within all beings. Since he was the first to elaborate the esoteric Buddhist doctrines that were to pervade religious practice
to the extent that the Heian period was eventually recognized as the stage
of the "esotericization" *(mikkyōka)* of Japanese religion, his formulation
must be considered very influential. Thus it is important to note that he
carefully balanced his theory of immanence with requisite practices.

One of the interesting features of Kūkai's treatment of the "original
enlightenment" idea is that he not only asserted that humans are intrinsically endowed with the virtues of the Buddha, but also attributed to the
ultimate Buddha (specifically to his most refined spiritual essence known as
the Dharma-body) qualities of an actively divine body, speech, and mind—
features that were denied of this highest reach of reality by most Buddhists.
One of Kūkai's most celebrated doctrines was the assertion of the "preaching" of this Dharma-body *(hosshin seppō)*. Consequently, Kūkai presented a
vision not only of a human realm replete with seeds of perfection but also
of a Buddha-realm comprised of miraculous activity. The esoteric Buddhist
practice of the Three Mysteries is thus intended to be the practice of what
buddhas do (note my comments below on the similarity to Dōgen's assessment of seated meditation). It is considered a "sudden" teaching and practice both because it claims to make complete enlightenment attainable in
this body *(sokushin jōbutsu)* as opposed to many lifetimes, and because its
practice is based on the goal.[5]

Hongaku Thought in the Founders of the New Kamakura Schools

Compared to the optimism that characterized *hongaku* thought, the attitudes of the Kamakura founders (especially Hōnen, Shinran, and Nichiren)
were in general less sanguine about the human condition. There was a pervasive sense that Japan was entering a period of decline, which Buddhists
identified as *mappō*. This idea plays a determining role in Kamakura Buddhism, though it is rejected by Dōgen, as it subjects the Buddhist path to
historical relativism. Shōshin does not invoke the idea of *mappō* in his
defense of the efficacy of Buddhist practice, though he strikes a grim note
as he reprimands excessive exuberance. Shinran's embrace of the *mappō* concept led him to reject the contemporary efficacy of any Buddhist practice
aiming at enlightenment. Not only were "originally enlightened buddhas"
dismissed as fictions, but even the hard-earned, "real time," traditional
enlightenment esteemed by Shōshin was also regarded as a thing of the
past. To aspire to such a goal was to subscribe to the "teaching of the way

of the saints" *(shōdōmon),* which could no longer be followed by the beings of inferior capacity of the latter age.

Each of the major Kamakura founders singled out one particular well-defined practice as the core of Buddhist living, a practice that in each case was seen not as a means to an end, but as the expression of a deep faith in a particular vision of salvation. This selectivity *(senjaku)* is often contrasted with the more eclectic and catholic vision of Buddhist practice characteristic of the Tendai school throughout most of the Heian period. The spirit embodied in these new exclusive approaches may be representative of transformations that were taking place in Japan at the time. Social conditions were changing as the center of political and cultural life shifted from Kyoto to the new capital of Kamakura, headquarters of the new military government *(bakufu)* of Minamoto Yoritomo from 1185, and the rule of the courtiers gave way to a rule by samurai warrior-administrators. At the same time, people in Japan were becoming conscious of a new cultural and political independence from the continent. On various levels, the Japanese had not only demonstrated their ability to successfully adopt elements of Chinese culture, but were growing confident as well in their ability to jettison previously revered foreign models in favor of newly emerging indigenous patterns. There was a new individualism, which the new systems of religious practice reflect. The darker side of this time of upheaval was a sense of insecurity and frustration, acerbated when the changes were interpreted as symptomatic of decline, as in the prevalent *mappō* schema. The selection of one relatively simple practice from among a menu of numerous often complicated practices may have been a response to this insecurity. Even Shōshin's emphasis on fact and actuality over and against theory and principle may be read as a response to the needs of historically determined individuals.

However, the traditional historical narratives may have unduly stressed the purported relationship between the new social circumstances, *mappō* thought, and the practices promoted by the Kamakura founders. While the physical transferal of the capital from Kyoto to Kamakura did clearly mark the beginning of a new era of military rule, the extent to which this shift in government was a direct cause of general feelings of malaise and inadequacy has perhaps been overstated. For the many people intimate with courtier society, the loss of Kyoto as the seat of government after four hundred years surely made for difficult adjustments. But it is well known that real political power had already slipped from the hands of the imperial family to other aristocratic and provincial elites in various ways by the tenth century. So the traditional alignment of "social changes" with a "reformation" may be considered in part a product of sectarian reconstruction of history that renders more dramatic the emergence of new forms of Buddhism and diminishes the appearance of continuities with pre-Kamakura traditions.

Despite all these differences between Heian and Kamakura Buddhism, it would be a mistake to discount the influence of *hongaku* doctrines on the Kamakura founders and on all subsequent periods. It is frequently noted that Dōgen, the founder of the Sōtō Zen school, was led to pursue the study of Zen in China by the driving force of a paradox embodied in a central tenet of *hongaku* thought: if we all possess the Buddha-nature, why is it that all the patriarchs of the past found it necessary to engage in the practice of meditation and to cultivate the Buddhist path? Dōgen's famed response to this question, apparently arrived at only through the assiduous practice of *zazen* (seated meditation), was that meditation did not constitute a means to an end; it did not precipitate enlightenment; rather, it was an expression, the only true expression, of one's inherently enlightened nature. Thus when we engage in *zazen,* we manifest our Buddha-nature. In fact, when we engage in any of the traditional practices of preserving the precepts or meditating, we are buddhas by virtue of doing what all the buddhas of the past did. This attainment is not as simple as it sounds, though, because Dōgen adds the condition that our practice must not be tainted with the intention to "make a Buddha" but must remain free of such dualistic thinking. Thus his celebrated motto of "just sitting" *(shikan taza)* embraces both wisdom and meditation: as long as it is "just" sitting, without any presumption of causal efficacy or any self-congratulation—having dropped off all attachment to both body and mind *(shinjin datsuraku)*—it is the Buddha-body and Buddha-mind that are present in full. The twist to Dōgen's radical affirmation of our inherent enlightenment is the exhortation to traditional forms of cultivation that it entails. His advocacy of diligent effort in the pursuit of the way *(kufū bendō)* thus stands in stark contrast to the kind of spiritual complacency that Shōshin attributed to *hongaku* proponents. Dōgen's handling of the premise of original enlightenment possesses a subtlety that Shōshin does not find in the ideas of his adversaries.

For Shinran, too, there is an important sense in which a concept of "inherent salvation" operates at the heart of his soteriological vision. One difference between Shinran and his master Hōnen is his idiosyncratic interpretation of the role of uttering the Buddha's name *(Namu Amida Butsu)*. For Shinran, there is no element of efficacy involved in the *nenbutsu* whatsoever. The reason is that our salvation has already been guaranteed by Amida; our utterance of his praise in the *nenbutsu* is to be regarded simply as an expression of our profound gratitude for the Buddha's great compassion. As such, it is an expression of the fact that we have already been saved. By chanting the Buddha's name we manifest our faith in the truth of Other-Power. The *nenbutsu* does not assure our salvation, it verifies it.

Nichiren, the founder of the school bearing his name, emphasized the power of chanting the title of the *Lotus Sūtra (Myōhō renge kyō)* and made this practice his central one. He shares with the Pure Land and Zen founders an exclusive reliance on one simple practice, coupled with a rhetoric that downplays the importance of abstract theory and privileges practice. Yet in spite of the efforts of many Nichiren scholars to portray him as completely free from the influence of *hongaku* thought, he affirms the immediacy of ultimate reality when he teaches that the chanting of the holy phrase (the *daimoku*) in and of itself embodies buddhahood.

The One-Vehicle Teaching

Much more important than *hongaku* thought is another Tendai doctrinal formulation that loomed large in the awareness of the Kamakura founders, namely the theory of the One Buddha Vehicle, which happens to represent a strong undercurrent of continuity with Heian-period Buddhist thought. The One Vehicle *(ichijō)* teaching of the *Lotus Sūtra*, presented as the final, most reliable teaching of Śākyamuni Buddha's career, dismisses all previous doctrines about the paths of the *arhat* and *pratyekabuddha* (two versions of Buddhist sainthood that represented, along with buddhahood, ultimate goals for religious aspirants) as having been expedient devices aimed at bringing spiritually weaker listeners onto the Buddhist path. Once converted to the path, they would be informed (by the teaching of the *Lotus Sūtra*) that the *arhat* and *pratyekabuddha* are inferior goals (of the "lesser vehicle," or Hīnayāna), surpassed by the sublime buddhahood to which they are entitled, and that they are in fact already on the "greater vehicle" (or Mahāyāna). So the central message of the sūtra is that the true purpose of the Buddha's teaching is nothing less than to help all beings advance to the exalted stage of buddhahood.

While many Buddhists were under the impression that there were three vehicles or paths for Buddhists to follow, the sūtra reveals that two of them (or depending on the interpretation all three, with the new vehicle being a fourth) were mere fictions fabricated out of the Buddha's compassion for beings who would have lost interest in Buddhist practice had they been told from the beginning that the goal was so high. Thus all practitioners are destined to become buddhas and nothing less; this is the upshot of the One Buddha Vehicle. This view of the Buddhist teachings obliged any system of Buddhist practice to align its methods with the principle of the teaching of the One Vehicle. In other words, the practice must be suitable for beings who possess the Buddha-nature; it must avoid too dualistic a depiction of the practitioner's condition (opposing ignorance to enlightenment), in order to reflect the proximity of the goal. Philosophically speaking, such practices are referred to as "sudden," not just because they are supposed to engender awakening quickly (although this may be a claim), but rather because they are based on the goal as being already immanent; such a distinction existed also in Indian Buddhism between practices or vehicles based on the *cause (hetuyāna)*, or the actual benighted condition of sentient beings, and those based on the *effect* or *goal (phalayāna)*, which is the purity and wisdom of enlightenment.

Insofar as many forms of Mahāyāna Buddhism considered themselves to represent the One Vehicle doctrine, they were also "sudden" teachings that possessed an inherent tension in terms of how to articulate the subtle relationship between cause (practice) and effect (Buddhahood). The T'ien-t'ai school (Tendai's precursor in China) was not alone in claiming to represent the Supreme Buddha Vehicle: Hua-yen, Ch'an, and esoteric Buddhism all saw themselves as expounding the One Vehicle. In Heian Japan the Tendai school was the foremost representative of One Vehicle Buddhism, and in the various practices developed within its ranks—including classical meditations based on T'ien-t'ai precedents, Pure Land, Zen, and esoteric Buddhist disciplines—it wrestled with the same basic problematic: how to find a practice appropriate to the One Buddha Vehicle.

The same concern was apparent in the esoteric Shingon school founded by Kūkai, and most of the esoteric practices of both Tendai and Shingon were informed by this theoretical sensitivity. The Kamakura founders may have differed greatly in the styles of their practice, and perhaps also in their historical sensibilities, from their Heian predecessors, but the underlying theory of the supreme and sudden One Buddha Vehicle remained a constant and effective force in the articulation of their respective religious visions.

The selectivity of the Kamakura founders was more than a mere preference for one particular style of Buddhism over another; it was a commitment to one practice as *the only true* Buddhist practice, as the best possible expression of the One Buddha Vehicle, and a candid dismissal of other practices as inadequate. In contrast to this emphasis on simplicity, the dominant Tendai and Shingon schools had practices that were not only complex but also multiple both in terms of variety and in the sense that gradations of practice were recognized. Whether it was the concentration and insight contemplations of Tendai or the esoteric Three Mysteries practices of both schools, diligence, memory, and plenty of free time were required of anyone intending to become proficient at the practices so as to reap their benefits. This was particularly so in the case of esoteric practice, which by the late Heian period had so engulfed the monastic and even aristocratic court culture by virtue of its attractive theory and enchanting liturgy that it had become the regnant Buddhist paradigm. Just as Shōshin singled out the excesses of practitioners of *mantra* in his critique of *hongaku* abominations, it was partly in response to the extravagance and perhaps even pomposity of aspects of esoteric practice that Kamakura reformers formulated their Buddhist systems in such unadorned terms. Again the social context should be noted: it has been argued that the new forms of Buddhism addressed the needs of the many commoners and soldiers now interested in Buddhist practice who could not easily identify with the noble ends and elaborate means of the classical Buddhist path as modeled in Heian monasteries.

The Unity of Medieval Japanese Buddhism

Just as the Tendai tradition on Mt. Hiei provided the soil out of which the new schools grew, so also did certain general features of Heian religion serve as the ongoing basis for Kamakura religion. Kuroda Toshio has developed a powerful theory about these continuities that sees all the schools of Kamakura and Heian Buddhism (including the schools established in the earlier Nara period) as heirs of deeply ingrained patterns of religious thought and action that he has labeled the "exoteric-esoteric system" *(ken-mitsu taisei)*. Characteristics of this system would include a fundamental proclivity toward models of practice formulated in the esoteric systems of Shingon and Tendai, even within the so-called exoteric schools, that utilize thaumaturgic methods for pacifying spirits, averting calamity, and assuring material well-being. Kuroda argues that pre-Kamakura chanting of the *nenbutsu*, for example, was commonly used to pacify spirits and that this apotropaic orientation was never completely jettisoned.

Another example of a pervasive characteristic of medieval Buddhist spirituality noted by Kuroda is the coalescence of native (so-called Shintō) deities with Buddhist ones in systems of worship. In fact he has argued that the term Shintō is not even found in medieval texts as a designation for a tradition that is doctrinally and liturgically distinct from Buddhism. The conflation of Buddhist and native objects of worship (known in Japanese as *shinbutsu shūgō*), which crosses sectarian as well as temporal boundaries, was partially concealed by efforts made during the Meiji period (late nineteenth century) to clearly demarcate the bounds of the native and foreign traditions for nationalistic purposes. This successfully obfuscated the realities of medieval religious belief and practice by creating in effect a myth of the parallel maintenance of two distinct traditions throughout Japanese history. This early modern achievement, coupled with the earlier division of Buddhism into clear sectarian ecclesiastical divisions by the Tokugawa shogunate at the beginning of the seventeenth century, are two major events in Japanese history that Kuroda holds responsible for much of the modern misconceptions about religion in premodern times.

Furthermore, Kuroda's theory includes a comprehensive view of the relationship between religion and the broader political world, where the strong structures of mutual support developed in the Nara period continue in force throughout the medieval age. Kuroda's perspectives have a potential to extend as well into considerations of doctrinal affinities that permit an understanding even of Zen practice in ritual terms that reveal strong resonances with esoteric Buddhist theories. In sum, Kuroda has challenged traditional Buddhist histories by envisioning a unity of religious ideology in medieval Japan that encompassed different periods, schools, doctrines, and practices. Like many theories, its propensity toward comprehensiveness may open it to some criticism, but it has provided a potent catalyst for rethinking traditional narratives.[6]

Conclusion

Finally, let us pose a question much discussed in recent years: How are we to evaluate the role played by *hongaku* thought in Japanese religion and culture? According to Shōshin, *hongaku* theorists believed that the One Buddha Vehicle had long ago transported everyone to its glorious destination, that universal buddhahood is an already accomplished fact, and that for those who realize this fact the world at once appears as a field of enlightened beings. As we have seen, the kind of self-righteous complacency that can result from this facile affirmation was foreign to the likes of Saichō and Kūkai. Although the esoteric Buddhist traditions did urge a creative visualization that sees all beings and even all phenomena as manifestations of the cosmic Buddha, this vision provided a context for practice, not an excuse for its neglect. The old Japanese saying, "even the grasses and the trees attain Buddhahood" *(sōmoku jōbutsu)*, reflecting *hongaku* thought, gives poetic expression to an aesthetic of perfection, to a vision of participating in a world that is essentially good and that is sacred. Critics such as Shōshin saw *hongaku* theories as ruining Japanese Buddhist practice by providing people with doctrinal supports for a kind of spiritual megalomania. But it seems implausible that such a scholastic textual tradition, rooted in sophisticated

Mahāyāna metaphysics, and grounded primarily in a monastic setting, could have been responsible for widespread decadence, as has sometimes been charged. Some may have hid behind a banner proclaiming their "original enlightenment," hoping thereby to legitimize unethical lifestyles. But it is clear that the authors of many *hongaku* texts were aware of the dangers of uncritical affirmation of the relative world and were anxious to mark out a delicate middle way. Many Heian and Kamakura authors combine allegiance to the *hongaku* theory with care for the preservation of prescribed religious practices. Critics of *hongaku* theories need to go beyond insinuation to demonstrate actual instances of the purported causal relationship between these doctrines and unsavory behavior.[7]

Tamura Yoshirō celebrates the philosophical heights of *hongaku* thought and interprets its pervasive influence in Japanese culture in terms of an affirmative attitude towards the particulars of the everyday.[8] Thus Japanese religious philosophy would differ from Chinese thought in that the latter, though also very concerned with concrete applications to the human world, has a profound interest in discerning universal principles or norms (J. *ri*). It seems that the ultimate value of *ri* was of less moment in Japan than the concern to verify that any given system of doctrine or praxis was the best possible expression or instantiation (J. *ji*) of a universal truth. The careful balance between principle and expression in China was tilted in Japan in favor of the latter. One might conclude that what animated the Buddhist traditions of Heian and Kamakura Japan was a desire to find the most perfect expression of the principle of the One Buddha Vehicle. This would bring out even more continuities between the two periods. It might also, like many generalizations, prove to be an essentialist reduction of a complex reality, but this should not prevent us from employing it for its heuristic value, particularly when seeking to overcome the distorting effect of prejudices embodied in particular historical narratives.

Notes

1. For perspectives that counter the traditional narratives, see James H. Foard, "In Search of a Lost Reformation: A Reconsideration of Kamakura Buddhism," *Japanese Journal of Religious Studies* 7 (1980) 261–91, and Robert E. Morrell, *Early Kamakura Buddhism: A Minority Report* (Berkeley: Asian Humanities Press, 1987).

2. On Shōshin, see Tamura Yoshirō, "Critique of Original Awakening Thought in Shōshin and Dōgen," *Japanese Journal of Religious Studies* 11 (1984) 243–66.

3. Hurvitz, Leon, trans., *Scripture of the Lotus Blossom of the Fine Dharma* (New York: Columbia University Press, 1976) 237, 244.

4. On Saichō and Kūkai's approaches to esoteric Buddhism, see Paul Groner, *Saichō: The Establishment of the Tendai School* (Berkeley: University of California Press,

1984); Ryūichi Abe, "Saichō and Kūkai: A Conflict of Interpretations," *Japanese Journal of Religious Studies* 22 (1995) 103–37; and my dissertation, "Kūkai and the Beginnings of Shingon Buddhism" (Stanford University, 1995), esp. 169–225.

5. On Kūkai's theory of the preaching of the Dharma-body, see my dissertation, "Kūkai and the Beginnings of Shingon Buddhism." This doctrine is the focus of the dissertation and is analyzed from philosophical as well as historico-political perspectives throughout the work.

6. See Kuroda's seminal piece, "The Development of the *Kenmitsu* System as Japan's Medieval Orthodoxy," *Japanese Journal of Religious Studies* 23 (1996) 233–69. For more on the combinative nature of Japanese religious practice, see Allan C. Grapard, *The Protocol of the Gods: A Study of the Kasuga Cult in Japanese History* (Berkeley: University of California Press, 1992). On Dōgen and the act of meditation as a ritual, see Carl Bielefeldt, *Dōgen's Manuals of Zen Meditation* (Berkeley: University of California Press, 1988) 133–60, 169–70.

7. For treatments of some Tendai *hongaku* texts that clearly do not negate the need for religious practice, see Jacqueline Stone, "Medieval Tendai *Hongaku* Thought and the New Kamakura Buddhism: A Reconsideration," *Japanese Journal of Religious Studies* 22 (1995) 17–48; Paul Groner, "A Medieval Japanese Reading of the *Mo-ho chih-kuan*: Placing the *Kankō ruijū* in Historical Context," *ibid.*, 49–81.

On the critiques of *hongaku* thought see Ruben L. F. Habito, "The Logic of Nonduality and Absolute Affirmation: Deconstructing Tendai *Hongaku* Writings," *Japanese Journal of Religious Studies* 22 (1995) 83–101. The "critical Buddhism" of Hakamaya Noriaki and Matsumoto Shirō has made the *hongaku* tradition its chief target; see Jamie Hubbard and Paul L. Swanson, eds., *Pruning the Bodhi Tree: The Storm Over Critical Buddhism* (Honolulu: University of Hawai'i Press, 1997).

8. Tamura Yoshirō, "Japanese Culture and the Tendai Concept of Original Enlightenment," *Japanese Journal of Religious Studies* 14 (1987) 203–10.

Sources

Commentary on the Profound Meaning of the Lotus Sūtra (Hokke gengi shiki). A commentary by Shōshin on the *Fa-hua hsüan-i* of Chih-i. In *Nihon bukkyō zensho*, vol. 22.

Profound Meaning of the Lotus Sūtra (Fa-hua hsüan-i) by Chih-i (T 68 no. 1716). Partial translation in Paul Swanson, *Foundations of T'ien-t'ai Philosophy*, 157–256. Berkeley: Asian Humanities Press, 1989.

Regulations for Students of the Mountain School (Sange gakushō shiki) by Saichō (T 74 no. 2377). In *Dengyō Daishi zenshū*, vol. 1. Excerpts translated in Wm. Theodore de Bary, et al., eds., *Sources of Japanese Tradition*, vol. 1, 127–32. New York: Columbia University Press, 1958.

Treatise on the Ten Stages of the Mind (Jūjū shinron) by Kūkai (T 77 no. 2425). In Katsumata Shunkyō, ed., *Kōbō Daishi chosaku zenshū*, vol. 1. Tokyo: Sankibō Busshorin, 1969.

Hakeda, Yoshito S., trans. *The Awakening of Faith Attributed to Aśvaghoṣa*. New York: Columbia University Press, 1967.

21

Pure Land

I. *Early Pure Land Leaders*

TAMARU NORIYOSHI

THE FIRST MENTION in Japan of the *Larger Sukhāvatīvyūha Sūtra*, one of the basic texts of Pure Land Buddhism, occurs in writings attributed to Prince Shōtoku (574–622). There is a tradition that he believed in the Tuṣita heaven of Maitreya, which in those days was not clearly distinguished from Amida's Pure Land. A famous painting dedicated to his memory, the *Tenjukoku mandara* (Maṇḍala of the heavenly land of longevity), is an early testimony to this belief. During the Nara period, too, there are scattered testimonies to belief in the Pure Land. For instance, the monk Chikō of the Sanron (Mādhyamika) school created a well-known representation of the Pure Land, the *Jōdo mandara*, and the basic texts of the Pure Land school were studied by many monks on different occasions.

However, it was not until the Heian period, especially its latter half, that Pure Land came to play an important role, establishing itself gradually at the Tendai headquarters on Mt. Hiei. The abbot Ennin (794–864), upon returning from China, established on Mt. Hiei the practice of *jōgyō-zammai*, perpetual chanting of the name of Amida with musical accompaniment.[1] This was one of the four forms of *samādhi* practiced in the Tendai tradition. Ennin had a special hall built for this purpose within the temple compound, enshrining a large golden statue of Amida and adorned with paintings of the Pure Land. Several temples in the vicinity of the capital followed this example. Abbot Ryōgen (912–985), too, who enjoyed great prestige as the restorer of the Mt. Hiei center after damage by fire, was a devotee of Amida and wrote a commentary on the Pure Land texts.

By far the most influential promoter of Pure Land Buddhism was Ryōgen's disciple Genshin (942–1017). He disliked the mundane atmosphere

of Mt. Hiei and retired to nearby Yokawa to devote himself to the practice
of *nenbutsu*. He advocated meditation on the image of Amida and the landscape of the Pure Land as a means to achieve birth in that wonderful land.
In 985 he composed the *Ōjōyōshū* (Essentials of birth in the Pure Land), a
collection of passages of Buddhist scriptures referring to the Pure Land.[2]
This was the first important theoretical work in Japan dealing with Pure
Land ideas, and it also exerted a far-reaching influence on literature and art
by its vivid description of the Pure Land and of hell.

Throughout the Heian period Mt. Hiei maintained close links with the
aristocracy, the Fujiwaras in particular, and the cult of Amida spread rapidly
in these circles. Perhaps the best-known example is the case of Fujiwara
Michinaga (966–1027) and his son Yorimichi. Michinaga, as regent to the
emperor, was the virtual ruler of the country. When he or his relatives were
threatened by sickness and death, he resorted rather indiscriminately to
various magical means, including the cult of Amida (as he understood it).
He also believed in *raikō* (or *raigō*), the appearance of Amida and his attendant bodhisattvas to welcome the dying, and is said to have had a special
ritual performed at his deathbed. His son Yorimichi built the famous
Byōdō-in temple in which the western Pure Land was depicted in all its
glory in sculpture and painting.

Parallel to this aristocratic line of development, there was a popular dissemination of Pure Land ideas, in which the monk Kūya (or Kōya,
903–972) took the lead. Born into the imperial family by a non-Fujiwara
mother, he underwent initial ordination in the Province of Owari and took
up the life of a wandering *shami* (S. *śrāmaṇera*, novice). He traveled the
countryside, performing such social works as the construction of roads,
bridges, and wells. In 938 he entered the city of Kyoto to preach *nenbutsu*
to the inhabitants, and accordingly he came to be known as *ichi no hijiri*
(holy man of the marketplace) or Amida *hijiri* (holy man teaching Amida).
Hijiri were people having no formal ordination but leading the Buddhist
way of life, and there seems to have been a considerable number of them in
those days. Pure Land thought gave direction to the amorphous *hijiri* tradition, which in turn became a powerful vehicle of its spread among the
common people.[3] Especially characteristic of Kūya was that he combined
nenbutsu, chanting the name of Amida, with popular forms of dancing, so
that his teaching is sometimes called the dancing *nenbutsu*.[4] In 948 he
received formal Tendai ordination at Mt. Hiei, taking the new name Kōshō,
but he preferred to be called Kūya for the rest of his life and to keep the
title of *shami*. Later, another itinerant Tendai monk, Ryōnin (1072–1132),
used his vocal talent to propagate the *nenbutsu* in songs.

The Amida devotion within the traditional Buddhist schools, notably in Tendai, as well as its popular version represented by Kūya and Ryōnin, paved the way for Hōnen (1133–1212), the founder of the Jōdo (Pure Land) school. To account for the popularity of Pure Land at the close of the Heian and the beginning of the Kamakura periods, another factor must also be noted, namely the doctrine of *mappō*. This doctrine, whose Indian origin is obscure, and which was further elaborated in China, envisaged a gradual decline of the Buddhist Dharma in three successive stages.[5] It held that the genuine teaching lasted for a period of a thousand years after the death of the Buddha, followed by another thousand years in which Buddhism won only external adherence, leading to the final stage when there no longer was any practice or attainment. In one count, this last stage of *mappō* was believed to commence in the year 1055. The fact that the late Heian society was plagued by earthquakes, famines, and warfare between powerful groups seemed to be in keeping with the doctrine. By its pessimistic outlook on humanity and history, the doctrine both fostered the desire for a Buddhist reform and provided it with a theoretical basis. The *mappō* doctrine was a pervasive feature of nearly all the Buddhist schools in the late Heian period, and it is against this background that many of the new movements of the Kamakura period must be interpreted.

Hōnen: His Life and Teaching

Among the eminent religious leaders of the Kamakura period, the first to appear was Hōnen. Born in Mimasaka Province (today Okayama Prefecture) in 1133, he had to experience the tragedy of human life early in his childhood. When he was nine years of age, his father, Uruma Tokikuni, an imperial gendarme of the locality, became involved in a struggle with the manager of a nearby estate and was mortally wounded during a night raid by the latter. This event epitomizes the situation at the end of the Heian period, a time when power was passing from the nobility to the warrior class. After his father's death, the family dispersed. Hōnen fled to an adjacent temple and entrusted himself to the priest in charge. Undoubtedly this experience greatly influenced his career. The hagiography by Shunjō (d. 1335) gives his father's dying words as follows:

> Don't let this rankle in your breast and lead you to avenge my enemy.... This misfortune was the result of some sin of mine in a former state of existence. If you harbor ill-will towards your enemy, you will never be free from enemies. So don't do it, my boy, but without delay forsake the worldly life and become a priest.[6]

Accordingly, at the age of thirteen, the boy was sent to Mt. Hiei for Buddhist training.

There he first studied under Jihōbō Genkō (otherwise unknown), who was astonished at his rapid mastery of the *Shikyōgi* (On the four doctrines; T 46, no. 1929), Chih-i's compendium of Tendai teachings.[7] Two years later he became a disciple of Kōen (d. 1169), a noted scholar, and was formally ordained as a monk. He was unable, however, to adjust himself to the prevailing atmosphere of Mt. Hiei, where the riots of Enryaku-ji's warrior monks and the struggles for the abbot's seat took center stage. The monastery had turned into a showplace of fame and wealth for monks of noble birth, and had quite lost its former excellence as a place of religious practice. One day Hōnen expressed the desire to retire into the solitude of the forest, but Kōen advised him first to read the sixty volumes of the T'ien-t'ai canon. Between fifteen and eighteen, Hōnen accomplished this gigantic task. He is said to have read the Tripiṭaka four more times in the course of his life. At the end of the three years, he retired to the Kurodani area of Mt. Hiei, a base of *nenbutsu hijiri* who practiced the Pure Land meditation advocated by Genshin in his *Ōjōyōshū*. Here Hōnen joined a group led by Jigenbō Eikū (d. 1179), the successor of Ryōnin, and was given the name Hōnenbō Genkū, of which the popular designation Hōnen is an abbreviation.

While staying at Kurodani, he also had a chance to visit Nara to study the teachings of the Nara schools, meeting Zōshun (1104–1180) of Kōfuku-ji, Keiga of the Kegon school (1103–1185), and some Sanron scholars. His later comment was: "There are many doctrinal systems in Buddhism, but when all is said and done, there are only the three disciplines of precepts, concentration, and wisdom."[8] On this occasion he probably came across the Pure Land devotion which had been taught at Nara by Yōkan (1033–1111), Chinkai (1091–1152), and Jippan (d. 1144). Whereas Tendai tradition used *nenbutsu* as a meditative practice, and Genshin had stressed visualization of the Pure Land, these teachers, inspired by Shan-tao (613–681), placed greater emphasis on Other-Power and the assurance of salvation contained in the primal Vow of Amida.

Hōnen during these years strenuously sought a teaching that would meet his spiritual needs and bring him peace of mind. He was tormented by the awareness that the more he applied himself to the three disciplines, the more he found himself to fall short: "I, for one, cannot observe even a single precept, cannot deepen my concentration, and cannot obtain wisdom by cutting off my passions." Of this long search he later wrote:

How pitiful! What should I do? It has become clear that a man like me is not a suitable vessel for the three disciplines. Does there exist, beside the three disciplines, a path suited to me, a discipline practicable by one of my character? I inquired of countless wise men; I paid visits to numerous scholars, yet there was none to teach me, no friend to show me the way. Therefore, in my distress, I buried myself in the Tripiṭaka and in sadness took up the sacred writings.[9]

At the age of twenty-four his distress impelled him to spend a week at the Shaka Hall in Saga on the outskirts of Kyoto. This was a center of devotion, frequented by *hijiri*, where many nameless people came in search of solace and healing. Hōnen, it appears, had discovered that his own problems could not be solved by a merely individual liberation. They were connected at the root with the sufferings of the people coming to look for salvation in this place.

The decisive turning point in Hōnen's life came only many years later, in 1175, when he happened to read the following passage in Shan-tao's (613–681) *Kuan-ching shu*, a commentary on the *Meditation Sūtra*:

Whether walking or standing, sitting or lying, only repeat the name of Amida with all your heart. Never cease the practice of it even for a moment. This is the very work which unfailingly issues in salvation, for it is in accordance with the Original Vow of that Buddha.[10]

As he himself relates in the last chapter of *Senchaku-hongan-nenbutsu-shū* (commonly known as *Senchakushū,* Treatise on the selection of the *nenbutsu* of the Original Vow),[11] the passage brought Hōnen to the realization that the *nenbutsu* itself was the thing he had long been seeking. By the grace of this encounter with Shan-tao's words, the forty-two-year-old Hōnen was drawn into a light that enabled him to find a true religious life, marked by spiritual growth. He abandoned other forms of practice and concentrated instead exclusively on chanting the name of Amida. This is the *senju nenbutsu* (exclusive practice of *nenbutsu*), central to Hōnen's teaching. In the same chapter he extols Shan-tao as his true teacher, urging his readers to depend on Shan-tao alone and calling his *Kuan-ching shu* "a guide to the Western Land" and "the eyes and feet of practitioners."[12]

At this time Hōnen left Mt. Hiei and settled in Ōtani in the eastern outskirts of Kyoto, where he spent the rest of his life, except for the years of exile at the end of his career. After this move nearer to the city area, he began to propagate his ideas in public and to attract followers from all walks of life: monks, nobles, warriors, and commoners. His growing fame seems to have caught the attention of the traditional schools. This led to a dogmatic debate, held in 1186 at Ōhara, a suburb of Kyoto, between Hōnen and some leading Buddhist monks including Kenshin (1131–1192), a later abbot of the Tendai school. Meanwhile, Hōnen had succeeded in gaining a number of aristocratic patrons, of whom the most prestigious and influential was the Fujiwara regent Kujō Kanezane (1147–1207), who served at the imperial court during the turbulent years of civil strife between the Taira and Minamoto families until, in 1196, he was removed from his influential position by a political intrigue. His support must have added to Hōnen's prestige. It was at his request that Hōnen compiled the *Senchakushū* in 1198.

However, these successes aroused the suspicion of the traditional Buddhist groups, who sought to repress the movement by means of government pressure. As a result Hōnen's last years were marked by a series of violent events. In 1204, the Mt. Hiei Tendai group presented a petition to the authorities to officially prohibit the exclusive practice of *nenbutsu*. Hōnen tried to appease his opponents by presenting a Seven-Article Pledge, signed by himself and a number of his major disciples, in which he disclaimed any intention to oppose the tenets of the established schools.[13] Though this brought about a temporary peace, in the following year a similar attack was made by the Kōfuku-ji temple in Nara. These criticisms, combined with misconduct on the part of some of his followers, led finally to catastrophe in 1207, when the imperial court was forced to take drastic steps: his movement was prohibited, some of his major disciples were executed or banished, and Hōnen himself was exiled to the island of Shikoku. Though in 1211 pardoned and allowed to return to Kyoto, he died in January of the following year.

Hōnen's most important contribution is the teaching of *senchaku* (selection; read as *senjaku* in the Jōdo Shinshū tradition) and *senju* (exclusive practice).[14] *Senchaku* meant, he declared, to adopt and to discard: to adopt *nenbutsu* and to discard other forms of Buddhist practice. This selective attitude had few if any precedents in Buddhism, which in both China and Japan had been predominantly syncretic, harmoniously combining various forms of training. The Tendai tradition, for example, combined meditation, *nenbutsu,* and a stress on the precepts. Hōnen emphasized instead the need to choose. A similar selectiveness may be found in other leaders of the Kamakura period such as Dōgen and Nichiren.

The *Senchakushū*, in which this teaching is put forward, is one of the classics of Japanese Buddhism. Though it is composed in a conventional manner as a collection of passages from various scriptures followed by a commentary, this work exhibits a consistent logic: the logic of either-or. First, Hōnen divided all Buddhism into the Holy Path *(shōdō),* as he called the teachings of the established schools, and the Pure Land. He urged his readers to choose the latter. It was a choice between a difficult practice and an easy one, between reliance on one's own power and reliance on another's power, between various practices *(zōgyō)* and the True Practice *(shōgyō)*. This is clearly stated in the first two chapters, which are based on the writings of Shan-tao and his predecessor Tao-ch'o (d. 645).

Release from the cycles of births and deaths, which is the aim of Buddhism, may be achieved by means of two splendid teachings, that of the Holy Path and that of Rebirth in the Pure Land. In the former, one exerts oneself to gain awakening in the present life. However: "In these days it is difficult to attain Enlightenment through the Holy Path. One reason for this is that the Great Enlightened One's passing has now receded into the far distant past. Another is that the ultimate principle is profound, while man's understanding is shallow."[15] But since this method is based on profound and difficult philosophical principles, it is hard to realize by one's own ability in these times so distant from the historical Buddha.

Opposed to this is the easy way of the Pure Land school, followed by having faith in Amida Buddha, relying on his power, and sincerely wishing to be born into his Pure Land. In practical terms, this distinction corresponds to that between the varied practice and the True Practice. There are many ways of practicing Buddhism, such as reciting the sūtras, contemplation and reverence of the Buddha, invocation of the Buddha's name, making offerings, giving alms, observing the precepts. As long as these are performed with the aim of gaining birth into the Pure Land, they constitute the True Practice, whereas on all other occasions they are nothing but varied practices. Furthermore, even in the True Practice, only the *nenbutsu* fixes the cause of birth into the Pure Land while all other deeds are merely auxiliary.

This teaching that declared all practices hitherto advocated by the established schools to be merely auxiliary, and urged the choice of the invocation of Amida as the exclusive practice, was revolutionary at that time. But to Hōnen there was nothing arbitrary about it, for it had solid scriptural foundation in the *Larger Sukhāvatīvyūha Sūtra*, in which the future Amida Buddha singles out this practice in his eighteenth vow:

> May I not gain possession of perfect awakening if, once I have attained buddhahood, any among the throng of living beings in the ten regions of the universe should single-mindedly desire to be reborn in my land with joy, with confidence, and gladness, and if they should bring to mind this aspiration for even ten moments of thought and yet not gain rebirth there. This excludes only those who have committed the five heinous sins and those who have reviled the True Dharma.[16]

Hōnen, following Shan-tao, interprets this to mean that he vows to save all those who invoke his name. If the Buddha thus selected *nenbutsu* himself, then certainly we must do so too. Hōnen concedes that "the Buddha's holy intention is difficult to fathom and impossible to understand fully,"[17] but suggests that in a degenerate age such as ours the practice of the Holy Path

25. Amida Coming over the Mountains. Hanging scroll, Kamakura Period, Japan.

is not possible for the ordinary person. He summarizes the essentials of his teaching in the concluding chapter of *Senchakushū* as follows:

> If you wish to separate at once from births and deaths, of the two superior methods, set aside the Saintly Way [Holy Path] and choose the Pure Land and enter into it. If you wish to enter into the Pure Land, of the two practices, the varied and the True, throw away the varied and choose the True and convert to it. If you wish to carry out the True Practice, of the two, the True and the auxiliary deeds, put the auxiliary aside, select the practice that correctly fixes the cause of birth, and concentrate on it exclusively. The practice that correctly fixes the cause of birth is to call on the name of the Buddha. If you call on his name you will with certainty be born into the Pure Land. This is so because of the vow of the Buddha.[18]

Hōnen's Disciples

Though his teaching implied a potential threat to the existence of the established schools and, accordingly, gave rise to much controversy in the subsequent decades and centuries, it is improbable that Hōnen intended to found a new school of his own in opposition to the old ones. Despite the radicalism of his ideas he himself lived as a traditional Buddhist monk, remaining a Tendai priest throughout his life and strictly observing the *vinaya* precepts. He enjoyed the reputation of an erudite scholar versed in the doctrines of different schools, and an exemplary ordination master and celebrant of esoteric rites. Though he stressed the importance of invoking the name of Amida instead of the visualizing meditation after the manner of Genshin, he seems to have entertained a keen interest in this trance-like meditation to the end of his life, for he left a record of his own visions of Amida and the Pure Land known as *Sanmai Hottokuki*.[19] He embodied in his personal life old and new elements, maintaining a rather ambivalent relationship to the established schools. One can detect in his teaching a similar ambiguity and a number of crucial issues that are not clearly resolved, such as the relationship between *nenbutsu* and other practices and means of gaining birth; whether only one invocation was enough or whether many invocations were advisable; and exactly when the birth into the Pure Land was assured. The clarification of these points was left to his disciples, and this favored the emergence of a wide variety of viewpoints among them, as did the fact that his following was not a rigid organization but a loosely knit movement in which people of different types could freely participate.

The foremost representative of Jōdoshū orthodoxy among Hōnen's successors is Shōkōbō Benchō (1162–1238), who is generally regarded as the second patriarch of the Pure Land school. He became a disciple of Hōnen in 1199. He was the direct recipient of Hōnen's teachings for five years, and one of the first to be allowed to make a copy of the *Senchakushū*. Later he returned to his native Chinzei (present-day Fukuoka) and founded a powerful base of Pure Land devotion there. Emphasizing the central importance of *nenbutsu*, he also admitted the possibility of being born into the Pure Land by a number of other practices, basing himself on Amida's twentieth vow, which promises rebirth to all who "fix their thoughts on rebirth in my land, cultivate all the roots of virtue, and single-mindedly dedicate this virtue desiring to be reborn in my land."[20] This moderate, ecumenical position allowed him to maintain the link with Tendai. His group, called the Chinzei-ha, later became the most important branch of the sect.

Zennebō Shōkū (1177–1247) also built bridges with Tendai. Shōkū, born of an aristocratic family, joined Hōnen's group at the age of fourteen. Because of his outstanding talent he was chosen as one of the assistants in the composition of the *Senchakushū*. In the time of persecution in 1207 and 1227, he escaped exile thanks to his relationship with the Tendai authorities. He entertained a close connection with the aristocracy in Kyoto throughout his life. Though stressing the significance of *nenbutsu* and of personal faith, he interpreted in a philosophical manner other practices as variations of *nenbutsu*. The branch he founded was the Seizan-ha, whose most famous scion is the "wayfaring saint" *(yugyō shōnin)*, Ippen (1239–1289), founder of the Ji sect of Pure Land and preacher of dancing *nenbutsu* in the style of Kūya.

Kakumyōbō Chōsai (1184–1266) was one of Hōnen's youngest disciples. He joined Hōnen's group in 1202 and five years later accompanied his master in exile. After Hōnen's death he continued to study under many prominent masters of other schools, including Dōgen. Influenced by Tendai and Hossō views, he proposed that practices other than *nenbutsu* are also in accord with the Original Vow of Amida and are of equal value. This seems quite distant from his master's position and was not considered by later generations to be orthodox Pure Land teaching.

On the question of one invocation or many, contrasting views were held by two of Hōnen's outstanding disciples. Ryūkan (1148–1227), born in Kyoto and educated on Mt. Hiei, associated himself with the movement rather late in his life, probably around 1204. He advocated the view of "many invocations" *(tanengi)* and is said to have chanted *nenbutsu* 84,000 times a day. In fact, it was Hōnen himself who gave the first example of the practice of many chantings. In addition, Ryūkan held that the birth into the Pure Land was fixed only at the moment of death, so that the state of mind at that moment became quite important. Practice during one's lifetime, accordingly, was a preparation for this decisive instant. His spirited defense of Hōnen's teachings in a work no longer extant became the pretext for the second persecution of the movement, again prompted by the powerful Mt. Hiei establishment, in 1227.

The proponent of the opposite view, called *ichinengi*, was Jōkakubō Kōsai (?1163–?1247). He is alleged to have been a Tendai priest before coming into contact with Hōnen. Already during Hōnen's lifetime Gyōkū and others had advocated a similar view. But as some of them tended to go to extremes—abandoning the fundamental precepts on the ground that birth into the Pure Land was assured—their behavior gave the opponents of the movement a pretext for the persecution of 1207. It is alleged that Hōnen expelled Gyōkū from the sect. The same allegation is made about Kōsai, who is not regarded as an orthodox Jōdo thinker.[21] But Kōsai's view was more philosophically oriented than Gyōkū's. Probably influenced by the Tendai teaching of enlightenment in this lifetime, he insisted on the assurance of birth here on earth and by means of one invocation. His approach exhibits undeniable similarities to that of Shinran (1173–1262), Hōnen's most famous disciple, who was also disowned by the orthodox mainstream of the Jōdoshū.

Notes

1. For the scriptural foundation of this practice, see Luis O. Gómez, *Land of Bliss: The Paradise of the Buddha of Measureless Light* (Honolulu: University of Hawai'i Press, 1996) 19, 148.

2. For the text, see Allan A. Andrews, *The Teaching Essential for Rebirth: A Study of Genshin's Ōjōyōshū* (Tokyo: Sophia University, 1973).

3. See Dennis Hirota, trans., *Plain Words on the Pure Land Way: Sayings of the Wandering Monks of Medieval Japan* (Kyoto: Ryukoku University, 1989) x. An important study is Ichiro Hori, "On the Concept of *Hijiri* (Holy Man)," *Numen* 5 (1958) 128–60; 199–232.

4. See Ōhashi Shunnō, *Odori nenbutsu* (Tokyo: Daizō Shuppansha, 1974) 51–70; Gorai Shigeru, *Odori nenbutsu* (Tokyo: Heibonsha, 1988) 79–94.

5. On the origins of this doctrine, see Jan Nattier, *Once upon a Future Time: Studies in a Buddhist Prophecy of Decline* (Berkeley: Asian Humanities Press, 1991).

6. Harper Havelock Coates and Ryugaku Ishizuka, *Hōnen: The Buddhist Saint* (Kyoto, 1925; repr. New York-London: Garland Publishing, 1981) 103–4. See *Hōnen Shōnin gyōjō ezu (Zoku nippon emonogatari taisei 1–3: Hōnen Shōnin eden)*, (Tokyo: Chūō Kōron, 1981).

7. Coates, *Hōnen*, 131.

8. See Coates, *Hōnen*, 185.

9. See Coates, *Hōnen*, 186.

10. Coates, *Hōnen,* 187.

11. An English translation of the *Senchakushū* by Tesshō Kondō and Morris J.

Augustine has been published in *The Pure Land* 5(1983); new series 1–4 (1984–87).

12. *The Pure Land* n.s. 4 (1987) 123–24.

13. Summarized in Daigan and Alicia Matsunaga, *Foundation of Japanese Buddhism*, II (Los Angeles-Tokyo: Buddhist Books International, 1976) 63–64.

14. On the many senses in which the *nenbutsu* is chosen, by Śākyamuni, by Amida, by the three sūtras, and by the believer, see *The Pure Land* n.s. 4 (1987) 115–18.

15. *The Pure Land* 5:1 (June 1983) 2–3.

16. Gómez, *Land of Bliss*, 167.

17. *The Pure Land* 5:2 (December 1983) 21.

18. See *The Pure Land* n.s. 4 (1987) 118–19.

19. *Hōnen Shōnin zenshū*, ed. Ishii Kyōdō (Kyoto: Heiraku-ji, 1974) 863–67. An English translation is given in Winston L. King, "Hōnen's Visualizations of the Pure Land," *The Pure Land* n.s. 4 (1987) 126–41.

20. Gómez, *Land of Bliss*, 168.

21. Coates, *Hōnen*, 784.

II. *Hōnen's Spiritual Legacy*

FUJIMOTO KIYOHIKO

THE UNFOLDING of Hōnen's spiritual life relies on the profound dynamism of his contact with "Amida (the Immeasurable)," revealed particularly in the following two distinct kinds of experience. First are his encounters with Shan-tao in dreams, which he experienced twice, at age forty-three and at age sixty-five. The first dream occurred shortly after the spiritual breakthrough he experienced on reading the Chinese master's *Commentary on the Meditation Sūtra*. This dream indelibly impressed on him that Shan-tao was his human master and savior. He had the second dream when writing the *Senchakushū*, the fruit of the maturation of his faith in the recitative *nenbutsu*. These two dream-state encounters with his teacher allow us to sense the vital pulse that throbbed in Hōnen's Pure Land doctrine, in other words, the way in which in his life the doctrine gradually blossomed into spiritual events.

Second are Hōnen's *nenbutsu zanmai* experiences. His practice of reciting the *nenbutsu* upwards of sixty thousand times a day gave rise at times to spiritual events in the depth of his psyche. These events are crystallized in his *Senchakushū*, which can be read as a cipher of his lived spiritual reality. Nicholas Cusanus (1401–1464) remarks: "It is said that the term 'God' comes from the verb *theoro* (I see); because God himself is present in our realm, as it were, as vision is in the realm of color." One speaks of the attainment of *samādhi* (J. *sanmai*) when, after the mind has become calm and quiet through the *nenbutsu*, and true wisdom and insight have arisen, one feels and sees the realm of the Buddha before one's very eyes. *Samādhi* is thus an extremely intense experience of our faculty of vision. Such vision, arising spontaneously and unbidden, as a result of repeated *nenbutsu* recitation, is central to Hōnen's religious experience.

The Record of Hōnen's Samādhi Experience

In the *Saihō shinan shō* (Written instructions on the West), of which there exists a handwritten copy alleged to be in his hand (the so-called *Takada-bon*), there is a chapter that records Hōnen's *samādhi* experiences. In statements such as "the Shōnin wrote this down during his life" (at the outset of the chapter) and "this is a record from the hand of the Shōnin himself" (end of chapter), the text claims to be based on a record of Hōnen himself, and it is printed among Hōnen's works as the *Sanmai hottokuki*. The record spans the period from 1198, when the sixty-five-year-old Hōnen composed the *Senchakushū*, to 1206, when he was seventy-three.

The record for 1198 reads:

> On the seventh day of the first month I started my *nenbutsu* practice as usual. During that day I had some clear visions [of the Pure Land]. It was all so natural and clear. On the second day I naturally realized the visualization of the water. On the seventh day of my *nenbutsu* practice, I had a view of the lapis lazuli section of the visualization of the ground. On the morning of the fourth day of the second month the lapis lazuli ground appeared to me in detail. Six days later at night I had a vision of the jewelled pavilions. These appeared to me again on the morning of the seventh day. From the first day of the first month to the seventh day of the second month, for thirty-seven days, I recited the *nenbutsu* constantly, seventy thousand times a day. On the strength of this I obtained the five visualizations of the water, the ground, the jewelled trees, the jewelled ponds, and the jewelled pavilions.... On the morning of the twenty-second day of the ninth month, the ground appeared to me clearly and distinctly. Around it the ground was terraced in about seven or eight levels. Afterwards, in the late night and morning of the twenty-third day, I had again this clear and distinct vision.

This is a detailed report of the various elements of paradise appearing naturally of themselves during the practice of the *nenbutsu*, when the continuation of the *nenbutsu* had produced a state of serene and calm concentration. These spiritual experiences were thus not obtained by Hōnen's own power, but supernaturally appeared from beyond. They were not sought as a fruit of his repetition of the *nenbutsu*, but were spontaneous, unbidden manifestations of his deep contemplative life.

The record for 1200 has the following accounts:

> In the second month, five visions of the Pure Land, among which the *chisōkan* (vision of its earth) appeared freely, in accordance with my mental states, whatever I was doing.

> On the fourth day of the first month, the great bodies of the three Honored Ones appeared to me.

From this we learn that, in his constant *nenbutsu* practice, Hōnen obtained a state of playfully dwelling in the Pure Land and meeting there the Buddha. "While applying myself solely to saying the Name of Amida, I see the glories of the Pure Land. How delightful!"

The year 1201 brings the following:

> In the later part of the night of the eighth day of the second month, I heard
> the voices of birds and the music of harps, flutes, and the like. Later, day by
> day, I could listen at will to these sounds, and heard, for instance, the sounds
> of a court flute. All kinds of sounds. On the fifth day of the first month the
> face of Mahāsthāmaprāpta Bodhisattva, big enough to be the face of a figure
> about five meters tall, appeared behind the statue of the Bodhisattva. And
> on the sixth day, I had again that vision, but now, for the first time, there was
> a ground of blue lapis lazuli on the four sides of my seat, for about one level.

Finally, in 1206 there is a record of the following *samādhi* experience: "On the
fourth day of the first month, while practicing the *nenbutsu*, the great bodies of the three Honored Ones appeared. It happened again the next day."

For Hōnen, *samādhi* experiences sealed his religious conviction, as he himself testified when he wrote in the *Senchakushū*: "I rely solely on Shan-tao,
since he is the one who appeared to me in *samādhi*." These *samādhi* experiences follow a pattern. The visions of the adornments of paradise, described
above, belong to what are called "the dependent and proper rewards" and
"the true and provisional views." Their content and order hark back to the
thirteen visualizations of the contemplative good in the *Meditation Sūtra*.

These experiences produced in Hōnen a state of joy and certitude, in
which the Pure Land as experience and the Pure Land in an ontological
sense can be said to come together. Words from his last years attest how
vivid the Pure Land heaven was to him:

> I rejoice in the years piling up and ready to topple over, since I see it as the
> Pure Land finally having come near. Feeling my life getting weaker with
> every night makes me see that I shall soon be able to leave this defiled land
> behind. I reckon the end of life to be the end of sorrowful birth-death, and
> expect the time of death to be the end of all troubles. I look forward to that
> moment, for then I shall go to the Pure Land and sit on the lotus throne of
> Kannon Bodhisattva come to welcome me. Birth in the Pure Land is some-
> thing that cannot come soon enough, you know. I am in a hurry to finish
> with this life. How I love Paradise! May this life end quickly!

These words manifest his joy in the expectation of birth in the Pure Land.
They are like a bubbling over of his ardent desire for the paradise of Amida
Buddha. To his disciples, the very existence of the founder is a stirring of
the spirit of life; it was because he sensed this life welling up within him
that he could declare: "I shall certainly go back to Paradise, since I am
somebody who was originally there."

Exclusive recitation of the Name means that human life every moment,
in each of its breaths, is the passageway to the experiential Pure Land of

Namu Amida Buddha; and in the seeing of the "adornments of the Pure Land" the ontological character of the Pure Land is intimated. This is not merely an explained Pure Land; with the continuation of the *nenbutsu* recitation, Namu Amida Butsu, as its locus, the call-and-answer relationship between the self that pronounces the *nenbutsu* and Amida Buddha is realized, and it can be said that it is precisely this "locus" that manifests the Pure Land. This is why Hōnen's *nenbutsu* experience crystallized into the state of mind he described in these words: "When alive, the merits of the *nenbutsu* pile up; when I die, I go to the Pure Land. In either case there is nothing to worry about in this world; both life and death are thornless."

When banished to Shikoku at the age of seventy-four, Hōnen was able to console his disciples with the words: "Mountains and seas may divide us, but we are sure to meet again in that Pure Land. Man is a being who goes on living even when he grows weary of life and dies even when he loves life." Here, he clearly expressed his idea of "reunion in the Pure Land." For all the people he came into contact with on his journey to the place of exile he found words that reverberated in their hearts: "All places where the sound of *nenbutsu* recitation, Namu Amida Buddha, is heard, be they lofty or lowly, even including the huts of pearl divers and fishermen, are sacred to me." Such words attest a serene awareness that every place where the *nenbutsu* is heard is in tune with the life of Amida Buddha, the blowing of the spirit. It was because they could intuitively sense this attitude of his that people came to find in Hōnen the image of a savior.

The Doctrinal Legacy

All this tells us that the doctrine of the Pure Land, as inwardly attested to by Hōnen, gradually took shape by way of his *samādhi* experiences. In other words, it was with Hōnen's *nenbutsu* experience as its inner reality, and from there out, that the doctrinal system of the recitative *nenbutsu* found expression. It is from the womb of the *samādhi* experience that Hōnen's doctrinal legacy was born.

The content of the doctrine of the recitative *nenbutsu*, as Hōnen established it on the basis of the three Pure Land sūtras, can be summarized as follows: Ordinary people, who cannot cut off their passions, obtain birth in the Pure Land paradise through the Vow Power of Amida Buddha, if they recite the *nenbutsu*.

1. The goal of faith is the Pure Land, that is, the world of the fulfillment of Amida's vows, as taught in the *Sūtra of Immeasurable Life* and the *Amida Sūtra* (the Longer and Shorter Pure Land sūtras). This world,

which lies innumerable countries to the West, has "form," namely, the three kinds of adornments.

2. The object of faith is Amida Buddha, that is, the fulfilled body of the Buddha that was perfected as a result of the fulfillment of the vows of Dharmākara Bodhisattva, as taught in the *Sūtra of Immeasurable Life*.

3. The means of faith is the *nenbutsu*, that is, the form of *nenbutsu* selected in Amida's Primal Vow for the salvation of common mortals *(bonbu)*, namely, the recitative *nenbutsu*.

Hōnen taught that it is precisely the eighteenth vow, the "vow of birth through *nenbutsu*, that was intended for the salvation of common mortals. He called it the "King Primal Vow." Through Hōnen, who was deeply conscious of himself as a common mortal, the Pure Land school is characterized by a doctrine and a salvific practice adapted to the capabilities of common mortals. Common mortals always concretize their thought in things that have a shape and they live within a project characterized by the imaginative (thinking in concrete images), the responsive (answering to a call), and the vocal (voicing their thoughts). To have a reality rooted in that essential project of the common person, the doctrine must indicate a direction and present a form. This is exactly what the doctrine of birth by *nenbutsu* into the Western Paradise of Amida does. Hōnen, adapting himself to the nature and capacities of ordinary people, strongly underlined the "having-form" character of the Pure Land, the historico-personal character of Amida Buddha, and the responsive and vocal character of the *nenbutsu.* He used to tell his disciples to recite the *nenbutsu* "in the midst of passion, if passion arises"; "as you are by birth: if a good man, as a good man; if a bad man, as a bad man." For it was with common mortals in view that Amida chose the *nenbutsu* as the practice for becoming "rightly settled."

The *Senchakushū* explains the excellence and easiness of the recitative *nenbutsu* in five points:

1. *Nenbutsu*, as the practice for Birth, has priority over all else.

2. *Nenbutsu* is the practice, indicated in the Primal Vow, that leads all sentient beings to Birth in complete equality, since it can be practiced whenever, wherever, and by whomsoever, without hindering other practices.

3. Amida's Holy Name embraces all inward and outward powers and virtues of Amida Buddha.

4. Thought (remembrance) and voice (recitation) are one.

5. Responding without fail to the acts in thought, word, and deed of those who say the *nenbutsu*, Amida Buddha will save all and, when they are dying, will come to meet them and take them to his Pure Land.

What the recitative *nenbutsu* taught by Hōnen offers is this: equality of all people within the personal relationship with Amida Buddha; the possibility of living in a world of call-and-response, wherein thought and voice correspond and an answer comes when one calls; and, when present life comes to an end, the prospect of birth in the Pure Land, guided there by Amida himself. This doctrine of salvation pulsates with a deep and universal insight into the reality of the human condition.

Jōdoshū: The Heirs to the Legacy

As the roots of grass spread naturally in the earth, so Hōnen's *nenbutsu* entered the hearts of nameless common people. The doctrine was greeted as a grace of salvation, like rainfall after a dry spell, for people living in this world of sin and defilement, burdened still more by the consciousness of the advent of the Latter Days. It injected a spiritual richness into their lives in the midst of political and economical upheaval. Those who placed their trust in Hōnen ranged from courtiers and advisors to the emperor, nobles and warriors, to courtesans, fisher folk, and the like. We can see the figure of Hōnen, moving among these people, recommending to them the *nenbutsu* practice in a conversational atmosphere, and offering them the means of salvation. These beginnings naturally led to the formation of a religious "sect" in the form of a community of people sharing the same faith.

Along with doctrinal divergences among the leading disciples—Shōkō Benchō, Kōsai, Ryūkan, Zennebō Shōkū, and Shinran—Hōnen's *nenbutsu* doctrine branched out into different schools, each of which emphasized different aspects. This diversity may be said to testify to the greatness of Hōnen's personality and doctrine, but it also proves that the *nenbutsu* experience can take on different forms according to the person.

The orthodox mainstream of the Jōdoshū derives from Benchō. In his *Tetsu Senchakushū*, a commentary on the *Senchakushū,* he attempted to bring the doctrine of his master in line with general Buddhism, by defining its basic concepts on the basis of Nāgārjuna's treatises. Despite these efforts at accommodation, the work indeed grasps Hōnen's doctrine and practice in a thoroughgoing *(tetsu)* way. Ryōchū (1199–1287), who became Benchō's disciple in 1236 and studied under him, and who was active in the Kantō region as an orthodox representative of the Hōnen community, followed Benchō's example in interpreting Hōnen's doctrine in the light of general

Buddhist concepts. Ryōchū's disciple, Ryōe Dōkō (?–1330/1), collected Hōnen's doctrinal tracts, sermons, letters, and so forth in his *Kurodani Shōnin gotōroku* (Record of words by the Saint of Kurodani), with the intention of conserving them for posterity. In this way there gradually took shape a lineage of the Jōdoshū, with Hōnen as founder, Benchō as second patriarch, and Ryōchū as third patriarch, within which Hōnen's writings and sermons were preserved and catalogued.

The seventh patriarch, Shōgei (1341–1420), by establishing within the doctrine of the Jōdoshū the two branches of "precepts" and "doctrines," aimed at elevating his school from an "inhabiting" status to an autonomous one. He established a system for the education of the school's priests and organized a code of rituals proper to the school in his *Gojū sōden* (Fivefold Transmission). In this way Hōnen's spiritual legacy came to be transmitted and developed systematically as the doctrinal system of an independent school.

In the Edo period, the basic code of the modern Jōdoshū, called *Genna jōmoku* (Regulations of the Genna Era) was formulated and, under the patronage of the Tokugawa regime, the structure of the sect and its temples was systematized, with the temples of Zōjō-ji in the Kantō area and the Chion-in in the Kansai area as strongholds. However, under the umbrella of this political and economic patronage, the doctrine gradually became complicated and intellectualistic. It moved away from the doctrine that had been able to captivate the hearts of the ordinary people in their actual lives. The "bouquet" of Hōnen's recitative *nenbutsu*, in other words, the practice of a means of salvation made to the measure of ordinary mortals, was lost. This problem has everything to do with the question of how Hōnen's Pure Land doctrine has been transmitted and developed during the "closed country" (*sakoku*) period and in the maelstrom of Japan's modernization in the Meiji period and beyond.

The Legacy in Modern Times

During the three hundred years of the national isolation policy, the Jōdoshū was efficiently organized as a religious body, but with this consolidation as a sect its doctrine tended to take on a conservative and apologetic character. However, a movement to revivify the mummified Pure Land doctrine was initiated by people such as Ninchō (1645–1711), Munō (1683–1719), and Tokuhon (1758–1816). This revival movement of the so-called Shase-ha and Jōdoritsu groups stressed the practice of the precepts and promoted a normative lifestyle for *nenbutsu* practitioners.

At the beginning of the Meiji years an anti-Buddhist iconoclastic movement *(haibutsu kishaku)* was unleashed against Buddhism and its temples in the whole of Japan, and the influence of State Shinto soon became strong. Meanwhile, the newly enacted "open country" policy allowed Western thinking and religion to stream into Japan as if a dam had been broken. The task of modernizing Buddhism became the order of the day. Concretely speaking, this happened mainly through the meeting with Christianity. In this encounter, two opposite reactions quickly surfaced: one of rejection, and one of eager absorption, of Western thought, including Christian thought. An ecclesiastical leader of the Jōdoshū at the time, Ugai Tetsujō (1804–1891), convinced that the eagerness to adopt Western culture would spell the rejection of Buddhism, preached the exclusion of foreign doctrine and promoted, along with others, anti-Christian polemics *(haijaron)*.

However, a number of new faith movements, keen to breathe new life into the transmission of Hōnen's teaching, chose to go in the same direction as Japan's modernization. Around 1920 Yamazaki Bennei's (1859–1920) "Illuminism" *(kōmyōshugi)* and Shiio Benkyō's "Symbiotism" *(kyōseishugi)* emerged within the Jōdoshū. Yamazaki Bennei stressed as the gist of Hōnen's Pure Land doctrine the adoption of the believer into the light rays of Amida Buddha. A life of light thus became the central theme: to go through the present life in a spiritual way, believing in Amida as the only "Great Parent" and obtaining Amida's spiritual light of mercy and wisdom, to finally enter into the eternal light. Noteworthy is his adoption of Christian terms: he invokes Amida with the words "Oh, Great Parent," translates Buddha-nature as "spirituality," Buddha's compassion as "grace," the Primal Vow as "the Holy Will," and also uses terms such as "the Spirit" or "the Great Spirit." On his side, Shiio Benkyō drew Hōnen's Pure Land doctrine in the direction of social action. Religion, he taught, does not aim merely at the liberation of the individual, it must liberate socially and realize a Pure Land of true symbiosis.

These two visions are far apart: while Illuminism focuses on the core of Jōdoshū, promoting the *nenbutsu* experience of the individual, Symbiotism reads the realization of social symbiosis into Hōnen's Buddhism. Yet they share an important point: the idea that Hōnen's doctrine is not merely about a future world after death, but rather a guide to living rationally and efficiently as an individual and in society. Especially in the Taishō era (1912–1926) and up to the middle of the Shōwa era (1926–1989), both movements drew much attention as modern forms of Jōdoshū faith and acting as a strong stimulus to revise the traditional understanding of Hōnen's Pure Land doctrine. They attracted many talented people, and are still alive today.

From 1964 onwards, the Chion-in head temple of the school has been promoting the so-called *otetsugi* ("from hand to hand") movement: activities aiming at adapting and reanimating Hōnen's *nenbutsu* in our present culture. This is noteworthy as a faith movement backed by the organization itself. In the above three faith movements, we can see a contribution of Hōnen's *nenbutsu* doctrine to the modernization of Japanese Buddhism, and the creative significance of Hōnen's spiritual legacy in the present.

Bibliography

Hattori Shōon. *Hōnen Shōnin and Buddhism.* Tokyo: Jodo Shu Press, 1992.

Ishii Shinpo. *Hōnen: The Luther of Japan.* Tokyo: Executive Bureau of the Jōdo-Sect and the International Buddhist Society, 1940.

Jōdoshū shi (History of the Jōdoshū). Kyoto: Jōdoshū Kyōgakukyoku, 1965.

King, Winston L. "Hōnen's Visualizations of the Pure Land." *The Pure Land* n.s. 4 (1987) 126–41.

Saihō shinan shō. Teihon Shinran Shōnin zenshū, vol. 5. Kyoto: Hōzōkan, 1980.

Shiio Benkyō zenshū (Collected works of Shiio Benkyō). Tokyo: Sankibō Busshorin, 1974.

Shimazaki Bennei. *Shūso no hizui* ("Skin and marrow" of the founder). Osaka: Kōmyō Shūyōkai, 1990.

Wakimoto Tsuneya, ed. *Kindai Nippon no shūkyō undō shisō* (The thought of modern Japanese religious movements). Tokyo: Monbushō Kakenhi Hojokin Hōkokusho, 1980.

{translated by Jan Van Bragt}

III. *Shinran's Way*

ALFRED BLOOM

SHINRAN (1173–1262) is revered as the founder of Jōdo Shinshū. The name means the school of the true teaching (the essence) of the Pure Land (tradition). The Chinese Pure Land teacher Shan-tao (613–681) used the same term to describe his teaching.

Shinran's Life and Character

Shinran's career unfolded amid the turmoil attending the decline of the effete, aristocratic Heian age (794–1185) and the onset of the more vigorous, at times brutal, warrior epoch of Kamakura (1185–1333). Born into the Hino family, a branch of the Fujiwara clan, Shinran entered monastic life at the age of nine, along with his father and two brothers, as a result of the changing social and political fortunes of the family. He began his studies and practice as a monk on Mount Hiei, reputedly receiving ordination under the tutelage of the abbot Jien. Aristocrat and poet, Jien (1155–1225), like his elder brother Kujō Kanezane, was sympathetic to Hōnen's Pure Land movement. Shinran, in addition to acquiring the Buddhist erudition later displayed in his writings, also had experience of traditional Pure Land practices on Mt. Hiei, for he served as a *dōsō*, a temple priest, in the Hall of Perpetual *Nenbutsu* (*jōgyō-zammaidō*) that Ennin had established and in which were held memorial services on behalf of deceased royalty and aristocracy.

After twenty years of discipline and practice, Shinran experienced deep spiritual anxiety for his future deliverance or enlightenment. To resolve his crisis, he undertook a period of intense meditation in the Rokkakudō in Kyoto. It was popularly believed that Prince Shōtoku had established this temple, which enshrined Kannon (Avalokiteśvara), the Bodhisattva of Compassion. For one hundred days Shinran contemplated his life. On the ninety-fifth day he had a dream-vision in which Kannon appeared to him, announcing that he would take a feminine form as his helpmate.

As a consequence of these experiences, in 1201 Shinran left Mount Hiei and entered the Pure Land community of Hōnen in Yoshimizu in the heart of Kyoto. His motive for leaving was a deep awareness of his own spiritual inadequacy and failure. Though he had practiced and studied for some twenty years, he realized that he could not fulfill the rigorous ideals of Tendai practice. He had no more assurance of his final enlightenment than when he began. He sought relief from the pain of this disillusion with himself in the Pure Land teaching, and was greatly encouraged when Hōnen personally assured him that even the most evil person, even a sinner such as himself, was embraced by the unconditional compassion of Amida Buddha. Shinran spent the remainder of his life plumbing the deep implications of Hōnen's principle of sole practice of *nenbutsu (senju nenbutsu)*.

Shinran studied for six years with Hōnen. During this time he resolved his doubts and became a leading disciple. Hōnen permitted him to copy his epochal work *Senchakushū*, the manifesto that established the Pure Land teaching as an independent sect. Shinran also drew a portrait of the master. At this time Hōnen, as a result of a dream, changed Shinran's name, Shakku, which he had earlier given him, to Zenshin. It was later that Shinran adopted the name by which he is now known. The changes in name reflect development in spiritual status or understanding. Hōnen's high esteem for Shinran was fully reciprocated. Shinran constantly maintained in his writings that he was merely a faithful disciple of Hōnen, transmitting the true meaning of his teaching, and when he took issue with other disciples, it was on the basis they had misinterpreted the master.

In 1207 apparent indiscretions of some of Hōnen's disciples led to the abolition of the community and exile from Kyoto for Hōnen and his major disciples, including Shinran. Shinran's keen sense of justice appeared in his outspoken criticism of the government authorities, the Buddhist establishments in Mt. Hiei and Nara, and the Confucian scholars, who had colluded in inflicting this persecution. He pointed out that there had been no serious investigation of the charges. Hōnen was sent to Tosa in Shikoku, while Shinran went to Kokubu in Echigo in the region of present Niigata. They never met again.

It was perhaps at this time that Shinran married Eshin-ni. His dream-vision of Kannon may have been a presage of this marriage, for while there are various theories about the identification and number of Shinran's wives, Eshin-ni is the only one clearly known to history and her role in his life was that of a faithful helpmate. Their marriage produced a family with six children and set the pattern for Shin Buddhist clergy thereafter. We possess a collection of letters written by Eshin-ni that contain much information about their living conditions, state of health, and family relationships. These letters, discovered in 1921, confirm Shinran's presence on Mount Hiei, and

26. Shinran (1173–1262).

his discipleship with Hōnen. They are significant in the absence of any record of Shinran's association with Hōnen in Jōdoshū sources, the tradition claiming direct lineage from Hōnen.

In his dream Shinran had also seen the suffering masses in the distant eastern provinces of Japan. This vision became reality when after five years in exile the banishment was lifted and Shinran moved with his family to the village of Inada in Kashima (Ibaraki Prefecture today). Here he spent more than twenty years, from 1212 to 1235, propagating Pure Land teaching among the peasants and townspeople far from the centers of cultural and political power. He lived quietly, cultivating his spiritual insight and thought. Gradually, however, he acquired several disciples, creating a nascent community. Some scholars have suggested that during his long period of residence in this area his followers numbered in the thousands.

He spent the last thirty years of his life in Kyoto, surviving at first on modest means. He lived for a while with a brother and received donations from followers who came to visit him. His wife in later years returned to Echigo, her native home, to spend her last years there. It was Shinran's daughter Kakushin-ni (1224–1283) who tended to him towards the end. During the last years of his life, in order to keep faith with his followers, Shinran was forced to disown his eldest son, Zenran, who apparently misrepresented Shinran in a dispute among the disciples in the east. Still, some of Shinran's most significant teaching was articulated in this final period. Shinran passed away quietly in 1262 at the advanced age of ninety years.

Shinran was held in the highest esteem by those who knew him well. In a letter to her daughter Eshin-ni relates that she once saw him in a dream as a manifestation of Kannon Bodhisattva. Further, according to the third abbot Kakunyo's biography *(Godenshō)*, a disciple, Ren'i, saw him in a dream as a virtual incarnation of Amida Buddha. Perhaps the most illuminating source for assessing Shinran's character is his own writings. His major scholarly work, the *Kyōgyōshinshō*,[1] along with his commentaries, exhibits a wide knowledge of the tradition and a penetrating critical insight. Versed in the use of language, he drew subtle shades of meaning from Buddhist terms to express his new insights and to justify his reinterpretation of Buddhism. He was a poet, giving lyrical expression to his teaching in *wasan* (hymns in Japanese style). People could sing or recite them as an aid to memory and thereby receive the teaching in a form comprehensible to unlettered people.

Shinran's letters show his thoughtful responses to disciples' questions and to problems of heresy. He wrote to his disciples in honorific terms, showing them high respect, regardless of social status. He was egalitarian, using the terms *dōbō dōgyō*, which mean brother companion and practitioner (on the way). His teaching betrays no class distinctions, for all people receive their faith equally from Amida Buddha. He was not aggressive or strongly assertive in spreading his teaching, but showed great sympathy and empathy for people, weeping on hearing of the death of a disciple, or laboring to make the teaching accessible to the ordinary person through careful explanations. He affirmed tradition, but his personal religious experiences opened his eyes to new possibilities of interpretation. His thought embodies a universal vision of Amida Buddha's unconditional compassion and non-discriminating wisdom, transcending all social, sexual, moral, and religious distinctions.

His Teaching

As we turn to consideration of Shinran's teaching, we should note that his interpretation challenged Buddhist tradition as a whole, represented chiefly by the Tendai tradition, which he studied in his earlier years, and the various strands of Pure Land teaching propagated by the successors of Hōnen, as well as the general Pure Land teaching that is a part of all major Mahāyāna schools. He particularly stressed the term "true teaching of the Pure Land" (Jōdo Shinshū). He did not treat this as the distinctive name of his movement, since he had no explicit intention to start a new sect. Nevertheless, the distinctive, critical character of his teaching naturally gave rise in later times to an independent sect claiming to promote the true Pure Land teaching among the other representatives of that tradition.

Shinran claims in his writings, as already mentioned, that his interpretation represents the true meaning of Hōnen's teaching, rooted in the history of Buddhism from India, to China, through Korea to Japan. This teaching is presented as an alternative to all other forms of Buddhism, which are essentially elitist in character and generally inaccessible to the ordinary person, both in the style of practice and the complexity of the teaching. That is, they are not truly universal in establishing the layperson as equal to the monk.

In order to legitimate his teaching, Shinran set out a spiritual lineage that provided a basis for his own position. He designated seven great teachers: Nāgārjuna (second or third century) and Vasubandhu (fourth century) in India; T'an-luan (476–542), Tao-ch'o (562–645), and Shan-tao (613–681) in China; and Genshin (942–1017) and Hōnen (1133–1212) in Japan as the links in the transmission of Pure Land doctrine, culminating in his own teaching. According to Shinran, each teacher had significant insights into the meaning of Amida Buddha's Primal Vows and confirmed the way to rebirth in the Pure Land and enlightenment through the *nenbutsu* of true faith as the central meaning of Śākyamuni's teaching. Shinran did not believe that he was inventing this tradition. He saw himself as sharing the correct understanding of it, on the basis of his own experience and study. Historically there had been several strands in the transmission of Pure Land teaching from China to Japan. However, Shinran goes beyond the historical data to give a buddhalogical meaning to the transmission as the manifestation of Amida's Vow in human history. He expresses this in his Hymn of True Faith *(Nenbutsu-shōshinge)* in the *Kyōgyōshinshō*.

Shinran's teaching mirrors his religious experience during his long residence in the monastery on Mount Hiei and his association with Hōnen, as well as his subsequent life among the peasants and townspeople in the eastern provinces. As a result of his varied experiences, Shinran developed a distinctive interpretation of traditional Buddhism and the Pure Land teaching that transformed the meaning of religious life and opened a new alternative in the unfolding of Buddhist religious insight through history.

Essentially, Shinran based his interpretations on his strong conviction that one's final enlightenment could not be attained by any self-motivated, self-striving (self-powered) practice or discipline. It was his perception, resulting from his own despair and disillusionment, that the pervasive, ineradicable egoism and passion that drove his life also rendered religious practices ineffective. He learned from his own experience that all human activity is entangled with ego interest, putting it fundamentally at odds with the goal of Buddhist spirituality—to rid the self of such ego interest. He declared:

> Even though I take refuge in the Jōdo Shinshū
> It is difficult to have a mind of truth.
> I am false and untrue,
> Without the least purity of mind.
>
> We men in our outward forms
> Display wisdom, goodness and purity.
> Since greed, anger, evil and deceit are frequent,
> We are filled with naught but flattery.
>
> With our evil natures hard to subdue,
> Our minds are like asps and scorpions.
> As the practice of virtue is mixed poison,
> We call it false, vain practice.[2]

Shinran held that it was impossible for the ego to purify itself sufficiently to achieve enlightenment as defined by the various Buddhist traditions to his time. As a consequence, he rejected the Tendai institutions of Mount Hiei, where the variety of approaches to practice were premised on this effort.

Shinran's search led him to Hōnen, who proclaimed that the *nenbutsu* (here recitation of the name of Amida Buddha) had been given by the Buddha for such defiled people of the Last Age *(mappō)* in order to enable them to be born in the Pure Land, where they could attain perfect purity and enlightenment. Nevertheless, Shinran came to understand that this practice had the same premise as the general Buddhist approach. Therefore, it may itself be undertaken as a self-striving effort to gain purity.

He saw that if deliverance were to be truly sure and universally available, as Hōnen had taught, it must be completely the result of the Buddha's effort and owe nothing to finite, unstable human striving. Therefore, Shinran stressed the principle of absolute Other-Power, expressed through the fulfillment of Amida Buddha's forty-eight primal vows and their associated ideals portrayed in the *Larger Pure Land Sūtra*. These vows state that if the

Buddha fails to establish a particular spiritual condition for all beings, then he will not accept the highest enlightenment only for himself. According to the Sūtra, all the vows were brought to perfection. Hence, the spiritual fulfillment of all beings is assured, thanks to the power of the Buddha's realized vows.

Shinran carried this insight to its logical conclusion: every aspect of religious experience and reality results from the power of Amida's vows. His writings aim at clarifying this understanding and giving a comprehensive interpretation of religious existence. As a consequence, following the general perspective of Mahāyāna Buddhism, he viewed Pure Land soteriology from two standpoints, namely, the aspect of going (to the Pure Land, ōsō) and that of returning (from the Pure Land, gensō). The aspect of going focuses on the way to rebirth in the Pure Land, emphasizing trust in Amida and the recitation of the nenbutsu. The aspect of returning deals with the final fulfillment or the goal and end of the soteriological process. Shinran placed a strong emphasis on this aspect in order to show that the pursuit of enlightenment is not merely a selfish effort, but ultimately ends in working for the deliverance and enlightenment of all beings. Still, the entire process is based on absolute Other-Power, which is rooted in the Buddha's vows.

Within the context of the process for going to the Pure Land, Shinran reinterpreted Buddhism and Pure Land teaching in accord with this insight into Other-Power. He indicated that religious experience and trust are characterized by two dimensions commonly termed Two Types of Deep Faith (nishujinshin). On the one hand, there is the awareness and understanding of the spiritual defilement and incapacity of the person and, on the other, the corresponding unconditional compassion and wisdom of Amida Buddha, who embraces beings and never abandons them. In effect, the deeper the awareness of one's evil self, the more absolute and embracing is the assurance of Buddha's compassion.

In the dialectic of the Two Types of Deep Faith, the issue of faith is central. The concept of faith or entrusting is, perhaps, Shinran's most distinctive contribution to the development of Pure Land thought. It is crucial for the understanding of practice and soteriology in his thought.

Shinran interpreted the Larger Pure Land Sūtra (which follows the pattern of traditional Buddhism with regard to practice) in accord with his view of absolute Other-Power. He read the reference to faith in the eighteenth vow and its fulfillment passage to indicate that the three minds: sincerity, faith, and aspiration for birth in the Pure Land are a unity resulting from Amida Buddha's giving (transferring) his infinite virtue to the person. He also read the Chinese text of the Sūtra in a Japanese linguistic fashion, by adding the honorific verb ending *seshimetamaeri* to the term *ekō*, which normally indicates the transfer of the merit of an act made by believers toward their goal. This change in grammatical reading alters the import of the text, making all transfer of virtue to be only that from the side of the Buddha. Ordinary persons cannot contribute any virtue or merit toward their deliverance. Faith may be described as single-minded trust endowed by Amida.

In addition to the principle of absolute Other-Power based on this passage, Shinran elevated the conception of Amida by asserting that he is the Eternal Buddha, on the basis of the fulfillment of the twelfth and thirteenth vows, in which the Bodhisattva Dharmākara pledged that he would become the Buddha of measureless life and light, compassion and wisdom. By virtue of these vows, the Bodhisattva became Amida Buddha. The name Amida is a Japanese transliteration of the Sanskrit name Amitāyus, or Amitābha, names that mean Eternal Life and Infinite Light, respectively.

However, Shinran used the term *kuonjitsujō*, a Tendai term indicating the absolute eternity of Śākyamuni of the *Lotus Sūtra*, chapter 16, in reference to Amida. This word indicated that Śākyamuni Buddha in this chapter was without beginning or end, in contrast to other buddhas who had either a beginning and an end, or a beginning and no end. In applying this tenet of the *Lotus Sūtra* to Amida Buddha, Shinran was aware that he was going beyond the view of the *Larger Pure Land Sūtra*, as the following *wasan* indicates:

> Since Amida became a Buddha,
> Ten kalpas have passed. So (the Sūtra) says.
> But He seems to be a Buddha
> Older than the innumerable mote-dot kalpas.[3]

The Sūtra itself teaches that Amida attained Buddhahood through his sincere and pure practice in five kalpas or aeons of time, and ten kalpas have passed since then in the ancient mythic past. Shinran sees the Sūtra story as revealing the true nature or meaning of formless, inconceivable reality. Amida Buddha symbolizes the eternal Buddha-nature that pervades the cosmos and is evident in the aspiration for enlightenment or fulfillment in all beings. Amida is, consequently, the universal, unimpeded light/wisdom that breaks through spiritual darkness, though itself being without form or color. In effect, Amida has form, represented in images or pictures, but simultaneously, as ultimate wisdom, has no form. Faith/trust is the realization of Buddha-nature that expresses itself in the aspiration to become Buddha for the deliverance of all beings.

In this way Shinran secures the soteriological process as the dynamic working of reality itself. It is not an external force toward which one directs trust. Rather, it is a spontaneous movement within the person, whereby trust in Amida is aroused in the moment that one sees the futility of self-striving efforts and intuitively realizes that deliverance is only possible through the Buddha's vow. For Shinran, in accord with his understanding of Other-Power, faith/trust is the realization of the Buddha-nature or the Tathāgata's true mind.

Though Shinran does not deny the conscious experience of faith as "my" faith or believing, he is placing it in a more fundamental spiritual context, in which the true mind of Amida's compassionate intention and promise to deliver all beings, as expressed in his vows, is manifested in human experience as the source of one's personal trust. Shinran regards this as a "turning of the mind" or conversion whereby one's spiritual eyes open to the truth of the vows and Other-Power. The Pure Land tradition generally taught that the belief in the meritorious recitation of the name was efficacious in attaining birth in the Pure Land. Shinran, however, speaks of an inner transformation of one's mind, whereby a firm trust arises that the Buddha has embraced us and assures us of our deliverance. It is not merely belief as intellectual assent, but strong, inner conviction as awareness of the self-evident truth of the vows.

This conversion and conviction are not brought about in abstraction. They arise from religious existence and from encounters with teachers and the teaching. Here Shinran has again transformed traditional understanding. In the general Buddhist view, Pure Land teaching was regarded as an *upāya*, that is, as a device given by the Buddha whereby people who could not engage in the more demanding, rigorous spiritual disciplines could attain birth in the Pure Land by the easy practice of reciting the name. The essential practices leading to enlightenment were the meditations and life of the monastery. Consequently, Pure Land practice was a subsidiary and subordinate path to enlightenment.

Shinran, however, reversed this relationship. He held that the traditional "Saintly Path" practices of the monastery, that is, meditation and morality, were the *upāya*. As in his own case, such practices, resulting in spiritual frustration, failure, and despair, open people's eyes to their true spiritual state and enable them to trust fully in Amida's vows.

Reviewing his own experience, Shinran speaks of this as "turning through the three vows" (*sangan tennyū*). He saw himself as having lived through three of the vows, which symbolized the variety of spiritual approaches in Buddhism. The nineteenth vow, for one who "resolves to seek awakening, cultivates all the virtues, and single-mindedly aspires to be reborn in my land," is the vow that teaches the path to birth in the Pure Land through cultivating meditation and morality. This may correspond to his experience as a monk on Mount Hiei. The twentieth vow, for those who "hear my name, fix their thoughts on rebirth in my land, cultivate all the roots of virtue, and single-mindedly dedicate this virtue desiring to be reborn in my land," is viewed as attaining birth through the practice of *nenbutsu*, and may correspond to his service in the Hall of Perpetual Nenbutsu as a *dōsō*. The eighteenth vow, for those who "bring to mind this aspiration for even ten moments of thought," corresponds to the stage of true faith, the stage at which Shinran's his eyes were opened to the fact that the vow, and not one's self-generated practice, was the cause and basis for deliverance.[4] In this process, the practice-oriented paths of traditional Buddhism are all preliminary to, and preparation for, the realization of trust in Amida's vow.

On the basis of this understanding, Shinran positioned his teaching in relation to other sects of contemporary Buddhism. He followed the general Buddhist practice of critical classification of doctrines, developing a system called "two pairs and four levels" *(nisōshijū)*. The two pairs are: crosswise *(ō)*, which symbolizes Other-Power, and vertical *(shu)*, which is self-striving. The second pair is "lengthwise going out" *(shutsu)* or gradual, and "transcending" *(chō)* or sudden, immediate. Through various combinations of these terms Shinran classified all forms of Buddhism, highlighting his teaching of absolute Other-Power. Accordingly, in his view, (1) the Hossō sect represents the self-striving gradualist approach to enlightenment *(jushutsu)*; (2) the general Pure Land tradition and the other disciples of Hōnen, whose interpretations Shinran disputed, employ the Other-Power based practice of *nenbutsu* in a gradualist, self-striving way for purification and merit—that is, the practice is given by the Buddha, but it is employed in a self-striving way *(ōshutsu)*; (3) the Zen, Tendai, Shingon, and Kegon sects are self-powered direct or sudden traditions *(juchō)*; (4) in contrast to all the others, Shinran's teaching is absolute Other-Power and transcending or immediate *(ōchō)*.

We can observe Shinran's critical approach to the religion of his time in the *Kyōgyōshinshō*. The initial five chapters of the work clarify and substantiate Shinran's interpretation of the path to enlightenment and the believer's final fulfillment. They present the truth of the Pure Land teaching. The sixth chapter focuses on Shinran's evaluation of alternative paths. Where the five chapters proclaim Shinran's Pure Land faith, the sixth chapter mounts a critique of the contemporary religious environment.

Through the use of a variety of texts from Buddhist tradition, Shinran employs Pure Land symbolism to show that self-striving practices lead to inferior levels of fulfillment. He rejects reliance on folk religious practices of prayer and divination or seeking magical benefits. He shows that the gods of the cosmos are subordinate to Buddha and are his supporters. According to Shinran, it is important to understand the spiritual character of the age. Therefore, he quotes at length the *Mappō tōmyōki*, traditionally attributed to Saichō (Dengyō Daishi). Delineating the conditions of the last age in the decline of the Dharma, the text states that even though monks do not keep precepts, they are to be respected because they represent the dharma. Shinran uses the text to criticize the contemporary Buddhist Order, and perhaps also to defend his own decision to marry publicly and give up keeping monastic precepts.

In this chapter he also presents his perspective on the unity of the Pure Land teaching despite its diversity in expression and conflicting interpretations. He distinguishes the surface, manifest teaching *(kenshō)* from the implicit, hidden teaching *(onmitsu)*. While the Pure Land Sūtras differ in their approaches to practice, they are unified in being based on the fulfillment of Amida's vows, which aim at the deliverance of all beings.

Throughout his writings Shinran asserts that his understanding of Pure Land teaching offers immediate assurance of Amida Buddha's embrace of absolute Other-Power in this life, through the transforming experience of entrusting in the vow. The guarantee of this status is the eleventh vow: "May I not gain possession of perfect awakening if, once I have attained buddhahood, the humans and gods in my land are not assured of awakening, and without fail attain liberation." In Shinran's interpretation, this means that the believer immediately enters the company of the truly assured *(shōjōju)*, and attains the stage of non-retrogression (in the bodhisattva path of traditional Buddhism), as well as immediate attainment of nirvāṇa upon death.

He also affirms that upon reaching this status the person is "equal to the Tathāgata" (Buddha) or to Maitreya the future Buddha. In these expressions equality does not mean present identity. Rather, they indicate that the causes for our future enlightenment have been firmly established and are certain to be realized. In effect, we are virtually buddhas. He illustrates this by pointing to the figure of Maitreya who, though still a bodhisattva, is commonly referred to as Maitreya Buddha since the cause for his becoming the next buddha is already established. With these concepts Shinran transformed the futuristic orientation of birth in the Pure Land to a present certainty made known through the faith experience. In addition, he implies the spiritual equality of all the faithful, who themselves are virtual buddhas. He maintained that he had no disciples, because they all had received their faith equally from Amida Buddha.

The elevated status of the believer counters the principle in Shingon and Tendai Buddhism that we become buddhas in this very body *(sokushin jōbutsu)* as a result of the practices of those sects. According to Shinran, we gain our spiritual status and assurance through Amida's vows and not by our own strivings.

In line with his emphasis on the altruistic nature of religious existence, Shinran devotes the fourth section of his work to showing that human fulfillment means that we return to this world after death to work for the deliverance of others, like the bodhisattvas who refuse to enter nirvāṇa, unless all other beings share it with them. This is based on Amida's twenty-second vow, which refers with special favor to "those who, because of the vows they took in the past to effortlessly bring all living beings to spiritual maturity, don the armor of the Great Vows, amass the roots of virtue, and liberate all these beings."

Further, in line with his perspective on the altruism of religious existence, Shinran also teaches in the fifth section that we become Buddha immediately on entry into the Pure Land of True Reward established by the twelfth and thirteenth vows. In essence both aspects of fulfillment are altruistic, since on becoming Buddha and attaining Nirvāṇa, one is identified with the salvific reality that constantly works for the deliverance of all beings.

The altruism of faith, however, is not merely a matter of the future for Shinran. Though he denies that we can become buddhas in this life, he constantly describes the Buddha's true mind, which is the essence of faith, as the compassionate mind that seeks the welfare and deliverance of others. He states that true entrusting/faith is the adamantine mind (a mind of strong conviction). The adamantine mind is the mind that aspires to become Buddha, and this mind desires to save all beings and bring them to birth in the Pure Land.[5] He expressed the altruistic spirit of faith in a phrase borrowed from the Chinese teacher Shan-tao: to repay the benevolence of the Buddha, he teaches people the faith that he has received *(jishinkyōninshin)*.[6]

As we have seen, the soteriological process established by Shinran's interpretation of Pure Land teaching stresses its absolute Other-Power foundation. Though individuals cannot contribute to their final fulfillment by their own efforts, Shinran did not mean that they are simply to be inactive or passive in religious life. The issue is the meaning of religious activity. For Shinran, religious life is an expression of gratitude for the Buddha's compassion and the assurance of our final enlightenment through our faith/trust in the Buddha's vows. The concrete manifestation of this gratitude is the recitation of the name of Amida Buddha *(nenbutsu)*. However, gratitude is not exhausted with that recitation. Rather, faith/trust is marked by a compassionate concern to share the teaching and live positively with others. For Shinran, ethical existence is not in order to acquire merit but a means by which the compassion of the Buddha becomes real in the world.

Shinran himself was very sensitive to issues of justice. He also took note of the unequal distribution of justice, stating in a verse that when a rich person goes to court, it is like throwing a stone into water, while for a poor person it is like throwing water into a stone. He criticized Buddhist institutions and clergy for being lackeys of the state and promoting folk magical practices. Hence, they were outwardly Buddhist but inwardly heathen (gedō). In effect, they did not represent Buddhist compassion and wisdom. Despite the apparent other-worldly character of Pure Land teaching, Shinran gave more attention to religious life in this world, urging his followers to respect other faiths; to be compassionate to opponents; to say the nenbutsu for the welfare of society and not to obstruct the spread of the dharma by antisocial action.

In conclusion, there are numerous features of Shinran's understanding of religion that are historically and religiously significant for the study of religion and spirituality. In the first place, Shinran's interpretation of religious reality is comprehensive. It offers a cosmic basis for the soteriological process, insight into the human condition, and aspiration of people for ultimate fulfillment, and it establishes a foundation for religious subjectivity and experience, yielding self-understanding as well as assurance and confidence of the truth of the teaching.

Shinran rejected traditional Buddhist practices, including the quantitative recitation of nenbutsu, as means to attain final enlightenment. He realistically observed the pervasive egoistic, defiled nature of human existence, which permeates religious practice itself. While attempting to overcome the egocentric character of religious endeavors, highlighting the ultimately altruistic nature of the soteriological process, Shinran also taught that all people, no matter how evil, are embraced by the Buddha's compassion and therefore have a hope they can live by. His understanding of the universality of the Vow maintains that access to religious reality is not dependent on the accidental aspects of life, such as social status, gender, intellectual or physical abilities, or even moral and spiritual achievements. Shinran was concerned more with the kokoro or state of mind that underlies all human activity than with the externals that can give rise to self-righteousness and attitudes of superiority.

Shinran's approach involves an egalitarian relationship with his followers, though they highly esteemed him as their teacher. He was authoritative, rather than authoritarian. He rejected the use of magical practices as a means to gain some benefit and security in life, though he sympathized with the people who felt the need for such methods. He attempted to liberate people from religious fears and exploitation. He comforted those who felt their spiritual weakness deeply, noting that it was for such people that the Buddha made his vows with unconditional compassion. He is, perhaps, most notable for his success in shifting religious emphasis from the form of practice to the spirit of practice. He transformed Japanese traditional religion from a largely utilitarian quest for self-benefits, material and spiritual, to an expression of gratitude for the assurance of enlightenment and a challenge to make compassion real in society.

Rennyo

Shinran's writings provided the foundation of a new movement. However, he did not designate a specific successor. Some disciples were already leaders of sizable bands of followers. Kakushin-ni, his daughter, established a mausoleum-shrine where all followers could come and share memories of the teacher. In bequeathing the shrine to the whole Shin community, she stipulated that the caretaker was to be a lineal descendant of Shinran. This initiated the practice of hereditary succession of the abbacy. Her grandson Kakunyo (1270–1351) worked strenuously to unify and institutionalize the movement, under the control of the Hongan-ji, as the shrine came to be called when it was transformed into a *jiin* or temple. Ten branches emerged, but the Hongan-ji, through Kakunyo and later Rennyo, became the major proponent of Shin Buddhism, eventually outdistancing other important branches such as Bukkōji-ha and Takada-ha in numbers and influence.

Though Shinran did not inspire a mass movement in his own time, his spirit passed down through the centuries to the eighth abbot, Rennyo (1415–1499), who distilled the essence of Shinran's thought and eloquently propagated it in simplicity. Whereas Shinran claimed to represent the true understanding of Hōnen, his master, against other claimants or successors, Rennyo, as scion of the Hongan-ji tradition, maintained that he was carrying on the true teaching and spirit of Shinran among the various factions that had developed in Shin Buddhism. Shinran's legacy underwent transformation as a result of the passage of time, institutionalization, and changing conditions facing the Shin community. Rennyo aimed to revive the fortunes of the lagging Hongan-ji, which suffered strong competition from other segments of Shin Buddhism.

Often called the "Restorer of Shinshū," Rennyo consolidated Shinran's work of opening a new path in Buddhism, one designed for ordinary country folk or townspeople, who could not devote themselves to the rigorous monastic discipline and practices that were the means to enlightenment in traditional Buddhism, since they were bound to their land, labors, or families. This path brought hope into the lives of vast numbers of people and became the basis of an influential, highly elaborate, ecclesiastical institution that has endured to the present day in Japan and in branches in the West.

Rennyo traveled to villages and towns, attracting large numbers of followers, and converting Tendai, Shingon, or variant Shin temples to the leadership of the Hongan-ji branch. The major vehicle for his transmission of the teaching was his letters, which dealt with many issues facing the evolving Shin Buddhist institution. These letters attest the clarity and earnestness of Rennyo's instruction. Like Shinran, he had a deep feeling for the common person. While he was not, perhaps, as scholarly as Shinran, he was a thinker who could articulate the teaching and adapt it to the minds of his listeners.

Rennyo followed his predecessors in upholding the universal embrace of Amida's compassion beyond anyone's deserving, and the nonmagical character of Shin teaching. Nevertheless, he had to institute rules *(okite)* to restrain the antisocial tendencies or licensed evil (antinomianism) that may result from misunderstanding the place of ethical life in Shinran's teaching of Other-Power deliverance through faith/trust alone. For Shinran and Rennyo, ethics is an important postfaith condition, as a grateful response to the deliverance received.

Rennyo, however, gave ethics a clearer definition by distinguishing between the level of *buppō* (buddha-dharma), that is, the spiritual dimension of faith and birth in the Pure Land, and *ōbō* (royal dharma), the secular, worldly dimension of Confucian ethical requirements promoted by clan, family, and government. Through our religious faith we aspire to, and are assured of, birth in the Pure Land, while in society we conform to the laws and principles of human relations transmitted through the culture.

This dualism has pervaded Shin teaching and its role in society to modern times. Rennyo was decidedly more other-worldly in his emphasis than Shinran, highlighting the brevity and fragility of life, most eloquently depicted in his letter on White Ashes, which is used in Shin funeral services. In its view of the human condition, it stresses the need to rely on the Buddha for deliverance.

In contrast to the more technical, scholarly character of much of Shinran's writing, Rennyo's letters simplified Shinran's understanding of faith, employing more frequently the term *anjin* (serene, peaceful, or tranquil mind), rather than *shinjin* (the trusting, believing mind). According to some scholars, *shinjin* is more individualistic, while *anjin* reflects a more communal perspective whereby the embrace of Amida's Vow is assured by one's participation in the community. In the understanding of the relation of the believer and Buddha, Rennyo employed the formula *ki-hō-ittai*, which indicates the unity or union of the person and the dharma (or the Buddha). *Anjin* is based on the oneness of the believer and the Buddha in the context of the community. It is symbolized and expressed in the *namu-amida-butsu* (I take refuge in Amida Buddha) or *nenbutsu*, in which *namu* refers to the passion-ridden being who takes refuge, and to *Amida-butsu*, the Buddha who embraces. Faith is the attitude of dependence and reliance indicated in the phrase much used by Rennyo: *tasuke-tamae-to-tanomu*. Rennyo interpreted this popular plea for the Buddha to save, as a reflection of the yearning heart moved by Other-Power to aspire for birth in the Pure Land. *Nenbutsu* recitation voices our gratitude for the faith we have received.

Shinran's teaching, though not aiming at institutionalization, laid the basis for a popular Pure Land movement whose power rested in the conviction of the members rather than in great landholdings or political connections. It is characterized by a warm piety which nurtures a lively hope of ultimate fulfillment through birth in the Pure Land, a deep gratitude to Amida Buddha's compassion and the tradition that transmitted the teaching, as well as respect toward all powers, divine and human, that order and secure worldly life. This piety and devotion has nourished the movement through many challenges and changes in Japanese history and continues to sustain the community to the present day.

Notes

1. The full name of the text is *Ken-jōdo-shinjitsu-kyō-gyō-shō-monrui*, which means "A Collection of Passages on the True Teaching, Practice and Realization of the Pure Land (Tradition)."

2. Alfred Bloom, *Shinran's Gospel of Pure Grace*, 28–29 (*Shinran shōgyō zenshō* 2.527).

3. *Jōdo Wasan*, No. 88. *Shinshū Seiten* (San Francisco: Buddhist Churches of America, 1978) 190.

4. For the text of the vows, see Luis O. Gómez, trans., *Land of Bliss: The Paradise of the Buddha of Immeasurable Light* (Honolulu: University of Hawai'i Press, 1996) 167-68.

5. Faith Chapter, *Kyōgyōshinshō* (Jōdo Shinshū Seiten) (Kyoto: Hongan-ji Shuppanbu, 1988) 252.

6. Faith Chapter, *Kyōgyōshinshō*, 261.

Bibliography

Sources

Shinran shōgyō zenshō. Kyoto: Kōkyō Shoin, 1953.

Hirota, Dennis, trans. *Tannisho: A Primer*. Kyoto: Ryukoku University, 1986.

Ueda Yoshifumi, ed. *The True Teaching, Practice and Realization of the Pure Land Way: A Translation of Shinran's Kyōgyōshinshō*. Shin Buddhism translation series. 4 Volumes. Kyoto: Hongwanji International Center, 1983–1990.

Studies

Bloom, Alfred. *The Life of Shinran Shōnin: The Journey to Self-acceptance*. Berkeley: Institute of Buddhist Studies, 1994.

———. *Shinran's Gospel of Pure Grace*. Tucson: University of Arizona Press, 1965.

Dobbins, James C. *Jōdo Shinshū: Shin Buddhism in Medieval Japan*. Bloomington: Indiana University Press.

Gira, Dennis. *Le sens de la conversion dans l'enseignement de Shinran*. Paris: Maisonneuve et Larose, 1985.

Kikumura Norihiko. *Shinran: His Life and Thought*. Los Angeles: Nenbutsu Press, 1972.

Nihon Bukkyō Gakkai, ed. *Bukkyō ni okeru shin no mondai*. Kyoto: Heiraku-ji Shoten, 1973.

Rogers, Minor L., and Ann T. Rogers. *Rennyo: The Second Founder of Shin Buddhism*. Berkeley: Asian Humanities Press, 1991.

Takahatake, Takamichi. *Young Man Shinran: A Reappraisal of Shinran's Life*. Waterloo, Ontario: Wilfrid Laurier University Press, 1987.

Ueda Yoshifumi and Dennis Hirota. *Shinran: An Introduction to His Thought*. Kyoto: Hongwanji International Center, 1989.

22

The Spirituality of Nichiren

LAUREL RASPLICA RODD

T HE CENTRAL RELIGIOUS change of the Kamakura period "resulted from a new affirmation: that an individual of any social or ecclesiastical standing could immediately reap the full benefits of Buddhist salvation, or such lesser benefits as health and prosperity, through some form of direct, personal devotion to a particular buddha, bodhisattva, sūtra, or saint."[1] One of the individuals who practiced and preached the new religious life was Nichiren, born in 1222 to a humble family in eastern Japan, far from the centers of political and religious influence. When one thinks of Nichiren's role in Japanese religious history, it is the blustering, challenging personality that led to a life of conflict with the government and other branches of Buddhism that springs first to mind, but he himself saw these skirmishes as the consequence of his spiritual life, a spirituality so important to him that he felt the responsibility to work to establish it throughout Japan regardless of the opposition and danger to himself.

As we trace the changes in Nichiren's understanding of his religious role, we are fortunate in the large amount of autobiographical material Nichiren left, material by which we may follow the progress of his spiritual life. Especially in his later years, he wrote copiously to followers, describing and interpreting the events that led him ultimately to the belief that he himself had inherited the role of the bodhisattva Jōgyō (Viśiṣṭacāritra), whose mission it was to protect the *Lotus Sūtra* and to propagate it in Japan. These accounts reveal a man grappling with contradictory religious texts and the turbulent events of his life and times, seeking to reconcile them. Even where facts may be debated, we are left a vivid record of Nichiren's continuing interpretation and reinterpretation of his own religious role and spiritual stance. The focus of Nichiren's spirituality was his personal reading of the *Lotus Sūtra (Saddharmapuṇḍarīka Sūtra)* and his increasing certainty as the events of his life unfolded that the sūtra was a revelation of the destiny of the world and that he himself was reenacting the events told in the sūtra. He came to believe that he was in fact a *gyōja*, one who "read the sūtra with his life."

Tendai, Shingon, and Nichiren

As a young boy Nichiren had been sent to study at the local Tendai sect temple, Kiyosumi-dera, where he learned to pray to the Buddha Amida and the esoteric deities and to understand the basic Tendai doctrines. The Tendai sect is based on a system by which the contradictions in the various Buddhist scriptures are explained as partial truths or accommodations meant to lead audiences of differing abilities to understanding. The *Lotus Sūtra* and *Nirvāṇa Sūtra* are seen as the culmination and the essence of the teaching, but all the other sūtras are also studied and practiced as appropriate to individuals at different stages of enlightenment. The Tendai priests at Kiyosumi-dera taught Nichiren a variety of practices, including Amida worship and the secret esoteric practices. Conflict between his growing faith in the *Lotus Sūtra* and worship of Amida soon led Nichiren to abandon his prayers to Amida, but the influence of esoteric ideas and practice was to dominate his personal syncretization of Tendai philosophy and determine the method of worship Nichiren advocated to his followers.

In the thirteenth century Kiyosumi-dera belonged to the esoteric San-mon branch of Tendai, and the chief object of worship was the bodhisattva Kokuzō (Ākāśagarbha), the central figure of the Taizōkai maṇḍala. This bodhisattva of wisdom vast as space, sitting upright upon a lotus and holding the sword of wisdom and the jewel of cessation of desires, played the central role in the visions and dreams of the young Nichiren, who later wrote: "From the time I was very young I prayed to the bodhisattva Kokuzō to make me the wisest man in Japan."[2] Meditating upon this bodhisattva, Nichiren felt the stirrings of his vocation early in his life.

Nichiren's affinity for the esoteric tradition is clear from several aspects of his thought. The exoteric Buddhist doctrine is that which was preached by the historical buddha and was tailored to his audiences' level of understanding, while the esoteric doctrine is that preached by the eternal Buddha without the use of pedagogical simplifications or modifications. The founder of the Japanese esoteric tradition, Kūkai, had traced its transmission from the Buddha Dainichi to himself, and Nichiren later came to believe that he had received the teaching directly from the Buddha Prabhūtaratna, the eternal Buddha introduced in the *Lotus Sūtra*. The exoteric doctrine states that the experience of enlightenment transcends language, while the esoteric states that a linguistic conveyance is possible via "true words" or mantras. The exoteric tradition believes that enlightenment is a gradual process taking aeons of lifetimes to achieve. In the esoteric tradition, proper practice enables a person to instantly unite with the eternal Buddha-nature and attain enlightenment. In the exoteric tradition sentient beings are classified according to their spiritual capability. In the esoteric tradition all sentient beings are deemed able to realize enlightenment, aided by mantras, works of art, and various mental and physical practices. The esoteric schools of Buddhism taught that one could attain buddhahood or enlightenment in this very body and this very lifetime (sokushin jōbutsu), without having to undergo the semblance of death and rebirth into nirvāna. The means to achieving this enlightenment were mudrās and postures of meditation, mantras, mandalas, and meditative techniques, and the reason sokushin jōbutsu was possible was that all sentient beings already possess an original, spiritually enlightened character (hongaku) that they must only realize. While he did not accept all the esoteric teachings and practices, Nichiren did incorporate a mantra, a mandala, and the concept of sokushin jōbutsu into his faith and practice.

Mantras, mandalas, and mudrās are used to inculcate habits of esoteric thinking. The mantra is an instrument for evoking or producing something in the mind, a holy formula or magic spell for bringing to mind the vision and inner presence of a god. It is used to help the practitioner experience the presence of the absolute, or Dharmakāya. In the mantra one hears the voice of the Dharmakāya from one's own body. Mandalas (schematic illustrations), like mantras, assist toward suprarational levels of experience and are employed to assist students to penetrate levels of awareness. Nichiren chose the title of the Lotus Sūtra as the basis for both mantra and mandala, instructing his followers to recite "Namu Myōhōrengekyō" (Homage to the Lotus Sūtra), and creating a mandala consisting of the title of the Lotus surrounded by the names of various buddhas, bodhisattvas, and religious figures.

In the Tendai tradition there is a long history of title exegesis, beginning in India with Vasubandhu, but developing especially in China. Efforts were made to depict the entire doctrinal content of a sūtra within the title itself. The tradition was continued in Japan by Saichō, Ennin, and Enchin and was the foundation of Nichiren's conviction that all the merits and teachings of the Lotus are expressed within the five Chinese characters forming the title, with mere vocalization of the title being equivalent to chanting the entire sūtra.

Another aspect of Lotus exegetical studies was critical division of the sūtra into halves called honmon and shakumon. The first half, the shakumon, treats of the historical or manifestation Śākyamuni Buddha. The second half, which speaks of the eternal Śākyamuni, was labeled the *honmon*. Each section contains a key chapter believed to express its essence. In the *shakumon*, this chapter is the second, "Expedient Devices," in which the historical buddha reveals his method of teaching approximations or partial truths to lead sentient beings gradually to enlightenment. The essence of the *honmon* is the sixteenth chapter, "The Life Span of the Tathāgata," wherein the eternal Buddha reveals his existence from the beginning of time and shows that the historical buddha is but one of his manifestations.

The theory of original enlightenment *(hongaku shisō)*, emphasizing that all sentient beings are intrinsically Buddha, was influential among all the new movements of Kamakura Buddhism and was fundamental to Nichiren's philosophy. The "emphasis on direct experiential encounter with the Dharmakāya was a contributing factor to the subsequent radically empirical tenor of many schools of Japanese Mahāyāna Buddhism,"[3] including that of Nichiren. "The innermost spiritual experience is not an experience of another world but an experience grounded in this world."[4] The focus on this world and the individual as already enlightened encouraged in Nichiren a habit of introspection and of attention to himself and the events of the life he lived.

The *hongaku* concept was introduced in Japanese Tendai by Saichō and was later associated with the second half of the *Lotus Sūtra*, the *honmon*, in contrast to the *shakumon*, which presents the theory of gradual enlightenment. Nichiren, of course, emphasized the teachings of the *honmon*, as did the esoteric Tendai tradition. Nichiren placed his entire faith in the absolute or eternal Śākyamuni and his words as recorded in the *Lotus*. After Nichiren's death a dispute over the emphasis on *honmon* alone versus emphasis on the two sections equally was one source of division among his followers.

Nichiren's emphasis upon the absolute or eternal Buddha resembles the Shingon idealization of Dainichi. Both represent not a drive to an Other but a search within—for the absolute in both Shingon and Nichiren's thought is actually the ground of one's own being. Nichiren believed enlightenment possible for all beings because they need only recognize their own nature, and, as a result, the world those beings live in, this very world, can be transformed into paradise. He interpreted the concept of *sokushin jōbutsu* on a grand scale, telling his followers often that the nation could become paradise if all its citizens turned to the *Lotus* and its teachings. Conversely, he felt urgently that all other faiths and practices should be cast aside to achieve this end.

Early Study and Convictions

After his ordination in 1237 Nichiren had set off on a study tour determined to learn "all the teachings of the Buddha which had been brought to Japan, all the discussions by bodhisattvas and commentaries by teachers."[5]

But as he studied he became uncomfortably aware of the contradictions among the sūtras and among the claims of each to superiority:

> Each of these sects teaches that certain sūtras and certain commentaries will provide understanding of the whole Buddhist scripture and complete comprehension of the Buddha's meaning.... But my doubts are difficult to dispel. When I look at this world, I see each sect praising itself, but a country has only one king.... Is not the Buddhist scripture the same? What sūtra should one believe? Which is the king of all sūtras?[6]

Finally he discovered two scriptural passages that allayed his doubts. In the *Nirvāṇa Sūtra* he read: "Follow the teaching, not men; the meaning, not the word; true wisdom, not shallow understanding." Nichiren realized that he could rely on the doctrine he learned from the sūtras and that he did not need a human teacher to interpret them. The *Nirvāṇa Sūtra* convinced him of the truth of Buddha Śākyamuni's words in the introduction to the *Lotus Sūtra*, when he announced that he had preached the law "variously" according to the varying natures and needs of living beings, but that he was now, in the *Lotus Sūtra*, revealing the Truth.

As Nichiren read the *Lotus*, he found what must have been a surprising announcement for the students of the historical buddha: "I have preached the Law in many ways, devising many means, but in these more than forty years, I have not yet revealed the truth." In other words, all the teachings prior to the *Lotus* had been teaching vehicles or expedient devices (*hōben*) designed to lead the disciples gradually closer to the truth. The *Lotus* itself is a vast religious allegory: in it the Buddha sits in meditation. Finally a light is emitted from his forehead and spreads to illuminate the ten directions of the universe. This illumination is received as a sign that a great teaching, revealing the truth of all life in the universe, is about to be preached. Each world sends a representative to hear it, and they arrive at the place called Vulture Peak where they are presented with the supreme truth, one large enough to explain the causal law in existence before time began, but yet specific enough to be relevant to the cause and effect of one person's short subjective lifetime.

Nichiren returned home to begin preaching the truth of the *Lotus Sūtra* and to compose the first of his doctrinal essays summing up his religious studies. The "Essay on Attaining Buddhahood with This Very Body"

(Kaitai sokushin jōbutsugi)[7] shows how profoundly he had been influenced by the esoteric teachings. The concept of attaining buddhahood with this body was to become a cardinal feature of his later philosophy. However, his insistence on one truth and one practice quickly antagonized the followers of Amida in his home district and he was forced to flee to Kamakura.

Early Preaching in Kamakura

In Kamakura Nichiren began to attract disciples, including the first whom he ordained himself. The established sects had designated ordination halls *(kaidan)* where new monks were officially accepted into the community, but Nichiren—who was by no means part of the religious establishment—taught that it was internal evidence, strength of faith, and efforts in proselytization and in "living the *Lotus Sūtra*" that mattered, and often he wrote that he and his disciples were priests "without vows" *(mukai)*. Nevertheless, Nichiren believed the doctrine he was preaching was a return to the original Tendai teachings and that his movement belonged within the Tendai order.

To his followers Nichiren explained that all other sūtras were accommodations and preliminary teachings that prepared the way for the *Lotus Sūtra*. He reminded them that in the *Lotus Sūtra* the Buddha Śākyamuni promised that the *Lotus* would be taught to all during the *mappō*, the final age of the Dharma, an era that many in Japan believed had already begun. As he read the *Lotus*, Nichiren chose the name by which we now know him: *nichi* (sun), suggesting the bright light that "lightens the darkness of all beings" (Chapter 21, "Supernatural Powers of the Tathāgata") and *ren* (lotus), for the bodhisattva who rises untainted by the world like the lotus rising from the muddy water (Chapter 15, "Welling Up out of the Earth"), making clear his desire to function as a bodhisattva in spreading the truth of the *Lotus Sūtra* to others.

Like Kūkai, who brought the esoteric Shingon teachings to Japan, Nichiren could not help identifying in part "with an earlier era of Japanese history in which natural phenomena, such as the light, wind, and heavens, were glorified as objects of worship."[8] He believed that gods *(kami)* permeated nature, and he participated in and encouraged ceremonies seeking their favor. Yet both he and Kūkai were intellectuals whose intellectual analytic abilities enabled them to systematize doctrine and excel in their studies. Theirs was a blend of archaic and intellectual, for they internalized the traditional Shinto notion that *kami* were embodied within various features of the landscape and elements of nature. Like Kūkai, Nichiren felt a special tie to Amaterasu, the sun goddess and progenitor of the Japanese people, "who participates in and shares the same reality as that upon which she shines."[9] The estate on which Nichiren had been born belonged to the Ise Shrine, the grand shrine of Amaterasu. Where Kūkai associated Amaterasu with Dainichi, who, as the manifestation of the Dharmakāya, permeates all things, Nichiren saw a link with the eternal Buddha revealed in the *Lotus Sūtra*.

The early tie with the Japanese gods and their continued importance for Nichiren is related to the ways in which Buddhism incorporated local gods as it spread: they were viewed as protectors of the true teaching and of the faithful, and they were sometimes seen as alternate manifestations of Buddhas and bodhisattvas. The latter concept is known in Japan as *honji-suijaku*. *Honji* is the "fundamental ground" or the "fundamental nature" of all things. *Suijaku* is the "trace" or the phenomenal manifestation of the fundamental nature. Chapter Sixteen of the *Lotus Sūtra*, the central chapter of the *honmon*, forms the basis for the development of the *honji-suijaku* theory in Japan. It speaks of the eternal Buddha, who is conceived as *honj,* and the historical buddha, who is conceived as *suijaku*, the emanation of the eternal buddha. In the course of Buddhism coming into contact with Shinto deities, Japanese folk religion conceived of buddhas and bodhisattvas as appearing in this world in the form of Shinto deities to save all beings.

Nichiren, as he became convinced of the truth of the *Lotus Sūtra*, refused to grant other forms of Buddhism even the right to exist. There is no indication that he himself engaged in sacrilegious actions against Amida and Kannon as was charged in 1271, but there is no doubt that some disciples took such action. However, in respect to the native gods, Nichiren was confronted with a problem. Instinctively he identified the *kami* with Japan itself and he was keenly aware of their importance to the masses. Using the *honji-suijaku* theory, Nichiren treated every Shinto god as a manifestation of the eternal buddha of the *Lotus*, and he believed the gods had an obligation to protect followers of the *Lotus* and to punish their enemies as was described in the sūtra. Faced with heresies throughout the land, Nichiren could only conclude that the gods had abandoned the nation and returned to their heavenly abodes. Nichiren's attitude toward the *kami* was ambivalent: he sought their help yet chastised them for neglect of their duties, wavering between resentment at their dereliction and certainty that they protected him and believers in the *Lotus* against evil. This ambivalence in Nichiren's own thought was the source of still another split among his followers after his death.

The very year Nichiren arrived in Kamakura, 1254, an onslaught of calamities began: plagues, droughts, famines, typhoons, fires, earthquakes, political plots and uprisings, and terrifying eclipses and comets. Nichiren,

27. Portrait of Nichiren, painted by Fujiwara Chikayasu in 1282.

with his literal belief that all beings could attain buddhahood and paradise in this very life, looked on in horror. Buddhism seemed to be flourishing. Public ceremonies and services were common; philanthropy was increasing. The common people were more involved in Buddhist practice and faith than ever before. Yet still there was such suffering.

From Buddhism's introduction into Japan in the sixth century, it had been accepted as a political tool as well as a means to individual salvation, as a means to better this world as well as a means to achieve a better state in the next life. Several of the sūtras, including the *Lotus Sūtra*, were known as "nation-protecting sūtras" *(chingo kokka kyō)*. Each of these sūtras promises the protection of various gods to the country that reveres the sūtra. Nichiren dreamed of the accession of an ideal ruler, a wise Confucian-Buddhist who believed in the Dharma and would lead the country to faith. Two obligations coalesced for him: the Confucian duty of putting his wisdom to the use of the ruler, and the bodhisattva course of working for the salvation of all. He set about composing a memorial to the shogunate in which he would recommend the nation-protecting sūtra that promised to be most effective for the times: the *Lotus Sūtra*.

This was the confirmation of Nichiren's sense of mission. He began to preach that the Tendai sect represented true Buddhism and that, during the age of *mappō*, the *Lotus* alone could offer salvation. He announced that the reason the imperial family had been forced to suffer political and military humiliation was the fact that Japan failed to pay homage to the *Lotus* and had allowed heretical teachings to dominate the land, causing the protector gods to abandon it. This was a message Nichiren was to transmit the rest of his life.

In Kamakura Nichiren preached in the homes of laymen or at public meeting places and began to attract disciples as he continued his own reading and meditation. To warn the rulers of the cause of the disasters the country was suffering Nichiren submitted the *Risshō ankokuron* of 1260 to Hōjō Tokiyori, former regent and still a power behind the throne. In it Nichiren argued that the calamities befalling the nation were due to the return to heaven of the protecting gods as a result of the popularity of teachings unsuited to the times. To save Japan, the rulers must put a stop to the Amidist heresy and give homage to the *Lotus*. If no action were taken, Nichiren predicted, foreign invasion and civil disturbances would result. Although he avoided denouncing the Zen sect, which the Hōjō practiced, Nichiren was officially ignored. However, his hut was attacked by Amidist faithful and Nichiren fled the city, returning to Kamakura the following year to resume preaching. The Amidists then appealed to the Kamakura government to have Nichiren charged with slander, a crime punishable by death or imprisonment. Nichiren was exiled to Izu, but Hōjō Shigetoki fell ill and died within the year, which Nichiren interpreted as divine punishment. In 1263 Hōjō Tokiyori died and Nichiren was pardoned and again returned to Kamakura. The next year there appeared a great comet, which Nichiren interpreted as another portent of disaster.

The "Practitioner of the *Lotus Sūtra*" in Exile

During his exile in Izu Nichiren found in the scripture the strength he would need to face persecution for his teaching. He was impressed by two passages from the *Lotus Sūtra* that seemed to apply to his life. In one the Buddha warns, "This scripture has many enemies even now when the Tathāgata is present. How much worse it will be after his nirvāṇa."[10]

The other tells of three types of enemies to appear "after the Buddha's passage into extinction, in a frightful and evil age": "ignorant men," "monks of twisted wisdom, their hearts sycophantic and crooked," and "prideful hermits, who say of themselves that they are treading the True Path, holding mankind cheap because they covet profit and nourishment."[11] Nichiren recognized these among his enemies and felt the prophecy of the sūtra was being realized in his life, that he was "reading" the sūtra with his every action. He exulted in his role:

> For more than 240 days, I have lived the *Lotus Sūtra* each day and night. It is for the sake of this scripture that I was born into the world and suffer exile. It is precisely being born and suffering for the sūtra which is called reading and practicing the sūtra while walking, sitting, standing, and lying down.... Though others who were born as men exert themselves to waken the *bodhi* mind and hope for salvation in the next life, common men are diligent in their practice only two to four hours of every twenty-four. However, even when I am not conscious of thinking of the sūtra, I am reading the sūtra. Even when I am not looking at the sūtra, I am living its words. During the *mappō* there has rarely been a person who practiced the teachings of the sūtra twenty-four hours of the day, even if that practice was without conscious effort, as mine is.[12]

Nichiren had discovered himself to be a *gyōja* of the *Lotus Sūtra*, a practitioner "who lives the sūtra, fulfilling its predictions in his life." Reading in the *Lotus* the story of the bodhisattva Jōfugyō (Sadāparibhūta) who was despised and abused, "beaten with sticks and staves, with tiles and stones,"[13] for practicing the *Lotus*, Nichiren took heart. As he examined his own life in light of the narrative, Nichiren gradually came to identify with Jōfugyō. Soon he was proclaiming that "there is no one else who is punished because he reveres the *Lotus Sūtra*. None of those who claim to keep the precepts of the sūtra have lived the predictions it contains. Only I read the sūtra with my life."[14]

Identification with this bodhisattva and with other figures and events described in the *Lotus* became a major factor in Nichiren's interpretation of his own experiences and the shaping of his activities. In Jōfugyō he found another who had suffered persecution with heroic perseverance. He had read again the portions of the sūtra which promise protection for its propagators, puzzled because the *kami*, who under the *honji-suijaku* theory were seen as bodhisattvas, should have protected him and punished those who persecuted him. By the time he wrote the *Risshō ankokuron* Nichiren had resolved this inconsistency:

> Because everyone turned his back on the truth, and all the people reverted to evil, the good *kami* abandoned the country and left, and the sages departed and did not return. On account of this, evil spirits and demons came, and calamities and difficulties occurred.[15]

While in exile on Izu Nichiren set forth his own analysis of the *Lotus* and redefined what he considered to be his mission on the basis of his religious realization. This later became the basis for the creation of Nichiren sects by his followers. In Nichiren's view there are five aspects to the *Lotus*: the teaching *(kyō)*—the doctrine; the object *(ki)* of teaching—heretics; the time *(ji)*—the present moment of the *mappō* era, the crucial moment for salvation; the master *(shi)*—Nichiren came to feel he must be the master with the responsibility to preach to the heretics, a belief confirmed by the persecutions he experienced, which he interpreted as fulfilling the prophecies of the sūtra; the country *(kuni)*—Japan, the one country where the other four components were present, filled with heresy during the *mappō*, but possessing the *Lotus* and Nichiren, and therefore the chosen land.[16] This formulation was the basis of Nichiren's sense of destiny as well as what has been viewed as his nationalism. Japan was the sacred soil because of the potential it had for reformation, but it was threatened with destruction if it should ignore his warnings. Nichiren's nationalism thus was confined to the dream of establishing a Buddhist state, thereby making Japan the nucleus of a world community of *Lotus* followers, as India had once been the center of the Buddhist world.

The Daimoku, or Mantra

As the number of lay converts increased, Nichiren began to urge them to recite the title *(daimoku)* of the *Lotus Sūtra* as a substitute for recitation of the *nenbutsu* (invocation of the name of the Buddha Amida), which was being encouraged by the Amidists. Like the *nenbutsu* chanters, Nichiren contended that salvation was attainable solely by chanting the sacred title of the *Lotus*. Despite the overt affinity with the *nenbutsu* movement in the choice of the practice of chanting, Nichiren's application is based on Tendai tradition and can be viewed as evolution of Tendai thought. Two fundamental Tendai concepts lie at its base: the theory of original enlightenment *(hongaku shisō)* and the tradition of exegesis of the *Lotus Sūtra*.

The Tendai concept *ichinen sanzen* (one thought equals three thousand worlds) was another factor in the development of Nichiren's thought. Nichiren was convinced that his personal belief that the *Lotus* was to be propagated in his time was in fact the subjective awareness of the eternal buddha of the sūtra. He conceived the universe of the eternal buddha to be revealed within his individual awareness. The metaphysical doctrine of *ichinen sanzen* was expressed in the religious practice of chanting the five characters of the title. Those five letters were seen to contain the three thousand worlds or the absolute. Self-reflection was the means to stripping away layers of ignorance to reveal original enlightenment. And the chanting of the title of the *Lotus* was to act as a medium between ignorant man and the object of his veneration, the absolute within him.

In keeping with the concept of *ichinen sanzen*, Nichiren saw the fate of the individual as inseparably linked to the destiny of society. His effort to realize the ideal world was based on the notion that the evil and sufferings of society could be reduced to the evil and sufferings of the individual, and vice versa. If the individuals could be saved, the result would be a perfect harmonious society. Attain buddhahood with this body and make this world the ideal Buddha-land: this teaching extended hope of salvation to those outside the established church, including warriors, lower-class peasants, and women, as it lessened the distinction between priest and lay person.

The Mongol Threat and Exile to Sado

The year 1268 saw the first threat from the Mongols, who had already pushed the Chinese court into exile and taken control of Korea, seemingly in fulfillment of the prophecy Nichiren had sent the shogunate in 1260. His reputation grew, as did his own conviction of the reliability of his reading of the *Lotus Sūtra*. Again he memorialized the shogunate, adding a preface: "I submitted this six years ago. So far my predictions have proven true. Will the future not bear me out as well? This essay contains prophecy."[17] He renewed his attack on the Amidists, and added the Zen and Ritsu practices to his list of heresies that were causes of the disaster Japan faced. By 1271 the frenzied efforts of Nichiren and his followers to rid Japan of heresy led to a second arrest and exile, this time to the remote northern island of Sado, while his followers were imprisoned and dispersed. The road from Kamakura led by the execution grounds, and Nichiren was convinced that his journey would end there. When he and his guards passed by, he felt a miracle had happened and that he had been reborn. During the exile in Sado Nichiren turned again to the scripture to decipher the meaning of these events:

> As the sūtra explains, "Again and again he will be cast out and many times censured, and by that his grave sins will be erased and he will achieve buddhahood. Therefore, I must suffer. It is through my punishment by the government that my faith in the *Lotus Sūtra* is revealed. When the moon disappears, we know it will fill again; when the tides wane, there is no doubt they will wax. Just so do I know that if I am persecuted, I have virtue.[18]

Nichiren's brush with death was traumatic and after his escape he felt spiritually reborn and found his convictions stronger than ever.

He arrived on Sado in early winter of 1271. Confined to a small abandoned temple during the cold snowy winter, he gradually won converts who helped him survive. His essay *Kaimokushō* includes the famous words: "I will be the pillar of Japan; I will be the eyes of Japan; I will be the ship of Japan,"[19] Nichiren's proclamation of his acceptance of his role as Japan's savior. His reading of the *Lotus* began to focus on the descriptions of the bodhisattva Jōgyō, who had vowed to protect and preach the *Lotus*. Jōgyō was a leader of the myriad of bodhisattvas who welled up out of the earth to hear the historical buddha reveal that he was actually enlightened from the beginning of time and that the life of the historical Śākyamuni was merely a show of expedient means to lead beings to enlightenment. The bodhisattvas who welled up from the earth were revealed to be those converted by the eternal buddha in the inconceivable past, and the Buddha entrusted them with the task of propagating the sūtra in the future.

Nichiren had declared that the *Lotus* was the only true sūtra for the era of the *mappō* in Japan. Now he asserted that, although the historical Śākyamuni was the leader of all sentient beings during his lifetime, in the age of *mappō* Nichiren (who read the sūtra with his life and acted the role of Jōgyō) was the leader of the faithful.

In spring Nichiren was allowed to take up residence with a farm family at Ichinosawa, and his followers on Sado increased. In 1272 a second prophecy of Nichiren appeared to be fulfilled when a leading member of the Kamakura bakufu, Tokimune's half-brother, Tokisuke, was charged with conspiracy to revolt. While on Sado in 1273 Nichiren first created the principal image of his movement in the form of the *daimandara* (great maṇḍala), or *honzon* (chief object of worship and meditation). This was a calligraphic representation of the characters "Namu Myōhōrengekyō" (Homage to the *Lotus Sūtra*) surrounded by the names of the buddhas Śākyamuni and Prabhūtaratna in company with those of the bodhisattvas who rose from the earth to protect the *Lotus* led by Jōgyō. At the next level are various saints and Mahāyāna bodhisattvas. Finally in the lower level are arrayed the Japanese gods Amaterasu and Hachiman and various other deities, along with Chih-i and Saichō. Here is seen the final crystallization of Nichiren's thought. Earlier he had considered himself the spiritual successor of Chih-i and Saichō, but now in the maṇḍala, as the embodiment of Jōgyō, Nichiren stands directly in the company of Śākyamuni. Nichiren had come to see himself as a central figure in religious history, with a mission foretold in the *Lotus Sūtra* centuries before. In 1272 he wrote to a disciple:

> I say that when the two buddhas, sitting side by side in the many-jeweled stūpa, commissioned Jōgyō Bodhisattva, it was as if Nichiren were [himself

commissioned] to propagate the five characters of the *daimoku*. Isn't Nichiren the emissary of Jōgyō Bodhisattva? You also, following Nichiren, as a practitioner of the *Lotus Sūtra*, relate it to the people.[20]

This is the culmination of Nichiren's increasing tendency to interpret the *Lotus* literally as prophecy for his life and times, which he came to see as the climax of the drama unfolded in the sūtra. In identifying with the bodhisattva Jōgyō, Nichiren established a sense of himself as having a uniquely important role in the reestablishment of the Dharma in Japan and the world.

Retreat to Minobu

Facing the Mongol threat, the shōgun perhaps felt he needed all the support he could find. Even prior to the pardon, a member of the ruling family, Tokimori, had sent a sword to Nichiren and requested him to perform rituals, and Nichiren had replied encouraging his faith. In 1274 Nichiren was pardoned and allowed to return to Kamakura, but after a third attempt to convert the shogunate to his beliefs, he retreated to a mountain hermitage to build his flock and prepare for the paradise to come after the heretical sects had been destroyed and all were converted. Mt. Minobu is surrounded by steep peaks and densely forested. To Nichiren it represented Vulture Peak, where Śākyamuni had preached the absolute truth of the *Lotus Sūtra*, and he consoled the faithful with assurances that they would be reborn in the paradise of Vulture Peak if this world were not transformed into that paradise in their lifetimes.

In the winter Mt. Minobu was nearly inaccessible and Nichiren suffered greatly during the first year in the hermitage with a small band of disciples. Soon after Nichiren's retreat to Minobu, in the tenth month of 1274, the Mongols attempted their first invasion of Japan, but were turned back by typhoons. Nichiren interpreted this as a further warning and began to see the Mongols as instruments of the Buddha, "messengers of heaven [who] will punish those people who are the enemies of those who live the *Lotus*."[21] The number of disciples grew, and by 1278 forty to sixty were living on Minobu. Eventually the community developed into a center for lay followers as well, with memorial services and rites conducted for laity as well as for the monks. The famous Kuon-ji temple developed from these beginnings. After a second thwarted invasion attempt in 1281, Nichiren fell silent. He had been ill since a dysentery epidemic in 1278. In October of 1282 he died on his way to the Hitachi hot spring near his old home. He was cremated and his ashes returned to Minobu.

The Legacy

Buddhism in the Kamakura period was moving from a spirituality reclusive in nature and individual in tone to one calling for a "corporate spirituality" in which participation in the ministry necessitated direct involvement in the world; from a spirituality that viewed salvation as liberation from the world to one of liberation for the world. Nichiren participated in this shift as he moved from the concept of spiritual development taught by the older forms of Buddhism with their focus on individual discipline to the interrelated and even interdependent spiritual progress that Nichiren came to envision for himself, his disciples, and all citizens of his land.

Nichiren's sense of destiny and the intensity of his convictions have been transmitted to the adherents of the Nichiren and *Lotus* sects of the twentieth century. Their practices variously include shamanism and semi-magical practices, quest for perfection of the individual through altruistic living and reformation of society, and practices modeled on the *Lotus Sūtra* and the life and writings of Nichiren. Individual efforts to extend faith and practice Buddhism are emphasized. Some sects have emulated Nichiren's sense of crisis and mission, strongly rejecting other forms of Buddhism and proselytizing vigorously. Nichiren's model of introspection and meditation has left a legacy of personal spirituality and faith for all his followers.

Notes

1. James Foard, "In Search of a Lost Reformation," 261.
2. "Zenmui sanzō shō," *Shōwa teihon Nichiren Shōnin ibun* (hereafter *Ibun*), 473.
3. David Edward Shaner, *The Bodymind Experience in Japanese Buddhism*, 79.
4. Shaner, *The Bodymind Experience*, 79.
5. "Myōhō amagozen gohenji," *Ibun*, 1535.
6. "Hōonshō, 1193–1194.
7. *Ibun*, 1–15.
8. Shaner, *The Bodymind Experience*, 68.
9. Shaner, *The Bodymind Experience*, 69.
10. Hurvitz, *Scripture of the Lotus Blossom of the Fine Dharma,* ch. 10, "Preachers of Dharma."
11. Hurvitz, *Scripture of the Lotus Blossom*, ch. 13, "Fortitude."
12. "Shionshō," *Ibun*, 246–47.
13. Hurvitz, *Scripture of the Lotus Blossom*, ch. 20, "The Bodhisattva Never Disparaging," 281.
14. "Nanjō Hyōeshichirō dono gosho," *Ibun*, 327.
15. *Ibun*, 209–10.
16, "Kyokijikokushō," Liun, 241–46.
17. "Ankokuron okugaki," *Ibun*, 443.
18. "Toki dono gohenji," *Ibun*, 503.

19. *Ibun*, 535–609.
20. *Ibun*, 673.
21. *Ibun*, 830.

Bibliography

Anesaki Masaharu. *Nichiren the Buddhist Prophet*. Cambridge: Harvard University Press, 1916.

Ch'en, Kenneth. *Buddhism in China*. Princeton: Princeton University Press, 1972.

Foard, James H. "In Search of a Lost Reformation: A Reconsideration of Kamakura Buddhism." *Japanese Journal of Religious Studies* 7/4 (1980) 261–91.

Hurvitz, Leon. "Chih-i: An Introduction to the Life and Ideas of a Buddhist Monk." *Mélanges chinois et bouddhiques* 12 (1960–1962) 1–372.

—————. *Scripture of the Lotus Blossom of the Fine Dharma*. New York: Columbia University Press, 1976.

Kabutogi Shōkō. *Hokkekyō to Nichiren Shōnin*. Kyoto: Heiraku-ji Shoten, 1956.

Katō Bunnō et al., trans. *The Threefold Lotus Sūtra*. New York: Weatherhill, 1975.

—————. *Nichiren*. Tokyo: Chūō Kōronsha, 1970.

Kino Kazuyoshi and Umehara Takeshi. *Eien no inochi*. (Bukkyō no shisō 12). Tokyo: Kadokawa Shoten, 1969.

Kirk, James. "Nichiren Reads the Lotus." Unpublished paper, 1983.

Kiyota Minoru. *Shingon Buddhism: Theory and Practice*. Tokyo: Buddhist Books International, 1978.

Kubota Shōbun. *Nichiren: Sono shōgai to shisō*. Tokyo: Kōdansha, 1967.

Masutani Fumio. *Nichiren: Shokan o tōshite miru hito to shisō*. Tokyo: Chikuma Shobō, 1967.

—————. *Shinran, Dōgen, Nichiren*. Tokyo: Shibundō, 1956.

Matsunaga, Alicia and Daigan Matsunaga. *Foundations of Japanese Buddhism* II. Tokyo: Buddhist Books International, 1976.

Miyazaki Eishū. *Nichiren to sono deshi*. Tokyo: Mainichi Shinbunsha, 1971.

Miyazaki Eichū and Motai Kyōkō, eds. *Nichiren Shōnin kenkyū*. Kyoto: Heiraku-ji Shoten, 1972.

Mochizuki Kankō, ed. *Kindai Nihon no hokke bukkyō*. Kyoto: Heiraku-ji Shoten, 1963.

—————. *Nichiren kyōgaku no kenkyū*. Kyoto: Heiraku-ji Shoten, 1968.

Risshō Daigaku Shūgaku Kenkyūjo, eds. *Shōwa teihon Nichiren Shōnin ibun*, 4 volumes. Minobu: Minobu Kuon-ji, 1959–1965.

Rodd, Laurel Rasplica. *Nichiren: Selected Writings*. Honolulu: University Press of Hawai'i, 1980.

Shaner, David Edward. *The Bodymind Experience in Japanese Buddhism: A Phenomenological Perspective on Kūkai and Dōgen*. Albany: SUNY Press, 1985.

Suzuki Ichijō. *Nichiren Shōnin ibun no bungakuteki kenkyū*. Tokyo: Sankibō, 1965.

Takagi Yutaka. *Nichiren: Sono kōdō to shisō*. Tokyo: Hyōronsha, 1970.

—————. *Nichiren to sono montei*. Tokyo: Kōbundō, 1965.

Tamura Yoshirō. *Kamakura shinbukkyō shisō no kenkyū*. Kyoto: Heiraku-ji Shoten, 1965.

—————. *Nichiren shū*. (Nihon no shisō 4). Tokyo: Chikuma Shobō, 1969.

Tamura Yoshirō and Miyazaki Eishū, eds. *Kōza Nichiren,* 5 volumes. Tokyo: Shun-jūsha, 1972–1973.

Tokoro Shigemoto. *Kamakura bukkyō.* Tokyo: Chūō Kōronsha, 1967.

———. "Nichiren." *Gendai shūkyō kōza,* vol. 1. Tokyo: Sōbunsha, 1954.

———. *Nichiren no shisō to Kamakura bukkyō.* Tokyo: Fuzanbō, 1965.

Tokoro Shigemoto and Takagi Yutaka. *Nichiren.* (Nihon shisō taikei 14). Tokyo: Iwanami Shoten, 1970.

23

Zen

I. *A Historical Sketch*

PHILIP YAMPOLSKY

ALTHOUGH ZEN flourished in China during the T'ang period and several Zen teachers came to Japan during this time, it was not until the Kamakura period that Zen became established in Japan as an independent school of Buddhism. Three men in particular can be credited with the early introduction of Zen to Japan: Myōan Yōsai, usually known as Eisai (1141–1215), Dainichi Nōnin (died ca. 1196), and Dōgen (1200–1253). Eisai is revered as the founder of the Rinzai school, Dōgen as the establisher of Sōtō Zen. Dainichi Nōnin remains a shadowy figure, although for a brief period he played a significant role in early Kamakura religious history.

Eisai and Dainichi Nōnin

The *Genkō shakusho* (1322), the first Japanese collection of biographies of Buddhist figures, gave Eisai prominence and ensured his reputation as the first to bring Rinzai Zen to Japan, but within the history of that tradition his contributions are of relatively slight account. He entered Mt. Hiei in 1154, where he studied the Tendai teachings, including the esoteric doctrines. He went to China in 1168, where he made a brief visit to the holy places of the T'ien-t'ai (Tendai) school and collected T'ien-t'ai texts. On his return he worked for the revival of Tendai, with particular emphasis on the maintenance of the precepts. He was convinced that Zen, which he found to be the dominant school in China, was essential for this purpose. In 1187, presumably after extensive study of Chinese in Kyūshū, he went to China again, with the intention of proceeding to India, but he failed to receive the

256

permission of the Sung court to travel through Central Asia, a journey that was in any case scarcely possible at the time. Instead he studied Zen under Hsü-an Huai-ch'ang of the Huang-lung (Ōryō) line of Rinzai Zen, a line that at the time was of lesser importance than the Yang-chi (Yōgi) line to which all later Rinzai monks, both Chinese who came to Japan and Japanese who studied in China, traced their lineage.

Having received Hsü-an's sanction, Eisai returned to Japan in 1191, established a temple in Kyūshū, and proceeded to propagate Zen teachings. In 1194 he attempted to establish a Zen temple in Kyoto but met with opposition from the Tendai school on Mt. Hiei, who regarded his emphasis on *zazen* as a deviation. He made unsuccessful efforts to persuade the Tendai establishment of the value of Zen, in the *Shukke taikō* (Essentials of monastic life, 1192) and *Kōzen gokoku ron* (Propagation of Zen in defense of the country, 1198). The latter work is a kind of memorial to the throne. Its principal theme is that the precepts must be maintained in this present degenerate world. Eisai calls for a return to the Zen of the Buddha, for a pure Zen. This is not the "separate transmission outside the scriptures" (*kyōge betsuden*) that other schools of Zen proclaimed. Eisai quotes generously from scriptural writings, but he mentions no Zen works except the *Ch'an-yüan ch'ing-kuei* of 1103 (*Zen'on shingi*) and the *Tsung-ching lu*. These works are not typical Zen compilations: the first deals with precepts and monastic regulations; the latter is a huge compendium of miscellaneous works, some of which are from Zen sources.

In 1199, Eisai moved to Kamakura, where he won the support of the newly established shogunate. Assisted by the shōgun Minamoto Yoriie, he established Zen temples in Kamakura (the Jufuku-ji) and Kyoto (the Kennin-ji). But it would be a mistake to see him as simply a founder of Zen temples. He was a Tendai priest who was determined to restore his school to its former eminence and to revive a strict adherence to the Buddhist precepts. He was a prolific writer, but only one of his works, the *Kōzen gokoku ron*, centers on Zen. The Yōjōryū, the school that he established, is solely in the Tendai tradition. The Kennin-ji, which he founded in 1202, is today a Zen temple. In Eisai's time both Tendai and Shingon teachings were offered together with Zen. Eisai's disciples all taught a combination of Tendai esotericism and Zen.

While Eisai was in China, a priest by the name of Dainichi Nōnin was active in Settsu and the Kyoto area. His school was called Nihon Darumashū. We know little of Nōnin except that he had studied at Mt. Hiei and advertised himself as a self-enlightened Zen master. Since he had no lineage to proclaim, he was vulnerable to attack from the Buddhist establishment.

In 1189 he sent two of his disciples, Renchū and Shōben, to China to Fo-chao Te-kuang (1121–1203), a noted priest of the Ta-hui school of Rinzai Zen, with a written statement of his understanding of Zen. The Chinese master sent back a portrait of Bodhidharma and an official statement sanctioning Nōnin's understanding. In 1194, according to the *Hyakurenshō*, the establishment at Mt. Hiei succeeded in having both Nōnin's Zen and that of Eisai banned. Eisai was enraged that his Zen should be equated with that of Nōnin, and this, according to a recent study, was what inspired him to compose the *Kōzen gokoku ron*, which accompanies the exposition of Eisai's views with severe criticism of the Zen taught by Nōnin. In section three, we read:

> It is asked: some people recklessly call the Daruma-shū the Zen sect. But they themselves say there are no precepts to follow, no practices to engage in. From the outset there are no passions; from the beginning we are enlightened. Therefore we do not practice, do not follow precepts. We eat when we are hungry, rest when we are tired. Why practice nenbutsu, why give offerings, why give maigre feasts, why curtail eating? How can this be?

Eisai's answer is that the adherents of Nihon Daruma-shū are the ones the sūtras describe as having a false view of emptiness; one must not speak with them and must keep as far from them as possible.

Until recently we have had little knowledge of what Dainichi Nōnin's school taught, but several years ago two works came to light that can be attributed to the Daruma School. They are short pieces that give few details. One is known as the *Kenshō jōbutsu ron* (Seeing into one's own nature and becoming Buddha); it details in simple fashion the enlightenments of the early patriarchs and warns against depending on words and phrases. It quotes frequently from canonical works, explicating the essential meaning of seeing into one's own nature and thus becoming Buddha. The second work, known as the *Shōtō shōkaku ron* (To attain to the awakening of the bodhisattva), seems to be intended for ceremonial use, and contains transmission verses and various formulas for salutations.

The text refers to Te-kuang as fiftieth in the line of succession from Bodhidharma of those who have seen into their own natures and become Buddhas; this identifies it as a Daruma-shū composition. The work gives detailed information about Bodhidharma, derived from the most recent Chinese biographical sources, and announces that Bodhidharma's teaching has been transmitted through 618 years until the present year (1189) when it came to Japan. A second doctrinal claim is that all the names of Buddhas and sages, all sūtras, and indeed all things, are different names for the mind, and that sentient beings are themselves Buddhas. A third major claim is that the Daruma-shū has the power to lessen crimes, to produce good fortune, to ward off disaster, and to bring ease and pleasure; there is a distinct coloration of the concept of rewards and benefits in the present life.

The contents of these two books, the comments in Eisai's *Kōzen gokoku ron,* and occasional mention in contemporary literature—Nichiren for example in his *Kaimokushō* specifically condemns Nōnin along with Hōnen—are all we know of Nōnin's Daruma-shū. It emphasized a Zen that made few demands on its practitioners and that catered to the needs of the populace. We do not know what happened to Nōnin. One story has it that he was a member of the Taira family, an uncle of Taira no Kagekiyo, also known as Akubyō, who is said to have come to Kyoto to kill Yoritomo and thus wipe out the disgrace that had befallen his family; when Yorito-mo discovered the plot, Kagekiyo took refuge with his uncle. When Nōnin left the house to purchase sake, Kagekiyo, suspecting a plot, killed him.

Nōnin left one disciple of note, a priest by the name of Kakuan who directed a temple in Tōnomine (present-day Sakurai in Nara). What happened to this temple is not definitely known; it may have been destroyed by monks from the Kōfuku-ji in Nara. Kakuan's heir, Ekan, moved to the Hajaku-ji in Echizen. It was from there that he later led a group of monks to join Dōgen at the Kōshō-ji in Fukakusa. Thus it was that a group of monks, once associated with a school famous for its lack of concern with training and the precepts, was to join the strictly-regulated community established by Dōgen.

Dōgen and Sōtō Zen

Dōgen is today perhaps the most revered figure in Japanese Zen. Founder of Sōtō Zen, he is honored as a religious genius and a thinker of deep philosophic insight. He was of aristocratic birth. His father was a high government official, and his mother was a daughter of the distinguished Fujiwara family. As a child he was given a thorough literary education. But his father died when he was two and his mother died when he was seven. His mother had wanted him to take up a religious life, and despite attempts by an uncle to turn him towards an academic career he entered the Tendai school on Mt. Hiei when he was twelve. Bothered by such doctrinal problems as the contradiction between innate and acquired enlightenment, he went to the noted monk Kōin at Onjō-ji, who directed him to Eisai at the Kennin-ji, where at that time esoteric studies were taught along with a strict Rin-zai school of kōan Zen. Eisai may already have left Kyoto for Kamakura; in any case it is not likely that he would have concerned himself with a young acolyte. It was under Eisai's student, Myōzen (1185–1225), that Dōgen pursued his studies. In 1223, together with Myōzen, Dōgen set out for China. His initial encounters with several Lin-chi (Rinzai) masters were a disappointment to him; he was not able to find a master to whom he was properly attuned. On the verge of returning to Japan, he was told that a new priest had been appointed abbot at the T'ien-t'ung temple where he had first studied upon arriving in China. The new abbot, T'ien-t'ung Ju-ching (Tendō Nyōjō, 1163–1228), and this youthful Japanese disciple hit it off at once. The practice at this monastery was extremely strict, which Dōgen found to his liking. Dōgen received his teacher's sanction, but stayed for a further two years to perfect his understanding.

On his return from China in 1227, Dōgen practiced at first in Kennin-ji, but he found himself dissatisfied with its mixture of Zen and esoteric teachings. In 1231, threatened by the monks at Mt. Hiei, he moved to Fukakusa, south of Kyoto, where he set up a Sung-style meditation hall, the Kōshō-ji, in which Zen practice and the strict observation of the precepts were emphasized. He appears to have attracted only a few students, virtually all of whom had belonged to Dainichi Nōnin's school. Koun Ejō (1198–1280) was the first to arrive, in 1234. He had been a Hiei monk, studying a great variety of teachings, and had become a disciple of Kakuan at Tōnomine. Another group of Nōnin's former disciples, led by Kakuzen Ekan (d. 1251), had gone to the Hajaku-ji in Echizen, which was a center of Hakusan Tendai, a mountain ascetic group, and which served as a refuge for the displaced Daruma-shū school. In 1241 this group, led by Ekan, Tettsū Gikai (1219–1309), Gien (d. 1314), and Gijun (n.d.), came to study with Dōgen.

In 1243 Dōgen suddenly turned over his temple in Kyoto to an obscure disciple and set out for the remote regions of Echizen, with the support of Hatano Yoshishige, an official of the Kamakura shogunate in Kyoto, who offered him a site on the family estate there. There has been much debate about his reasons for leaving Kyoto. The motive—along with pressures from older Buddhist sects—probably was that the Tōfuku-ji, a Rinzai temple, had been established on a grand scale in Higashiyama, virtually in his own backyard. It was sponsored by the Fujiwara family, with which Dōgen himself was associated, and Enni Ben'en (1202–1280), also known by his posthumous title Shōitsu Kokushi, a noted priest of the Yōgi branch of Rinzai Zen, was invited to be its first abbot. Enni had studied in China and gained the sanction of a famed master, Wu-chun Shih-fan (1178–1249), returning to Japan in 1241. He was one of the first of many Japanese priests who studied in China in the thirteenth century, who were, together with Chinese priests who came to Japan, to form the basis for the elite Zen of Kyoto and Kamakura that later came to be organized into the Gozan or Five Mountain system.

In Echizen, where a large number of his disciples had previously studied, Dōgen stayed first at various temples and eventually settled at Eihei-ji, the temple with which he is most closely associated. Although still fairly young, Dōgen was in failing health, and he turned over the conduct of temple affairs to his learned disciple Koun Ejō, in order to concentrate on his writings, particularly the *Shōbōgenzō,* the work for which he is justly famous. Each chapter of this work has an individual title and very often a dated colophon, so we can tell to which period of his life it belongs. Ejō assisted Dōgen throughout the compilation, and may well after Dōgen's death have amplified the text. At the time Dōgen moved to Echizen about forty chapters, roughly half of the work, had been completed. There is an abrupt change in the tone of his writings after this point. He had once praised lay Buddhism and advocated the study of Zen by women; now he found that Zen could only be studied by monks who had left their homes. He had deliberately ignored sectarian distinctions in Zen; now he began to champion the Sōtō school.

Around the time of his move from Kyoto he had received from China a copy of the *yu-lu,* or recorded sayings, of his master Ju-ching. The work infuriated him because he felt that it had been carelessly put together and did not truly represent his master's teachings. He wrote scathingly of the incompetent Sung monks and added rather intemperate attacks on the Rinzai school and the famous Ch'an master Ta-hui. Ordinarily such comments would have brought a quick response from Rinzai partisans; however, they did not hear of Dōgen's attack, because manuscript copies of the *Shōbōgenzō* were handed down in private, and the work remained unpublished until late in the Tokugawa period. Publication of the ninety-five chapter version began in 1796 and was completed in 1811. Dōgen's sayings, recorded under the title *Eihei kōroku,* were given fairly wide distribution and did not contain the violent attacks on Rinzai Zen that are found in the *Shōbōgenzō.*

Dōgen passed away during a visit to Kyoto in 1253. Ejō, who was two years Dōgen's senior, took over the Eihei-ji. Because of failing health he delegated the affairs of the temple to Tettsū Gikai in 1267. Gikai was in charge of the kitchen, an important post, at both Kichijō-ji and Daibutsu-ji, the temples at which Dōgen stayed prior to the establishment of Eihei-ji, and at Eihei-ji he also held an official post. In 1251 his old teacher Ekan, on the verge of death, handed to Gikai the certificate of succession in the

Nihon Daruma school. At that time, the story has it, he asked to be shown the certificate Dōgen had received from Ju-ching but was refused this privilege. When Dōgen went to Kyoto for medical care he promised Gikai that he would show him the certificate and transmit the dharma on his return; but Dōgen died in Kyoto, leaving the promise unfulfilled. Gikai now turned to Ejō as his teacher, and Ejō had sent him to study at various Rinzai temples in Kyoto and Kamakura. In 1259 he went to Sung China, traveled widely and brought back architectural designs for Eihei-ji temple buildings. In 1267 Ejō became ill and turned over the temple to Gikai.

Gikai's appointment was opposed by a faction centering on Gien (d. 1314) and Chi-yüan (Jakuen, 1207–1299), who objected to his attempts to engage the temple and to gain a local following by adding elements of esoteric Buddhism. They claimed that the simple and austere style that Dōgen had established was being violated. This quarrel, known as the *sandai sōron,* or third-generation dispute, continued for five years until Gikai with his followers finally left Eihei-ji for Kaga (present-day Ishikawa), where, under the protection of Togashi Iehisa, in 1283 he changed a former Tendai temple, the Daijō-ji, into one of the Sōtō sect. Meanwhile Gien and Chi-yüan maintained a precarious hold on Eihei-ji. From this time until the end of the Muromachi period there was no communication between the descendants of Gikai and those of Gien and Chi-yüan. Eihei-ji lost the support of the Hatano family and fell into disrepair, virtually ceasing to exist. However, the school stemming from Gikai and his descendants spread throughout Japan, dominating the Sōtō school, which grew enormously in prosperity and popularity throughout the centuries.

Keizan Jōkin (1268–1325), Gikai's heir, is spoken of as one of the two founders of Sōtō and was until recently revered as a patriarch equal in status to Dōgen. Born in Echizen, he became a monk under Ejō at Eihei-ji; he took Gikai as his teacher after Ejō's death. At eighteen he left to study under a variety of masters associated with different Rinzai schools. In 1295 he received sanction from Gikai and in 1302 became the second abbot of Daijō-ji. In 1311 we find him at Jōjū-ji in Kanazawa; in 1313, with the sponsorship of Shigeno Nobunao, he founded Yōkō-ji in Kaga and Sōji-ji in Noto, but soon turned these temples over to his disciples Meihō Sotetsu (1277–1350) and Gazan Jōseki (1275–1366). He died at age fifty-eight in 1325.

It may be noted that almost none of these early Sōtō masters or their successors went to China, contrary to the practice in the Gozan schools. Thus the great emphasis on Chinese literature and the Chinese heritage was largely lacking. A large number of them studied under Rinzai masters for brief periods of time, indicating more a freedom of movement among various Zen temples than the influence of Rinzai teachings. Quite a few Sōtō masters seem to have been associated with the Hattō school of Rinzai Zen that was located at Kōkoku-ji in Wakayama. This school, founded by Shinchi Kakushin (Hattō Kokushi 1207–1298), had many esoteric elements in its teachings. It had the misfortune to have been associated with the Southern court and thus did not survive the displeasure of the Ashikaga rulers in the Muromachi period.

Keizan made no attempt to preserve Dōgen's austere style, but rather sought to enlarge his religious group. As it spread it incorporated elements of old Buddhism and gained a distinct esoteric coloring. Many of the early monks had begun their religious careers at the Tendai stronghold on Mt. Hiei. The area around Eihei-ji was a center of Hakusan Tendai beliefs; some of the temples taken over by Sōtō monks were originally Hakusan temples, and they continued the forms of worship locally practiced. For example, at Yōkō-ji Hakusan gongen is worshiped and the principal statue is that of Kannon, as in other Hakusan temples. Keizan incorporated elements from mountain religions, Hakusan beliefs in Kannon, various local Shinto guardian deities, and ascetic practices of the Shugendō mountain monks. Temples associated with older forms of Buddhism were gradually converted into Sōtō temples. A similar pattern was followed by later Sōtō leaders, with the result that Sōtō attracted members from all schools of Buddhism and revitalized temples as attractive new places of worship. Sōtō also won popular support by the emphasis it placed on public works and services: the building of bridges, digging of hot springs, irrigation projects, the curing of diseases, and the expulsion of evil spirits and wicked dragons. A conscious effort was made to educate the people and render them service.

The few Sōtō sect *goroku* of this period reflect this popular approach; they consist largely of homilies uttered at funerals, memorial services, brief passages, and verse. Written in simple, readable language, they are addressed not only to the warrior class but to the people at large. They differ completely from the elaborate elegance of the *goroku* and other literature of the Gozan temples. Of the seven volumes of Sōtō *goroku* in the *Sōtōshū zensho* and its continuation, only one dates back to the Muromachi (1333–1467) and Sengoku (1467–1568) eras. Although a few Sōtō authors are known for their literary skill, there was little concern with written expression in this period. Printed works used in the temples included such standard Sōtō works as *Sandōkai, Hōkyō zanmai,* and *Goi kenketsu,* as well as books common to Rinzai and Sōtō such as *Hekiganroku, Daie sho, Keitoku dentō roku, Zenrin-ruiju.* Parts of Dōgen's *Shōbōgenzō* and Keizan's *Denkōroku* were in some instances circulated in manuscript.

Until the middle of the Muromachi period a strenuous lifestyle was maintained in Sōtō temples, a style that probably differed little from that of other Zen temples. The day was divided into three periods of work and four of *zazen*. Each year there were two three-month periods, summer and winter, of intensified practice, a yearly gathering of monks from all over the country known as *gokōe*, and an eight-day period at the start of the twelfth month, known as *rōhatsu sesshin*, in which meditation was continued day and night. The practice of *sanzen*, or visiting the Zen master for an interview, had by mid-Muromachi deteriorated. As in the Gozan schools and in Daitoku-ji and Myōshin-ji, kōan answer books circulated widely. Practicing monks knew what answers their predecessors had made and they memorized these answers; kōan practice developed into a fixed form, lacking all vitality. Meanwhile, assemblies such as *gokōe* and *jukaie* (receiving precepts), which were originally designed as aids in the practice of meditation and *sanzen*, and in which as many as a thousand monks might participate at one time, became extremely popular throughout the country. Since the general public was allowed to attend, these meetings assisted in the restoration or maintenance of a temple, and at the same time imparted to the people a general knowledge of the forms of Zen, the practice of *sanzen*, and ceremonial functions. In the *jukaie* a temple would invite a famous priest or *vinaya* master to confer precepts on the people, from daimyō to commoner; with hundreds receiving the precepts, such occasions were an effective vehicle of education and promotion of the Sōtō school.

In the Sengoku period Sōtō was protected by the Imagawa and Tokugawa families and spread still more widely. In late Muromachi the descendants of Keizan's school had begun to take an interest in Eihei-ji, with which they had had no connection since the third-generation struggle. From around 1490 Eihei-ji was named a *kompon dōjō* (basic place of practice and was assigned abbots descending from the Keizan line.

Rinzai Zen and the Gozan Schools

During the thirteenth and early fourteenth centuries Rinzai Zen, with the support of the Kamakura shogunate, flourished in Kyoto and Kamakura. Many of the Japanese monks who went to China came from Tendai or Shingon backgrounds and advocated a Zen tinged with elements of esoteric Buddhism, while others brought back a strict Sung kōan Zen. The Chinese monks who arrived often exhibited the literary orientation of Sung Zen, reinforced by their frequent recourse to written communication because of the language barrier. Zen monks soon gained the patronage of both the

Imperial Court and the Shogunate, enabling them to withstand the pressures exerted by the established schools of Buddhism.

Monks traveled freely between Kyoto and Kamakura, residing in temples built with imperial and shogunal support. In Kyoto, Zen tended to be combined with esoteric doctrines with which the educated courtiers were familiar. In Kamakura, Chinese monks, at the invitation of the Hōjō regents, conveyed a simplified teaching. These early priests were associated with temples in Kyoto and Kamakura that later, in the Ashikaga period, were organized into a temple hierarchy known as the Gozan or Five Mountains, in imitation of a system that had been established in Sung China. A prominent early transmitter of Zen was Enni Ben'en, who had gone to China in 1235 and become the heir of Wu-chun Shih-fan. In 1241 he returned to Japan, bringing with him a thousand books dealing with both Buddhism and Confucianism. At the Tōfuku-ji temple complex he taught Zen with a strong admixture of esotericism. His contemporary Shinchi Kakushin went to China in 1249 and became the heir of Wu-men Hui-k'ai (1185–1260), the compiler of the *Wu-men kuan* (*Mumonkan*; The gateless barrier). Returning in 1254 he established a temple in Wakayama, but was often summoned to Kyoto by the Emperor to lecture on Zen. He, too, combined Zen and esotericism. His school flourished for several generations, but, because it supported Emperor Godaigo during the Kenmu restoration, it was suppressed by the Ashikaga shogunate.

Lan-hsi Tao-lung (Rankei Dōryū, 1213–1278) had studied in China under several famous Zen masters. In 1246 at the age of thirty-three he came to Japan with a group of fellow monks. He was installed as the first abbot of Kenchō-ji in Kamakura in 1253, and gained a large following among the Kamakura warrior class. He taught a strict Zen, devoid of esoteric elements, that stressed adherence to monastic regulations. In 1259 he was called to the Kennin-ji in Kyoto, which he brought into line with his purer style of Chinese Zen. Two years later he was back in Kamakura, but was twice exiled to the provinces because of slanders by disgruntled followers. During his thirty-three years in Japan he contributed significantly to the establishment of Zen as an independent school.

Another Chinese priest who had a significant impact on Japan was Wu-hsüeh Tsu-yüan (Mugaku Sogen, 1226–1286). In China he had a distinguished career, gaining the sanction of the famous master Wu-chun, and later visiting many teachers in order to deepen his understanding. When in 1279 Hōjō Tokimune sent monks to China to invite a learned master, Tsu-yüan was chosen to go to Japan. Arriving in Kyūshū in 1282, he was welcomed by Enni Ben'en, who also had studied under Wu-chun, and went soon to the Kenchō-ji in Kamakura. Tokimune studied under him and built the Engaku-ji, making Tsu-yüan its abbot. Tsu-yüan's numerous disciples were active in developing the Gozan Zen of the Ashikaga period.

Kamakura Zen, associated with the Hōjō regents, and Kyoto Zen, associated with the imperial court and the aristocracy, grew in popularity, especially among the elite classes. As it gained recognition and overcame the hostility of the older schools of Buddhism, Zen came to wield great political and literary influence and was gradually organized on the basis of the Gozan system, which was imported from China to Japan in the late Kamakura period, attaining a fixed form during the Muromachi period. Within this hierarchical ranking of the principal Rinzai temples of Kamakura and Kyoto, each temple had its own hierarchy or line of descent of the temple head or abbot. In addition, the literary schools so prominently associated with the Gozan each had its own lineage, frequently with subordinate or branch schools. Very often famous priests played significant or dominant roles in all three of these separate hierarchies.

When Japanese Zen monks began to arrive in China in the early thirteenth century, Sung Zen was dominated by the school that had descended from Ta-hui Tsung-kao (1089–1163). Many of the Chinese priests who had come to Japan in the Kamakura period belonged to the lesser rival school deriving from Hu-ch'iu Shao-lung (1077–1136). When they in turn sent their students to China it was usually under priests of this school that they worked. The Hu-ch'iu school, however, itself was divided into two factions, those of P'o-an Tsu-hsien (1132–1211) and Sung-yüan Ch'ung-yüeh (1132–1202), and the disputes between these factions were carried over to Japan and underlie certain antagonisms in the Gozan schools. Enni Ben'en and Musō Soseki (1275–1351) belonged to the school of P'o-an, whereas the Ōtōkan school, associated with Daitoku-ji and Myōshin-ji, temples outside the Gozan system, descended from the Sung-yüan school.

By this time the Ta-hui school of Sung Zen had become closely associated with the Sung court, high officials, and the literati. On occasion Neo-Confucianists who had passed the civil service examination became students of Zen, and it is probable that a good number who had studied but failed to pass these examinations also turned to Zen. With the establishment of the Wu-shan (Gozan) system during the Southern Sung the school of Ta-hui took precedence. The Chinese bureaucratic system entered into Zen temples throughout the country, and a highly organized system of temple rank and administration developed. Although the Ta-hui school dominated Chinese Zen when Japanese monks first arrived, most of these monks studied under teachers associated with the Hu-ch'iu school. This school, however, with the appearance of Wu-chun Shih-fan, had itself gained access to aristocratic circles. The aristocratic atmosphere of this Zen held much appeal for the ruling families of Japan, the Hōjō and Ashikaga.

The Ashikaga shogunate, established by Takauji (1305–1358) after the fall of the Hōjō regime in 1333, found this highly organized Zen ideal for its purposes and adopted it almost in its entirety. Not only were its institutions adaptable to the Zen temples of Japan, they also served a political purpose, in that not only the city temples but the provincial ones as well served to add dignity and authority to the Ashikaga house. A variety of measures were taken in order to organize Zen and to promote the interests of the shogunate. Initially, following the suggestion of the Rinzai Zen master Musō Soseki, Takauji and his brother Tadayoshi, beginning in 1338, set up official temples in the sixty-six provinces and two islands. Officially named Ankoku-ji by Emperor Kōgon in 1345, these temples served to emphasize the political presence of the Ashikaga in the provinces and to lend importance to the provincial lords. In addition to the Ankoku-ji, which were all Zen temples, pagodas known as rishō-tō were also established in the provinces. Dedicated to the spirits of warriors who had died since the civil strife of the Genkō era (1331–1333), these pagodas were located within the precincts of Tendai, Shingon, and Ritsu temples and served further to accentuate the power of the Ashikaga. Here the Ashikaga were directly following the Chinese model, for the Sung government had established official Zen temples in all provinces. After the death of Takauji the significance of the Ankoku-ji and rishō-tō was lost, and when Yoshimochi became shōgun they were allowed to wither away. Many of them became designated temples within the newly-adopted Gozan system.

Occasional mention of the Gozan system is found in the late Kamakura period (before 1333). Not until the Muromachi period did it come into full official use. The first mention of it occurs in 1299, when the Jōchi-ji in Kamakura was given official rank. In 1310 three other Kamakura temples—Kenchō-ji, Engaku-ji, and Jufuku-ji—gained Gozan ranking, indicating a certain official acceptance of this system before the end of the Kamakura period. The early rankings of Gozan temples in both Kyoto and Kamakura were often disputed and frequently changed as shogunal preference shifted or prominent priests exerted their influence. In 1334 the ranking was: (1) Nanzen-ji, (2) Tōfuku-ji, (3) Kennin-ji, all of Kyoto, (4) Kenchō-ji, and (5) Engaku-ji, of Kamakura. When the Ashikaga shogunate was fully established, temples were ranked to suit immediate purposes. Musō Soseki persuaded Takauji to establish the Tenryū-ji in honor of Emperor Godaigo (r. 1318–1339), and it was ranked within the Gozan system. In

1341 Takayoshi revised the ranking again, adding two temples to the original five, so that the Chinese model was effectively abandoned and Gozan became simply a means of indicating temple rank. Further revisions were made in 1377 and in 1382, when for the first time the Kamakura temples were ranked above their Kyoto counterparts.

Ranking just below the Gozan were the Jissetsu, or "ten temples." Here again the Sung organization was imported into Japan, also in the later Kamakura period. These ten temples were located in the provinces, and their rankings were frequently changed during the Muromachi period. In 1341 Tadayoshi set up a ranking of ten temples, which in 1358 was revised to provide for an equal division of temples between Eastern and Western Japan. Over the years there were numerous shifts in the position of temples, and in 1380 Yoshimitsu revised the ranking drastically, adding six new temples to make a total of sixteen. Again the original Chinese concept of ten temples was abandoned, and the Jissetsu became merely a temple rank. This encouraged the powerful temples in the provinces to rush to claim Jissetsu status, and their number gradually increased. Around 1486 there were forty-six Jissetsu; eventually some sixty temples attained this rank.

Below the Jissetsu was a further classification of temples known as the *shozan*; here again the Sung Chinese system was used as a model. When the Ashikaga bakufu first gained power it established officials to supervise the major temples throughout the country. For Zen, with which the Ashikaga had an especially close connection, special officials were assigned to administer the temple complexes. Initially officials with a military background were assigned as supervisors, but as the Ashikaga consolidated their position the control of Zen temples was gradually turned over to the priests themselves. With the emergence of Shun'oku Myōha (1311–1388), the central figure in the dominant Musō school of Gozan Zen, administration was consolidated in the hands of the priests. Myōha was appointed head of the *sōroku,* the highest administrative position in the Gozan, and this office controlled all Gozan Zen affairs. The Ashikaga intention appears to have been to control all Zen affairs, including the Sōtō and the non-Gozan temples associated with Daitoku-ji and Myōshin-ji, but this broad central control was never achieved. The *sōroku* was located within the temple grounds of the Shōkoku-ji in Kyoto. In 1383 a temple known as the Rokuon-in was established in the Shōkoku-ji precincts, and the *Rokuon-sōroku,* as it came to be called, oversaw the appointment of all chief priests, passed raises in rank, and regulated all ceremonial procedures. Furthermore, the priests were frequently required to prepare documents relating to trade and foreign affairs.

Among the priests associated with the Gozan are many famous names,

largely of literary figures or of men who were closely associated with the
Ashikaga shogunate. Of these none was more famous than Musō Soseki.
Born to an aristocratic family, Musō entered Buddhism at an early age. A
talented student, he steeped himself in Buddhist texts and also read widely
in Confucian and Taoist works. At eighteen he went to the Tōdai-ji in Nara,
where he received the precepts. Dissatisfied with scholastic Buddhism, he
turned to Zen, visiting several teachers in Kyoto and Kamakura, including
priests from China, but he was unable to find anyone with whom he felt an
affinity. Eventually he came to Kōhō Kennichi (1241–1316), who attempted
to wean him from his concern with scriptural and literary texts. Failing in
his efforts, Soseki spent three years in isolation in a distant province and
eventually returned to Kennichi in 1305. This time he received his teacher's
sanction. Soseki made no attempts to travel to China for study.

Representing a literary Zen, Soseki came under severe criticism from
some of his contemporaries. The diary of Emperor Hanazono (r. 1308–
1318) retails some unflattering criticism of Soseki by Shūhō Myōchō (Daitō
Kokushi, 1282–1338), who held Soseki's understanding to be on a on a
level with that of the teaching schools. Myōchō remarks that if a priest of
Soseki's caliber were to become abbot of an important temple, Zen would
indeed be ruined. Soseki had a tremendous following and had free access to
the Imperial Court and to the shogunate. His style of Zen sought an
accommodation between Zen and the teaching schools, particularly the
esoteric teachings. This set the style for all the Gozan temples and contributed greatly to the Gozan emphasis on literary compositions. Gradually the teaching of Zen became highly formalized as the literary and political functions of the Gozan priests took precedence.

Ōtōkan

Among the temples in Kyoto were some in which a strict kōan Zen imported
from China was taught and where admixtures from other forms of Buddhism were avoided. Chief among these were the Daitoku-ji and the
Myōshin-ji. The type of Zen taught here, known as the Ōtōkan school
(after the names of its three founders, Daiō Kokushi, Daitō Kokushi, and
Kanzan), dominated the Rinzai school from the seventeenth century on,
and is the only form of Rinzai that exists today. The founder of the line is
Nanpo Jōmyō (Daiō Kokushi, 1235–1309). He began his studies under
Lan-hsi Tao-lung in Kamakura, going to China in 1259. There he studied
under Hsü-t'ang Chih-yü (1185–1269), who had close connections with
the Sung imperial court. Receiving his sanction, he returned in 1267 to his

former master in Kamakura. He spent over thirty years in Kyūshū and was later called to Kamakura by the Hōjō as chief abbot of the Kenchō-ji. His teaching followed the strict kōan style of his Chinese master and did not include elements of esoteric Buddhism. His principal heir was Shūhō Myōchō (Daitō Kokushi). Myōchō maintained a strict Sung style of Zen (although he never went to China) and probably was the first to make a systematic program of kōan study in Japan. After receiving his master's sanction he spent some twenty years in isolation, eventually emerging as a teacher. He was the founder of the Daitoku-ji and had close connections with Emperor Hanazono and the Imperial Court. It was he who was so highly critical of the Zen understanding of Musō Soseki.

Shūhō was followed at Daitoku-ji by Tettō Gikō (1295–1369), who enlarged the temple, worked closely with his parishioners, and established branch temples in the area around Kyoto. Emperor Godaigo had given Daitoku-ji Gozan rank in 1333, but this was withdrawn because of objections by other Gozan temples, who pointed out that the Daitoku-ji method of appointing successors to the abbotship differed from theirs. Since the style of teaching at Daitoku-ji differed considerably from that of the Gozan temples it did not receive the support of the Ashikaga bakufu, and was for a while in a very dilapidated condition. It prospered again when Ikkyū Sōjun (1394–1481) became abbot.

Ikkyū is one of the most famous of Japanese priests, noted for his eccentricities. He was the son of Emperor Gokomatsu, but his mother, for unexplained reasons, was required to leave the court before his birth, so he never became an imperial prince. He became an acolyte at five, showed an aptitude for composing Chinese poetry, and gave himself to energetic study. At twenty he went to practice Zen under Kasō Sōdon (1352–1428) at Daitoku-ji and after a severe period of training attained enlightenment at twenty-six, awakened, as the story goes, by the cawing of crows while seated in meditation in a small boat. Ikkyū was a persistent critic of what he saw to be the venality and corruption of the monkhood. His *Jikai shū* (Self-admonitions) is filled with vilifications of Yōsō Sōi (1379–1458), Kasō's successor as abbot of Daitoku-ji, written in Chinese poetic form. Yōsō is accused of trafficking in Zen, of selling certificates attesting to parishioners' enlightenment, of seducing women within the temple compounds. Ikkyū was outraged that Yōsō received the title of *zenji*, Zen master, from the emperor when his own teacher had not received this distinction. Ikkyū himself would have nothing to do with the formalities of Zen. He rejected the highly-esteemed certificate of enlightenment and lived a life of freedom, although he spent the last eight years of his life as abbot of Daitoku-ji. His poetry is collected under the title *Kyōun-shū* (Crazy cloud collection), the name he took as his sobriquet. Many of the verses contain double-entendres or extol a life of debauchery. Ikkyū openly frequented the gay quarters and cultivated deep attachments to women, all of which he speaks of in his verse.

The Daitoku-ji was destroyed in 1468, during the Ōnin War, as were most of the temples in Kyoto. Reconstruction was begun in 1473. In late Muromachi and the Sengoku period branch temples of the Daitoku-ji spread throughout the country, often taking over temples that had once been connected with the Gozan. Meanwhile, a school centering around Kanzan Egen (1277–1360) at the Myōshin-ji was attracting students disenchanted with the literary fads and lack of Zen practice at the Gozan temples. Kanzan was an extremely simple man, living in great poverty. Late in life he became the chief disciple of Shūhō Myōchō, and Emperor Hanazono on Myōchō's recommendation studied Zen under him. Whereas the disciples of Daiō and Daitō Kokushi compiled *goroku* or records of their masters, Kanzan left none, because he refused to lecture and thus left no materials to be recorded.

The Myōshin-ji was not a major temple at first, but merely a subtemple of Daitoku-ji. Furthermore, when the Ōuchi family rebelled against the Ashikaga in 1399, Yoshimitsu, because the incumbent abbot of Myōshin-ji had close connections with the Ōuchi family, confiscated all the property of the temple and transferred the buildings elsewhere, and the monks scattered throughout the country. For a period the temple ceased to exist, but in 1432 a portion of the precincts was returned to the temple, the monks were recalled, and the temple was finally restored. The chief architect of the restoration was the seventh abbot, Nippō Sōshun (1368–1448), who was called to Kyoto from the area around present-day Nagoya, to which many of the temple priests had dispersed. A succession of able abbots who put the temple on a sound fiscal basis and gained the support of local daimyōs throughout the country followed, and the temple continued to prosper and expand. From the beginning of the sixteenth century a quarrel developed between Daitoku-ji and Myōshin-ji, and for a time all contact between the two temples ceased. Because Myōshin-ji was now more powerful than Daitoku-ji, the latter felt threatened and acted in self-defense. In 1509, when the Myōshin-ji was designated by the Imperial Court as a temple whose abbots were permitted to wear the purple robe, the Daitoku-ji, which had already been so honored, protested vehemently, but to no avail. The Myōshin-ji continued to gain the support of the various Sengoku daimyōs and began to take over, one after the other, the Gozan, Jissetsu, and *shozan* temples. Its successes in the provinces also included attracting poets, actors, and other people in the arts, merchants and doctors, and people from every rank. As had the Sōtō sect before it, it took pains to present itself to the common people, to adopt the local beliefs, and to conduct Buddhist services and offer prayers that catered to the masses. The traditional Zen practice that had been so characteristic of the school was neglected, the question-and-answer session was formalized, and *missan-chō*, secret records of kōan interviews, were circulated widely, as they were in Gozan temples. The temples came more and more to resemble Tendai and Shingon establishments, and the spirit and qualities of Zen became more and more difficult to discern.

With the advent of the Tokugawa bakufu in the early seventeenth century, Buddhism as a whole came under strict government control, a system of main and branch temples was established, and all phases of Buddhist life were strictly regulated. The Tokugawa government was Confucian in its orientation and Buddhism was exposed to frequent attack. Though the period is often pictured as one of precipitate decline for Buddhism, it is marked by a creative reassessment of their faith by Buddhists and by an emphasis on scholarly concerns. Zen was no exception. Both the Rinzai and the Sōtō schools produced several figures of great distinction who were able to revitalize the teachings, and either to lead them in new directions or to restore to them some of the vigor they possessed when first brought to Japan.

Bibliography

Works Consulted

Akamatsu Toshihide and Philip Yampolsky. "Muromachi Zen and the Gozan System." In *Japan in the Muromachi Age,* ed. John W. Hall and Toyoda Takeshi, 313–29. Berkeley: University of California Press, 1977.
Furuta Shōkin. "Kangen gannen o kyō to suru Dōgen no shisō ni tsuite." In *Furuta Shōkin chosakushū,* I, 479–97. Tokyo: Kōdansha, 1981.
———. *Zen shisō shiron: Nihon Zen.* Tokyo: Shunjūsha, 1966.
Imaeda Aishin. *Chūsei zenshūshi no kenkyū.* 2nd edition. Tokyo: Tōkyō Daigaku Shuppankai, 1982.
———. *Zenshū no rekishi.* Tokyo: Shibundō, 1962.
Ishii Shūdō. "Busshō Tokkō to Nihon Daruma shū." *Kanazawa Bunko Kenkyū* 20:11–12 (1974).
Ogisu Jundō. *Zenshūshi nyūmon.* Kyoto: Heiraku-ji Shoten, 1983.
Suzuki Taizan. *Zenshū no chihō hatten.* Tokyo: Yoshikawa Kōbunkan, 1983 (reprint).
Tamamura Takeji. *Gozan bungaku.* Tokyo: Shibundō, 1955.
———. *Musō Kokushi.* Kyoto: Heiraku-ji Shoten, 1958.

Yanagida Seizan. "Kūbyō no mondai." In *Bukkyō shisō*, vol. 7. Kyoto: Heiraku-ji Shoten, 1982.

Further Reading

Bodiford, William M. *Sōtō Zen in Medieval Japan*. Honolulu: University of Hawai'i Press, 1993.
Collcutt, Martin. *Five Mountains: The Rinzai Monastic Institution in Medieval Japan*. Cambridge: Harvard University Press, 1981.

II. *The Monastic Spirituality of Zen Master Dōgen*

Tsuchida Tomoaki

ŌGEN (1200–1253) was one of the reformers and founders of Japanese Buddhist tradition as it went through reinvigoration and reform around the turn of the thirteenth century. Along with Pure Land Buddhism shaped by Hōnen and others, the meditation-centered Zen introduced by Eisai and Dōgen helped Buddhist faithful to fathom the transcendental dimensions of human spirituality that Buddha and great masters of history had pointed to. Among the most respected spiritual masters Japan has ever seen, Dōgen continues to command admiration today, and his religious and philosophical thought to merit serious study.

Dōgen's Life

Dōgen was born in January 1200 into an aristocratic family. His father was said to be Lord Kuga Michichika, and his mother a daughter of the chief advisor to the Emperor, Kujō Motofusa. When he was three years of age, his politically active father died, and when he was eight his mother passed away—facts not mentioned by Dōgen anywhere in his writings. Like other aristocratic males of his age, he most likely received an education in the Chinese classics and in Japanese *waka* poetry.

His background would seem to have dictated a political career for him, but at the age of thirteen he entered the novitiate at one of the temples in the Enryaku-ji complex on Mt. Hiei. In 1214, he seems to have visited the temple Kennin-ji in Kyoto, the first Zen monastery inaugurated by Myōan Eisai (1141–1215) in 1203.[1] Dōgen became a student of Myōzen (1184–1225), a disciple of Eisai, in 1217 at Kennin-ji and was eventually confirmed as his successor. In 1223 Myōzen took Dōgen and others to China to pursue further study at Zen monasteries. Dōgen sojourned at several monasteries with Myōzen, and after the latter's death continued to seek out various masters until he visited T'ien-t'ung Ju-ching (1163–1228) for the second time at the Ching-te-ssu temple of Mt. T'ien-t'ung. There he was certified by Ju-ching as a right successor in the Ts'ao-tung (J. Sōtō) line of Zen tradition.

Dōgen returned to Japan in 1227, carrying with him the ashes of his master Myōzen and a collection of Buddhist literature, as well as the great aspiration to convey what he considered the authentic tradition of the Bud-dha-Way. While still at his port of landing, Kawajiri in Higo (present-day Kumamoto Prefecture) in Kyūshū, he wrote a treatise entitled *Fukanzazen-gi*, exhorting people to *zazen*, or sitting (cross-legged) meditation. In the following year, he returned to Kennin-ji in Kyoto, but in 1230 was forced to move out—under pressure from Enryaku-ji, it is believed—to a small temple in the south of Kyoto, where he wrote the *Bendōwa* (A Lecture on Studying the Way). In 1233 he opened Kōshō Hōrin-ji, a new temple where he began to instruct and to write for monks coming to study and practice under him. Among those who joined his inchoate order were Koun Ejō (1198–1280), who was to become Dōgen's most trusted assistant and the second abbot of Eihei-ji after Dōgen's death,[2] and later Ejō's peer Tettsū Gikai (1219–1309), the future third abbot of Eihei-ji.

Over the course of the next ten years, Dōgen was active in teaching and writing at this temple and at Ropparamitsu-ji, also in Kyoto. His order con-tinued to grow until, in 1243, after the completion of the summer retreat, he and his disciples suddenly had to evacuate Hōrin-ji. This time they moved out of Kyoto into a remote place deep in the mountains of Echizen (present-day Fukui Prefecture). The move was supposedly forced on them by Enryaku-ji, the head of all the Buddhist institutions in the Imperial Cap-ital, where it policed new and reformatory Buddhists. (Enryaku-ji was also instrumental early on in penalizing Hōnen and his followers, among them Shinran.) Dōgen himself makes no mention of the reasons given for this difficult relocation or its background. In any case, the exodus from Hōrin-ji was facilitated by a warrior lord, Hatano Yoshishige, who had heard Dōgen's sermon *(Shōbōgenzō zenki)* in the previous year and offered a place within his fiefdom. This was obviously an important moment in Dōgen's life, but it also marks a watershed in the history of Japanese Buddhist tra-dition: for the first time a vigorous, full-fledged monastery for contempla-tive life was established outside of the large cities. The warrior lord sup-ported Dōgen and his order, donating a temple, Daibutsu-ji (*daibutsu* means "great Buddha"), and a set of Buddhist scriptures (*tripiṭaka*).

In his new monastery Dōgen gave sermons and lectures continually and laid out a monastic rule. In 1246 he renamed the temple Eihei-ji (*eihei* means "eternal peace").[3] This was the start of a new Buddhist order or, in

Dōgen's view, the inauguration of the genuine Way of the Buddha in Japan. To this day Eihei-ji is the head temple of the Sōtō sect, one of the largest of Buddhist sects in Japan.

In August 1247 Dōgen traveled to Kamakura at the behest of the lord regent Hōjō Tokiyori (1227–1263), there to teach the lord and others. He returned to Eihei-ji in March of the following year to take care of his own monastery; in 1249, the embodiment of the true monastic spirit that he was, he pledged never to leave Eihei-ji again. His health began to decline from around 1252, and he died in August of the following year at the age of fifty-three. As he was abbot of Eihei-ji, he has been called Eihei Dōgen; he is sometimes also referred to by his posthumous name, Kigen. In 1879, he was conferred the honorary title Jōyō Daishi by Emperor Meiji.

Dōgen was a contemplative monk who insisted on meditation in silent sitting, yet he left many writings behind. The most important among them are the *Shōbōgenzō* (The Essence of the Buddha's True Dharma), which, together with several handwritten manuscripts, still extant, seems to represent Dōgen's original writing; and the *Eihei kōroku*, a collection of sermons, lectures, and comments, recorded and edited by his disciples. In addition we have the *Hōkyōki*, memoirs from his days in China, *Fukan-zazengi, Gakudō yōjinshū* (Advice on Learning the Way), *Tenzo kyōkun* (Instructions for the Chief of the Monastery Kitchen), and a number of monastic regulations to whose composition Dōgen must have devoted much of his later days in order to give Zen monastic life a firm grounding for the first time in Japan.

Dōgen's Buddhacentric Practice

Dōgen's spirituality as revealed in the *Shōbōgenzō* and other writings revolved around three points. First, it is a thoroughly Buddha-oriented practice. The kind of meditation practiced by the Buddha and his followers through many generations is meant to be a witness to the truth of being. Speech acts or verbal communications about the truth between master and disciple are meant to be transcendental, as between a buddha and a buddha; and fidelity to the routine activities of everyday monastic life is understood as part of the pursuit of Buddhism. In short, Dōgen's Buddha-Way is for each individual to realize and embody buddhahood, to become a buddha.

Against the backdrop of the Japanese Buddhist tradition, where founders of sects tend to be the primary focus of veneration (sometimes even eclipsing the figure of Śākyamuni Buddha), Dōgen's spirituality stands out for its focus on the Buddha. For Dōgen the Buddha had lived not so long ago, and indeed is still visible in the great masters. Through the genealogy of the masters tracing their origins to the Buddha, the rightful heirs of succession—such as Dōgen also considered himself—could feel a close kinship with the Buddha himself.

Second, Dōgen's spirituality is rooted firmly in the *Lotus Sūtra* and other scriptures that he felt transmitted the words as well as the spirit of the Buddha. This differs markedly from many a Chinese Zen master who boasted of "heart to heart transmission" and of a position "not dependent on the words and letters of the scriptures" (phrases rarely used by Dōgen) and tended to slight, if not scoff at, the role of scriptural formulations and explanations of transcendence. That Dōgen was well-versed in the *Lotus Sūtra* is obvious from the way the *Shōbōgenzō* is studded with phrases and words from its text. Moreover, he spent his early years at Enryaku-ji, the center of Tendai (C. *T'ien-t'ai*) Buddhology based on the writings of T'ien-t'ai Chih-i (538–597) about the *Lotus Sūtra*. (T'ien-t'ai Buddhology was a religio-philosophical synthesis of doctrine and practice that included Zen meditation.)

Third, Dōgen was emphatically committed to a form of transcendental monism that dynamically united transcendence and immanence (as well as knowledge and faith) in action. This action centered on meditation in the cross-legged or "lotus" position, and in life in the monastery, which, in Dōgen's appreciation, was of a kind with the life the Buddha and his early disciples as well as the great Zen masters in China had lived. Every inclination to make the Buddha or his word an object for one's own use needs to be transcended by acting like the Buddha, that is, by meditating and speaking as Buddha had. (This alone must never be transcended.)

The Meaning of Practice

Dōgen began his quest for truth at an early age. As a rank novice he had his doubts about the meaning of religious ascesis: if beings are endowed with innate Buddha-nature, why in the past, in the present, and in the future do buddhas turn away from the world and seek bodhi? It was a question about being a Buddhist, but more than that, a question about the meaning of a human life that decays and passes away so quickly. Not only the lives of his own parents but the lives of hundreds of people around him were under constant threat during the tumultuous years at the beginning of the Kamakura period (1200–1333). It was a great turning point in Japanese history, when the ancient regime of aristocracy was falling apart. In its place there arose a warrior class under the leadership of Minamoto Yoritomo

28. Dōgen (1200–1253).

(1147–1199), who around 1192 formed the shogunate at Kamakura, far from the seat of the old regime in Kyoto.

Spiritually, too, a new era was dawning for institutional Buddhism. Once firmly established Buddhist schools in Nara and Kyoto, although still officially recognized and supported, were on the decline. For example, in 1193 one of the most highly regarded religious figures of the day, Jōkei of the Hossō-shū (*Vijñānavāda,* Consciousness-Only school) left Kōfuku-ji, the most powerful temple in Nara, disgusted with its moral and religious degeneration. Numerous holy men *(hijiri)* experimented with all sorts of asceticisms away from the large temples. In 1191 Myōan Eisai (or, Yōsai) had introduced a new school of Buddhism from China, the Lin-chi (Rinzai) line of Zen, which, under the patronage of the Shogunate, gradually found acceptance in Kyoto as well. The most notable change, however, was the rise of the Amida-faith movement under Hōnen (Genkū, 1133–1212) and his followers. Despite official suppression that included the exile of Hōnen, Shinran, and others in 1207, the movement spread both among the establishment and among the common people. This idea of faith aimed at a "quietistic" and total dependence on the saving powers of Amida Buddha, sometimes to the point of disregarding Buddhist studies and religious practices, and sometimes even bordering on antinomianism. Objections were voiced to this mass movement, especially by learned scholars and strict ascetic practitioners like Jōkei and Myōe (Kōben, 1173–1232) of the Kegon School. But for all the opposition, a new era was dawning, questioning old ways and seeking a more existential, easy-to-understand religiosity.

In this environment the perceptive mind of the young Dōgen continued to seek an answer to his problem, but none around him was able to provide a satisfactory answer. He went to China in 1223, during the time of the Great Song, as an attendant to his Rinzai master Myōzen. While they were still aboard the ship at Ming-chou (Ning-po in Che-chiang Province) waiting for a landing permit, Dōgen met an old monk of sixty-one years, chief of the kitchen at a temple some nineteen kilometers away. He had traveled the distance in search of a special vegetable being transported by this ship from Japan. Dōgen was impressed by this monk and begged him to stay a while so that they might attend him, but the monk declined, explaining that despite his advanced years he had been placed in charge of this important work in service of the Buddha-Way. Dōgen was deeply moved and realized that not only meditation and study, but even cooking for one's fellow monks, was part of Buddhist life.

Later, during his stay at the Ching-te-ssu temple of Mt. T'ien-t'ung near Ningbo, Dōgen was to meet a similar monk. On a hot summer's afternoon, the chief of the kitchen, a sixty-eight-year-old monk, was out in the scorching sun drying sea vegetables. Dōgen felt sorry for him and asked why he did not let his underlings do the work. The old man replied, "What other time should I wait for?" In other words, the right time to do what must be done is at this very moment.

Dōgen included these two episodes in his *Tenzo kyōkun*, written in 1237 for his own monks at Kōshō-ji in Kyoto, to show not only that kitchen work is an important form of Buddhist practice, but also that to live as a disciple of the Buddha is to embrace the Buddha-Way in all the aspects of life—even in cooking, serving, and eating. In 1239 Dōgen composed detailed instructions for his disciples on how to wash one's face and mouth (*Shōbōgenzō senmen*) and on toiletry (*Shōbōgenzō senjō*), as even these daily tasks should be done in a way befitting a follower of the Buddha. If done religiously, even these acts can help one to transcend the mundane and to see the Buddha.

A phrase cited by Dōgen frequently in his writings as suited to his spirituality is taken from the exchange between the Sixth Patriarch, Hui-neng (638–723), and his successor Huai-jang (677–744):

> "Does one yet resort to Buddhist practices and testimony of enlightenment?"
> "It is not that there are no practices and enlightenment, but that these cannot be defiled."

Dōgen expands on this idea in the *Bendōwa* (1231), an early treatise that is a kind of manifesto written after he had returned from China and settled in a Kyoto temple. In a general outline of his approach to the True Way to Buddhahood, he says:

> It will be a heretical view if one would think that practices and testimony of enlightenment are not one; in Buddha's truth, practices and enlightenment are one and same. Practicing at this very moment is done in enlightenment; thus the beginner's striving in the Way is the whole of the innate enlightenment. That is why we teach not to expect enlightenment outside practices.

Fundamental to Dōgen's Buddha-Way is the conviction that every act as a disciple of the Buddha and the ultimate testimony (of enlightenment)[4] are one and inseparable.

There is a chapter in the *Shōbōgenzō* entitled *Gyōbutsuigi* (Practice is the Buddha's Majesty). The title contains a striking term coined by Dōgen, *gyōbutsu*, which can mean "putting buddhahood into action," or "Buddha in action." The idea is that the moment one knows and comprehends *bodhi* as *bodhi*, one is bound by the insight. In fact, buddhas in the Buddha-Way do

29. Sōtō nuns seated in meditation at Nisōdō, Nagoya, Japan.

not await *bodhi*; only the acting buddha will truly understand the acts in the Buddha-transcending Way. Mere comprehension, no matter how lofty the notions of buddha or dharma that it contains, may be no more than a trap or temptation. It is in this spirit that Sōtō Zen proclaims that "dignified manner *(igi)* is Buddha-dharma, and proper manner *(sahō*, as in ritual) is the tenet [of the Sōtō school]." Each and every act must be regulated to aid in transcendence. Everything one does must testify to the truth of being that the Buddha revealed. All is to be sacramental.

Striving in the Way with Body and Mind Together

Given Dōgen's emphasis on appropriate action and the implied transcending of dualism between the Buddha realm and the realm of this world, it follows naturally that his idea of learning the Way should entail the body as well as the mind and heart. This is just what we find in the *Shinjin gakudō* (Body-Mind Learns the Way) chapter of the *Shōbōgenzō*.

The body-mind as Dōgen understands it has two aspects: it is the whole being of the seeker after truth who follows the Buddha-Way and it is the realization of the true self as one with all beings in the universe. It means that what I perceive as my body and my mind have first to be "dropped" in order for the body-mind to become real. This is what takes place in the learning of the Way, or rather when the Way is *realized* in the body-mind.

(As we see below, this learning of the Way, with body and mind/heart in order to realize oneself along with others, resonates with other Japanese notions of "ways," or specialized vocations.)

This realization of self and beings together ("the earth and sentient beings realize *bodhi* simultaneously with the Buddha-seeker's realization of the truth") draws one's attention to the voices of a stream, to the changing colors of a mountain, to learning from the blossoming of a plum flower, and so forth—all beings disclose and speak of the Buddha-dharma as part of its continued realization.[5] Only in our sin, when we are sunk in idleness without faith, are we hindered from seeing this oneness between our life's truth and that of other beings. Dōgen's Zen opens up horizons on the unity of beings in the universe that are consonant with the traditional Japanese ethos and at the same time conducive to sharpening the aestheticism appreciative of "flower and birds, winds and moon."

Seeing the Buddha

For Dōgen the official certificate of transmission of the dharma (*shisho*: written certificate of master-disciple succession) that he had received from the Chinese master Ju-ching—a Zen practice found in China and elsewhere to verify the authenticity of dharma-heirs—was of utmost importance for him. It was not just a legitimation of his right in the Sōtō line. It meant that in the lineage that begins with Śākyamuni Buddha and continues in unbroken succession from one master to one disciple down to Ju-ching and finally to himself, there was a transmission of Buddhahood that gave him a warm, personal, and direct communication with all his predecessors, including Śākyamuni. This should be understood as part of Dōgen's broader insistence that living and striving like the Buddha enables one to meet the Buddha himself.

The *Shōbōgenzō kenbutsu* (Seeing the Buddha) thus rejects, and the rejection is repeated elsewhere, the tendency in China and especially in Japan to exalt founders of particular sects, like Lin-chi or Yün-men (or, for that matter, Kōbō Daishi [Kūkai] of the Shingon sect, Shinran of the Jōdo Shin sect, and so forth in Japan), to positions of honor sometimes even exceeding that of Śākyamuni Buddha. Dōgen's Buddha-Way was primarily an "imitation of the Buddha," a living and acting as the Buddha Śākyamuni had, in particular, as the Lord of the *Lotus Sūtra*. This seeing of the Buddha as he understood it differed from the Jōdo (Pure Land) Buddhists' visualization of the Amida Buddha, as we see it depicted in so many pictures around Dōgen's time and after. In the devotional practice of calling on the name "*namu-amida-butsu*," Pure Land Buddhists believed that at their deathbed

Amida Buddha would appear with his holy retinue to receive the faithful into his paradise in the West. Dōgen's "seeing" is somewhat more mystical, but it is a mysticism located in the concrete practice of Buddha-like practices and in the interpersonal exchange with one's master rather than in an anticipated deathbed apparition.

Among the chapters in the *Shōbōgenzō* touching on the blossoming of a flower as a symbol of the manifestation of the truth of being there is one entitled *Kūge* (literally, "empty, or illusory, flower"). The metaphor is found in a number of Buddhist sūtras, but it became widely known through its appearance in the *Shou-leng-yen-ching*, a scripture that enjoyed an enormous popularity in China from the eighth century on, though at an early stage Dōgen, among others, doubted its authenticity. In the sūtra, *kūge* (C. *k'ung-hua*), an illusory flower that to the eyes of the deranged would appear in the air, was likened to the search for enlightenment outside of one's own mind, even though all along one is endowed innately with a pure, Buddha-like mind. We are reminded here of the young Dōgen struggling against the kind of immanentism that would eclipse true transcendence.

If, as some Buddhists contend, things around us are empty and without any independent being of their own, so too, Dōgen says, is "innate enlightenment." One has always radically to examine what one believes oneself to be seeing to know if it is illusory or not, to know if it is really seen or only imagined. The flowering of beings, though not necessarily visible to the physical eye, can be distorted by bias and conditioning at the notional level. Or again, in the practicing and progressing on the Buddha-Way, one may find that one is acting blindly, and knowing what blindness means, learn to see oneself as being in this world while ever transcending it. In this way one can see the Buddha in the flowering of beings that coexist with the seer, with the one who walks the Buddha-Way.

Buddhacentric Practice

The question arises, and rightly so, why Dōgen insists on seated meditation *(zazen)* when there are many other approaches to the Buddha's truth. In Dōgen's time, for instance, we see the Shingon synthesis of ritualistic practices, meditation on maṇḍalas, and concentration on the utterance of holy words *(mantra)*, as well as Amida Buddhism's exclusive concentration on the vocal chanting of Amida's name. Between these two lay a whole spectrum of other supposedly efficacious or merit-accumulating acts.

Dōgen's response was simple: *zazen* is the true gate to the Buddha's truth because Śākyamuni the Great Teacher practiced it, testified to it, and transmitted it as the supreme method. Not only buddhas in the past and present, and buddhas to be, but also great masters in the West (India) and in the East have practiced it and attained *bodhi*. What is more, meditation in this posture is the most peaceful *(Shōbōgenzō bendōwa)*.

Properly seated meditation is the core of what has been passed down from the Buddha to his disciples, from one master to another down through the generations, without interruption and without modifications. In seeking to adhere to the Way of the Buddha in every aspect of life, Dōgen even turned to "Hīnayāna" texts dealing with Buddhist precepts—texts that were largely ignored by other Japanese "Mahāyāna" Buddhists—for concrete rules and forms of practice. To live as Buddha did was of such supreme importance for him that, even though he held monastic life in such high esteem, he insisted that no regard should be given to status, age, or sex among the Buddha's children in their quest for truth. One thinks here, for example, of the *Shōbōgenzō raihai-tokuzui* (Bowing and Attaining the Quintessence [of what master has to transmit]).[6] Citing actual instances of nuns and lay faithful being great masters, he writes:

> Those who have attained the truth [dharma] are each of them none other than an authentic buddha, and others should not see in them the persons they formerly were. They see me in a wholly new way, and I see them just as the "here and now [of testifying to the ultimate truth] surely enters into here and now." For instance, a nun who has received and keeps the essence of the True Dharma should receive homage from all ranks of saints and bodhisattvas who would come, do reverence to her, and ask her about the truth. How can a male be superior? Just as the firmament is what it is, just as earth, water, fire and wind [the four elements] are what they are, and just as [material] form-perception-notion-volition-consciousness [the five aggregates that make up the body and mind of all sentient beings of the world] are what they are, so are women. Those who have attained the truth can see this to be so. In any case, what should be respected is the attainment of the truth: there is no point to quibbling about whether one is a man or a woman. This is the ultimate law of the Buddha-Way.

Buddhatā and Attainment

Dōgen did not use the word *go* (C. *wu*; J. *satori*; awakening, enlightenment) as often as *shō* (C. *cheng*; certify, witness, testify). The phrase from the *Great Nirvāṇa Sūtra*, "All sentient beings are possessed of Buddha-nature," has been cited often in China and Japan in support of the idea that all beings are equally endowed with the same potential to become Buddha. This idea, in turn, has tended to reify that potentiality and identify it as the power of perception innate to each individual. Such a "gnostic" view of the psyche would, however, lead to a denial of transcendence, which is why Dōgen considers it heretical. For him, the notion of "all sentient beings" itself already points to a transcendent dimension revealed by the Buddha. All living beings are, through and through, beings of the Buddha. That is, beings are transcendent and ever transcending. They are in transcendence *in act,* not merely in our perception or understanding of what Buddha-nature might be or what enlightenment is like.

The truth that the Buddha and other masters discovered and testified to is open to us insofar as it is realized in and through beings. Our existence, acting, and knowing—that is, our openness-in-faith to the transcendental dimension—is realized in time. Beings are existent in time; they exist as time. The Buddha and other masters are also known by us in time in that all beings are copresent in time and communicate among themselves through the action of the Buddha. As we participate in the concrete action of the Buddha-Way, our existence, just as it is, entails a transcending, a participation in an External Now. There is no turning away from the realization of the Buddha's truth, whatever one's state in life. All beings are bathed through and through with the light that the Buddha's time continually provides.

In this sense, there is no end to the Buddha-Way, there is no fixing buddhahood with words and concepts. There is only continuous, ever transcending life as a traveler on the Buddha-Way, in communion with the buddhas and masters and all beings about us who always and ever speak the Buddha's truth and make it manifest, drawing us actively into it.

To Speak

Dōgen's lectures, sermons, and reflections were compiled in the *Shōbōgenzō* (75 original fascicles, plus 12 new, and 8 or so others). They were written down in Japanese in the form in which he delivered them orally to his congregation in Kyoto and later in Echizen. In those days, most of the formal writings by Japanese intellectuals were regularly rendered in Chinese. (Not only had Dōgen been trained to read Chinese, he was also proficient in spoken Chinese. He also wrote works in Chinese, among them *Eihei kōroku, Fukanzazengi, Gakudō yōjinshū,* and his memoirs of China, the *Hōyōki.*)

Yet, like the Zen masters in China who instructed in the everyday vernacular tongue, Dōgen prepared his lectures in Japanese, since most of them were intended for oral presentation to his congregation. Still, the *Shōbōgenzō* is notoriously difficult to understand.[7] In part this is due to the fact that his sentences are sprinkled with vernacular Chinese Zen phrases.

But more basically, it is a result of his attempt to give fresh expression in his own "language" to the transcendental dimension that the Buddhist scripture and Zen masters' sayings are trying to convey, while at the same time considering the speech acts of bodhi-seekers as themselves acts in and of transcendence, that is, as participatory testimonies to ultimate truth. In this regard we read in the *Shōbōgenzō bukkyō* (The Buddhas' Teachings):

> The realization of the *dō* of the buddhas, that is, of the words or Way [or: the Way expressed in words[8]], constitutes the buddha's teachings. As *dō* is by buddhas for buddhas, [the act of] teaching is transmitted correctly for [acts of] teaching. This is the turning of the wheel of Buddha-dharma. Within the quintessence of this dharma turning like the wheel, buddhas have been realized as such and ordained to attain nirvāṇa.

This verbal act of transcendence pushes words to their limits, almost to the point of violating ordinary Japanese syntax. Even when a sentence makes sense, one quickly gets lost trying to comprehend its connection with what follows. Dōgen takes each phrase, however well known it may be, and pulls it apart piece by piece, turning it upside down, reshuffling the terms, imagining new juxtapositions—all in the effort to rethink it radically. In this way he tries to elicit hidden dimensions of the text and engage his listeners in the search for new meanings that can be tested and validated in one's own life as a Buddha-seeker, leading one toward transcendence.

In wrestling with the words of the scriptures, the buddhas, and the masters of the past, Dōgen has an idea of the kōan that goes beyond what has been formulated into textbooks and employed over many generations of Zen masters in China. Virtually every utterance, every gesture or action made by buddhas and masters, and ultimately even the mountains and waters, the flowers and trees are kōan that can speak of the Buddha turning the dharma-wheel and revealing the transcendent. For example, in the *Shōbōgenzō sokushinzebutsu* (This Mind Itself Is the Buddha-Mind), Dōgen questions this illustrious phrase *sokushinzebutsu* that had been formulated by Ma-tsu Tao-i (709–789) and seems to have been conducive to a certain "mind-only" subjectivism prevalent in Chinese Zen of later generations. Dōgen criticizes this tendency roundly in many of the chapters of his *Shōbōgenzō*. He not only examines the meaning of each of the four characters *soku-shin-ze-butsu*, he even jumbles them in every possible combination to see if this might elicit fresh insight.

In the *Dōte* (Right Saying) chapter of the *Shōbōgenzō* Dōgen says:

> All buddhas and masters have their say. Thus, when buddhas and masters tested buddhas and masters, they always questioned the latter whether they have had their words [say] or not. This question was asked with mind/heart,

with physical action, with staff and whisk, and even with pillars and lanterns.[9] Those who are not buddhas and masters do not question, do not have their say, as they have not met buddhas or masters yet.

One does not gain one's own say [i.e., recognition as rightly testifying to buddhahood] by following someone else, nor by one's own power and strength. If one verily pursues the buddhas and masters and strives to examine them as being oneself a buddha and master [i.e., both in fact and in orientation], one has one's say as a buddha and master. As they have always been in the past, Buddha-seekers are now in the present toiling and testifying to the truth in the [act of] right saying [i.e., communicating or testifying verbally to ultimate truth].

As buddhas and masters strive with might and main to become buddhas and masters [through following them by transcending them], examining and affirming the acts of saying [words] of the buddhas and masters, this saying will itself be a striving and examining over three years, eight years, thirty years, or forty years, and will say it out with all its own might [i.e., the word will bear fruit of itself]. Over so many decades, there is in this case no interruption in one's say [which, however, involves non-saying or striving in silence as well, for the striving in silence is itself an act according to and in the Buddha's word].

In the above passage, Dōgen seems to be saying, in line with his basic approach, that from the moment one sets out on the Buddha-Way one is already testifying to the truth at each moment. The first steps to conversion already entail the last, namely, seeing the Buddha, testifying to *bodhi*, becoming a Buddha together with other buddhas and masters. The beginning and the end are united in living and striving on the Buddha-Way without ceasing. Or, more precisely put, since there is no final end but only constant transcending, as long as one does not deviate from the Buddha-Way or object to its path of life and truth, one is already living as a Buddha-seeker and testifying to Buddhahood, verbally or otherwise, in everything one does.

Dōgen Rediscovered

After Dōgen's death the strict order he had set up at Eihei-ji was maintained by his disciple Ejō and then by Gikai. The monastery remained small, although Gikai opened Daijō-ji (located in present-day Kanazawa, Ishikawa Prefecture) toward the end of the thirteenth century. Gikai's disciple Keizan Jōkin (1268–1325) studied mystic Buddhism and Tendai doctrine, traveled widely around the country, and was active in making the Sōtō sect known. Thanks to his efforts and those of his successors, the sect spread among the common people and eventually grew to a large institution nationwide. Nonetheless, for centuries Dōgen and his writings were revered without being much studied. During the Edo period (1600–1868) several Sōtō scholar monks wrote commentaries on the *Shōbōgenzō*, and in 1815 most of it was published, finally, for the first time. During our own century Dōgen has drawn the attention not only of Sōtō scholars but also of intellectuals in general.

Dōgen and the Ways

Zeami Motokiyo (1363?–1443?), the Noh playwright, actor, and theorist, who together with his father, Kan'ami, perfected Noh *(sarugaku)* as an important performing art, was ordained a Zen priest in the Sōtō line around 1422 at the Nara temple of Fugan-ji and given the name Shiō Zenhō. He was around sixty years of age at the time and had handed the leadership of his troupe over to his son Motomasa. Zeami continued to produce plays and wrote one treatise on Noh after the other. We have no reliable account of the circumstances under which he formally assumed a Buddhist name, nor can we find any trace, in all his writings, of his familiarity with Dōgen's own words. Still, Zeami's writings reveal a close affinity to Zen teachings in general, at least on a popular level.

Zeami is remarkable for his single-minded, lifelong quest for beauty in Noh plays—a notion he crystallized in what he called "the flower" or *hana*. The *hana* blooms and withers in ways that differ from flower to flower, from season to season. Yet there is something common to all flowers that fascinates, charms, and enhances the joy of life. Zeami's aim was for playwright, actors, and audience to construct the *hana* together by pursuing its beauty not only in the performance of a particular play on a particular stage at a particular time, but permanently by approximating the quintessence of beauty, the true *hana*. To attain the *hana* required constant selfless striving and rigorous study, free of all conceits and self-authentication. Through collaborating with the audience in individual plays, the actor will draw near, on a metaphysical level, to the true and ultimate *hana*, and in so doing carry on the Way of Noh. The *hana* and the dedication of one's life to it are consonant with the Buddhist quest for the Way.

Dōgen's emphasis on dignified deportment *(igi)* and proper manners *(sahō)* was heeded not only by Zen monks at Sōtō monasteries, but also honored in the phrase *gyōgi-sahō* (well-mannered activity) in all sorts of traditional *michi* (or *dō*, ways), arts, and disciplines.[10] The terms *gyōgi* and *sahō* entered common speech, bringing a kind of formalism to Japanese decorum and aestheticism. The *michi*-endeavors share the common characteristics of being action-centered (participants performing together, with body and mind engaged in the act), process-oriented (focused less on the result than on the collaborative constitution of the act, aesthetic or spiritual, or the conviviality of performing it together), and stressing an impeccable mastery of form. The way, *michi*, is necessarily a multiplicity of ways in that it involves concrete action in concrete situations and engages the body and mind of the individual. For this reason it can be pursued in all sorts of particular disciplined endeavors or arts. By striving in this way, one is able not only to arrive at the pinnacle of the art one is practicing but also at spiritual mastership.

Dōgen rejected the term *Zenshū* (Zen sect). For him there can be but one genuine, ever-transcending Buddha-Way, and meditation, acting, and speaking like the Buddha is its essence. His was a rigorous yet peaceful way of living in faith. Although some of the traditional Zen Buddhist symbolism that Dōgen embraced—for example, the legendary succession of masters from Śākyamuni down to the present—may be considered "mythical," as today's historical research confirms, his meditation-centered spirituality is remarkably free of historical and ethnic baggage, and points to a universal human quality of faith and the capacity for transcendence.

Notes

1. Eisai had introduced the Rinzai (C. Lin-chi) line of Zen Buddhism from China in 1191 and since then was active in an attempt to restore Buddhism in Japan through Zen meditation.

2. Ejō wrote down Dōgen's sayings in these early years from around 1235 into 1238, and compiled them into a work known as the *Shōbōgenzō zuimonki* (The Quintessence of the True Dharma As I Heard It).

3. Eihei is also the era title (C. Yung-p'ing) in China in whose eighth year (A.D. 65), according to legend, Buddhism was introduced to China for the first time.

4. Dōgen almost always uses the word *shō* to point to the attainment of *bodhi*, rather than *satori* or *go* (C. *wu*). The latter term, however, is addressed in the *Shōbōgenzō daigo* (Great Enlightenment), where the all too common view of *go* as a one-time experience is countered. "Buddhas and masters leap out of the sphere of the great enlightenment *(daigo)*, and great enlightenment is the quintessence that leaps transcendently out of the buddhas and masters." In this way Dōgen redefines *satori* or *go* as an ever-transcending process in and towards *bodhi* that a disciple of the Buddha pursues, rather than as an ultimate end of Buddhist practice.

5. There are several chapters in the *Shōbōgenzō* dealing with this, such as *Keisei sanshoku* (The Sounds of the Stream, The Colors of the Mountain), *Sansuikyō* (Mountains and Rivers as the Buddha's Sūtra), and *Baika* (Plum Blossom), in which the encounter with beings in "nature" helps the seeker realize the truth of the Buddha.

6. This title refers to the legendary episode in which the second-patriarch-to-be, Hui-k'o, was asked by Bodhidharma what he as a disciple had attained; he silently

bowed, thus being confirmed by Bodhidharma as having gotten the very essence (*zui,* marrow) of the Master.

7. See Tamaki Kōshirō, *Dōgen* (Tokyo: Shunjūsha, 1996). Tamaki, a renowned Buddhologist who has long been studying Dōgen in addition to other major Buddhist writings, insists that Dōgen is far more difficult to read and make sense of than any other philosophical works from the West or the East.

8. *Dō* (C. *tao*) means primarily "way," as in the terms *butsudō* (Buddha-Way) or Tao-chiao (Taoism, the Way's teaching), but as a verb it means "to say." In addition, the word was also employed at times to translate *bodhi*.

9. Dōgen has a chapter in the *Shōbōgenzō* titled *Mujōseppō* (Non-Sentient Beings Proclaim Buddha-Dharma). The staff and whisk were used by the master symbolically when giving lectures and instructions; pillars and lanterns were also familiar objects in the meditation hall and elsewhere, representing, in the Zen context, non-sentient beings.

10. *Michi* was a generic term for various specialized, disciplined enterprises and occupations, such as *chadō* (the way of tea), *kadō* (the way of the floral arts), *kendō* (the way of the sword), *budō* (the way of the martial arts), *bushidō* (the way of the warrior), or even Shintō (the way of the gods).

Bibliography

Translations

Shōbōgenzō. Trans. by Thomas Cleary. Honolulu: University of Hawai'i Press, 1986.

Zen Master Dōgen: An Introduction with Selected Writings. Trans. by Yūhō Yokoi with Daizen Victoria, New York: Weatherhill, 1976.

Shōbōgenzō-zuimonki: Sayings of Eihei Dōgen Zenji. Kyoto: Kyoto Soto Zen Center, 1987.

General References

Abe Masao. *A Study of Dōgen: His Philosophy and Religion.* Albany: SUNY, 1992.

LaFleur, William. *Dōgen Studies.* Honolulu: University of Hawai'i Press, 1985.

III. *Three Zen Thinkers*

MINAMOTO RYŌEN

IN A PERIOD OF increasing secularization and intellectualization, three remarkable seventeenth century Zen thinkers reshaped their tradition, each creating a distinctive and concentrated brand of Zen wisdom, which was an antidote to dualistic and rationalistic tendencies in the culture and a powerful response to the spiritual needs of Japanese people of that time. Besides being striking personalities and teachers, these three—Takuan Sōhō (1573–1645), Bankei Yōtaku (1622–1693), and Shidō Munan (1603–1676)—were real thinkers. Their writings reveal a modern Zen that is not only a path of monastic spiritual practice but also a major social and cultural presence and a resource for radical philosophical questioning.

Takuan and the Self

Takuan came from a samurai family. He was a scholar, poet, tea master, calligrapher, ink painter, and teacher of swordsmanship in the Zen spirit of no-mind, and his name is a household word as the inventor of the *takuan* (pickle).[1] Formed in Rinzai Zen at Daitoku-ji, his real teachers were the Gozan scholar-monk Monsai Tōnin (d. 1603), whose library he inherited, and the rugged Ittō Shōteki (d. 1606), his spiritual master, who brought him to that experience of enlightenment that underlies many of the passages we shall be reading. Saddled with the abbotship of Daitoku-ji in 1609 at the remarkably early age of thirty-five, Takuan preferred to roam the country, enjoying nature and art in rural temples. Because of his resistance to pressures on Buddhism from the shogunate, he was banished to northern Japan in 1629. Later he was back in favor. He lectured on Tsung-mi's *Treatise on the Origins of the Human (Yüan-jen lun)* in the presence of the retired emperor Go-Mizunoo. The shōgun, Iemitsu, admired him greatly and summoned him to Edo. He founded Tōkai-ji in Shinagawa in 1638, and his grave there is adorned with a *takuan*-shaped stone.

Amid all these activities, Takuan, as a Zen thinker, was preoccupied with the question: "What is the true self?" In the first chapter of his *Anjin hōmon*

(Gateway to calming the mind), he speaks of the true self from several perspectives. Commenting on Bodhidharma's words, "In confusion a person
goes after things; in enlightenment things come to the person," he writes:

> The confusion that is far from truth consists in chasing after deception. What
> is true is the self *(jiko)*. The self is mind *(kokoro)*. In mind there is deluded
> mind *(mōshin)* and true mind *(shinshin)*. The self is true mind.... The person
> is self *(ga)*. Within the self there is a delusory self and the true self. The delu-
> sory self is a provisionally assembled body of the four great elements. The
> true self is the one true subject *(shutai)* within this body of the delusory
> self.... Enlightenment is enlightenment with regard to the truth. The truth
> is the self. The self is self-nature *(jishō)*. Self-nature is the above-mentioned
> true mind. To understand true mind is to see that mind and nature are one.
> (Ichikawa, 121–22)

Notice the radical theory of truth proposed in the identification of the true
with the self. Note also, however, that there is a true self in the depths of
this self. Later in the same work we read:

> In the self there is the true self and the delusory self. Because we attend to
> the delusory self we fail to attain the path *(michi)*. Even the true self should
> be forgotten, how much more so the delusory one....

> The self is not limited to my individual body, but extends to all living crea-
> tures.... Understanding that the self is no thing is to realize no-self. (155,
> 161, 162)

Takuan identifies truth with the self as absolute subject, as opposed to surface objectifications of selfhood. This absolute subject, however, transcends
self-consciousness and is not confined to what we ordinarily understand by
selfhood; that is the point of the remark, "the true self should be forgotten."

In the *Riki sabetsuron* he writes:

> As soon as there is one thought or discriminative fixation *(nen)*, mind has
> come into being. Nature is that which exists before any thought or discrim-
> ination arises. (Ichikawa, 105)

To break through "the confused or human mind" to the "great mind," the
"Tao mind," or the "direct and unmediated mind," we must follow this
"nature," which appears to be identical with what has traditionally been
called Buddha-nature.

Later, in the *Fudōchi shinmyōroku*, he approaches the issue from a different
angle, referring to the mind that "concentrates on one thing and dwells on it
exclusively" as *henshin* (a biased mind) or *mōshin* (forgetful mind), or even as
ushin (conscious mind), whereas the mind that has expanded to encompass

30. Takuan Sōhō (1573–1645)

everything is called *shōshin* (true mind), *honshin* (fundamental mind), and *mushin* (no-mind), or "the true mind that appears when the mind has no place to abide" *(Diamond Sūtra).* These designations are reached through a discussion of the relation between the mind and physical freedom, whereas in the *Anjin hōmon*, *ushin* and *mushin* are contrasted in terms of the relation between the mind and things:

> *Ushin* is to place things directly in contact with mind, and *mushin* is to exclude things from mind. When things continually take up their residence in the ordinary mind, this is called *ushin*, and when things are always apart from the ordinary mind, this is *mushin*. (Ichikawa, 128)

This state of things maintaining their abode in the mind is called *shinshiki* or *shikishin* (discriminating mind), and he refers to it as "blind thought or blind discrimination." In contrast, no-mind is compared to a mirror, which reflects all things but on which the things it reflects leave no trace.

The *Treatise on the Awakening of Faith* had taught that "the birth of the discriminating mind is like the birth of waves on the ocean due to the wind," and that "true mind and true intelligence" are nirvāṇa: "When the wind dies down, the waves subside." Similarly, when Takuan says that if we understand the true mind, "mind and nature are one," the nature he is talking about is nothing other than nirvāṇa. The true mind is the realm of nirvāṇa (*jakumetsu*). "Nirvāṇa in Buddhism is a symbol for self-nature, the embodiment of the world of dharmas (*hokkai*)" (Ichikawa, 159); in other words, a symbolic expression for the Buddha-nature. The world of nirvāṇa is not one of destruction (annihilation, *metsubō*), but of light (hope, *kōmyō*). When one arrives at this world of light, what is the nature of the psychological landscape that is revealed? It can be described only in the language of paradox:

> When the light of one's mind is revealed, the moon is not the moon, and flowers are not flowers. We ourselves take the measure of and create the moon and the flowers. For an enlightened one, the eye may be on the flower, but there is no form of a flower in the mind. The eye may be on the moon, but there is no form of the moon in the mind. (128)

He expresses the character of this enlightenment-landscape in more general terms as follows: "The world and all the mountains and rivers simply are one dharma mind. The whole of the world of dharmas is the essence of my mind" (152). Here the mind is fully one with the world of dharmas, but enlightenment completely obliterates the discriminated forms of the individual things seen by the mind.

In this emptiness, what becomes of the world of things for Takuan? A careful investigation of the notions of emptiness and seeing is requisite to grasp what is being said here. He warns us against an annihilationist interpretation: "If all people and things are determined to be empty, then since that determinate emptiness is itself empty, it is crucial to avoid establishing the view that simply negates." As long as emptiness remains mere emptiness it becomes a new form of bondage. Emptiness must always be negated. As to seeing (*ken*), it refers to the last constraint or impediment in this process of the thorough emptying of emptiness. We try not to be caught up in the *u* (existent) aspect of the world. But if that desire not to be constrained remains in our hearts and minds, it itself becomes *ken*. Thus he says:

> If one separates oneself to some extent from existents, one is left with non-existence, non-ens, which itself becomes a view. If one rejects *mu* (nothingness), then non-nothingness too becomes a view. Even if one tries to avoid both non-ens and non-nothingness, one merely gets non-non-ens and non-non-nothingness, which is to say another limited perspective, another view. No matter how many times one repeats this process, as long as the

original position remains to any extent, one is constrained by another limited perspective.... View is still present when one has separated oneself to some extent from considerations of existence or non-existence in the normal sense, while remaining a captive of thinking in terms of the existence or non-existence of the Buddha-nature. (Ichikawa, 165)

This penetrating analysis of view shows how delusions become ever deeper as one approaches enlightenment. One who argues for the standpoint of emptiness and remains there cannot be free in the fullest sense.

How is one liberated from this curse of "perspective" *(ken)?*

If one realizes that there are no things apart from nature *(shō)*, and that there is no nature apart from things, then neither of the two perspectives (the denial of existence and the denial of non-existence) will be established. If you try to perceive nature apart from things, you will immediately be setting up such a limited perspective. (165-66)

In other words, the way to free oneself from the curse of limited perception is to view nature through objects. Elsewhere he recommends that one adopt a variety of perspectives in order to attain this realization of emptiness or nothingness through objects, events, and modes of being *(usō)*. He stresses the necessity of staying close to things and events, in both epistemological and practical contexts. As he pursued his two great questions— "What is the true self?" and "What is true freedom?"—Takuan related himself constantly to things and events, dwelling securely in a spiritual realm which he categorically identified with the ordinary world *(hokkai)*.

Bankei and the Unborn

Bankei, born in Hamada on the shore of the Inland Sea, near Himeji, came of a family of physicians of samurai rank. He was a boy of turbulent temperament. Shortly after his father's death, he was struck by the opening statement of the Confucian classic, the *Great Learning:* "The way of great learning lies in clarifying bright virtue *(meitoku)*." His questions about the meaning of this term, indicating the fundamental nature of human beings, became so obsessive that his exasperated elder brother threw him out of his home at age eleven. Eventually his quest led him into the world of Rinzai Zen. He received training in *zazen* from Umpo Zenjō (1568–1653) for three years, then wandered the country for four years, living with beggars under the Gojō bridge in Kyoto and beside the Tenmangu shrine in Osaka. He then secluded himself in a hermitage and pursued his austerities with such intensity that he became critically ill of tuberculosis. But one day, as he spat out a mass of black phlegm, the answer he had so long sought suddenly

31. Bankei Yōtaku (1622–1693).

flooded his mind: *"All things are perfectly resolved in the Unborn"* (Waddell, 10). This was his first *kenshō* (enlightenment). He was twenty-six years old.

For the rest of his life he preached the answer as persistently as he had sought it in fourteen years of hardship. During a stay in the hills of Yoshino, the haunt of mountain ascetics, he first taught the doctrine of the unborn to the local peasants in simple songs. Obtaining formal affiliation with the Myōshin-ji branch of Rinzai Zen, he gave talks and retreats to great numbers of people, most often at the Ryūmon-ji, a big temple built for him in his native village. He worked incessantly to improve the condition of Zen in Japan. His two most devoted disciples were his mother, who became a nun, dying in his arms at the age of ninety, and the nun Teikan (Den Sutejo), a popular poet, who celebrated the last ten years of Bankei's ministry in her detailed diary.

Bankei expressed his enlightened experience in such phrases as "The Buddha mind is unborn and spiritually clear *(reimei)*." He forged a mode of philosophical expression that radically unified three concepts: "the unborn" *(fushō; anutpāda;* the innate), "the Buddha mind," and its "spiritually clear" activity. Of these three core concepts of his mature philosophy, "the unborn" plays the leading role. In later years he deliberately used the term "unborn" in place of the more traditional Buddhist term "unborn and undying" *(fushō fumetsu;* no creation and no annihilation). He claimed that since it is logically impossible to say that something which has not been created has been destroyed, "undying" is redundant and one need only say "unborn." But his concern was not only for logical coherence.

> That which I speak of when I use the term "unborn" is not merely the term that is used in the phrase "unborn and undying." The unborn mind can discriminate things and respond appropriately without knowing or having even the slightest tinge of consciousness.

In this way he was promoting a concept of "unborn" which had all the dynamic force of reality itself and which was not fragmented by consciousness or discriminating intellect, in place of the "unborn" of *fushō fumetsu,* which was imbued with the quality of tranquility and thus was taken in a static sense.

"Since the Buddha mind arranges all things simply by virtue of its being unborn, those who do not consciously strive, but let things take their natural course, those who stand, sit, stay, go, sleep, wake, and act in all ways while remaining in this unborn state, are those that have perfect, unwavering faith" (BZG 87). If one were to replace "unborn" here with "neither created nor destroyed," the passage would make no sense. It is only as the "unborn" that the self can be aware of itself as the Dharmakāya Buddha; it is only when it identifies with reality and is fully active that the *zenkigen* (total working of reality) can be expressed. In addition to this aspect of eternal dynamism, the concept of the "unborn" also displays the character of an absolute source, the fundamental reality which is the basis even for the Buddha, who is taken to be the most universal and ultimate reality:

> Since "Buddha" is the designation for something which was born or delimited, there must be an unborn ground for all the Buddhas. The unborn is the foundation and beginning of all things, and there is nothing more fundamental or earlier. (BZG 59)

In Mahāyāna, *kū* (emptiness) is the concept which is usually said to have all these characteristics, but Bankei preferred the terms "the unborn" or "the "uncreated Buddha mind," probably because he wanted to indicate in the most lively manner the absolute, fundamental nature and the eternal dynamism of enlightenment *(satori)*.

Let us now consider the question of "mind" and its relation to the notion of "Buddha mind" in Bankei. He treated the unborn and the Buddha mind as identical:

> The unborn is the Buddha mind, and the Buddha mind is spiritually clear *(reimei)* since it is the unborn. (BZG 21)

> If one constantly... lives with the unborn Buddha mind, when we sleep, we sleep in the state of the Buddha mind, and when we wake, we awaken in the state of Buddha mind. The Buddha mind is active in all affairs and is never absent. (BZG 30)

He argues that since the mind is unborn it cannot be destroyed, even though the body becomes earth and ashes. Moreover, "All the former and later Buddhas share the same single transmitted Buddha mind" (BZG 46), and "the mind of the enlightened Buddha and the ordinary person are not different" (BZG 128).

In this philosophy of mind the distinction between subject and object disappears. Here the subject and the true self that the subject is seeking are fundamentally the same mind *(kokoro)*. Only when the two are one does the self truly become the self:

> My sect is the Buddha mind sect; there is no dichotomy between the one who sees and hears and that which is the object sought.... The one unborn mind is the master or lord of each person, perceiving color in the eye and sound in the ears. This unborn mind is illuminated fully and without residue through the activity of the six senses. (BZG 133)

These words reflect the logical structure of self-consciousness in Buddhism, not that of so-called objective knowledge in the Western philosophical tradition. Bankei's view seems quite similar to that of Nishida Kitarō (1870–1945), who speaks of the "self-conscious determination of nothingness."

Bankei thinks of spiritual clarity *(reimei)* as the proof of "unbornness":

> While you face this way listening to me now, if a sparrow chirps behind you, you don't mistake it for a crow; you don't mistake the sound of a bell for that of a drum, or hear a man's voice and take it for a woman's, or take an adult's voice for a child's. You hear and distinguish those different sounds, without making a single mistake, by virtue of the marvelous working of illuminative wisdom. This is the proof that the Buddha mind is unborn and wonderfully illuminating. (Waddell, 35; BZG 4)

The attention of the audience is absorbed by the speaker, yet without conscious effort they are able clearly to distinguish the various sounds in the background. The discriminatory function that operates in the unconscious state before there is any differentiation of subject and object, the state Buddhists refer to as non-discriminatory discrimination, is proof that the Buddha mind is unborn, and shows the spiritual clarity of the unborn Buddha mind. What Bankei wants to say here is quite close to what Nishida says about pure experience in *An Inquiry into the Good*.

Bankei's illustrations strike one as a trifle too common, and may be thought inappropriate to the uncreated nature of the miraculous functioning of this spiritual clarity, which is nothing other than the future and eternal dynamic Tathāgata. But they have the merit of rooting Buddhist insight in everyday being-in-the-world. We live in a world of discrimination, always pondering the various things in this world, and we allow our cares and concerns to link together and entangle our spirit, as flies are caught in a web. Yet on rare occasions the power of non-discriminatory discrimination—what D. T. Suzuki calls "spirituality" *(reisei)*[2]—manifests itself within us, and we realize that a dynamic spiritual power is operating within us in all circumstances, and that the human spirit is essentially unborn, unrestrained.

Bankei backs up his auditory illustration of this marvel with a visual one:

> The unborn is like a clear mirror. Since everything is reflected in a mirror, even though you might not want to see it, anything brought in front of the mirror will necessarily be reflected in it. Furthermore, if you remove that reflected thing, it will not be reflected in the mirror, but not because the mirror does not want to reflect it; this is the activity of the uncreated spirit *(ki)*. No matter what the thing in question is, as long as you want to see or hear it, the result is an act of seeing or hearing, not the action of the Buddha mind. That things are seen and heard without one's trying to see or hear

them is due to the efficacy of the Buddha mind. This is what is meant by the "unborn mind".... The spiritually clear efficacy *(reimei)* of the Buddha mind is as different from the function of an ordinary mirror as the clouds are from the mud below. (BZG 65, 69)

How does the spiritually clear efficacy of the Buddha mind so far outstrip the function of a mirror? A mirror can do no more than reflect and distinguish objects five or ten feet away, while the Buddha mind can distinguish a person at more than a thousand feet. The Buddha mind even surpasses the sun and the moon, for they illumine only the earth and the sky while the spiritually clear Buddha mind illumines people through language and makes all people seek the true self. The image of the mirror was frequently used by Buddhists and Confucians to indicate the basic nature of human beings, the most famous example perhaps being Shen-hsiu's poem in *The Platform Sūtra of the Sixth Patriarch*:

> This body is the Bodhi-tree
> The mind is like a mirror bright;
> Take heed to keep it always clean
> And let not dust collect upon it.[3]

Bankei has no equivalent of the last two lines of this. His point rather is that even though the mirror has no desire *(ki)* to see a thing, it will reflect any object placed in front of it. We can interpret the mirror as the unborn Buddha mind, the "*dharmakāya* considered as nothingness," which all human beings possess and which manifests its power spontaneously when it comes in contact with tangible objects. The unborn has two aspects: the hidden *dharmakāya* nature which is the root of all things, and dynamic adaptability or the power of the total working *(zenkigensei)* which manifests itself on these occasions.

It is instructive to examine the interchange between Bankei and his audience on the concept of the unborn. For most people of the time Bankei's doctrine of the unborn was nothing more than an affirmation, overly simple and without substance. In fact one of the priests to whom Bankei was lecturing stated his puzzlement quite clearly. He said that, as he understood it the injunction to be as the unborn could be thought of in terms of "emptiness," but if this is correct then it seems that indifference *(muki)* would become a serious problem. The term *muki* here means a total negation of human feeling *(jōnen)* and sensation *(kankaku)*. Bankei replied, "If someone should suddenly thrust a flame at you from the rear when you are intently listening to me speak, you would surely feel the heat, wouldn't you?" The priest agreed that he would, and Bankei continued:

Well, then, that would not be emptiness. Can something that is sensed as hot be utterly neutral or mere emptiness? Could you be utterly indifferent? Clearly not, you would sense it as heat, not nothingness. The Buddha mind is not mere emptiness, it is to know heat and cold without consciously trying to perceive or know. (BZG 25)

This too is an explanation of the spiritual activity and total working *(zenki-gensei)* of the unborn Buddha mind.

Bankei stresses the uniqueness of his "unborn" Zen:

Because even in China ... the true tradition of the unborn has not been transmitted, one can these days not find any instances of it; and there is nothing written in the records *(goroku)* about the unborn Buddha mind. (BZG 72)

In the records of the Buddhist patriarchs the word "unborn" does appear, but the old masters did not use this single term to refer to all living things. Since the time of the Buddha no one but I have used it as the sole key to practice. (BZG 286)

Whatever the validity of this bold claim from the historical point of view, it seems that Bankei's Zen, despite its simple form, captured the essence of Mahāyāna teaching in an orthodox fashion. It is a self-awareness of the *dharmakāya* and an absolute affirmation of the self based on that.

However, it is clear that our actual daily lives do not reach that state, and thus while on the one hand he states, "The self is the true unborn just as it is" (BZG 130), he will on the other hand claim that this awareness is to be attained through "self-criticism," instead of through meditation on Zen kōans. What is of particular interest in this form of Zen is the notion of the liberation of the self from illusion *(mayoi)* and dualistic thought or fixations *(nen)*. Bankei thought illusion arose because of "selfish desire" and "favoring oneself." Accordingly, he argues, it is not innate in humans. Only the Buddha mind is inborn or innate, and illusion exists only when one allows oneself to be deluded. After birth we learn, through both sight and sound, various illusions, and build our own prejudiced, tendentious personalities. We then come to think of these traits as the fundamental nature of human beings. Sometimes we go so far as to place a high value on these illusions and take pride in them. This is simply a perversion of the human spirit, and Bankei declares that no matter how grand and exalted an illusion may appear, no one could be stupid enough to prefer it to the one Buddha mind.

The most central of Bankei's arguments on the question of illusion concerns *nen* (discriminative fixation). In Buddhist philosophy, *nen* refers generally to the process of remembering or, on occasion, to deliberation and rational thought. It also refers to what is created by these fundamental

processes, that is, to our attempts to make sure that something is committed to memory so it will not be forgotten, and even to that instant when
the mind's activities are minimal. Bankei says that *nen* (fixations) are images
of things seen and heard, reflected on our mental screen in accordance with
the actual experience of visual and auditory phenomena (BZG 32-33). This
is a conception of *nen* that could have come directly from Yogācāra.

He does not say that *nen* are bad; his concern is rather with the way people relate to these fixations. If someone becomes concerned about a particular fixation or image and tries to struggle free, he may succeed; but it well
immediately be replaced by another. If people become caught up in such
fixations and thereby engender cravings, anger, and stupidity, they will be
reborn in one of the three lower realms: hell, the world of hungry ghosts,
or the world of beasts. If they should try to put an end to these fixations,
he argues, it will avail them little, for

> As soon as they have the notion of trying to stop this endless generation of
> fixations, they give birth to another. To use an analogy, it is like trying to use
> blood to wash out a bloodstain. Even if the earlier blood is washed away it
> will be replaced by the later and the red spot will never disappear. (BZG 63)

What then should we do if we have fallen into such a trap? Bankei advises:

> Even if one should become angry all of a sudden, almost without realizing it,
> or if one should be attacked by depression or cravings, there is a solution. If
> one handles these as they come, without piling on new fixations and without
> becoming attached, that is, if one detaches oneself, neither trying to prevent
> nor trying to encourage further thought,... they will certainly stop of them-
> selves.... One mind continues to be one mind, unfragmented. (BZG 63)

This little speech is quite sensitive and refreshing, like a hand scratching an
itch. It reveals that Bankei was extremely concerned with the problem of
"mental cramps" in the process of searching for enlightenment. How
important this is appears in his next remark:

> When one does not hang on to those fixations and neither tries to eliminate
> them nor attempts to continue them, this is the state I call the unborn Bud-
> dha mind. (BZG 65)

As long as people insist on these fixations, they will be eternally bound to
the wheel of karma, ever repeating the cycle of birth and death: "If someone cannot detach from cravings and attain the wondrous wisdom, they
will create karma keeping them on the wheel of life and death" (BZG 138).
For Bankei, it was the aim of Zen to bring about release from craving and
the attainment of "wondrous wisdom," as which he details as follows:

This wondrous wisdom is detached from views of existence and non-existence, and there is nothing it cannot penetrate. It is like a bright mirror that clearly and distinctly reflects all things as they are. This being the case, how could any discrimination arise? Discriminations are necessary because there is confusion and uncertainty. Once one achieves non-discriminatory wisdom, this wisdom will fully illumine all things before dualistic thought has a chance to begin, and thus there will be no confusion. Thus it is that we hold this wondrous wisdom in such high regard, and why we say that the *zazen* of unborn wondrous wisdom is the highest form of practice. (BZG 139)

Bankei's Zen has a psychological emphasis that contrasts with the logical turn of Takuan's thought. Yet both agree on the necessity of detaching from dualistic knowledge, which involves thinking in terms of objects, to live in world of non-dualistic wisdom. Bankei's interpretation of Zen is surprisingly simple and direct, especially since most of us amateurs expect that Zen masters will express themselves in translogical and recondite terms. Bankei stresses the fundamental unity of the everyday world and the absolute, but this does not necessarily make it any easier for an ordinary practitioner to make Bankei's "unborn Zen" his own. Its very simplicity seems to have become the greatest stumbling block for many. Nonetheless, according to the *Record of the Great Master Bankei*, in addition to those who specialized in Zen practice, "over fifty thousand people, ranging from the highest levels of the aristocracy to lower-class warriors, women, and townspeople, pledged themselves as his disciples"—a testimony to the level of religious consciousness in the mid-Edo period. After his death his doctrines were used by Tejima Tōan (1718–1786), a disciple of Ishida Baigan, in the development of Ishida's Shingaku, or Philosophy of the Heart.[4]

Shidō Munan and the Mind

Shidō Munan, the former commander of a way station at the Battle of Sekigahara who became a Zen monk at the age of fifty, speaks of enlightenment (*satori*) as the "original mind" or the "real heart" (*honshin*) or as "one's own heart" (*waga kokoro*). In explanation of this notion of original mind he merely says that "it is treasure worth more than heaven and earth" and that "it is not any one thing (*muichibutsu*)." "With further practice, the body, fixations, knowing, and not knowing should all disappear."[5] His "not any one thing" is moving to a state of "no-mind" (empty mind; mental openness). He takes enlightenment to be the starting point of Zen, yet he also is careful to point out the danger involved in enlightenment: "Enlightenment is the Buddha's greatest enemy." What he seems to be saying here is that a person may reach enlightenment of a sort, achieve a state of indifference (*muki*) that puts one beyond considerations of good and evil, but if that person still has a smidgen of self-consciousness, he may succumb to a pride that leads him to protect a self-centered lifestyle. It is clear that he was concerned with self-criticism in the practice of Zen.

If pitfalls of this sort are to be found on the path to enlightenment, how can one avoid them? Munan maintains that what is important is that after enlightenment one stresses practical application and observance (*risenkufū*), which concretely means a thoroughgoing self-denial in the world of ordinary behavior. He speaks of this in some detail in *Dōka* (Songs of the Way):

> Kill, kill, kill your self, only when it has died and nothing is left can you
>   become a teacher of men.
> What remains after the self or body has been thoroughly exterminated is
>   called the Buddha.
> When one has thoroughly and utterly died (to oneself), free and sponta-
>   neous activity appears.

What emerges as a result of such thoroughgoing self-denial and rejection of the ego is "heart or mind" (*kokoro*) or "original mind" (*honshin*), and this is ultimately "Buddha." For Munan the heart is the truth of truths, but since it exhausts mere verbal truth he tries to explain the experience of *kokoro* or *honshin* through a discussion of its relation with "fixations" (*nen*), "body" (self), "things," and "selfish ego" (*jikoshin*). A fixation (*nen*) is a "petrifaction of *kokoro*." Just as ice is the same substance as water but in a different form, so when *kokoro* hardens it loses its essential flexibility. He contrasts the "evil" of the body with the "purity" of the heart: "The Buddha is *kokoro* and hell is the body. Expose the evil of the body to the Buddha and when you have done so it will be purified."[6]

Clearly Shidō Munan's is a philosophy that doggedly concentrates on the heart or mind (*kokoro*), and this is also reflected in the way he speaks about "things." Thus he says: "It is easy to avoid things but difficult to be such that they avoid you."[7] "Things" here refers to external objects or circumstances, which lead us astray. It is possible to rid oneself of those, but it is no easy thing to live in such a way that distractions do not come upon us. Munan thought that if we could free ourselves from fixations, renounce our concern for our bodies and our little selves, and thoroughly become one with *kokoro*, then we could indeed reach that state of complete tranquility. A heart thoroughly become heart and nothing else is what he called *honshin*, and it has purified itself completely of any taint of self-mind (*jikoshin*).

Such a mind is identical with "Buddha," and this "Buddha" "neither goes thither nor remains here. There is no *nen* and it is identified with the void."[8] Yet the self which is originally the Buddha that is one with the void must, as long as it lives in this world, respond to a variety of things and be limited in a multiplicity of ways. What is the lifestyle of such a Buddha? Such a one, he says, "acts in accord with affirmation and negation but remains aloof; abides amidst desire but remains aloof; dies without dying; lives without living; sees without seeing and hears without hearing; moves without moving; seeks without searching; receives criticism without attachment; and falls into the karmic cycle without producing karmic effects."[9]

Shidō Munan's Zen, centered on *kokoro*, was a world that transcended value judgments, where "good and evil, correct and incorrect had no place," a world of pure spirituality. This spirituality was to be realized through a thoroughgoing self-criticism. His Zen was simple, clear, and easily understood, but also very deep and rewarding, all in all an accurate reflection of his personality. I should like to add that in consonance with this emphasis on *kokoro*, Munan proclaimed the ultimate identity of the three belief systems: Buddhism, Confucianism, and Shinto.

Conclusion

Each of the three famous Zen masters we have studied was trying to give an answer from the Buddhist viewpoint to fundamental questions of the human condition like: "What is a human being?" "What is the self?" and "What is human freedom?" Each had his original style of expressing the spiritual vision of Zen in the new context of Tokugawa culture: Takuan centered everything about the question of the self; Bankei preached "unborn Zen" and tried to uncover a fundamental realm of the "unborn" that would be the ground for even the Buddha, while showing that living naturally (*sono mama no ikizama*, BZG 63)—living itself when uncluttered by external influences—was the essence of the "unborn"; and Shidō Munan concentrated on the realm of the heart or mind and identified *kokoro* with the Buddha.

All three believed that the self could realize its true nature, reveal the true self, through pulverizing the "selfish desire" (*gasho*) that prevents the heart or mind (*kokoro*) from being itself and acting naturally. It must be admitted that in terms of its relation to actual social conditions their spirituality was limited by its incapacity to overcome the premodern character of their society. Yet the core of their spiritual vision—their conviction that it is only by thoroughgoing rejection of the "selfish, narrow self" that human beings can realize the true self and taste true freedom—has manifest relevance even for today's society.

Notes

1. For Takuan's cultural achievements, see D. T. Suzuki, *Zen and Japanese Culture* (Princeton University Press, 1959). Another Zen cultural hero of this time is the fiercely independent Suzuki Shōsan (1579–1655), who was close to the Sōtō school; see Winston L. King, *Death Was His Kōan: The Samurai-Zen of Suzuki Shōsan* (Berkeley: Asian Humanities Press, 1986) and *Zen and the Way of the Sword* (Oxford University Press, 1993). Takuan's achievements bring to mind his predecessor as abbot of Daitoku-ji two centuries earlier, the astonishing Ikkyū Sōjun (1394–1481); see Sonja Arntzen, *Ikkyū and the Crazy Cloud Anthology* (Tokyo: University of Tokyo Press, 1973); Jon Carter Covell, *Unraveling Zen's Red Thread: Ikkyū's Controversial Way* (Elizabeth, NJ: Hollym International., 1980); James H. Sanford, *Zen Man Ikkyū* (Chico, CA: Scholars Press, 1981).

2. Suzuki Daisetsu, *Nihonteki reisei* (Japanese spirituality), *Suzuki Daisetsu zenshū*, vol. 8 (Tokyo: Iwanami).

3. In D. T. Suzuki, *The Zen Doctrine of No-mind*, 179.

4. See Minamoto Ryōen, "Bankei Zenji to Tejima Tōan" (Zen Master Bankei and Tejima Tōan), *Shunjū* 155/104 (1974–1975).

5. *Jishōki* (On self-nature, 1672), 62.

6. *Jishōki*, 57.

7. *Sokushinki* (On the mind, 1660), 13.

8. *Sokushinki*, 34.

9. *Sokushinki*, 12.

Bibliography

BZG = *Bankei Zenji goroku* (Tokyo: Iwanami, 1941)

Dumoulin, Heinrich. *Zen Buddhism: A History, II: Japan*. New York: Macmillan, 1990.

Haskel, Peter. *Bankei Zen: Translations from the Record of Bankei*. New York: Grove Weidenfeld, 1984.

Ichikawa Hakugen, ed. *Takuan* (Nihon no zengoroku 13). Tokyo: Kōdansha, 1978.

Minamoto Ryōen. *Kinsei shoki jitsugaku shisō no kenkyū* [Studies in early modern Japanese practical learning]. Tokyo: Sōbunsha, 1980.

———. "Bankei ni okeru 'fushō' no shisō" (Bankei's concept of the Unborn). *Tōhoku Daigaku Nihon Bunka Kenkyūjo hōkoku* 17 (1981) 29–58.

———. "Shidō Munan ni okeru 'kokoro' no shisō to shin ju butsu no ittchi" (The concept of mind and the coalescence of Shinto, Confucianism, and Buddhism in Shidō Munan) (unpublished).

Waddell, Norman. *The Unborn: The Life and Teachings of Zen Master Bankei (1622–1693)*. San Francisco: North Point Press, 1984.

Wilson, William Scott, trans. *Takuan Sōhō:The Unfettered Mind*. Tokyo-New York: Kodansha International, 1986.

{translated by Robert Wargo}

IV. *Hakuin*

MICHEL MOHR

THE HUNDREDTH ISSUE of the review *Zendō* (The Zen Path) appeared on November 1, 1918, a few days before the end of World War I. It was dedicated to a presentation of Hakuin Ekaku (1686–1769), who had died a century and a half earlier.[1] This unobtrusive cultural event occurred at a time when overconfidence in the achievements of the country was encouraged by many Japanese politicians and intellectuals. The fact that Japan, having been victorious in the Russo-Japanese conflict, now sided with the Allies was perceived as confirming its rise to the rank of a "first-class country" *(ittōkoku)*.[2] This pride transpires in some of the *Zendō* articles, in particular the one by Satō Kokyū, a priest at Engaku-ji, who elaborates on the traditional association between Mount Fuji and Hakuin: "Mount Fuji expresses the immovability of the national polity *(kokutai)* of Japan and rises in the Eastern sky. The Zen master (Hakuin) represents the spiritual radiance of the superior Japanese people *(yūshū naru Yamato minzoku)* and makes it shine in the whole world" (34).

The use of terminology with such heavy nationalist connotations is, however, not the exclusive tone of this publication. Although the overall trend is laudatory, some critical opinions are also voiced. Sōtō priest Kohō Useki (1879–1967) denounces the formalization of practice after Hakuin (53–55). Among the forty contributors are some of the most prestigious figures of the time, such as Shaku Sōen (1860–1919) and Suzuki Daisetsu (1870–1966), the chief editor. It appears to be one of the first attempts to assess the place of Hakuin in Japanese Buddhist thought. It is also noteworthy that at least ten of the authors were certified masters *(rōshi)* directly stemming from Hakuin's line and that the articles come from representatives of the three obediences of Zen Buddhism, namely the Sōtō, Rinzai, and Ōbaku schools.[3]

Despite obvious shortcomings, this publication is valuable for at least two reasons. First, it presents a spectrum of views by Zen Buddhist leaders of the Taishō era before the escalation of military dictatorship. Second, it provides us with a midway point to look back onto the Tokugawa period, helping us to put into perspective the progress and stagnation of studies centered on Hakuin and his successors during the twentieth century. Most of the contributors were born in the Tokugawa period and some experienced the transition to Meiji as adults, witnessing transformations in the Buddhist world that are now difficult to piece together given the scarcity of documents.

In the following study I shall begin with current perceptions of Hakuin, then examine the problems of his biography and the reorganization of Zen practice that was implemented in Hakuin's school, with some final remarks on the school's outreach to a wider audience.

The Image of Hakuin Today

Hakuin's abundant literary output is one of the factors slowing the study of his thought. While some teachings in vernacular language (kanahōgo) are still widely read, his more difficult writings in classical Chinese remain almost untouched. This is particularly true of *Kaian kokugo* (T 81, no. 2574, and HZ 3), Hakuin's commentary on the *Record of Daitō Kokushi*, first published with a postface dated 1750. This can be considered Hakuin's lifework and an elaborate expression of his intent to return to the sources of Rinzai Zen.[4] The various sayings and writings of Hakuin collected in *Keisō dokuzui* (HZ 2.1–301) are likewise largely unexplored.

The main purpose of Hakuin's activity was to revive his school, an endeavor that obliged him to go back to the pivotal phase in which the Zen tradition was transmitted from Sung China to Kamakura-period Japan during the thirteenth century. To do so, Hakuin needed to stress his affiliation to the main stream of the Myōshin-ji line, which had emerged as the most dynamic lineage at the beginning of the Tokugawa period. This would link him to the Ōtōkan tradition, which since Tokugawa times has increasingly represented the Rinzai orthodoxy. Although the question of Hakuin's ties with this lineage needs to be investigated further, suffice it to say that at present he is generally regarded as the legitimate heir to the Ōtōkan legacy and as the teacher who revitalized it.

Despite the esteem in which Hakuin is held, there has been surprisingly little scholarly research on his thought and works. There is, nevertheless, an enormous amount of literature *about* Hakuin in Japan, albeit of uneven quality. Legends surrounding his life and the methods of health inspired by his teachings are many, and the fact that a series of comics depicting his life has recently been completed[5] shows the degree of popularity he still enjoys.

The first step toward a better knowledge of Hakuin's writings was taken with the publication of his complete works (*Hakuin oshō zenshū*, here abbreviated as HZ) between 1934 and 1935, under the editorship of Kōson Isan (Gotō, 1895–1953), abbot of Hōrin-ji in Kyoto. Since then the major publications have been the extensive study of Hakuin's biography and related issues by Rikugawa in 1963, followed by the annotated edition of the biography in 1985 by Katō Shōshun (*Hakuin oshō nenpu*, here abbreviated as HN). For Hakuin's thought, the contributions of Yanagida Seizan and Tokiwa Gishin have been most important. Several authors have contributed to a better understanding of particular aspects of Hakuin's biography, especially Akiyama and Machida, but a few postwar Japanese historians have also proposed to examine Hakuin from a more critical perspective that underlines Hakuin's submission to the religious policy of the bakufu.[6]

Research on the institutional history of the Rinzai school during the Tokugawa period has been undertaken by Takenuki (1989 and 1993), but much remains to be investigated in that area,[7] as well as in the study of the impact Hakuin's movement had on popular religion. Reception of the Rinzai school teachings in the less-educated sectors of Tokugawa society is similar—and in some cases related—to the success of the Shingaku movement, a connection that has been clearly demonstrated by Sawada Anderson (1993). Regarding other Western publications, the important anthology provided by Yampolsky (1971) has been followed by a series of translations by Waddell. Considerable labor is still required to translate and analyze the vast corpus of texts composed by Hakuin and his disciples. In order to have a balanced view of Hakuin and his spiritual legacy, it is necessary to take into account not only the different facets of his personality, as far as they are revealed by the remaining documents, but also to examine the extent to which he was the product of his time and how his work was carried further by his successors.

Problems of Hakuin's Biography

The details of Hakuin's life are chiefly known through biographical[8] and autobiographical accounts.[9] The biography was composed by Hakuin's disciple Tōrei Enji (1721–1792), at Hakuin's own request, and then revised by Taikan Bunshu (1766–1842), one of Tōrei's successors. Fortunately, both Tōrei's manuscript and Taikan's remolded version remain, showing the evolution of this document. A comparison of the two versions shows that Tōrei's text relies heavily on Hakuin's own autobiographical accounts. Furthermore, a letter from Tōrei to Hakuin dated 1757 establishes that the redaction of the biography was already under way when Hakuin was aged seventy-three, and that Hakuin himself had given instructions in that respect.[10] The first manuscript by Tōrei was completed in 1789, but the final version amended by Taikan was printed only in early 1821.[11]

Since Tōrei became Hakuin's disciple when Hakuin was fifty-five, in 1743, he necessarily depended on information provided by his master, and Hakuin presumably wrote at least the first part of his biography himself.[12] Contradictions remain, however, in several places in the story. The efforts made by Tōrei and Taikan in their successive versions to eliminate the discrepancies contribute to present an idealized image of Hakuin, and the account as a whole leaves many points in obscurity. This document should therefore be used with caution and cannot be taken at face value. On the other hand, beyond the inevitable fact that the literary genre of such chronological biographies *(nenpu)* is characterized by a hagiographical tone, it is most instructive to see how Hakuin shaped his personal history in order to use it as a teaching device.

The title of the biography uses the honorific title Shinki Dokumyō Zenji, bestowed on Hakuin in an imperial edict shortly after his death, in 1769. A second title, Shōjū Kokushi, was conferred in 1884, the last time an emperor has awarded the title "national master." The 1918 special issue of *Zendō*, discussed above, loftily reproduces this proof of recognition on its first page, and the chief Abbot *(kanchō)* of Daitoku-ji, Sōhan Genpō (1848–1922), further glosses it by stating that the title is in itself "the confirmation of the master's virtue" (18-19).

Besides its few discrepancies, there are two notable problems concerning Hakuin's biography. Their importance lies less in the historicity of the facts than in the indication they provide of Hakuin's will to emphasize certain aspects of his life so as to furnish a model for future generations. The first problem concerns the story of the young Hakuin meeting a hermit called Hakuyūshi. The second, quite consequential in the perspective of Rinzai orthodoxy, has to do with the relation between Hakuin and the priest he recognized as his teacher, Dōkyō Etan (1642–1721), alias Shōju Rōnin.[13]

The issue of Hakuyūshi is not very complicated. Since his tomb is located on the Yoshida hill of Kyoto and his death is recorded in the register of the Jōgan-in, his historical identity can scarcely be doubted.[14] His real name was Ishikawa Jishun (1646–1709), and he was a disciple of the poet Ishikawa Jōzan (1583–1672). Hakuin's first account of his encounter with Hakuyūshi appears in his commentary on Han-shan's poems, the *Kanzan-shi sendai kimon*, published in 1746 (HZ 4.109). Hakuin declares that he was twenty-six when he visited Hakuyūshi, and all his subsequent autobiographical works confirm this.

The problem is, when Hakuin was twenty-six, in 1710, Hakuyūshi had already been dead for a year. The evidence shows that Hakuin used the somehow enigmatic character of Hakuyūshi to enhance the interest of his story and to transmit Taoist ideas about health, breathing, and the care of vital energy. Hakuin had assimilated these notions by reading Taoist classics. He quotes, for instance, the *Chuang Tzu* saying that "common people breathe with their throats, true men breathe from their heels" (HZ 1.216). Hakuin also frequently mentions the Yellow Lord (Huang Ti), referring in particular to the *Su Wên*. He liked the passage describing the sage: "Composed and satisfied in nothingness, true vital energy follows him; innate nature and spiritual force being preserved within, from where could illness come?"[15]

The use of Taoist sources by Hakuin is a poorly explored and thus promising topic for research. However, Hakuin's narration of his encounter with Hakuyūshi is definitely a fiction. The fact that this story does not fit well in the biography apparently caused his disciples some unease, and the year assigned to this event was changed from 1715 in Tōrei's version to 1710 in Taikan's (HN 19-21). The attempt to insert the Hakuyūshi episode into the chronicle is awkward and, although Taikan presumably was not aware of the date of Hakuyūshi's death, this may have been another reason for the delay of the biography's publication. From Hakuin's perspective, however, there was no intent to deceive. With his customary sense of humor, he may have felt that the message was clear enough when he claimed in the *Yasenkanna* that Hakuyūshi was aged more than 180 or 240 years, three or four sexagesimal cycles (HZ 5.350). The title *Yasenkanna* probably alludes to the "night boat of Shirakawa" *(Shirakawa yobune),* a synonym for talking knowingly about nonexistent subjects. Indeed, Hakuin explicitly confesses his literary artifice in the postface to *Yasenkanna*, dated 1757, saying that this work "has not been set up *(mōkuru)* for those gifted persons who have already realized [the essential] in one hammer stroke" (HZ 5.365).[16]

The second problem, which is more delicate, is related to the story of another hermit, Dōkyō Etan, who spent his life in a small temple called Shōju-an (literally, Samādhi Retreat).[17] Hakuin's stay with Dōkyō was extremely short, probably little more than six months, and he never met him again, although he traveled in nearby areas and could easily have done so. The historicity of Dōkyō is questioned, and with it the authenticity of Hakuin's claim to derive his Zen lineage from him. This twofold problem was already brought up in the 1918 issue of *Zendō*.

Dōkyō's historicity is difficult to assess, since he lived in almost complete retirement and since there are no documents external to Hakuin's milieu that establish his whereabouts with certainty. The obscurity of Dōkyō's profile could, however, be attributed to the circumstances of his birth. Apparently born from the union of the aging lord Sanada Nobuyuki (1566–1658) with one of his young maids, Risetsu (1622–1707), the future Dōkyō was sent away with his mother and entrusted to the house of Matsudaira Tadatomo, lord of Iiyama castle, where he was raised. Patient research conducted by Nakamura Hiroji (1914–1985) and other Iiyama residents on local archives have finally shed some light on the origins of Dōkyō. One of the most convincing of Nakamura's arguments concerns the first biographical record about Dōkyō, the stone inscription *(Saishō no tō)* left by Tōrei and his disciples on the occasion of their stay at the Shōju-an in 1781. After commemorating the sixtieth anniversary of Dōkyō's death, they erected this stone, explicitly stating that Dōkyō was "the child from a certain lord Sanada and a concubine."[18] If this story had been invented, Tōrei and his followers would have incurred enormous risks in mentioning such a powerful family. They must have had solid evidence to support this written assertion. The existence of Dōkyō is further documented by investigations concerning his disciples, in particular the second abbot of the Shōju-an, Dōju Sōkaku (1679–1730) (Rikugawa 1964 and HN 107).

In the absence of further information concerning Dōkyō, we can only hypothesize. It seems that Hakuin's own account can be trusted and that he first visited Dōkyō at the age of 24, when he was still elated by the decisive breakthrough he had experienced upon hearing the sound of a distant bell (HN 92). The stay under Dōkyō's stern fist made him aware for the first time that his initial realization was not wrong, just incomplete. Remaining scoria of pride were further swept away when he passed the kōan Dōkyō had assigned him, a crucial moment that led him to be more modest about his own attainments. After he left Dōkyō's hermitage, illnesses served as reminders of remaining constraints. After almost twenty years of further struggle another major inner transformation took place at the age of forty-two, as he read the *Lotus Sūtra*. This event apparently led Hakuin to realize the importance of the short period spent under the guidance of Dōkyō, persuading him to consider himself Dōkyō's heir in the Dharma, a choice that was also strategically justified. Evidence to support this view is provided by the fact that, on inscribing his new surname "Hakuin" on the register of Myōshin-ji at the age of thirty-four, in 1718, he still noted the name of his predecessor at the Shōin-ji, Tōrin Soshō (d. 1754), as his master and did not mention Dōkyō (HN 160).

Currents of Reform

Without minimizing the contribution of Hakuin to the revival of Rinzai Zen, we must place the myth of his uniqueness in historical perspective. The linkage between Zen monasteries and patrons belonging to the warrior class had been a factor of prosperity during the Kamakura and Muromachi periods. After the Ōnin War (1467–1477), however, this source of income started to decline and, in an age characterized by "the ascendancy of individual interest,"[19] the support obtained from the merchant class became increasingly important. This shift led to a reversal in the comparative strength of the monastic branches in the Rinzai school: the temples that had enjoyed official recognition within the Gozan system weakened, while the hitherto relatively marginal Daitoku-ji and Myōshin-ji lines rose to preeminence. This tendency is particularly important for understanding the success of Hakuin's movement, which emerged from the Myōshin-ji branch.

Neither this reshuffling of positions of the monasteries nor their economic backgrounds fully explains the transformations that took place in most schools. There were other factors, both external and internal, that induced an in-depth mutation of religious institutions. Chief among the external factors was the new influx of Chinese monks in the seventeenth century and the bakufu ordinances regulating Buddhist schools. Interactions and rivalries with the various increasingly influential Neo-Confucian currents, followed by National Learning, must also be taken into account. The internal factors are the reformist tendencies that emerged from the beginning of the Tokugawa period, in particular within the Myōshin-ji line.

As early as 1606, seven young priests of Myōshin-ji decided to form a group that would visit all the living masters in the country and have personal consultation with them *(ketsumei hensan)*. Among them was Gudō Tōshoku (1577–1661), who was to become engaged in a movement to restore the true Dharma *(shōbō)* in his school, and whose successor, Shidō Munan (1603–1676), is regarded as Hakuin's spiritual grandfather. Gudō, who was acutely aware of the lack of vitality in his school, attempted to reform Myōshin-ji by proposing to return to the spirit of the founder, Kanzan Egen (1277–1361).[20] The strictness of Gudō's views on how reforms should be accomplished by reviving the past permitted no accommodation with circumstances, and he is remembered as having refused to meet Yinyüan Lung-ch'i (1592–1673), who had wanted to visit Myōshin-ji after his arrival in Japan in 1654. Gudō did not recognize Ming-style Ch'an Buddhism as genuine. Gudō's position, however, was not the only tendency represented within the Myōshin-ji. For instance, the faction led by Ungo Kiyō

(1582–1659), a colleague of Gudō who had also participated in the 1606 expedition, favored reforms accommodating the new trend of incorporating the use of *nenbutsu* in the Rinzai practice.

Attitudes resulting from the arrival of Chinese Ming Buddhism on Japanese soil tended toward either rejection or assimilation. Ironically, the rejecting faction ultimately assimilated much of the new Chinese influence, sometimes without knowing it. This is particularly the case with monastic regulations. Despite protests by the Myōshin-ji abbot Keirin Sūshin (1653–1728), who sided with the Sōtō school reformers, many customs introduced through the Ōbaku rules were adopted in Rinzai monasteries, such as the convenient habit of using two different buildings for practicing monks, one for *zazen* and sleep (the *zendō*), and the other as dining hall (called *saidō* in Ōbaku, *jikidō* in Rinzai). The institutional aspect of reforms was on the point of being implemented a few months before Hakuin's birth. The concretization of this first phase of reforms can be seen in the publication in 1685 of the *Shōsōrin ryaku shingi* (T 81 no. 2579) by Mujaku Dōchū (1653–1745), the Rinzai monastic codes that still constitute the basis for today's rules.

New trends introduced by Ōbaku strongholds in Kyūshū had an impact on the Rinzai lineage represented by Kogetsu Zenzai (1667–1751), a teacher who caused a considerable stir in the whole western part of Japan. Kogetsu's master, Kengan Zen'etsu (1618–1696), had consulted several of the Chinese Ōbaku priests, who had strongly influenced his conception of the precepts. Kogetsu was Hakuin's elder by eighteen years; at a certain point the two seem to have been regarded as the most prominent teachers of the country. The rather simplistic slogan, "Kogetsu in the West and Hakuin in the East," epitomizes the competition between the pro-Ōbaku faction (Kogetsu's followers) and the moderate anti-Ōbaku party (Hakuin's followers). Their areas of influence are, however, not so conveniently divided. For instance, one of Kogetsu's second-generation successors, Seisetsu Shūcho (1745–1820), played an important role in reviving the Engaku-ji of Kamakura, converting one of the monastery buildings into a monks' hall (*sōdō*).[21] Although affiliated to Kogetsu through his principal teacher, Gessen Zenne (1701–1781), Seisetsu consulted Hakuin and several of his disciples, which indicates emulation rather than hostility between the two groups. Many of Kogetsu's disciples subsequently turned to Hakuin when Kogetsu retired; Tōrei was one of them. Such shifts eventually resulted in the convergence of Kogetsu's and Hakuin's dynamism, under the single banner of Hakuin's movement.[22]

Reorganization of Practice

One of the most publicized aspects of Hakuin's contribution to the Rinzai revival is the "kōan system" *(kōan taikei)* attributed to him and his successors.[23] Unfortunately, this is also one of the most indistinct features of the changes that took place in Rinzai practice between the eighteenth and nineteenth centuries. The word "system" obviously does not appear in any traditional source, being the translation of a Western concept, and its use seems to coincide with efforts made to present Zen Buddhist teachings in a way that would be compatible with modern rationality.[24] What we know about methods used for teaching kōans is that the transformations experienced by Chinese Ch'an during the Sung dynasty, especially in the circle of Wu-tsu Fa-yen (1024?–1104) and his followers, were imported into Japan by the pioneers. Three varieties of kōans, namely *richi* (principle), *kikan* (functioning), and *kōjō* (going beyond), are already mentioned in the writings left by priests who journeyed to China, like Enni Ben'en (1202–1280) and Nanpo Jōmyō (1235–1309).[25] There are antecedents of these terms in Chinese sources, but it seems that the returning Japanese were eager to clarify the teachings they had received by arranging them in such categories. However, apart from the idea that certain kōans correspond to certain stages of cultivation, this early classification can hardly be considered a "system."

Before examining further the way kōans were rearranged in Hakuin's lineage, a word should be added concerning their practical objective. Kōans are questions taken from ancient records or devised by modern masters, which are used for focusing the mind. They are also further used for testing the student's understanding. For instance:

> Without thinking "good" or "bad," at this very moment, what is your original face before your parents were born?[26]

One is supposed to struggle with the specific question with one's whole psyche, and it accompanies one in every activity, whether sitting in *zazen*, walking, or engaged in manual work or other activities. Kōan practice is not confined to the Rinzai school, but in the Rinzai context much emphasis is laid on the occasions to have personal consultation *(dokusan)* with the master, in order to present one's understanding, verbal or nonverbal. This "answer" *(kenge)* is in turn evaluated by the master, usually by a brief comment, a grunt, or some other means. The kōan is thus used as a particular tool for communicating, in a way that goes as close as possible to the expression of prereflexive states of mind. It can be likened to a screen on which students project their understanding. The master in turn looks at the screen and can assess the depth of the student's meditative absorption. The function of the first kōan in particular is to coincide with a crystallization of the existential doubt: "Who am I?" There is nothing mysterious about this interrogation and it is shared by most religious traditions. Making the decisive leap to the resolution of a kōan is an act that can only be realized by the practitioner, but the peculiar kind of dialogue accompanying kōan practice may be conceived as a subtle educational device.[27] This type of pedagogy is characterized by an emphasis on oral tradition, even if classics are highly valued and their study is encouraged. Moreover, the formal aspect of kōan practice could anthropologically be described as a kind of "rite of passage."

Hakuin and his followers precisely sought to revive a kōan practice that would avoid the pitfall of becoming a mere intellectual game. For this purpose, one of the Chinese masters who was suited as a model was Ta-hui Tsung-kao (1089–1163), the advocate of a spirited style of practice. Hakuin refers to this paradigm of active cultivation in his *Orategama*, telling us that "Master Ta-hui too said that [meditative] work in movement is infinitely superior to that in stillness" (HZ 5.111).[28] The quote is faithful to the spirit of Ta-hui, who frequently uses the expression "[meditative] work" *(kung-fu; J. kufū),* stressing the necessity of "not letting the [meditative] work be interrupted" (T 47.868c)—of continuing it in all activities. However, Hakuin does not reproduce Ta-hui's exact wording. Ta-hui says in one of his Letters:

> If you really like stillness and dislike agitation it is suitable to exert your force (= make efforts). When you clash head-on against agitation with the state [acquired in] stillness, the force [you acquire] is infinitely superior to what [is obtained by sitting] on a bamboo chair or a cushion. (T 47.918c)

The word for "agitation" *(nao)* suggests a noisy and busy environment. Ta-hui, writing to a layman, alludes to the activities of a person involved in public obligations. The difference admittedly is minor, and the intention of the author is not betrayed, but the fact that Hakuin attributes to Ta-hui a sentence that he has himself devised is indicative of the liberty he sometimes takes with the Chinese tradition. Despite his vast learning, or perhaps because of it, he does not scruple to reinterpret his predecessors' thought to make it more accessible. Put in other terms, he likes to tell stories. Still, there is a gap between the Sung style and the style advocated in Hakuin's school, in particular in regard to stages in the practice after awakening.

The reorganization of kōan practice attributed to Hakuin involves the extension of the three aforementioned categories *(richi, kikan, and kōjō)* into a curriculum including the progression through five successive types of kōans: *hosshin* (Dharmakāya), *kikan* (functioning), *gonsen* (verbal expressions), *nantō* (difficult to penetrate), and *kōjō* (going beyond).[29] It should be added that, although this resembles a graduation course, the actual use of kōans in private consultations is something that varies according to individuals, even if specific patterns are followed by teachers belonging to the same lineage. The above reflects the way kōan practice is generally presented, and it mirrors a scheme still in use. Still, one may wonder to what extent it was developed by Hakuin himself and to what extent by his direct disciples.

In the writings of Hakuin, the necessity of realizing one's true nature *(kenshō)* is indeed emphasized, and this emphasis is even surpassed by the frequency of reiterated exhortations not to be satisfied by such realization. The kōans "difficult to penetrate" are, for example, cited as efficient tools for avoiding this danger of stagnation. In *Sokkōroku kaien fusetsu* Hakuin advises his students:

> Individuals of strong resolve, you must fiercely mobilize your energy and see your nature once. As soon as you realize an unequivocal *kenshō*, drop it and resolve [this matter] by practice on the cases difficult to penetrate. (HZ 2.389)

According to this passage, *kenshō* (corresponding to *hosshin kōan* in the above categories) would be directly followed by the *nantō kōan*. Despite this basic linking in the steps of cultivation, no text by Hakuin mentions a sequence of five categories of kōans that should be practiced one after the other. Two reasons for this silence may be conjectured.

First, given the emphasis on oral transmission and direct guidance from teacher to disciple, even if Hakuin did actually use these categories to teach disciples, he may have chosen not to express such a rigid pattern in written form, as it could impede an optimal adaptation to individuals and circumstances. If written traces related to a peculiar sequence of kōans existed, they were individually noted down, and these notes were not intended to be disclosed. Such information on how Hakuin taught his direct disciples has not yet come to light, if it indeed exists at all. The idea commonly held by living masters, that these transformations are to be attributed to Hakuin himself cannot be entirely discarded either, as this judgment is the result of convictions carried by the oral tradition.[30]

Alternatively, it could be that successors of Hakuin devised this sequence of kōans, drawing on their master's teachings. Here again, the lack of documents does not allow us to draw conclusions. By a process of elimination, it is possible to ascertain that nothing close to a "system" appears in Tōrei's writings. His central work, the *Shūmon mujintō ron* (Treatise on the inexhaustible lamp of our lineage, T 81 no. 2575) published in 1800,[31] does describe in detail stages on the path of cultivation, but carefully avoids furnishing a rigid structure governing the use of kōans. One could consider, as Kajitani Sōnin puts it, that the aim pervading the whole kōan "system" is to avoid stopping halfway through, to avoid being satisfied with one's accomplishments, to keep going beyond *(kōjō)*.[32]

The few published sources on this topic give precious information on the actual use of kōans, but they are from a later period. Akizuki Ryōmin has, for example, disclosed the "notebook for practice" *(anken)* listing the sequence of two hundred kōans followed in the lineage of Ekkei Shuken (1810–1884), the founder of the monks' hall of today's Myōshin-ji, and his successor Kasan Genku (1837–1917).[33] Fearing that the tradition he has inherited from his masters might disappear, the same author has also published another collection, giving the sequence of 268 cases used in the Bizen branch of the Rinzai school.[34]

At this point, a word should be said about Hakuin's direct successors. There has been some confusion concerning this matter, because of the ambiguous designation used in the biography, where the word for "Dharma heir" *(hassu)* signifies a successor in the temple lineage *(garanbō)* (HN 33–34). Although contemporary usage generally considers a *hassu* a fully acknowledged successor, this technical term is used more loosely in the biography, so that no specific term permits identification of the numerous disciples who received Hakuin's certification *(inka)*. This aspect seems to have been voluntarily left out of the biography, perhaps to avoid giving a restrictive list that might omit disciples unknown to the redactor. Furthermore, Hakuin had given his recognition to many lay persons, and it was not customary to mention nonordained practitioners on Dharma charts. Kawakami Kozan (1874–1932), who wrote a history of the Myōshin-ji, provided a list of the forty-one successors he considered the most important. There are omissions, however, and the criteria chosen for his classification are unknown.[35]

To focus on only eight among the figures most active after Hakuin's demise, we should begin with the names of Tōrei and Suiō Genro (1717–1790) (see HZ 1.123-26). Suiō inherited the Shōin-ji from Hakuin and his activity also involved remarkable art works. Shikyō Eryō (1722–1787) founded a new monastery, the Enpuku-ji, at Yawata on the outskirts of Kyoto (see HZ 8.267-69). Daishū Zenjo (1720–1778) had studied Neo-Confucianism; he later became abbot of the Jishō-ji, in present Ōita Prefecture, and was the main redactor of *Keisō dokuzui* (see HZ 1.119-21). Kawakami calls the above four masters the "four heavenly kings" in Hakuin's succession.[36] A lesser-known disciple, Tairei Shōkan (1724–1807), revived the Shōrin-ji of Hashima, in present Gifu Prefecture. Reigen Etō (1721–1785) played a considerable role in introducing Hakuin's line at the Tenryū-ji. Although relegated by Kawakami in his list to the grade of "guest disciple," Daikyū Ebō (1715–1774) is regarded as one of Hakuin's most talented followers, as shown by the words of his colleague Suiō, who reportedly said that "the only one who followed Hakuin since he was young, exhausting and grabbing his treasures of the Dharma *(hōzai)*, is Tōrei; the only one who penetrated to the source of his Dharma *(hōgen)* is Daikyū" (HZ 1.139).

Special mention must be made of Hakuin's last disciple, Gasan Jitō (1727–1797). Coming from Kogetsu's line, through his first master Gessen Zenne, Gasan is not even mentioned in Hakuin's biography. There is nothing surprising about this, considering that Gasan had not completed his training under Hakuin. According to Gasan's own account, he consulted Hakuin during four years and, upon Hakuin's death, completed his kōan practice under Tōrei (HZ 1.134-35). This is confirmed in Tōrei's biography, which mentions the certification he gave to Gasan in 1777.[37] Gasan nevertheless chose to consider himself the direct heir of Hakuin and he is recorded in all Dharma charts as such. Surprisingly, although Gasan was the last to enter the community of Hakuin, he appears from today's perspective to be the main figure connecting later generations with Hakuin's teachings. This is due to the fact that almost all present teachers belong to a lineage derived from two of Gasan's heirs, Inzan Ien (1751–1814) and Takujū Kosen (1760–1833). In other words, despite the prosperity of Hakuin's descendants until the end of the eighteenth century, almost all the lines that did not belong to Inzan and Takujū's successors had disappeared by the end of the nineteenth century. There is at least one exception, a lineage stemming from Suiō that is reported as subsisting today, but it seems marginal.[38]

The consequences of these developments for the transmission of Hakuin's legacy to Rinzai teachers today are far-reaching. While at the moment of the inauguration of the Ryūtaku-ji in 1761, when Hakuin was still alive, expectations that this current of teaching would flourish were well founded, the position of Rinzai representatives became increasingly defensive toward the end of the Tokugawa period. Was this phenomenon the result of a lowering in the quality of practitioners, or did it happen under increasing pressure from external factors? This is a major issue for future research. There is as yet almost no Japanese scholarship on the last decades of Zen Buddhism during the Tokugawa, and this difficult period is further obscured by the destruction that occurred at the beginning of the Meiji era.

32. Brush drawing of
   Bodhidharma by
   Hakuin.

The Outreach to a Wider Audience

Besides the purely monastic environment, the other facet of the reforms implemented by Hakuin and his followers regards their efforts to make Zen practice and teachings more accessible. Among the followers of Hakuin, the number of lay persons who consulted him and reached a deep insight is noteworthy. When his lay disciples' attainment was unmistakable, Hakuin sometimes composed commemorative paintings, often in the form of a dragon-like whisk, with an inscription appended. Two of these paintings have been rediscovered in recent years, showing the successive certifications given to a doctor named Sugiyama Yōsen (d. 1779) and to his wife Juhō (d. 1796).[39]

A marked characteristic of these certifications is that they acknowledge a breakthrough occurring upon meditative work on the "sound of a single hand" kōan. This signifies that the meaning given to such attestations was devised differently for lay persons and for monks. In the case of lay persons, it could be conferred upon realization of *kenshō*, while for monks it supposed the completion of the whole kōan training.

This appears to be another aspect of the endeavor to facilitate access to Zen practice by engaged lay practitioners, while further means were used to vulgarize the teachings for the masses. Popularization through writings in vernacular language, songs, or miraculous tales, and nonverbal teachings in the form of art works are often regarded as the key to Hakuin's success.[40] Already in the 1918 issue of *Zendō*, Suzuki Daisetsu commented on the ability of Hakuin to use Chinese classics while making people "feel that Zen had always been Japanese" (18). Again, the obsession with getting rid of the Chinese flavor, which had become a leitmotiv since Motoori Norinaga, is conspicuous. Besides this emphasis on national identity, the rural flavor and the language used in Hakuin's writings has contributed to make his teachings more compatible with local beliefs and customs.[41]

Besides using popular preaching, which appears to be partially a concession to the trends of the time, Hakuin worked to express the fundamentals of training in a way that would be understandable and attractive for anyone. This type of openness to worldly preoccupations can be seen, for instance, in the emphasis put on filial piety, although this cannot be reduced to skillful means and has deeper roots in Buddhist thought. Another distinctive feature of Hakuin's perspective is his attempt to achieve a synthesis. His teachings are not characterized solely by openness, as he can condemn without mercy the "false Zen" propagated by some of Bankei's followers, but he mentions Dōgen in a very respectful way (HZ 1.221; 2.25; 4.116; 5.359), and he had acquaintances among Sōtō priests.

(He met, for example, the young Ōryū Genrō [1720–1813] in 1749.) Moreover, he often quotes Buddhist thinkers of other schools, for instance T'ien-t'ai (HZ 1.220-21; 4.115), and he generally admits the non-duality between the teachings of Zen masters and those belonging to classical Buddhism. One notices as well a propensity on his part to defend the idea of the fundamental unity between the three teachings (Shinto, Confucianism, and Buddhism), although Zen Buddhism is generally presented as the deepest.

We have seen that the originality of Hakuin's legacy lies precisely in his success in integrating his school with historical circumstances and responding to the needs of the time, while imposing subtle transformations. Like most reformers, Hakuin searched for the roots rather than trying to innovate. One indication of this tendency is the emphasis he places on the basic exercise of mindfulness of breathing *(susokkan and zuisokkan)*, a meditative practice derived from Indian origins *(ānāpāna-smṛti)*. More than conceptual grounds, the deep attention to breath, which facilitates the calming of body and mind, condenses the commencing point of Buddhist practice, which is not separate from its ultimate goal. Hakuin's exhortations as recorded by Tōrei in the *Rōhatsu jishu* begin with the following passage, which may also serve as my provisional conclusion:

> First place a thick cushion and sit in full lotus posture; loosen your clothing. Straighten your spine and adjust evenly your body. Begin by contemplating the count of your breaths. Among the innumerable *samādhi* this is the unsurpassable one.
>
> Having filled your lower abdomen *(tanden)* with vital energy, take one kōan. It is essential to cut the very root of life [with this *samādhi*]. As time passes on this way, assuming you are not lazy, even if [there is a faint possibility of] missing the ground when you hit it, *kenshō* [will occur] inevitably and without fail. Keep working! Keep working! (T 81.615a; HZ 7.233)

Notes

1. The dates of Hakuin are still inaccurately given in most publications, which usually do not take into account the gap between solar and lunar calendar. According to his biography, Hakuin was born in the second year of the Jōkyō era, twelfth month, twenty-fifth day. This corresponds to 19 January 1686. He died at the end of the fifth year of the Meiwa era, twelfth month, eleventh day. This corresponds to 18 January 1769 (HN 39 and 248). The counting of age followed in Hakuin's biography is, however, based on the lunar years, making him one year old in 1685. In 1695, for example, he is eleven years old.

2. Imai, *Taishō demokurashī*, 217. For critical studies depicting the links of certain Zen teachers with nationalism or militarism see Ichikawa (1975) and Sharf, "The Zen of Japanese Nationalism."

3. At the time of Hakuin, the Ōbaku movement was designated by speaking of the Ōbaku branch of the Rinzai school *(Rinzai shū Ōbaku ha),* while its members considered themselves to represent the "True Rinzai school" *(Rinzai shōshū).* This stream acquired the status and denomination of an independent school *(Ōbaku shū)* in 1876 *(Zengaku daijiten,* 123d).

4. For Daitō kokushi (Shūhō Myōchō 1282–1338), see Kraft, *Eloquent Zen,* and my review of the work in *Japanese Journal of Religious Studies* 20 (1993). The main publication concerning Hakuin's *Kaian kokugo* remains the record of the oral teachings *(teishō)* given by Iida Tōin (1863–1937), a layman who had been certified by several masters of the Rinzai and Sōtō schools, including Kōgaku Sōen, Nantenbō, and Taiun Sogaku (Iida, *Kaiankokugo teishōroku).* Titles used by Hakuin for his works generally play upon several layers of meaning, alluding to ancient stories. It is therefore often better not to restrict their signification and I shall avoid translating them. In the case of *Kaian kokugo,* Yampolsky explains the title as "the locust-tree land of tranquility, a never-never land of dreams" *(Zen Master Hakuin,* 226). The title is inspired from the novel *Nan-k'e T'ai-shou chuan* by the T'ang writer Li Kung-tso (n.d.); its hero falls asleep in broad daylight and dreams that he visits this chimerical country, marries the king's daughter, and becomes governor. The peace (of mind) obtained after napping under a Chinese scholar tree (scientific name Sophora Japonica [sic]) suggests, however, that Hakuin's title emphasizes the awakening from the dream.

5. Tsujii, *Hakuin oshō monogatari.*

6. This stance has been explored chiefly by Funaoka in "Hakuin zen no shisōshi teki igi," and developed by Muneyama in his "Hakuin no gohōron to minshūka."

7. An introduction to the institutional aspect is provided by Foulk, *The "Ch'an School" and Its Place in the Buddhist Monastic Tradition.*

8. I shall not paraphrase here the biography of Hakuin, so frequently quoted in Western publications. See the bibliography for Waddell's translation and his rendering of the autobiographical *Itsumadegusa.* The complementary document to HN is the biography of Tōrei (Nishimura, *Tōrei oshō nenpu).*

9. The first autobiographical account is in the appendix to *Orategama,* written in 1747 when Hakuin was sixty-three (HZ 5.196–209). It is the most concise story, lacking the episodes telling about his discovery of the *Ch'an-kuan ts'e-chin,* the visit to Hakuyūshi, and his stay at Iwatakiyama. The second one, a text called *Sakushin yōchi monogatari,* is recorded in some versions of *Yaemugura,* a neglected work of Hakuin that has not been included in HZ. Concerning this complicated issue, see Katō Shōshun, *"Yaemugura* no ihon ni tsuite," and HN 5–6. It was printed in 1761. The third autobiographical record is the one published in 1766, *Itsumadegusa.*

10. This letter is recorded in the miscellanea called *Taiyō zatsudokkai* (HZ 7.40–41). The same letter is found in the more comprehensive manuscript in Tōrei's own hand, called *Zatsudokkai,* that is kept at Ryūtaku-ji (folio 66b). See also HN 6.

11. The particulars that led to this publication are explained by Taikan in his postface to the biography (HN 295–96). At the end of this postface, the date of publication is given as the third year of the Bunsei era, twelfth month, eight day, corresponding to 11 January 1821.

12. Rikugawa, *Kōshō Hakuin oshō shōden,* 25.

13. For the reading of this name, I follow Katō (HN 17). The appellation *rōnin* appended to the name of his hermitage, Shōju, forms the nickname that Dōkyō Etan was given, apparently by the villagers in the countryside where he resided. The Buddhist reading *nin* of the character for "person" seems to have a more respectful connotation than the more usual reading *jin*, as it evokes the "true person" *(shinnin)*. The reading of this name in the bibliography has adjusted accordingly. Nakamura (who is not a priest) nevertheless uses *rōjin* (*Shōju rōnin to sono shūhen*, preface, and *Shōju rōnin no shi to geju*, 13).

14. See Itō, *Hakuyūshi*, 6–12. New developments have been presented by the same author in *Zenbunka* 24 (January 1962), 42–47; 54 (September 1969) 46–55. The more critical approach by Rikugawa (*Hyōshaku*, 140–203) is essential.

15. *Huang Ti Nei Ching Su Wên*, ed. Jen Ying-ch'iu (Beijing: Renmin weisheng chuban, 1986), 8. Compare the translation by Ilza Veith, *The Yellow Emperor's Classic of Internal Medicine* (Berkeley: University of California Press, 1966), 98. Hakuin quotes this passage in *Itsumadegusa* (HZ 1.221), *Kanzanshi sendai kimon* (HZ 4.108, 116) and *Yasenkanna* (HZ 5.359).

16. See also HN 21. The expression "realized in one stroke of hammer" is common in Ch'an sources, e.g. the *Transmission of the Lamp of the Ching-te Era* (T. 51.319b9–10).

17. This temple was restored in the Meiji period and is now located in present Nagano Prefecture, near the city of Iiyama. A description can be found in Koga ("Koji tanbō").

18. A photograph of the stone is included in *Zenbunka* 30–31 (January 1964) 19–20. A reproduction of the text with the reading is provided in Imakita (1935, 34–37), and the reading only in Rikugawa (*Kōshō Hakuin oshō shōden*, 42) and Nakamura (*Shōju rōnin to sono shūhen*, 34).

19. Berry, *The Culture of Civil War in Kyoto*, 13.

20. The life of Kanzan has been surrounded by mist, as there are few reliable documents about his biography (see Katō, "Kanzan Egen den no shiryō hihan"). This situation is improving with the efforts of historians like Takenuki ("Kanzan Egen to Getsurin Dōkō").

21. A special issue of *Zenbunka* (60, March 1971) is devoted to this figure.

22. Hakuin once attempted to meet Kogetsu, but gave up on his way. Concerning these two priests and their indirect relationship through their disciples, see Akiyama, who provides a list of disciples who shifted from Kogetsu to Hakuin (*Shamon Hakuin*, 146–153).

23. This locution is frequently used, for instance, by Akizuki (*Kōan*, 77 and 82; *Hakuin Zenji*, 138). Suzuki Daisetsu uses a similar expression in the 1918 issue of *Zendō*: "Hakuin brought kōan Zen to completion *(kanna zen o taisei shita)* and at the same time Japanized Chinese Zen to a certain extent" (12; also in *Suzuki Daisetsu zenshū*, vol. 28, 93).

24. Besides the above use of the word *taisei*, Suzuki in 1942 employs the expression *kōan seido*, which precisely means "kōan system" (see *Suzuki Daisetsu zenshū* vol. 4, 212). Shibayama, writing about the same time, describes Hakuin's contribution in terms of a "system" *(soshiki)* consciously devised ("Hakuin kei kanna no ichikanken," 6).

25. See, for example, T 80.20b17–20 for Enni, and *Zenmon hōgoshū* vol. 2, 438 for Nanpo.

26. The prototype of this question is attributed to the Sixth Patriarch in the *Transmission of the Lamp* (T 51.232a), but it does not include the expression "before your parents were born." The same text is reproduced as case 23 of the *Wu-men-kuan (Mumonkan)*. The more elaborate version I give is based on the text most currently used in Japanese monasteries, as it appears in the kōan collection *Shūmon kattōshū* (Kajitani, *Shūmon kattōshū*, 5). This version seems to be based on the *Wu-chia cheng-tsung tsan*, a Southern Sung dynasty text completed in 1254 (Z 135.906b–907a).

27. For a description of education as conceived in today's monasteries, see Hori, "Teaching and Learning in the Rinzai Monastery."

28. See also Izuyama, *Hakuin zenji,* 36 and 38, note 6; and Yampolsky, *Zen Master Hakuin*, 33.

29. A detailed exposition of these categories can be found in Akizuki, *Hakuin Zenji*, 138–88; Fuller Sasaki, *The Zen Kōan* and *Zen Dust*, 46–76; and Shimano, "Zen Koans." The five categories mentioned form the main bulk of post-Hakuin practice, and they are generally followed by the kōan dealing with the *goi* (five positions), *jūjū kinkai* (the ten essential precepts), and *matsugo no rōkan* (the last barrier).

30. For example, this idea is clearly expressed by Kajitani, the former abbot of Shōkoku-ji monastery, who states that Hakuin "created *(tsukutta)* a kōan system" including five categories ("Kōan no soshiki," 263).

31. Translation in Mohr, *Traité sur l'Inépuisable Lampe du Zen.*

32. Kajitani, "Kōan no soshiki," 266.

33. Akizuki, *Kōan*, 262–332.

34. Akizuki, *Zen no shugyō*, 163–308. The Bizen branch is the current that emerged from the area of Okayama, since Taigen Shigen (1769–1837) and his successor Gisan Zenrai (1802–1878) resided at Sōgen-ji. Concerning this current see Zenbunka Henshūbu, *Meiji no Zenshō* (271–90).

35. Kawakami, *Zōho*, 663–65; HN 29–32.

36. Kawakami, *Zōho*, 663–64; HN 29.

37. Nishimura, *Tōrei oshō nenpu*, 240.

38. See Tanaka Kōichi, "Suiō no hōkei."

39. Machida, "Hakuin no kosui kō."

40. Hakuin and his school as seen from the point of view of art history will not be treated here, despite the interest of this topic. The study by Kameyama Takurō *(Hakuin Zenji no ga o yomu)* is notable for its pioneering use of the methods of iconology. It denounces in particular the fakes that have been taken for Hakuin's works by previous authors. Classical publications include Naoki, *Hakuin Zenji*; Takeuchi Naoji, *Hakuin*; Tanahashi, *Hakuin no geijutsu*; Yamauchi, *Hakuin* and *Hakuin san no e seppō*; Yanagida and Katō, *Hakuin*. The relation between Hakuin and the painter Ike no Taiga (1723–1776) has been studied by Takeuchi Naoji in "Hakuin to Taiga." Addiss provides a synthesis on the topic of art by Zen masters, with an annotated bibliography (*The Art of Zen*, 214–18).

41. Yanagida uses the expression "indigenous handwriting" *(dochaku no sho)* for Hakuin's brush works, and speaks of a movement toward the native soil that started with Shidō Munan (*Hakuin*, 55 and 67).

Bibliography

Primary Sources

Chokushi Shinki dokumyō zenji Hakuin rō oshō nenpu. Manuscript by Tōrei Enji in the archives of the Hōrin-ji, Kyoto. Japanese reading *(yomikudashi)* version in Rikugawa 1963, 444–546.

Ryūtaku kaiso Shinki dokumyō zenji nenpu, the revised version of Tōrei's manuscript by Taikan Bunshu, printed in 1821, included in HZ1.

HN = *Hakuin oshō nenpu,* ed. Katō Shōshun (Kinsei zensōden 7). Kyoto: Shibunkaku, 1985.

HZ = *Hakuin oshō zenshū*, 8 vols., ed. Gotō Kōson and Mori Daikyō. Tokyo: Ryūginsha, 1934–1935 (reprint 1967).

Kinsei zenrin sōbōden (Ogino Dokuon, 1890) and *Zoku Kinsei zenrin sōbōden* (Obata Buntei, 1936), 3 vols., facsimile edition. Kyoto: Shibunkaku, 1973.

Hyakugō kinen: Hakuin kenkyū. Zendō no. 100. Tokyo: Kōyūkan, 1918.

Zenmon hōgoshū, 3 vols. Yamada Kōdō et al., eds. Tokyo: Shigensha, 1973.

Secondary Sources (in Japanese)

Akiyama Kanji. *Shamon Hakuin*. Shizuoka: Akiyama Aiko, 1983.

Akizuki Ryōmin. "Hakuin ka kōan Inzan Bizen ha: shitsunai issan no tomoshibi." In *Zen no shugyō*, ed., Akizuki Ryōmin, 163–308. Tokyo: Hirakawa Shuppan, 1986.

———. *Hakuin Zenji*. Tokyo: Kōdansha, 1985.

———. *Kōan: Jissenteki zen nyūmon*. Tokyo: Chikuma Shobō, 1987.

Funaoka Makoto. "Hakuin zen no shisōshi teki igi." In *Kinsei bukkyō no shomondai*, ed. Tamamuro Fumio and Ōkuwa Hitoshi, 345–66. Tokyo: Yūzankaku, 1979.

Ichikawa Hakugen. *Nihon fashizumuka no shūkyō*. Tokyo: Enaesu, 1975.

Iida Tōin. *Kaiankokugo teishōroku*. Kyoto: Kichūdō, 1954.

Imai Seiichi. *Taishō demokurashi* (Nihon no rekishi 23). Tokyo: Chūōkōron, 1974.

Imakita Kōsen. *Shōju rōnin sugyōroku*. Nagano: Shinano Kyōikukai, 1935.

Itō Kazuo. *Hakuyūshi: shijitsu no shintankyū*. Kyoto: Yamaguchi Shoten, 1960.

Izuyama Kakudō. *Hakuin zenji: Yasenkanna*. Tokyo: Shunjūsha, 1983.

———. *Hakuin zenji: Orategama*. Tokyo: Shunjūsha, 1985.

Kajitani Sōnin. "Kōan no soshiki." In *Zen no koten: Nihon* (Kōza Zen 7) 263–70. Tokyo: Chikuma Shobō, 1968.

———, ed. *Shūmon kattōshū*. Kyoto: Hōzōkan, 1982.

Kamata Shigeo. *Hakuin*. Tokyo: Kōdansha, 1977.

Kameyama Takurō. *Hakuin zenji no ga o yomu*. Kyoto: Zenbunka Kenkyūsho, 1985.

Katō Shōshun. "Kanzan Egen den no shiryō hihan." *Zenbunka kenkyūsho kiyō* 4 (1972) 1–30.

———. "*Yaemugura* no ihon ni tsuite." *Zenbunka kenkyūsho kiyō* 12 (1980) 213–42.

Kawakami Kozan. *Zōho: Myōshin-ji shi*. Kyoto: Shibunkaku, 1975.

Koga Hidehiko. *Zengo jiten*. Kyoto: Shibunkaku, 1991.

———. "Koji tanbō: Hakuin yukari no tera." *Zenbunka* 83 (1976) 46–51.

Machida Zuihō. "Hakuin no kosui kō." *Zenbunka* 63 (January 1972) 39–43.

Mōru Missheru. "Tōrei no chosaku ni kansuru shomondai." *Zengaku kenkyū* 73 (1995) 143–89.

Muneyama Yoshifumi. "Hakuin no gohōron to minshūka." In *Futaba Kenkō hakase koki kinen: Nihon bukkyōshi ronsō*, 305–22. Kyoto: Nagata Bunshōdō, 1986.

Nakamura Hiroji. *Shōju rōnin to sono shūhen*. Nagano: Shinano Kyōikukai Shuppanbu, 1979.

———. *Shōju rōnin no shi to geju*. Nagano: Shinano Kyōikukai Shuppanbu, 1985.

Naoki Kimihiko. *Hakuin zenji: minshū no kyōke to shoga no shashinshū*. Tokyo: Ryūginsha, 1957.

Nishimura Eshin. *Tōrei oshō nenpu* (Kinsei zensōden 8). Kyoto: Shibunkaku, 1982.

Ōtsuki Mikio, Katō Shōshun, and Hayashi Yukimitsu, eds. *Ōbaku bunka jinmei jiten*. Kyoto: Shibunkaku, 1988.

Rikugawa Taiun. *Hyōshaku: Yasenkanna*. Tokyo: Sankibō Busshorin, 1961 (1982).

———. *Kōshō Hakuin oshō shōden*. Tokyo: Sankibō Busshorin, 1963.

———. "Shōju rōnin monka shihō no hitobito." *Zenbunka* 30–31 (January 1964) 14–24.

———. "Ōkami Genrō to Hakuin oshō." *Zenbunka* 40 (March 1966) 51–53.

Shaku Sōen. "Yo ga mitaru Hakuin rōso." *Zendō* 100 (1918) 5–9.

Shibayama Zenkei. "Hakuin kei kanna no ichikanken." *Zengaku kenkyū* 38 (December 1943) 1–30.

Shinano Kyōikukai. *Shōju rōnin shū*. Nagano: Shinano Kyōikukai, 1937.

Takenuki Genshō. "Kanzan Egen to Getsurin Dōkō." *Zenbunka* 153 (July 1994) 104–115.

———. *Nihon zenshūshi*. Tokyo: Daizō Shuppan, 1989.

———. *Nihon zenshūshi kenkyū*. Tokyo: Yūzankaku, 1993.

Takeuchi Naoji. *Hakuin*. Tokyo: Chikuma Shobō, 1964.

———. "Hakuin to Taiga." *Zenbunka* 45 (June 1967) 32–45.

Tanahashi Kazuaki. *Hakuin no geijutsu*. Tokyo: Geijutsu Shuppan, 1980 (Eng. trans., Tanahashi 1984, below)

Tanaka Kōichi. "Suiō no hōkei." *Zenbunka* 55 (January 1970) 12–22.

Tokiwa Gishin. *Hakuin*. Tokyo: Chūōkōron, 1988.

———. "Hakuin Ekaku no 'Sekishu no onjō' o *Orategama* to *Tōzan goi jū* to ni kiku." *Zenbunka kenkyūsho kiyō* 16 (1990) 1–25.

Tsujii Hirohisa. *Hakuin oshō monogatari*. 5 volumes. Kyoto: Zenbunka Kenkyūsho, 1989–94.

Yamauchi Chōzō. *Hakuin: sho to ga no kokoro*. Tokyo: Gurafikku sha, 1978.

———. *Hakuin san no e seppō*. Tokyo: Daihōrinkaku, 1984.

Yanagida Seizan. "Chūgoku zenshūshi." In *Zen no rekishi: Chūgoku* (Kōza Zen 3) 7–108. Tokyo: Chikuma Shobō, 1963.

———. Yanagida Seizan (with Katō Shōshun). *Hakuin*. Kyoto: Tankōsha, 1979.

Zenbunka Henshūbu. *Meiji no zenshō*. Kyoto: Zenbunka Kenkyūsho, 1981.

Zengaku Daijiten Hensansho. *Zengaku daijiten*. Tokyo: Taishūkan, 1978.

Secondary Sources (in Western languages)

Addiss, Stephen. *The Art of Zen: paintings and calligraphy by Japanese monks, 1600–1925*. New York: Harry N. Abrams, 1989.

Berry, Mary Elizabeth. *The Culture of Civil War in Kyoto*. Berkeley: University of California Press, 1994.

Foulk, Griffith. *The "Ch'an School" and Its Place in the Buddhist Monastic Tradition*. Ph.D. Dissertation, University of Michigan, 1981.

Fuller Sasaki, Ruth and Miura Isshū. *The Zen Kōan*. New York: Harcourt Brace Jovanovich, 1965.

———. *Zen Dust*. Kyoto: The First Zen Institute of America in Japan, 1966.

Hori, G. Victor Sōgen. "Teaching and Learning in the Rinzai Monastery." *The Journal of Japanese Studies* 20 (1994) 5–35.

Kraft, Kenneth. *Eloquent Zen: Daitō and Early Japanese Zen*. Honolulu: University of Hawai'i Press, 1992.

Mohr, Michel. "Examining the Sources of Japanese Rinzai Zen." *Japanese Journal of Religious Studies* 20 (1993) 331–44. A review article on Kraft 1992.

———. "Vers la redécouverte de Tōrei." *Cahiers d'Extrême-Asie* 7 (1993–1994) 319–52.

———. *Traité sur l'Inépuisable Lampe du Zen: Tōrei (1721–1792) et sa vision de l'éveil*. Brussels: Institut Belge des Hautes Études Chinoises, 1997.

Sawada Anderson, Janine. *Confucian Values and Popular Zen: Sekimon Shingaku in Eighteenth-Century Japan*. Honolulu: University of Hawai'i Press, 1993.

Sharf, Robert H. "The Zen of Japanese Nationalism." *History of Religions* 33 (1993) 1–43.

Shimano Eidō T. "Zen Koans." In Kenneth Kraft, ed., *Zen: Tradition and Transition*, 70–87. London: Rider and New York: Grove Press, 1988.

Tanahashi Kazuaki. *Penetrating Laughter: Hakuin's Zen and Art*. Woodstock: The Overlook Press, 1984.

Waddell, Norman trans., *Zen Words for the Heart: Hakuin's Commentary on the Heart Sutra*. Boston: Shambhala, 1996.

———. "Wild Ivy." *The Eastern Buddhist* 15:2 (1982) 71–109; 16:1 (1983) 107–139.

———. *The Essential Teachings of Zen Master Hakuin*. Boston and London: Shambhala, 1994.

———. "A Chronological Biography of Zen Priest Hakuin." *The Eastern Buddhist* 27:1 (1994) 96–155; 27:2, 81–129.

Yampolsky, Philip B. *The Zen Master Hakuin: Selected Writings*. New York: Columbia University Press, 1971.

24

Tokugawa Period

I. *Buddhist Responses to Confucianism*

MINAMOTO RYŌEN

HE GROWTH OF secularization and intellectualization in the Tokugawa (Edo) period (1603–1867) brought about a positivistic way of thinking—marked by dichotomies of subject and object, self and other, spirit and matter—that was inimical to spiritual awareness. Confucianism increasingly became a politically serviceable orthodoxy, which strengthened the authority of the shogunate government. Buddhism, lacking any important political role, maintained its spiritual tradition as a vital social force, especially among the common people. Many Buddhists, threatened by the superiority of Confucianism, took a defensive posture toward it and resorted to sophistical arguments. This approach is well represented by the *San'ikun* (Teaching of the three laws, 1758; NST 57.7–33) of the Jōdoshū priest Daiga (1709–1782), in which he claims that Buddhism possesses teachings on political economy common to itself, Shinto, and Confucianism. Of more interest are the attitudes adopted by the most vigorous sects of the time—Jōdo Shinshū, Nichirenshū, and Zen.

Jōdo Shinshū

Endowed with an intense faith in Other-Power by its founder, Shinran, Jōdo Shinshū had in the Muromachi period been faced with the task of reconciling this inviolable and transcendent faith with secular power and secular morality. An accommodation between faith and morality was proposed by Rennyo (1415–1499):

> Take the laws of the state as your outer aspect, store Other-Power faith deep in your hearts, and take the principles of humanity and justice as essential.

329

Bear in mind that these are the rules of conduct that have been established within our tradition.[1]

This text determined the attitude of religious communities to secular power and ethics. Unlike Dōgen's *datsuzoku* (emancipation from the secular) or Nichiren's *shakubuku* (subduing evil), Rennyo's doctrine consisted of conforming with the principles of secular living while keeping the world of faith intact. Thus Shami Ganjō (d. 1869) writes:

> Outwardly, to observe the laws of the state completely, and not to forget the way of benevolence, righteousness, ritual propriety, wisdom, and good faith [the Confucian "five norms" of the Tokugawa ideology]; in one's inner heart, to believe in the Original Vow deeply; to ascribe good and evil fortune in this world to karmic destiny from the past; and to make the occupation of one's family, whether of samurai, farmer, artisan, or merchant, one's primary concern—this is what we call good companionship of the Pure Land.

Here, along with the "five norms," a concern with family occupation makes its appearance, but the basic principle enunciated by Rennyo and Saigin (1605–1663) is unaltered.

Thus the purity of faith characteristic of Jōdo Shinshū was preserved in the Tokugawa period by a dualism between the original vow of Amida maintained in the inner world of faith and a Confucian code of secular conduct, an approach that might be called "externally soft and internally hard." The coexistence of Buddhism and Confucianism did not entail any profound mutual interaction. Even though it looks as if Jōdo Shinshū here forswears independent ethical thinking and simply adapts to its environment, the sect did follow a policy of "not having a Shinto altar or hanging up a single talisman" (*Myōkōnin-den*; NST 57), which suggests that it remained a potential adversary both to secular administrators and to Shintoists.

Nichirenshū

In contrast to the accommodating attitude to secular power adopted by other branches of the Nichiren sect, Nichiō (1565–1630) of the Fujufuse branch, in his *Shūgiseihōron* (On the meaning and laws of our sect, 1616; NST 57.255–354), adhered to Nichiren's teaching that it was wrong to conduct services for or accept alms from nonbelievers in the *Lotus Sūtra*. Nichiō was persecuted by the Tokugawa authorities for his persistence in this view. Holding to the primacy of the *Lotus Sūtra*, he placed Confucianism and Taoism in a lower position, but nonetheless believed that

Confucianism was a necessary first step in the study of Buddhism. "He who would study Buddhism should first know the moral obligations of the world" (NST 57.272). As people's knowledge was shallow and Buddhism extremely profound, study of the secular Way provided an approach to the latter. Nichiō's rejection of services for nonbelievers could appeal to Confucian principles, and he quotes Mencius's words: "If it is not right to do so, one should not accept even a spoonful of food from another." "Life is what we desire; righteousness is also what we desire. If we cannot have both, we should abandon life and cleave to righteousness" (the *Mencius*). Nichiō adds: "Secular moral obligations are as binding as this. How much more so are the Buddhist ones!" (NST 57.273). It seems safe to conclude that he found a congruence between Confucian morality and Fujufuse principles, and that in his mind there were no obstacles to incorporating Confucianism within the structure of his Buddhism.

Zen

In contrast to China, debates between Zen and Confucianism are rare in Japan. Nevertheless, it was Zen monks among Tokugawa period Buddhists who met the challenge of Confucianism most directly, to some extent compelling the Confucians to respond. The reason for this is that they shared with the Confucians a concern with psychological techniques *(shinpō)*.

Takuan

In the early Tokugawa period, when the Neo-Confucianism of Chu Hsi (1130–1200) was becoming an object of serious study and practice in Japan, Takuan was the only Zen monk of his time to realize the importance of Confucianism for Buddhists. He proceeded to study it intensively and to criticize it from a Buddhist perspective. He made it part of his conceptual repertoire, using Confucian vocabulary to develop Mahāyāna philosophy. In his early work, *Sennan gūkyo roku* (Record of residence south of Izumi), he criticized the theory of the Korean Confucianist Yi T'oegye (1501–1570) concerning the "four beginnings and seven emotions." Yi saw Mencius's "four beginnings" as principles of goodness issuing from *li* (the noumenal realm), while the "seven emotions" are products of *ch'i* (material force). Takuan held that, from the Buddhist standpoint, both categories belonged to the physical rather than the noumenal aspect of the world. He also tackled the Confucian understanding of Buddhist nirvāṇa and, basing his arguments on the *Ssu-chu cheng-i k'ao* (Study of the correct interpretation of the

Four Books) of the Ming syncretic thinker Lin Chao-en (1517–1598), defended Buddhism against the charge of being a heterodoxy. He refuted the Confucian notions that one could make oneself into Yao or Shun by self-cultivation and that one could achieve "the extension of knowledge and investigation of things" simply by reading books.

The clearest and most complete expression of Takuan's early views is in his *Riki sabetsuron* (On the distinction between principle and force). Here he developed a theory of *li* (principle) and *ch'i* (force) from a Mahāyāna Buddhist perspective. Unlike Chu Hsi, he did not maintain the ontological identity of *ch'i* and *li*, the non-ultimate and the supreme-ultimate, but separated them as self-sufficient independently existing categories. There is nothing unusual about his concept of *ch'i*, but of *li* he wrote: "The substance of *li* fills heaven and earth. Because it exists in the mode of non-activity, it is described as 'empty' and 'void'." Takuan proceeded to criticize Chu Hsi's view of the relationship between *ch'i* and *li* as that of salt added to food to enhance its flavor. He denied that *li* had a will and was the cause of activity and quiescence in *ch'i*, or that *ch'i* had a will and was subordinate to *li*. However, since the motion of *ch'i* was always unregulated, one was forced to adopt the form of words that *ch'i* was subordinate to *li*. Takuan's separation of *li* from *ch'i* and his designation of the former as "empty" and "void" are based on the Buddhist doctrine of non-self *(muga)* and used to argue against the heterodox belief in a substantial self *(gedō shinga)*. His theory of *li* and *ch'i* reflects Buddhist thought on mind and nature, founded on the non-self doctrine.

In the *Fudōchi shinmyō roku* (Record of immovable wisdom and divine mystery) Takuan advances philosophical criticisms of Chu Hsi's doctrine of *ching* (respect). He praises the Confucian understanding of *ching* as "making oneness the ruler of all things and not letting go." This, he says, is considered the best method of disciplining the mind by Confucians; but from a Buddhist point of view it is not the ultimate state, but only an intermediate stage of training. As such, it is necessary for beginners to prevent disturbances to the mind, but in itself it involves what might be described as a lack of freedom. One should aim at true freedom which comes only when "the mind resides nowhere and pervades the whole person," a state described in the *Diamond Sūtra* as "having no abode and gaining a proper mind."

Behind Takuan's view of Chu Hsi's *ching* lies his criticism of Chu Hsi's attitude to the mind *(hsin)*. In the *Anjin hōmon* (Gateway to calming the mind) Takuan wrote:

> Confucians have misunderstood the mind, holding that it is the master of the whole self, and that if the master is lost, a person will become mad. This is a

wholly mistaken view. All enterprises start with the mind as their master and are retained firmly in the mind. When they are perfectly completed, the mind is forgotten and a state of working with no mind is reached. If this is not so, the action cannot be described as skillful. The Buddhist perfection of the perfect is "no-mind and no-working."

He claimed that this notion of "no-working" was congruent with Confucius's idea that "the sage does not act, yet transforms society." Chu Hsi's commentary on the words "Was it not Shun who did not act, yet the Empire was well ordered?" from the Wei Ling-kung chapter of the *Analects*, "lacks stature. It shows a grasp of the sage's mind, but reflects the limitations of the annotator." In the *Tōkai yawa* (Evening conversation at Tōkai-ji), Takuan compares the government of Yao and Shun to a single cloud in the Great Void:

> The sage's heart is like the Great Void: it is utterly empty. Just as one clears a room and awaits a guest, so one clears one's heart and awaits whatever may occur, like a single cloud floating on the Great Void.

Whereas Chu Hsi had expounded "non-activity" from the point of view of a governor who promotes and rewards ability but does not himself participate in administration, Takuan adopted the perspective of an administrator who responds to each administrative event with an attitude of no-mind.

Imakita Kōsen

At the end of the Tokugawa period, another Zen Buddhist, Imakita Kōsen (1816–1892), engaged in a creative critique of Confucianism. Kōsen initially studied the works of the great Confucian philologist Ogyū Sorai (1666–1728) and then went on to Chu Hsi. He gradually became less and less satisfied with Chu. After coming into contact with the more subjective philosophy of Wang Yang-ming (1472–1529), he reinvestigated Chu Hsi from the point of view of his own subjective existence. Once again, however, he felt his own requirements as a subject were not satisfied. Finally, at the age of twenty-four, he embraced Zen and became a Rinzai monk. Yet even after his experience of Zen enlightenment, he still retained a Confucian manner of thinking, for instance verifying his own enlightenment by reference to the Confucian concept of "utmost sincerity."

Of all Zen monks of the Tokugawa period, it was Kōsen who became most seriously involved with Confucianism at the intellectual level. He sought to realize Confucian aims from a Buddhist standpoint. He found much evidence in the Confucian classics of a concern with and a search for ultimate value, for instance in expressions such as: "My way is one of unity" (*Analects*); "to be watchful over oneself is solitude" (*Doctrine of the Mean* 1.3); "all-pervading energy" (Mencius); "utmost sincerity without ceasing" (*Doctrine of the Mean*). He recognized the validity of the Confucian belief that the ultimate source of value was in the self, and of the psychological techniques Confucians had developed for reaching that source. For him, therefore, the "scholarship" (*gakugei*) that had preoccupied Confucians since Sorai was merely a preliminary step to that learning. In light of these beliefs, Confucianism and Buddhism had much in common. The "illustrious nature" of Confucianism and the "Buddha-nature" referred to the same reality; Confucius talking of the "unity" was the same as the Buddha turning a flower in his hand. The ultimate reality and ultimate values at which the two traditions aimed were thus the same, and, he also claimed, they shared a concern with the achievement of good government.

Yet though he venerated Confucius as "a person who belongs to the rank of bodhisattva," Kōsen was far from discounting the differences between the two traditions, and as a Zen Buddhist he inevitably valued Buddhism more highly than Confucianism. Most of his comparisons refer to the psychological techniques they had in common. He criticized Chu Hsi's dualism between the "human mind" (*jen hsin*) and the moral mind (*tao hsin*) and his requirement that the latter overcome the former. The two minds, Kōsen claimed, were identical and formed a unity whose realization could be achieved by grasping the mean (*chung*), of which both traditions spoke. But the mental condition of grasping the mean required various procedures before it could be achieved. It was here that Kōsen found Confucianism most deficient, for it lacked the subtle and mysterious techniques commanded by the Zen sect. It seems likely that, as a follower in the tradition of Hakuin, Kōsen had the kōans compiled by the latter in mind here.

The deficiency of Confucianism in the realm of psychological techniques was illustrated by its concept of meditation. Kōsen praised the introductory passage of the *Great Learning* as "the main principles of the learning of the sages and a true method of refining the mind" and argued that the five stages of "stopping, settling, quieting, calming, and reflecting" expounded there shared the same objectives as Zen. Yet, for him, Zen meditation differed essentially from its Confucian counterpart, for the former was concerned with "correct thought" and did not involve formal questions of posture.

Again, Kōsen thought highly of Mencius's notion of "knowing one's nature" but at the same time expressed regret that Mencius had not spoken of "seeing one's nature." This was because "when one knows one's nature one merely knows Heaven; but when one sees one's nature, one then grasps

Heaven." But it is his interpretation of Confucius's reply to Yen Yuan's question concerning benevolence in the *Analects* that best illustrates Kōsen's concept of psychological techniques. Confucius has said: "Overcoming self and returning to ritual is what I call benevolence." Kōsen's comment on this was that the Confucian procedure of merely "overcoming self" was insufficient, for it was like the proverb, "chasing flies off food"— the deluded aspects of the self would simply reappear the next day. Buddhism therefore spoke rather of slaying one's deluded mind with the sharp sword of the kōan once and for all.

Underlying Kōsen's assessment of Confucian psychological techniques is a difference in assumptions between Confucianism, which is humanistic, and Buddhism, which paradoxically tries to affirm reality through radical denial of the self. Kōsen's criticisms of Confucian psychological techniques derive their persuasiveness from the stimulus he himself must have received from the Confucian studies he pursued before enlightenment. His *Zenkai ichiran* (The world of Zen surveyed), written in 1862 and printed in 1874, analyzes thirty Neo-Confucian ideas from the Zen Buddhist standpoint. It represents the first systematic intellectual response by a Tokugawa period Buddhist to the challenge posed by Confucianism, and the richest Buddhist contribution to the interaction of the two traditions during the period. But from the side of the Confucians, during the rush to modernization in the Meiji Restoration, there came nothing in reply. Nonetheless the enterprise of Zen apologetics that produced its finest result here may well have been a source of Zen intellectual self-confidence and energy after the Restoration.

Notes

1. Minor L. Rogers and Ann T. Rogers, *Rennyo: The Second Founder of Shin Buddhism* (Berkeley: Asian Humanities Press, 1991) 180.

Bibliography

NST = *Nihon shisō taikei* 57. *Kindai bukkyō no shisō* (Modern Buddhist thought). Tokyo: Iwanami Shoten, 1973.

Berling, Judith. *The Syncretic Religion of Lin Chao-en*. New York: Columbia University Press, 1980.

Imakita Kōsen. *Zenkai Ichiran*, ed. Morinaga Sōkō. Tokyo: Hakujusha, 1987.

Kashiwabara, Yūsen. "Kinsei no haibutsu shisō" and "Gohō shisō to shominkyō-ka." In *Nihon shisō taikei*, vol. 57. Tokyo: Iwanami.

Minamoto Ryōen. "Kinsei jusha no bukkyōkan" (Tokugawa Confucianists' views on Buddhism). In *Bukkyō no hikakushisōronteki kenkyū*, Tamaki Kōshirō, ed. Tokyo: Tokyo University Press, 1979.

————. "Bakumatsu-ishinki ni okeru 'gōketsu'-teki ningenzō no keisei" (The formation of a "heroic" view of the human at the end of the Tokugawa period and the beginning of the Meiji restoration). *Tōhoku Daigaku Nihon Bunka Kenkyūko hōkoku* 20 (1984) 53–78.

————. "Edo kūki ni okeru jukyō to bukkyō to no kōshō" (The interaction between Confucianism and Buddhism in the late Edo period), in *The Study of the Late Edo Period from the Viewpoint of Comparative Culture* (Tokyo: Perikansha, 1990).

Suzuki Daisetsu. *Imakita Kōsen*. Tokyo: Shunjūsha, 1992.

Yi T'oegye. *To Become a Sage*. Trans. by M. C. Kalton. New York: Columbia University Press, 1988.

{translated by James McMullen}

II. *The Buddhist Element in Shingaku*

PAUL B. WATT

IN TOKUGAWA JAPAN (1600–1868), as in earlier periods, the ideals and values of Buddhism were disseminated in works of literature and art and in intellectual and religious movements which, though not primarily concerned with the propagation of the religion, embraced important aspects of it. One of the most influential religious movements that functioned in this way is Shingaku, or "the Learning of the Heart."

Founded in the early eighteenth century by Ishida Baigan (1685–1744), Shingaku initially spread among the *chōnin*, or townsmen, a group consisting of merchants and artisans. Merchants in particular were attracted to the Learning of the Heart, since it spoke to their needs at a time when they were groping their way toward a new understanding of their place in Japanese society. In traditional Confucian theory, which served as the chief ideology of state, merchants had been relegated to the bottom of a four-tiered social structure. That ranking reflected both the predominant agricultural basis of the Tokugawa economy and the antipathy that Confucians generally felt toward a class they regarded as "unproductive." Samurai, farmers, and even their fellow townsmen the artisans, all held a higher status.

In reality, however, in the course of the seventeenth and eighteenth centuries, merchants had become the central figures in an expanding money economy, and many within the ruling samurai class had fallen deeply into their debt. Having achieved a level of material well-being and influence theoretically inappropriate to their station in society, merchants were often the target of criticism by defenders of the old order and of sumptuary edicts issued by the government.

Ishida Baigan was one of several individuals in this period who came to their defense. Drawing upon Shinto, Confucianism, and Buddhism—as well as on an established syncretic tradition—he articulated a way of life for the merchants which, while based on traditional values, imbued their work with new and, ultimately, religious significance. But the appeal of the Learning of the Heart soon reached beyond the merchant class, and by the latter half of the eighteenth century it was attracting followers from all social orders.

A Brief Life of the Founder

Ishida Baigan was born into a farm family in the small mountain village of Tōge, located just west of Kyoto. He was the second of three children. While the Ishida family was not poor, neither was it wealthy, and with the eldest son destined to inherit the family home, Baigan was apprenticed to a merchant family in Kyoto at about the age of eleven. After he had been there several years, however, it was learned that his employer was unable to properly compensate his workers and Baigan was brought home.

At twenty-three, Baigan was again sent to Kyoto as an apprentice, this time to a more successful firm. He quickly established himself as a valued and trusted employee, but during his recent stay at home, he had become interested in Shinto. Serious and introspective as a young man and anxious to correct certain faults he had discovered in his character, he had apparently concluded that Shinto embodied the true "way" for mankind. After his return to Kyoto he devoted whatever free time he had to its cultivation. As we read in *Ishida Sensei jiseki*, the biography written by his students:

> When going on business to the lower city, he carried a book in his pocket and studied whenever he had leisure. In the morning before his companions arose he read by the second story window, and at night he read after they had fallen asleep. (IBZ 2, 613)[1]

Baigan is also remembered as having exhibited a special concern for his fellow employees during these years. Even after he had achieved the position of head clerk, in winter he would leave the warmest sleeping places to others and on summer nights he made sure that the boys in the shop did not kick off their blankets (IBZ 2, 613). This marked consideration for others continued to be characteristic of Baigan throughout his life.

During his twenties and early thirties, Baigan read not only Shinto but also Buddhist and, particularly, Confucian works. The precise content of his studies is unclear, but through them he seems to have arrived at an understanding of the true way for mankind that incorporated aspects of all three religions and that stressed selfless devotion to one's appointed task, honesty, frugality, and compassion. When Baigan was thirty-five or six, however, he began to have doubts. In particular, he had become unsure about the character of human nature *(sei)*, an issue that bore directly on his estimate of the individual's capacity to realize the way. After seeking out several teachers without success, he met Oguri Ryōun (d. 1729), a man who had once served as a domain official and who had retired to Kyoto to live out his days as a teacher. Oguri was versed not only in Neo-Confucianism but in Taoism and Buddhism as well. Their first meeting was little more than a failed attempt on Baigan's part to initiate a discussion of the problem of human nature; nevertheless, Baigan's spirits were buoyed by the encounter, for he felt that at last he had found someone to whom he could turn for help.

Yet even under Oguri's guidance, Baigan's uncertainties were not quickly resolved. After a year and a half of intense reflection and study, some progress was unexpectedly made during a visit home to care for his ailing mother. On one occasion when he left her side and opened a door to go out, he had the sudden sensation that all of his doubts had been dispersed. According to his *Recorded Sayings*, in that moment he realized "that his own nature *(jisei)* was the parent of Heaven and earth and all things" (IBZ 1, 438), and he was overcome with joy. To this, the *Jiseki* adds that at the same time he came to know that "the way of Yao and Shun [legendary rulers revered in the Confucian tradition] is only filial piety and obedience" (IBZ 2, 615).

When Baigan informed Oguri about this experience, his teacher recognized that he had made a breakthrough of sorts, but he pointed out that Baigan had another step to take. "The eye with which you saw that our nature is the parent of Heaven and earth remains," Oguri told him. "Nature truly exists when there is no eye. Now just once set that eye aside" (IBZ 2, 615). Baigan worked conscientiously for more than a year before he could accomplish this, but he finally attained full illumination, or *hatsumei* as the Shingaku people refer to the experience, early one morning just after dawn. The *Jiseki* gives the following account:

> Late one night he lay down exhausted and was unaware of the break of day. As he lay there, he heard the cry of a sparrow. At that moment, a feeling comparable to the serenity of a great sea or cloudless sky pervaded his body. His experience of the cry of that sparrow was like a cormorant's breaking the surface and entering the water of a great serene sea. From that time on, he set aside the conscious observation of his own nature. (IBZ 2, 615)

His confidence restored, Baigan, now forty-two or three, left his place of employment and began to give occasional lectures. Shortly thereafter, in 1729 when Baigan was forty-five, his teacher died. Just before his death, Oguri had offered Baigan his books, replete with his notations, but Baigan refused, explaining that as he encountered new circumstances, he would expound the teaching anew (IBZ 2, 616). In that same year, Baigan opened his first lecture hall in Kyoto and formally began his career as a teacher. He neither charged his students a fee nor asked for any special introductions. Over the remaining fifteen years of his life, which he passed unmarried, he lectured in Osaka as well as Kyoto and produced the two works for which he is most often remembered: his *Tohimondō* (City and country dialogues,

1739) and his *Kenyaku Seikaron* (Frugality: essays on household management, 1744). These, along with his *Recorded Sayings* and the *Ishida Sensei jiseki*, which were completed after his death, constitute the chief sources for an
understanding of his thoughts.[2]

Baigan's Teachings and Buddhism

Although early in his life Baigan had stated that his chief aim was to propagate Shinto, and although Buddhism, too, had a place in his thought,
there is little doubt that Confucianism—especially the Neo-Confucianism
of the Ch'eng-Chu school—had the greatest influence upon him. Several
aspects of his life and teachings indicate that this is the case. First, at the
core of his teachings lay the traditional Neo-Confucian emphasis on the
importance of knowing one's nature. Thus he writes in his *Tohimondō:*

> The highest aim of learning is to exhaust one's heart and know one's nature.
> Knowing one's nature, one knows Heaven. Knowing Heaven, one knows the
> heart of Confucius and Mencius, which is identical with Heaven. Knowing
> the heart of Confucius and Mencius, one knows the heart of the Sung literati,
> which is the same. (IBZ 1, 71)

Moreover, as Baigan's illumination experience shows, to know one's
nature is to know the nature of all things and to attain an experience of
unself-conscious union with them. Although Baigan's illumination in particular has often been interpreted in a Buddhist light, as de Bary has indicated both the general thrust of his teaching and his illumination experience
fall within the mainstream of the Neo-Confucian tradition.[3]

Secondly, for Baigan the ethical implications of knowing one's nature are
also typically Confucian. In his first illumination experience, Baigan realized not only that his nature was "the parent of Heaven and earth and all
things," but also that when that nature manifests itself in action, filial piety
and obedience are the result. In the *Tohimondō* he makes the connection
between knowing one's nature and Confucian ethics explicit: "When one
knows one's nature, one also knows that the five constant virtues [benevo-
lence, righteousness, decorum, wisdom, and good faith] and the five human
relationships [between father and son, ruler and subject, husband and wife,
elder and younger brother, friend and friend] are endowed within it" (IBZ
1, 5). Thirdly, the methodology that Baigan followed in realizing his nature
and that he later taught his students is the common Neo-Confucian one. It
involved primarily three activities: study, reflection, and the conscientious
application of what one had learned to everyday life situations.[4] Finally,
both the texts that Baigan cites in his writings and those upon which he

lectured were predominantly Confucian. Baigan does in fact cite sūtras and other Buddhist material, and he lectured upon the *Tsurezuregusa,* a work of Buddhist coloration. But it was the *Analects,* the *Mencius,* and the writings of the Sung Neo-Confucians that most often held his attention.

Even given this close connection between Baigan and Neo-Confucianism, however, it would be wrong to view him as a self-conscious transmitter of that tradition. As Shibata Minoru has pointed out, Baigan was not related to any specific lineage of teachers nor did he belong to any currently popular school (IBZ 1, 10). In the end, his teachings can only be understood as the result of his personal reflections on his own experience. Although, on the one hand, this approach led to the appearance of inconsistencies, for which he was criticized by Confucian, Shinto, and Buddhist adherents alike; on the other, it enabled him to move freely among the religious traditions popular in his day, selecting from each that which his own experience had confirmed. In Baigan's view, Confucianism, Shinto, and Buddhism—and indeed, even Taoism—were all "whetstones for polishing the mind" (IBZ 1, 121) and he "neither clung to one nor discarded any" (IBZ 1, 120).

The interpretive key upon which Baigan relied as he moved from tradition to tradition was the experience of self-transcendence he had undergone at the time of his illumination. Baigan later sought to indicate the nature of this state through such terms as "no selfish heart" *(shishin nashi)* and "no self" *(muga),* and it is clear that, for Baigan, selfish desire was the fundamental problem all human beings had to conquer. He saw Shinto addressing this issue through its stress upon the virtue of honesty, or *shōjiki,* which he understood as reflective of a pure and unselfish heart (IBZ 1, 218). In Buddhism, as one might expect, it was its own teaching of no self or no mind to which he was drawn. Baigan granted, as did many of his contemporaries, that Confucianism was better suited as a philosophy of government than Buddhism (IBZ 1, 56), but he also believed that there was no difference between the heart attained through the Buddhist Dharma and that attained through the Confucian way (IBZ 1, 120). Further, he held that all Buddhist sects taught the achievement of this same state of mind. He writes in his *Tohimondō:*

> In the Tendai sect, they speak of concentration and insight; in the Shingon sect, of the original unborn mind symbolized by the Sanskrit letter *A;* in the Zen sect, they speak of one's original face; in the Nenbutsu sect, of the interpenetration of self and Self *(nyūga ga'nyū)*[5] and the union of the believer's heart and Amitābha's Dharma; and in the Nichiren sect, they speak of the Wondrous Dharma. Although the terminology thus differs, the goal achieved is the same. (IBZ 1, 116-17)

It was this teaching of knowing one's nature and of unselfish living, upon which Baigan believed all traditions agreed, that he spread among the merchants. Since for him the difference among the four classes was not one of value but merely one of function, he encouraged merchants to regard their everyday activities as the place where they might come to know their natures and realize the way. Profit gained through the honest and frugal pursuit of these activities, he argued, was no different from the stipends received by the samurai, the model citizens of Tokugawa society (IBZ 1, 78).

As regards the specifically Buddhist element in his teachings, while his attitude toward the religion was in most respects positive, Baigan could not fully embrace it on its own terms; rather he interpreted Buddhism in the light of his fundamentally Neo-Confucian vision and discarded those aspects that did not permit such an interpretation. Indicative of this is his view of the Buddhist precept of non-killing. Baigan personally could go to great extremes to avoid needlessly harming living things, but he rejected Buddhism's prohibition of killing out of hand. "It is a principle of nature," he states flatly, "that the noble eat the humble" (IBZ 1, 54).

Buddhism and Later Shingaku

Buddhism continued to occupy a prominent position in the teachings of later Shingaku masters. Indeed, at times it appears to displace Neo-Confucianism as the dominant element in the syncretist thought of Tejima Tōan (1718–1786) and Tōan's disciple, Nakazawa Dōni (1725–1803). The former was Shingaku's chief organizer; the latter, the movement's most famous preacher. These were the men chiefly responsible for the organization of Shingaku into a recognizable movement and its dissemination to many areas of the country in the half century after Baigan's death.

Tōan, the son of a wealthy Kyoto merchant family, joined Baigan's group when he was eighteen and within three years had his *hatsumei* experience. As a result of the deaths of other early disciples, by 1760 he had emerged as Baigan's principal heir. In that year Tōan completed the compilation of the *Jiseki*, and in the following year he commenced his activities as a full-time teacher. His most important contributions to the movement were (1) his founding of the first permanent lecture halls, including the three that became the main Shingaku schools: the Shūseisha, Jishūsha, and Meirinsha; (2) his establishment of a system for the instruction of Shingaku followers and the certification of individuals who had achieved illumination; and (3) his systematization of some of Baigan's teachings[6] and his composition of numerous popular tracts for the education of women and children.

Dōni was also a native of Kyoto and came from a family that for genera-tions had produced the famous Nishijin brocade. His family was affiliated with the Nichiren sect, and consequently he had an acquaintance with its teachings from his youth. In his early forties, he also had contact with the Rinzai Zen master Tōrei, a disciple of Hakuin. Dōni entered Tōan's circle in his mid-forties and quickly became his leading student. When Dōni was fifty-five, Tōan sent him to Edo, the seat of the Tokugawa government, where he founded the Sanzensha, the school that became the center of the Shingaku movement in eastern Japan. In Edo, Dōni spoke to day laborers and high-ranking samurai alike, winning a vast following and forging the close link between Shingaku and the government that lasted until the end of the Tokugawa period.

Tōan and Dōni followed closely in Baigan's footsteps and taught a syn-cretism of Confucianism, Shinto and Buddhism. Like Baigan, Tōan stressed the importance of attaining a state of selflessness, which he characterized as a condition in which one "has no self-centered preoccupations" *(shian nashi)*, and he often chose to explicate this state in Buddhist terms. In particular, he was attracted to Zen Buddhism as it was transmitted by two well-known Tokugawa masters, Suzuki Shōsan (1579–1656) and Bankei Yōtaku (1622–1693).[7] From the perspectives of biography and personality, Suzuki and Bankei were strikingly different individuals, but both men sought to simplify Zen and to make it more accessible, and it was to this simplified Zen that Tōan was drawn.

Suzuki was the more radical of the two Buddhist masters, even going as far as to discourage people from entering the clergy; he asked instead that they look upon their ordinary activities as their practice. Tōan indicated his approval of Suzuki's views by writing an introduction to one of his works, the *Mōanjō* (A safe staff for the blind).

Unlike Suzuki, Bankei never disavowed traditional Buddhist practice, although he was critical of aspects of Zen as it existed in his time. Still, in his own attempt to set forth Zen's essence—maintaining above all that its goal was simply the realization of the unborn *(fushō)* Buddha-mind—he made statements that could be understood to imply a position similar, if not identical, to Suzuki's. Tōan interpreted Bankei precisely in this manner. Thus, when he was asked by an observer, who had noticed the apparent similarities between Tōan's and Bankei's teachings, about the relationship between the two, Tōan replied that there was not the slightest difference.[8] "It is just that since there are people who are not familiar with the word 'unborn,' I tell them about having no self-centered preoccupations."[9] More-over, Tōan took Bankei's occasional references to the term *meitoku*—a key concept in the Confucian classic, the *Great Learning*—as evidence that the Zen monk also taught a syncretism similar to his own. In fact, it is clear that Bankei believed Buddhism to be superior to Confucianism.[10] Be that as it may, from Tōan's time on, Bankei was held in high regard in the Shingaku movement.

In Dōni's case, the influence of Zen, transmitted indirectly through Tōan and directly through Tōrei, is still evident, but more striking in his presentation of Shingaku teachings is his use of the language of the Nichiren sect, with which his family was affiliated. Dōni summarized the insight attained in an enlightenment experience he had while still with Tōrei in the words, "All under Heaven and within the four seas takes its refuge in the Wondrous Dharma." The words "Wondrous Dharma" *(myōhō)* form part of the full title of the *Lotus Sūtra* (*Myōhō Rengekyō*, Lotus sūtra of the wondrous dharma), upon which the Nichiren sect is based. In Dōni's later *dōwa*, or "talks on the way," the phrase "wondrous Dharma" appears with regularity. Here one example will have to suffice:

> If one knows one's heart, one knows one's nature. If one knows one's nature, one knows Heaven.... All things have empty Heaven *(kokūten)* as their heart. The sparrow chirps and the crow caws. Since it is something marvelous beyond expectation, we call it both the wondrous Dharma and ultimate reality *(jissō)*.[11]

Further illustrations of the prominence of Buddhism in later Shingaku could be given: Fuse Shōō (1725–1784), for example, drew on a variety of Buddhist sectarian teachings, and Shibata Kyūō (1783–1839) gave "talks on the way" that show traces of Pure Land, rather than Zen, influence. In all cases, however, their orientation toward the tradition did not differ fundamentally from Baigan's. Tōan could, from his perspective, argue that his teachings were identical to those of Bankei, but when he went about setting up a curriculum for Shingaku schools, he limited the works upon which lectures could be given to the Four Books (the *Analects*, the *Mencius*, the *Great Learning*, and the *Mean*), *Reflections on Things at Hand* (writings and sayings of Sung Neo-Confucians compiled by Chu Hsi and Lu Tsuch'ien), the *Elementary Learning* (a manual for the instruction of children compiled under Chu Hsi's direction), and the writings of Baigan. Similarly, while Dōni could borrow the vocabulary of Zen and Nichiren Buddhism, his teaching never went beyond the limits of what might be termed Neo-Confucian ethical naturalism. "What is the Way?" he asks. "The sparrow chirps and the crow caws. The kite has its way and the dove, its way; 'the gentleman acts in conformity with his position and desires nothing beyond it' [a quotation from the *Mean*]. To act in accordance with one's form *(katachi)* is called the way of harmony of Heaven and earth."[12] Thus, although Shingaku could impart new meaning to the activities of the merchant class, for the rest, it simply affirmed the existing social and moral order. As Dōni himself stated, "The way lies merely in conforming *(junnō)*."[13]

In spite of the close resemblance of Shingaku to Buddhist teachings, what Shingaku lacked from a strictly Buddhist point of view was the radical critical spirit embodied in the Mahāyāna Buddhist doctrine of emptiness and in its teaching regarding the nature of the mind. Kashiwabara Yūsen has written of Fuse Shōō that "even if he taught no self, his message was the ethical one of abandoning selfish desires within the context of social life; in Buddhism, he sought spiritual sustenance for practical living that to the end had, *as its immediate premise*, the affirmation of the human being."[14] This evaluation could be extended to include the entire Shingaku tradition. Although Mahāyāna Buddhism, too, had a message of ultimate affirmation of the human being, it held that such a stance could only be taken after an initial negation and transformation of ordinary human consciousness had been carried out.

Thus, the Buddhism transmitted within Shingaku was not Buddhism in its most philosophically consistent form. Nevertheless, since an unalloyed transmission of its teachings was the exception rather than the rule wherever Buddhism spread, and since Tokugawa Buddhism itself often failed to exhibit the above-mentioned critical spirit, the significance of Shingaku's role as a disseminator of the religion should by no means be underestimated. It could be argued that, because of the similarity of Shingaku and Buddhist teachings, Shingaku's popularity created subtle barriers to a genuine encounter with the Buddhist tradition. Yet the popularity of the Shingaku interpretation of Buddhism, even among Japanese with no direct ties to the movement, cannot be denied.

Notes

1. IBZ = Shibata Minoru, ed., *Ishida Baigan zenshū* (Kyoto: Meirinsha, 1957). A complete translation of the *Jiseki* can be found in Robert Bellah, *Tokugawa Religion: The Values of Pre-Industrial Japan* (Boston: Beacon Press, 1957) 199–216.

2. Another short work traditionally attributed to Baigan and couched almost entirely in Buddhist language is the *Makumōzō*. Questions have been raised about its authenticity, however, and it has been excluded from consideration here. A copy of the text can be found in Shibata Minoru, ed., *Sekimon Shingaku* (Nihon Shisō Taikei, 42) (Tokyo: Iwanami, 1971).

3. Wm. Theodore de Bary, *Neo-Confucian Orthodoxy and the Learning of the Mind-and-Heart* (New York: Columbia University Press, 1981) 207.

4. Although Bellah includes meditation among the essential practices in which Baigan engaged, it actually appears to have been of only secondary importance to him. See Shibata's discussion of this point in *Ishida Baigan* (Jinbutsu Sōsho) (Tokyo: Yoshikawa Kōbunkan, 1962) 71. The Neo-Confucian practice of "quiet sitting" *(seiza),* however, was systematically incorporated into Shingaku practice by later teachers.

5. Although this concept is also associated with Shingon, here Baigan uses it in reference to Pure Land Buddhism; in meaning, it is virtually identical to the phrase following it.

6. Most important in this regard is Tōan's consistent use of *honshin,* or "true heart," for Baigan's *sei,* or nature; it was only after this change had been made that the movement was commonly referred to as Shingaku.

7. On Suzuki, see Winston L. King, *Death was his Kōan: The Samurai-Zen of Suzuki Shōsan* (Berkeley, CA: Asian Humanities Press, 1986), and Royall Tyler, *Selected Writings of Suzuki Shōsan,* Cornell University East Asian Papers, 13 (Ithaca: Cornell China-Japan Program, 1977). On Bankei, see Norman Waddell, *The Unborn: The Life and Teaching of Zen Master Bankei (1622–1693)* (San Francisco: North Point Press, 1984), and Peter Haskel, *Bankei Zen: Translations From the Record of Bankei* (New York: Grove Weidenfeld, 1984).

8. Shibata, *Sekimon Shingaku,* 118.

9. Shibata, *Sekimon Shingaku,* 119.

10. See Kinami Takuichi's article on Bankei and Tōan, "Bankei rikai no ippōto: Tōan no Shingaku kara," *Zen bunka* 10-11 (April 1958) 75–86.

11. Shibata, *Sekimon Shingaku,* 224.

12. Shibata, *Sekimon Shingaku,* 210.

13. Shibata, *Sekimon Shingaku,* 211.

14. Tamamuro Taijō, ed., *Nihon Bukkyō shi III: Kinsei kindai hen* (Kyoto: Hōzōkan, 1967), 150 (emphasis added).

Bibliography

Bellah, Robert. *Tokugawa Religion: The Values of Pre-Industrial Japan.* Boston: Beacon Press, 1957.

Brocchieri, Paola Beonio. "Some Remarks on the Buddhist Elements in the Philosophy of Ishida Baigan." *The Transactions of the International Conference of Orientalists in Japan,* vol. 3, 1958, 32–45.

Furuta Shōkin. "Shingaku to Bukkyō: Baigan, Tōan, Dōni no Zen ni tsuite." *Shingaku* 6 (1942) 1–40.

Ishikawa Ken. *Shingaku: Edo no shomin tetsugaku.* Tokyo: Nihon Keizai Shinbun, 1964.

Izuyama Kakudō. "Zen to Shingaku." *Kōza Zen 5* (Zen to Bunka), 239–55. Tokyo: Chikuma Shobō, 1968.

Kashiwabara Yūsen. "Bukkyō shisō no tenkai." In Tamamuro Taijō, ed., *Nihon Bukkyō shi III: Kinsei kindai hen,* esp. 148–51. Kyoto: Hōzōkan, 1967.

Kinami Takuichi. "Bankei rikai no ippōto: Tōan no Shingaku kara." *Zen bunka* 10–11 (April 1958) 75–86.

Sawada, Janine. *Confucian Values and Popular Zen: Sekimon Shingaku in Eighteenth-Century Japan.* Honolulu: University of Hawai'i Press, 1993.

Shibata Minoru. *Ishida Baigan*. (Jinbutsu Sōsho). Tokyo: Yoshikawa Kōbunkan, 1962.

————. *Shingaku*. Tokyo: Shibundō, 1967.

————, ed. *Ishida Baigan zenshū*, 2 vols. Kyoto: Meirinsha, 1957.

————, ed. *Sekimon Shingaku*. (Nihon Shisō Taikei, 42). Tokyo: Iwanami, 1971.

Yamamoto Shichihei. *Kinben no tetsugaku*. Kyoto: PHP, 1979.

III. *Jiun Sonja*

PAUL B. WATT

IN THE TOKUGAWA period (1600–1868), Buddhism continued to exert widespread influence in Japanese society, but it also faced serious challenges to its traditional position of strength. Within, the Buddhist establishment suffered from a divisive sectarianism and a decline in discipline among the clergy. From without, it was challenged by new developments in the world of thought. Confucianism, a renewed interest in Shinto and nativist learning, and a less influential although burgeoning strain of rationalist thought, all came to the fore in the Tokugawa period, and proponents of these various points of view were often harshly critical of Buddhism.

Jiun Sonja stands as one of the leading Buddhist reformers, scholars, and apologists of this period. Although attracted to Confucianism as a boy, he was converted to Buddhism in his teens and went on in his adult years to formulate a comprehensive response to the challenges that Buddhism faced in his day. Underlying his response was his commitment to reviving what he sometimes called "Buddhism as it was when the Buddha was alive" *(Butsu zaise no Bukkyō)* or, more simply, the "True Dharma" *(shōbō),* by which he meant the suprasectarian fundamentals of Buddhist thought and practice.

Biography

Jiun was born in 1718 in Osaka, one of the great commercial cities of Tokugawa Japan. His father, Kōzuki Yasunori (1665–1730), was a rōnin or masterless samurai who had found employment at one of the many domain granaries located in the city. His mother, an adopted daughter of the official in charge of the granary, was a devout Buddhist. Jiun was the last son and seventh of eight children born to the couple. Although Jiun's father was sympathetic to both Buddhism and Shinto, he seems to have been most attracted to Confucianism. Jiun tells us that a follower of the Chu Hsi school of Confucianism lectured at their home. As a boy, Jiun adopted the Confucian position as his own, and also embraced the traditional Confucian criticism of Buddhism as an antisocial religion that encouraged people to withdraw from family and society; thus he "hated monks and the Buddhist Dharma" and regarded Śākyamuni as a "deceitful leader" (JSZ 11.479-80).[1] Ironically, however, when Yasunori died in Jiun's thirteenth year, his last wish was that his son enter the Buddhist clergy. Almost immediately Jiun's mother entrusted the boy to the care of Ninkō Teiki (1671–1750), a monk of the Shingon Vinaya sect (Shingon Risshū) who had periodically visited the Kōzuki home in Osaka and who was the head of Hōraku-ji, a temple located just east of the city.[2]

Jiun arrived at Hōraku-ji in 1730, and Teiki began his training in 1731 with rudimentary instruction in Sanskrit. Jiun's conversion did not take place, however, until 1732 when, at Teiki's direction, he undertook a series of four meditations (the *shido kegyō*) designed to prepare the practitioner for ordination as a Shingon monk. The first of these meditations had such a powerful effect upon him, he reports, that at its conclusion he found his entire body covered in sweat and he wept uncontrollably; thereafter, he threw himself into his Buddhist studies and practice and "day by day became increasingly aware of the Dharma's profundity" (JSZ 11.481).

In 1733 Teiki gave Jiun's training a new direction. Concerned that he have a sound knowledge of Confucianism, Buddhism's chief rival in the Tokugawa period, Teiki sent Jiun to Kyoto to study at the school of the famous Confucian scholar, Itō Jinsai (1627–1705). A leader in the Ancient Learning *(kogaku)* movement, Jinsai had been critical of the abstract philosophical tendencies of Neo-Confucianism and had urged a return to the original teachings of Confucius and Mencius. Jinsai had died by the time Jiun arrived, but the school was still flourishing under the leadership of his son, Tōgai (1670–1736). Jiun studied Confucian texts and Chinese prose and poetry there for three years.

Jiun returned to Hōraku-ji in 1736. In that year, he spent time at the Shingon Vinaya center Yachū-ji, there receiving the precepts for novices. In 1738 he was again at Yachū-ji to receive the 250 rules that guide the life of the mature monk. When Jiun was twenty-two, Teiki ordained him as a full-fledged Shingon master *(ajari),* and shortly thereafter he made him abbot of Hōraku-ji. During this period Jiun also studied Mahāyāna Buddhist thought generally and received instruction from Teiki in *Ryōbu,* or Dual, Shinto, a form of Buddhist-Shinto syncretism transmitted within the Shingon sect.

After his return from Kyoto, Jiun gave special attention to meditation. While abbot of Hōraku-ji, he took up one of the most basic forms of Shingon meditation, the "meditation on the Sanskrit letter *A*" *(ajikan).* Progress came slowly, however, and apparently dissatisfied for the moment with the

Shingon approach, Jiun turned over Hōraku-ji to a fellow disciple and in 1741 set off to practice Zen under the guidance of the Sōtō Zen master Hōsen Daibai (1682–1757) in Shinshū. Jiun stayed with Daibai until 1743 and seems to have benefited greatly from the experience; he later wrote that it was while he was in Shinshū that he "first felt right" (JSZ 14.750). Moreover, although Jiun remained a Shingon monk throughout his life, from this period on he held Zen in particularly high regard. Still, if at this time Jiun had reservations about the tradition in which he had been raised, he was also not entirely comfortable with Zen. He writes of a "divergence of opinion" between himself and Daibai (JSZ 14.750). The reason for the tension is not clear, but it may well have been a result of Daibai's narrow dedication to Zen and Jiun's growing awareness of the need for a more broadly defined revival of the essentials of Buddhist thought and practice, if the religion were successfully to meet the challenges confronting it.

Jiun returned to Hōraku-ji in 1743 in a state of uncertainty about the prospects for such a revival and seriously considering a retreat to a life of solitary contemplation. Waiting for him at the temple, however, were young disciples of Teiki who pleaded convincingly with him to take action. Jiun was particularly moved by the appeal made by Gumoku Shinshū (1728–1751), who became his leading disciple at this time and who was a constant source of inspiration. From 1744 to 1758 Jiun and a small band of followers made their first concentrated efforts at a restoration of the True Dharma. They began at Chōei-ji, a dilapidated temple just east of Osaka that had been under Teiki's supervision. There, in his *Konpon sōsei* (Basic regulations for monks, 1749), Jiun expressed for the first time his view of what life according to the True Dharma entailed (JSZ 6.70–75). These regulations, which set the tone for life at Chōei-ji, mandated strict observance of the vinaya, stressed the importance of meditation and study, and, affirming that all followers of the Dharma and the vinaya were "brothers in this school," prohibited any expression of sectarian prejudice. Much later in his career, Jiun received official recognition from the Tokugawa government for his Shōbōritsu, or "Vinaya of the True Dharma," movement, but it is clear that the movement had its beginning in the 1740s at Chōei-ji.

In 1750 Jiun took over Keirin-ji, another temple located in the Osaka area, and it became the center of his activities for the next eight years. At Keirin-ji, he produced his first major piece of scholarship, the *Hōbuku zugi* (Explanation of monastic attire with illustrations) in 1751 (JSZ 1.87–324; abridged version 1.1–83). Jiun regarded the wide variation in styles of robes worn by the clergy as indicative of the fragmented character of the Japanese Buddhist community, and in this work he sought to reestablish the correct standard in monastic apparel. He also lectured on numerous occasions in this period on such texts as the *Vinaya in Four Parts, The Recorded Sayings of Lin-chi, The Platform Sūtra of the Sixth Patriarch,* and the *Vimalakīrti Sūtra* (the lectures are not extant, but he refers to them in JSZ 17.26–27). The list reflects well the great value he attached to monastic discipline and Zen, as well as the suprasectarian quality of his movement. Further evidence of his special interest in the vinaya is the commentary he wrote in 1758 on I-ching's (635–713) *Nan-hai-chi-kuei-nei-fa ch'uan* (Record of the inner law sent home from the southern sea), a report on Buddhist discipline as it was practiced in South Asia in I-ching's day (JSZ 4.39–555).

Jiun lost many of his closest supporters during the Keirin-ji years, including his teacher, Ninkō Teiki, and his leading disciple, Gumoku Shinshō. Although talented people continued to enter the movement, by 1758 Jiun had resolved to move to a small hut on Mt. Ikoma, east of Osaka, for a period of reflection and study. The dwelling was called Two Dragon Hut (Sōryūan), after the image it enshrined, a small statue of Śākyamuni seated in meditation with two dragons coiled around its base. Here Jiun devoted much of his time to meditation, and many of the portraits of Jiun still extant show him seated in meditation on a large rock at nearby Nagao Falls.[3] He also gave talks on the Dharma from time to time and wrote sermons at the request of individual followers (many of which can be found in JSZ 14.287–778). However, the most important development of these years was his Sanskrit studies. Convinced of the need to reach beyond Chinese Buddhist texts to the Sanskrit originals in his quest for the True Dharma, and stimulated by the parallel example of scholars in the Ancient Learning school of Confucianism, who in their own reform movement emphasized the importance of a thorough knowledge of the earliest Confucian texts (JSZ 9b.3–4), Jiun spent long hours in the study of the language. He brought his work to a culmination in his *Bongaku Shinryō* (Guide to Sanskrit studies). A thousand-fascicle work that includes Sanskrit texts, grammars, dictionaries, and background information on Indian geography, history and customs, it represents the high watermark of Japanese Sanskrit studies in the premodern period.[4]

Jiun's lengthy stay at Two Dragon Hut came to an end in 1771. In that year, four lay followers in Kyoto purchased Amida-dera, a temple located in the city, and after repeated requests finally convinced him to take up residence there. Although up to this point in his career Jiun had concentrated more on matters of concern to the clergy, during the short time he resided at Amida-dera, he became an apologist for Buddhism to Japanese society as a whole.

The major product of his efforts in this regard was a series of sermons given at Amida-dera between the eleventh month of An'ei 2 and the fourth month of An'ei 3 (1774). They were recorded by his disciples and have been known to later generations as the *Jūzen hōgo* or Sermons on the Ten Good Precepts.[5] Jiun gave these sermons at the request of certain women in the Imperial Family, most notably Kaimeimon'in (d. 1789), the surviving consort of the long deceased Emperor Sakuramachi, and Kyōraimon'in (d. 1795), the mother of the reigning emperor. Shaken by the death of a young prince and having heard of Jiun's presence in the capital, they turned to the now famous monk for an explanation. The result was one of the classics of Tokugawa Buddhism. Through a discussion of a widely accepted formulation of Buddhist morality and thought—the ten good precepts—Jiun presented his understanding of the essentials of the religion and its relevance to humankind. In these sermons he also set forth his most complete response to Confucian critics and made an indirect reply to the rationalists. Jiun himself is reported to have said of the work, "Those who would know me and those who would criticize me, both must rely on the *Sermons on the Ten Good Precepts*" (JSZ, introductory volume, 46).

Jiun completed the editing of his sermons in 1775 and in 1776 he set off for the quiet mountain temple of Kōki-ji, located in the district of Kawachi, southeast of Osaka. This temple became his home for the last twenty-eight years of his life.

During this period, the Shōbōritsu movement continued to grow. In Kyoto, for example, the first nunneries of the movement were founded by Kyōraimon'in and Kaimeimon'in. The former established Chōfuku-ji in 1784; the latter, Mizuyakushi-ji in 1793. Jiun frequently traveled to these and other temples in the Kyoto-Osaka area to speak or officiate at ceremonies. Also during these years the lord of nearby Kōriyama castle, Yanagisawa Yasumitsu (1753–1817), became his lay disciple.

Jiun's chief concern at this time, however, was the establishment of Kōki-ji as the central training ground for monks of the Shōbōritsu movement. During the late 1770s and early 1780s work was done on the temple and rules were set down regarding temple finances and monastic conduct. Then, in 1786, the Tokugawa government recognized Kōki-ji as the main Shōbōritsu temple. In that year Jiun issued yet another set of regulations, known as the *Kōjiki kitei* (JSZ 6.83–90), a document that, in its demand for dedication to the True Dharma, observance of the vinaya, and suprasectarian unity, echoes many of the themes first articulated in the *Konpon sōsei* of 1749. This and other products of these years, such as his short *Hito to naru michiai* (The way to be truly human, 1781; JSZ 13.21–46)—

an abridgement of his *Sermons on the Ten Good Precepts*—testify to fundamental continuities in Jiun's thought.

Yet in this last phase of his life, Jiun also widened the scope of his studies. Both Shinto, Japan's native religion, and Shingon Buddhism, the sect
to which he belonged, increasingly came to occupy his attention.[6] His aim
in taking up these topics was to show the relationship of each to the True
Dharma he had spent a lifetime advocating. Moreover, in setting forth his
own unique interpretation of Shinto, known as Unden Shinto, he was also
responding to the revival of the religion then taking place.

In the summer of 1804 Jiun became ill and moved from Kōki-ji to
Amida-dera in order to receive medical attention. In spite of his failing
health, he gave periodic lectures at the temple on the *Diamond Sūtra* until
his death in the twelfth month of that year.

Thought

Throughout Jiun's long career, reviving the True Dharma remained the
consistent rationale behind all of his activities. Even his calligraphy, yet
another aspect of his work for which he is still remembered, was undertaken
with this purpose in mind. He usually defined this Dharma in general
terms; at one point he describes it as "simply acting as the Buddha acted
and thinking as he thought" (JSZ 14.331). His frequent references in his
sermons and writings to the "three branches of Buddhist learning" *(sangaku)*—i.e., morality, meditation, and wisdom—suggest that it, too, served
as a handy guide. However, the most comprehensive statement of Jiun's
thought in this regard is his *Sermons on the Ten Good Precepts*. A product of
his mid-fifties, the work brings together the fruit of decades of scholarly
inquiry into the essentials of the Buddhist religion and of attempts to realize the ideal of the Buddha-like life in his own experience and in that of the
communities he led.

The focus of these sermons is, of course, the *jūzen*, or ten good precepts,
a formulation of Buddhist ethics and thought that prohibits killing, stealing, adultery, lying, frivolous language, slander, equivocation, greed, anger,
and wrong views. For Jiun, this simple code, which Buddhists had acknowledged in all periods of their history and wherever Buddhism spread, represents the essence of the Buddhist path. All progress toward enlightenment
depends upon its observance, and all more detailed statements of Buddhist
morality and thought can be subsumed within it.

However, beyond encapsulating the heart of Buddhism, in Jiun's mind the
jūzen stand as a universal guide for humankind. They are in effect wherever

human beings exist, "whether or not a Buddha appears in the world" to identify and expound them (JSZ 11.25, 46, 55). They encompass "all countries, the past as well as the present, the wise as well as the foolish, the clever as well as the slow, the noble as well as the humble, and men as well as women" (JSZ 11.56). And in long sections in his *Sermons*, Jiun points out the relevance of the *jūzen* for all aspects of human existence, secular as well as sacred. Thus, on the one hand, they constitute a path that, if followed, results in stability in the family, success in business, and a well-governed state; on the other, they lead finally to the attainment of buddhahood, which Jiun characterized as the full realization of our true human nature.

The universalistic ethical vision that Jiun offers in his *Sermons* is inextricably linked to the Mahāyāna Buddhist understanding of ultimate reality, an understanding most fully expressed in the concept of emptiness. As is well known, Buddhism generally holds that the common condition of the unenlightened person is one of suffering. That suffering is seen as arising from attachments to persons and things falsely believed to possess a "self," or abiding, unchanging essence. Through the concept of emptiness, the Mahāyānists sought to point, in a radical way, to the lack of such an abiding essence in all things, thus undercutting the structure of consciousness that posits "self" and "other" as absolute categories and that inevitably leads to attachments and suffering. Thus, from the perspective of the emptiness doctrine, reality is fundamentally dynamic, and all particulars in the phenomenal order exist, not autonomously, but only in a vast net of interdependencies. Indeed, as Jiun indicates, the experiential consequence of having attained insight into emptiness is that one sees all sentient beings as one's children and all things as one's very own body (JSZ 11.6, 9).

Although Jiun prefers to use synonyms for emptiness—most commonly, Buddha-nature *(busshō)*, the *dharmatā*, or true nature of the phenomenal order *(hosshō)*, and Principle *(ri)*—the claims for the *jūzen* that he makes in his *Sermons* stem directly from the conception of reality built upon the emptiness doctrine. In short, the ten good precepts represent the implications that this view of reality has for human conduct. To live in complete accord with the *jūzen* is nothing less than to live in accord with the *dharmatā*, the true nature of the phenomenal order. Thus, Jiun writes in chapter one of his *Sermons*, "Although I preach the ten good precepts, there is just the one Buddha-nature, the one *dharmatā*. Keeping your mind in harmony with the *dharmatā* is called good; going against it is called evil" (JSZ 11.15–16).

Proper conduct, therefore, depends ultimately on the attainment of insight into the *dharmatā*. In Jiun's view, this is the insight that the historical

Buddha achieved, and his conduct—passed on as a model for the clergy in the vinaya and in simpler codes like the *jūzen*—flowed naturally from his wisdom. It was to this high ideal of the unity of wisdom and morality, transcending all sectarian boundaries, that Jiun summoned the Tokugawa Buddhist clergy. And should this ideal be too lofty for lay followers, to them he held out more immediate goals: the joys and benefits of a life lived in conformity with the *jūzen* to whatever degree their individual circumstances permitted, for to the extent they observed the ten good precepts they were also living in conformity with the *dharmatā* and would experience the rewards of that way of life.

Jiun's response to Confucianism was also presented from this perspective. Although his first concern in his *Sermons* was to provide guidance to the Buddhist community, by making clear the relevance of the *jūzen* for life in the secular world, he was also demonstrating that Buddhism was not, as many Confucians had contended, a socially, harmful religion. But Jiun's response to Confucianism went further than this. On the one hand, Jiun attested to the merits of Confucian morality; to the degree that it approximated the *jūzen*—and he found abundant evidence to this effect in the Confucian classics—it also contributed to the growth of the individual and the well-being of society. Thus, Jiun could speak of filial piety as the foundation of all virtue and embrace the Confucian values of benevolence, righteousness, decorum, wisdom, and good faith as part of the Buddhist Dharma (JSZ 14.416, 489). On the other hand, however, he did not hesitate to point out what he considered to be the limitations of Confucianism: first, its failure to discern the true, empty nature of reality, and hence its inability to appreciate the way of life that stemmed from such a view, i.e., the way of life exemplified by the Buddha and followed by the clergy; and second, an elitism reflected in the predominant scholarly character of the Confucian tradition and in an overreliance on the intellect, which operates properly only within the conventional realm of subject and object. We may also note that Jiun made a similar charge of intellectualism against the rationalists, as he knew them in the figure of Tominaga Nakamoto (1715–1746).[7] A brilliant student not only of Buddhism but of Confucianism and Shinto as well, Nakamoto had argued that the truth claims of all three traditions were brought into question by the effects of cultural and historical conditioning. Jiun by no means rejected this position out of hand, since his own studies of Buddhism had made him painfully aware of the aberrations that had crept into the tradition. Indeed, given the critical character of his scholarship, Jiun himself might be cited as another example of the rationalistic tendencies apparent in eighteenth-century Japanese thought. But his conviction regarding the supreme value of Buddhism did not rest on intellectual considerations alone; rather, it was grounded ultimately in experience attained through the practice of meditation. From Jiun's perspective, the overemphasis on the role of the intellect that he saw in Confucianism and in the thought of Nakamoto constituted a crucial barrier to their full spiritual development.

Although in his later years Jiun turned to the study of Shinto and Shingon Buddhism, there was no change in his commitment to the True Dharma. Through his studies of the native religion, he sought to further demonstrate the universality of his vision. If leanings toward the True Dharma, understood in terms of the *jūzen*, could be seen in Confucianism, they could also be found in Shinto, and his examination of the earliest Japanese sources, particularly the *Kojiki* (Record of ancient matters) and *Nihon shoki* (Chronicles of Japan), revealed a people naturally predisposed to the ethical ideal he embraced. Moreover, finding at the base of that predisposition a purity of heart *(sekishin)* not evident in the Chinese materials, he argued, with a sense of national pride shared by many writers and thinkers of his age, that the Japanese were even closer to that ideal.

In his Shingon studies, Jiun sought to emphasize the best of that sect's tradition as judged from the viewpoint of the True Dharma. While he advocated a return to the suprasectarian fundamentals of Buddhism, Jiun never seems to have envisioned the disappearance of Buddhist sects. Therefore, as a reformer his task became to identify "that which is in accord with the True Dharma" *(zuibun no shōbō)* within each sect (JSZ 14.38–39). As regards Shingon, Jiun stressed two points in particular: (1) its characteristic emphasis upon "the attainment of enlightenment in this very body" *(sokushin jōbutsu)*, which for Jiun had immediate ethical implications, and (2) its unique form of meditation, which through the use of *mudrās* (hand gestures), *mantras* (incantations), and *maṇḍalas* (religious art that served as the object of meditation) provided a structure for the transformation of the individual—in body, speech, and mind—that could be adapted to the needs of all.[8]

Influence

The significance of Jiun's effort's to revive the True Dharma was widely recognized in his own day. Myōdō Taiju, Jiun's disciple and first biographer, tells us that during Jiun's lifetime he had several hundred close disciples and that over ten thousand people "inquired after the Way and received the precepts" (JSZ, introductory volume, 46). In addition, information available on Jiun's followers indicates that they came from all segments of Japanese society and from a wide variety of Buddhist sects. The number of temples affiliated with the Shōbōritsu movement is not precisely known, but there seems to have been at least a few dozen.

Jiun's influence extended into the Meiji period (1868–1912) as well. In addition to problems of sectarianism, moral laxity within the clergy, and competition from rival worldviews, Buddhism in early Meiji Japan also faced efforts by both national and regional governments to weaken its position in Japanese society. An effort was made to elevate Shinto to the position of sole state religion as part of a program to mobilize the nation for modernization, and for a brief period in the early 1870s, Buddhism was actually persecuted, although this was not the official policy of the national government. As the Buddhist community worked to rebuild itself in the following decades, several Buddhist leaders turned to Jiun's writings for guidance, attracted by his pan-Buddhist conception of the True Dharma and the emphasis he placed on both ethics and practice. Among those leaders were the Shingon monk Shaku Unshō (1827–1909), Fukuda Gyōkai (1806–1888) of the Pure Land Sect, and the one-time Sōtō monk turned journalist, Ōuchi Seiran (1845–1918).[9]

Notes

1. JSZ = *Jiun Sonja zenshū*.

2. The Shingon Vinaya sect had its origins in the Kamakura period (1185–1333) and gained its identity from the special importance it attached to the vinaya or monastic discipline in addition to Shingon doctrine and practice.

3. Miura Yasuhiro, *Jiun Sonja*, 155.

4. The work exists only in manuscript; tables of contents are given in JSZ 9b.383–491. For a brief description of the work, see Ono Genmyō, comp., *Bussho kaisetsu daijiten* (Tokyo: Daitō Shuppansha, 1933–36).

5. There are two versions of the *Jūzen hōgo*. The difference between them is the style of language used. One is recorded in a colloquial style reflecting Jiun's actual speech (JSZ 11.1–453); the other is written in a literary style (JSZ 12.1–471).

6. Among Jiun's most important works on Shinto are his *Shinju gūdan* (JSZ 10.1–190), *Nihongi shindai origamiki* (JSZ 10.441–580), and *Mudaishō* (JSZ 10.581–640); see also his *Hito to naru michi daisanpen* (JSZ 13.388–407). On Shingon, see his *Ryōbu mandara zuimonki* (JSZ 8.68–342; abridged version 8.371–457), *Kongō satta shugyō giki shiki* (JSZ 8.1–53), and *Rishukyō kōgi* (JSZ 9b.247–382).

7. On Jiun and Nakamoto, see Okamura Keishin, "Tominaga Nakamoto to Jiun Onkō: Kinsei Mikkyō no ichidōkō," *Mikkyōgaku Mikkyōshi ronbunshū*, 1965, 141–60.

8. Although these points are usually thought to date from an earlier period, see Jiun's *Shingonshū anjin* (JSZ 14.328–30) for a convenient statement of them.

9. On Jiun's impact on Meiji-period Buddhism, see Ikeda Eishun, *Meiji no shin Bukkyō undō* (Tokyo: Yoshikawa Kōbunkan, 1916) 1–122, *passim*.

Bibliography

Hase Hoshū, ed. *Jiun Sonja zenshū*. 19 vols. Kyoto: Shibunkaku, 1974. Originally published 1922–26.

Jiun Sonja zenshū hoi. Comp. by the Jiun Sonja Hyakugojūnen Onki Hōsankai. Osaka, 1955.

Kinami Takuichi. *Jiun Sonja: Shōgai to sono kotoba*. Kyoto: Sanmitsudō, 1961.

Miura Yasuhiro. *Jiun Sonja: Hito to geijutsu*. Tokyo: Nigensha, 1980.

Okamura Keishin. "Jiun Sonja no shōgai to shisō." *Bokubi* 5, no. 127 (1963) 2–11.

———. "Jiun Sonja kenkyū josetsu." *Kōyasan Daigaku ronsō* 2 (1966) 35–79.

Watt, Paul B. "Jiun Sonja (1718–1804): A Response to Confucianism within the Context of Buddhist Reform." In Peter Nosco, ed., *Confucianism and Tokugawa Culture*. Princeton: Princeton University Press, 1984.

———. "Sermons on the Precepts and Monastic Life by the Shingon Vinaya Master Jiun." *The Eastern Buddhist* 25:2 (1992) 119–28.

25

Kiyozawa Manshi's "Spiritualism"

GILBERT JOHNSTON AND WAKIMOTO TSUNEYA

AMONG JAPANESE Buddhists of the Meiji period, Kiyozawa Manshi (1863–1903) is one of the few whose influence is still being felt today. Known throughout his youth by his own family name of Tokunaga, he acquired the name Kiyozawa through adoption at the time of his marriage in 1888. To avoid confusion, he is commonly referred to by his given name, Manshi. Shortly before his untimely death from tuberculosis, Manshi had found his most prominent role as the guiding spirit of a movement called *Seishinshugi* (literally "Spiritualism," not of course in the parapsychological sense), which aimed to put into practice the Other-Power faith of Shinran, the thirteenth-century founder of Jōdo Shinshū, and to renew this tradition by demonstrating its applicability to the modern situation. Manshi and his associates promoted the *Seishinshugi* through classes and regular Sunday lectures at the movement's center in Tokyo, the Kōkōdō; and their magazine, *Seishinkai* (Spiritual World), carried the message and the energetic spirit of the movement to readers throughout Japan.

Of the numerous articles Kiyozawa Manshi wrote to elucidate the meaning of *Seishinshugi*, none expresses his faith more clearly and succinctly than "Waga Shinnen" (My Faith), written five days before his death. The following quotation illustrates the earnestness of his pursuit of faith:

> [My] study finally led me to the conclusion that human life is incomprehensible. It was this that gave rise to my belief in Tathāgata (Buddha). Not that one must necessarily undertake this kind of study in order to acquire faith. One might ask if it wasn't just an accident that I came to faith after engaging in strenuous study, but I would say it was not an accident. It was essential that I should do it this way. My faith has within it a conviction that all my self-power efforts are futile. But in order to be convinced of this futility of self-power, it was necessary to exhaust all my intellectual resources and get to the point where they would not reassert themselves. This was a most strenuous business. Before I reached the end of it there were quite a few

times when I thought I had acquired a religious faith. Yet, time and again my conclusions were shattered. As long as one tries to build up a religion on the basis of logic and intellectual study, one cannot escape this difficulty. What is good? What is evil? What is truth? What is untruth? What is happiness? What is unhappiness? Every one of these questions is beyond our understanding. At the point when it came home to me that I didn't know anything, I began to trust in the Tathāgata for everything. And this is the essential point of my faith. (KMZ 6.229–30)

This final stage of Manshi's career has to be understood against the background of his earlier life. Manshi was born five years before the start of the Meiji Period, the eldest son of Tokunaga Eisoku, a lower-rank samurai in Nagoya. The fall of the Tokugawa shogunate deprived Manshi's father of his livelihood and plunged the family into poverty. Fortunately, Manshi's talents saved him from obscurity. In elementary school he was so good at mathematics that his teacher made him a tutor to some of the younger children. At the age of eleven he moved on to a language school where he acquired the knowledge of English that was to prove essential to his later studies. After a brief, abortive move toward a medical career, Manshi happened upon an educational opportunity that was to determine his future direction. The Ikuei School had been founded by the Higashi Hongan-ji in Kyoto for the purpose of educating talented young men for the Jōdo Shinshū priesthood. Manshi entered this school in order to acquire an excellent secondary education at the temple's expense, though he had not previously been interested in a priestly career. It was at the Ikuei School that he was first exposed to Buddhism as a subject of serious study. He threw himself into his studies with characteristic diligence, acquiring a reputation among the other students for his recitation of sūtras during his free time.

In 1881, aged eighteen, he was selected by the Higashi Hongan-ji to study at the newly established University of Tokyo, where he stayed for six and a half years, completing a four-year course in philosophy and an additional year of advanced work in philosophy of religion. It was a time of tremendous intellectual stimulation for him as he came to grips with the panorama of Western thought for the first time. Under the guidance of Ernest Fenollosa and others he gave particular attention to the writings of Spinoza, Kant, Hegel, Spencer, and Lotze. He made the discovery that Buddhism could be seen as a system of thought capable of taking its place among these Western systems.

In the summer of 1888 Manshi returned to Kyoto at the request of the temple authorities to become the principal of a middle school operated by the Higashi Hongan-ji. He left behind him the stimulating intellectual environment and the relative freedom of Tokyo, as well as the promise of worldly advancement, so strong was his sense of obligation and gratitude to the Higashi Hongan-ji. From this point his career as an educator, reformer, writer, and man of faith was confined to the world of the religious order. Yet he was always to carry with him the breadth of view he had attained during his university days in Tokyo.

It was at this time that a marriage was arranged for Manshi with a daughter of Kiyozawa Genshō, head priest of the Saihō-ji near Nagoya. His adoption into the Kiyozawa family enabled him to succeed his father-in-law as head of the influential temple. He seems to have viewed family matters and temple business as a distraction from his real purpose, and devoted most of his time to religious and educational affairs unconnected with Saihō-ji.

His first years in Kyoto following his university education were a time of dramatic change in Manshi's lifestyle. At first, he cultivated and took pride in his image as a modern, up-to-date gentleman; but in the summer of 1890, in a sudden about-face, he gave up the trappings of modern sophistication and devoted himself to a life of rigorous self-denial and austerity. The motto he adopted at this time, "Minimum Possible," perfectly expressed his intent, which was to show by his own example that the religious life depended upon inner faith and commitment, not on the externals of modern civilization. He hoped that through his own experiment he might help reverse a deteriorating trend in the lifestyle of Shinshū priests. The next change in his life came when a severe attack of pulmonary tuberculosis in the winter of 1894 forced him to discontinue his work and spend a year in recuperation. Narrowly escaping death, he spent this year quietly in reading and writing. What he wrote at this time reveals the deepening influence of Shinran's Other-Power faith on his mind.

Before the onset of this illness he had already become involved in a movement for educational reform. Protesting the diversion of Higashi Hongan-ji's resources to the reconstruction of temple buildings and the repayment of debts at the expense of the educational program, Manshi and his colleagues succeeded in persuading the authorities to adopt a new educational plan. Almost immediately, however, the new plan had to be scrapped, mainly because of adverse reaction on the part of students to new rules imposed upon them and lack of support by the chief administrative officer of the Higashi Hongan-ji. This setback revealed the essentially authoritarian character of the Higashi Hongan-ji organization. Manshi's group embarked on the next step: a campaign for administrative reform. Under the name Shirakawa Party, they published a magazine called *Kyōkai jigen* (Timely words for the religious world), which gave the reform movement national exposure. The resulting resignation of the chief administrative officer and the establishment of a relatively powerless representative assembly fell far short of the movement's goals. Moreover, Manshi himself was expelled from the priesthood. He abandoned any further reforming efforts and devoted himself to reading and contemplation.

Toward the end of 1898, Manshi entered the most productive stage of his career. His priestly status restored, he returned to Tokyo the following year to serve as tutor to the son of the head priest of Higashi Hongan-ji. Shortly afterwards he was appointed president of Shinshū College and was asked to super-

33. Kiyozawa Manshi, 1943 (age 41).

vise the removal of the college to Tokyo. His home became a meeting place for students and colleagues, and the *Seishinshugi* movement was born in the fall of 1902. Failing health forced him to resign from Shinshū College before he could see the fulfillment of his educational plans. At the same time he suffered the loss of his eldest son and his wife. Returning in low spirits to his temple in Ōhama, he spent the last months of his life there and died in June 1903.

Those who knew Manshi personally testified in various ways to his impressive character. He seemed to have a natural gift for leadership. His keen mind and articulate command of ideas made him a stimulating conversationalist. Argument, he confessed, was his first love. Apart from the exchange of ideas in reading, writing, and speaking, he had few other cultural or avocational interests. Like Epictetus, whose writings he read with deep appreciation, he made a sharp distinction between the internal and the external spheres of life. In his relations with other people and with the things of the world he was broad-minded and easygoing, while in matters that pertained to his inner self he was severe and rigorous in his self-imposed demands. His strong sense of responsibility made him more inclined toward self-criticism than criticism of others. As he matured in faith, he developed the capacity to face with stoic equanimity the worst misfortunes—the threat of death, the loss of loved ones, physical pain, the frustration of his dedicated efforts, and strains in his domestic relationships. The direction of Kiyozawa Manshi's religious thought is clearly shown in his *Shūkyō tetsugaku gaikotsu* (KMZ 2.1–44). He penned this work in 1893 as a resumé of his lectures on the philosophy of religion at Shinshū College and in 1894 supervised the English translation (2.45–100). The titles of its six chapters suggest the nature and scope of his concerns: (1) Religion, (2) Finite and Infinite, (3) The Soul, (4) Becoming, (5) Good and Bad, and (6) Peace of Mind and Culture [cultivation] of Virtue. The first four chapters expound his basic conceptions and the last two deal with their application to ethics and personal religious practice. The structure of the work is based on the terms finite and infinite. Manshi explains that it is the nature of all things in the universe to be finite or limited; but the universe itself, since it is the whole and is unlimited by anything outside itself, is infinite. The relation between the two terms is a dynamic one: the infinite is to be seen in contrast to the finite, and yet, at the same time, in complete identity with it. This principle of identity in contradiction enables one to look upon the infinite as both "other" and "the same" in relation to the self or any finite thing. The infinite thus conceived becomes the divine reality of religion, and religion is defined as "the Unity of a Finite with the Infinite" (KMZ 2.53).

In agreement with much of the German metaphysical thought he had studied, Manshi conceived of the universe as a great organic whole. His characteristic term for this totality was *banbutsu ittai* (the oneness of all things). Essential to this conception was the notion of mutual interdependence, similar to the teaching of the Kegon school of Buddhism. The organic totality of the universe is in a constant state of evolution and dissolution. The two processes together constitute what he calls "becoming." Manshi interprets the Buddhist notion of flux as a twofold process of evolution of the finite toward the infinite and dissolution of the infinite toward the finite (KMZ 2.70). Change occurs in a way analogous to the Hegelian dialectic, except that Manshi substitutes for the terms thesis, antithesis, and synthesis the terms cause, condition, and effect (77–78). Following Spinoza, he claims that for change to occur from one state to another there must be "an identity of substance persisting through the two states" (70). In this way he comes to regard the human soul as an identical substance that persists through changing mental states, and as the synthetic function of apperception in consciousness. Not only the soul, but all things in the universe, have the capacity to develop into the infinite, in accord with the Buddhist maxim: "Herbs, trees, and even lands can attain the Buddhahood" (64). "The real nature of the finite," he says, "is also originally the Infinite" (81). The human soul, because of its ability to perceive the relationship between finite and infinite, is in a uniquely favorable condition to realize the infinite. The typical progress of an individual in acquiring religious faith starts from the perception of the distinction between the finite and the infinite, then goes on to the discovery that finite and infinite cannot be separated. Finally, one comes to the point where the two terms are seen as identical.

The final chapter of the *Gaikotsu* shows the relation of the foregoing ideas to the Shinshū form of faith, called *anjin* (peaceful mind or mind at rest). When one realizes a knowledge of the infinite the mind is set at rest and can go about the business of cultivating virtue without undue exertion. Followers of the "self-power gate," on the other hand, feel that they must exert themselves more strenuously because they have not yet realized the actuality of the infinite and feel that they must engage in arduous labors in order to achieve an infinite goal. *Anjin* and the active cultivation of moral goodness should go hand in hand like "the head and heart of a single body" (KMZ 2.93).

The *Gaikotsu* was only a "skeleton" of rational notions; it needed to be tested in actual experience before it could become a living body of religious faith. Such a time of testing came to Manshi in the form of the near-fatal illness that overtook him in 1894. He began to face the stark reality of death: "The Tokunaga who existed up until now has died; from now on this corpse will be entrusted to my friends to do with it as they please" (KMZ 3.755). From this point on he began to develop a deeper understanding of Shinran's Other-Power faith, especially through his reading of the *Tannishō* and the writings of Rennyo. Still, there remained a strong tendency to try to attain *anjin* through his own effort rather than, in accord with the logic of the *Gaikotsu*, to simply accept it as something freely given.

During a second period of recuperation, Manshi devoted himself to reading the *Āgamas* of the Hīnayāna tradition, which at that time were little read by Buddhists in Japan, and also the works of Epictetus. Particularly in regard to the problem of death, these works helped him to find the peace of mind that had eluded him until then. After reading Epictetus, he wrote in his journal:

> To put it plainly, we are helpless in the face of death. We cannot prevent it. We must die! And yet, though we die, we do not perish. Life alone is not the whole of ourselves; death is also part of us.... We are not to be controlled by life and death. We are spiritual beings, apart from life and death. (KMZ 7.418)

Again, reflecting on his reading of Epictetus, he wrote:

> Our coming into life and our going out of life at death are not things that we can control by our own will or desire. It is not just that we cannot make things before birth and after death conform to our will; even right now the appearance or disappearance of a single thought in our minds is beyond our control. We are absolutely in the hands of the Other-Power. (417)

Once more, in 1902, reworking some ideas from his journal for publication in the *Seishinkai*, he wrote:

> The self is nothing but this: something that happens to be here in these present circumstances, upheld, according to the law that determines its destiny, by the wonderful efficacy of *zettai mugen* (Absolute Infinity).
>
> It is simply upheld by the *zettai*. Therefore, matters related to life and death are not worth grieving about; even life and death themselves should not cause us grief. Why, then, should we be worried about lesser things? Banishment and imprisonment are things that we can accept and endure with ease. And as for slander, ostracism, and insults, why should we be concerned? Let us rather be happy with just what the *zettai mugen* provides us. (KMZ 7.380 and 6.49)

Kiyozawa's spiritual quest can be seen as illustrating a particularly pressing problem for Shinshū Buddhists in the modern period. In the Meiji period, when educational attainments had come to be held in high esteem even by the Shinshū denominations, there was undoubtedly a common difficulty on the part of many educated young priests in reconciling the traditional Shinshū views of faith with the standards of intellectual activity they were taught to follow in the secular world. The problem was to find a way of understanding the Shinshū Other-Power faith as a suitable religious expression for persons who could not pretend to be ignorant of secular learning or devoid of personal talents and resources. Or, to put it differently, the problem was to reconcile the modern view of self—a self that was at least partly emancipated from the group structures and values of traditional society and at least somewhat aware of its individual capacities and options—with a faith that placed a high value on self-negation. Kiyozawa Manshi never fully resolved this conflict but rather held the two sides together in tension by the force of his personality, stressing absolute Other-Power faith at one time and rational self-assertion at another. It was difficult for others who had not shared his distinctive experience to attain to this view of the Shinshū faith. And yet those who followed the course of Manshi's spiritual development most closely were left in awe at the triumphant spirit of this dedicated man of faith.

Bibliography

KMZ = *Kiyozawa Manshi zenshū.* 8 vols. Kyoto: Hōzōkan, 1953–55 (repr. 1967–1968).

Tajima Kunji and Floyd Shacklock, trans. *Selected Essays of Manshi Kiyozawa.* Kyoto: The Bukkyō Bunka Society, 1936.

Wakimoto Tsuneya. *Hyōden Kiyozawa Manshi.* Kyoto: Hōzōkan, 1982.

Johnston, Gilbert L., et al., "The Significance of Kiyozawa Manshi's *Seishinshugi*: A Modern Expression of Jōdo Shinshū." *Proceedings of the Sixth Biennial Conference of the International Association of Shin Buddhist Studies* (Kyoto: Ōtani University, 1994) 169–202.

26

Philosophy as Spirituality

The Way of the Kyoto School

J AMES W. H EISIG

I N THE FIRST OF A series of talks delivered on Basel radio in 1949, Karl Jaspers described philosophy as "the concentrated effort to become oneself by participating in reality."[1] For the historian of the Western intellectual tradition, the description may seem to exaggerate the importance of only one ingredient in the practice of philosophy, but it applies well to the group of Japanese thinkers known as the Kyoto school. Their pursuit of philosophical questions was never detached from the cultivation of human consciousness as participation in the real. Drawing on Western philosophy ancient and modern as well as on their own Buddhist heritage, and combining the demands of critical thought with the quest for religious wisdom, they have enriched world intellectual history with a fresh, Japanese perspective and opened anew the question of the spiritual dimension of philosophy. In this article I would like to focus on this religious significance of their achievement.

It might be thought that the philosophy of the Kyoto school is inaccessible to those not versed in the language, religion, and culture of Japan. Read in translation, there is a certain strangeness to the vocabulary, and many of the sources these thinkers take for granted will be unfamiliar. They presuppose the education and reading habits of their Japanese audience, so that many subtleties of style and allusion, much of what is going on between the lines and beneath the surface of their texts, will inevitably be lost on other audiences. Still, it was not their aim to produce a merely Buddhist, much less Japanese, body of thought, but rather to address fundamental, universal issues in what they saw as the universally accessible language of philosophy. That is why their work has proved intelligible and accessible far beyond Japan, and why it is prized today by many Western readers as an enhancement of the spiritual dimension of our common humanity.

Opinions differ on how to define the membership of the Kyoto school, but there is no disagreement that its main pillars are Nishida Kitarō (1870–1945) and his disciples, Tanabe Hajime (1885–1962) and Nishitani Keiji (1900–1990), all of whom held chairs at Kyoto University. Similarities in interest and method, as well as significant differences among the three, are best understood by giving each a brief but separate treatment.

Nishida Kitarō: The Quest of the Locus of Absolute Nothingness

For Nishida the goal of the philosophical enterprise was self-awakening: to see the phenomena of life clearly through recovering the original purity of experience, to articulate rationally what has been seen, and to reappraise the ideas that govern human history and society with reason thus enlightened by reality. Since reality is constantly changing, and since we are part of that change, *understanding* must be a "direct experiencing from within" and *articulation* of what has been so understood must be an internalized, "appropriated"[2] expression. Accordingly, Nishida's arguments are often *post hoc* reconstructions of a path of thinking he had traversed intuitively, led as much by a Buddhist sense of reality as by the Western philosophies he was absorbing.

He is said to have been struck one day while on a walk by the buzzing of a fly near his ear. Lost in his thoughts, he only "noticed" it later, but this confirmed in him the ordinariness of the experience where things happen and are later noticed according to biased habits of thought. "I heard a fly" brings the event to mind, but in the process distorts it into a relationship between an "I" and a "fly."[3] The event itself is pure actuality. Somehow, he saw, actualities constitute subjects and objects, but then mind is immediately distracted to analysis and judgment, never to find its way back to the purity of the original experience. To recover that purity would be to unfetter mind from the distorting constraints of being reasonable or of communicating the experience to those who did not share it. This does not mean that mind leaps free of the senses to some privileged inerrant state, but simply that within the limits of its skinbound, bodily existence, mind reaches what can only be called a kind of boundlessness.

This idea of experience prior to the subject-object distinction was Nishida's starting point and courses through the pages of his collected works like a clear stream. In the opening pages of his maiden work, *A Study of the Good*,

Nishida calls it "pure experience," borrowing a term from the American philosopher William James. His attraction to the idea, however, stems less from James, or indeed from any Western thinker, than from his own Sino-Japanese tradition. We read, for instance, in the eleventh-century Buddhist *Record of the Transmission of the Lamp* that "the mental state having achieved true enlightenment is like that before enlightenment began"; or again, the great Noh dramatist Zeami (1363–1443) comments on how the *Book of Changes* deliberately omits the element for "mind" in the Chinese glyph for "sensation" to indicate a precognitive awareness.[4] Such was the tradition out of which Nishida stepped into his study of philosophy and forged what he was later to call his "logic of locus."[5]

The Logic of Locus

In its forward, rational construction, the process of restoring experience to its purity—the aim of the logic of locus—may be described graphically as a series of concentric circles.[6] The smallest circle, where the center is most in control of the periphery, is that of a judgment where something is predicated of a particular subject. (Japanese does not suffer the ambiguity of the term "subject" here as Germanic and Latin languages do, where the grammatical subject is easily confused with the subject who makes the judgment.) Thus "The rose is red" is like a small galaxy with the rose at the center and redness revolving about it like a planet. Nishida interpreted Aristotle's logic of predication as focused on the subject, which provides a stable center of gravity for its attributes and the comprehension of which grows as more and more attributes are given orbit about it. Nishida sought for his own logic the same solid foundation that Aristotle's "subject that could not become a predicate," provided, but without the metaphysical nuisance of "substance." To do so, he reversed the emphasis by following the predicates. In other words, he shifted his attention away from expanding description or analysis of the object to releasing predication from the subject-object framework in order to see where the process itself "takes place."

As reported by his students, he would then draw a second circle on the blackboard surrounding the first, opening the field for other predicating judgments. The galaxy of particular judgments is now seen to rest in a larger universe where the original, grammatical subject has forfeited its position of centrality to the thinking subject who makes the judgment in the first place. This is the locus of reflective consciousness. It is not the world; nor is it even experience of the world. It is the consciousness where judgments about the world are located—indeed where all attempts to know and control reality by locating it within the limits of the thinking processes of human beings find their homeground.

The predicate "red" is no longer bound to some particular object, and particular objects are no longer limited by their satellite attributes or the language that encases them. Everything is seen as relative to the process of constructing the world in mind. The move to this wider circle shows judgment to be a finite act within a larger universe of thinking.

This gives rise to the next question: And just where is this consciousness itself located? If mind is a field of circumstances that yield judgments, what are the circumstances that define mind? To locate them deeper within the mind would be like Baron Munchausen pulling himself out of the swamp by his own pigtail. Recourse to the idea of a higher subject for which ordinary consciousness is an object is a surrender to infinite regress. Still, if the notions of subject and object only set the boundaries for conscious judgment, this does not preclude the possibility of a still higher level of awareness that will envelop the realm of subjects and objects.

To show this, Nishida drew another circle about the first two, a broad one with broken lines to indicate a location unbounded and infinitely expandable (though not, of necessity, infinitely expanded), a place he called "nothingness." This was his absolute, deliberately so named to replace the absolute of being in much Western philosophy. Being, for Nishida, cannot be absolute because it can never be absolved from the relationships that define it. The true *ab-solutum* had to be—as the Japanese glyphs *zettai* indicate—"cut off" from any and every "other." Absoluteness precludes all dichotomy of subject and object, all bifurcation of one thing from another, all individuation of one mind or another.

Thus "defined" by its unboundedness, this place of absolute nothingness is the locus of salvation, of deliverance from time and being. It is the fulfillment of the philosophical-religious quest where the action of intuition and consciousness take place without an acting subject and in the immediacy of the moment, where the self working on the world yields to a pure seeing of reality as it is. It is the moment of enlightenment that is right at hand in the here-and-now, all-at-once-ness of experience. The final circle is thus one whose circumference is nowhere and whose center can be anywhere. The image was taken from Cusanus, but the insight behind it was there in Nishida from the start.

In fact, over the years Nishida employed a number of idioms to express self-awareness at the locus of absolute nothingness, among them: "appropriation," "acting intuition," "seeing without a seer," and "knowing a thing by becoming that thing." In his early writings he is somewhat inhibited by Neo-Kantian epistemological conundrums, but he advances steadily to an integrated view of how consciousness takes shape, with a Hegelian emphasis on its embeddedness in the historical praxis of a bodily agent. He comes to see knowing not as the activity of a self-empowered subject but as "acting intuition" in which the very idea of the subject grasping objects has been superseded. This intuition is no longer a spying on reality as the ultimate "other," but a participation in the self-actualization of reality itself. In other words, awareness of the unbounded, absolute character of nothingness which arises out of reflection on immediate experience is not meant to detach the subject from the real world but to insinuate its presence still deeper there. "True reality," he writes, "is not the object of dispassionate knowing.... Without our feelings and will, the actual world ceases to be a concrete fact and becomes mere abstract concept."[7]

This idea of participating in reality by overcoming the subject-object dichotomy was given logical form by Nishida in a deliberately ambivalent formula that can be read "an absolute self-identity of contradictories" or "a self-identity of absolute contradictories." The Japanese apposition allows for both and he made free use of the *double-entendre*, depending on whether he wished to stress the radical nature of the identity achieved or the radical opposition of the elements that go into the identity. A further ambiguity in the formula, less transparent in the texts, is the qualification of the identity as a *self*-identity. For one thing, the identity is *automatic*. It is not induced from without, nor is it forced on a stubborn, resistant reality. It takes place when the limitations of the narrow circles of subject-predicate and subject-object are overcome. Here "identity" refers to the way reality is, minus the interference of reflective mind, and the way the mind is when lit up by reality. At the same time, the true identity of reality is not independent of that of the true, awakened self. It is not that the self is constructed one way and the world another; or that the deepest truth of the self is revealed by detaching itself from the world. The apparently absolute opposition between the two is only overcome when the individual is aware that "every act of consciousness is a center radiating in infinity"[8]—that is, out into the circumferenceless circle of nothingness.

In all these reflections Nishida is pursuing a religious quest, a summation of which he attempted in a rambling final essay, "The Logic of Locus and a Religious Worldview." We see Nishida, on the one hand, at pains to clarify the roots of his logic of locus in Buddhist thought; on the other, to clarify his understanding of religion as not bound to any particular historical tradition. Religion is not ritual or institution, or even morality. It is "an event of the soul" which the discipline of philosophy can enhance, even as religion helps philosophy find its proper place in history. This "place" is none other than the immediacy of the moment in which consciousness sees itself as a gesture of nothingness within the world of being. For consciousness does not see reality from without, but is an act of reality from within and therefore part of it. This is the fountainhead of all personal goodness, all just societies, all true art and philosophy and religion for Nishida.

Absolute Nothingness

Nishida's idea of absolute nothingness, which was later to be taken up and developed by Tanabe and Nishitani each in his own way, is not a mere gloss on his logic of locus. His descriptions of historical praxis as "embodying absolute nothingness in time,"[9] and religious intuition as "penetrating into the consciousness of absolute nothingness"[10] are intended to preserve the experiential side of the logic and at the same time to assert a distinctive metaphysical position. But at a more basic level, the idea of nothingness itself is the stumbling block for philosophies which consider being as the most all-encompassing qualification of the real, and which see nothingness as the class of everything excluded from reality.

In his search for the ultimate locus of self-awakening—the point at which reality recognizes itself, through the enlightened consciousness of the human individual, as relative and finite—Nishida could not accept the idea of a supreme being of ultimate power and knowledge beside which all else was no more than a pale analogy. He conceived of his absolute as an unbounded circumstance rather than as an enhanced form of ordinary being. The "locus" of being in reality could not itself be another being; it had to be something that encompassed being and made it relative. Being was by its nature a form of codependency, a dialectic of identities at odds with one another, defining one another by each setting itself up as non-other. As the totality of all such things, being could not be an absolute. Only against the all-embracing infinity of a nothingness could the totality of the world in which beings move exist at all.

At the same time, Nishida recognized that "God is fundamental to religion in any form."[11] This left him with two options: either to redefine what religion, and particularly Christianity, calls God as absolute nothingness; or to show that the absolute being is relative to something more truly absolute. Nishida found a third way: he took both options. Nishida's God was an "absolute being"-in-"absolute nothingness." The copulative *in* here is meant to signal a relationship of affirmation-in-negation (the so-called logic of *soku-hi* which Nishida seems to owe more to D. T. Suzuki than to the Buddhist sources on which Suzuki drew). The two terms are bound to one another by definition. In the same way that there cannot be a creator without creatures, or sentient beings without a Buddha, Nishida writes, there cannot be an absolute being without an absolute nothingness. On the one hand, he insists that the absolute is "truly absolute by being opposed to absolutely nothing." On the other, "the absolute is not merely non-relative.... It must relate to itself as a form of self-contradiction."[12]

Even his clearest remarks in this regard are something of a logical tangle and continue to perplex his commentators.[13] Insofar as I have been able to understand the texts, Nishida's reluctance to absorb God without remainder into absolute nothingness seems to stem from his need to preserve the element of pure experience in awakened selfhood. Metaphysically, he refused to pronounce on God's nature or existence. But "dropping off body and mind to be united with the consciousness of absolute nothingness"[14] is also a religious act, and one that transforms perception to "see eternity in the things of everyday life." As such, it is an engagement of one's truest, deepest self with a radical, absolute otherness. Nishida recognized this basic "spiritual fact" to be the cornerstone of religion, articulated in God-talk or Amida-talk as nowhere else in philosophical history. In other words, if the absolute *in itself* is "absolved" of all dependence on the relative, there is yet a sense in which the absolute *for us* must be nearer to our true selves than anything else can be. The very nature of absolute nothingness was bound to this contradiction: "In every religion, in some sense, God is love."[15] It is also the point at which logic must finally yield to experience, and hence where Nishida's perplexing prose can best be read as a philosopher's bow to religion.

Clearly Nishida's notion of absolute nothingness is different from the "beyond being" (ἐπέκεινα τῆς οὐσίας) of classical negative theology. If anything, his idea of locating nothingness absolutely out of this world of being may be seen as a metaphysical equivalent of locating the gods in the heavens. His point was not to argue for an uncompromising transcendence of ultimate reality, but to establish a ground for human efforts at self-control, moral law, and social communion that will not cave in when the earth shakes with great change or life is visited by great tragedy. True, the personal dimension of the divine-human encounter (and its reflection in Christological imagery) is largely passed over in favor of an abstract notion of divinity not so very different from the God of the philosophers that Pascal rejected. In general, Nishida alludes to God as an idiom for life and creativity minus the connotations of providence and subjectivity. But for one so steeped in the Zen Buddhist perspective as Nishida to have given God such a prominent place in his thought proved to be a decisive ingredient in opening Kyoto-school philosophy to the world.

On the whole, Nishida's "orientalism" is restrained to an ancillary role in his philosophy. Zealous disciples, less secure in their philosophical vocation and lacking Nishida's religious motivation, have been preoccupied with finding in him a logic of the East distinct from that of the West. Nishida himself did not go so far. Rarely, if ever, does he set himself or his ideas up as alternative or even corrective to "Western philosophy" as a whole. He was making a contribution to world philosophy and was happy to find affiliates and sympathetic ideas, hidden or overt, in philosophy as he knew it.

That said, his attempts to return the true self awakened to absolute nothingness to the world of historical praxis rarely touch down on solid ground. Even the most obvious progression from family to tribe to nation to world is given little attention. In principle he would hardly have rejected such an expansion of the self (though it must be said that during the war years, he came dangerously close to describing Japanese culture as a kind of self-enclosed world with the emperor as the seal of its internal identity). But this was not his primary focus, and in fact he never found a way to apply his search for the ultimate locus of the self to the pressing moral demands of his age. The bulk of his reflections on the historical world concerns general structures of human acting and knowing in time rather than the relation of particular nations and cultures to universal world order. The attainment of the true self ultimately lies beyond history; it happens in the "eternal now." Even the most immediate existential fact of the I-Thou relationship is assimilated virtually without ethical content into the abstract logic of the "self-identity of opposites" in which the I discovers the Thou at the bottom of its own interiority. These questions provided the starting point for the contributions of Nishitani and Tanabe.

Tanabe Hajime: Locating Absolute Nothingness in Historical Praxis

Like many of the young intelligentsia of his generation, Tanabe was attracted to the vitality and originality of Nishida's thinking. But his was a temperament different from Nishida's. His writings show a more topical flow of ideas and a passion for consistency that contrasts sharply with Nishida's creative leaps of imagination. If Nishida's prose is a seedbed of suggestiveness where one needs to read a great deal and occasionally wander off between the lines to see where things are going, Tanabe's is more like a mathematical calculus where the surface is complex but transparent. Nishida's work, it has been said, is like a single essay, interrupted as often by the convention of publishing limits or deadlines as by the end of a thesis. One problem flows into the next, not in the interests of a unified system of thought but in pursuit of clarity about the matter at hand. Tanabe—and for that matter, Nishitani also—were more thematic and produced essays that can stand on their own and be understood as such.

When Meiji Japan opened its doors to the world in the mid-nineteenth century after two hundred years of cloister, it immediately inherited intellectual fashions that had been nurtured during the European enlightenment and the explosion of modern science. Not having been part of the process, Japan was ill-prepared to appropriate its results critically. That the road should have been a bumpy one, very different both from the West and from its Asian neighbors, is understandable. As Japan was going through its restoration to the community of nations, the countries of Europe were struggling with the idea of national identity. National flags, songs, and other more ritual elements aside, we find for the first time a widespread concern with distinctive national literatures and philosophies, along with national psychologies. The human sciences, all in their infancy, were caught up in this fascination even as they tried to monitor it. While the cosmopolitan spirit of the enlightenment struggled to survive this test of its roots, the natural sciences and technology proudly marched in the van of a transnational, transcultural humanity. Throughout it all, Japan swayed back and forth between a total infatuation with the superior advances of Western culture and a rigid determination to carve out for itself a unique position in the world.

Nishida suffered this ambiguity as a man of his age. While he never sought translation of his thought into foreign languages, he did recognize the need for ties with the contemporary world of philosophical thinkers. To this end, Tanabe was sent by Nishida to study in Europe, where word of Nishida's work had already stirred interest. Whereas Nishida could calmly pen German phrases here and there in his diaries and skim through English and French books without the fear of criticism at home, the young Tanabe had to struggle with the daily life of a foreigner clumsily making his way in a tongue and culture he had so far only admired from a distance. In the course of time, a certain resentment seems to have built up in him over Nishida's insistence that he pursue neo-Kantian thought. His own interests turned him in the direction of phenomenology, but on returning to Japan he was met with a request of Nishida for a major paper on Kant for a collection celebrating the two hundredth anniversary of the latter's death. Its composition was a turning point for Tanabe.

In his essay Tanabe argued that Kant's third *Critique* lacked an important ingredient that Nishida's philosophy could supply. Specifically, he tried to wed the idea of self-awakening to Kant's practical reason in order to shift the foundations of morality away from a universal moral will in the direction of absolute nothingness. On the one hand, he saw that awareness of nothingness could provide moral judgment with a telos outside of subjective will. This "finality of self-awareness," as he termed it, could provide "a common principle for weaving history, religion, and morality into an insoluble relationship with one another." On the other hand, it dawned on him that Nishida's true, awakened self effectively cut the individual off from history. On completion of his essay, he turned to Hegel to fill the gap. In time he realized that Hegel's absolute knowledge was lacking content, and he set out to think through the possibility of praxis in the historical world grounded in the self-awareness of absolute nothingness. Nishida, for his part, was hard at work on his logic of locus, but Tanabe was not persuaded that it would solve his problem. During this period he developed his dialectic of "absolute mediation" as a way of establishing the bond between absolute nothingness and the historical world.[16]

Philosophical questions aside, two things should be noted with regard to Tanabe's attempts to draw the philosophical vocation closer to the historical world. First of all, the tendency to be abstract that Tanabe criticized in Nishida was very much his own problem. In fact, on his own account he recognized "a flaw in my speculative powers" as responsible for his abstractness.[17] Secondly, Tanabe's genius, as apparent as it was to his students, was no match for the overwhelming presence of Nishida, towards whom he took an ever more critical position even as he continued to measure his own philosophical progress as a Japanese working primarily with Western sources against Nishida's contributions. As Nishitani recalls, the dialectic that he was advancing "seems to give us a mirror-image of Tanabe himself desperately struggling to escape the embrace of Nishida's philosophy."[18]

Absolute Nothingness and the Logic of the Specific

On the occasion of Nishida's retirement, when the academic world was piling accolades on its first and greatest world philosopher, Tanabe wrote a self-serving piece deviously entitled "Looking Up to Nishida." Leaving Nishida to his logic of locus, Tanabe (who now held Nishida's chair at Kyoto University) prepared the way for his own "logic of the specific" by protesting that "the religious experience that goes by the name of the 'self-awakening of absolute nothingness'... belongs outside the practice and language of philosophy, which cannot put up with such a complete lack of conceptual definition.... Religious self-awareness must not be set up as the ultimate principle of philosophy."[19]

The religious bent in Nishida's philosophy was fed by his many years of sitting in *zazen* and his ongoing contact with Buddhist and Christian thinkers. Tanabe's religiosity was more bookish. No less than Nishida, he shied away from turning the philosopher's trade against organized religion and tried to get to the heart of religious and theological thinkers, but his religiosity was a more solitary one. No diaries and few letters remain to let us suppose otherwise. The irony is that Tanabe is remembered as the more religious figure because of a postwar book on penitential philosophy in which he criticizes the profession he had devoted his life to, himself included, for its moral timidity.

Tanabe's contribution to Kyoto-school philosophy as a religious way, as I have said, cannot be separated from his uneasy relationship with Nishida, which stimulated him to look closely at some of the questions Nishida had skimmed over in his creative flights and which also gave him the foundations for doing so. From Nishida he received the idea of approaching religious judgments in terms of affirmation-in-negation, as well as the conviction of absolute nothingness as the supreme principle of philosophy. Further, like Nishida, he did not consider anything in Japanese language or thought a final measure of what was most important in his philosophy. These attitudes he passed on, passionately, to the students. Finally, like Nishida he never argued for the supremacy of any one religious way over any other. What he did not take from Nishida, however, was a conviction of the primacy of religious experience as an "event of the soul" which philosophy may or may not try to explain but can never generate. For Tanabe, there is no unmediated religious experience. Either it is appropriated by the individual in an "existentially philosophic" manner or it yields to the specificity of theology, ecclesial institution, or folk belief.[20]

Tanabe's search for his own philosophical position began with a meticulous rethinking of Hegel's dialectic as applied to a philosophy of absolute nothingness. Along the way he became convinced that for nothingness to be absolute, it was not enough for it to serve as a principle of identity for the finite world from a position somewhere outside of being. It must be a dynamic force that sustains the relationships in which all things live and move and have their being. He could not accept the idea that the historical world in which opposites struggle with one another to secure their individual identities is being driven inexorably towards some quiet, harmonious, beatific vision in absolute mind; neither could he feel at home in the private awakening to a true self within. Precisely because all things without exception are

34. Nishida Kitarō, age 46 (1916).

35. Tanabe Hajime, age 72 (1957).

36. Nishitani Keiji (1900–1991), age 89.

made to struggle with one another for their individuality, the dialectic is an absolute fact of being cannot be accounted for within the world of being alone. Only a nothingness outside of being can make things be the essentially interactive things that they are. But the reverse is also true: "Insofar as nothingness is nothingness, it is incapable of functioning on its own. Being can function only because it is *not* nothingness."[21]

If nothingness allows the world to be, awakening to this fact serves as a permanent critical principle in all identity, whether in the sense of a lofty philosophical principle like Nishida's self-identity of absolute contradictories or in the sense of the ordinary psychological self-composure of the individual mind. It is the fire in which all identity is purged of the fictions of individuality and substantiality that mind attaches to it, leaving only the pure awakening to that which has itself no conflict, no otherness: nothingness. This purification of the mind was Tanabe's test of religious truth. In its terms he appreciated the great figures of the Buddhist and Christian religious past.

The logic of the specific is testimony to the fact that Tanabe never made peace with his own tendency to distance himself from the historical world in the way Nishida did. Many of the latter's young disciples had turned the sharp analysis of Marxism against Nishida's fixation on self-awareness, but to little avail. Tanabe, in contrast, from his critical reading of Kant, had come to see that the subject of consciousness is not a mere individual who looks at the world through lenses crafted by nature for the mind without consultation. It is also a by-product of specific cultural, ethnic, and epochal conditions. In its purgative function, the awareness of absolute nothingness demands that even our most treasured theories be seen as bundles of relationships not within our control. We cannot speak without a specific language nor think without circumstances with a history. We are not individuals awakening to universal truths, but stand forever on specificity, a great shifting bog of bias and unconscious desire beyond the capacity of our mind to conquer once and for all. Nothingness sets us in the mire, but it moves us to struggle against it—never to be identified with it, never to assume we have found an identity of absolute contradictories that is not contaminated by specificities of history. This "absolute negation" is the goal of religion.[22]

Philosophical Metanoia

The problem for Tanabe was to salvage a meaning for self-awakening in this logic of the specific and not resign oneself to the cunning of history. It was not a lesson he taught himself in the abstract but rather one that was forced on him by his own injudicious—and probably also unnecessary—support of state ideology at the height of Japan's military escapades in Asia. The logic that he had shaped to expose the irrational element in social existence was now used to set up against the "clear-thinking gaze of existential philosophy" something more engaging: the "praxis of blessed martyrdom" in a "war of love." Proclaiming the nation as the equivalent of Śākyamuni and that "participation in its life should be likened to the *imitatio Christi*,"[23] Tanabe lost touch with the original purpose of his logic of the specific.

While these sentiments frothed at the surface of Tanabe's prose, a deep resentment towards the impotence of his own religious philosophy seethed within him, until in the end it exploded in the pages of his classic work *Philosophy as Metanoetics*. It was no longer enough to posit absolute nothingness as a supreme metaphysical principle grounding the world of being. It must be embraced, in an act of unconditional trust, as a force liberating the self from its native instinct to self-sufficiency. The notion of faith in Other-Power as expressed in the *Kyōgyōshinshō* of Shinran (1173–1262) gave Tanabe the basic framework for his radical metanoia and reconstruction of a philosophy from the ground up.

It is no coincidence that the heaviest brunt of his penitential attack on overreliance on the power of reason fell on the head of Kant's transcendental philosophy, but from there it reaches out to a reassessment of virtually all his major philosophical influences, from Hegel and Schelling to Nietzsche, Kierkegaard, and Heidegger. Woven into this critique is a positive and unabashedly religious insistence on what he calls "nothingness-in-love" or compassionate praxis in the historical world. The principal model for this ideal is the Dharmākara myth of ascent-in-descent in which the enlightened bodhisattva returns to the world in order to certify his own awakening, but frequent mention is also made of the Christian archetype of life-in-death, which was to dominate certain of his later works.[24] In any case, his aim was not to promote any particular religious tradition over any other but to bridge the gap between absolute nothingness and concrete reality in a way that a simple leap of self-awareness could not accomplish. He drew on religious imagery because it seemed to keep him focused on the moral obligation of putting the truth of enlightened mind to work for the sake of all that lives.

As it turned out, the purgative, "disruptive" side of his metanoetics overshadowed the practical, moral side and left him on shaky ground when it came to taking his new "philosophy that is not a philosophy" beyond its initial statement. Tanabe was aware of this, and devoted his late years to reinforcing the foundations of his logic of the specific, fusing elements from Zen, Christianity, and Pure Land in the forge of a loving, compassionate self-awakening. But when all was said and done, Tanabe, like Nishida, remained aloof from the concrete problems of science, technology, economic injustice, and international strife that were shaking the foundations of the historical world outside the walls of his study. His was to the end a philosophy committed to uncluttering the mind of its self-deceptions, but forever haunted by the knowledge that only in the hopelessly cluttered specificity of history can moral praxis exert itself. The vision he left us is a portrait of his own struggles with the intellectual life: a seamless robe of ideals tattered by experience but not rent, whose weave remains a testimony to the weaver's dedication to the philosophical vocation as a spiritual way.

Nishitani Keiji: From Nihility to Nothingness

With Nishitani, the philosophical current that flowed from Nishida through Tanabe spread out in fresh, new tributaries. Not only did he carry over Tanabe's concern with historical praxis; he also drew the ties to Buddhism closer than either of his senior colleagues had done and closer, as well, to the lived experience of the philosophical quest. In addition, Nishitani took up in his philosophy two major historical problems, each pulling him in a different direction. He was preoccupied, on the one hand, with facing the challenge that modern science brought to religious thinking; on the other, with establishing a place for Japan in the world. All of this combines to give his writing a wider access to the world forum.

More than Nishida and Tanabe, Nishitani turned his thought on a world axis. He actively welcomed and encouraged contact with philosophers from abroad, and in his final years many a foreign scholar beat a path to his small home in Kyoto.[25] He, too, studied in Germany as Tanabe before him, and later was to travel to Europe and the United States to lecture. The happy combination of the publication of his major work, *Religion and Nothingness*, in English and German translation, the rising number of Western scholars with the skills to read fluently in the original texts, and the great human charm of Nishitani as a person, helped bring the work of the Kyoto philosophers to a wider audience. Still, given the trends in Continental and American philosophy at the time this was happening, it was unsurprising that it was the theologians and Buddhologists who were most attracted to Nishitani's work. Only after his death did neighboring Asian countries like Korea, Taiwan, and Hong Kong begin to show an interest in him and other of the Kyoto-school philosophers. But for all his cosmopolitan sentiments, Nishitani followed his predecessors in showing favoritism towards the West—as had virtually all Japanese philosophers since the Meiji period.

In defending himself against the Inquisition, Galileo presented what has become the central assumption of modern science. "I am not interested," he said, "in how to go to heaven, but in how the heavens go." This dichotomy was one that Nishitani never accepted. Not only had the West got it wrong in separating philosophy from religion, its separation of religious quest from the pursuit of science also seemed to him fundamentally flawed. Anything that touches human existence, he insisted, had its religious dimension. Science is always and ever a human enterprise in the service of something more, but when the existential element is sacrificed to the quest for scientific certitude, "what we call life, soul, and spirit—including God—find their 'home' destroyed." Nishitani's response was not to retreat into preoccupation with the true self, but to argue that only on the self's true homeground do the concrete facts of nature "manifest themselves as they are, in their greater 'truth'."[26]

In Nishitani the concern with true self reaches its highest point in Kyoto philosophy. He saw this as the focal point of Nishida's work and interpreted Tanabe's philosophy as a variation on that theme. In his own writings he drew to the surface, through textual allusions and direct confrontation with the original texts, many of the Zen and Buddhist elements in Nishida's work. D. T. Suzuki's efforts to broaden Zen through contact with Pure Land Buddhism also reverberate in Nishitani's writings, though not as deeply as they do in Tanabe's. In addition, he turned directly to Christian theology both for inspiration and to clarify his own position as distinct from the Christian one.

But perhaps the single greatest stimulus to Nishitani's broadening of Nishida's philosophical perspective was Nietzsche, whose writings were never far from his mind. The deep impression that *Thus Spoke Zarathustra* had made on him in his university years left him with doubts so profound that, in the end, only a combination of Nishida's method and the study of Zen Buddhism was able to keep them from disabling him. As a scholar of philosophy he had translated and commented on Plotinus, Aristotle, Boehme, Descartes, Schelling, Hegel, Bergson, and Kierkegaard—all of whom left their mark on his thought. But Nietzsche, like Eckhart, Dōgen, Han-shan, Shih-te, Zen poets, and the New Testament, he seems to have read through the lenses of his own abiding spiritual questions, resulting in readings of arresting power and freshness.

The fundamentals of Nishitani's own approach to the true self as a philosophical idea are set forth in an early book on "elemental subjectivity." This term (which he introduced into Japanese from Kierkegaard) is not one that Nishida favored, but Nishitani's aim is not substantially different from that of his teacher: to lay the philosophical foundation for full and valid individual existence, which in turn would be the basis for social existence, cultural advance, and overcoming the excesses of the modern age. Written at the age of forty and under the strong influence of Nishida, the work contains in germ his own mature philosophy.

As with Nishida, the Achilles' heel of Nishitani's highly individual approach to historical questions was its application to questions of world history. In the attempt to lend support during the war years to elements in the Navy and government who wanted to bring some sobriety to the mindless antics of the Japanese Army in Asia, his remarks on the role of Japanese culture in Asia blended all too easily with the worst ideologies of the period, and the subtle distinctions that made all the difference to him—as they did to Nishida and Tanabe caught up in the same maelstrom—earn him little sympathy today in the light of subsequent events. Nishitani suffered a purge after the defeat of Japan and never returned to these questions in print. While he continued to write on Japan and the culture of the East, he did so at a safe distance both from his own earlier opinions and from the relentless pummeling of Marxist critics.

The Standpoint of Emptiness

To Nishida's logic of locus and Tanabe's logic of the specific, Nishitani added what he called the standpoint of emptiness. He saw this standpoint not as a perspective that one can step into effortlessly, but the achievement of a disciplined and uncompromising encounter with doubt. The long struggle with nihilism that lay behind him was far from merely academic. As a young man, not yet twenty years of age, he had fallen into a deep despair in which "the decision to study philosophy was, melodramatic as it might sound, a matter of life and death for me."[27] This was to be the very starting point for his description of the religious quest: "We become aware of religion as a need, as a *must* for life, only at the level of life at which everything else loses its necessity and its utility."[28]

For Nishitani, the senseless, perverse, and tragic side of life is an undeniable fact. But it is more than mere fact; it is the seed of religious awareness. The meaning of life is thrown into question initially not by sitting down to think about it but by being caught up in events outside one's control. Typically, we face these doubts by retreating to one of the available consolations—rational, religious, or otherwise—that all societies provide to protect their collective sanity. The first step into radical doubt is to allow oneself to be so filled with anxiety that even the simplest frustration can reveal itself as a symptom of the radical meaninglessness at the heart of all human existence. Next, one realizes that this sense of ultimate is still human-centered and hence incomplete. Now one gives oneself over to the doubt entirely, and the tragedy of human existence shows itself as a symptom of the whole world of being and becoming. At this point, Nishitani says, it is as if a great chasm had opened up underfoot in the midst of ordinary life, an "abyss of nihility."

Whole philosophies have been constructed on the basis of this nihility, and Nishitani threw himself heart and soul into the study of them, not in order to reject them but in order to find the key to what he called the "self-overcoming of nihilism." The awareness of nihility must be allowed to grow in consciousness until all of life is transformed into a great question mark. Only in this supreme act of negating the meaning of existence so radically that one becomes the negation and is consumed by it, can the possibility of a breakthrough appear. Deliverance from doubt that simply transports one out of the abyss of meaninglessness and back into a worldview where things make sense again, Nishitani protests, is no deliverance at all. The nihility itself, in the fullness of its negation, has to be faced squarely in order to be seen through as relative to human consciousness and experience. In this affirmation, reality discloses its secret of absolute emptiness that restores the world of being. Or in his philosophical terms, "emptiness might be called the field of 'be-ification' *(Ichtung)* in contrast to nihility, which is the field of 'nullification' *(Nichtung)*."[29]

In other words, for Nishitani religion is not so much a search for the absolute as one of the items that make up existence, as an acceptance of the emptiness that embraces this entire world of being and becoming. In that acceptance—a "full-bodied appropriation" *(tainin)*—mind lights up as brightly as mind can. The reality that is lived and died by all things that come to be and pass away in the world is "realized" in the full sense of the term: one shares in reality and one knows that one is real. This is the standpoint of emptiness.

Because it is a standpoint, it is not a terminus ad quem so much as a terminus a quo: the inauguration of a new way of looking at the things of life, a new way of valuing the world and reconstructing it. All of life becomes, he says, a kind of "double-exposure" in which one can see things just as they are and at the same time see through them to their relativity and transience. Far from dulling one's critical senses, it reinforces them. To return to the case of science, from the standpoint of emptiness, the modern infatuation with explanation and fact is disclosed for what it is: a sanctification of the imperial ego that willingly sacrifices the immediate reality of its own true self for the illusion of perfect knowledge and control. To personify or humanize the absolute, to rein it in dogmatically with even the most advanced apparatus and reliable theories, is at best a temporary cure to the perpetual danger of being overwhelmed by nihility. Only a mysticism of the everyday, a living-in-dying, can attune our existence to the empty texture of the absolutely real.

In general, it may be noted, Nishitani favored the term *emptiness* (S. *śūnyatā*) over Nishida's "absolute nothingness," in part because its corresponding Chinese glyph, the ordinary character for *sky*, captures the ambiguity of an emptiness-in-fullness that he intends. In this seeing that is at the same time a seeing-through, one is delivered from the centripetal egoity of the self to the centrifugal ex-stasis of the self that is not a self. This, for him, is the essence of religious conversion.

In principle, Nishitani always insisted that conversion entails engagement in history. While he appreciated, and often repeated, the Zen Buddhist correlation of great doubt with great compassion (the Chinese glyphs for both terms are pronounced the same, *daihi*), his late writings contain numerous censures of Buddhism for its "other-worldly refusal to enter into the affairs of human society," for its "lack of ethics and historical consciousness," and for its "failure to confront science and technology."[30]

In his principal philosophical discussions of history, however, Nishitani tends to present Christian views of history, both linear and cyclical, as a counterposition to the fuller Buddhist-inspired standpoint of emptiness— despite the greater sensitivity of the former to moral questions. Emptiness or nothingness did not become full by bending time back on itself periodically, like the seasons that repeat each year, or by providing an evolutionary principle that points to an end of time when all the frustrations of nihility will be overturned, as is the case in Christian eschatology. He envisaged deliverance from time as a kind of tangent that touches the circle of repetitive time at its outer circumference or cuts across the straight line of its forward progress. Like Nishida, he preferred the image of an "eternal now" that breaks through both myths of time to the timelessness of the moment of self-awakening. What Christian theism, especially in its personalized image of God, gains at one moment in its power to judge history, it often loses at the next in its failure to understand the omnipresence of the absolute in all things. For Nishitani the standpoint of emptiness perfects the personal dimension of human life by the addition of the impersonal, non-differentiating love, which was none other than the very thing that Christianity reveres in the God who makes the sun to shine on the just and the unjust alike, and who empties himself kenotically in Christ.[31] Yet here again, we see Nishitani in later writings reappraising the I-Thou relationship and the interconnectedness of all things, even to the point of claiming that "the personal is the basic form of existence."[32]

In the foregoing pages much has been sacrificed to brevity and a certain forced clarity of exposition. Perhaps only the *askēsē* of struggling with the original texts can give one a sense of the complexity of the Kyoto school thinkers. Philosophically, many problems remain with the "logics" of Nishida, Tanabe, and Nishitani. Some of them have been superseded by more recent philosophy; others will benefit from further study and comparison; still others are perennial. The task of formulating philosophical questions as religious ones belongs, I am convinced, among the latter.

Notes

1. Karl Jaspers, *The Way to Wisdom* (New Haven: Yale University Press, 1954), 14. Translation adjusted.

2. These two ideas are present from Nishida's earliest writings. See his two brief essays on Bergson in *Nishida Kitarō zenshū* (hereafter NKZ) 1:317–27; The idea of "appropriation" *(jitoku)* appears in *An Inquiry into the Good*, 51 (where it is translated "realizing with our whole being").

3. Nishitani, *Nishida Kitarō*, 55.

4. *On the Art of the No Drama: The Major Treatises of Zeami*, trans. by J. Thomas Rimer and Yamazaki Masakazu (Princeton: Princeton University Press, 1984), 133, 136.

5. This term is sometimes translated as "logic of topos," but the connections to Aristotle which the term suggests seem to conflict with his own position.

6. See *Kōsaka Masaaki chosakushū* 8:98–101.

7. NKZ 1:60; see *An Inquiry into the Good*, 49.

8. *Last Writings*, 54. In order to capture the philosophical sense, the translator has taken some liberties with particular passages. A more literal translation was prepared by Yusa Michiko in *The Eastern Buddhist* 19:2 (1986) 1–29, 20/1 (1987) 81–119.

9. Textual references to this idea may be found in Jacinto, *La filosofía social de Nishida Kitarō*, 208–12.

10. NKZ 5:182.

11. *Last Writings*, 48.

12. *Last Writings,* 68–69.

13. The long-standing debates among Takizawa Katsumi, Abe Masao, Yagi Seiichi, and Akizuki Ryōmin over the reversibility or irreversibility of the relationship between God and the self, as well as the wider debate over the obscure notion of "inverse correspondence" *(gyakutaiō)* that appears in Nishida's final essay, leave little hope of a final word on the subject.

14. NKZ 5:177. The allusion, of course, is to Dōgen's *Genjōkōan*.

15. NKZ 11:372, 454, 435.

16. *Tanabe Hajime zenshū* (hereafter THZ) 3:7, 78–81.

17. THZ 3:76–77.

18. Nishitani, *Nishida Kitarō*, 167.

19. THZ 4:306, 318.

20. THZ 8:257–58.

21. THZ 7:261.

22. THZ 6:147–53.

23. THZ 7:24, 99.

24. Regarding his relation to Christianity, Tanabe referred to himself in 1948 as a permanent Christian-in-the-making, *ein werdender Christ* who could never become *ein gewordener Christ* (THZ 10:260). The distinction is more commonly associated with Nishitani, who adopted it to describe his own sympathies with Tanabe's position.

25. See the special issue of *The Eastern Buddhist* devoted to the memory of Nishitani, 25:1 (1992).

26. "Science and Zen," *The Buddha Eye*, 120, 126.

27. *Nishitani Keiji chosakushū* (hereafter NKC) 20:175–84.

28. *Religion and Nothingness*, 3.

29. *Religion and Nothingness*, 124.

30. See NKC 17:141, 148–50, 154–55, 230–31.

31. See especially *Religion and Nothingness*, ch. 2.

32. NKC 24:109.

Bibliography

Primary Sources

Franck, Frederick, ed. *The Buddha Eye: An Anthology of the Kyoto School*. New York: Crossroad, 1982.

Jacinto Zavala, Agustín, ed. *Textos de la filosofía japonesa moderna* (Zamora: El Colegio de Michoacán, 1995), vol. 1.

Nishida Kitarō zenshū (Collected works of Nishida Kitarō). 19 vols. Tokyo: Iwanami, 1978.

Nishida Kitarō. *An Inquiry into the Good*. New Haven: Yale University Press, 1990.

―――. *Last Writings: Nothingness and the Religious Worldview*, trans. by David Dilworth. Honolulu: University of Hawai'i Press, 1987.

Nishitani Keiji chosakushū (Collected works of Nishitani Keiji). Tokyo: Sōbunsha, 1986–. 26 vols. to date.

Nishitani Keiji. *Religion and Nothingness*. Berkeley: University of California Press, 1982.

―――. *The Self-overcoming of Nihilism*. Albany: State University of New York Press, 1990.

Ōhashi Ryōsuke, ed. *Die Philosophie der Kyōto-Schule: Texte und Einführung*. Freiburg: Karl Alber, 1990.

Tanabe Hajime zenshū (Collected works of Tanabe Hajime). 15 vols. Tokyo: Chikuma Shobō, 1964.

Tanabe Hajime. *Philosophy as Metanoetics*. Berkeley: University of California Press, 1986.

Secondary Sources

Heisig, James W., and John Maraldo, eds. *Rude Awakenings: Zen, the Kyoto School, and the Question of Nationalism*. Honolulu: University of Hawai'i Press, 1994.

Jacinto Zavala, Agustín, ed. *La filosofía social de Nishida Kitarō, 1935–1945*. Zamora: El Colegio de Michoacán, 1995, vol. 1.

Kōsaka Masaaki chosakushū. Tokyo: Risōsha, 1965, vol. 8.

Laube, Johannes. *Dialektik der absoluten Vermittlung*. Freiburg: Herder, 1984.

Unno, Taitetsu, ed. *The Religious Philosophy of Nishitani Keiji*. Berkeley: Asian Humanities Press, 1989.

Unno, Taitetsu, and James W. Heisig, eds. *The Philosophy of Tanabe Hajime*. Berkeley: Asian Humanities Press, 1990.

"Nishida Kitarō," "Tanabe Hajime," "Nishitani Keiji," and "The Kyoto School" in the *Encyclopedia of Philosophy*. London: Routledge, 1998.

Nishida Kitarō Memorial Issue. *The Eastern Buddhist* 28:2 (1995).

Nishitani Keiji Memorial Issue. *The Eastern Buddhist* 25:1 (1992).

Part Six

ART, SOCIETY, AND NEW DIRECTIONS

27

Buddha's Bodies and the Iconographical Turn in Buddhism

MIMI HALL YIENGPRUKSAWAN

ANY QUESTIONS have been asked about what we see when we see Buddha. On the face of it a simple matter, this query raises the most challenging proposition of Buddhist discourse: that Buddha is at once present and absent. Buddha has a body, what the Yogācāra philosopher Asaṅga called a "support" (āśraya), and Buddha as that body takes up space, has a location, is seen or felt or heard. But Asaṅga made clear that the "support" that is Buddha's body is ultimately the Dharma body, which—empty, imageless, wishless, silent—is the state of enlightenment itself and not a body at all. As Malcolm David Eckel puts it, the body of Buddha, its location, is "a place where an absence is present."[1]

This type of paradox is fundamental to the Buddhist episteme and informs all aspects of Buddhist discourse. There is the "tension between a buddha's transcendence and immanence—his location within both *nirvāṇa* and *saṃsāra*," John D. Dunne writes, and "Śākyamuni Buddha's involvement in the world as a teacher and his detachment from the world as an awakened being."[2] Buddha has "omnilinguality" even as "Buddha *in se* does not speak," Paul J. Griffiths writes, and "is not implicated with language."[3] Eckel considers such paradoxes, and specifically the implications of Buddha's absence, as "points of incongruity that challenge the stability of conceptuality itself" yet lead to insight, knowledge, and "the ability to perceive and respond to the absence." He uses Foucault's model of the heteroclite as a way of understanding the operation of paradox in Buddhist thought as a radical challenge to figuration itself: "things are 'laid,' 'placed,' 'arranged' in sites so very different from one another that it is impossible to find a place of residence for them, to define a common locus beneath them all."[4] On these terms it is possible to argue that the double binds of Buddhist discourse arise from the fundamental condition of Buddha as outside the space of representation.

This ground zero of emptiness and its figuration, on which the edifice of Buddhism stands, is a realm whose gateways are vision and recollection. The process of awakening is one of seeing: to understand is to see (darśana) or to have insight. It is a process dependent on images, without which, Asaṅga said, "there is nothing to understand."[5] The ultimate image is Buddha, whence derive the words and images of sacred texts, and insight itself. This is image in an elemental sense: a figure that recalls "a concrete but currently absent perceptual experience."[6] A language of memory sustains such figuration. By reflection (anusmṛti) the physical properties of Buddha are recalled and remembered, his life represented in the most literal sense, his teachings heard once more.[7] In these ways, vision and memory work to recover Buddha but prove also that he is gone.

Of course recollections and visions, indeed all expedient means along the path to enlightenment, come from Buddha. There is Buddha; and then there is everything else as the predicate. It is not so much that Buddha is seen, or represented, but that he makes it possible to see. As Eckel notes, "the Buddha's crucial characteristic is not his own seeing. It is his ability to illuminate the minds of others who have not yet seen." In this sense vision becomes an exchange, "a form of communion, like touching." Seeing Buddha "is not just the cool, analytical vision that allows a person to take the structure of reality apart... but also the emotional vision of a beloved object."[8]

The high iconicity that characterizes Buddhism, where a multiplicity of forms renders Buddha visible, is the logical issue of so fraught an enterprise of pursuit and union. It is a project touched by melancholy: every image is a reminder that Buddha is elsewhere, beyond representation. The Chinese pilgrim Fa-hsien, at the temple Jetavana in the early fifth century C.E., was saddened when he saw places where Buddha had once been (T 51.860c3–4; Legge, 58).[9] Images of Buddha can be likened to that temple: they are the site of transient localizations of Buddha for the benefit of sentient beings. Thus images are not so much graphic pictorializations as they are likenesses of Buddha in the many forms through which he affects the minds of those who seek him. Such an image is an icon in the literal sense that it "is a sign which would possess the character which renders it significant, even though its object had no existence."[10]

It is logical that Buddhism as a signifying practice without an object or a referent allows for the development of a vast system of iconic, indexical, and symbolic signs and a complex iconography addressed to making the non-pictorial perceptible to the senses. Indeed, the process of awakening turns on the ability to gain insight into such signs. Iconography here is not simply a record or list of images, although that is part of its function. Iconography is more importantly an inscription, "to write icons," by which images are plotted (or imagined) along the coordinates they share with the words of scripture in the field of representation. It is also the table on which Buddhist imagery is sorted—a taxonomy—to make possible the orderly negotiation of a realm of signification where the referent constantly shifts its ground like a shadow on the wall.

The following essay briefly outlines Buddhist iconography as a practice, a system of representation, and a history. It explores how and under what conditions an iconographical turn of mind came to dominate Buddhist thinking and examines the implications of such a paradigm shift. It surveys Buddhist iconography in its taxonomic aspects of category and type, with emphasis on the nature of Buddha's body. In conclusion it considers the social consequences of iconography as ideology on the Buddhist assumption that, to borrow a phrase from the singer Johnny Cash, "in your mind... it all goes down in your mind."[11]

Beginnings

As Gautama Śākyamuni prepared for final cessation he asked his disciples to look at his body and showed them the major and minor characteristics that identified it as a Buddha body *(Tathāgatakāya)*. Viewers saw the thirty-two major characteristics *(lakṣaṇa)* and eighty minor marks *(anuvyañjana)* of a "great person" *(mahāpuruṣa)*.[12] Among the major characteristics were long fingers, broad heels, soft and delicate hands and feet, a sheathed penis, a straight and rounded body, golden skin, blue eyes, white teeth. He displayed himself this way out of compassion because such a body is "difficult to see." Then he said, "Things are like this, conditioned phenomena have no existence," and was gone (T 6.968a–969a). Subsequently the physical body *(kāya)* of Śākyamuni was cremated and its corporeal relics *(śarīra)* distributed for deposit in stūpas.[13]

This account, from the *Śatasāhasrikā-prajñāpāramitā Sūtra,* postdates the life of Gautama Śākyamuni by hundreds of years and cannot be taken literally. Nonetheless it articulates the basic facts of Buddha's figuration. First of all, Buddha causes his own representation to be seen; he is its originator and shows his followers its marks with himself both the sign and the ground of the sign. The representation is that of a beautiful human male. It is divisible into parts—marks, signs—that make up the whole. Buddha can be seen as that whole, or in its discrete parts: as icon, then, but also as symbol or index. One does not preempt the other; each is a strategy by which Buddha is imagined after the fact as a body, or "standpoint," where enlightenment happened or was contained.[14] At the final cessation Buddha is reabsorbed but leaves a remainder: his body as image and memory, as relic, and, ultimately, as place or standpoint.

The systematic way in which the body of Buddha is described in the *Mahāparinirvāṇa Sūtra* presupposes the existence of a model, perhaps a painting or a sculpture. There were legends that a statue of Gautama Śākyamuni was made and honored while he was still in the world. Fa-hsien recorded the story of King Prasenajit of Kosala, who had a sandalwood statue carved in the likeness of Buddha as a stand-in while Buddha, whom Prasenajit longed to see, was away in the Trāyastriṃśa Heaven. The statue was placed where Buddha usually sat at Jetavana. When Buddha returned, the image rose to meet him, but Buddha ordered it back to its seat. After the final cessation, he said, the statue would serve as a model for his disciples; Buddha then left to take up residence elsewhere at the temple complex. "This was the first of all the images," Fa-hsien wrote, "and that which men subsequently copied" (T 51.860b18–23; Legge, 56–57).[15]

Initial representations of Buddha probably did not follow such a model, and indeed the earliest images tend not to be anthropomorphic at all. Rather, Buddha appears as symbols—a wheel or a stūpa, footprints, an empty space on a throne—and not as a person, as in the stūpa carvings at Bhārhut that date to the second century B.C.E. Such depictions can be likened to the epithets by which Buddha was known: "titles of dignity and power" such as "Awakened" (Buddha), "Thus-Gone" (Tathāgata), "Blessed" (Bhagavat). These epithets are used by writers of scripture "to gesture lexically at what they take to be ultimately and finally real," knowing that the finally real "is inaccessible to discourse." Like relics, depictions of Buddha in the manner of epithets denote a significant absence that is held dear through remembrance.[16]

Alfred Foucher introduced the term "aniconic" to describe the ways in which Buddha was rendered as symbol, not person, in the earliest examples of Buddhist art.[17] This notion has been questioned by Susan Huntington, who argues that such "aniconic" imagery (empty thrones, wheels, stūpas) is not intended to represent Buddha at all but rather to denote the places at which Buddha was worshiped, the "sacred nuclei" of ritual activity. The case is a good one but does not necessarily prove that a wheel or a stūpa is not a "surrogate" for Buddha, only that, at the initial stage of interpretation or understanding, it shows a thing or place associated with Buddha but from which he has withdrawn.[18] That such a thing or place (like a human body) can also be Buddha—can make an absence present—is logically consistent on philosophical and doctrinal grounds.

The idea that some representations of Buddha are aniconic, whether symbolic (stūpa) or indexical (footprints), follows from the notion that Buddha also has an iconic form, a "likeness," which is that of a human male. That aniconic and iconic depictions of Buddha coexisted in early Buddhist art is certainly plausible but to date only rare examples have been documented.[19] As Griffiths has noted, the "resolutely aniconic" presentation of Buddha in early Buddhism came from a doctrinal need "to avoid predicating change of Buddha."[20] In later times other needs prevailed, and fully anthropomorphized figures of Buddha became the norm. However, aniconic imagery continued to figure in Buddhist iconography like a deep grammar at the semantic core of Buddhism's language of vision.

Representation of Buddha in human form has been linked to the consolidation around the beginning of the common era of the diverse system of teachings later called Mahāyāna Buddhism. Indeed, the iconographical turn in Buddhism, toward increasingly complex anthropomorphic and zooanthropomorphic imagery, occurred in close conjunction with the spread of Mahāyāna practices from India into Central Asia and then China.[21] Hirakawa Akira has identified three main sources for this emergent "religion of many facets" with its deep roots in lay devotion: specific doctrinal developments in the Mahāsānghika, Sarvāstivāda, and other Buddhist sectarian movements of the time; a growing trans-sectarian literature on the biography of Buddha; and veneration of stūpas.[22]

As the Mahāyāna movement gained acceptance new scriptures were compiled from the second through the fifth centuries: the *Prajñāpāramitā* sūtras on wisdom; the *Avataṃsaka* sūtra on Buddha's enlightenment and the bodhisattva nature; the *Lotus* sūtra on the purity of mind and Buddha nature; the *Sukhāvatīvyūha* on Amitābha and the power of faith; and others.[23] While these texts are complex philosophical tracts on the wisdom of non-substantiality or emptiness, the nature of Buddha and mind, and other critical issues of doctrine, they also contain vivid accounts of a variety of Buddhas and Buddha-fields (*buddhakṣetra*) with literally hundreds of bodhisattvas and other saviors described in intense detail. As such they are ample testimony, not only to Mahāyāna devotionalism, but also to its ideal of compassionate Buddhas and bodhisattvas manifest in infinite bodies to inhabitants of the realm of suffering. The importance of seeing these figures, of making contact with them through vision and contemplation, is everywhere apparent in the texts.

The case for iconic as opposed to strictly symbolic or indexical representation of Buddha, and by extension of bodhisattvas as Buddha-beings who have deferred their final cessation out of compassion, follows from Mahāyāna roots in biography and stūpa worship and from scriptural emphasis on visual engagement with Buddha and bodhisattvas. It is easy to see how biography would have prompted anthropomorphic representation of Buddha. Asaṅga's idea of the body as a support, with the corollary notion that a body is a container, helps to explain how a stūpa might be conflated with Buddha. As Gustav Roth shows, early descriptions of Buddha's body might as well refer to a stūpa. "The figure of my body should be made circular," Buddha says, "as far as the measure of the two extended arms goes, the measure of the body should be equally extended (regarding height and width)."[24]

One outcome of the need to conceive of Buddha as having a human body, and to make likenesses of that body for the purposes of worship, was early commentary on how to make a Buddha image.[25] It also gave rise to a discourse on the nature of the Buddha body, out of which Asaṅga's theory of the body as a support derived. Philosophical analysis pivoted on the notion that the Buddha body is "numerically single but functionally multiple."[26] In early Mahāyāna thought Buddha was seen as having a twofold body, namely, the Dharma body (dharmakāya), which is formless, absolute, real; and the Form body (rūpakāya), which, colorful and tangible, is accessible to the senses. Asaṅga and other Yogācāra masters subsequently held that Buddha has a threefold body: the Dharma body; the Enjoyment body (saṃbhogakāya); and the Manifestation body (nirmāṇakāya). This has been the principal Mahāyāna position since the fourth century.

Like the unified field in particle physics, the Dharma body is understood as basically inconceivable in space and time. It is Buddha's essential or "first" body, Griffiths writes, and it supports the other bodies as Asaṅga maintained. Properly speaking, the Dharma body is neither a body nor gendered; Griffiths refers to Buddha as "it."[27] Eckel writes of the Dharma body as a "state of awareness that makes the Buddha an enlightened being" and that is free from all concepts.[28] It might also be described as the root directory of Buddhism's virtual realities.

The Enjoyment body is how Buddha becomes apparent—virtually—to those who have reached an advanced stage of understanding. There are many Enjoyment bodies, as there are many Buddhas. Each Enjoyment body exists as a Buddha in a Buddha-field, or "heavenly realm not directly or easily accessible to embodied living beings in a world-realm like ours,"[29] where it lectures to a group of listeners. An Enjoyment body has an individualized name—Amitābha, Akṣobhya, Bhaiṣajyaguru, Vairocana—and displays recognizable physical features by which it can be distinguished from other Enjoyment bodies, such as a bluish body (Akṣobhya) or light streaming from its pores (Vairocana).

Gautama Śākyamuni exemplifies the "body of magical transformation" that is the Manifestation body, which, like the Enjoyment body, has multiple forms. Eckel describes the Manifestation body as a "conceptual expression" of the Dharma body, for it speaks and "produces a teaching that fits the needs of the disciples."[30] Griffiths says that Manifestation bodies all have a career: "they are born, they renounce the world, they attain awakening, they preach the doctrine, found the monastic community, teach, gather followers, and eventually die." Strictly speaking, a Manifestation body need not be human: it can be an animal, or a hungry ghost, so long as it "appears as whatever is most salvifically beneficial."[31]

The Enjoyment and Manifestation bodies can be likened to the shadow Fa-hsien saw on the wall of a cave temple in Nāgara. From a distance "it seemed to be Buddha's real form, with his complexion of gold." But the closer you approached the shadow, the fainter it became, "as if it were only in your fancy" (T 51.859a; Legge, 39). This interactive aspect, a play of shadow and mind in the figuration of a Buddha, was important to meditative practices that became prominent in the Mahāyāna culture. Whereas older types of meditative activity were largely directed toward states of absorption or trance that resulted in sensory withdrawal, Mahāyāna practice drew also on traditions involving visualization exercises that were intended to produce states of heightened sensory awareness of a Buddha or bodhisattva.

Alan Sponberg has identified a variety of meditational practices in Mahāyāna—he lists nine types—and distinguishes among them two basic modes: enstatic and ecstatic. He calls "enstatic" those classes of meditation, such as *dhyāna* and *samādhi*, that seek "a state of stasis, the complete cessation of sensory processing." Classes of meditation that require visualization exercises, most prominently *anusmṛti*, he calls "ecstatic." In ecstatic meditation "the practitioner seeks a state of enhanced sensation by throwing himself into an alternative reality rich in aesthetic and emotional detail." Ecstatic meditation is "eidetic" in that it necessitates total recall of a visual image through mental projection. For the most part ecstatic visualization exercises are directed at recollection of Enjoyment bodies and their Buddha-fields, most famously Amitābha in Sukhāvatī. They are understood as highly emotional experiences that produce beautiful visions and are psychologically transformative.[32] If visualization exercises mark "just the beginning" of meditation proper, Eckel notes in view of standard practice, they nonethe-less prepare the ground for what follows.[33]

Enjoyment bodies and mental projections have in common the fact that they do not really exist. They are intended rather to exercise salvific effects on the minds of those who perceive them. In this way they are a function of how the experience of seeing Buddha is also one of being illuminated. The valorization of icons—of painted and sculpted likenesses of Enjoyment bod-ies and other saviors—follows logically from the emphasis on vision and memory (or recollection) as points of entry into deeper areas of medita-tion and understanding. Icons have the added dimension, quite literally, of physically existing in space and providing a purchase for the insatiable gaze that is awakened by meditation and devotion as the fundamental paradigm of Buddhist practice. Icons, like mental projections and Enjoyment bodies, in the end have no more substance than Buddha. But their expediency is unas-sailable in a discursive order that needs to see something in nothing.

Iconography

By the sixth century a great manifold of Buddhas and Buddha-beings had appeared in tandem with doctrinal explorations into non-substantiality and mind. Thousands of iconic possibilities had been generated by early Mahāyāna scripture and practice for Buddha alone, the representative example of this trend toward multiplication being the *Avataṃsaka Sūtra* with its myriad Buddha-fields emanating out of the resplendent Vairocana. A way of managing a potentially unwieldy situation was developed by the Vajrayāna movement, or tantrism, which appeared as a distinct tradition within the Mahāyāna framework in the sixth century.

Tantrism emphasizes, among other things, a high level of interactivity with Buddha and a systematic (even tabular) understanding of the Bud-dhist universe. The interactivity comes by way of initiation into secret teachings transmitted directly from Buddha and accessible only to adepts; and through expertise in a complex of ritualistic behaviors including hand gestures *(mudrā),* magical syllables *(mantra)* and formulas *(dhāraṇī),* and concentration on maṇḍalas and other visual aids that leads to union with Buddha. Vajrayāna practitioners in effect gain direct access to Buddha as though they were entering a dense power grid, which they are able to manipulate to various ends.

The Buddha that generates that grid, the Buddha prime, is Mahāvairocana as revealed in the *Mahāvairocana Sūtra* (J. *Dainichikyō*) and *Vajraśekhara Sūtra* (J. *Kongōchōkyō*) in his own voice. (He is not expounded by Gautama

Śākyamuni or some other Buddha.) Described as a *Buddha solaris* radiating intense light, Mahāvairocana is understood as the interior to which all other Buddhas and Buddha-beings in the Mahāyāna manifold are homeomorphic; all emanate from him. He is also the mapper of the universe: everything in the noumenal and phenomenal realms emerges from him, is spun out like a great web from his complete presence. The two sūtras set forth the principal teachings on Mahāvairocana and on the maṇḍala rituals proper to his celebration. In some sections they are as much an exercise in ekphrasis as they are a systematic articulation of doctrinal and ritual protocols, for the plastic arts, and painting in particular, are absolutely critical to the revelations that Mahāvairocana generates.

The *Mahāvairocana Sūtra* and *Vajraśekhara Sūtra* contain accounts of diagrammatic pictorializations—maṇḍalas—of the noumenal and phenomenal realms emanating from Mahāvairocana as Buddhas, bodhisattvas, and other beings to form the Womb world (Garbhadhātu) and Diamond world (Vajradhātu) respectively. The second and ninth chapters of the *Mahāvairocana Sūtra* present the Womb maṇḍala, or Mahāvairocana as ultimate wisdom, in the form of a field containing 414 emanations arranged around a figure of Mahāvairocana at center (T 18.4a–12c, 31a–36a). Similarly, the second section of the *Vajraśekhara Sūtra* presents the Diamond maṇḍala, or Mahāvairocana made manifest to those reaching the ultimate (fifth) realm of praxis, as a field containing some 1,461 emanations, each the result of a mental projection against the oval of the new moon (T 18.216c–217b). Both maṇḍalas are described as pictures on a two-dimensional plane, which is to say, as constructions of line and paint (T 18.11c17, 31a29). The *Vajraśekhara Sūtra* instructs practitioners to measure out wisdom with lines (T 18.217a2).

Strong emphasis on visual materials in meditative or ritual activity follows standard Mahāyāna practice and does not in itself make the Vajrayāna movement unique. However, when the *Mahāvairocana Sūtra* and *Vajraśekhara Sūtra* stress the importance of beautifully drawn maṇḍalas, in other words when art becomes critical to the process of ritual conduct, a line is crossed from text to picture in the instantiation of doctrine. The Japanese monk Kūkai, who introduced Vajrayāna teachings to the Japanese monastic community in the ninth century, articulated this shift in memorable words:

> In truth, esoteric doctrines are so profound as to defy their enunciation in writing. With the help of painting, however, their obscurities may be understood. The various attitudes and mudrās of the holy images all have their source in Buddha's love, and one may attain Buddhahood at sight of them. Thus the secrets of the sūtras and commentaries can be depicted in art,

and the essential truths of the esoteric teaching are all set forth therein....
Art is what reveals to us the state of perfection.[34]

The iconographical turn of Buddhist doctrine finds its proper maturity
here, where icons, as art, but also as containers of "perfection," lead the way
into the matrix of wisdom and illumination.

When practitioners are told in the sūtras to "see" Mahāvairocana, then,
what is understood is that they are looking at a picture or icon as they initiate meditative or ritual activities. That such pictures existed along with
the scriptures and were used in their elucidation is clear. The Vajrayāna
master and sūtra-translator Śubhākarasiṃha, in Ch'ang-an from 716, had
brought a maṇḍala with him from India in order to help explicate the
Mahāvairocana Sūtra (see T 39.636–41). It is also apparent that there were
rules governing how any given Buddha or Buddha-being was drawn.
According to the *Mahāvairocana Sūtra*, for example, Śākyamuni was to be
painted with a body of purplish gold that displayed the thirty-two marks
(T 18.7b28–29); Mahāvairocana with a high topknot and crown and colored lights streaming from his body (5a13–15); Trailokyavijaya in furious
aspect, with three eyes and four fangs, his body the color of a rain cloud in
summer (7b7–9).

Such details of appearance suggest that, by the time that the *Mahāvairocana Sūtra* was in circulation, a system for the description and classification
of images existed and was utilized by its compilers. This would suggest that
iconographic manuals were also in circulation by the sixth and seventh centuries. With the spread of Vajrayāna teachings into China and Japan, these
kinds of manuals proliferated as an adjunct to textual study and for accuracy in the preparation of ritual environments. The manuals were called
"illustrated icons" (C. *tuxiang;* J. *zuzō*), a term found in the *Mahāvairocana
Sūtra* (T 18.5a13) as well as in Kūkai.[35] They combined pictures with cita-
tions from texts and various instructions.

A number of Japanese manuals of this type survive from the twelfth and
thirteenth centuries.[36] Prepared for the most part by monks of the
Vajrayāna tradition belonging to the Shingon school, the manuals systematically classify and describe the Buddhas and Buddha-beings of the
Mahāyāna manifold. Respective rituals are carefully elucidated; all appropriate precedents listed; and scripture quoted at length to further fix the
pictorial and doctrinal meaning of any given Buddha representation. In the
orderly arrangement of pictures and texts a sense of control prevails: over
images, how they are manipulated, where they stand in the world of praxis. It is a progression that both originates and ends in the figure of Mahāvairocana (fig. 1) as "the order of things" in the full sense of Foucault's term.

Taxonomy

The typical iconographical manual, be it a twelfth-century Japanese text such as *Besson zakki* or a modern equivalent like Sawa Ryūken's *Butsuzō zuten*, takes each figure of the Mahāyāna manifold and provides relevant iconic, scriptural, and liturgical data in a combination of words, symbols, and pictures. The format is encyclopedic and taxonomical. For example, the section on Śākyamuni (J. Shaka) in *Besson zakki* is found under "Buddhas" (Tathāgata; J. Nyorai); includes a drawing of Śākyamuni seated on a lotus in an attitude of preaching (fig. 2); and provides written information on physical appearance, mantras, mystical syllables, scriptural sources, common bodhisattva attendants, and so forth.[37]

The compilers of these manuals were concerned to address two aspects of reception in regard to icons and viewers: initial engagement with the figure (how is it identified, where has it come from); and interaction and exchange (what does it communicate, what can it do, how are its powers reached through ritual or prayer). A hierarchical system of classification, using four orders of beings, was developed to serve the first purpose of typing and identification. The scheme seems to have been based in part on Buddhist cosmology, with its multiple levels of existence, and in part on the hierarchies of the Womb and Diamond maṇḍalas. On a descending scale of awareness and wisdom, the four orders consist of Buddhas, bodhisattvas, wisdom kings, and gods. Virtually every iconographic manual, ancient and modern, follows this hierarchical model.

The second purpose, to establish what the icon is doing and why, is addressed by attention to hand gestures and to implements (and other objects) held in the hands. Hand gestures *(mudrā*; J. *inzō)* take many forms and have broad implications in a system of signing that alerts viewers to what the icon intends (an attitude) or represents (a state of awareness). Some hand gestures indicate deep meditation or trance; others show that the icon is engaged in some exchange—preaching, comforting—with the viewer; others signal hostility or anger. Objects held in the hands are called attributes and, like gestures, relay useful information about the icon in its relationship with the viewer. The thousand implements held in the thousand arms of one of the forms of Avalokiteśvara (J. Kannon) is an extreme example of such armamentaria; iconographic manuals laboriously list and illustrate each item (fig. 6). Perhaps the most common attribute is the lotus, with its implications of purity and the blossoming of wisdom out of impurity.[38]

Diversity of type, gesture, and implement, indeed of body language, is crucial because it establishes difference where there is in fact significant

Fig. 1

Fig. 2

Fig. 3

Fig. 4

Fig. 5   Fig. 6

Fig. 7   Fig. 8

Fig. 9

Fig. 10

Fig. 11

Fig. 12

Fig. 13   Fig. 14

Fig. 15

sameness in morphology. Most representations of Buddhas and Buddha-beings are anthropomorphic: they look like human beings or take the human form as their point of departure. They are often gendered in favor of the human male, but this derives, not so much from scriptural instructions, but from the androcentrism that accompanied the institutionalization of Buddhism.[39] It is well known that "female" Buddhas are not uncommon in the literature and that some "male" Buddhas originated as females in a past life.[40] Indeed, most figures of Buddhas and bodhisattvas—the upper echelon of the Buddhist manifold—are distinctly androgynous in appearance. This is consistent with the insignificance of gender in higher states of awareness. That practitioners and commentators have understood Buddhas and bodhisattvas as gendered is both force of habit (literally) and evidence that the play of illusion remains a fact of life.

While it is true that anthropomorphism is the rule in representations of Buddha and other beings, there are many variations on human anatomy. Bodies come in a variety of colors: gold (e.g., Amitābha), blue (Akṣobhya, Acalanātha), red (Kuṇḍalī, Rāgarāja), yellow (Mañjuśrī), blue-black (Yamāntaka). They might have multiple heads, or eyes, or arms, like any number of bodhisattvas, wisdom kings, or gods; or they might look like an ordinary monk, like most representations of Buddha, or a figure of the bodhisattva Kṣitigarbha (J. Jizō). Zooanthropomorphic forms are also seen but for the most part avoided, as also human figures with multiple legs. Such examples, albeit rare, are striking: the human-peacock "female" wisdom king, Mahāmāyūrī (J. Kujaku; fig. 11); the form of Avalokiteśvara that has a horse's head (Hayagrīva; J. Batō Kannon); six-headed, six-armed, six-legged Yamāntaka (J. Daiitoku; fig. 10).

The taxonomic structure of Buddhist iconography, with its four orders of beings, is the net that holds the various forms in place for Buddhist practice. Each category of representation has its own particular conventions. These seem to have been in place by the time that the *Mahāvairocana Sūtra* was written: the sūtra, in explaining the Womb maṇḍala, works its way through Buddhas, bodhisattvas, wisdom kings, and gods in relatively that progression. However, it does not explicitly cite the orders, nor is there any general commentary on what entails membership in any given order. Iconographical manuals such as *Besson zakki* classify images according to the orders but again do not address how any given order is defined. That task has fallen to modern compilers of Buddhist iconographical dictionaries, among them Sawa Ryūken and Louis Frédéric, whose characterizations of the four orders are outlined below.[41]

The category "Buddhas" proceeds from the idea that Buddha has three bodies: Dharma, Enjoyment, and Manifestation. Thus the singularity of Buddha becomes a multiplicity, and many Buddhas appear in iconographic manuals as Buddha. For example, Mahāvairocana (J. Dainichi; fig. 1) and Buddhalocanī (J. Butsugen Butsumo) represent Dharma bodies; Śākyamuni (fig. 2) is a Manifestation body; and Amitābha (J. Amida; fig. 3) and Bhaiṣajyaguru (J. Yakushi) are Enjoyment bodies in respective Buddhafields to west and east. There is also a Buddha subcategory called "Wisdom peaks" (Uṣnīṣa; J. Butchō-son), after the cranial protuberance that is one of the thirty-two signs that identify a Buddha body; it includes Ekākṣaroṣnīṣa-cakra (J. Ichiji-kinrin) and Vikīrnoṣnīṣa (J. Shijōkō Butchō).

Representations of Buddha follow two conventions: either the figure is shown in the guise of a monk (but with a full head of hair); or it is shown as a king. As a monk, Buddha wears a simple robe thrown over the left shoulder to leave the chest and sometimes shoulders bare, and a dhoti (Figs. 2,3). There is no ornament or jewelry shown. Buddha in the form of a king is shown wearing a crown and high topknot of hair; a dhoti; and a sash or scarf and jewelry over a bared chest. Such royal costuming is reserved, interestingly enough, for Mahāvairocana, Ekākṣaroṣnīṣa-cakra, and other representations of the Dharma body (fig. 1). It is related to the early association of Buddha with the Indian ideal of righteous kingship as embodied in the notion of the Cakravartin-rāja (Wheel-Roller King).[42]

All Buddha depictions include at least a few of the more obvious marks unique to the Buddha body: a cranial protuberance; elongated ears; a whorl of hair on the forehead between the brows; curly hair in the distinctive "snail shell" configuration. It is understood on the basis of scripture that Buddha is a colossus, whether Vairocana (J. Birushana) or Amitābha, and that the Buddha body is greater than any other.[43] Typically a Buddha is shown seated in meditation, as befits the state of awareness that is represented, but there are many examples of seated and standing figures engaged in acts of instruction, comfort, or succor. Buddha images tend to be enstatic in appearance, symmetrical, and generally of reserved aspect despite occasionally dynamic hand gestures. For example, Mahāvairocana sits still even as its hands form the "militant" fist of wisdom—a violent and sexually charged gesture—that signifies its adamantine and all-possessing powers as a form of hyperknowledge.[44] In a manner entirely consistent with the paradigmatic function of an icon, Buddha images are always shown in place: seated or standing on a diamond-like promontory, on a throne, on a lotus, occasionally on a lion.

The category "Bodhisattvas" (J. Bosatsu) is the largest of the four orders and proves the importance of this being to Mahāyāna practice. A bodhisattva, it is well known, is a creature in transit, somewhere between a postponed Buddhahood and the realm of sentient beings whence it has emerged. Bodhisattvas embody compassion but also change: the awakening of the human heart to Buddha nature, a slow progress toward enlightenment, the contingency of wisdom as it unfolds. Typically a bodhisattva is depicted in humanlike form and appears androgynous; many bodhisattvas have multiple heads and arms. The clothing worn by a bodhisattva is appropriate to a prince and resembles that of Mahāvairocana: crown, high topknot, earrings, bare chest covered with a sash and necklaces, dhoti, ankle bracelets, and so forth (fig. 4). An exception is Kṣitigarbha, who is dressed as a monk for journeys along the six paths of existence to help those trapped in the coils of *saṃsāra*.

Bodhisattvas are understood to be extroverted, ready to grant aid to those in need, and so their representations often suggest that the figure is moving in space with eyes looking at the beholder. A bodhisattva may stand in languorous *contraposto* with hips swaying; may sit in relaxation with one leg bent at the knee; may seem to walk toward the viewer; may even raise multiple arms to fan cobra-like around the upper body. In the majority of cases a bodhisattva also has a place to stand or sit on, usually a lotus blossom, but sometimes an animal "vehicle" *(vāhana)*. For example, Mañjuśrī (J. Monju) rides a lion, Samantabhadra (J. Fugen), an elephant (fig. 7).

The category "Wisdom kings" (Vidyārāja; J. Myōō) derives from Vajrayāna belief that *dhāraṇī*—magical or mystical sounds—are supercharged with the vast energies of Mahāvairocana and, ultimately, wisdom.[45] Wisdom kings are *dhāraṇī* embodied, which is to say that they are manifestations of the great forces of the secret teachings. They exist to protect and disseminate the teachings of Buddha by forcefully obstructing evil and by awakening the lay community to Buddhism. In essence wisdom kings are a form of bodhisattva, but their distinctive characteristics give them unique status in the iconographical manifold.

With one or two exceptions, wisdom kings look frightening and belligerent. They are depicted with angry faces and muscular male bodies that take a variety of dynamic poses; their flesh bristles with hair; they have multiple arms and heads; some have many legs like an insect (e.g., Yamāntaka) (Figs. 8, 9, 10). Even their costumes are intimidating. Although wisdom kings typically are shown in the same princely garb as bodhisattvas, they also wear animal skins (Trailokyavijaya, Kuṇḍalī) and sometimes even human skulls (Kuṇḍalī) (Figs. 9, 10). Usually they stand atop outcroppings of rock or crystal (Acalanātha) (fig. 8); some ride a buffalo or cow (Yamāntaka) (fig. 10); some squash creatures representative of desire and other evils (Trailokyavijaya) (fig. 9). Wisdom kings are also called "Angry kings" (Khodharāja; J. Funnuō) in keeping with this aggressive body language.

The category "Gods" (Deva; J. Ten) contains the benevolent riffraff of the Mahāyāna universe. These are beings not much different from humans in that they inhabit, with people and animals, the world of illusion. As distinguished from Buddhas, bodhisattvas, and wisdom kings, who guide sentient beings toward enlightenment, gods are charged with the mundane task of tutelary protection for Buddhism and its community of practitioners. Most gods are Indian in origin, for example, Brahmā (J. Bonten) and Indra (J. Taishakuten). They are fully gendered and have either an aristocratic or a military bearing. The majority, whether aristocratic or military, have something on which to sit or stand: a lotus blossom, a rock, often a pair of demons. There are even some animals who are gods, for example, the elephant Gaṇeśa (J. Shōden; fig. 15).

The aristocratic types are so designated for their relatively polite demeanor, fancy dress, and quiet poses. A male god in this category, such as Brahmā or Indra, wears a suit of decorated armor or a costume like that of a bodhisattva. Female gods, such as Sarasvatī (J. Benzaiten; fig. 12) or Śrī (J. Kichijōten), appear in the noble raiment of queens and princesses. In sharp contrast are the rough types, the body guards and bouncers, who make up the military gods. Some wear suits of armor and brandish weaponry, such as Vaiśravaṇa (J. Bishamonten) and others of the Four Heavenly Kings (J. Shitennō; Figs. 13, 14). Others are virtually naked, among them the Vajradhāra (J. Niō), who pose like weight lifters to display musculature and attitude. These military figures usually trample grotesque creatures reminiscent of gargoyles. They seem worlds away from peaceful beings such as bodhisattvas, and soteriologically they are. But military gods are no less compassionate than any other member of the Mahāyāna manifold, and, like the aristocratic gods, they serve Buddha as protectors of people, temples, sūtras, and Buddhism itself.

The taxonomy of Buddhas, bodhisattvas, wisdom kings, and gods is just that: a classification that provides a table on which to sort the various images that come about in the drive to see and gain insight. As a system of data it is akin to a nautical chart superimposed on the shifting expanse of the sea. Where the chart renders the sea in discrete units—currents, channels, depths, banks, shoals, islands—the sea itself is all of these things taken together and (as a bluewater fisherman would admit) ultimately beyond the reckoning of charts. The chart is a filter by which the vast indivisibility of things (the sea) is negotiated.

Similarly, the Mahāyāna taxonomy charts a world of interrelations, unities, potentialities, and constant shifts of identity. Whether in scripture or ritual, Buddhas and Buddha-beings rarely appear as alone or discrete as the taxonomic order might imply. They are usually presented in the company of other Buddhas and Buddha-beings; with crowds of humans and sometimes animals around; entertained by various magical creatures, such as the Apsarās (J. Hiten), a beautiful celestial nymph, and the Kimnara (J. Kinnara), a human bird of melodious voice. Typically, a Buddha is attended by two bodhisattvas: Mañjuśrī and Samantabhadra with Śākyamuni, for example, or Avalokiteśvara and Mahāsthāmaprāpta (J. Seishi) with Amitābha. In most cases there are some body guards as well, such as the Four Heavenly Kings, who encircle the place where Buddha is, or the Vajradhāra, who stand sentry nearby.

Some Buddhas and bodhisattvas appear with retinues so large they resemble armies. Sahasrabhūja (J. Senju Kannon), the thousand-armed version of Avalokiteśvara, has twenty-eight rather fearsome-looking servants. Śākyamuni heads a contingent that, in addition to Mañjuśrī and Samantabhadra, includes Mahākāśyapa (J. Daikashō), Ānanda (J. Anan), Śāriputra (J. Sharihotsu) and other of his ten disciples; five hundred arhats; and the Four Heavenly Kings. Bhaiṣajyaguru, the Healer Buddha, is attended by the bodhisattvas Sūryaprabha (J. Nikkō) and Candraprabha (J. Gakkō); by Mañjuśrī, Avalokiteśvara, Mahāsthāmaprāpta, and others of a group called the Eight Great Bodhisattvas (J. Hachi Daibosatsu); by Khumbīra (J. Rubira), Vajra (J. Bazara), Mihira (J. Mekira), Andira (J. Anteira), and others of the Twelve Yakṣa Generals; and by seven emanations emerging like clones from his own body in his own image.

Emanation, of course, is as basic a paradigm as the play of absence and presence. Fundamentally speaking, the whole of the Mahāyāna manifold itself emanates from Buddha as the Dharma body (understood as Mahāvairocana in the Vajrayāna tradition). In this sense there are no stable iconic identities but rather various states of multiplicity and intersubjectivity. Amitābha may appear in nine identical forms, for example, Kṣitigarbha in six. In a more complex articulation of the same principle, Mahāvairocana gives rise to what are called the Five Wisdom Buddhas, namely, Mahāvairocana, Akṣobhya (J. Ashuku), Amitābha, Ratnasambhava (J. Hōshō), and Amogasiddhi (J. Fukujōju). Each in turn produces respective bodhisattva and wisdom-king emanations that simultaneously have their own distinct identities separate from any role as an emanation. For example, Mahāvairocana (fig. 1) is also the bodhisattva Samantabhadra (fig. 7) and the wisdom king Acalanātha (J. Fudō; fig. 8), Amitābha is also Avalokiteśvara (fig. 4) and Yamāntaka (fig. 10), even as each of these bodhisattvas and wisdom kings has a unique personality apart from Mahāvairocana or Amitābha, as well as its own scriptures and rituals.

A remarkable collection of emanations occurs in the case of Avalokiteś-vara. There are at least thirty-three forms of Avalokiteśvara, "the all-seeing," a number so large that iconographers have occasionally assigned it a sepa-rate order in their manuals: "Avalokiteśvaras" (J. Kannon). The forms range from human to animal and across gender, as befits a bodhisattva who embodies the Mahāyāna ideal of compassion and understanding through expedient means. Āryāvalokiteśvara (Lokeśvara) is the prime and usually appears in the guise of a human with monstrous or magical features (eyes in the palms of the hands) not immediately evident (fig. 4). Others are memorable for the imaginative shapes that they take: eleven heads with some frowning and others laughing (Ekadāśamukha; J. Jūichimen Kannon; fig. 5); a thousand arms and eleven heads (Sahasrabhūja; fig. 6); a horse face with an angry expression (Hayagrīva). Still others, with four and six arms, hold attributes or make gestures that set the context of worship. Amoghapāśa (J. Fukūkenjaku), for example, grasps the rope and hook that enables it to capture humans like fish from the sea.

These emanations and transformations can only destabilize a system, be it a taxonomy or a doctrine, that seeks to establish some level of perma-nence for a subject that in effect does not exist yet is patently present. Any reading of Mahāyāna iconography must take into account the strength of this dichotomy, for it reaches to the core of the Buddhist episteme. If there are orders and classifications—Buddhas, bodhisattvas, wisdom kings, gods—there are also all the ties that bind them together as one in the moment of unification that seeing, ultimately, grants and destroys.

"Where it came from"

What we see when we see Buddha turns out to be a lot and entirely con-tingent. Seeing is active, not passive: we see what we want to see. The par-adox and incongruity of Mahāyāna iconography, where the fundamental condition is that Buddha is outside the space of representation, make the act of seeing as charged, as laden, as any philosophical rumination on non-substantiality. In pictures and icons, as in words, realization comes about through illusion, which might be the whispered insinuation of Māra at

Buddha's ear, or the boundless enterprise of ekphrasis that the voices of the sūtras call out to us so we can see.

Mahāyāna iconography celebrates figuration as a *mysterium tremendum et fascinans*. Its army of bodies, each with a place to stand on, offers a practical means to visualizing a referent that constantly shifts and finally does not exist. There is a body for everyone, and a social order: kings and vassals, servants, laborers. There are visions, filled with Buddha bodies, that make ignorance into bliss. But these are like the grapes of Zeuxis, a counterfeit truth in the field of representations: they are decoys, lures, the perfect illusion. When Sudāna asks Maitreya where the vision has gone, the one that fills the *Avataṃsaka Sūtra* like a vivid hallucination, the answer is blunt: where it came from (T 9.782b). There could be no better way than that to answer the biggest question of all, why is there something rather than nothing.

Notes

1. Malcolm David Eckel, *To See the Buddha: A Philosopher's Quest for the Meaning of Emptiness* (Princeton: Princeton University Press, 1992) 65; Paul J. Griffiths, Noriaki Hakamaya, John P. Keenan, Paul L. Swanson, *The Realm of Awakening: Chapter Ten of Asaṅga's Mahāyānasangraha* (New York and Oxford: Oxford University Press, 1989) 49–56. For seeing Buddha, see Eckel, *To See the Buddha*, and Paul J. Griffiths, *On Being Buddha: The Classical Doctrine of Buddhahood* (Albany: State University of New York Press, 1994).

2. John D. Dunne, "Thoughtless Buddha, Passionate Buddha," *Journal of the American Academy of Religion* 64:3 (1996) 525.

3. Griffiths, *On Being Buddha*, 116, 160–61; see also Eckel, *To See the Buddha*, 65–66.

4. Eckel, *To See the Buddha*, 63–65; see also Michel Foucault, *The Order of Things: An Archaeology of the Human Sciences* (New York: Vintage Books, 1994) xvii–xviii.

5. Griffiths et al., *The Realm of Awakening*, 10.

6. Gilbert Durand, "The Imaginal," in *The Encyclopedia of Religion*, ed. Mircea Eliade (New York: Macmillan, 1987) 7.109.

7. For recollection see Eckel, *To See the Buddha*, 135, 137; Griffiths, *On Being Buddha*, 93, 100, 194.

8. Eckel, *To See the Buddha*, 1, 138–39, 146. Griffiths writes of Gautama's career as a manifestation consisting "solely in 'representations' *(vijñapti)*, 'appearances' *(pratibhāsa)*, or 'reflections' *(pratibimba)* in the minds of others"; see Griffiths, *On Being Buddha*, 93.

9. *Kao-seng Fa-hsian chuan* (T no. 2085); James Legge, trans., *A Record of Buddhistic Kingdoms: Being an Account by the Chinese Monk Fa-Hien of His Travels in India and Ceylon (A.D. 399–414) in Search of the Buddhist Books of Discipline* (New York: Dover, 1965; orig. pub. 1886).

10. C. S. Peirce, "Logic as Semiotic: The Theory of Signs," in *Semiotics: An Anthology*, ed. R. Innis (Bloomington: University of Indiana Press, 1985) 9.

11. Johnny Cash, "In Your Mind," *Dead Man Walking*, Columbia Pictures, 1995.

12. See Griffiths, *On Being Buddha*, 68, 99–100.

13. For *kāya* as a physical body and as a collection or combination, and *śarīra* as a physical body as well as a remnant or relic, see Eckel, *To See the Buddha*, 99, and Gustav Roth, "The Physical Presence of the Buddha and its Representation in Buddhist Literature," in *Investigating Indian Art* (Berlin: Museum für Indische Kunst, 1987) 291, 293–94.

14. For Buddha's body as a "standpoint," see Eckel, *To See the Buddha*, 105.

15. A similar story was recorded by the Chinese pilgrim Hsüan-tsang in 629 about the king of Udayana and a statue of Buddha, which Hsüan-tsang saw in an old temple in Kosāmbi; see *Ta-t'ang hsi-yü chi* (J. *Daitō shiyūki*), T 51.898a6–16 (no. 2087), and Samuel Beal, trans., *Si-yu-ki: Buddhist Records of the Western World* (New York: Paragon Book Reprint Corp., 1968; orig. pub. 1884) I, 235–36.

16. Frank E. Reynolds and Charles Hallisey, "Buddha," in *The Encyclopedia of Religion* 2.326. For epithets, see Griffiths, *On Being Buddha*, 60, 173.

17. See Alfred Foucher, *The Beginnings of Buddhist Art and Other Essays in Indian and Central Asian Archaeology* (Paris: Paul Geuthner, 1917), 1–29.

18. See Susan L. Huntington, "Early Buddhist Art and the Theory of Aniconism," *Art Journal* 49 (1990) 401–8.

19. Huntington, "Early Buddhist Art," 402. To distinguish between nonrepresentational (aniconic or symbolic) forms and representational (iconic) forms is not to accept Foucher's argument that iconic forms derived from Greek models.

20. Griffiths, *On Being Buddha*, 94.

21. Gregory Schopen and others have shown that concern "with images and the cult of images" was already evident in the Theravāda schools of early Buddhism; see Gregory Schopen, "Mahāyāna in Indian Inscriptions," *Indo-Iranian Journal* 21 (1979) 16. Such interest in icons, especially in icons as cult objects, needs also to be considered as one of the determining factors in the development of Mahāyāna Buddhism.

22. Hirakawa Akira, *A History of Indian Buddhism from Śākyamuni to Early Mahāyāna*, trans. Paul Groner (Honolulu: University of Hawai'i Press, 1990) 4, 260–74.

23. For a history and summary of these scriptures, see Hirakawa, *A History of Indian Buddhism*, 275–95.

24. Roth, "The Physical Presence of the Buddha and its Representation in Buddhist Literature," 295. Circularity or roundness of form is also the eleventh of the thirty-two major characteristics of Buddha's body: "He is round, like a banyan tree" (T 6.986). See Griffiths, *On Being Buddha*, 99.

25. See for example the final two chapters of Lokakṣema's second-century translation of the *Aṣṭasāhasrikā-prajñāpāramitā Sūtra*, the *Dōgyō hannya kyō* (C. *Tao-hsing pan-jo ching*), T 8 (no. 224) 476b–78a.

26. Griffiths, *On Being Buddha*, 134.

27. Griffiths, *On Being Buddha*, 81, 89.

28. Eckel, *To See the Buddha*, 75.

29. Griffiths, *On Being Buddha*, 129.

30. Eckel. *To See the Buddha*, 75.

31. Griffiths, *On Being Buddha*, 82, 90–91. For an important examination of the three-body theory, see Nagao Gadjin, *Mādhyamika and Yogācāra: A Study of Mahāyāna Philosophies* (Albany: State University of New York Pess, 1991) 103–22.

32. Alan Sponberg, "Meditation in Fa-hsiang Buddhism," in *Traditions of Meditation in Chinese Buddhism*, ed. Peter N. Gregory (Honolulu: University of Hawai'i Press, 1986) 17–19, 21–22, 26–27.

33. Eckel, *To See the Buddha*,135.

34. William Theodore de Bary, ed., *Sources of Japanese Tradition* (New York: Columbia University Press, 1964) I,138; *Goshōrai mokuroku*, in Bussho Kankōkai, ed., *Dai Nihon Bukkyō zensho* (Tokyo: Bussho Kankōkai, 1914) II, 25b (see also 27a). On his return from study with Vajrayāna masters in China, Kūkai brought with him a large collection of maṇḍalas and iconographical drawings from Ch'ang-an to the Kyoto capital. For a study of these maṇḍalas, see Elizabeth ten Grotenhuis, *The Sacred Geography of the Japanese Maṇḍala* (Honolulu: University of Hawai'i Press, 1998).

35. *Goshōrai mokuroku*, 25b.

36. The iconographies are collected in twelve supplementary volumes to T. They include *Zuzōshō* (ca. 1135), *Besson Zakki* (ca. 1160–1180), *Kakuzenshō* (between 1176 and 1219), *Asabashō* (ca. 1249–1269); see Sawa Ryūken, *Butsuzō zuten* (Tokyo: Yoshikawa Kōbunkan, 1982) 14–15.

37. *Taishō shinshū Daizōkyō Zuzōbu* (Tokyo: Daizō Shuppansha, 1933–1934) III, 103-105.

38. For hand gestures and implements, see E. Dale Saunders, *Mudrā: A Study of Symbolic Gestures in Japanese Buddhist Sculpture* (Princeton: Princeton University Press, 1985). The ninth chapter of the *Mahāvairocana Sūtra* presents the primary hand gestures associated with the Womb maṇḍala and its rituals (T 18.24a-30a).

39. See Alan Sponberg, "Attitudes toward Women and the Feminine in Early Buddhism," in *Buddhism, Sexuality, and Gender*, ed. José Ignacio Cabezón (Albany: State University of New York Press, 1992) 3–36.

40. Examples of "female" Buddhas are Prajñāpāramitā (J. Butsumo, "Mother of Buddhas") and Buddhalocanī (J. Butsugen Butsumo, "Eye of Buddhas, Mother of Buddhas"); see Sponberg, "Attitudes toward Women," 26–27, and Sawa, *Butsuzō zuten*, 50. According to the *Suvarṇaprabhāsottama-rāja Sūtra* even Śākyamuni was at one time female (T 16.417a14–15).

41. See Sawa, *Butsuzō zuten*, and Louis Frédéric, *Flammarion Iconographic Guides: Buddhism* (Paris and New York: Flammarion, 1995).

42. See Roth, "Physical Presence of the Buddha," 293–96. As Roth notes, the body of a Cakravartin-rāja was also seen to have thirty-two identifying characteristics.

43. In Tibet various iconometric systems were developed after the thirteenth century; see David and Janice Jackson, *Tibetan Thangka Painting: Methods and Materials* (Ithaca, NY: Snow Lion Publications, 1984) 50–57, 144–48. Buddhist painters and sculptors in Japan of the eleventh and twelfth centuries used an iconometric system based on scriptures such as the Pure Land *Kanmuryōjukyō*, which described the Buddha as having a giant body, "filling up the sky," or as having the linear measurements one *jō*, six *shaku*, and eight *shaku* (T 12.344b–c). There were ten *shaku* to one *jō*; and one *shaku* is thought to have been about thirty centimeters. In other words, Buddha is understood as having a body length that is infinite or that measures from two and a half to five meters. For Japanese iconometrics, see Ōta Koboku, *Butsuzō chōkoku gihō* (Tokyo: Sōgeisha, 1980).

44. See Saunders, *Mudrā*, 102–107.

45. Wisdom kings for this reason might also be called Dhāraṇī kings, in that
the term *vidyā* (J. *myō*) indicates knowledge, or wisdom, attained at the deepest
levels of invocation; see Mochizuki Shinkyo, *Mochizuki bukkyō daijiten* (Tokyo:
Sekai Seiten Kankō Kyōkai, 1960–1963) V, 4779, and Ariga Yoshitaka, *Butsuga no
kanshō kiso chishiki* (Tokyo: Shibundō, 1996) 109.

28

Buddhist Spirituality in Modern Taiwan

HENG-CHING SHIH

TAIWANESE Buddhism originally came from mainland China. Most historical records indicate that it was gradually imported into the island after the arrival of Cheng Ch'eng-kung, a general during the end of the Ming (1368–1644) Dynasty who had been fighting against Ch'ing (1644–1912) soldiers along the southern coast of Fujian Province and who retreated to Taiwan after failing to occupy the lower reaches of the Yangtze River. He expelled the Dutch, who had been occupying Taiwan, and along with his son made the island a base of rebellion against the Ch'ing Dynasty. Taiwan gradually became prosperous and attracted many immigrants who brought Buddhism with them.

Taiwanese Buddhism can be divided into three periods: (1) from the end of the Ming Dynasty to the end of the Ch'ing Dynasty; (2) during the Japanese occupation (1895–1945); and (3) from the recovery of Taiwan (1945) to the present. The first group of Buddhist monks who came to Taiwan with Cheng Ch'eng-kung were mostly from the Lin-chi school of Fujian Province. Initially small, their number continued to grow, and by the end of the Ch'ing Dynasty, four major lineages had developed, with the following centers: (1) Ling Ch'uan Monastery at Mt. Yueh Mei in Chi Lung; (2) Ling Yun Monastery at Mt. Wu-ku Kuan-yin in Taipei; (3) Fa Yun Monastery at Ta Hu in Miao Li; and (4) Ch'ao Feng Monastery at Mt. Ta Kang in Kaohsiung.

During the first period, the Pure Land and Ch'an, especially the Lin-chi and Ts'ao-tung schools, enjoyed the greatest popularity. Practice was primarily a combination of Pure Land and Ch'an, supplemented by Dharma-teaching and Precepts. Because of the emphasis on personal practice, there was little activity in the field of preaching and writing, though there were a few monks who were very knowledgeable in the Dharma. This deficiency signifies that Ch'ing-period Taiwan did not yet have a fully mature Buddhist culture. A very special lay Buddhism was transmitted from the mainland, the so-called Chai-chiao (vegetarian sect), which emphasized purification of body and mind, control of craving and desire, and abstention from nonvegetarian and stimulating food, and from sexual indulgence, alcohol, and gambling. Most of its female followers were celibate. Actually, Chai-chiao was not pure Buddhism but a popular amalgam of Buddhist teaching, Confucianism, and Taoism. However, because it satisfied the religious needs of the general public, its influence was great. During the Japanese occupation, for convenience of management, the government placed all Chai-chiao organizations under the South Seas Buddhist Association and classified them as lay Buddhist associations under different monasteries. There were three major groups of Chai-chiao in Taiwan: Chin Chuang, Lung Hua, and Hsien T'ien. In addition to its religious importance, it was a close-knit social organization that made great contributions to society and the economy.

The Japanese were the colonial rulers of Taiwan from 1895 to 1945, when Taiwan was recovered. Although the relationship between Taiwanese Buddhism and Chinese Buddhism was not severed during this period, there was a tremendous influence from Japanese Buddhism. Japan pursued its colonial policy of Japanizing Taiwanese Buddhism gently and slowly. The tactics included appointing Japanese monks to preach in Taiwan, registering all local Taiwanese monasteries under different Japanese Buddhist sects, sending chosen Taiwanese monks to study in Japan, and publishing Japanese Buddhist periodicals. Taiwanese monks wore Japanese monastic attire, and they were allowed to marry and to eat meat. The monasteries followed the Japanese architectural design and setting, and were under the management of Japanese Buddhist sects. Lay surnames were added to the Dharma-names of the monks and nuns. Some monks received training from the Japanese Buddhist Association and no longer took full precepts in the Chinese way.

The Japanese Sōtō (Ts'ao-tung) school was the earliest group to make contact with the Taiwanese Buddhists. In 1912 the Sōtō school set up a Patriotic Buddhist Society through the Chai-chiao in Tainan, in order to recruit Taiwanese Buddhists to its organization for easier monitoring. Their efforts were helped by the Hsi Lai Temple incident in 1915 that occurred shortly afterwards. Hsi Lai Temple was an important Chai-chiao temple in Tainan City. A certain Yü Ch'ing-fang used this temple as a liaison center for resistance activities against the Japanese occupation, seeking to arouse people's patriotism through religion. As a result of the disturbance this caused, many conservative Chai-chiao organizations applied to join the Patriotic Buddhist Society in order to be protected by the Japanese Sōtō school. The orthodox Buddhist saṃghas reluctantly followed the Chai-chiao devotees and applied to belong to the Japanese Buddhist sects for their own safety. They founded the Buddhist Youth Association of Taiwan in 1918 and the South Seas Buddhist Association in 1921. The latter was a Buddhist organization for the whole of Taiwan. It gathered almost all the best people in the Buddhist circle of the time, such as Dharma-master Shan Hui of Ling Ch'uan Monastery, Dharma-master Pen Yuan of Ling Yun Monastery, and Dharma-master Chueh Li of Fa Yun Monastery. Although these two Buddhist associations were under Japanese supervision, they were free to preach the Dharma.

The Buddhist Youth Association of Taiwan engaged in teaching and preaching by sponsoring lectures and publishing journals for its members, while the Nan Ying Buddhist Association made its greatest contribution by conducting Buddhist lectures around the whole island and holding study seminars regularly in monasteries. These were substantial in content, including a specifically Buddhist curriculum (e.g. *Diamond Sūtra*, *Vimala-kirti Sūtra, Lotus Sūtra*) and general subjects such as Chinese and history. It is worth mentioning that, of the sixteen study seminars, two were for women.

In 1925 the Nan Ying Buddhist Association and the Fa Yun Institute of Buddhist Studies (founded by Dharma-master Chueh Li) together sponsored a seminar that lasted for six months for the Buddhist nuns in Taiwan. That was the first opportunity for women in Taiwan to study Buddhism in public officially and systematically and indeed marked the beginning of formal education in Buddhism for Buddhist women in Taiwan. In 1923, the Nan Ying Buddhist Association started to issue the *Nan Ying Buddhist Journal*, which published essays on the reforms of Taiwanese Buddhism, explanations of Buddhist teachings, accounts of Japanese Buddhism and culture, and discussions of Taiwanese folk religions. This publication is a valuable source of historical information on Taiwanese Buddhism and folk religion during the Japanese occupation.

Four major sects of Taiwanese Buddhism during the Japanese occupation were separately engaged in preaching the Dharma and in education. The K'ai Yuan Monastery founded the Saṃgha School. The Fa Yun Monastery established the Fa Yun Institute of Buddhist Studies for the education of monks and nuns. Dharma-master Shan Hui of Ling Ch'uan Monastery and Dharma-master Pen Yuan of Ling Yun Monastery together established the Taiwan Buddhist Middle School for both laymen and monks. However, because the education of monks and nuns was not well organized and Buddhist institutes were few, the quality of the monks and nuns was not high. Since very few monks or nuns preached the Dharma, the lay devotees were unable to establish right belief. Thus the modernization of Taiwanese Buddhism did not really start until the third period.

This period extends from the recovery of Taiwan (1945) to the present. As internal self-awakening matched external social changes, Taiwanese Buddhism progressed on many fronts and is today recognized in international Buddhist and academic circles as one of the Buddhist cultures with the greatest vitality and potential for development. The development over the last fifty years can be further divided into three stages: from 1945 to 1960, from 1961 to 1980, and from 1981 to the present.

After the Japanese occupation ended in 1945, the Kuomintang (Nationalist Party) regime took over Taiwan. Over the next fifteen years, because of oppressive political rule, economic hardship, and social ignorance, Buddhism developed slowly. However, a few measures taken by Buddhists at this time laid the foundation for future development. The rebuilding of Chinese Buddhism in Taiwan should be attributed to two groups of monks who came to Taiwan from mainland China.

The first group came in 1949, in the wake of the Nationalist government that moved to Taiwan after the communist takeover of the mainland. It included Dharma-masters Pai Sheng, Chih Kuang, Nan T'ing, and others. Their main contribution was the reconstruction of the Buddhist precepts, so that the traditional Chinese system of Buddhism could be restored. Dharma-master Pai Sheng and others also founded the Buddhist Association of the Republic of China, with branches all over Taiwan. All monasteries and individuals could become members. Although the Buddhist Association of the Republic of China had the function of uniting and structuring Buddhism in Taiwan, it became merely a mouthpiece of the government because of government control and because it was led by conservative people like Pai Sheng and others for decades.

The second group consisted of those who fled to Hong Kong and then to Taiwan after the mainland fell to the communists. It included Yin Shun, Yen P'ei, Tao An, and others. Their main contributions were their work on Buddhist education and Buddhist philosophy.

After Taiwan was returned, the Chinese Buddhist tradition of transmitting the precepts was restored. During the Japanese occupation, some monasteries had conducted the transmission of precepts, and some monks and nuns even went to Japan or mainland China to receive the precepts, but their number was extremely small. At that time there were many "home-leaving" women belonging to Chai-chiao. Unlike Buddhist nuns, they did not shave their hair or take precepts. Although they really had left their families and stayed in monasteries all the time to practice, they did not conform fully to the Buddhist rules and regulations of monastic life. Furthermore, under the influence of traditional Japanese Buddhism, many Taiwanese "monks" married and ate meat, which was even more incompatible with the Buddhist regulations. These situations gradually improved with the establishment of precept-transmission. In 1953, the Dharma-masters who had come from the mainland held the first transmission of the Full Precepts in Three Platforms at Ta Hsien Monastery in Tainan County. After that, various monasteries took turns yearly to transmit the full precepts of bhikkhus and bhikkhunīs. In the past four decades, tens of thousands of monks and nuns have been formally ordained and taken the full precepts. Even though some problems have arisen in the transmission of precepts, the establishment of rules and regulations for precept-transmissions effectively extricated Taiwanese Buddhism from the influence of Japanese Buddhism. It also strengthened the saṃgha's ideology and practice of precepts, and established the positive and pure image of the saṃgha in the minds of the Buddhist lay devotees.

Besides the transmission of precepts, the active establishment of institutes of Buddhist studies was also an important factor in the development of Taiwanese Buddhism. During the Japanese occupation Buddhist education in Taiwan was not common, and some monks and nuns chose to go to Japan to receive more systematic Buddhist education. After 1945 Yuan Kuang Monastery at Chung Li was the first to establish a Buddhist institute. Its abbot, Venerable Miao Kuo, invited Dharma-master Tz'u Hang from mainland China to Taiwan to run the school as early as 1948. Tz'u Hang first toured the whole island to talk about his ideas of education; this kindled a new hope of reviving Taiwanese Buddhism and made monks and nuns eager to attend schools. In the next twenty years, about twenty Buddhist schools were founded one after another; the number had probably reached about thirty by the nineties, despite the persistence of numerous insurmountable problems connected with the education of the saṃgha, on both the conceptual and organizational levels.

The second phase lasted from 1961 to 1980. During these years the Taiwanese economy was about to take off, and education was becoming popular. These timely conditions provided great impetus for Buddhism. The greatest accomplishment within the religion in this period was the founding of Buddhist societies in colleges and universities, and these have helped to raise the level of Buddhist culture among both monks and lay people.

Credit for this goes to Upasaka Chou Hsuan-te, a pioneer in preaching the Dharma to college students. In 1958, on his sixtieth birthday, he gave money for the publication of one thousand copies of the *Pa-ta ren chueh ching* (Sūtra of Eightfold Enlightenment) and *The Characteristics and Values of Buddhism*, and donated them to college students, encouraging them to write essays after studying them. On the Buddha's birthday in 1960, thanks to his unstinting efforts, National Taiwan University formed the first college Buddhist society—the Ch'en Hsi Buddhist Society. Soon afterward, National Normal University formed the Chung-tao Society. After that, Buddhist societies were formed in succession in colleges all over Taiwan, over seventy in all, and there is now one in virtually every college or university. These societies have guided innumerable students to intensive engagement with Buddhist doctrine and practice. After graduation, some students have formed societies for lay devotees, which play their role in different professions and trades, and some have even become monks or nuns to preach professionally.

In addition, the organization of college Buddhist lectures and Buddhist summer camps and the establishment of college Buddhist scholarships were highly effective in bringing intellectuals to study Buddhism. Many monasteries sponsored summer camps that provided opportunities for young intellectuals to learn Buddhism and to experience Buddhist life. Besides sponsoring activities by various college Buddhist societies, the Wisdom Torch Publications (founded by Chou Hsuan-te) also sponsored and handled a variety of Buddhist scholarships, such as the Maitreya Scholarship, the Fan Tao-nan Scholarship, and some twenty others. Every year, about one to two hundred undergraduate and graduate students receive these scholarships. Since applicants have to submit a paper on Buddhism, it has helped to improve the understanding of Buddhism among college students.

In this period, Buddhist magazines, totaling about twenty to thirty, were very popular. Most of these magazines were general publications with an emphasis on faith. Although they were not highly academic, they served the purposes of preaching and teaching to the public. Popular editions of Buddhist scriptures made the latter available to the interested public. A major publishing project, a new edition of the Chinese Tripiṭaka Canon initiated and compiled by lay devotees, was eventually completed after more than twenty years.

The most important stage in the development of modern Taiwanese Buddhism is the one from 1981 to the present. Building on the foundation laid by the Buddhists of the previous two stages, and helped by the highly developed Taiwanese economy and a more open social and political environment,

Taiwanese Buddhism has achieved great things in the areas of preaching, Buddhist studies, social education, medical aid, and charitable work. Taiwanese Buddhism today is very active. Many Buddhists participate in indoor activities such as lectures and sessions of seven-day meditation and seven-day Buddha-recitation and outdoor activities such as making pilgrimage to monasteries. The social concern of Buddhists, academic research carried out by Buddhist scholars, and even the exploration of new Buddhist concepts are much more lively than at any previous time. These auspicious phenomena are linked to the promotion of a "Buddhism of humanity" or "society-oriented Buddhism." Taiwanese Buddhism has shed its previous image of being rigid, reclusive, passive, pessimistic, and superstitious and has developed life-oriented, popularized, modernized, and diversified approaches. The remainder of this article presents some of the most important features of contemporary Taiwanese Buddhism.

Preaching Activities

The style of preaching of Taiwanese Buddhism has changed from the traditional and nonaggressive style of "neither rejecting anyone who comes nor pursuing anyone who leaves" to become more positive and active. This has been achieved by sponsoring such religious activities as large- and small-scale Buddhist lectures, summer camps and winter camps, Buddhist talks in prisons, short-term monastic experience as a monk or nun, pilgrimage activities, preaching programs on radio and television, and sessions of seven-day meditation and seven-day Buddha-recitation. Many monks and nuns give Buddhist lectures regularly or irregularly. Some expound a certain scripture, while others explore in depth a specific topic of Buddhist doctrine. These are the main opportunities for the laity to learn Buddhism. Some Dharma-masters also hold large-scale lectures that usually attract thousands and even tens of thousands of listeners, and thus exert remarkable influence. Many lay people also lecture.

In the past, many monasteries held summer camps for college students, with a planned curriculum, to enable them to understand Buddhist teaching and to have a personal experience of monastic life. Recently, summer camps have been diversified for different groups, such as children, teenagers, and teachers. Curricula and activities are geared to the different participants, so as to increase their confidence, religious experience, and experience in life. For example, teachers learn how to relate Buddhist teachings to contemporary social issues and problems and how to apply Buddhist educational concepts in their teaching job.

In order to carry out the traditional Buddhist rules and regulations, and to allow lay Buddhists to experience the life of the saṃgha, some monasteries sponsor "short-term leaving home." "Leaving home" in Chinese Buddhism is for life. This differs from Theravāda Buddhism, which has a practice of "short-term leaving home." For those modern Buddhists who long for monastic life but are unable to undertake it for life, a short-term experience as monks or nuns can give them the opportunity to experience religious life without interfering with their social responsibilities. Thus, many Buddhists are drawn to participate.

Besides such traditional Dharma-assemblies as prostration to the Buddha, repentance, and so forth, "seven-day practice" is one of the most favored Buddhist activities in Taiwan. The aim is to find deeper religious experience or even enlightenment in a practice of seven days. In order to obtain better results in a short period, cultivators frequently do intensive and time-limited practice. If only the recitation of Buddha's name is practiced, it is called seven-day Buddha-recitation (fo-ch'i); if only Ch'an meditation is practiced, it is called seven-day meditation (ch'an-ch'i); if only Kuan-yin Bodhisattva's name is chanted, it is called seven-day Kuan Yin. At present, Dharma-master Wei Chueh of Ling Ch'uan Monastery in Taipei is the most respected of those who conduct sessions of seven-day meditation. His followers are from all walks of life, ranging from peddlers and civil servants to high officials and rich merchants, and many of them are able to obtain profound experience in meditation under his guidance. Nowadays, meditation has become so popular in society that many Buddhists meditate at home every day. Some even form organizations of different sizes to practice together at night or on weekends.

At the moment, lay Buddhism is also flourishing in Taiwan. The laity have their own organizations. They hold frequent and varied preaching activities, such as Buddhist lectures by lay Buddhists who are very knowledgeable in the Dharma. In the early years, the more influential lay organizations included the Wisdom Torch founded by Chou Hsuan-te, and the Taichung Pure-land Buddhist Society founded by Lee Ping-nan. The latter, a pious Pure-land practitioner, was well-versed in Buddhism and Confucianism. His life-goal was to nourish lay devotees' faith in the Pure Land. He founded Buddhist societies, conducted regular assemblies to chant Buddha's name, and expounded Pure Land Scriptures. He has taught innumerable lay Buddhists. In the last ten years, because the number of intellectual and young Buddhists has significantly increased, lay Buddhism has flourished even more. Such groups as Wei-man Hsueh-hui (Vimalakīrti and Śrīmālā Study Society), Hsin-yu Buddhist Cultural Center, and Modern

Ch'an have developed distinctive views and styles in interpreting and practicing the Buddhist doctrines. A group of Buddhist scholars has formed the Modern Association for Buddhist Studies, which aims to give consideration to both faith and an academic study of Buddhism. Recently many public figures—high officials, people's representatives, actors and performers—have become Buddhists. This has imperceptibly given an impetus to the study of Buddhism in society. Some lay Buddhists have even set up foundations to promote the preaching of Dharma and Buddhist culture.

Academic Study of Buddhism

In recent years the number of intellectual Buddhists has increased, and the quality of monks and nuns also has significantly improved. However, the development of academic study of Buddhism has been slower. There are external and internal reasons for this. The external reason is that in the past few decades the Ministry of Education, far from encouraging academic studies in Buddhism, prohibited colleges and universities from having any curriculum of religion. Under this ignorant and inappropriate educational policy, academic research on religion, particularly Buddhist studies, could not be pursued within the regular educational system. It was only in 1991 that the ban was lifted.

The internal reason for the slower development of Buddhist studies in Taiwan is that Taiwanese Buddhist groups did not realize the importance of such studies. Consequently, there was no active training of qualified academic people. In early years, although many traditional monasteries ran Buddhist schools, they emphasized the training of monks and nuns, and rejected or even despised the modern academic method of investigating the Dharma. However, things have improved in recent years. At present, there are two graduate schools of Buddhist studies, founded by a nunnery and a monastery, which are of larger scope and higher standards: the Fa Kuang (Buddha Light) Institute of Buddhist Studies and the Chung-hua Institute of Buddhist Studies. Their graduate students are required to receive training in the canonical languages, to acquire a good command of research methods in Buddhism, and to have a broad understanding of the historical development of Buddhism and the important doctrines. However, because the institutes are not recognized by the Ministry of Education, they cannot grant a master's degree. Many graduates of these institutes are continuing their advanced studies in Japan, America, Europe, India, or other countries. Given the solid formation they have received in Taiwan and the additional research training abroad, it can be anticipated that a new generation of young Buddhist scholars will emerge in the next ten years. They will become a new force for the development of Buddhist studies in Taiwan.

Another turning point benefiting Buddhist studies is that the Ministry of Education has lifted the ban on the establishment of private colleges and universities. So far one fully accredited university and three colleges have been established by Buddhist organizations. In those schools graduate schools of religious studies were set up to enhance Buddhist studies. However, the establishment of the department or the graduate school of Buddhist studies is still banned by the Ministry of Education.

At present, Buddhist academic research in Taiwan mainly comes from the thirty to forty Buddhist scholars who are teaching in the departments of philosophy, history, or literature in various colleges and universities. Their expertise includes almost all areas of Buddhism, and each year brings a rich crop of publications. Although Buddhist studies are not taken seriously in public universities, Buddhist scholars at the National Taiwan Universities managed to set up a Center for Buddhist Studies in 1995. Even without any support from the University, the Center holds conferences on Buddhism, publishes an annual journal, and has set up a database on Buddhism for international use on the Internet. Recently the Center, with the help of some Buddhist organizations, has launched a five-year project of computerizing the Taishō Buddhist Canon, which it will make available free on CD and on the Internet.

A group of Buddhist scholars formed a Modern Society for Buddhist Studies in 1990. Its aims are: (1) to promote research in Buddhism; (2) to convene academic conferences on Buddhism; (3) to issue academic journals; (4) to accept inquiries from public and private organizations, or commissions to carry out research projects; and (5) to have cultural exchange with Buddhist research organizations overseas. For example, members of this society have organized a group to study Ta-li Buddhism in Yunnan in mainland China, resulting in a collection of monographs. Another important academic activity is the annual United Conference on Buddhism. The participants are graduate students at various Buddhist institutes in Taiwan. The purpose of this conference is to promote Buddhist research and to foster students' ability to write, discuss, and give verbal critiques of papers. These conferences are a valuable opportunity for students to exchange views and to learn from one another.

In the field of Buddhism in Taiwan, the most outstanding scholar is the ninety-three-year-old Dharma-master Yin Shun. A deep connoisseur of Buddhist tradition and a prolific author, he is praised as the most outstanding Tripiṭaka-master of Chinese Buddhism in recent centuries.

Although he says he has spent most effort on the *Āgama Sūtras* (the early Buddhist canon), the scope of his studies is extremely broad. His contributions to Buddhist research include:

1. An exposition of the meaning of *pratītyasamutpāda* (dependent origination) and *śūnyatā* (emptiness) in the study of Mādhyamika. Yin Shun is one of the very few scholars in the San-lun School since Chia-hsiang Chi-tsang (549–623) who has a profound understanding of its teaching (though he does not profess to belong to this school). His books in this area include *New Discussion on Mādhyamika, Commentary on the Mādhyamika-kārikā*, and *Studies on Śūnyatā*.

2. An original and critical view of the system of the Mahāyāna doctrines. Yin Shun distinguishes three systems in Mahāyāna Buddhism: "Name-only with empty-nature" (Mādhyamika), "Consciousness-only with illusion" (Yogācāra), and "Mind-only with true eternity" (Tathāgatagarbha). His account transcends sectarian bias and follows the record of historical development. Although he has reservations about Tathāgatagarbha thought, he affirms its distinctiveness. His book, *Studies on Tathāgatagarbha*, gives a fine exposition of Indian Tathāgatagarbha thought.

3. A clear and logical analysis of the development of Indian Buddhism and the process of formation of the Buddhist sūtras. In *The Origin and Development of Early Mahāyāna Buddhism*, he answers questions about the origin of Mahāyāna Buddhism, with special emphasis on the role played by "cherishing eternally the memory of the Buddha."

4. Historical studies of Chinese Ch'an, dealing with the formation and characteristics of the early Ch'an school. *The History of the Chinese Ch'an School* is the result of his studies.

The quality and quantity of Yin Shun's works are extraordinary. Burying himself in Buddhist texts for the past seventy years, he is one of very few Buddhist scholars in the world who have fully mastered the Chinese Buddhist Scriptures and their contents.

Buddhist Women in Taiwan

The most striking feature of Taiwanese Buddhism since 1945 has been the emergence of outstanding Buddhist women in large numbers in positions of leadership. This phenomenon is extremely rare in the Buddhist world of modern or ancient times, in China or elsewhere. Although there have been outstanding Buddhist women, as witnessed in the Scriptures (such as the senior nuns in the *Therīgāthā*, who attained arhatship; Queen Śrīmālā, who preaches the Dharma in the *Śrīmāladevī-siṃhanāda Sūtra*; or the goddess who teases Śāriputra in the *Vimalakīrti Sūtra)*, Buddhist women have been treated unfairly all along in the saṃgha and in society. They have been discriminated against by the "eight rules for bhikkhunīs" and the traditional view of women as inferior to men. However, now Buddhist women in Taiwan have broken the shackles of thousands of years. They not only stand up to men as equals but even exert more influence in society.

There are three main factors that have enabled the Buddhist women in Taiwan to break through the old structures. First, the social ideology is more open, with changes in values. Second, the standard of their education has risen considerably. Third, women are more independent financially. These three factors are related to macrocosmic changes within Taiwan in the past four decades. In recent years, Taiwanese society has changed from being narrow-minded and conservative to being more democratic and liberal. It allows women to expand their participation in the life of society beyond their traditional roles as wives and mothers. Thus, women can remain single and have their own careers, or they can give up family life and dedicate themselves to Buddhism without having to face as much social or family pressure as before. This is one of the main reasons that the number of single Buddhist women and bhikkhunīs is increasing.

The number of bhikkhunīs in Taiwan is about three times the number of bhikkhus. Many bhikkhunīs of this younger generation are college graduates. The greatest asset in the development of the saṃgha of bhikkhunīs is their high educational standard. Drawing on their strong educational background, some of the Buddhist women are active in preaching; some engage in educational work, such as running a college or a Buddhist institute; some devote themselves to philanthropic or cultural work; and some are zealous in social movements.

The most influential bhikkhunī in Taiwan is Dharma-master Cheng Yen, who is honored as the "conscience of Taiwan." She once witnessed an aboriginal woman suffer a miscarriage after being rejected by a hospital because she was too poor to pay the registration fee. This incident impelled Cheng Yen to form the Tz'u Chi kung-te hui (The association for meritoriously compassionate relief) with five nuns and thirty lay devotees in 1966. It now has over three million general members and four thousand committee members around the world, and is the largest and most influential private religious organization in Taiwan. The association has four main fields of action: charity, medical aid, education, and culture.

Tz'u Chi's charitable work includes assisting low-income households, supplementing medication in free clinics, relieving various disasters and crises, and assisting orphans and the poor in funeral needs. A unique feature of its charity work is that every case in which assistance is given involves a personal, sympathetic contact with the members, after which spiritual and material aid is given as needed. Every three months committee members reexamine the case, and decide to stop or continue assistance as the situation requires. Such intimate concern and direct contacts arouse the Buddhist spirit of compassion, kindness, joy, and equanimity in the minds of givers and receivers. Recently, Tz'u Chi has expanded this work of charity to active relief of international disasters, such as floods in Bangladesh and mainland China, famine in Ethiopia, and even an earthquake in southern California.

Cheng Yen believes that poverty and illness exist codependently. So, after many years of charity work, she started to combine it with the cause of medical aid to tackle poverty and illness at the root. In 1986 she built Tz'u Chi Hospital. Today it is a teaching hospital in eastern Taiwan with equal emphasis on clinical treatment and research. It has a medical research center, an aboriginal health research office, and a children's development and rehabilitation center. A unique feature of the hospital is the support of the Tz'u Chi Volunteer Service Team, consisting of over two thousand people, and of overseas members and college students who work in the hospital as volunteers in their vacation. Their work includes talking sympathetically with patients; bathing patients; bringing patients to register for examination; participating in recreational activities, such as singing for patients; and miscellaneous tasks such as delivering medical records, making cotton-balls and gauze, and mending bedsheets. They also help with the Concerned Discharge Plan, which allows chronic patients to spend less time in hospital and to receive care at home. The plan includes home care, home visits, and care for the dying. Through such continuous care, patient readmission rates are lowered. The support of volunteers makes the hospital's work much more humane, personal, and effective.

The third cause to which Cheng Yen is devoted is education. In order to implement her work of charity and medical aid, she founded the Tz'u Chi Nursing School in 1989 to train nurses for the hospital. In 1994 she also established the first accredited Buddhist medical school in history, to train doctors in both medical ethics and medical skills. Cheng Yen always emphasizes that medical staff should be humane in deed and spirit. At present, the medical school has five departments and four graduate schools. The final goal is to expand it to become Tz'u Chi University, which will consist of a

37. Cheng Yen awarding graduates of the Medical Institute of Tzu-chi College of
Medicine (March 1997).

medical school, a college of humanities, a college of religious studies, and a
college of arts.

The fourth cause is cultural work, which is the responsibility of the Tz'u
Chi Cultural Affairs Center. It issues the *Tz'u Chi Monthly* and *Tz'u Chi
Biweekly*, broadcasts radio and television programs, and publishes books on
literature, history, philosophy, medicine, and Buddhism. Preaching and
sponsoring activities for social welfare are also their work. For example,
they promote activities to protect and purify the environment, stressing
purity of mind as well as of the environment. The very imposing Tz'u Chi
Memorial Hall, which combines academic, artistic, technological, and educational functions in one, provides a venue for the promotion of culture to
academic, cultural, and religious organizations.

In pursuing these four causes Tz'u Chi practices socially oriented Buddhism, linked closely with the reality of human suffering and welfare. It has
won recognition from Buddhists and non-Buddhists alike. Probably
because Cheng Yen is a woman, the majority of the members of Tz'u Chi
are female, mostly housewives. Since they move freely between family and
the social work of Tz'u Chi, they can break through the confinement of
their traditional family roles and increase their independence, confidence,
and sense of accomplishment. More importantly, these housewives receive

religious and moral influence from Cheng Yen, and in turn they exert moral influence on their family members and communities. Cheng Yen, who has great religious charisma, is a spiritual leader who has tapped the Buddhist spirit of kindness and compassion to create a beneficial social movement to counterbalance the utilitarian atmosphere that has earned Taiwan the soubriquet "Island of Greed" in the foreign mass media.

The educational contribution of Buddhist women is also unprecedented. The first officially accredited college ever founded by Buddhists in history, the Hua Fan College of Humanities and Technology (now Huan Gan University), was established by Dharma-master Hsiao Yun. She is a dedicated educator and Buddhist artist, and has devoted herself to Buddhist education for thirty years. Although her idea of education tends to be conservative, it is bound to develop, since she is now expanding her scope from Buddhist schools to non-Buddhist higher education. She has repeatedly emphasized the combination of humanities and technology to nurture a new generation with a holistic vision of life. In Taiwan Buddhist women's high standard of education and their sense of mission facilitate their enthusiastic engagement in higher education. At present there are more than a dozen Buddhist nuns and lay women teaching at various universities. In addition to their academic contribution they are role models for Buddhist women of the younger generation.

Another reason for the prosperity of the Buddhist female saṃgha in Taiwan is that bhikkhunīs not only hold the financial power in monasteries but also have vast numbers of devotees. With abundant personnel and financial resources, they can choose to engage in preaching, education, charity, or cultural work with high success. Moreover, in the saṃgha of bhikkhunīs there are many virtuous and highly-respected elders and leaders who can attract women of the younger generation to study Buddhism, or even to join the saṃgha. In brief, Buddhist women in Taiwan are developing continuously in an auspicious cycle. They not only play an active role in society, but they have also changed the erroneous image of Buddhism as negative and rigid. What is more, they have broken away from the sexual discrimination in traditional ideology and are fully carrying out their religious and social functions. In the past decade, the rise of the female saṃgha in Taiwan, the general improvement of their status, and their great contribution to education, preaching, social work, and Buddhist economy are all very remarkable and without parallel in the female saṃghas in other Buddhist countries.

Rise of the Tibetan Esoteric Sect

Another feature of contemporary Taiwanese Buddhism is the presence of the Tibetan Esoteric Sect. After 1949, following the arrival of mainland monks, Tibetan esoteric Buddhism also came to Taiwan. The most famous teacher was the Chan-chia Living Buddha, who was President of the Buddhist Association of the Republic of China before Pai Sheng. Its earliest adherents were Ch'u Ying-kuang, Han Tung, and Shen Shu. Without lamas, monasteries, or regular organizations, they slowly went around to preach. This situation changed in the early eighties, when, for political reasons, the official Mongolian-Tibetan Affairs Commission and some nongovernmental Buddhist organizations started to invite Tibetan lamas to Taiwan to preach. Since then the Esoteric Sect has been developing fast. At present, all the four major schools of Tibetan Buddhism have monasteries or centers in Taiwan. For example, a branch of the Foundation for the Preservation of the Mahāyāna Tradition of the Gelugpa (FPMT) was established in Taiwan a few years ago, and it is planning to embark on the work of translating Tibetan Buddhist scriptures into Chinese. Although Tibetan Buddhism seems to be flourishing now, the real Tibetan Buddhist teachings and methods of practice need to be fortified. This is because the lamas or teachers are of mixed backgrounds and qualifications, and often engage in anointing and praying for blessings as their main religious activities without teaching in depth. In 1997 the Dalai Lama made a historic and very successful visit to Taiwan. It is foreseeable that after his visit Tibetan Buddhism will continue to grow in Taiwan.

The Latent Crises

One should not be misled into thinking that the picture of Buddhism in Taiwan is all rosy. The most serious of the latent crises are commercialization, secularization, and rapid overexpansion. Some monasteries, in the effort to raise funds, have become commercialized through the selling of religious objects, fixing prices for religious services, and so forth. Too much commercialization and secularization exposes Buddhism to the risk of losing its sacredness and spirituality.

The rapid development of Buddhism in Taiwan for the last couple of decades is a positive spiritual phenomenon, but it also has its negative side-effects. The incident of the Chungtai Monastery is a good example. Situated in Nantou County in central Taiwan, the monastery was founded by Ch'an Master Wei Chueh, a well-known and respected meditation master who has attracted many followers. Wei Chueh has established dozens of branch temples in cities all over Taiwan. The need for sufficient staff to manage the branch temples has led to the rapid ordination of many young Buddhists. On 1 September 1996 the Chungtai Monastery held a ceremony to ordain 110 young Buddhists, most of whom had been at the monastery as volunteer instructors for a summer camp for children. Many of them took the ordination without parental knowledge. Many parents of the new novices went to the monastery in disbelief after learning what had happened. Screaming, pushing, and shoving, they pleaded tearfully for their sons and daughters to return home, but the young people refused. This dramatic incident was played out under the glare of television cameras for all to see. Shocking scenes of novices being taken away by their families against their will made prime-time news throughout the country.

Three questions were foremost in the mind of the general public with regard to the incident. First, the young Buddhists had come largely from middle-class families. Many were college students and some had already earned a university degree. Why did these well-educated young people choose to dedicate their lives to Buddhism at such a young age? Second, among the 110 novices, eighty-nine were women. Why do highly educated women forsake the traditional Chinese roles of wife and mother to opt for a religious and spiritual path? What is the social significance of this phenomenon? And third, in a society where filial piety is valued highly, why did these young people disregard their parents' demands that they return to lay life? Why did the parents react so hysterically? Why could they not respect the decisions of their children?

All these questions were discussed by scholars, journalists, and the general public, resulting in a flurry of different theories and explanations for the events. At the least, we can say that this incident reflects one of the sideeffects of rapid overexpansion by Buddhist organizations. If the pace of ordaining people surpasses the time needed for proper training, and if the time spent for temple construction and management exceeds the time spent in the study and practice of Buddhist teachings, problems are certain to arise. This is an example of a crisis that the saṅgha must deal with if Buddhism is to deepen its profound spirituality instead of just appearing superficially to flourish and grow strong.

In conclusion, having become modernized, diversified, enterprised, popularized, and socially oriented, modern Taiwanese Buddhism not only has become part of the lives of many Buddhists, but has integrated itself deeply into society to become a vital force. Although Taiwanese Buddhism is sure to face its problems after a period of rapid development, it has certainly fulfilled its religious and social functions.

Bibliography

Chang Man-t'ao, ed. *Chung-kuo fo chiao shih-lun chi*. Taipei: Ta-cheng Press, 1979.

Chiang T'san-t'eng. *Tai-wan fo chiao you hsien tai she-hui*. Taipei: Tung Ta Press, 1992.

Chu Ch'i-ch'ang, ed. *Tai-wan fo chiao ssu yen t'ang tsung lu*. Kaohsiung: Fo Kuang Press, 1977.

Jones, Charles B. *Buddhism in Taiwan: Religion and the State, 1660–1990*. Honolulu: University of Hawai'i Press, 1998.

29

Sōka Gakkai and the Modern Reformation of Buddhism

SHIMAZONO SUSUMU

I N A WORLD OF rapid change, progressively urbanized and informa-tion-intensive, what transformations are taking place in Buddhist practice and in the community of practitioners that make up Bud-dhist congregations? In pursuing this question, one is instinctively drawn toward those Buddhist movements that have won popular accept-ance and shown a rugged vitality over the past fifty years, while many tra-ditional Buddhist groups appear to have fallen into decline. Esoteric Tibetan Buddhism and Zen attract an enthusiastic following in the United States, Europe, and Taiwan. The urban masses of Thailand flock to Tham-makai and Santi Asoke.[1] Among Japan's "new religions," Buddhist move-ments like Shinnyoen and those derived from Reiyūkai stand out for their dynamic appeal, but the most successful of all is Nichiren Shōshū/Sōka Gakkai, which has spread beyond Japan to attract a large number of fol-lowers worldwide.[2]

In the modern world of East Asia, the most significant change that has occurred in praxis-oriented groups within the Mahāyāna Buddhist tradition has been the rise of popular *Lotus Sūtra* (or Nichiren)-based Buddhist groups. In contrast to the widespread recession and fossilization of estab-lished temples and sects, these groups have completely altered the distri-bution of power and influence in the region. Here again, Sōka Gakkai, the largest active Buddhist group since the end of the war, stands out as repre-senting the dramatic transformation taking place within Mahāyāna Bud-dhism in the twentieth century.

Without wishing to minimize the kinds of changes that have gone on in faith-praxis, group activity, and organization, I would like to focus my remarks here on the doctrinal side of these movements, which—at least in the case of Japan—can be characterized as religions of "this-worldly salvation."[3]

In particular, I will try to account for the emergence of this notion in Sōka Gakkai's second president, Toda Jōsei, and his "theory of life-force."[4]

In Sōka Gakkai today, as the following excerpts attest, "life-force" is understood as the foundation of faith and practice:

> The greatness of the Buddhist teaching is that in trying to provide for the happiness of the human person, the subject of human life and society, it gets right to the root of the problem, namely *life-force*, and through scientific analysis emerges with a principle that can be practiced by ordinary people.
>
> Nichiren ... systematized the principle of life-force into a practical method to provide happiness for the masses.[5]

> Faith is firm belief in the universe and the life-force.... Only a person of sublime faith can live a good and vigorous life....
>
> Buddhist doctrine is a philosophy that has human life as its ultimate object, and our Human Revolution Movement is an act of reform aimed at opening up the inner universe, the creative life-force within each individual, and leading to human freedom. The Movement sees humanity poised on the summit of a new idea of life-force, surveying the twenty-first century and ready to build the future.[6]

Originally formed as a lay organization within Nichiren Shōshū, Sōka Gakkai assumed the doctrine of the sect by and large intact. But the idea of "life-force," not to mention what Sōka Gakkai has made of it, is not apparent in traditional Nichiren Shōshū.

The foundational ideas of Sōka Gakkai are found in Makiguchi Tsunesaburō's 1930 book, *Sōka kyōikugaku taikei*. Makiguchi himself does not speak so much of life-force as of "value theory" and "the life of great virtue." Toward the end of his life he also proposed a theory of dharmic retribution.[7] It was only after Makiguchi's death that the term came into ascendancy with Toda Jōsei, who was responsible for rebuilding the movement, giving it the name Sōka Gakkai, and overseeing its rapid growth in the postwar period. The opening chapter of *Shakubuku kyōten* (1951), the doctrinal compendium that Toda edited and that was the mainstay of the movement during these years, was entitled "The Doctrine of Life-Force." In terms of the doctrinal history of Sōka Gakkai, the idea of life-force marks a move away from Makiguchi's thought towards that of Toda.[8] What is of more interest to us here, however, is how this idea reshaped the traditional teachings of Nichiren Shōshū in the direction of a belief in this-worldly salvation that is typical of popular Buddhist movements in East Asia in the modern period.

Toda Jōsei's Doctrine of Life-Force

Toda's reflections on life-force go back to the experience of being imprisoned in 1943, along with Makiguchi, on a charge of *lèse majesté* for having refused to display a talisman from the Ise Shrine. Immersed in the study of Buddhist scriptures and teachings, Toda came to a firm conviction of belief within his prison cell. He seems to have had visions of the word *seimei* (life-force) flashing before his eyes and of himself seated among the assembly in the presence of the Buddha.[9] Years later, in response to a question from a Sōka Gakkai believer as to the meaning of *Namu myōhō rengekyō*, the chanted phrase popularized by Nichiren, Toda recalls:

> Ten years ago, absorbed in the search for who the Buddha was and whether he was real or not, I looked for help in books about Buddhism, but they were of no help. In the end, I came upon the *Muryōgi-kyō*, where I read: "Body neither is nor is not.... It is neither red nor purple, nor any other color." Reflecting on these words, it dawned on me, "The Buddha is life-force." After agonizing over the relation of the Buddha to the *Namu myōhō rengekyō* in light of the theory of the ten worlds, I realized that life-force is the name of the Buddha, and that this is the fundamental force in the universe, the *Kuon gansho,* which has the power to change the fate of every person. After that I was able to read and understand all the Buddhist scriptures.[10]

For Toda, this life-force, the essence of humanity and the universe, is an omnipresent, creative power emanating from the Buddha. The root of this universal, vital life-force is the "True *Honzon*," inscribed with the words *Namu myōhō rengekyō*. To receive the *honzon* and to chant the *daimoku* is to release that power. This is the source of happiness and ultimately leads to the attainment of Buddhahood. Hence the goal of the human person is to attain happiness personally and then to spread this happiness to others.

To break this down in further detail, we may single out six elements, referring to Toda's own words as much as possible.

1. The Eternal Nature of Human Life

Human life is more than this present existence: it includes life in its past, present, and future existences. This is not the same as saying that one's "spirit" survives through time in the form of great accomplishments or things passed on to one's descendants:

> Just as in life nothing can come between one sadness and another, one joy and another; or just as in sleep the mind does not go anywhere, so, too, at death the life-force is taken up in the Great Life-Force of the universe. No matter where you look for it, it is not something you can find.

When you wake up in the morning you remember the activities of the day before and pick up where you left off. In the same way, new life receives the karmic causes of past existences and continues to live their effects in the present existence.[11]

Toda traces this doctrine of the "eternal nature of life" back to Śākyamuni Buddha, but claims that Nichiren has taken it still further, to its "true form and origin,"[12] namely, the *Gohonzon*.

2. The Universe is the Life-Force

"Life coexists with the universe. It does not precede the universe; neither does it come later by accident or as someone's creation." The universe is life even before biological life appears. "If the universe itself *is* life, then primary life forms can appear wherever conditions allow."[13] In effect, for Toda all of existence, including non-life forms, participates in life.

At times Toda sets up a mutual self-identity of universe, life-force, and Buddha, but his arguments tend to be mystical and hard to follow. The "true reality of life-force" is equated with the Tathāgata *(nyorai)*, who at each moment "comes forth from its own suchness":

Every moment of this man Toda is the essence of life. When you stop to think about it, every moment of every single thing must be a *nyorai*. This is the meaning of the fundamental doctrine that all things in the universe are the activity of life itself.

For us, too, every second of life is true reality, and in the true reality of this moment past life for all eternity is included, giving birth in turn to future life on into eternity....This moment is the activity of the universe itself as well as the life and essence of the individual. This moment-to-moment activity of the universe is expressed as the ever-changing phenomena that make up the totality of all things in flux.[14]

In this idiom of "life-force" and "universe" we see reflected the doctrine of *ichinen sanzen* (three thousand existences contained in one thought) and *kanjin* (introspection into one's mind-essence) that Nichiren took over from Tendai Buddhism.

3. Becoming One with the Life-Force of the Gohonzon through Faith

The Three Great Esoteric Methods of Practice *(sandaihihō)* that Nichiren taught to sentient beings in the age of *mappō*—that is, the *Daimoku* of the *Honmon* section of the *Lotus Sūtra (Honmon no daimoku)*, the *Honzon* of the *Honmon (Honmon no honzon)*, and the *Kaidan* of the *Honmon (Honmon no*

kaidan)—can all be summarized in the *Gohonzon* (or
Great Maṇḍala), which is the
origin of the life-force of the
universe.

> The enlightenment of Nichi-
> ren, the true Buddha, and the
> life-force live continuously in
> the Great Maṇḍala.

> By embracing the life-force,
> everything is enjoyed, noth-
> ing is suffered. This is called
> liberation *(gedatsu)*... and it is
> attained through faith in the
> *Gohonzon*.... Therefore, when
> you sit before the *Gohonzon*
> and believe that there is no
> distinction among the *Gohon-
> zon,* Nichiren, and you your-
> self, when you allow this
> great blessing to permeate

38. Toda Jōsei, November 1956.

> your heart and offer thanksgiving, when you chant the *daimoku* fervently, you
> enter into harmony with the rhythm of the universe: the great life-force of
> the universe becomes your own life-force and gushes forth.[15]

Nichiren's awakening to the truth of the universal life-force *(ichinen sanzen),* is thus directly embodied in the *Gohonzon*. In contrast to the "ideal *ichinen sanzen*" taught by Śākyamuni in the first half *(shakumon)* of the *Lotus Sūtra*, Nichiren's Three Great Esoteric Methods of Practice represent the "practical *ichinen sanzen*" *(jigyō no ichinen sanzen)* that can be learned by ordinary people just as they are.

4. Varieties of Manifestation of Life-Force in Daily Life

Good fortune and bad can also be explained as states of the life-force:

> Two laws of cleansing *(senjō nihō)* exist in our lives. A life of pure innocence
> *(kiyorakana seimei)* accepts everything from the outside world meekly and in
> harmonious rhythm with the universe; for this reason, its transmigration is
> completely natural. Such a life manifests a tremendous life-force, and is thus
> able to enjoy existence. But in the course of its many transmigrations, life
> becomes tainted by the mistakes of daily life and falls into vice of all sorts.
> This is why we speak of a cleansing *(senpō)* of life... that has fallen out of har-
> mony with the rhythm of the universe and whose life-force has faded away.[16]

In the doctrine of *ichinen sanzen*, these fallen states are summarized as the "life of the ten realms" *(jikkai)* in accord with the *Kanjin honzonshō*. The following ten realms can be identified in our own life-force as well as in the Great Life-Force of the universe:

Anger (a life of affliction): hell

Covetousness (a life of desire for things): the realm of the hungry spirits

Foolishness (a life of being attracted to what is before one's eyes and losing sight of the overall meaning): the realm of animals

Flattery (a life of anger): the realm of *asuras* (demigods)

Tranquillity (a human life): the realm of human beings

Joy (a life full of joy, but limited in time): the realm of heavenly beings

Impermanence (the person who has realized that nothing is permanent in this world and seeks peace of mind in contemplation): the realms of *śrāvakas* and *pratyekabuddhas* (disciples of Buddha or Hīnayāna sages)

Virtue (virtuous human life): the realm of bodhisattvas

Faith (a life of belief in the *Namu myōhō rengekyō* of the Three Great Esoteric Methods of Practice): the realm of buddhas.[17]

Each of these life states, in turn, represents one of the "ten suchness aspects" *(jūnyoze)* of reality, which works its own effects on them. For example, people in the *asura* realm "are incited to more and more anger," whereas people in the state of the bodhisattva "are filled with the desire to help those who have fallen and an awesome energy wells up to support them in their effort."[18]

5. Happiness and the Attainment of Buddhahood as Manifestations of the Universal Life-Force

Happiness, for Toda, "springs forth from the relationship between our own life-force and the external world" and "an affirmation of inner truth." Religion, in particular Nichiren Shōshū, teaches this internal truth and leads humanity to happiness. Again, we let Toda speak in his own words:

Through belief in this great religion, life harmonizes with the rhythm of the universe and one feels completely the happiness of life.... But if the energy of the life-force energy is applied only to problems in the home, then the home will be taken care of, but what about problems in the neighborhood or in the city?...

The attainment of buddhahood is a state of absolute happiness. No one can attack you, there is nothing to fear, and each moment of life is like the clear blue ocean or the cloudless sky.

And what is the attainment of buddhahood? Impossible as it is for ordinary people like us to explain such things, I will try—realizing that it may amount to no more than one millionth of the insight of faith all of you have: It means the attainment of eternal happiness. Our life is not limited to this existence.... The attainment of buddhahood means being born full of vital life-force energy, accepting the mission given you at birth and acting freely in accord with that mission, achieving the task set out for you from birth, and possessing a happiness that no one can destroy. If one can enjoy such a life tens of times, hundreds of times, even thousands or millions of times, does that not make happiness all the greater? To forsake the search for such happiness for the greedy pursuit of lesser pleasures can only be called pitiful.[19]

6. Compassion and Life-Force

"Compassion is the characteristic of the Buddha, and Nichiren was compassion itself." Believers are called on to imitate this compassion:

If you would possess even one millionth of the compassion of Nichiren, you must be diligent in chanting the *daimoku* day and night.... You must engrave it on your heart, color your life with it; you must strive for the faith to change all of your daily actions into expressions of compassion.

All of the universe is in essence the Buddha, and all things without exception are the activity of compassion. Therefore, compassion is the innate form of the universe.... If the universe is the *Myōhō rengekyō* itself, the *Myōhō rengekyō* is none other than the original Buddha. And if, therefore, the universe is the form of the Buddha, the universe must also be the activity of compassion itself.

If the universe itself is compassion, it follows that our daily activities are acts of that same compassion. But since they are set in motion by the life-force unique to human life, the human being cannot remain at the level of common animals and plants. A higher level of activity is required of the true servant of the Buddha. As I said before, since the practice proper to the latter stage of the law (*mappō*) is the practice of Nichiren, we must chant the *daimoku* as he taught us to do; ...we must encourage others to chant, and thus help to produce more people whose actions are filled naturally with compassion.

Although in the age of *mappō* wicked people abound, which makes works of compassion absolutely essential, there is a great lack of compassion in the actual world.[20]

Only through the wisdom of the Buddha is true compassion put into action, and "only through faith can this wisdom be gained." Accordingly, "the implanting of pure life-force" through *shakubuku* is described as a particularly important concrete expression of compassion, while almsgiving is dismissed as less than true compassion.[21]

Such are the major elements in Toda's idea of life-force as he presented it when talking about his own faith or giving direction to others. Obviously he believed he was passing on the essence of the Buddhist teaching as he inherited it through Nichiren Shōshū: At the same time, he introduced innovations of his own, as will become apparent when we turn to a more traditional exposition of Nichiren Shōshū doctrine.

The Transformation of Nichiren Shōshū Doctrine

Nichiren Shōshū is the branch of Nichiren Buddhism that follows in the tradition of Nikkō (1246–1333), a disciple of Nichiren. Its center is located on Mt. Fuji at Taiseki-ji.[22] Nikkō was one of the "Six Elder Monks" (*rokurōsō*) named by Nichiren before he died to take over the control of the order. Following a clash with the other five elders, Nikkō left Mt. Minobu for Taiseki-ji to pursue his own path. The resulting branch of Nichiren Buddhism constructed a distinct doctrine based on books of teachings purportedly passed on to Nikkō by Nichiren—among them the *Honinmyōshō*, *Hyakurokkosōjō*, *Juryōbonmonteidaiji*, and *Ogikuden*—as well as on works written by Nikkō himself. Various schools of doctrine developed within the branch, for example, around Nishiyama Honmon-ji, Omosu Honmon-ji, and Yōhō-ji in Kyoto; but the school associated with Taiseki-ji, organized around the systematization of doctrine by Nikkan (1665-1726), predominated. In 1900 the sect was reorganized under the name Nichirenshū Fujiha, and in 1912 the name was changed again to Nichiren Shōshū. It was the doctrine of this Nichiren Shōshū, as formulated by Nikkan, that Makiguchi and Toda followed.

Nichiren Shōshū teaching revolves around the Three Great Esoteric Methods of Practice: the *Maṇḍala Honzon (Dai Gohonzon)* presented by Nichiren as the ultimate Buddhist teaching or the ultimate reality needed for salvation; the *Kaidan* where the *Maṇḍala Honzon* is enshrined; and the *daimoku*, or chant of *Namu myōhō rengekyō*. This forms the core of Buddhist faith in the age of *mappō* (Last Dharma). Taiseki-ji is believed to be the true *Kaidan* and the *Maṇḍala Honzon* enshrined there (the *Ita Maṇḍala* thought to have been inscribed in 1279) is regarded as the supreme presence.

The value set on Nichiren's *honzon* reflects the fact that Nichiren and his teaching are held in far higher regard than Śākyamuni Buddha and the message he preached in India so many centuries ago. In particular, the teaching of Nichiren is believed to surpass that of even the *Lotus Sūtra*, the supreme teaching of Śākyamuni. As a result, Nichiren is revered as *Nichiren Honbutsuron*, the rebirth of the ultimate Buddha *(Musa no honbutsu)* who is superior to Śākyamuni. Behind these claims lies a reading of history at odds with that normally held by Hokke Buddhism, to which we may now turn our attention. In doing so, I should like to avoid as far as possible the doctrinal terminology particular to Nichiren Buddhism.[23]

Nichiren Shōshū's Buddhological History

In the sixteenth chapter of the *Lotus Sūtra*, the *Juryōbon* (The lifespan of the Tathāgata), Śākyamuni, who was previously considered to be the highest enlightened being, is revealed to be merely one finite manifestation of a more universal Buddha. This universal Buddha is called the "True Attainment of the Remotest Past" *(Kuon jitsujō no shakuson)*, while *Jōgyō* and other bodhisattvas who spring out of the earth in chapter fifteen of the sūtra *(Jūji yujutsubon)* are presented as figures taught by various Buddhas in the past. In Nichiren Shōshū, however, while *Kuon jitsujō* is held to have achieved buddhahood in the eternal past, belief is focused on a supreme being that has existed from the beginning of the universe *(kuon gansho)*. This being reveals itself as the Dharma in the mantra *Namu myōhō rengekyō*, and as a person in the *Musa no honbutsu*. Nichiren is the rebirth of this latter. The period prior to the appearance of the *Kuon jitsujō* Buddha is described as the age of the true Buddha, when people who bear some relationship to the Buddha follow the law and can attain the state of Buddhahood.

Following the appearance of *Kuon jitsujō*, Śākyamuni Buddha makes his own appearance several centuries B.C.E., and the periods of *Shōbō* (True Dharma) and *Zōbō* (Semblance Dharma)—periods before the revelation of the true *honzon* and the *daimoku*—are described as a time of provisional teaching. The *Lotus Sūtra* itself is held to be a provisional teaching, and the people who were able to attain enlightenment through the sūtra are those who had in fact previously been implanted with the "seed" to become buddha by *Kuon jitsujō*. The material in the first fourteen chapters of the sūtra, the *Shakumon*, "ripened" the state of these people, and the latter fourteen chapters, the *Honmon*, brought them to liberation. However, for the "wild common person" *(arabonpu)* of the *mappō* period, such a teaching of ripening and liberation is not sufficient; a new "seed" for becoming a buddha must be revealed. This was where Nichiren enters history, in Japan at the beginning of the age of *mappō*. The very *Musa no honbutsu* who existed from the beginning of the universe and who appeared previously during the life of Śākyamuni as Jōgyō Bosatsu, has come again as savior for the age of *mappō*.

This reading of history is said to be present in Nichiren's writings and intimated in the *Lotus Sūtra*—absent from the text but hidden in the deeper meanings of the *Juryōbon*.[24] The doctrinal reinterpretation of the sūtra resulted in a hierarchical ordering of increased value from sūtras that preceded the *Lotus Sūtra*, to the first fourteen chapters of the *Lotus Sūtra*, to the latter half of the sūtra.

Nichiren Shōshū teaches that in addition to the apparent *Honmon (monjō no honmon)* there exists a deeper *Honmon (montei no honmon)*, with the most important elements of Śākyamuni's teaching being contained in the latter. It is there that the presentation of the *Gohonzon, Namu myōhō rengekyō,* and the *Musa no honbutsu* (that is, Nichiren) is foreshadowed; and it is because of this foreshadowing that the *Lotus Sūtra* maintains its relevance for the understanding of the *Gohonzon* and Nichiren's teaching. At the same time, the claim is made that this sūtra was previously proclaimed for the sake of those who could benefit from "ripening" and liberation, and is no longer suited to ordinary men and women in the age of *mappō* who seek a new "sowing."

Kanjinron in Nichiren Shōshū

Although there are the two aspects of Dharma and person in the true original Buddha *(Kuon gansho)*, it is the Dharma, namely the *daimoku (Namu myōhō rengekyō)*, that is of greater importance. This is the ultimate existence that is contained in the *Gohonzon*, and it is through the "reception" *(juji)* of this ultimate reality, that is, through belief in the *Gohonzon* and chanting of the *daimoku*, that the common masses living in the age of *mappō* can achieve buddhahood. Concentration on the *Gohonzon* as the object of faith gives profound significance to that act of "reception."

This view is expounded in Nichiren's *Kanjin honzonshō*. Basing his argument on the *ichinen sanzen* Tendai doctrine of Chigi (C. Chih-i, 538–597), Nichiren seeks to demonstrate that belief in the *honzon* and the chanting of the *daimoku* constitute the means to attaining buddhahood. The explanation of *ichinen sanzen* found here comes to occupy a central place in Nichiren Shōshū. Following the *Kaimokushō*, both Nichiren Shōshū and Sōka Gakkai consider this doctrine to be the ultimate teaching hidden in the depths of the *Juryōbon* of the *Lotus Sūtra* and the heart of Buddhist teaching. A quick look at the contents of the *Shakubuku kyōten* and *Sōka Gakkai nyūmon* make this plain. Chigi's *Makashikan* (C. *Mo ho chih kuan*), based on the doctrine of the *Lotus Sūtra* as the most sublime sūtra, lays forth both the theory and practice of meditation *(shikan, zazen, kanjin)*. An explanation of *ichinen sanzen* is presented here in the section where *kanjin* is described as a "mysterious state" in which "all spirit is possessed in one spirit." *Sanzen* refers to all living creatures and everything in existence, and it is explained in terms of the concepts of *jikkai*, *jūnyoze*, and *sanseken* (the three categories of realm).

Jikkai refers to the ten modalities of existence of all sentient beings (hell, realms of hungry spirits, animals, *asuras*, human beings, heavenly beings, *śrāvakas*, *pratyekabuddhas*, *bodhisattvas*, and buddhas). These realms are not isolated aspects of being, but each incorporates all of the others as potential existences. This state is called *jikkai gogu*, which confirms the reality of one hundred aspects of existence. Of these relationships, those of the realm of buddhas with the other nine realms are central: while humanity finds itself under the aspect of the other nine realms it is at the same time incorporated in the realm of the buddhas; and conversely, the Buddha is also incorporated in the other nine aspects of existence.

When these realms are multiplied by the *jūnyoze* (form, nature or quality, substance, function, action or motion, cause, indirect cause or condition, effect, reward or retribution, ultimate non-differentiation) and the *sanseken* (the realm of sentient beings, the realm of non-sentient beings, the realm of the five aggregates) that results in the *sanzen seken* or three thousand worlds. Just what the *jūnyoze* and *sanseken* refer to is not as easy to grasp as the concept of *jikkai*, which doubtless leaves many believers with only the vaguest impression of having understood it. Suffice it here to say that *sanzen seken* indicates the pluralistic modality and "complex totality" of existence, in particular of living beings. The state in which this totality is completely grasped at a single moment is *ichinen sanzen* and culminates in the realization that the Buddha is present within one's own spirit.

The realization by the masses of ordinary people that they are, each of them and within this present life, Buddha is captured in the phrase *sokushin jōbutsu*. In the *hongaku shisō* of Japanese Tendai Buddhism, where all sentient beings are taught to exist in the state of enlightenment in their present life, the link between *ichinen sanzen* and *sokushin jōbutsu* is dominant. Nichiren, too, presupposes this position in the *Kanjin honzonshō* and elsewhere. The influence of *hongaku shisō* on Nichiren Shōshū was even greater after Nichiren's death, which in turn reinforced the orientation towards *sokushin jōbutsu*.

In the development from Nichiren's *Kanjin honzonshō* to Nichiren Shōshū's doctrine, the *honzon* and *daimoku* are stressed as concretizations of *ichinen sanzen*, as is the conviction that *sokushin jōbutsu* can be realized through the practice of chanting the *daimoku* rather than meditation. This "experience of *ichinen sanzen*" contrasts with the "principle of *ichinen sanzen*" of Chigi. Differences between Nichiren Shōshū and the other sects of Nichiren Buddhism revolve about whether this "experience of *ichinen sanzen*" as attained through the *honzon* that embodies the *Kuon Jitsujō* Buddha from the latter half of the *Lotus Sūtra* is followed, or whether the accent is rather placed on the *honzon* that embodies the original Dharma-Buddha hidden in the sūtra.

In other words, for Nichiren Shōshū, belief in the *gohonzon* and chanting of the *daimoku* are themselves considered to be the realization of *sokushin jōbutsu*, and this is called *juji soku kanjin* (reception as meditation). This doctrine is offered to the masses in the age of *mappō* as an easy practice. But since ultimately it requires that one experience oneself as existing in the state of the Buddha, more is involved than a mere notional assent. Not only a small number of monks and doctrinal experts, but the masses of ordinary people also need to be convinced of the reality of the proposition. This is the problem that faced Toda in his prison cell, and that the concept of Buddha as life-force helped him solve.

Toda Jōsei's Innovation

Toda's life-force theory reshapes Nichiren Shōshū doctrine by providing a vitalistic interpretation of the *sokushin jōbutsu* attained in chanting *Namu myōhō rengekyō*. To single out the main elements: (1) Buddha and humanity, as well as (2) Buddha and the various beings of this world—since they share in the essential life-force—(3) can become one with the life-force of the *gohonzon* through faith; (4) the fortune or misfortune concretized in the life-force activity of everyday life (5) can be transformed into a state of achievement of buddhahood characterized by absolute happiness overflowing with life-force energy; (6) furthermore, it is the life that takes as its mission spreading this happiness to others that can be called a truly Buddhist life.

Understanding the life of faith and its purpose in this way, three possibilities emerge:[25]

1. *Buddhism can be conceived as the fervent pursuit of a way of life in the present world.*

The *gohonzon*-as-Buddha is the source of life-force energy and provider of this-worldly benefits. The attainment of buddhahood that Buddhism teaches to be the final goal of life remains absolute. But even if particular benefits are not considered to be the realization of that ultimate goal, they can be seen as a first step towards its achievement. One can see in these benefits indications of that ultimate goal. Thus one may link the easily understood goal of happiness in this life with the ultimate goal of Buddhism. Since happiness is the overflowing of life-force, it is in itself a manifestation of the Dharma and the Buddha (*gohonzon*), the origin of life, and not something vulgar or base. Conversely, the attainment of buddhahood does not imply a separation from life, as indicated by the word *nirvāṇa*, nor does it necessitate taking leave of this world. It is to be realized in this world, since life's ultimate purpose can only be achieved in the continuous rebirths into life in this world.

2. *The relationship with ultimate reality is perceived as pertaining to this-worldly existence, and hence is both practical and concrete.*

Life-force and its energy are realities that can be touched and affirmed through the senses, and the Buddha (Dharma) shares in the same substance of life in this world. No discontinuity between bodily sense experience and the experience of a connection with ultimate reality is emphasized. Rather the two are seen as continuous. Belief and the chanting of the *daimoku* are thought of in the same way as attempts to influence this-worldly existence or power. The *gohonzon* is often compared to a machine—a machine for manufacturing happiness—and the mutual relationship with the *gohonzon* is perceived as a process for drawing out energy that can be confirmed by the senses through physical activity. Thus faith and secular knowledge are not separate but are seen as overlapping domains. Just as ordinary knowledge of life is deepened through science, so, too, must it be deepened through religion. Through the mediation of life-force, science and religion are joined as mutually complementary undertakings.

3. *Personal religious transformation is perceived as inseparable from an active stance towards the present world, which is positively promoted.*

The achievement of buddhahood is not an inner event that involves temporary separation from everyday life; nor is it something to be experienced after death in some other world (*jōdo*). Rather, it is experienced in the very midst of daily life as a transformation of that life. This follows from the belief that life-force is manifested in the everyday just as the various states of *jikkai* are. The reception of the *gohonzon*, through belief and chanting of the *daimoku*, might be perceived as somehow other-worldly and distant from daily life. But insofar as it has to do with life-force, it entails daily life. Faith that does not effect progress towards greater happiness is regarded as imperfect. Nor is the advance of happiness restricted to one's own personal life; it must be extended to include others as well. In more immediate terms, this implies activity aimed at increasing the ranks of believers and also a reform of collective life.

The three points enumerated above are not to be found in the doctrine of traditional Nichiren Shōshū, except perhaps in germ. Strictly speaking, the reformulation of traditional doctrine does not follow from Toda's revelation that "Buddha is Life-Force," but it does allow for the incorporation of truly modern ideas and religious attitudes into that doctrine. It also affects the structure of the Japanese Buddhist idea of salvation. The reformation of religious ideas through the establishment of a this-worldly idea of salvation, conceived in vitalistic terms—as seen in new religious movements based on folk-religious or syncretic beliefs, as well as in Buddhist groups such as Honmon Butsuryūkō and Reiyūkai—has borne new fruit in Toda's transformation of Nichiren Shōshū doctrine.

Reformation of the Conception of Salvation

A host of new religious movements has emerged in Japanese society since the beginning of the nineteenth century. These movements have been stimulated by a wide variety of religious and intellectual sources, among them the various sects of Buddhism, Shintoism, the National Learning School, Confucianism, Christianity, folk religion—especially as it pertains to *shinbutsu* syncretism, modern sciences, and even nationalism. Despite this wide variety of influences, a certain commonality emerges in the basic structure of their concept of salvation. Recent scholars[26] have dubbed this structure a "Vitalistic Conception of Salvation" and singled out a number of claims that undergird it:

1. *The essence of the cosmos.* The cosmos is perceived as a living body or life-force possessed of everlasting, inexhaustible fertility. In human terms, this means that we are given life through nature and that the universe is the source of unlimited benefit for humanity.

2. *Primary religious being.* The new religions posit a central holy figure such as God or Buddha as the reality that unifies the universe. Conceived of as the primary religious being, it is symbolized as the "Source of Life" who gives birth to all beings and provides tender nurture to all.

3. *Human nature.* The human being is also thought to have an existence born of and nurtured by the Source of Life. Not only that, human beings are regarded as tributaries of the Life Source, possessing a divine, unpolluted nature that is able to return to or unite with this Source. Furthermore, in this way all human beings participate in the same life-force and are therefore all brothers and sisters.

4. *Life and death.* Due to the positive evaluation given life in this world, concepts of other-worldly salvation in a postdeath existence are rare.

Salvation is presented as the growth and efflorescence of life in this world, and rebirth as a return to this world is endowed with a positive meaning.

5. *Evil and sin*. If ties between the self and Life Source, or with others and one's environment, are severed, the harmonious development of life is hampered and life-force dries up. It is the attachment to self and selfish desires that causes this evil.

6. *Means of salvation*. One must restore harmony between the Life Source on the one hand, and oneself, others, and the environment on the other in order to overcome the state of evil. In addition to repentance and the recovery of the harmonious spirit, various practices are prompted to restore bonds to the Life Source.

7. *The saved state*. Salvation is defined as the state where the bonds with the Life Source have been restored and one is filled with the fertile life-force, a state of unity—or peace and harmony—between humanity and God, the living of a life suffused with joy. The image is this-worldly, sensate, even sensual. Although this is related to individual this-worldly benefits, it is represented as the total efflorescence of a life-force that transcends these partial benefits.

8. *Founders*. Founders are not merely regarded as instructors of ultimate truth but are represented as those within whom the Life Source resides, those from whom the Life Source flows, the ultimate mediators of this Life Source to humanity.

Toda Jōsei's life-force doctrine is typical of this "Vitalistic Conception of Salvation." Although it varies somewhat from the pattern in that there is little emphasis placed on a "harmonious spirit," and the *gohonzon* and Nichiren himself become the objects of veneration rather than a founder figure, in terms of overall structure it corresponds closely to the conceptual model. In commenting on the eight points listed above, the authors describe the vitalistic concept of salvation as "a this-worldly centered concept of salvation" in contrast to the pessimistic worldly view of liberative or other-worldly concepts of salvation. Furthermore, it is argued that this view rejects both the dualistic thought that sets up some ideal religious world cut off from the present reality and the logic of world-renunciation that preaches a total overcoming of the world and the separation of oneself from the world.

To say that the view of salvation presented by the New Religions is this-worldly, however, does not go far enough in describing the unique development that the idea of salvation has undergone in these groups. Other religions, such as Shinto or animistic folk beliefs, as well as the *hongaku shisō* characteristic of Japanese Buddhism, also take a positive attitude towards the present reality. But these differ from the concept of this-worldly salvation found in the new religious movements.

For example, the concept of "salvation" is rather weak in Shinto and animistic thought. Since *hongaku shisō* presents a typical case of premodern religious thought that is both this-worldly and directed towards salvation, it offers a more promising topic for comparison, especially given the fact that the basis of Sōka Gakkai's religious thought, Nichiren Shōshū, was strongly influenced by *hongaku shisō*. The various sects of Kamakura Buddhism exhibit the influence of *hongaku shisō* in their core beliefs,[27] though this influence is more marked in Shinran, Ippen, and Nichiren than in Hōnen or Dōgen. The influence of *hongaku shisō* is especially clear in arguments concerning the significance of the *honzon* in Nichiren's *Kanjin honzonshō*, and Nichiren Shōshū—among the branch sects of Nichiren Buddhism, the one where the *honzon* is venerated and the *Kanjin honzonshō* is considered authoritative to a greater degree—is especially close to *hongaku shisō*. Many valued texts of Nichiren Shōshū once attributed to Nichiren but now held to be of questionable authorship were also influenced by later *hongaku shisō*. It is therefore safe to conclude that Sōka Gakkai has transformed the *hongaku shisō* conception of salvation into the vitalistic concept found in the New Religions.

The Iwanami *Buddhist Dictionary* defines *hongaku shisō* as an inquiry into the undivided, absolute world that transcends the dualistic relativity of reality, and then returns to reality in order to affirm the varieties of dualistic relativity as expressions of the undivided *hongaku*.[28] In terms of the achievement of buddhahood, it constitutes a rejection of the dualistic way of thinking that opposes the Buddha and common humanity, and sees humans attaining buddhahood by rejecting their common nature. *Hongaku* is an absolute that transcends such a dualistic relativity. It is the true mode of being of the Buddha that returns one to the real world, thus demonstrating the enlightened insight that the lost masses are already the undivided unity of the Buddha and common humanity. "Evil passions are themselves enlightenment" *(bonnō soku bodai)* and "endurance is itself tranquil light" *(shaba soku jakkō)* are expressions of this affirmation of reality.

In its extreme application *hongaku shisō* affirms wandering from the path of virtue and completely rejects the importance of religious practice *(shugyō)*, landing it in a view that can hardly be called Buddhism any longer. Tamura argues that when Japanese Buddhism was being swept along in this direction of affirming an absolute monism, Kamakura Buddhism countered by reinforcing the dualistic element.[29] Hōnen's opposition of Amida to common humanity and the overcoming of reality through birth *(ōjō)* in the Pure Land is a classic example of this development. At the same time, as Tamura notes, *hongaku shisō* was the fountainhead of the Kamakura reform, and with Shinran and Nichiren regained its prominence.

In the doctrine of Nichiren Shōshū, common humanity already possesses within itself the realm of the Buddha, and through the reception of the *gohonzon* humanity immediately achieves buddhahood. Within Nichiren's thought one also finds the idea of *ōkei shisō* which holds that after death one is reborn in the Pure Land and there achieves buddhahood. This is closer to a dualistic salvation theory that presents the overcoming of this deviant reality on the other side, rather than the manifestation of buddhahood in our present state. Some scholars argue that this dualistic *ōkei shisō* was emphasized in Nichiren's latter years, when confrontation with society deepened.[30] No trace of *ōkei shisō*, however is to be found in Nichiren Shōshū, where the monistic salvation theory of the attainment of buddhahood through the reception of the *gohonzon*—within the framework of *shaba soku jakkō* and *bonnō soku bodai*—dominates.

Nichiren Shōshū's doctrine of salvation, emphasizing as it did the immediate attainment of buddhahood, was clearly this-worldly or world-affirming. But it did not encourage engagement with the world and the transformation of present reality. Salvation was not seen to entail participation in the transformation of reality. It remained rather at the level of an internal transformation of the self unaffected by everyday life. Despite a strong desire for reform in the national religion, tied to the ideals of Nichren's *Risshō Ankokuron*, the idea of a practical reform of one's own life extending to reforms on behalf of others was rather weak.

For Toda Jōsei, who had learned the importance of the practical transformation of daily life from Makiguchi Tsunesaburō, such a this-worldly, world-affirming concept of salvation was not easy to swallow. His idea of "life-force" gave him an alternative: the immediate attainment of buddhahood means salvation through engagement in the realities of daily life, through attaining benefits and happiness that involve all of life, and through extending this happiness to others. While affirming present reality, this idea of salvation does not simply accept reality as it is. It retains the hope that reality can be changed and may therefore better be described as reality-transformative. The transformation in question does not necessarily imply the reform of social structures or a dramatic change in communal life, as found in the *yonaoshi* concept. At certain times such a transformation may be advocated; at other times, not. What remains constant is the aspiration to transform the self and life around oneself, and the belief that these efforts have to do with salvation. As befits a faith community centered on the laity and teaching participation in reality, this contrasts sharply with the low esteem accorded present reality in historical religions centered on religious specialists and preaching separation from the world.

Notes

1. See Fukushima Masato, "Mō hitotsu no 'meisō': Toshi to iu keiken no kaidoku kōshi" (Yet another way of meditation: A framework for understanding the urban experience), Tanabe Shigeharu, ed., *Jissen shūkyō no jinruigaku* (The anthropology of practical religion) (Kyoto: Kyōto Daigaku Gakujutsu Shuppan, 1989).

2. For the expansion of Japanese New Religions abroad, see Inoue, *Japanese Religions Abroad*, and Nakamaki, *Japanese Religions in the New World*. See also the special edition of the *Japanese Journal of Religious Studies* on the subject, 18 (2/3) 1991.

3. For an explanation of the term "this-worldly salvation," see the introduction to Shimazono, *Studies in Contemporary Salvationist Religions*.

4. The translation "life-force" is meant to draw attention to the particular sense that has been given to *seimei*, one of the ordinary Japanese words for life.

5. Sōka Gakkai Kyōgakubu, ed., *Revised Introduction to Sōka Gakkai*, 77.

6. Seikyō Shinbunsha, ed., *Snatches of life: Proverbs of Ikeda Daisaku*, 109, 112.

7. Makiguchi's thought is treated in Seikyō Shinbun-sha, *Makiguchi Tsunesaburō*, and Miyata, *The Religious Movement of Makiguchi Tsunesaburō*. In "Practicality in Daily Life and Religious Movements," I have tried to lay out the characteristic ideas of Sōka Kyōiku Gakkai in its formative period. Asai, "The Emergence of Sōka Gakkai," argues that there are inconsistencies between Makiguchi's value theory and Nichiren Shōshū doctrine, as well as between Makiguchi's thought and the life-force theory of later Sōka Gakkai.

8. For Toda's life and thought, see Higuma, *Sōka Gakkai;* Tōkyō Daigaku Hokkekyō Kenkyūkai, ed., *The Doctrine and Practice of Sōka Gakkai;* Uefuji and Ōno, *The Story of a Revolution;* and Nishino, *The Biography of Toda Jōsei*.

9. Seikyō Shinbunsha, *The Human Revolution* 2: 235–55.

10. *Collected Works of Toda Jōsei*, vol. 2, 12. The original existence, in Nichiren Shōshū's doctrine, is thought to predate even the *Kuon jitsujō* or "True Attainment of the Remotest Past" of the Lotus Sūtra.

11. *Essays of Toda Jōsei*, 17, 19–20.

12. *Essays of Toda Jōsei*, 50, 52–53.

13. *Essays of Toda Jōsei*, 13–14.

14. *Essays of Toda Jōsei*, 450–52

15. *Essays of Toda Jōsei*, 339, 171–72.

16. *Essays of Toda Jōsei*, 36.

17. *Collected Works of Toda Jōsei*, vol. 7, 117.

18. *Essays of Toda Jōsei*, 266–67.

19. *Essays of Toda Jōsei*, 38–39, 351, 177–78.

20. *Essays of Toda Jōsei*, 44–45, 54–56, 48.

21. *Essays of Toda Jōsei*, 46–48.

22. Concerning the position of Nichiren Shōshū within the Nichiren sects see Shugyō, *A History of Nichirenshū Doctrine,* and Mochizuki, *A Study of Nichiren Doctrine.* Murakami also gives a concise treatment of this point.

23. In addition to the books by Shugyō and Mochizuki cited in the previous note, see Horigome, *The Teachings of Nichiren,* and Ōhashi, *Buddhist Thought and the Fuji Sect Doctrine.*

24. In Nichiren's *Kaimokushō* this is called the true law of *ichinen sansen* hidden in the deeper meaning of the *Juryōbon.*

25. Tōkyō Daigaku Hokkekyō Kenkyūkai's *The Doctrine and Practice of Sōka Gakkai* contains a penetrating analysis of the characteristics of Toda's life-force theory.

26. See Tsushima et al., "The Vitalistic Conception of Salvation in Japanese New Religions."

27. Tamura, *Studies in the thought of Kamakura Buddhism.*

28. Nakamura Hajime, *Iwanami bukkyō jiten* (Iwanami Buddhist Dictionary) (Tokyo: Iwanami Shoten, 1989).

29. Tamura, *Studies in the thought of Kamakura Buddhism.*

30. Mochizuki, *A Study of Nichiren Doctrine*; Tamura, *Studies in the thought of Kamakura Buddhism*, 601–11.

Bibliography

Asai Endō. "Sōka Gakkai no shutsugen to mondaiten" (The emergence of Sōka Gakkai and its problems). In Mochizuki Kanko, ed., *Kindai Nihon no hokkei bukkyō* (*Lotus Sūtra* Buddhism in modern Japan). Kyoto: Heiraku-ji Shoten, 1968.

Higuma Takenori. *Sōka Gakkai, Toda Jōsei.* Tokyo: Shinjinbutsu Ōraisha, 1971.

Horigome Nichijun. *Nichiren daishōnin no kyōgi: Nichiren shōnin to Hokkekyō* (The teachings of Nichiren: Nichiren and the *Lotus Sūtra*). Tokyo: Nichiren Shōshū Bussho Kankōkai, 1976.

Inoue Nobutaka. *Umi wo watatta Nihon shūkyō* (Japanese religions abroad). Tokyo: Kōbundō, 1985.

Inoue Nobutaka et al., eds. *Shinshūkyō jiten* (Dictionary of new religions). Tokyo: Kōbundō, 1990.

Makiguchi Tsunesaburō. *Sōka Kyōikugaku Taikei* (The system of value-creating education). Tokyo: Sōka Kyōiku Gakkai, 1930.

Miyata Kōichi. *Makiguchi Tsunesaburō no shūkyō undō* (The religious movement of Makiguchi Tsunesaburō). Tokyo: Daisan Bunmeisha, 1993.

Mochizuki Kankō. *Nichiren kyōgaku no kenkyū* (A study of Nichiren doctrine). Kyoto: Heirakuji Shoten, 1958.

―――. *Nichirenshū gakusetsushi* (The history of Nichirenshū doctrine). Kyoto: Heiraku-ji Shoten, 1969.

Murakami Shigeyoshi. *Sōka Gakkai=Kōmeitō.* Tokyo: Aoki Shoten, 1967.

Nakamaki Hirochika. *Shinsekai no Nihon shūkyō* (Japanese religions in the new world). Tokyo: Heibonsha, 1968.

Nishino Tatsukichi. *Denki Toda Jōsei* (The biography of Toda Jōsei). Tokyo: Daisan Bunmeisha, 1985.

Ōhashi Jijō. *Bukkyō shisō to Fujikyōgaku* (Buddhist thought and the Fuji Sect doctrine). Tokyo: Nichiren Shōshū Busshō Kankōkai, 1978.

Seikyō Shinbunsha, eds. *Makiguchi Tsunesaburō*. Tokyo: Seikyō Shinbunsha, 1972.

———. *Shosetsu ningen kakumei* (Human revolution). Tokyo: Seikyō Bunko, 1972.

———. *Jinseishō: Ikeda Daisaku Shingenshū* (Snatches of life: Proverbs of Ikeda Daisaku). Tokyo: Seikyō Shinbunsha, 1980.

Shimazono Susumu. *Gendai kyūsai shūkyōron* (Studies in contemporary salvationist religions). Tokyo: Seikyūsha, 1992.

———. Seikatsuchi to kindai shūkyō undō: Makiguchi Tsunesaburō no kyōiku shisō to shinkō (Practicality in daily life and religious movements: The educational philosophy and faith of Makiguchi Tsunesaburō). In Kawai Hayao, ed., *Iwanami kōza shūkyō to kagaku*, vol. 5, *Shūkyō to shakai kagaku* (Religion and science, vol. 5, Religion and the social sciences). Tokyo: Iwanami Shoten, 1992.

Shugyō Kaishū. *Nichirenshū kyōgakushi* (A history of Nichirenshū doctrine). Kyoto: Heiraku-ji Shoten, 1952.

Sōka Gakkai Kyōgakubu, ed. *Shakubuku Kyōten*. Tokyo: Shūkyōhōjin Sōka Gakkai, 1952.

———. *Kaiteiban Sōka Gakkai nyūmon* (Revised introduction to Sōka Gakkai). Tokyo: Seikyō Shinbunsha, 1980.

Tamura Yoshirō. *Kamakura shinbukkyō shisō no kenkyū* (Studies in the thought of Kamakura Buddhism). Kyoto: Heiraku-ji Shoten, 1965.

———. "Japanese Culture and the Tendai Concept of Original Enlightenment." *Japanese Journal of Religious Studies* 14 (1987) 203–10.

Toda Jōsei. *Toda Jōsei-sensei ronbunshū* (Articles by Toda Jōsei). Tokyo: Shūkyōhōjin Sōka Gakkai.

———. *Toda Jōsei zenshū*, vol. 7, *Kōgihen III* (Lectures, part III). Tokyo: Seikyō Shinbunsha, 1987.

Toda Jōsei Zenshū Shuppan Iinkai, ed. *Toda Jōsei zenshū* (The collected works of Toda Jōsei), vol. 2, *Shitsumonkai hen* (Answering questions from the believers). Tokyo: Seikyō Shinbunsha, 1982.

Tōkyō Daigaku Hokkekyō Kenkyūkai, ed. *Sōka Gakkai no rinen to jissen* (The doctrine and practice of Sōka Gakkai). Tokyo: Daisan Bunmeisha, 1975.

Tsushima Michihito, Nishiyama Shigeru, Shimazono Susumu, Shiramizu Hiroko. "The vitalistic conception of salvation in Japanese New Religions." *Japanese Journal of Religious Studies* 6 (1979) 139–61.

Uefuji Kazuyuki and Ōno Yasuyuki, eds. *Kakumei no taiga: Sōka Gakkai yonjūgo-nenshi* (The story of a revolution: The forty-five-year history of Sōka Gakkai). Tokyo: Seikyō Shinbunsha, 1975.

[translated by Robert Kisala]

30

Contemporary Buddhist Spirituality and Social Activism

SALLIE B. KING

P EOPLE IN THE West usually conceive of Buddhism as a religion of monks in which spirituality involves cutting oneself off from the world to pursue a detached life of meditation. Inaccurate for Buddhism at any time, this image is least adequate for Buddhism in the twentieth century. Today, Buddhist leaders travel from one capital to another, delivering position papers and addressing parliaments on issues of global importance; nuns and laypersons have come increasingly to the fore; and on occasions of national crisis, Buddhism has the power to move its adherents by the millions into the streets. I shall examine the spiritual foundations of this new Buddhism and some of its major forms of social activism, focusing throughout on the interface between spirituality and activism. We shall see that when Buddhist monks, nuns, and laypersons shift their focus from within to without in order to actively engage social issues, they are not leaving spirituality behind.

Spiritual Foundations

The intersectarian "Open Letter" issued by the "Network for Western Buddhist Teachers" in March 1993 well articulates the perspective of Buddhist social activists around the world. It gives the following as its first point of agreement among those present:

> Our first responsibility as Buddhists is to work towards creating a better world for all forms of life. The promotion of Buddhism as a religion is a secondary concern. Kindness and compassion, the furthering of peace and harmony, as well as tolerance and respect for other religions, should be the three guiding principles of our actions.[1]

The source of this concern to make a "better world for all forms of life" is found in the central teaching of Buddhism, the Four Noble Truths: (1) suffering; (2) the cause of suffering; (3) the cessation of suffering; (4) the path or way to bring about the cessation of suffering. Śākyamuni Buddha called himself a physician, and Buddhism a medicine or cure, for the suffering of the world. The conception of suffering, the analysis of suffering, and the means for its cure have been matters for varied interpretation in different sects, eras, and cultures, but the core idea that suffering is the problem and that Buddhism is a tool to be used to eliminate suffering has remained a constant. "Creating a better world for all forms of life" is perhaps a modern, a Western-influenced, and an ambitious way of expressing this, but it remains faithful to that foundational concern.

That the concern is spiritual, rather than merely well-intentioned and busybodyish, is shown by its basis in the venerable Buddhist teaching of selflessness and compassion. Buddhism finds the cause of suffering in a craving *(taṇhā)* expressible as "I want" that underlies all of our ordinary actions, thoughts, and feelings. Through Buddhist practice, one may come to experientially realize the ultimate emptiness or non-existence of this "I" and as a consequence one may become free of the constant drive to serve the "I." When the "I" and its wants have been erased from the picture, according to Buddhism, one ceases to identify solely with the contents of this "bag of skin." In one who has realized the fruits of Buddhist spiritual practice and eliminated the "self," the line between "self" and "other," essential to ordinary consciousness, may fade to complete obscurity.

Buddhist social activism has its basis here. If one who has eliminated the "self" becomes aware that "another" person (or sentient being) is in pain, the natural response is to take steps to relieve that pain, in the same way that one would naturally do what one could to relieve one's "own" pain; that is, "another's" pain is one's "own" pain. When the suffering becomes widespread and acute, as among the people of Vietnam during the war, then we witness hundreds of thousands of monks, nuns, and laypeople acting nonviolently to bring it to an end. As Thich Nhat Hanh said, the suffering caused by the bombing and the oppression "hurts us too much. We have to react."[2] Thus the monks and nuns left the peace and safety of the monasteries for the villages and cities to do what they could to help; the people's pain was their pain.

Compassion is perhaps the first identified and most consistently exalted Buddhist virtue, the defining mark of a Buddha, along with wisdom. Even for the beginner on the Buddhist path, or one whose spiritual aspirations are very modest, compassion has always been the absolute minimum required in order to be a Buddhist in more than name. For the layperson who thought meditation beyond his or her ken, daily acts of generous giving, of simple kindness, have always comprised the very stuff of Buddhist spirituality. In other words, one could (and most Buddhists historically did) forgo meditation and strenuous self-discipline without in the least threatening one's Buddhist identity; but without compassion and kindness, one could be no more than a nominal Buddhist.

The above "Open Letter" lists "kindness and compassion" as the first of three principles to guide action, and the other principles listed, "the furthering of peace and harmony" and "tolerance and respect for other religions" are further expressions of the same basic concern to avoid causing suffering and to relieve it when it occurs. Thus, in the spirituality that lies at its foundation, contemporary Buddhist social activism does not seem very new at first glance. Its novelty resides in factors proper to the twentieth century:

1. modern social, economic, psychological, and political analysis of Western liberal origin;

2. the great example of Gandhi, whose influence among most Buddhist social activists is vast (with the prominent exception of the Ambedkarites, who disdain him for his failure to attack the caste system in toto);

3. acute crises, many of which have hit the Buddhist world particularly hard: genocide (Cambodia); modern warfare (Japan, Vietnam, and much of Southeast Asia); the aftermath of colonialism (Sri Lanka in particular); foreign invasion and cultural genocide (Tibet); repressive governments (Burma, Thailand); and the ecocrisis; and

4. chronic crises, long-term ills coming to a head in our time: extreme social inequality, bigotry, and poverty (in particular among the ex-untouchables of India); and sexism.

Unique forms of Buddhist social activism have arisen in response to each of these crises.

Buddhist Spiritual Values in the Fight against Poverty

In contemporary Buddhism, spirituality and social activism are often so deeply intertwined that it is difficult to separate the two. Examples of this may be seen in the work of an individual Thai monk and abbot, Abbot Nan Sutasilo, and the large Sri Lankan organization, Sarvodaya Shramadana. Both apply Buddhist principles to overcome rural poverty while resisting

Western capitalist models of development. The combination of Western social analysis and Buddhist spiritual analysis demonstrates the causal inter-connections of the various influences in human life: material and economic conditions, cultural and social conditions, intellectual and psychological conditions, and finally spiritual conditions all act upon each other in causative ways. As a result, concern with spiritual development cannot be divorced from concern with economic development. However, Buddhist activists are concerned about material well-being only to the point where the real needs of individual and society are met. Thus, both Abbot Nan and Sarvodaya see Western-style development as harmful insofar as it fuels end-less wanting, consumerism, and ever deeper debt. The Middle Path of Bud-dhism is antipathetic to consumerism: the young Siddhartha discovered that human wants are intrinsically insatiable, that despite his harem, power, wife, child, and luxurious life, his wants continued to multiply and his deeper, spiritual, wants remained unfulfilled. Needs must be met, but insa-tiable wants avoided; this is the Middle Path in Buddhism today.

Abbot Nan seeks to help his villagers acquire "spiritual immunity" so that they can resist the lure of consumerism and its cycle of greater wants, doomed efforts to satisfy them, and greater debt. He took a group of vil-lagers to meditate in a graveyard "in order to give them a new life," telling them:

> When your mind is calm and clear, you can see through illusions and see sit-uations as they are. This realization helps cleanse the mind of selfishness and greed.... When greed stops, peace arises. Your mind will be imbued with compassion, which provides the best fertilizer to nourish your life.[3]

The monks who work with Abbot Nan or in Sarvodaya provide guidance and assistance but they may not make decisions and run the development projects. This principle is based upon a teaching strongly emphasized in Theravāda: self-reliance. In Sarvodaya, the monks may come into a village to help organize and inspire the villagers, but it is the villagers themselves who decide what is their first priority: a road or a sanitation system, a school house or a day care program. Neither do the villagers wait for the govern-ment to take action; they simply identify their needs and take immediate action themselves. Self-reliance applies to funding as well. Though Sarvo-daya does accept foreign contributions, in general, projects are funded by countless small donations from the villagers, and, of course, the labor is all donated. Sarvodaya makes a point of insisting that each village household that wishes, for example, to attend a communal meal as part of a workcamp donate at least a matchbox of rice. In this way, each person knows him or herself as a contributor to the project; no one leaves feeling diminished as the object of others' charity.[4] Buddhists who work with the poor recognize that the sense of personal worthlessness that often accompanies poverty is a psychological impediment to serious Buddhist practice, as well as an illness that requires healing.

Abbot Nan has made some creative changes in traditional practices to fund his projects. Throughout South and Southeast Asia, giving has always been one of the most important expressions of spirituality of the Buddhist laity, and monks and temples have been the single most prized object of such giving. Giving to monks and temples has not only served as the economic base of Buddhism, but it has also been an opportunity to practice virtue and earn merit ("good karma"). Traditionally, donations have been used for the temple's own welfare and the laypeople have wanted it so. But now most temples are financially secure and many are quite well-endowed with land and buildings. Declaring that "the temple's money is the people's money," Abbot Nan has begun taking money donated to his temple and applying it to his various projects, such as a Fertilizer Bank and a Village Rice Bank. He has inspired villagers to make a religious vow that they will resist consumerism, decrease unnecessary expenditures, and donate the money saved to a village savings group, the funds of which are used to set up a medical cooperative and to pay off the villagers' loans before the banks to whom they are indebted foreclose and take their land. He has transformed the annual three day robe-presentation ceremony, traditionally the major festival of lay giving to the Buddhist temple, into an occasion that raises money for village development projects rather than for the temple. In this way, giving, and the expression of selflessness that it embodies, remains a central practice, but transformed in such a way that it directly serves the development needs of the village.

Response to War, Genocide, and Invasion

The Buddhist world has experienced some of the most horrific suffering produced by twentieth-century warfare. The engaged Buddhist response has been one of deep, principled nonviolence, accompanied by efforts to prevent suffering and heal wounds, and to promote peace and reconcile enemies.[5] This is in accord with the principle of *ahiṃsā*, non-harmfulness or nonviolence, which is the first of the five Buddhist lay precepts, the foundation of ethical life for all Buddhists; indeed, all Buddhist ethics can be understood as a variety of expressions of this single, fundamental value. The other four lay precepts—not to steal, not to lie, not to engage in sexual misconduct, not to take intoxicants—are all explained as disciplines that the Buddhist undertakes in order to avoid causing harm to oneself or others. *Ahiṃsā* is also a spiritual value; indeed, ethics and spirituality are two sides of a single coin in Buddhism. It is the practical expression of selflessness and compassionate care for others.

Cambodia

In little more than three and a half years (April 1975 to January 1979) and as a direct result of Khmer Rouge policies and brutality, an estimated two to three million Cambodians died of starvation, disease, overwork, torture, and execution. During the same period, the Khmer Rouge destroyed virtually all of Cambodia's 3,600 Buddhist temples, while only an estimated 3,000 of what had been 50,000 monks survived (figures on female monastics are unavailable, though they were persecuted as well).[6] Temple remains were used for ammunition storage, manure dumps, torture and execution sites. To refer in any way to Buddhism was a punishable offense.

In response to this unspeakable human horror came the monk Maha Ghosananda. Having lived out the holocaust in a Thai monastery (where he had lived since 1965), Maha Ghosananda returned to Cambodia in 1978, shortly before the fall of the Khmer Rouge. Arriving at a refugee camp, he distributed copies of the *Mettā Sutta*, the Buddha's teachings on love and kindness. There is perhaps no more moving scene imaginable than the picture of this monk, who himself lost his entire family in the holocaust, seated in the refugee camp, in the utterly devastated land of the Killing Fields, surrounded by survivors of the holocaust, who themselves had gone through years of hell on Earth, reciting over and over again, as thousands prostrated themselves and loudly wailed, the verses from the Buddha's teaching in the *Dhammapada*:

> Hatred never ceases by hatred
> but by love alone is healed.
> This is the ancient and eternal law.[7]

Since that day in the refugee camp, Maha Ghosananda has worked tirelessly to heal the wounds of the Cambodian people in Cambodia and in diaspora, reconcile its still warring factions, and rebuild the Cambodian Buddhist church. He has been elected *Somteja*, Supreme Patriarch of Cambodian Buddhism, and is often called "the Gandhi of Cambodia." He established temples first in every refugee camp, then all over the world for Cambodian expatriate communities. In 1992 he began a series of Dhamma

Yietra, Walks for Peace and Reconciliation. The first accompanied many refugees returning home for the first time; the second, held just before the elections in 1993, is credited with helping to create the atmosphere in which Cambodians were able to vote in large numbers; the third, in which one monk and one nun were killed, was held in 1994 in an effort to spread *mettā karuṇā* (loving kindness and compassion) and bring reconciliation to the still warring factions.

Vietnam

In 1963 the regime of Ngo Dinh Diem, President of South Vietnam, was brought to an end by a combination of Buddhist and military forces, acting separately. Diem, a Catholic, was infamously oppressive of Buddhism. In a country which was eighty per cent Buddhist, this was his downfall. Having prohibited public celebration of the Buddha's birthday in May, government officials fired on a peaceful crowd that had gathered around a radio station when it failed to air an expected Buddhist program. This event outraged the Buddhist public and huge protest demonstrations followed. In June, the monk Thich Quang Duc, in a state of meditative trance and complete self-control, publicly burned himself to death in protest. Ever larger strikes, marches, protests, and fasts occurred, along with further self-immolations, which Madame Nhu mocked as "barbecues."

In August, Diem's forces raided Buddhist pagodas throughout South Vietnam, resulting in large numbers of monks being arrested. Protests and arrests continued through September and October. In November, Diem was ousted in an almost bloodless coup; Diem and his brother Nhu were executed. Until May 1966 there followed a period of short-lived South Vietnamese administrations, in which governments sympathetic to Buddhism and its anti-war stance were popular with the people but unacceptable to the South Vietnamese military and their American backers, while governments acceptable to the latter were unacceptable to the masses of South Vietnamese people and the Buddhist leadership that voiced their anti-war sentiment.[8]

In this way, from 1963 to 1966, protest for freedom of religion steadily widened into protest against political oppression and, especially, for peace. Buddhism became the people's voice and steadfastly called for an end to the war. Finally, in 1966, with strong American backing, the South Vietnamese government army of the Thieu-Ky regime crushed the military forces that had withdrawn their support from the government and arrested virtually the entire Buddhist activist leadership. This effectively ended the power of the Buddhist anti-war movement known as the "Struggle Movement" though protests continued throughout the war years.

At the same time that Buddhism represented the anti-war sentiment of the Vietnamese people, it was also developing a new social work emphasis. The monk Thich Nhat Hanh founded the School of Youth for Social Service in 1964 as a vehicle for social work in the countryside. Inevitably, the monks, nuns, and laypeople attracted to this dynamic new form of Buddhism found themselves engaged in efforts to protect the people from the war and to heal them from its destruction, while at the same time going about their social work of teaching, building public buildings, caring for the needy, and helping improve agriculture, sanitation, and roads.

The spiritual foundations of the Buddhist Struggle Movement contain features we have seen in other movements, though in a form that might be difficult to recognize here. First, despite the role played by the military in the above account, the Buddhist Struggle Movement itself was strictly nonviolent. While they invited members of the South Vietnamese army to withdraw their support from regimes determined to perpetuate or expand the war, they never sought military backing for themselves. Indeed, a large part of the Buddhist movement's efforts were dedicated to the aid and protection of deserters and draft resisters. Similarly, the self-immolations of Buddhist monks, nuns, and laypersons look violent indeed to the observer, but Buddhist theoreticians insisted that they should not be so understood. First, no Buddhist leadership ever endorsed or sanctioned the self-immolations; they were the actions of individuals who had made the kind of decision that is made without asking for approval. Second, the self-immolations were not acts of despair but were said to be the loving efforts of a selfless person sacrificing him/herself in an effort to teach, to reach deeply into the hearts of those propagating the war so as to make them psychologically and spiritually unable to continue doing so, and to make them want to stop. Those who immolated themselves willingly took unto themselves the bad karma of causing harm to a sentient being (themselves), abandoning their parents, and so on, in an effort to prevent the much greater suffering of a much greater group of sentient beings by bringing the war to an end.

The second characteristic feature of the spirituality of the Buddhist Struggle Movement was the refusal to take sides, either with North or South, communist or capitalist; they wished to be only on the side of the people and of life. This was, after all, a fratricidal civil war, in which brothers might be in opposing armies. In such a situation, Nhat Hanh expressed the sentiments of many in a poem entitled "Do Not Shoot Your Brother," which was sung throughout South Vietnam:

Our enemy has the name of hatred
Our enemy has the name of inhumanity
Our enemy has the name of anger
Our enemy has the name of ideology
Our enemy wears the mask of freedom
Our enemy is dressed in lies
Our enemy bears empty words
Our enemy is the effort to divide us.

Our enemy is not man.
If we kill man, with whom shall we live?[9]

This refusal to take sides with one party against another is based not only upon sympathy for all involved—the Buddhists were clear that in war, all are victims: combatants and noncombatants, victors and losers, the living and the dead—but also upon a keen Buddhist sense of karmic interconnection, with a consequent nonjudgmental ethical posture. The war was the massive karmic consequence of countless interconnected causal threads (including global geopolitics, the Cold War, Vietnamese history); it was a vast karmic knot in which the threads of countless individuals from North and South Vietnam, America and the Soviet Union were hopelessly tangled. Given the inexorability of the law of cause and effect, given the interconnectedness of causes and effects in the lives of all the individuals directly and tangentially involved, from the Buddhist perspective it would have been false to the reality of the situation to pretend to divide these tangled, interconnected threads, to sort them into two groups, us and them, and to justify one's own side while condemning the other. From this perspective, there was no place for blame, no place for negative judgment: humans are karmic beings who do what they do for reasons. Rather than judgment, blame, and side-taking, what was needed in this context was to understand the karmic forces that drove people and groups to do what they did and to remove the causes that would result in further suffering—prominently including separation and enmity between opposing "sides." Thus, to avoid taking sides and to make every effort to reconcile, to repair the rift in the human community, was not a matter of strategy or even of distaste for the various extant camps; it was a matter of fundamental necessity in the Buddhist analysis. The war was an expression of a divided humanity; the Buddhists would not contribute to that division, but heal it if they could.

The Buddhist effort to end the war did not succeed. Since the reunion of Vietnam under the communist government, Buddhism has continued to suffer oppression. Fearful of the power latent in Buddhism, the government keeps the church and its leadership under strict control, with many monks under house arrest and some still in prison. Buddhists are prohibited from performing social work and are limited to the most traditional kinds of religious services.

Thich Nhat Hanh lives in exile in France (the Vietnamese government refuses to grant him a return visa). He and his followers continue to work actively on behalf of the people of Vietnam. During the boat people crisis, they hired boats and picked up refugees from their flimsy crafts. Today they work in a variety of creative ways to send money to Vietnam to support war orphans and the poorest of the poor. They continue to train Buddhist social workers, poised for action the moment the government lifts its restrictions, as they believe it will. Nhat Hanh also travels around the Western world, a leader in the international Engaged Buddhism movement (this term was coined by Nhat Hanh to refer to socially activist Buddhism), a widely respected leader in the interreligious community of spiritual social activists, and a leader of workshops in Buddhist practice designed variously for social activists, expatriate Vietnamese, Western families, Vietnam war veterans, psychologists, artists, and other groups.

Tibet

The Chinese invaded Tibet in 1949, establishing complete control in 1959, at which time the Dalai Lama fled from Tibet to India. He continues to the present to live in Dharamsala, India, together with a community of about 100,000 Tibetan refugees. Chinese rule in Tibet has been catastrophic for the Tibetan people, their culture, their Buddhist religion, and for the physical land of Tibet. Suffering at all times strict political oppression, with severe punishment for any challenge or protest against the Chinese government or its policies, the Tibetan people's suffering was especially acute during the Cultural Revolution, when death from torture, inhumane prison conditions, execution, and especially famine reached its peak. It is estimated that over one million Tibetans have died as a direct result of the Chinese invasion, occupation, and mismanagement of Tibet; this is one-fifth of the population of Tibet.

Since the Cultural Revolution, the Chinese have changed their Tibet policy in a manner that remains devastating to the Tibetans. By means of a massive population transfer of ethnic Han Chinese into Tibet, the Tibetans are fast becoming a minority in their own country. Combine this with the destruction and repression of traditional religion and culture, especially as embodied in the foremost transmitter of traditional culture, the Buddhist religion (over 6,000 monasteries, temples, and historic structures have been destroyed; vast numbers of monks and nuns have been forcibly returned to lay life; the Buddhist leadership is in exile or effectively silenced), and it is obvious that Tibetan culture is engaged in a desperate struggle for survival. Many have called the present Tibet policy of China "cultural genocide" for this reason; indeed, much of the hope for the preservation of Tibetan culture and religion lies in what can be preserved outside of Tibet.

The Dalai Lama, regarded by Tibetan Buddhists as the incarnation of the bodhisattva Avalokiteśvara, was until 1959 the spiritual and temporal head of the Tibetan people. He continues as their spiritual head and as the head of a government-in-exile in Dharamsala. As the intensely beloved and deeply respected heart and soul of the Tibetan people, the fact of his survival has been of the first importance to the Tibetans. Not only has he survived, not only has he failed to be overcome by his plight and that of his people, but he has developed into a unique and remarkable leader who embodies in his person both the continuity of the Tibetan religion and its far-reaching reform, both profound spiritual guidance and deft secular leadership. He has consistently drawn on Buddhist spiritual resources to urge the Tibetans to avoid all violence in their response to the Chinese occupation. He has led the movement for the reform of the Tibetan government in exile and Tibetan ecclesial institutions, replacing hierarchical and authoritarian structures with representative and democratic ones. He has overseen efforts to preserve Tibetan culture and religion in Dharamsala and throughout the world. Most importantly, he has led the global effort to restore independence to Tibet through negotiation and diplomacy. His proposals, which have never received a positive response from the Chinese, consistently call for the demilitarization of Tibet, the restoration of human rights to the Tibetan people, abandonment of the population transfer policy, protection of the natural environment of Tibet, and a negotiated settlement of relations between Tibet and China. The Dalai Lama was awarded the Nobel Peace Prize in 1989.

Along with Maha Ghosananda and the Vietnamese Struggle Movement, the Dalai Lama is one of the foremost examples of the Buddhist practice of loving the enemy under conditions which might be expected to drive anyone to hate. In the Dalai Lama's understanding, the proper response to the enemy is gratitude. He quotes a verse and comments as follows:

> If one whom I've helped my best
> And from whom I expect much
> Harms me in an inconceivable way,
> May I regard that person as my best teacher.

Only when someone criticizes and exposes our faults are we able to discover our problems and confront them. Thus is our enemy our greatest friend. He provides us with the needed test of inner strength, tolerance, and respect for others. Instead of feeling anger toward this person, one should respect him and be grateful.

Reflecting on human suffering, he states, "many of our troubles are man-made, created by our own ignorance, greed, and irresponsible action."[10] Thus, while not flinching from criticizing Chinese treatment of Tibetans, as a Buddhist leader (and, the devoted would say, as an incarnation of the Bodhisattva of Compassion) he is incapable of leading the Tibetan people down a path which could only add to the suffering in the China-Tibet confrontation through the harboring of ill-will, anger, and hatred and the expression of these emotions in violence, and instead always reaches out in goodwill to the Chinese, seeking solutions that meet the real needs of both sides of the conflict, calling for peaceful third-party intervention, and urging the Tibetan people to be as forbearing as they possibly can. The Dalai Lama is absolutely certain that anger cannot solve the problems of Tibet, or any problems, in a deep and lasting way. Conversely, he is equally confident that only love and understanding can produce a real resolution. Though the path of love takes longer, he says, it is finally the only real alternative.

Japan

Japan is the only country in the world to have suffered nuclear attack. As a consequence, intense antipathy has been the dominant feeling of the Japanese towards nuclear weapons, and war in general, since the end of WWII. These feelings are expressed in a number of Japanese Buddhist activist groups.

Focusing almost exclusively upon an anti-war and anti-nuclear message is the Nihonzan Myōhō-ji sect of Nichiren Buddhism, founded in Japan by Nichidatsu Fujii, and with chapters in several countries throughout the world. Fujii was an anti-war activist well before WWII; he met and was deeply impressed by Mahatma Gandhi. Today the sect is best known for the construction of peace pagodas throughout the world and for its peace marches led by monks of the sect beating on drums and chanting the Nichiren sect's "Namu Myōhō Rengekyō" ("Praise to the *Lotus Sūtra*") and followed by long or short columns of supporters, both Buddhist and non-Buddhist. In addition, activist monks of the sect may be found sitting in protest or witness before such things as armament shipment sites or exhibitions of newly developed weapons, beating their drums and chanting. All these activities are expressions of their passionately held belief that war and the manufacture of weapons are criminal activities; and at the same time they are public actions intended to raise public awareness of and support for the imperative of global disarmament and peace.

Moved by similar concerns, the large Nichiren-inspired lay sects Risshō Kōseikai and Sōka Gakkai have ongoing programs designed to bring about a world in which peace is possible. Both sects have sponsored many dialogues, workshops, and cultural exchanges between persons of differing cultures and religions in order to promote simple understanding across the barriers erected by nations, ethnicity, language, and religion. This is an expression of a prominent theme in Buddhist activist thought, namely, that the divisions among humankind promote misunderstanding, and that the human ego tends to react to that which it does not understand, that which it suspects is "different" from itself, with fear and aggression. Thus in an effort to prevent violence and war these sects create opportunities for understanding by promoting simple contact and communication across the barriers erected among themselves by humankind.

With similar motivation, Risshō Kōseikai and Sōka Gakkai have also sponsored exhibitions in Japan graphically depicting the sufferings of WWII, particularly those caused by nuclear attack. Concerned that the younger generation of Japanese who did not suffer through the war lack the experiential knowledge that gave so many of their elders firm anti-war and anti-nuclear attitudes, these groups have sought to provide some understanding of the intensity of the suffering involved through the graphic portrayal of such things as nuclear wounds and destruction. Sōka Gakkai has published over one hundred volumes recording in their own words and in painful detail the wartime experiences of those who fought in or lived through WWII.

Underlying such activities are beliefs about human nature, beliefs largely formed by the concept of Buddha-nature. According to this view as applied in this context, and simplifying drastically, a human being is composed of a surface-level ego and a deeper-level Buddha-nature. The ego is the cause of the major part of human suffering. One of its propensities is to fear and feel aggressive towards that which is unknown or "different." But the ego causes suffering because it suffers itself. It knows, and indeed does not forget for a moment, that it is fundamentally exceedingly fragile, small, isolated, and mortal. Life for the isolated ego is quite dismal and hopeless. Fortunately, we are also, on a deeper level, Buddhas, that is, beings who may at any moment actualize their potential for Buddha-like behavior. These two functions are inversely related. That is, the greater the dominance of the ego in an individual, the less that individual will be able to express Buddha-like qualities, and vice versa.

Efforts by Buddhist activists to reach out to the public are invariably efforts to reach out to the Buddha within each person, or in other words, that within each person which has the ability to transcend the isolation of the ego through empathetic understanding, feeling-with, and bonding. The Buddha within is that which is capable of feeling the suffering of another as one's own suffering and spontaneously reaching out in an act of compassion. The Buddha within is that which is capable of bypassing the ego's fear of those who are "different" and constructing a bridge on the basis of our common humanity. It is the Buddha within that is capable of looking for the common good, rather than "my" or "our" advantage or victory.

Here again is the meeting ground of Buddhist spirituality and Buddhist social activism. How does one reach the Buddha within when it is so often completely concealed by the ego and its fears? The Buddhist answer is essentially *upāya*, skillful means: any and all effective, moral, nonviolent means should be used. On the one hand, the Buddha within may be nurtured and the ego weakened through Buddhist practice of meditation and mindfulness. But obviously not everyone is prepared to sit down today and start meditating. Clearly, other means must be found. In some cases, the example of a dignified Buddhist monk chanting before an arms shipment

39. Monks leading Dhammayatra Walk III for the protection of Sankla Lake,
southern Thailand (May 1998)

facility may succeed in touching the compassionate depths of an onlooker. In other cases, to meet the "enemy" and discover some common interests may weaken the ego's fear. In many cases, to directly witness the suffering of another delivers a powerful jolt to the Buddha within, producing an immediate bond of concern transcending the gulf between self and other. These are only some ways; in principle, there are countless ways in which the Buddha within might be nurtured and/or the dominance and fear of the ego reduced. To the activist, all these approaches reinforce each other, and the door is wide open to the creation of new ways capable of addressing the condition of human beings today.

Protection of the Environment

Though less headline-catching than Buddhist work for peace, protection of the environment is a prominent element in Buddhist activism in the West, throughout Southeast Asia, in Tibet, Japan, and Sri Lanka. In Asia, this seems to be a matter of historical necessity. As predominantly Third World people, many Asian Buddhists have tended to live in rural areas, with lives based upon subsistence farming or fishing. Suddenly, the modern world has caught up with this way of life and is rapidly overpowering it. Perhaps the two most acute cases are Thailand and Tibet.

In Thailand, Buddhists struggle against overwhelming odds to protect Thailand's trees from deforestation so rapid that in the space of only forty years Thailand has been transformed from a country 80% covered by forests to one only 20% covered by forests. The consequences have been devastating, including drastically reduced harvests, tremendous loss of topsoil, both flooding and aridity, ruined water sources, and ruined farmers. In addition to

40. Monks "ordaining" the community forest in Yasothon Province, northeast Thailand.

educational, protest, and petitionary responses, a unique response to this problem from the Buddhist leadership has been the ordination of threatened trees. Knowing that it would be extremely difficult for a Theravāda Buddhist to harm a monk, monks "ordain" trees by wrapping them in the robes of a Buddhist monk and conducting the ordination ceremony that transforms the trees into monks, thereby protecting them.

With the Chinese invasion, Tibet has also suffered environmental devastation with widespread deforestation and the wholesale wiping out of the wildlife of Tibet, including the apparent elimination of many rare species. For example, in the forties an observer reported,

> Every few minutes, we would spot a bear or a hunting wolf, herds of musk deer, kyangs, gazelles, bighorn sheep, or foxes.

Observers today report walking 100 miles over three weeks and seeing nothing.[11] This sudden transformation has come about through Chinese policies of wildlife slaughter (organized hunts using machine guns on entire herds), destruction of habitat, overgrazing through the forcing of nomads into communes, and deforestation (the clear-cutting of seventy percent of Tibet's forests).[12]

The Dalai Lama himself has a very strong commitment to the protection of the natural world, both in Tibet and globally. His Holiness's birthday, July 6, is celebrated every year as "Tree Planting Day"; seeds blessed by His Holiness are available for this purpose. Virtually every Buddhist publication related to environmental issues carries an article by His Holiness. His famous Five Point Peace Plan, which lists the minimal essential requirements for a free Tibet, lists as point four, "Restoration and protection of Tibet's natural environment and the abandonment of China's use of Tibet for the production of nuclear weapons and dumping of nuclear wastes." The Dalai Lama has also proposed that the entire Tibetan plateau be made into a wildlife sanctuary and a demilitarized zone of peace.

Is there a basis in Buddhist spirituality for this concern to protect the environment, or is Buddhist environmental concern an accidental consequence of the fact that some countries facing environmental devastation are Buddhist, and thus inevitably draw on the Buddhist resources that happen to be available? Some of the resources found in Buddhism to support the protection of nature include the following. (1) The most basic principles of Buddhist ethics are teachings of compassion and nonviolence; these are directed most immediately at the human and nonhuman animal worlds, but are always understood to embrace all forms of life and life itself. In the modern world, these teachings are easily interpreted to apply also to the matrix of life, the Earth. For example, in his effort to popularize and interpret for the modern world the five lay precepts of Buddhism, Thich Nhat Hanh rewords the first precept (not to kill) as: "Aware of the suffering caused by the destruction of life, I vow to cultivate compassion and learn ways to protect the lives of people, animals, plants, and minerals."[13] (2) The most basic cosmological principles of Buddhism, conditioned origination and interdependence, undercut tendencies to see reality in terms of separate and independent units and instead emphasize the dependence of every phenomenon upon countless other phenomena. Buddhists in the habit of thinking in terms of interrelationships and mutual causation readily understand the basic principles of an ecological worldview; indeed, they are one and the same. (3) Buddhism espouses a Middle Path way of life in which enough is, simply, enough—countering consumerism, waste, the drive to possess, and greed.

The Sarvodaya Shramadana Movement, founded by A. T. Ariyaratne, may be the best proactive example of Buddhist environmental concerns in Asia. Sarvodaya is a vast, Buddhist-inspired Sri Lankan grassroots development movement. Free of the necessity of reacting to environmental threat and disaster, this group has the opportunity to promote development based upon Buddhist principles, rather than capitalist or Marxist ones. Sarvodaya takes as its first objective the "total well-being" of the people—moral, cultural, spiritual, and economic.[14] It understands the Ten Basic Needs of humans to be: water; food; housing; clothing; health care; communication; fuel; education; a clean, safe, beautiful environment; and a spiritual and cultural life. These needs are interactive, rather than hierarchical; thus the needs for food, housing, and clothing cannot cancel the need for a clean and beautiful environment and, as Macy notes, "attention to the nonmaterial needs sets the material ones in perspective, as the support but not the purpose of life." Consequently, Sarvodaya seeks ways to develop work opportunities in the villages, thus eliminating the need for young men to move to the cities in order to work, which in turn helps prevent the ills of rapid urbanization and allows people to live on a humane scale in the villages with their community rootedness, support, and security. Sarvodaya practices the kind of "Buddhist economics" espoused by E. F. Schumacher[15] in which sufficiency is plenty, low technology and small-scale projects are always preferred, decisions impinging upon the community are made locally by those who will be impacted by them, and nature is a partner to be conserved and sustained.

Human Rights and Well-Being

Some Buddhist leaders and scholars have asserted that the notion of human rights is a Western concept, alien to Buddhism and potentially harmful in its implications. Their concerns have to do with the individualism that they believe is embedded in the concept and the selfishness and adversarial stance of insisting upon "my/our rights." These concerns are valid from a Buddhist perspective. However, against these points must be weighed the facts that (1) Buddhist activist leaders today—especially those most experienced in communicating in the international community—readily explain their own work using human rights language; and (2) Buddhist social activists in the modern world are already working for human rights by the millions. Taking these facts together, we conclude that, while the concept of human rights and the phrase "human rights" may require some adjustment from a Buddhist perspective, still the social and political objectives sought by many Buddhist activists are the same kind of objectives sought by Western human rights activists.

Ambedkarites

The most outstanding example of a Buddhist movement working for human social equality is the group of ex-untouchable new Buddhist organizations inspired in India by Ambedkar. Dr. B. R. Ambedkar, born a Hindu untouchable, rose to become one of the great statesmen and founding fathers of the postcolonial state of India. Despite his status as major architect of the Constitution of India, he continued to be treated as an inferior being by many more ordinary mortals because of his low caste status. Repulsed by the immorality and incorrigibility of the caste system, Ambedkar vowed he would not die a Hindu. Citing its roots in India, its tolerance, and its principles of social equality, Ambedkar converted to Buddhism shortly before his death in a massive public ceremony in which millions of other untouchables joined with him in a great mass conversion. Since that time, millions more of former untouchables have converted to Buddhism, expressly to leave behind their status as socially contemptible and to gain a new level of dignity as human beings spiritually and socially equal to anyone. In practice, since almost all Buddhists in India are ex-untouchables, the Buddhist label has by no means always helped them to escape social ostracism and disdain. Nonetheless, converts to Buddhism report a surge in self-esteem as they take a step for themselves that rejects the status imposed upon them by the larger society. Thus, to convert is to repudiate the caste system, to repudiate institutionalized inequality, and to insist upon being regarded as worthy.

The Ambedkarite movement poses a challenge to Buddhism as deep as any challenge from within may be. Their Buddhism is social and political first, spiritual second. They largely reject the "blame the victim" mentality of traditional Buddhism that claims that one's suffering is caused by one's own actions in this and past lives and insist upon the social and institutional causes of the suffering they experience as *dalit*, "oppressed" people. They by and large are exclusively interested in the betterment of their lot here and now, and have little patience with delaying gratification to a little understood *nirvāṇa*. Buddhism here is so thoroughly transformed that some Buddhists wonder out loud if it is still Buddhism at all. Nonetheless, this movement is heavily supported by Buddhist organizations from both East and West who contribute both money and labor to support this effort to overcome the economic, social, psychological, and spiritual wounds caused by millennia of oppression. Understanding the elimination of suffering to be the goal of Buddhism, and further understanding all forms of suffering to be interrelated, so that someone cannot be expected to overcome spiritual suffering (by attaining enlightenment) while bearing gaping wounds caused by poverty, ill health, and self-loathing, these Buddhists do not hesitate to see this movement as well within the parameters of the way of understanding and compassion founded by the Buddha. Some *dalit* groups themselves are beginning to see matters this way as well, and are beginning to reach out to embrace traditional Buddhist spiritual practices as tools that can help to heal their wounds—while social action helps to prevent new wounds from being inflicted.

Political Activism

The other great category of human rights work within Buddhism is work for freedom from political oppression. Countless Buddhists have died in the course of this work in Vietnam and in Tibet. Many Vietnamese and Tibetan monks and nuns remain imprisoned or under house arrest in their countries for their insistence upon religious freedom, a religious freedom that has in each case powerful political implications: a sovereign state in Tibet, and an open society in both countries. Aung San Suu Kyi spent six years under house arrest in Burma after her overwhelming success in the 1990 election, which the dictatorial military regime refused to recognize. She continues to lead the struggle that has seen monks and students by the tens of thousands filling the streets calling for democracy and for the military rulers to step down. Sivaraksa stood trial in Thailand, accused of lèse-majesté—treason—for his many criticisms of the autocratic tendencies of the Thai rulers.

Acquitted, he pursues his activist endeavors, notably on the environmental and "anti-consumerism" fronts.

Why do Buddhists so readily engage in this kind of political activism? In some cases, the need to practice their religion freely has pitted them against those in power; in others, the sheer brutality of rulers has caused suffering so intense and widespread as to make insurrection inevitable. In face of oppressive governments, the Buddhist *saṅgha* may become the *de facto* leadership and representative of the people because it is the only leadership available. However, the assumption of such political responsibility is also an expression of Buddhist spirituality, insofar as the monks, nuns, and laypersons accept the challenge of the people's suffering because they feel the suffering of others as their own.

Buddhist political leadership tends to be limited to crisis situations. Typically, the Buddhist monastic leadership tends to have an aversion to politics. They dislike the adversarial stance and the accusing voice it seems to require; they abhor the self-assertion and self-praise that seems to be intrinsic to political life. During the war in Vietnam, for example, the Buddhist leadership for some time held real power in their hands, the power to bring down regimes and install sympathetic leaders, the power to mobilize the people by the tens of thousands and the millions, but they did not know what to do with that power and were very unsure whether they wanted it at all. They agonized over the pros and cons of founding a Buddhist political party until the moment of opportunity passed and they were crushed. Even Aung San Suu Kyi has disavowed all interest in politics and declared that her willingness to act as she has was purely a matter of accepting her duty as daughter of a Burmese national hero and serving the people, itself an anti-political motivation harmonious with Buddhist spirituality. The one exception to this anti-political pattern is the Japanese Nichiren sect Sōka Gakkai which founded an expressly political party, the Kōmeitō. This party has been quite successful in getting itself elected but quite unsuccessful in making any significant change in Japanese politics or society.

The Nobel Peace Prize is a measure of the importance of Buddhist work within the political realm. Two Buddhist leaders have been awarded the Nobel Peace Prize in recent years, the Dalai Lama in 1989 and Aung San Suu Kyi in 1991. In addition, Maha Ghosananda, Sulak Sivaraksa, and Thich Nhat Hanh have all been nominated for the Prize. Considering how few Buddhists there are in the world, this represents vastly disproportionate peace leadership offered to the global community by Buddhists. It is, of course, an expression of the foundational role played by nonviolence in Buddhist spirituality and ethics. The spiritual tenor of Buddhist social activism is also having a disproportionate impact in global circles of nonviolent social activism, both interfaith and sectarian. Many activists cite the Buddhist emphasis upon the cultivation of spirituality—the notion that in order to "make peace" a person must "be peace"—as a new and vital contribution to the art of peacemaking.[16]

Women's Issues

A profound challenge to the *status quo* of institutional Buddhism has come from within, from Buddhist women. Buddhist women's challenges are basically two: (1) the challenge to make major improvements in the status of Buddhist nuns, including the reestablishment of the nuns' order in countries where it has died out; and (2) challenges from Western Buddhist feminists to rethink and reform all aspects of Buddhist thought, practice, and institutional life that partake of, or support, patriarchal thought or mores.

Concern about the status of Buddhist nuns, of course, has its roots in long-standing Buddhist institutionalization of nuns as inferior to monks. For millennia, the facilities, training, and popular support offered nuns has been far inferior to that offered monks. Today, women who want to ordain as nuns in Theravāda or Tibetan lineages cannot do so since, according to the rules of the Buddhist order, the ordination process requires existing nuns to ordain new nuns, and the nuns' order has died out in those countries. In Theravāda countries and in Tibet, women can only receive the vows of a novice, a situation that has led to the development of various quasi-nun categories. While their status varies from country to country, in many countries nuns and quasi-nuns fail to get the material support, the education, or the training they need.

In response to this situation, a new organization, "Sakyadhītā: International Association of Buddhist Women" ("Sakyadhītā" means "Daughters of the Buddha") was formed in 1987 at the first International Conference of Buddhist Nuns, to address the needs and concerns of Buddhist nuns and quasi-nuns. The progressive and activist wings of the male Buddhist world have joined with these women to research the *Vinaya*, the monastic rule, to find a way to restore the Theravāda and Tibetan nuns' orders. Meanwhile, some women simply ordain in an existing order and then return to practice in their own line. Simultaneously, the nuns and quasi-nuns continue to press for reforms in their support, education, and training, which are quite urgently needed in some countries.

Curiously enough, one group of quasi-nuns has little interest in ordaining as traditional nuns. In Sri Lanka, the *dasa sil matavo*, or "ten precept women," hold a status in between layperson and nun. They combine personal meditation practices for their own spiritual development with public service activities such as teaching, counseling, ministering to the sick, chanting Buddhist scriptures, and performing ceremonies for the laity.[17] Few of these women are interested in being placed under the control and supervision of the monks as they would be, by monastic rule, if they were ordained as nuns. Most of them prefer the situation they have at present, in which they train and practice independently of the monks. Some of Thailand's *mai ji* feel the same.

Two prominent groups of reform Buddhists have simply proceeded to directly institutionalize equality for women. In Taiwan, the large reformist temple Fo Kuang Shan provides equal opportunities for training and leadership to men and women. Men's and women's abilities are equally expressed in the temple's many activities, including extensive educational programs (preschool through high school, plus four Buddhist colleges), free medical clinics, homes for children and the elderly, a publishing house, wildlife preservation areas, prison visitation, and lecturing on Buddhist teachings in factories and on radio and television. Women, both nuns and laypersons, are very visible in these activities. Similarly, the reformist Wŏn Buddhist sect of Korea trains men and women equally to serve as priests. Female priests have equal status with male and can be seen independently establishing branch temples in Korea and wherever expatriate Koreans can be found. In Korea, their social services are very similar to those of the Fo Kuang Shan. In both of these dynamic and growing sects, women are given a thorough education, are encouraged to develop themselves spiritually, are given opportunity for extensive and varied leadership in religious work *per se* and in social services, and are very highly respected by the communities they serve.

Meanwhile, from the West comes the challenge of Western feminist women. Embracing Buddhism for its promise of spiritual liberation, they are very prepared to challenge any oppressive qualities or practices they find therein. Among other things, Western feminists have (1) sought out and highlighted aspects of Buddhist teachings, history, and training that might be especially helpful for women, and subjected to criticism aspects of Buddhism that might be harmful to women; (2) challenged hierarchical patterns of authority within the administration of practice centers, while leaving alone, for the most part, the spiritual authority of the teacher; (3) exposed the abuse of power by some male teachers, including sexual relations between male teachers and female students; these exposures have torn some practice centers apart and seen some teachers asked to leave by the members of their centers; (4) challenged misogynist attitudes when found among more conservative monks and in some cases established offshoot centers to elude control by such monks.

The West has also seen the emergence of impressive numbers of full-fledged female teachers, often with new emphases and creative approaches. For example, Joko Beck teaches an "everyday Zen" in which students take as the themes of their practice such things as love, work, emotions, and family life. Toni Packer teaches a Zen that attempts to tear away all labels and "isms," including the Zen label, all words and institutions that divide people, and focuses entirely on attending to the present moment. These are two examples of women who, while not labeling themselves as feminist, powerfully express the concerns of feminist Buddhist spirituality. Toni Packer rejects a traditional Buddhism in which "spirituality and ordinary existence are seen as antithetical to each other" and seeks a spirituality that can speak to women's concerns, one in which "housework, meditation, business, study, childcare, retreat, marriage, celibacy—all the dichotomies and hierarchies that seemed so clear—vanish." In such a spirituality, "no longer will a man who spends most of his life alone in caves attaining esoteric states of mind be regarded as so ideal," but "nor for that matter will a woman who raises many children without ever developing herself."[18] In quest of a spirituality that brings to ordinary life the conditions of calm, mindfulness, compassion, and wisdom that have traditionally been developed by meditation in retreat from ordinary life, feminist Buddhists seek to integrate their two deepest commitments: to spiritual self-development and to loving relationships lived out in the mundane sphere.

American Buddhist Activism

The Buddhist Peace Fellowship

The Buddhist Peace Fellowship is a network of American Buddhist social activists. The following sample of activities reported in the pages of the BPF journal will provide an idea of the concerns and ingenuity of American Buddhist activists:

1. "Making Peace with Animals" finds homes for retired racing greyhounds that would otherwise be destroyed or sold to labs;

2. San Francisco Buddhists open the Maitri AIDS Hospice in the heart of San Francisco's gay community, offering care to terminally ill people with AIDS and support to their family and friends, including meditation training as a skill for responding to life-threatening illness;

3. "Urban Agriculture for Violence Prevention" attempts to make a difference in the lives of inner-city youth through gardening and human presence;

4. Zen master Bernie Glassman and followers provide employment, permanent housing, and child care for homeless families, thereby offering them the opportunity to help themselves; he also offers weeklong "street retreats" in New York's bowery in which participants live for several days on the streets and experience homelessness, poverty, hunger, and begging;

5. anti-death penalty work emerges as an expression of the first lay precept, no killing;

6. Veteran's Day anti-gun vigils are held at gun stores;

7. the "Nuclear Guardianship Project" plans for long-term citizen surveillance of nuclear wastes; and

8. work with Asian refugee communities is widespread. Beyond such activities (which proliferate creatively and endlessly), many American Buddhists have taken the perspectives of activist Buddhism to heart and seek to express them daily in their interactions with others, their choice of vocation, their determination to live an environmentally sound lifestyle, and so forth.

The Naropa Institute Program in Engaged Buddhism

Beginning in 1995, Naropa Institute (a Buddhist-inspired college) is offering a new "Engaged Buddhism" concentration within its Master of Arts degree program in Buddhist Studies.[19] The program draws upon thought basic to Engaged Buddhism, seeking to prepare students to "address social issues in a manner which recognizes the interdependence of all things, such that the suffering of others is also one's own suffering, and the violence of others is also one's own violence." The program offers training that focuses on "meditation practice, awareness of suffering [see Bernie Glassman], ability to exchange self for other [see Thich Nhat Hanh], and appreciation of obstacles as opportunity [see the Dalai Lama]." This program well expresses the basic premises of Engaged Buddhism: social action requires the personal preparation of meditation, which yields calm, insight, and compassion; action lacking in such underlying personal peace will never be able to "make peace."

At the same time, personal spiritual development breaks down the boundaries between self and other and will thus naturally be expressed in action to enhance the well-being of others, which may be formalized in social service work or other forms. It should be noted that while this program is unique for the West, its heritage may clearly be seen in the School of Youth for Social Service, founded by Thich Nhat Hanh in the 1960s in Vietnam to train Buddhist social workers.

Conclusion

Twentieth-century Buddhist social activism is unprecedented as a Buddhist phenomenon. While all the needful spiritual and ethical foundations for such activism have always been present in Buddhism, it required phenomena of our time—Western liberal social analysis, Gandhi, acute and chronic crises—to bring these seeds to fruition.[20] But while this movement is unprecedented, it is so geographically widespread, so appealing to the millions upon millions of ordinary Buddhists who have embraced it in one form or another, indeed so inevitable as a phenomenon of the modern world, that it is certain to have pervasive and lasting influence on Buddhism as the latter strives to meet the challenges of the Western world and of modernity in the coming century.

Buddhist social activism, then, represents a major change in Buddhism. But is Buddhist spirituality itself changed in this movement? "Traditional" Buddhist spirituality already embraces vast diversity. Insofar as what we have here manifests the spirituality of selflessness, compassion, calm, and insight, it cannot be regarded as new. Rather, it should be regarded as a natural evolution of its heritage. Perhaps the greatest challenges to Buddhist spirituality in this movement come from the Ambedkarite groups and Western feminists, both of which question whether there may be something deficient in the traditional values of Buddhist spirituality themselves. But Buddhist spirituality is patient and pragmatic, highly tolerant of change and diversity. Buddhists are happy to nurture the questioning and experimentation in which these groups are engaged. Indeed, they see this seeking itself as a form of Buddhist spirituality and are entirely confident of the outcome.

Notes

1. "An Open Letter from The Network For Western Buddhist Teachers," *Turning Wheel: Journal of the Buddhist Peace Fellowship* (Summer, 1993) 40.

2. Thich Nhat Hanh in Daniel Berrigan and Thich Nhat Hanh, *The Raft is Not the Shore: Conversations Toward a Buddhist/Christian Awareness* (Boston: Beacon Press, 1975) 99.

3. All quotations and other information on Abbot Nan are taken from "A Buddhist Approach to Fighting Rural Poverty," by Sanitsuda Ekachai, March 11, 1989, distributed by the International Network of Engaged Buddhists, P.O. Box 1, Ongharak Nakhorn Nayok 26120 Thailand.

4. See Joanna Macy, *Dharma and Development: Religion as Resource in the Sarvodaya Self-Help Movement*, Revised Edition (West Hartford, CT: Kumarian Press, 1983, 1985).

5. There have also been right-wing responses, such as Japanese Buddhist churches' support for Japanese imperialism during World War II, but these things fall outside the scope of this essay.

6. Information on Cambodia is taken from "Editor's Introduction," *Step by Step* by Maha Ghosananda, edited by Jane Sharada Mahoney and Philip Edmonds (Berkeley: Parallax Press, 1992) 3–23.

7. "Preface" by Jack Kornfield in Maha Ghosananda, *Step by Step*.

8. For details, see George McT. Kahin, *Intervention: How America Became Involved in Vietnam* (New York: Alfred A. Knopf, 1986).

9. Thich Nhat Hanh, cited in James H. Forest, *The Unified Buddhist Church of Vietnam: Fifteen Years for Reconciliation* (International Fellowship of Reconciliation, published by Hof van Sonoy, the Netherlands, 1978) 12.

10. His Holiness the Dalai Lama XIV, "The Principle of Universal Responsibility" (pamphlet) (New York: Potala Publications, no date), no pagination.

11. Galen Rowell, "The Agony of Tibet," *Buddhist Peace Fellowship: Newsletter of the Buddhist Peace Fellowship* (Spring, 1990) 10; reprinted from *Greenpeace Magazine* 15:2 (March/April, 1990).

12. Rowell, "The Agony of Tibet," and Christine Keyser, "Endangered Tibet," *Buddhist Peace Fellowship* (Fall, 1990) 28.

13. Thich Nhat Hanh, *For a Future to Be Possible: Commentaries on the Five Wonderful Precepts*. (Berkeley: Parallax Press, 1993) 13.

14. This paragraph draws directly from Macy, esp. 27, 45–47.

15. E. F. Schumacher, *Small Is Beautiful* (New York: Harper and Row, 1973).

16. Thich Nhat Hanh's *Being Peace* (Berkeley: Parallax Press, 1987) is a widely-read modern classic.

17. On the *dasa sil matavo*, see Nancy J. Barnes, "Buddhist Women and the Nuns' Order in Asia," in Christopher L. Queen and Sallie B. King, *Engaged Buddhism: Buddhist Liberation Movements in Asia* (Albany, NY: SUNY Press, 1996).

18. All quotations in this paragraph from Rita M. Gross, "Buddhism After Patriarchy?" in Paula M. Cooey, William R. Eakin and Jay B. McDaniel, eds., *After Patriarchy: Feminist Transformations of the World Religions* (Maryknoll: Orbis Books, 1991) 79, 80, 85.

19. Information on this program comes directly from Naropa Institute and their promotional flyers.

20. There is one exception to this generalization: the large Japanese lay organizations Risshō Kōseikai and Sōka Gakkai find their inspiration for activism in Nichiren, a *sui generis* Buddhist reformer of the thirteenth century.

Bibliography

Books

Aitken, Robert. *The Mind of Clover: Essays in Zen Buddhist Ethics*. San Francisco: North Point Press, 1984.

Ambedkar, B. R. *The Buddha and His Dhamma*. Bombay: People's Education Society, 1984.

Ariyaratne, A. T. *In Search of Development: The Sarvodaya Movement's Effort to Harmonize Tradition with Change*. Moratuwa, Sri Lanka: Sarvodaya Press, 1982.

Buddhadasa, Bhikkhu. *Dhammic Socialism*. Edited by Donald Swearer. Bangkok: Komol Kimtong Foundation, 1986.

Dalai Lama. *The World of Tibetan Buddhism* (Part II: An Altruistic Outlook and Way of Life). Translated, edited, and annotated by Geshe Thupten Jinpa. Boston: Wisdom Publications, 1995.

Eppsteiner, Fred, ed. *The Path of Compassion: Writings on Socially Engaged Buddhism*. Berkeley: Parallax Press, 1985, 1988.

Jones, Ken. *The Social Face of Buddhism*. London: Wisdom Publications, 1989.

Kabilsingh, Chatsumarn. *Thai Women in Buddhism*. Berkeley: Parallax Press, 1991.

Kraft, Kenneth, ed. *Inner Peace, World Peace: Essays on Buddhism and Nonviolence*. Albany: SUNY Press, 1992.

Macy, Joanna. *Dharma and Development: Religion as Resource in the Sarvodaya Self-Help Movement*, Revised Edition. Introduction by A.T. Ariyaratne. West Hartford: Kumarian Press, 1983, 1985.

Nhat Hanh, Thich. *Vietnam: Lotus in a Sea of Fire*. New York: Hill and Wang, 1967.

———— *Love in Action: Writings on Nonviolent Social Change*. Foreword by Daniel Berrigan. Berkeley: Parallax Press, 1993.

Queen, Christopher L. and Sallie B. King, eds. *Engaged Buddhism: Buddhist Liberation Movements in Asia*. Albany: SUNY Press 1996.

Rahula, Walpola. *The Heritage of the Bhikkhu: A Short History of the Bhikkhu in Educational, Cultural, Social and Political Life*. New York: Grove Press, 1974. (First published 1946)

Sangharakshita (Dennis P. E. Lingwood). *Ambedkar and Buddhism*. Glasgow: Windhorse Publications, 1986.

Sivaraksa, Sulak. *Seeds of Peace: A Buddhist Vision for Renewing Society*. Foreword by the Dalai Lama. Preface by Thich Nhat Hanh. Berkeley: Parallax Press, 1992.

Suu Kyi, Aung San. *Freedom from Fear*. Edited by Michael Aris. London and New York: Penguin Books, 1991.

Tsomo, Karma Lekshe, ed. *Sakyadhītā: Daughters of the Buddha*. Ithaca: Snow Lion Publications, 1988.

Journals

Newsletter on International Buddhist Women's Activities, c/o Dr. Chatsumarn Kabilsingh, Faculty of Liberal Arts, Thammasat University, Bangkok, Thailand 10200.

Turning Wheel: Journal of the Buddhist Peace Fellowship, c/o Buddhist Peace Fellowship, P.O. Box 4650, Berkeley, CA 97404.

31

Theravāda Spirituality
in the West

EGIL FRONSDAL

WHILE WESTERN contact and study of the Theravāda tradition goes back to the earliest Christian missionaries in Sri Lanka in the sixteenth century and to European scholars in the early nineteenth century, the beginning of popular Western interest in and inspiration from Southeast Asian Buddhism began around 1870. Since that time, there have been two peaks in this interest, which we may take up in turn.

In the first, from 1870 to 1912, European and American intellectuals found in the early Buddhist texts an attractive alternative to Western religious beliefs.

The second, which took place a century later in the period from 1970 to the present, involved two separate demographic groups: one composed predominantly of Caucasians, the other of Southeast Asian immigrants. The former group is organized around specific Theravāda meditation practices, sometimes completely divorced from their doctrinal and religious context. The latter have built numerous temples in which the Theravāda Buddhism of their home countries is replicated. These traditional temples have had little impact outside of their respective ethnic constituencies.

With the exception of the partially Westernized Sri Lankan missionary Anagārika Dharmapāla (1864–1933), the introduction of Theravāda Buddhism has mainly been due to the efforts of Westerners. In the process of selection, translation, and adaptation, these Westerners have tended to define the tradition around their own concerns. What is most fascinating about this process is the fact that the twentieth-century Theravāda Buddhism that many Westerners are encountering in Southeast Asia has been profoundly changed by the nineteenth-century Asian contact with the West and with Western interpretations of Buddhism.

1873–1912

The first popular wave of Western interest in Buddhism occurred during the last quarter of the nineteenth century among educated middle- and upper-class Europeans and Americans. Offering for many an attractive alternative and contrast to Christianity, Buddhism played an important part in the public dialogue on religion that characterized much of the intellectual history of the times. During this period, articles on Buddhism, both favorable and critical, frequently appeared in popular English and American magazines at a rate that has not been matched since. The interest was sparked in 1879 by the publication of Sir Edwin Arnold's (1832–1904) epic poem *The Light of Asia*. The book became a best-seller that ran to more than one hundred reprints in England and the United States, not to mention numerous translations in other languages. It gave Western readers a biography of the Buddha that fitted in well with the humanistic and rational currents of Victorian thought. The presence of Buddhists at the 1893 World Parliament of Religions in Chicago further stimulated popular interest in Buddhism in the United States.

This primarily intellectual interest in Buddhism had little contact with the living spirituality of contemporary Asian Buddhists. In fact, the general consensus among the European scholars of Buddhism, who did much to define the late-nineteenth-century Western view of Buddhism, was that "pure" and "original" Buddhism was to be found in the earliest layers of the Pāli Canon before the tradition was contaminated by the popular, supernatural, and superstitious overlays of later centuries. Such influential books as T. W. Rhys Davids's *Buddhism* (1878) and Hermann Oldenberg's stillread *Buddha: Sein Leben, Seine Lehre, Seine Gemeinde* (1881; published in English as *The Buddha: His Life, His Doctrine, His Community*) did much to introduce a Western audience to a rational and humanistic view of the Buddha and his teachings. The preference given to "original" Buddhism over the living spirituality of the East resulted in great scholarly efforts at collecting, editing, printing, translating, and studying the Pāli canon. In 1881 Rhys Davids founded in London the Pāli Text Society, which by 1930 had succeeded in publishing most of the Pāli canon both in romanized Pāli editions and in English translations. The availability of these texts in English and other European languages contributed to a long-standing preference in Europe for the Theravāda scriptures over the literature of other Buddhist traditions. The contemporary Theravāda tradition, however, was seen as the custodian of these texts, not their authoritative interpreter.

This scholarship had an impact on modernist reform movements within the Theravāda tradition in Southeast Asia in that it encouraged a "return to the origins" through revising the tradition according to the teachings found in the Tripiṭaka, the three divisions of the Scriptural Canon.[1] In addition, the translation of the Pāli canon into English had a major impact on educated Southeast Asian Buddhists by making the sacred texts available to a wider audience than ever before. Only then were they translated into modern Southeast Asian languages. The availability of these translations did much to break the religious monopoly of the monks and to stimulate the rapid growth of lay Buddhist movements in Sri Lanka and Burma.

In the famous "Great Debate of Pānadura" between the monk Mohotti-vatte Gunānanda (1826–1890) and Christian missionaries in Sri Lanka in 1873, the well-educated Gunānanda was perceived as soundly refuting the Christians, reversing several decades of defeat at their hands. This event stimulated a resurgence of Buddhism in Sri Lanka, and accounts of it in American newspapers caught the attention of Colonel Henry Steele Olcott (1832–1907) and Madame Blavatsky (1831–1891), who were subsequent-ly to found the Theosophical Society. After corresponding with Gunānanda, they traveled to Sri Lanka on May 17, 1880, a date that marks the begin-ning of the modern Buddhist revival there. On May 25th, before a large audience, they participated in the Theravāda ceremony of taking the triple refuge and the five lay precepts. They were among the earliest, if not in fact the first, Westerners to formally declare themselves Buddhists in this solemn way.

The Theosophists, in addition to introducing their own esoteric under-standing of Buddhism to the West, played an important role in the mod-ern "reformation" of Buddhism in Sri Lanka and to a lesser degree other Asian countries. Olcott initiated an education movement that eventually created some four hundred Buddhist grade schools throughout Sri Lanka. On the international front, he attempted to unite the various Buddhist tra-ditions in a single association, designing a flag that is still recognized and flown as the international flag of Buddhism. On a visit to Japan in 1888 he received an enthusiastic welcome for his efforts on behalf of Asian Bud-dhists in their struggle with the challenges of Christianity, Western ration-alism, and science.

A young Sri Lankan disciple of Olcott and Blavatsky, Don David Hewav-itarne (1864–1933), was directed by Blavatsky to devote himself to his native Theravāda religion. Remaining a celibate layman and adopting the innovative religious title of Anagārika (homeless one) and the name Dharmapāla (guardian of the Dharma), he went on to become one of the most important reformers of modern Sri Lankan Buddhism. Through his trips to the United States and Europe Dharmapāla became the most influential Theravāda Buddhist missionary in the West. In 1893 he was one of the more charismatic speakers (second perhaps only to Swami Vivekananda) at the World Parliament of Religions in Chicago. There he met the publisher Paul Carus, who invited him back to the United States in 1897, at which time he opened an American branch of the Maha Bodhi Society, an international organization aimed at restoring the site of Buddha's enlightenment in Bodh Gayā. Individual Americans had declared themselves Buddhist before, but this was the first formal Buddhist organization in the West.

In 1898 an Englishman, Gordon Douglas, was ordained in Sri Lanka, becoming the first Westerner to join the traditional Buddhist monastic community. Little is known about Douglas, as he is often overlooked in historical accounts of modern Western Buddhism. He seems to have stayed in Asia and to have had little influence on the development of Buddhism in the West. Of more historical consequence was the work of Alan Bennet (1872–1923), the second Englishman to receive Theravāda ordination. Inspired by both *The Light of Asia* and Theosophy, Bennet spent three years studying Buddhism in Sri Lanka. Then, in 1902, he was ordained in Burma under the name of Ananda Metteya. Within the year he had formed the Buddhasasana Samagama (International Buddhist Society) for the purpose of propagating Buddhism in Europe. In 1908 he traveled to England together with three Burmese monks and was received by the Buddhist Society of Great Britain and Ireland. The Society, founded in 1907, was the first Buddhist association in England and was presided over by T. W. Rhys Davids. Its primary focus was the Theravāda tradition with its perceived atheism and ethic of nonviolence and renunciation. Partly because of ill health, Ananda Metteya had little success as a missionary, and within a year of his death in 1923 the Buddhist Society ceased to exist.

German interest in Theravāda Buddhism in the later nineteenth century was stimulated by Arthur Schopenhauer's (1788–1860) high regard for Buddhism. The translations of much of the Pāli Canon by Karl Eugen Neumann (1865–1915) did much to advance knowledge of Buddhism in Germany. Neumann was inspired by Schopenhauer to study both Pāli and Sanskrit, and in 1894 visited Sri Lanka for the first time.

In 1903 Karl Seidenstuecker founded the first Buddhist society in Germany, and in 1906 Germany hosted the first Buddhist Congress in Europe. In 1904 the German violinist Anton Geuth (1878–1957) was ordained in Sri Lanka and given the name Nyanatiloka. He subsequently founded a monastery in Sri Lanka on Polgasduwa Island, which has since housed many Western monks, several of whom were first-rate scholars. These scholar-monks produced a number of influential translations and studies. The *Visuddhimagga* (The path of purification) was translated into German by Nyanatiloka and into English by the British monk Ñāṇamoli (Osbert Moore, 1905–1960). The German monk Nyanaponika (Siegmund Feniger; 1901–1994) wrote on the practice of mindfulness as taught in the *Satipaṭṭhāna Sutta*. In 1950 he published *Satipaṭṭhāna, Der Heilsweg buddhistischer Geistesschulung*, and in 1954 the widely used English book *The Heart of Buddhist Meditation* (revised 1962).

1920–1970

The five decades between 1920 and 1970 saw little change in Theravāda Buddhism in the West. Owing to the influence of D. T. Suzuki, interest in Southeast Asian Buddhism was eclipsed by a fascination for the Mahāyāna tradition, especially in the United States. Even in England, which had had a long relationship with Sri Lanka and Burma, involvement with Theravāda spirituality grew slowly during this period, despite numerous visits by Buddhist missionary monks, some of whom were gifted scholars. The first English *vihāra*, or temple, was established by Sri Lankan monks in 1938. English interest in Buddhism tended to be eclectic and ecumenical rather than to align itself with any particular sect. After the Buddhist Society of England and Ireland closed in 1924, it was "absorbed" into the Buddhist Lodge of the Theosophical Society, which was then renamed the Buddhist Society in 1926. As the most important vehicle for Buddhism in England for the next forty years, the Buddhist Society fostered interest in all forms of Asian Buddhism.[2]

In contrast, the German interest in Buddhism during this time remained predominantly Theravāda in orientation. The writings of the Schopenhauer-inspired Paul Dahlke (1865–1928) and Georg Grimm (1868–1945) did much to support the German Buddhist movement. But differences of opinion between these two about the Buddhist teaching of no-self split the German Buddhist community. Grimm argued that the doctrine of *anattā* pertained only to the empirical world and that the Buddha believed in an eternal and transcendental soul. Dahlke had visited Sri Lanka in 1900 and doctrinally aligned himself closely with the modernist Buddhist reform movement there. Basing his position on the Pāli Canon, he argued in favor of the orthodox Theravāda understanding of no-self as denying the existence of any eternal soul. Though most German Buddhists sided with Dahlke, the small Buddhist association started by Grimm in 1921 still survives. In 1926 Dahlke completed construction of Das Buddhistische Haus in Berlin, which to this day houses Sri Lankan monks. It is the oldest surviving Theravāda structure in the West.

1970 to the Present

Two developments have marked the rapid Western growth of the Theravāda tradition in recent decades: a growing involvement in Theravāda meditation practices by Westerners, and the arrival of many Southeast Asian immigrants in the United States and to a lesser degree England. There are now about 175 ethnic Theravāda temples in the West, most of which have at least one Southeast Asian monk in residence. Serving as ethnic, cultural, and religious centers for their communities, few of these temples have made any effort to reach out beyond their ethnic constituents, and as a result have had little impact beyond these communities. Furthermore, as these temples serve to maintain for their members the religio-cultural practices and identities associated with their home countries, there tends to be little contact among Thai, Burmese, and Sri Lankan temples in the West.

During the late 1950s and 1960s there was little significant change. The first American *vihāra* was built in 1966 by Sri Lankans in Washington, D.C. Meanwhile, many Europeans, Americans, Australians, and New Zealanders were becoming familiar with the Theravāda tradition in Southeast Asia. Some were Americans in Thailand and Vietnam with the Peace Corps or on military assignment; others were young travelers searching for alternatives to Western cultural norms and worldviews. Some of them immersed themselves deeply enough in the Theravāda tradition, both as monastics and as lay people, to be able to return to the West as meditation teachers. Whereas Tibetan and Zen Buddhism was introduced to the West mainly by Asian teachers, most of them monastics, the modern importation of Theravāda practice is largely the work of these Westerners who returned from Asia as lay teachers. As a result, the movement has remained almost entirely a lay movement, which has led it in directions dramatically different from those of the monastic-centered forms of Theravāda Buddhism that predominate in Asia. Even Dhiravamsa and Achaan Sobin, two of the more successful Thai meditation teachers in the West, disrobed soon after coming to England and America.

Of the large repertoire of meditation practices found in Theravāda Buddhism, practice in the West is dominated by forms of *vipassanā*, a practice based on the *Satipaṭṭhāna Sutta* (The discourse on the four foundations of mindfulness), and often known in English as "insight meditation" or simply "mindfulness." The preference given to this practice reflects its great popularity in Southeast Asia after its "rediscovery" at the end of the nine-teenth century. In Sri Lanka the resurgence in meditation practice is attributed to Anagārika Dharmapāla, who in 1892 came across an old Sinhalese med-itation manual, *Manual of a Mystic* (English translation by F. L. Woodward, 1906), dating back one or two centuries. Since the practice of meditation seemed to have largely disappeared in Sri Lanka, Dharmapāla turned to this manual, the *Visuddhimagga*, and the *Satipaṭṭhāna Sutta* for guidance. His efforts, together with the reissuance of the texts in modern translations, did much to foster interest in meditation in Sri Lanka. In Burma, where medi-tation practice had also come to the brink of extinction, the revitalization of meditation may be traced to the efforts of U Nārada (also known as Min-gun Jetawun Sayadaw, 1868–1954) and Ledi Sayadaw (1846–1923), both of whom championed the practice of *vipassanā* based on the *Satipaṭṭhāna Sutta*. In each of these countries, what had previously been thought the reserve of monastics was now being opened up to lay participation.

The most significant figure for the modern *vipassanā* movement in South-east Asia was the Burmese Monk Mahāsi Sayadaw (also known as U Sob-hana, 1904–1982). In 1938 he began teaching a streamlined and system-atic style of *vipassanā* meditation that involves the careful labeling of one's experience together with a high level of sustained concentration known as "momentary concentration" *(khaṇika samādhi)*. A unique feature of his method is that it dispenses with the traditional preliminary practices of con-centration or tranquilization *(śamatha,* involving fixed concentration or *appanā samādhi)*. A practitioner begins immediately with *vipassanā* practice, the idea being that until one attains the first stage of sainthood (stream entry, *sotāpatti)* the practice of dedicated mindfulness contains within it whatever level of concentration is needed. After stream entry, however, Mahāsi would sometimes teach concentration practices based on *mettā*, or loving-kindness, in order to prepare the practitioner for further deepening of the meditation practice.[3]

As the head of a large lay-organized meditation center in Rangoon (known now as the Mahāsi Sāsana Yeiktha) from 1949 to his death in 1982, Mahāsi Sayadaw oversaw the explosive growth in popularity of his medita-tion technique throughout Southeast Asia and eventually in the West.[4] By 1985 the center had seen the establishment of over three hundred branches throughout Burma. Mahāsi-trained Burmese monks traveled to Sri Lanka in the 1950s and to Thailand in the 1960s, popularizing *vipassanā* practice in general and the Mahāsi technique in particular. There are now over two hundred Mahāsi-inspired meditation centers (Thai, *samnak vipassanā)* in Thailand, a few of which have attracted numbers of Westerners.

By 1972, Westerners who had studied at the Mahāsi Center in Rangoon or who had trained in Bodh Gayā, India, under Anagārika Munindra, an Indian student of Mahāsi Sayadaw, had begun teaching *vipassanā* in the West. The two teachers who have done most to popularize this practice in the United States and Europe are Joseph Goldstein and Jack Kornfield. By 1976 they had established, together with Sharon Salzburg and Jacqueline Mandell, the Insight Meditation Society (IMS), a large meditation center in Barre, Massachusetts, that attracts students from all over the Western world. IMS is particularly known for an annual "three-month course" held every autumn for about ninety participants. This is an intensive retreat with twelve to fifteen hours of meditation a day. In 1987 Jack Kornfield, with three other Western teachers, cofounded Spirit Rock, a sister center to IMS, in Marin County, California. By the mid-1980s these teachers were in turn training other Western teachers, some of whom had never practiced in Asia. While the growth of Zen and Tibetan Buddhism in the United States has slowed down in the 1980s and early 1990s, thanks to the loosely knit Insight Meditation movement, Theravāda Buddhism has enjoyed great success. The large numbers of people attracted to the practice and the indirect cultural influence it has had attest to the fact.[5]

By conservative estimates, about 100,000 Westerners have been involved in *vipassanā* meditation retreats between 1964 and 1994, with about 20,000 people attending one-day to three-month retreats in 1994.[6] Most of this has only minimal connection with the Theravāda tradition, as the participants focus on the practice rather than on its historical origins. They think of themselves as *vipassanā* students rather than as students or followers of Theravāda Buddhism. Indeed, the *vipassanā* resurgence in Southeast Asia itself has shifted the emphasis away from the doctrinal, ritual, faith, and monastic elements of Theravāda Buddhism to personal insight and transformative experiences of *nibbāna* (awakening). Of course, the wider Theravāda context that is taken for granted there is absent in the West, where the practice of meditation has tended to be self-contained. Furthermore, teachers like Goldstein and Kornfield have consciously attempted to present mindfulness practice in a relatively nonsectarian manner so to make it available even to those who have no interest in Buddhism as such.

A second *vipassanā* tradition that has taken root in the West stems from the unique practice of the Burmese lay meditation teacher U Ba Khin (1899–1971). Here the focus is mainly on cultivating deep concentration through mindfulness of body sensations. To this end, U Ba Khin has developed a practice known as "body sweeping," in which attention is systematically directed throughout the body. As in the Mahāsi tradition, the practice relies on intensive retreats with a schedule of at least fourteen hours of meditation a day. Aiming for transformative meditation experience, the practice is taught independently of much of the cultural and ritual context of Theravāda Buddhism. The most successful international teacher of this practice is the Indian businessman Satya Narayan Goenka (1924–), who, like Munindra, returned from Burma to India in the late 1960s to teach *vipassanā*. Goenka's success in attracting Western students in India led him to open a number of meditation centers in the United States and England. The first of these, the Vipassana Meditation Center, opened in 1982 in Shelburne Falls, Massachusetts. Aside from Goenka there are a few Western disciples of U Ba Khin teaching in the West, among them Ruth Dennison, the material elder of the American *vipassanā* community who has integrated sensory awareness and movement exercises into her retreats.

The Monastic Sangha in the West

While the Mahāsi and U Ba Khin traditions in the West have had a decidedly lay orientation, there have been some stirrings of interest in Theravāda monasticism, the traditional center of Theravāda spirituality. The most viable monastic communities in the West are in England under the direction of Achaan Sumedho (Robert Jackman, 1934–), an American disciple of the Northeast Thai forest monk Achaan Chah (1918–1992). Though Westerners have been ordained throughout Southeast Asia, the biggest concentration of Western monks was found studying under Achaan Chah during the period from the late 1960s through the 1980s. In contrast to the emphasis on intensive meditation retreat in the Burmese *vipassanā* movements, Achaan Chah stressed a more integrated practice centered on the disciplined life of the forest monk. Formal meditation was not ignored, but mindfulness—especially of one's thoughts and mental states—throughout daily activities was his main practice. He taught his monks to strengthen their mindfulness by adhering strictly to the *Vinaya* code.

In 1977 Achaan Chah instructed Achaan Sumedho, his senior Western student, to move to England. Achaan Sumedho attracted many other Westerners who had either been ordained in Asia or whom he ordained in England. In 1979 he founded Chithurst monastery in West Sussex, and by 1990 he had founded three other monastic centers, including Amaravati just north of London, and was making plans, along with more than sixty monks and more than twenty nuns in these four centers, to start additional monastic communities in Switzerland, Italy, and the United States. Although a number of senior monks have disrobed and left his centers in recent years,

Sumedho seems to have established the first viable monastic community in the West. Insofar as the presence of a monastic community is traditionally taken to be the criterion for the arrival of Theravāda Buddhism to a new country, this is an event of some significance.[7]

Since the Theravāda tradition has not had a valid lineage of nuns (bhikkhunī) since the thirteenth or fourteenth century, strictly speaking the only monastics in Achaan Sumedho's community are the male monks. In an attempt to improve the religious opportunities and status of women, however, the "nuns" in Sumedho's community live a more traditional monastic life than that of most lay-nuns in Thailand. For example, in Thailand the "nuns" wear white robes and do not go out on alms-rounds, while in England their robes are the same brown-to-saffron color as those of monks and they participate actively in alms-gathering. Achaan Sumedho has petitioned the monastic leaders of Thai Buddhism for permission to ordain women as real Buddhist nuns, but to date permission has been denied.

Another Westerner to attempt to reinstate the traditional nuns' order is Ayya Khemma (Ilse Ledermann; 1923–1997). Ordained as a nun by Narada Mahathera in Sri Lanka, she founded a nunnery for Western and Sri Lankan women on Parappunduwa Nuns' Island in Sri Lanka near Nyanatiloka's Island Hermitage. Ayya Khemma frequently traveled to the West to teach, but did not take part in legitimizing female monastics in the West. She is one of the few Western teachers to emphasize the importance of concentration or samatha meditation. Instead of teaching vipassanā alone, she follows the more traditional path of first developing a strong foundation in the concentrative absorptions (jhāna).[8]

Of potential importance for the future of the Theravāda nuns' order was the 1988 ordination of twelve Theravāda nuns from Sri Lanka, Burma, Thailand, and the United States at Hsi-lai temple in Southern California by the Taiwanese monk Hsing Yun. Since the Chinese nuns' ordination was transmitted to China from Sri Lanka in the fifth century, it has been argued that the Theravāda lineage of nuns could legitimately be reintroduced from Chinese Buddhism. So far the Theravāda orthodoxy in Southeast Asia has been unwilling to accept this argument, leaving the future status of the women uncertain. Apart from the nuns at Achaan Sumedho's community in England, there seems to be little impetus in the West for establishing a nuns' order within Western Theravāda Buddhism. The growing Theravāda movement in the West remains predominantly a lay movement associated with vipassanā practice.

Recent Developments in the West

As noted earlier, the growing lay interest in *vipassanā* meditation may be the most significant aspect of the Western Theravāda tradition. In the 1970s and early 1980s, the network of *vipassanā* or Insight Meditation practitioners consisted mostly of young adults attending intensive meditation retreats. Since the mid-1980s the practice has spread beyond the confines of the retreat. As participants return to life with their families and as an increasing number of older, working people with families became attracted to mindfulness practice, efforts are being made to integrate the *vipassanā* practice into daily life. As a result there are currently at least three hundred weekly *vipassanā* groups throughout the United States in which people sit together in an effort to support each other in the ongoing practice of meditation.[9] While most of these groups are small, a few have up to a hundred or more weekly participants. Twenty or more of these weekly groups are led by teachers. The smaller, teacherless groups usually substitute for a teacher's presence by playing Dharma talks on tapes or by reading Dharma books.

While mindfulness practice *(sati)* is at the heart of this lay movement, loving-kindness *(mettā)*, ethics *(śila)*, and generosity *(dāna)* are also central elements. Taught as a complement to mindfulness meditation, loving-kindness meditation is practiced both for the stabilizing effects it has on the mind and in order to infuse mindfulness practice with a spirit of friendliness. Much as compassion is the primary spiritual emotion of Mahāyāna Buddhism, it is loving-kindness that is emphasized in the Western *vipassanā* movement. The practice of loving-kindness in the West has often been combined with a forgiveness practice that seems to be absent in the formal *mettā* practices found in Southeast Asia.[10]

Until the mid-1980s *vipassanā* was taught in the West with much less emphasis on the ethical dimension than it is given in Southeast Asia. Since then, and particularly in the United States, there has been an increasing stress placed on ethics and on the traditional Buddhist precepts for the laity. The change was to a great extent in response to the significant number of accusations of ethical impropriety leveled against Asian and Western teachers of Tibetan, Zen, and Theravāda Buddhism. At the instigation of Jack Kornfield, the collective of teachers affiliated with the Insight Meditation Society and Spirit Rock formulated a teacher's code of ethics.[11] In September 1993 Kornfield, together with the San Francisco Zen Center, hosted at Spirit Rock the first joint conference of American teachers of Tibetan Buddhism, Zen Buddhism, and *vipassanā*. Ethical issues were the dominant subject of the meeting.

The teachings of Western *vipassanā* instructors tend to be less dualistic than those of the Southeast Asian Theravāda tradition, stressing not world-renunciation but engagement with and freedom within the world. Rather than focus on ultimate spiritual goals such as nirvāṇa, ending the cycles of rebirth, or attaining the various stages of sainthood *(ariyasāvako)*, the immediate benefits of mindfulness and untroubled equanimity amid the vicissitudes of life are stressed. Spiritual purification is less emphasized than purification of one's relationship to one's inner and outer world. Instead of aiming at the elimination of destructive emotions, the practitioner is directed to see the emotion clearly without either acting on it or suppressing it. Some of these Western teachers are reevaluating the ultimate goal posited by the modern Theravāda tradition.

Egalitarianism, democracy, feminism, and contact with other Buddhist traditions have wrought great changes in the Western Theravāda movement. In contrast to the predominance of male teachers in Southeast Asia, almost half of the *vipassanā* teachers in the United States are women.[12] It is not clear whether the orthodox Theravāda saṅgha or monastic community will recognize the evolving Western lay-centered movement as Theravāda Buddhism. In any case, the boundaries that define Theravāda Buddhism are far from clear even in Southeast Asia. Whether the tradition be defined scholastically on the basis of certain texts, monastically as a particular lifestyle and discipline, practically as particular practices and goals, or geographically, there is no final authority accepted by all. Thus, as Theravāda practices and teachings find a place in the West, it is not clear yet whether we are seeing the transplantation of the Asian Theravāda tradition or the evolution of new traditions of (Western) Buddhism. Most likely we will have both as some teachers and communities retain their Theravāda affiliation and others renounce it.

The Impact of Theravāda Spirituality in the West

The influence of Theravāda spirituality on Western culture has been strongest in the United States. Since the early and mid-1980s, the application of mindfulness practice in various styles of *vipassanā* has spread beyond its original Buddhist context. Perhaps the most successful of these applications is that initiated by Jon Kabat-Zinn at the University of Massachusetts Medical Center. A meditation student at IMS in Barre, Kabat-Zinn distanced the mindfulness practice so completely from its Buddhist context that the patients at his Stress Reduction Program are not even aware of its Buddhist roots. Dramatically successful in alleviating pain and stress, the

Kabat-Zinn program has prompted the inauguration of mindfulness-based stress reduction programs in a number of other hospitals and medical clinics around the United States.[13] In addition to training people to teach mindfulness in medical settings, Jon Kabat-Zinn has also trained social workers to bring awareness meditation and practices to prisons and to those living in the inner city.

Similarly, *vipassanā*-derived mindfulness practices have been integrated into the work of some American psychotherapists, most notably those associated with the Association of Transpersonal Psychology. The therapeutic effect of *vipassanā* has supported the trend away from psychoanalysis toward therapies centered more on present awareness. Psychotherapists are by far the best represented profession among students at American *vipassanā* retreats, and many of the American *vipassanā* teachers are also psychotherapists. The excessive degree to which some Western *vipassanā* teachers have been influenced by Western psychological concepts, however, has become a matter of some debate in Western Theravāda circles.

Whereas Zen Buddhism, especially during the 1950s and 1960s, was influential in intellectual and artistic circles, the primary influence of the Theravāda tradition in the West seems to be in the areas of medicine, therapy, and social work. In this way, awareness meditations and systematic training in mindfulness have won a place in American life outside of any formal Buddhist context.

Notes

1. For a study of the Sinhalese Buddhist reformation at the end of the eighteenth century, see Richard Gombrich, *Theravada Buddhism: A Social History from Ancient Benares to Modern Colombo* (London: Routledge & Kegan Paul, 1988) 172–97.

2. For a history of the Buddhist Society and of Buddhism in England between 1908 and 1968, see Christmas Humphreys, *Sixty Years of Buddhism in England* (London: The Buddhist Society, 1968).

3. The Mahāsi method of *vipassanā* meditation is described in Mahāsi Sayadaw, *Practical Insight Meditation: Basic and Progressive Stages* (Kandy, Sri Lanka: Buddhist Publication Society, 1971).

4. For an account of practice at the Mahāsi Center, see E. H. Shattock's *An Experiment in Mindfulness: An English Admiral's Experiences in a Buddhist Monastery* (London: Rider, 1958).

5. Jack Kornfield and Joseph Goldstein have expounded their mindfulness practice in a number of popular books; see Joseph Goldstein, *The Experience of Insight: A Simple and Direct Guide to Buddhist Meditation* (Boston: Shambhala, 1983); Joseph Goldstein and Jack Kornfield, *Seeking the Heart of Wisdom: The Path of Insight Meditation* (Boston: Shambhala, 1987).

6. These figures are calculated from the number of well advertised or listed retreats offered each year in the United States and Europe. Estimating that half of the retreatants have attended previous retreats, only half of the participants were counted in these calculations.

7. For Achaan Sumedho's teaching, see his *Cittaviveka: Teachings from the Silent Mind* (Hemel Hempstead, England: Amaravati Publication, 1984).

8. For Ayya Khemma's teaching, see her book, *When the Iron Eagle Flies: Buddhism for the West* (London: Arkana, 1991).

9. This figure was conservatively estimated by doubling the number of sitting groups listed in *Inquiring Mind*, the international journal of the Western *vipassanā* community. Probably the majority of sitting groups in the United States are not listed in the journal. (*Inquiring Mind*, PO Box 9999, North Berkeley Station, Berkeley, California 94709.)

10. For a Western presentation of loving-kindness practice, see Sharon Salzburg, *Loving-kindness: The Revolutionary Art of Happiness* (Boston: Shambhala, 1995).

11. The *vipassanā* teacher's code of ethics is found in the appendix of Jack Kornfield, *A Path with Heart: A Guide through the Perils and Promises of Spiritual Life* (New York: Bantam Books, 1993) 340–43.

12. For an example of feminist influence on a Western *vipassanā* teacher, see Christina Feldman, *Women Awake* (London: Arkana, 1989). An account of women in American Buddhism is found in Sandy Boucher, *Turning the Wheel: American Women Creating the New Buddhism* (San Francisco: Harper & Row, 1985).

13. See Jon Kabat-Zinn, *Full Catastrophe Living: Using the Wisdom of Your Body and Mind to Face Stress, Pain, and Illness* (New York: Delta, 1990).

Bibliography

Almond, Philip C. *The British Discovery of Buddhism*. Cambridge: Cambridge University Press, 1988.

Batchelor, Stephen. *The Awakening of the West: The Encounter of Buddhism and Western Culture*. Berkeley: Parallax Press, 1994.

Fields, Rick. *How the Swans Came to the Lake: A Narrative History of Buddhism in America* (3rd ed.). Boston: Shambhala, 1992.

Tweed, Thomas. *The American Encounter with Buddhism: 1844–1912*. Bloomington: Indiana University Press, 1992.

Zen in the West

Franz Aubrey Metcalf

> "Zen and the Art of Root Canal Therapy"
> — One of 92 listings for "Zen and the Art of..."
> found on the WorldCat library database
> "Oooh, that was so zen!"
> — Overheard at a Hollywood party, in reference
> to the movement of a balloon.
> "Stuck at the top of a 100' pole? Call: 976-KOAN"
> — Found on the Internet

IN MOST OF THE Western world, in the 1990s, one simply cannot escape the word "zen." One hears it in conversation, sees it in advertisements, finds it even in cartoons. But this "zen" one encounters, what is it? "Zen," to a prospective Western student, inevitably denotes a vague and alluring, unsystematic, mysterious collection of attitudes and impressions epitomized by the quotes above. It is significant that the word now probably functions more often as an adjective than as a noun: Westerners may not know what Zen Buddhism is, but they feel they can somehow intuit what is "zenlike." Zen has thrived in a kind of cultural playground, between Asia and the West, since the 1940s. Especially in places like California, it has become a mood more than a religion. Yet California, on the Pacific Rim, has also become one of the most active Buddhist regions in the world, Zen Buddhist not least. This pattern recurs throughout the West, but is especially marked in California's exotic climate.

While Zen-the-adjective flourishes, Zen-the-religion puts down roots. We might see them as two levels of one process: the transmission of Zen Buddhism from Asia to the West.[1] The playground is the first level, cultural presence. After this comes the second level, spiritual practice. In this article I shall focus on that Western Zen which, though it may challenge and radicalize its root tradition, remains in continuity with Zen Buddhism in Asia.

Still, we cannot neglect the creativity of the "Zen playground." Play gives birth to culture and all its achievements. A prospective Western Zen practitioner, Student Z, will likely discover Zen through some sort of cultural play. The Zen merry-go-round might pick her up at a lecture on Asian art, or an avant-garde concert, but it might set her back down in a New Age bookstore or the alt.zen discussion group on the Internet. Many are attracted after taking such a ride, and begin to play with "Zen" ideas. In their interchanges they continue a cultural give-and-take, a sort of teeter-totter between Zen philosophical and artistic ideas and Western lifestyles, businesses, and art forms. This creative play can yield lasting benefits for Western culture, though it is not in itself Buddhist spirituality. That begins only when individuals embark on Zen practice.

Suppose Student Z decides she wants to practice Zen; she now faces a basic choice. She can practice in an Asian context or a Western context. Most Western practitioners opt for the latter, which Jan Nattier has called "elite Buddhism," the preserve of relatively privileged people, in contrast to "ethnic Buddhism," the kind practiced almost exclusively by Asian immigrants. To understand why Westerners choose elite Zen, we need to look at these two forms of religious practice.

Ethnic Zen and Elite Zen

What would Student Z do on a day of strong practice at an ethnic Zen temple? Let us imagine her driving to the temple, in the old part of the city, where the immigrants clustered. This kind of Zen is only available in large cities because only in cities were there enough Asian immigrants to found a traditional temple and keep it running over the decades. She walks into the building, with its striking architecture and its elaborate interior, evocative of the old country. The smell of incense reaches her as she looks for the temple priest to ask him to give her an introduction to the practices of the temple. She looks for people meditating, but doesn't see anyone. Perhaps she is there on a day of making special celebratory visits to honor deceased family members. In that case, the temple grounds are swarming with families all there to pay their respects to their ancestors and to the priest who sees to their spirits' needs. But she has no family memorialized at the temple, so she feels excluded. She stays for a service, offering incense or chanting to earn merit; this she can do. At the service she hears the priest lecture on a Zen theme such as the power of mindful action or the original enlightenment of all beings. She feels she has intruded into a whole complex of religious culture; a rich sense of history pervades the day. She cannot understand the language, but she realizes that if this were her heritage she could learn the rituals and participate—there is little need to understand the ancient words. She bows, she chants, and she knows that her family would do this for her if she too became an ancestor. This continuity of devotion is what matters,[2] but she wonders if she has a part in it.

One cannot read such a description without an overpowering impression of cultural embeddedness and familial focus. The idea of our lone, Western Student Z turning to such a practice as a spiritual path makes little sense. Such practice must be familial and does not speak to the reasons Westerners turn to unusual religious options. If Student Z is typical, she is looking to non-Western religions for a spiritual path she can follow with dedication and effort, a path that responds to her inner need to do real spiritual work on her private (though perhaps universal) questions. She is not looking for practice embodied in a complex of rituals reinforcing links to the family and to traditional social roles in an Asian culture.[3] Such a spirituality expresses Asian, more than Western, needs.

Student Z's other choice is to practice in a Western Buddhist context, and this means taking part in the evolution of a new spiritual form, created (to use a classic American idiom) of, by, and for the laity. This is elite Zen, and it contrasts powerfully with traditional ethnic Zen, yet it grew out of it. Importantly, this new form of spirituality collapses the monastic-lay distinction so important to traditional (or "ethnic") forms of Buddhism. This means we can view all of Western Zen practice at once, rather than focusing on the religious virtuosi of the bhikkhu saṅgha (monks and nuns), at the expense of the laity (who form the rest of the greater Buddhist saṅgha, or community).

We return to Student Z as she tries out a day of strong practice at an elite Zen center. In this case it begins almost at night. She wakes up in her apartment and heads to the converted house or shop or barn to begin an all-day sitting. Many students live nearby in buildings owned by the Zen center, but she must drive some distance to gather with one or two dozen others in the chilly zendō where they all silently bow to their cushions and each other, then sit for half an hour in zazen meditation, following their breath or wrestling with kōans. They walk a bit, then sit again. Now they chant and perform a service at the altar; though Student Z is not actively involved in the altar rituals she still feels a part of the ceremony as she chants the powerful words. Though many are in a language she cannot understand, others have learned their meaning over the years. Perhaps they eat breakfast now and are able to greet each other with friendly talk, but soon the sitting begins again, and the hours pass. Student Z may spend a period cleaning the center or working in the garden, but this too is meditation. Throughout the day, sitting, speaking, eating, or working, she tries to preserve her mindful and meditative state. She strives mightily to simply sit and stop the chatter of her mind, and she learns that others are doing this, too, or are grappling with the kōans they must solve to open them to the experience of insight. This work never stops, even outside of the four or six hours of *zazen*. The day ends with announcements and the business of running the center. Student Z drops some money into the donation box and, her body aching, she drives home wondering if she would want to do this her whole life.

Such is the emphasis of Zen in the West as it is practiced. How did such a level of intensity and such a focus on meditation become the rule rather than the exception for Western Zen? Reviewing the history of Zen's development here will give us a clearer picture of Zen in the West and help us understand both its power and its dangers.

History and Development

Buddhist ideas and descriptions of its practices had filtered into the West by the early nineteenth century. These first Western notions of Buddhism were highly colored by their reporters (often missionaries) and further distorted by Western interpreters. In the early twentieth century, Chinese Ch'an and Japanese Zen priests came to minister to immigrant communities, but these priests had little or nothing to do with Western converts or the formation of a Western form of Zen practice. We can date the latter to the World Parliament of Religions, in Chicago, in 1893. Shaku Sōen represented Zen there, and it was his lineage that formed the Rinzai side of the first, tiny Western Zen sitting groups, beginning in the 1920s. Not coincidentally, these pioneering Rōshis, on both Sōtō and Rinzai sides, came from lineages already promoting lay *zazen* practice in Japan.[4] Such lineages still exist there, but as a tiny minority. In the West, however, they have come into their own. These Rōshis wanted to promote their vision of an active saṅgha, practicing *zazen*. In the words of one of them, they held the lotus to the rock, and though it took longer than their lives, it has taken root.

Despite these efforts, Zen in the West remained insular for several decades. The immigrant communities held to an Asian spirituality and the tiny elite centers failed to capture the attention of mainstream Western culture. World War II further alienated the Asian communities from their host societies. But by the 1950s things began to change. D. T. Suzuki's books had introduced the West to a romanticized but highly alluring vision of Zen

41. D. T. Suzuki, 1958.

spirituality. Alan Watts followed Suzuki, promoting the joyous freedom of Zen and setting the stage for the wild growth of religious experimentation in the next decades. The Beat writers, notably Jack Kerouac, began to narrate a new form of iconoclastic and individualized practice, calling for a generation of "lunatic bhikkhus," a "rucksack revolution." These intellectuals and Beat wanderers alike questioned core values of Western culture, so that as the idea of an intense Zen spirituality took hold it was associated with the counterculture, one of whose fundamental qualities is a kind of mystical yet worldly "Zen" enthusiasm.

In the 1950s differing movements within Japanese Buddhism desired not to simply service the spiritual needs of a passive laity but to engage the laity in active practice. Several committed Zen teachers looked outside of Japan for opportunities to spread the dharma (sometimes expressing discomfort with the collusion of the Zen schools in the war effort). A similar dissatisfaction with his own country's institutions prompted the Korean teacher Seung Sahn (Soen Sa Nim) to come to Japan and the West, after the Korean War. Meanwhile the radical Beat questioning of Western values continued and an increasing portion of the middle classes began to join it. This process, beginning in America, extended to all industrialized nations not under totalitarian ideological rule, in tandem with an openness to new religious ideas and forms.

By the fabled 1960s a mixed lot of Asian spiritual teachers were flocking to the West. They came to spread the dharma in new lands and, in the case of the Tibetans and Vietnamese, to escape political persecution at home. With the arrival of this generation of teachers, Zen in the West entered a new phase, a phase of cross-cultural transmission as profound as the one initiated by Bodhidharma and his successors when they brought the *dhyāna* school to China. Some of these Asian Zen teachers, like Shunryu Suzuki Rōshi and Taizan Maezumi Rōshi, came to minister to immigrant communities and were seduced away by the enthusiasm of elite Western students. Some, like Thich Nhat Hanh and Hsuan Hua, came as political exiles; some, like Thich Tien-an, came as scholars. But all these creative teachers began to devote their attention to Western congregations. They founded "Zen centers." In hindsight it seems these centers tended to walk a common path, but their stumbling actually *created* the path, inventing something truly new. Robert Aitken Rōshi, himself a powerful force in Zen in the West, comments that Suzuki Rōshi, founder of the San Francisco Zen Center, would say he didn't know what he was doing.[5] His students didn't believe him, but it was the truth: they were recreating Zen in a highly unstable environment; no one knew how it would turn out. At Suzuki's center; at Maezumi's center, four hundred miles down the coast; at Thich Nhat Hanh's Plum Village in France; at Taisen Deshimaru's centers in Europe; at Sheng-yen's in New York City; at Seung Sahn's around the world, an Asian teacher, with his Western students, was creating a new form of Buddhism, of, by, and for the laity. Even at centers like Philip Kapleau's Rochester Zen Center and Aitken's Hawaiian centers, where the overseeing Asian teacher was not resident, he retained a vital role in creating a culture-bridging practice.

Zen Redefined

This new form of Buddhism has changed the normative mode of being religious. For the overwhelming majority of Zen Buddhists, from T'ang China on, Zen spirituality was chiefly confined to offerings for priests, listening to sermons on Zen subjects, devotion to ancestors, and, finally, being ordained into the saṅgha *after one's death*. This last, through the mediating power of the priest and temple, conferred upon the devotee the reward of enlightenment without the trouble of working on it in this lifetime.[6] But this passive mode of spirituality could not attract Western students. Not content with posthumous ordination, they wanted active participation in soteriological activity in this lifetime. In fact, they wanted to transform themselves into a new form of the saṅgha, participating in meditation normally reserved for monks, indeed monks in advanced training. Zen in the West became a Buddhism for laypersons, but for laypersons who wanted to act in important ways like bhikkhus and bhikkhunīs.

Buddhism, over the millennia, has never finally resolved the question of what or who is the saṅgha. Is it only the monks and nuns? Or is it the whole of the "Four Assemblies": monks, nuns, male, and female laypersons? Both answers have been common, but here a new answer emerged, one that continues to evolve today: the saṅgha is those who meditate regularly and follow the basic precepts of Mahāyāna Buddhism. Within this saṅgha, distinctions of priest, monk, nun, and layperson carry relatively little weight. What matters is practice. Thus, in this new form of Buddhism, everyone who wished practiced together in an urban center or perhaps went on retreat together at a remote mountain center. This new form of convivial practice generated great enthusiasm in its students, who were mostly young, well-educated, middle class people with intellectual and spiritual horizons wide enough to consider this foreign spiritual path, and with the time and financial means to devote themselves to it.[7] Monks and nuns usually stayed at the mountain centers (when these were available) and were celibate; priests (both male and female) took vows of commitment to Zen but were allowed to be sexually active and continue their lives outside the centers; laypersons took the bodhisattva vows and were ordained Buddhists in the Zen lineage, but also maintained their outside lives. The great majority of practitioners chose the lay path, and some of these devoted as much time to practice as those becoming priests or monastics.[8]

All these new types of practitioners followed the same general pattern of practice: they sat zazen, usually every day, counting breaths at first, then moving on to shikan taza (just sitting, minimizing thinking) or to kōan practice. They worked closely with a teacher, who would guide their practice, helping them to meditate better or solve their kōans. Most attended sesshins (intensive meditation retreats) at least once a year and as often as once a month. This practice was open-ended, and students knew it. In many centers, especially in the Japanese and Korean lineages, over the years students would work through a system of hundreds or even thousands of kōans. In pure Sōtō lineages and in the Vietnamese and Chinese lineages this was less practiced, but the student would work with her teacher just as closely. Students with years of experience were expected to take positions of responsibility in the centers and some were groomed for teaching positions. Most, even if they did not want to teach, wanted dharma transmission, the official reception of the mind-to-mind transfer of Zen understanding, the Buddha's enlightenment. They were willing to practice all their lives to get it.[9]

This practice has broken down traditional sectarian divisions in Zen. Some Western centers follow Yasutani Rōshi's Rinzai emphasis on breaking through the Mu kōan to a kenshō experience, yet they also do shikan taza; some follow the Sōtō spirituality of slowly realizing enlightenment in sitting, yet they also work with kōans; some calm the mind with recitation of Buddhas' names, yet they also do pure zazen; and all these various styles of practice call the practitioners to manifest their Buddha-mind in their everyday activities. This balance of practice retrieves a freedom inherent in the traditions of each imported lineage of Zen, a freedom that often lay neglected in Asia (especially in the Japanese lineages; all three other countries' traditions preserved more latitude for combining practices, such as name-recitation and *zazen*). But some lineages here have also expanded on that freedom by intentionally borrowing practices from other lineages. In fact, even the Sōtō/Rinzai distinction has been broken down by the mixed lineage of many prominent teachers (e.g., Kapleau, Maezumi, Aitken, and Sheng-Yen).

These new saṅghas grew around charismatic, usually Asian, teachers, but the Western students' values, too, have formed them. Though the head teacher stood in unquestioned authority (at first), the remainder of the saṅgha hierarchy collapsed. Where in Asia monks always outranked nuns, and senior monks outranked junior monks, and all were governed by the 250 or more rules of conduct, in the West all this immediately fell away. Boards of directors replaced councils of elders, and though an informal hierarchy remained, it was based more on time given to the center, than time spent in the saṅgha. With policies developing from trial and error, and with the freer atmosphere of the 1960s as the social context, these Zen centers came to embody many of the leitmotifs of the time: communal living, cottage industries, egalitarian order, experimentation with drugs and sex. Most important and formative of these developments was this new egalitarianism, especially regarding women.

Though Mahāyāna's emphasis on non-duality and the inherent enlightenment of all things has undercut gender bias, the history of Buddhism nevertheless remains a history of androcentrism. Now, in two decades, two thousand years of patriarchy were thrown out and replaced by what Rita Gross calls "androgynous Buddhism." Women and men began to participate equally in practice, in decision-making, and in high saṅgha positions. This change is taking some time to actualize, but by the 1980s women often constituted more than half the centers' members, had attained dharma transmissions in several schools of Zen, were on the boards of nearly every Zen center in significant numbers, and were head teachers at several Zen centers (though still vastly outnumbered by men at this, the highest, level).

The full participation of women is probably the most radical and creative development in Western Buddhist spirituality in general, not only in Zen. Women's equal participation was a theoretically necessary base for a Buddhism centered on laypersons ("householders," to use the traditional Buddhist term) trying to establish Buddhist spiritual paths in the modern West. But, more than that, women's active presence has changed Buddhism's style and emphasis in fundamental ways, not only mitigating the sometimes military harshness of traditional, monastic Zen training but also opening Buddhist philosophy to new practical and theoretical insights. This opening may permanently alter Buddhist spirituality, both in the West, directly, and in Asia, through dialogical influence.[10]

This enthusiasm and experimentation has not been without dangers. As teachers faced new challenges, for which their training had not prepared them, inevitable scandals ensued—not everywhere, but in enough places to call into question the very strengths which gave Western Zen its greatest successes. These trials illustrate some of the deep problems involved in the cross-cultural transmission of religion, and throw light on the direction of Zen's development in the West. Though the explosive growth of Zen slowed somewhat in the 1970s, centers often had hundreds of active students and some even had waiting lists owing to the shortage of qualified teachers.

The presence of women at all levels of practice made for new and close relationships between male teachers and a large and growing number of female lay students. The relationship of teacher and student had always been close in Zen, whether in the privacy of *dokusan* (face-to-face interviews), or in the intimacy of long-term training together. But these relationships had been same-sex. With powerful male teachers working with liberal female students, temptation to sexual interaction was sometimes irresistible. Despite efforts to work against it, sexual liaisons occurred, sometimes with the female students feeling coerced by the hierarchy of the teacher-student relationship. Nor was such behavior confined to Zen schools; all the imported Asian religions have repeatedly suffered from it, with several major scandals occurring in the single year of 1997. Exact numbers of incidents are unavailable, since many continue to be unreported or dealt with in-house, but the problem remains.

In addition to sexual scandals, Western Zen has, equally inevitably, had more purely power-based struggles in its evolution. Just as teachers had no training in working with women, so they had none in running the business of a Zen center. Even in Japan, where the Zen temple priest has to maintain solvency, there is a social net to support the institution. In the West, the Zen teacher typically had to come up with new ways of funding the center, and new modes of leading the center. This could lead him to assume too much power, even if he (all the first-generation teachers were men) didn't originally covet it. Several centers began businesses; some were quite successful. Success obliged teachers to make decisions about money and livelihood for which they were ill-prepared. Further, the creation of the new saṅgha forced the creation of politics which had no parallel in the Asian system. Teachers and centers had to struggle mightily to define their roles in this new order. Finally, the teacher found himself in a new and totally alienated position in Western society. Deprived of everything he had cherished in his old environment, he had to define a new role for himself in a culture disinclined to grant him very much respect, assistance, or forgiveness. He could not lean even on normal patterns of behavior, let alone the experience and assistance of others who had gone before. Some teachers faltered under the weight of this burden. At the same time, Western students tended to idealize their teacher, assuming that his spiritual elevation also conferred equivalent moral and psychological elevation. For this reason, students in the 1960s and 1970s wanted to give their teachers very great powers and responsibilities. Only through the de-idealizing experience of teachers' failures were teachers and students able to begin working toward a balance of authority. But in this process several centers were torn apart by disclosures of abuses and the bitter struggles that followed.[11] These scandals ended the boom years of Zen in the West.

In the 1980s the experimentation of the 1960s and 1970s and the youth of the Baby Boom generation were over. Conservatism both in economic and religious choices, the busier lives of its most active practitioners, and the scandals which deeply wounded some centers and dulled the reputation and growth of all the others, caused Zen practice to dwindle. Some deflation was inevitable: Zen had grown with the 1960s counterculture and suffered with its demise. But a core group of practitioners had gone beyond the Zen playground of popular culture, and they continue their work now. By the early 1980s Zen groups began to exhibit more self-reflective criticism. Further questioning of cultural patterns (both Asian and Western) led to further refinements of practice. One overarching question was how much assimilation to Western culture was the right amount, in matters of rules, ritual, and ceremony. This issue, apparently superficial, touches on the question of the essentials of Zen. To replace, say, an ancient and unintelligible Japanese chant with English changes the whole character of its ritual. Arguments occurred over whether such changes were destructive. There is more than age to religious forms; to tamper with them is to wrestle with the sacred. Several new teachers actually broke with their old teachers over these issues. To cite the example of one center, Kapleau Rōshi broke with his Japanese teacher over translating the *Heart Sūtra*, and his chosen successor, Toni Packer, broke with him, in turn, over the many changes she wanted to make in her own teaching.

By this time, centers that were originally under the guidance of Asian teachers began to acquire their independence, both through the deaths of those teachers and through the granting of teaching authority to a new,

Western, generation during the Asian teachers' lifetimes. This process continues, and may open the door to still more radical changes in the old tradition. The centers of Maezumi Rōshi's first two dharma heirs could hardly be more different: Tetsugen Glassman Rōshi's New York City center devotes its energy to practice while sheltering and retraining the homeless, running a bakery, and doing retreats on the street; Genpo Merzel Rōshi's centers give their attention to retreat and strong *shikan taza*, as well as international outreach. Maezumi Rōshi's other dharma heirs, meanwhile, pursue their own visions, emphasizing art in a monastic setting (Daido Loori Sensei), attending to the ordinariness of the moment and dropping most Buddhist trappings (Joko Beck Sensei), and so forth. And now, with Maezumi Rōshi's death, the styles of his twelve dharma heirs will, no doubt, diverge still further.[12]

While confusing, this divergence may be healthy for Zen in the West. The development of widely different styles of practice has been compensated by greater dialogue between centers and lineages. Even the difficulties of teachers have led to gatherings of Western teachers both to support one another and to arrive at shared statements of policy on ethical conduct. Various Buddhist groups have also been drawn together in addressing the sangha's responsibility for social and environmental action. Zen teachers Thich Nhat Hanh and Robert Aitken have been leaders in this movement, which continues to gain ground and may be central to the Western sangha in the next decades.

This attention to its social context has also led Western Zen to the beginnings of dialogue with other Buddhist forms by supporting the work of Asian Buddhists abroad and at home. It remains to be seen how far this will go toward healing the rift between "elite" and "ethnic" forms of Buddhism. Some elite lineages of Zen, such as the Vietnamese, have maintained fairly close ties to their ethnic communities in the West. Hsuan Hua's lineage, in Northern California, has remained in contact with the Chinese community, partially due to his greater adherence to traditional forms of practice, including his emphasis on monastic ordination. Yet it also runs a large educational institution, a strongly Western form of outreach. In Los Angeles, Thich Tien-an's lineage has been strong in working with the more traditional Vietnamese temples (which are also Thien [Zen]), and seeks actively to increase cooperation between Buddhist schools of all kinds. This contrasts starkly with the Zen Center of Los Angeles, just a few blocks away, which maintains almost no relationship with the traditional Japanese Zen community. Both sides of the ethnic/elite split need to learn from each other to discover how best to create forms of practice that can endure in Western culture. This rift, whether wide or narrow, has obstructed the mutual enrichment of both sides' forms of practice, but there are recent signs that it may be narrowing.[13]

Emphasis on lay householder practice continues to be virtually a constant in Western Zen, though nearly every center also has monastic practice options. But it is by no means clear if this kind of lay practice can be made self-sustaining. Zen's boom occurred during a time of great experimentation in Western societies. That cohort of once new practitioners now is running most centers. Despite a rebound in membership after the decline of the early 1980s, new converts are not coming as quickly as before. Further, Zen spirituality requires great commitment of time and energy, and methods of enticing children of practitioners to serious practice have yet to bear much fruit. It may be that having a variety of available styles of practice may inspire a new generation of practitioners who would not have responded to the more traditional styles of their parents. I have heard enthusiasm for diversity expressed by more than one Western Zen teacher. One told me of the freedom of second-generation teachers, saying the first generation had to bridge Asian and Western cultures, but the new generation has the opportunity to use their native cultural familiarity and their weaker ties to Asian hierarchies to build new centers where creativity has new presence.

Work has recently begun to formalize an American Sōtō Zen organization. Although this would apply only to one school of Zen, the school is by far the most represented and influential in the West. The proposed organization would highlight the centrality of the teacher-student dharma transmission without imposing a hierarchy of temples or centers, and it would allow for accreditation of recognized teachers, yet allow them to cooperate in moving students to centers appropriate to their interests. Such a flexible and transmission-based organization would well fit the teacher-oriented (rather than temple-based) structure of American Zen. If the Sōtō school can organize in this way, other schools may wish to follow its lead. This sort of organization may help stabilize and coordinate Zen's development over the next generation.

Given the disparate styles of teaching in elite Zen, and the creative changes that will certainly continue, can we still say that elite Zen centers are Zen, or even Buddhist? Joko Beck Sensei still clearly leads a Zen center, though on her altar sits not Mañjuśrī Bodhisattva or Śākyamuni Buddha, but a rock. If the students are meditating, but without the rituals, without the statues, without the robes, can one still call their practice Zen? Toni Packer has dispensed with all that and no longer calls her center Buddhist at all, yet she remains the first dharma heir of Kapleau Rōshi. So, is she still a Zen teacher? Without reference to the thousand-year tradition of teacher-student transmission of the dharma, without reference to the philosophies that lie behind it, without reference even to Śākyamuni Buddha and his experience, what would be taught and learned and practiced? These questions trouble all concerned, since particular Zen lineages want to preserve their reputations of holding the original dharma and yet be free both to experiment and discard.

What is Zen? This is the root question underlying elite Zen and its development. Yet the Zen tradition has asked such questions of its own forms and essence from the very first. All schools of Zen over the centuries have repeated the (supposed) words of Bodhidharma, advertising Zen as without forms, pointing directly to one's own mind. Yet all schools of Zen over the centuries have repeated that they have the true dharma transmission and one needs to practice with them to realize it in oneself. We can look at Western Zen as a noble attempt to free Zen from the tension between its philosophical freedom and its institutional rigidity, and to allow travelers on its path to shed their baggage. Some part of Zen's truth may be transmitted without the old forms; but perhaps the forms *are* the truth and the core is emptiness.[14] Zen in the West has been an experiment in uncovering the root values of a religious tradition and transplanting them to the soil of a new culture. The fruition of this process took hundreds of years in China; despite the acceleration of modern culture, a mature Zen in the West will unfold only with further generations to blossom in ways we have yet to imagine.

Notes

1. I should add that what holds true for the word "Zen," holds true for "Ch'an" and "Sŏn" and "Thien," the Chinese, Korean, and Vietnamese varieties. Following a standard Western practice, I will use "Zen" to refer to all of these.

2. For descriptions of Japanese Zen practice, see the works of Reader and Bodiford in the bibliography.

3. Buddhist forms emphasizing meditation have garnered the most attention and publicity (not always good) in the West, especially Theravādin *vipassana*, various Tibetan forms, and the several varieties of Zen. In the 1970s, Nichiren Shōshū, in its Sōka Gakkai guise, began to outstrip the meditational forms in popularity, but its time demands and its emphasis on chanting put it, too, in the active lay category of Buddhism. All these forms of Western Buddhism continue to grow, especially attracting Europeans and European-Americans. On the other hand, it seems Asians in the West may be losing enthusiasm for more traditional sorts of practice. Membership in the Buddhist Churches of America (Jōdo Shinshū School) is down, though it is becoming more heterogeneous, and Paul Numrich (in a paper presented to the annual meeting of the American Academy of Religion, November 18–22, 1994) reported not a single fully ordained Asian-American bhikkhu

(monk) in an American Theravādin temple. Without new bhikkhus from within the community to form a field of merit, one wonders how traditional forms of Buddhism will survive in the West.

4. Taizan Maezumi Rōshi, personal communication. For an excellent, journalistic account of the process of the transmission of early lineages to America, see Fields, *How the Swans Came to the Lake*, chapters 10–12.

5. Aitken, *Encouraging Words*, 115. Aitken Rōshi then goes on to follow Suzuki Rōshi in saying he himself does not know how his center will evolve. He accordingly asks his students to experiment with him. Aitken Rōshi's book, and his other writings, provide a humane and intelligent source for the study and creation of Western Zen, especially its devotional forms and its ethics. For more from the well-loved and influential Suzuki Rōshi, see his *Zen Mind, Beginner's Mind*, where he compassionately introduces Sōtō Zen spirituality and first raises many ongoing questions about the development of Zen in the West.

6. See Bodiford, especially 185–208.

7. For sociological examinations of California Zen centers, see Tipton, *Getting Saved*, and Preston, *Social Organization of Zen Practice*.

8. Different lineages have differently addressed the difficulty of promoting non-lay practice in Western societies. A few teachers, Hsuan Hua for example, have emphasized creating monastic communities with fully ordained monks and nuns. Much more common, though, is the practice described above, which fosters serious students on the cusp of the lay/priest distinction. Maezumi Rōshi ordained dozens of priests, but this was within a lineage where celibacy was not expected and community involvement unavoidable. This pattern holds true for most of the Japanese lineages. On the other hand, Seung Sahn aroused unease in (the much more strict) Korean Zen circles when he created the "Bodhisattva Monk" ordination, not requiring celibacy. Still, the teacher remains the deciding factor; some teachers, even in Japanese lineages, Kyogen Carlson for example, require years of intensive training in a monastic setting before they will ordain someone as a priest. Revealingly, as of this writing, Kyogen Sensei has no priests among his successors.

9. Lacking space to describe the excitement, the dedication, and the travails of these students, I refer the reader to the following excellent accounts: the books by Robert Aitken and Shunryu Suzuki for the teacher's perspective; Peter Matthiessen's touching *Nine-Headed Dragon River* for an insightful view of both Rinzai and Sōtō practice; Tworkov's examination of several Western teachers and their spiritual journeys, *Zen in America*; Preston's more scholarly, but practice-based account of the process of learning Zen; and for an acerbically humorous, but ultimately moving, account of practice in Japan and America, van der Wetering's two memoirs (he is reportedly at work on a third).

10. Rita Gross carefully explores all these issues, from historical, feminist, and doctrinal perspectives, in her important book, *Buddhism after Patriarchy*.

11. The most celebrated scandal involved Richard Baker Rōshi, successor to Suzuki Rōshi in San Francisco. This scandal included both power and sex and ended with Baker's ouster as abbot. See Fields and Tworkov for further details. The center then spread some of the powers of the abbot to the board of directors, and took years before installing another full abbot. When it did, it split the abbotship, giving responsibilities to Reb Anderson and Mel Weitsman (never a supporter of Baker Rōshi). The split abbotship, though growing out of the mud, has proven

popular and continues to bloom. A less destructive resolution took place at the Zen Center of Los Angeles, where Maezumi Rōshi went through a period of alcoholism and several affairs. He took a leave of absence and came back with new attitudes about both women and the role of Zen teachers in the West. One of his senior female students commented to me that this process changed and deepened his teaching and played a crucial role in the ongoing growth of the center.

12. Tworkov devotes a stimulating chapter of her book to Glassman Rōshi. For further perspectives on Zen practice in the West, see Kraft's excellent collection of essays, *Zen: Tradition and Transmission*, where the issues are taken up by Zen teachers in addition to scholars.

13. For measured and accessible examinations of this situation, see Prebish, "Ethics and Integration," and Nattier, "Politics of Representation."

14. Here I am playing on the *Heart Sūtra*, cherished in Zen, which proclaims: "form is no other than emptiness, emptiness no other than form." Bernard Faure has brilliantly deconstructed Zen's inherent and effaced tension between freedom from forms and the sanctity of tradition in his groundbreaking recent works. In its evolution, Zen in the West will continue this exploration.

Bibliography

Aitken, Robert. *Encouraging Words*. New York and San Francisco: Pantheon, 1993.

Bodiford, William M. *Soto Zen in Medieval Japan*. Kuroda Institute Studies in East Asian Buddhism No. 8. Honolulu: University of Hawai'i Press, 1993.

Faure, Bernard. *The Rhetoric of Immediacy*. Princeton: Princeton University Press, 1991.

——— *Ch'an Insights and Oversights*. Princeton: Princeton University Press, 1993.

——— *Visions of Power: Imagining Medieval Japanese Buddhism*. Princeton: Princeton University Press, 1996.

Fields, Rick. *How the Swans Came to the Lake*. 3rd ed. Boston: Shambhala, 1992.

Gross, Rita. *Buddhism after Patriarchy*. Albany: State University of New York Press, 1993.

Kraft, Kenneth, ed. *Zen: Tradition and Transmission*. New York: Grove Press, 1988.

Matthiessen, Peter. *Nine-Headed Dragon River*. Boston: Shambhala, 1986.

Nattier, Jan. "The Politics of Representation." *Tricycle* 5:1 (1995) 42–49.

Prebish, Charles. "Ethics and Integration in American Buddhism." *Journal of Buddhist Ethics* (electronic journal) 2 (1995) 125–39.

Preston, David. *The Social Organization of Zen Practice*. New York: Oxford University Press, 1991.

Reader, Ian. "Images in Sōtō Zen." *Scottish Journal of Religious Studies* 10:1 (1989) 5–21.

Suzuki, Shunryu. *Zen Mind, Beginner's Mind*. New York: Weatherhill, 1970.

Tipton, Steven. *Getting Saved from the Sixties*. Cambridge: Harvard University Press, 1979.

Tworkov, Helen. *Zen in America*. 2nd ed. San Francisco: North Point Press, 1994.

van der Wetering, Janwillem. *The Empty Mirror*. New York: Houghton Mifflin, 1974.

———. *A Glimpse of Nothingness*. London: Routledge & Kegan Paul, 1975.

Glossary of Technical Terms
[Sanskrit (S), Pāli (P), Chinese (C), Korean (K), Japanese (J)]

Acalanātha S.; Fudō-myōō 不動明王 J. One of the *myōō* (q.v.).

abhiṣeka S. Ritual initiation into Shingon meditative techniques.

ācārya S.; *ajari* 阿闍梨 J. Monastic teacher; title Achaan, Ajahn in Theravāda Buddhism. Also a rank in the Japanese priesthood.

āgama S.; *agonkyō* 阿含經 J. One of the early collections of Buddhist scriptures.

ahiṃsā S. Non-killing; first of the five lay precepts.

ajikan 阿字觀 J. Shingon meditation on the letter A.

Akṣobhya S.; Ashuku 阿閦 J. The immovable buddha, whose Pure Land is in the East.

ālaya-vijñāna S.; *ariyashiki* 阿梨耶識 J. Store-consciousness, underlying the other consciousnesses in Yogācāra.

Amitābha S.; Amita 阿彌陀 C.; Amida J. The Buddha of measureless light; also called Amitāyus, the Buddha of measureless life. Before becoming a buddha, he was a monk called Dharmākara (Hōzō 法藏 J.), who vowed to welcome into his Pure Land in the west all who called on his name.

anātman S.; *anattā* P.; *muga* 無我 J. No-self. One of the three marks of existence, along with impermanence (*anitya* S.; *mujō* 無常 J.) and suffering (*duḥkha* S.; *ku* 苦 J.).

anjin, anshin 安心 J. Serene mind. In Pure Land, contrasted with practices (*kigyō* 起行).

anusmṛti S. Reflection, recollection, mindfulness. Meditation that involves visualization.

arhat, arahat S.; *rakan, arakan* 阿羅漢 J. An enlightened saint, one who has reached the fourth and highest stage of the Buddhist path (after stream-enterer, once-returner, and non-returner). Regarded by Mahāyāna as inferior to a *bodhisattva*.

āśraya S. Support. The body of the Buddha, or the ground of our existence, in Yogācāra.

asura S. *ashura* 阿修羅 J. The fourth class of sentient beings, belligerent beings. One of the six courses of rebirth (*rokudō* 六道): hell, *preta*, animal, *asura*, human, heaven.

Avalokiteśvara S.; Kuan-yin 觀音 C.; Kannon J. Bodhisattva of compassion.

Avataṃsaka S.; Hua-yen 華嚴 C.; Hwaŏm K.; Kegon J. "Flower-adornment"; name of Mahāyāna sūtra and school; one of the Nara schools in Japan.

bendō 辨道 J. Earnest pursuit of the Buddhist path.

Bhaiṣajyaguru S.; Yakushi 薬師 J. Buddha of healing.

bodhi S.; *bodai* 菩提 J. Enlightenment, awakening, and the accompanying wisdom of insight.

bodhicittotpāda S.; *bodaishin* 菩提心 J. The mind of enlightenment (the aspiration to enlightenment), the first step on the bodhisattva path.

bodhisattva S.; *bosatsu* 菩薩 J. Future buddhas, who vow to work for the enlightenment of all beings.

bonnō 煩悩 J.; *kleśa* S. Passionate afflictions; mental defilements.

buddhakṣetra S.; *setsudo* 刹土 J.; *butsudo* 佛土 J. Buddha-field.

buddhatā, buddhadhātu, buddhagotra S.; *bulsŏng* K.; *busshō* 佛性 J. Variant possible terms for "Buddha-nature": the seed of buddhahood possessed by all sentient beings, enabling them to become buddhas.

busshin 佛心 J. Buddha-mind; the Buddha-nature.

busshō. See *buddhatā.*

Ch'an. See *dhyāna.*

ching C. Reverence, in Neo-Confucianism.

chong/yo 宗要 K. Doctrine/essence.

ch'uan fa chieh C.; *denpōge* 伝法偈 J. Transmission verse, epitomizing a Ch'an master's teaching.

daihi 大否 J. Great negation

daihi 大悲 J. Great compassion.

daimoku 題目 J. Title of the *Lotus Sūtra*, in the Nichiren schools.

daishi 大師 J. Title meaning "Great Teacher."

darśana, dṛṣṭi S.; *ken* 見 J. Seeing; doctrinal viewpoint; (false) view.

deva S. Deities, the sixth class of sentient beings; gods who have become protectors of Buddhism.

dhāraṇī S.; *t'o-luo-ni* C.; *darani* 陀羅尼 J. Lit. "that which sustains": ritual formulas that sustain the religious life of those who recite them; similar to *mantra.*

dharma S.; *fa* C.; *hō* 法 J. Teaching; element, phenomenon. Dharma: the law that governs all things; the ultimate truth as taught by the Buddha.

dharma-dhātu S.; *hokkai* 法界 J. The realm of cosmic law; the world of phenomena.

dharmakāya S.; *hosshin* 法身 J. The collection of teachings or sūtras. Dharmakāya: Truth-body; cosmic body; the eternal nature of the Buddha.

dharmatā S.; *hosshō* 法性 J. True nature of the phenomenal order, interpreted by some Mahāyānists as "emptiness" or "thusness."

dhyāna S.; *jhāna* P.; *ch'an* 禪 C.; *sŏn* K.; *thien* Vietnamese; *zen* J. Meditation aiming at enstatic absorption. Four *dhyāna*s = four stages of concentration.

dokusan 獨參 J. Personal meeting with the master, in Zen.

ekayāna S.; *ichijō* 一乘 J. The One Vehicle revealed by the *Lotus Sūtra* to underlie the three vehicles *(triyāna)* used by the Buddha as skillful means *(upāya)*, namely *śrāvaka-yāna, pratyekabuddha-yāna,* and *bodhisattva-yāna* or Mahāyāna. It is often identified with the Mahāyāna.

ekō 廻向 J. Transfer of merit, esp. the transfer of Amida's boundless merit to sentient beings so that they can enter his Pure Land.

Fa-hsiang C.; Hossō 法相 J. East Asian Yogācāra Buddhism, based on the writings of Dharmapāla (530–561).

Four Beginnings: *ssu-tuan* 四端 C.; *sadan* K.; *shitan* J. The moral qualities that give rise to the original goodness of human nature, according to Mencius; their relation to the Seven Emotions mentioned in the *Doctrine of the Mean* is discussed in Neo-Confucianism.

Fudō-myōō. See Acalanātha.

fushō fumetsu 不生不滅 J. Unborn, undying; the state of *nirvāṇa*.

gedō 外道 J. Lit. "outside the path": heresy or non-Buddhist teaching.

gedatsu 解脱 J. Release, *nirvāṇa*.

goi 五位 J. The five ranks of insight according to Tung-shan; levels of training in the Rinzai kōan curriculum.

gozan. See *wu-shan.*

gyōja 行者 J. A practitioner.

haibutsu kishaku 廃佛毀釈 J. "reject and destroy Buddhism"; anti-Buddhist slogan of the Meiji Period in Japan.

hassu 法嗣 J. Dharma heir; a priest who takes over from his master.

hatsumei 発明 J. Illumination; the experience of insight in Shingaku.

hijiri 聖 J. Wandering ascetics.

hokkai J. See *dharma-dhātu.*

hongaku 本覺 J. Original enlightenment (of all beings), a teaching developed particularly in the Japanese Tendai school.

hongan 本願 J. Original Vow (of Amida Buddha).

honji-suijaku 本地垂迹 J. Original ground (= Buddhist bodhisattvas) and trace manifested below (= Japanese kami).

honzon 本尊 J. Chief object of veneration. In the Nichiren tradition, *Dai-go-honzon*: a *maṇḍala* composed by Nichiren, serving as a focus of veneration.

Hossō. See Fa-hsiang.

hsin 心 C.; *shin* J. Mind, heart.

hsing 性 C.; *shō, sei* J. Nature.

hua-t'ou 話頭 C.; *hwadu* K.; *watō* J. Lit. "head of the statement": the critical phrase in a kōan.

ichinen sanzen 一念三千 J. One thought includes all three thousand worlds; a Tendai doctrine derived from the *Lotus Sūtra*.

ichinengi 一念義 J. Single-invocation theory, Kōsai's theory that one invocation of Amida assures rebirth; as opposed to Ryūkan's many-invocation theory *(tanengi)*.

inka 印可 J. Sanction or certification of enlightenment in Zen.

jakkō 寂光 J. Tranquil light.

jakumetsu 寂滅 J. Tranquil extinction; *nirvāṇa*.

jikkai 十界 J. Ten worlds: the six realms in which sentient beings transmigrate (*rokudō* 六道 J.), plus the four realms of *śrāvakas, pratyekabuddhas*, bodhisattvas, and buddhas.

jinshin 深心 J. Deep faith, in Jōdo Shinshū.

jissetsu 十刹 J. "Ten temples"; temples ranking below the *gozan* (q.v. *wu-shan*) in the Chinese and Japanese ranking systems.

Jizō 地蔵 J.; Kṣitigarbha S. Bodhisattva of travelers, children, pregnant women, and hell-beings.

jōdo 浄土 J.; *ching t'u* C.; *chŏngt'o* K. A pure land, the dwelling of a Buddha.

Jōgyō 上行 J.; Viśiṣṭacaritra S. Bodhisattva mentioned in the *Lotus Sūtra*, chapter 15; one of the four leaders of the bodhisattvas who emerge from the earth to propagate the sūtra.

jōgyō-zammai 常行三昧 J. Pure Land *samādhi* practice of perpetual walking.

jūnyoze 十如是 J. The ten "such-like" factors of existence: form, nature, substance, power, activities, primary causes, environmental causes, effects, rewards and retributions, and the totality of the above nine; from the *Lotus Sūtra*.

jūzen 十善 J. The ten good deeds, an ancient formulation of Buddhist ethics.

kaidan 戒壇 J. Lit. precept-platform; ordination platform.

k'an-hua 觀話 C.; *kanhwa* K.; *kanna* J. Observing the kōan; the style of practice characteristic of Rinzai Zen since the time of Ta-hui. Opposed to *mo-chao* (q.v.).

ken J. See *darśana*.

kenshō 見性 J.; *chien-hsing* C.; *kyonsŏng* K. Lit. "seeing the nature"; Zen enlightenment (= *satori* 悟 J.)

kenmitsu 顯密 J. The exoteric (*kengyō* 顯教) and esoteric (*mikkyō* 密教) teachings; the former are taught by the Buddha in his enjoyment and transformation bodies, the latter by his Dharma-body.

kihō-ittai 機法一體 J. The unity of the person and the Dharma (identified with Amida Buddha), in Pure Land Buddhism.

Kogaku 古学 J. "Ancient Learning" movement of the Neo-Confucian school in the Tokugawa period.

kokoro 心 J. Mind or heart. See *hsin*.

kokushi 國師 J. National Teacher, a posthumous honorific title conferred by an emperor.

kōmyō 光明 J. Radiant light, symbolizing the wisdom of buddhas and bodhisattvas.

k'ung 空 C.; *kū* J.; *śūnyatā* S. Emptiness.

kung-an 公案 C.; *kongan* K.; *kōan* J. Paradox, riddle, theme for focusing the mind, often taken from ancient dialogues, used as teaching device in Zen training.

kung-fu 工夫 C.; *kufū* J. Strenuous application in the practice of *zazen;* the work of cultivation in Zen's daily practice.

kuonjitsujō 久遠實成 J. "having realized Buddhahood in the remote past": a phrase from the *Lotus Sūtra* used in Tendai to indicate the eternity of the Buddha.

Kusha 俱舍 J.; *kośa* S. One of the Nara schools, based on the *Abhidharma-kośa*.

lakṣaṇa S.; *hsiang* 相 C.; *sō* J. "Mark"; identifying characteristic.

li/ch'i 理/気 C; *ri/ki* J. Noumenal principle/material force.

Mādhyamika, Madhyamaka S. The "middle path" school of Buddhism, founded by Nāgārjuna.

Mahākāśyapa S.; Mahākassapa P.; Makakashō, Kashō J. He became an *arhat* after only eight days as the Buddha's disciple. According to the Zen legend, when the Buddha raised a flower and blinked his eyes without speaking, Kāśyapa showed his understanding by a smile. The Buddha thereupon declared to him, "You have the treasury of the eye of the true

Dharma" (正法眼蔵 *shōbōgenzō* J.) and the "wondrous mind of *nirvāṇa*" (*nehan myōshin* J.); this "transmission from mind to mind" (*ishin denshin* 以心伝心 J.) made him the first patriarch of Zen Buddhism.

Mahāyāna S.; *ta-sheng* 大乗 C.; *daijō* J. "Great Vehicle"; the path of those Buddhists who choose to strive for Buddhahood rather than arhatship, as opposed to Hīnayāna ("little vehicle") Buddhism.

Mahāvairocana S.; Dainichi 大日 J. The cosmic Buddha, identical with the Dharmakāya, who is revered in Shingon. All other buddhas and bodhi-sattvas are generated from him.

Maitreya S.; Miroku 彌勒 J. The future Buddha dwelling in the Tuṣita paradise.

maṇḍala S.; *mandara* 蔓荼羅 J. Diagram illustrating Buddhist cosmology and used as aid in meditation.

Mañjuśrī S.; Monju 文殊 J. Bodhisattva of wisdom.

mantra S.; *shingon* 真言 J. Ritualistic formula or incantation that symbolically embodies the truth.

mappō 末法 J.; *mo-fa* C. Decline of the Buddhist Law in the Latter Days; the third and last period in the East Asian tripartite dating system.

mārga S.; *magga* P.; *tao* 道 C.; *dō, michi* J. Path; way.

mayoi 迷い J. Illusion.

meitoku 明德 J. Illuminating virtue, a Confucian term.

metsubō 滅亡 J. Annihilation.

metsudo 滅度 J. *Nirvāṇa*.

mettā P.; *maitrī* S. Love, friendliness. First of a group of four meditative states called *brahma-vihāra*, followed by *karuṇā* (pity, compassion), *muditā* (sympathetic joy), and *upekkhā* (equanimity).

milgyo K.; *mikkyō* 密教 J. Esoteric or tantric Buddhism.

missan-chō 密參帳 J. Secret records of kōan interviews.

mo-chao 黙照 C.; *mokushō* J. Silent meditation; opposed to *k'an-hua* (q.v.).

mondō 問答 J.; *mundap* K. Question and answer; Zen dialogue; exchange between Zen master and student (or between two masters) that reveals their degree of understanding.

mudrā S.; *inzō* 印相 J. Ritual hand-gesture.

muga 無我 J. See *anātman*.

mushin 無心 J. No-mind; freedom from discriminative thinking, in Zen.

myōhō 妙法 J.; *miao-fa* C. Wondrous Dharma.

Myōhō rengekyō 妙法蓮華經 J.; *Miao-fa lien-hua ching* C. Title of the *Lotus Sūtra*, used as a mantra in the Nichiren tradition.

myōō 明王 J.; *vidyārāja* S. Deities of ferocious aspect who destroy evil spirits at Dainichi's behest.

nen 念 J. Thought, fixation, remembrance.

neng-so 能所 C.; *nung-so* K. Subject-object (distinction).

nien-fo 念佛 C.; *nyŏmbul* K.; *nenbutsu* J. Recollecting the Buddha; reciting the name of Amida Buddha.

Niō 二王 J. A guardian deity on either side of a temple gate: *Kongō-misshaku* on the left and *Naraen-kongō* on the right.

nirmāṇakāya S.; *keshin* 化身 J. Transformation body of the Buddha.

Nirvāṇa Sūtra S.; *Nieh-p'an ching* 涅槃經 C.; *Nehangyō* J. A Mahāyāna *sūtra* (full title: *Mahāparinirvāṇa Sūtra*) that recounts the Buddha's last journey (entirely different from the *Mahāparinibbāna Sutta* in the Pāli Canon). This was the scripture of the Nirvāṇa school in China and is one of the sources for the idea of the universal Buddha-nature.

Ōbaku-shū 黃檗宗 J. Japanese Zen sect, introduced from China in the seventeenth century.

ōbō 王法, *buppō* 佛法 J. Royal law and Buddha law, the secular and the spiritual (in Rennyo).

ōjō 往生 J. Birth in the Pure Land.

ōsō/gensō 往相/還相 J. The two phases of going to the Pure Land and returning to this world.

p'an-chiao 教判 C.; *kyōhan* J. Classification of doctrines.

paramārthasatya/samvṛtisatya S. Ultimate and conventional reality, the twofold truth.

prajñā 般若 S.; *po-jo, pan-jo* C.; *hannya, e* 慧 J. Wisdom, insight.

Prabhūtaratna S.; Tahō 多寶 J. A Buddha who appears and praises Śākyamuni after his exposition of the first ten chapters of the *Lotus Sūtra*.

pratyekabuddha S.; *engaku* 縁覺, *byakushi-butsu* 辟支佛 J. A self-enlightened Buddha. Beings thought to attain enlightenment by their own power and for themselves alone.

preta S.; *gaki* 餓鬼 J. Hungry ghosts, the inhabitants of the world of the same name; one of the six courses of rebirth (*rokudō* 六道): hell, *preta*, animal, *asura*, human, heaven.

rōshi 老師 J. A Zen master, who has completed the training and is regarded as being enlightened.

ryōbu shintō 両部神道 J. Dual Shinto: a form of Buddhist-Shinto syncretism transmitted in the Shingon sect.

Sadāparibhūta S. Jōfugyō 常不軽 J. "Never Despising": a bodhisattva who revered everyone, even his enemies, as future Buddhas; Śākyamuni himself in a former existence, according to the *Lotus Sūtra*.

samādhi S.; *san-mei* 三昧, *ting* 定 C.; *sanmai, zanmai, jō* J. State of meditative absorption. Meditation, the second of the three disciplines (*sangaku* 三学 J.), along with *śila* (precepts) and *prajñā* (q.v.).

Samantabhadra S.; Fugen 普賢 J. Bodhisattva of teaching.

śamatha S.; *chih* 止 C.; *shi* J. Serenity; calming.

saṃbhogakāya S.; *hōjin* 報身 J. One of the three bodies *(trikāya)* of a Buddha, the enjoyment body or reward body.

sanmaya-kai J. Esoteric precepts taught by Kūkai.

san-chü 三句 C.; *sanku* J. Three phrases of Lin-chi used in Ch'an meditation.

san-hsüan 三玄 C.; *sangen* J. Three "mysterious gates" of Lin-chi; stages on the way to Zen understanding.

San-lun 三論 C.; Sanron J. The Three Treatise school of Buddhism (Mādhyamika), based on the Chinese translations of Nāgārjuna's *Middle Treatise* and its companion texts, the *Hundred Treatise* and the *Twelve Topics Treatise*.

sanmitsu 三密 J. Three Mysteries of body, speech, and mind, in Shingon.

sanzen 參禪 J. Meeting the Zen master.

Sarvāstivāda S.; Setsu-issai-ubu 説一切有部 J. Early Buddhist school teaching the real existence of all dharmas, past, present, and future.

śāstra S.; *lun* 論 C.; *lon* K.; *ron* J. Treatise; the third basket of the Tripiṭika.

sati P.; *smṛti* S. Mindfulness.

seimei (inochi) 生命 J. Life; in Toda Jōsei, "life force."

Seishi 勢至 J.; Mahāsthāmaprāpta S. Bodhisattva of wisdom; in Pure Land iconography, Amida's right-hand attendant; Kannon, bodhisattva of mercy, is on the left.

senchaku, senjaku 選択 J. Selection: Amida Buddha's prescription of a single practice for attaining salvation.

sesshin 接心 J. Intensive Zen retreat.

shaba 娑婆 J.; *sahā* S. The samsaric world in which Śākyamuni teaches.

shakubuku 折伏 J. To conquer and overcome evil aggressively; the aggressive method of converting, as contrasted with the gentle (*shōju* 攝受) method.

shakumon / honmon 迹門・本門 J.; *chi men/pen men* C. The two divisions of the *Lotus Sūtra* (provisional teaching and fundamental teaching). The Buddha reveals his eternal nature only in the *honmon*.

shami 沙彌 J.; *śrāmaṇera* S. A novice who has vowed to observe ten precepts: the five lay precepts forbidding killing, stealing, lying, sexual misconduct, and intoxicants, plus precepts against decorating one's body, listening to songs and seeing dances, sleeping in a big bed, eating at the wrong time, and keeping money and jewels.

shana-gyō, shana-gō 遮那業 J. Esoteric teachings and practices in the Tendai school.

shih-shih wu-ai 事事無礙 C.; *sasa muae* K.; *jiji-muge* J. Hua-yen doctrine of the unobstructed interpenetration of all phenomena.

shikan 止觀 J.; *chih-kuan* C.; *śamatha-vipaśyanā* S. Concentration and insight, or, cessation and contemplation; the style of meditation taught in the Tendai school. *Shikan-gō* and *shana-gō* are the two practices (*ryōgō*) decreed by Saichō for Tendai monks.

shikan taza 只管打坐 J. "Just sitting"; the style of meditation practice of Sōtō Zen.

Shingaku 心学 J. The "Learning of the Heart" movement founded by Ishida Baigan.

Shingon 真言 J. Lit. "true word"; *mantra*; the tantric Buddhist sect founded by Kūkai.

shinjin datsuraku 身心脱落 J. "Dropping off body and mind": the enlightenment Dōgen learned from his teacher Ju-ching.

Shinto (*shintō*) 神道 J. Lit. "way of the gods," indigenous religion of Japan.

shinjin 信心 J. Believing mind; trust in Amida Buddha.

shinpō 心法 J. Psychological techniques.

shinshiki 身識 J.; *kāya-vijñāna* S. Somatic-awareness consciousness; consciousness dependent on the perception of touch.

shōbō 正法 J. The true Dharma. In the tripartite *mappō* schema, the age of the true Dharma is followed by that of the semblance Dharma (*zōhō*).

shōdōmon 聖道門 J. The "teaching of the way of the saints," relying on self-power, as opposed to the Pure Land path of trust in Other-power.

shōjōju 正定聚 J. Fully assured of birth in the Pure Land.

shōnin 聖人 J. Title meaning "Saint."

shozan 諸山 J. Temples of the third rank, below *gozan* and *jissetsu*.

shugendō 修験道 J. A movement that focuses on ascetic practice in the mountains.

soku-hi 即非 J. The paradoxical logic of affirmation-in-negation from the *Diamond Sūtra*: "A is not A, therefore it is called A."

sokushin jōbutsu 即身成佛 J. To become a Buddha in this very existence; the realization of buddhahood with this very body.

śrāvaka S.; *shōmon* 聲門 J. Hearer, Hinayāna disciple.

stūpa S.; *sotoba* 卒都婆, *tō* 塔 J. Burial mound of a secular or religious hero, notably one enshrining Buddha relics.

Sukhāvatī S. The Pure Land, the Western paradise of Amitābha Buddha.

sūtra S.; *ching* 經 C.; *gyŏng* K.; *kyō* J. Lit. "thread"; scripture, authoritative text; the first basket of the Tripiṭika.

taizō 胎蔵 J.; *garbha* S. Matrix; womb; *taizōkai*: name of Shingon maṇḍala.

ta-li 他力 C.; *tariki* J. Other-power (of Amida Buddha) as opposed to self-power (*tzu-li* 自力 C.; *jiriki* J.).

tantra S. A type of religious literature that deals with incantation, divination, iconographic, and/or sexual devices to symbolically represent what the writers conceive as the truth.

tathāgata S.; *nyorai* 如来 J. Lit. "thus-come" or "thus-gone"; an epithet of a Buddha.

tathāgatagarbha S.; *nyoraizō* 如来蔵 J. Embryo, womb, or store of buddha-hood in all sentient beings; see *buddhatā*.

tathatā S.; *shinnyo* 真如, *nyojitsu* 如實 J. Suchness, the true reality of things as empty; identified with the *dharmakāya*.

Ten worlds; ten realms. See *jikkai*.

tengo 轉語 J. "Turning word": an utterance that comes at the decisive moment and brings the hearer to enlightenment in Zen Buddhism.

T'ien-t'ai 天台 C.; Ch'ont'ae K.; Tendai J. School founded by Chih-i, who systematized a vast array of Buddhist teachings and practices, based on principles from the *Lotus Sūtra*.

ti-yung 體用 C.; *ch'e-yong* K. Essence/function, substance/operation.

ti-hsiang yung 體相用 C.; *ch'e-sang-yong* K. Essence/attributes/function.

t'ong pulgyo 通佛教 K. Buddhism of total interpenetration.

tonŏ chŏmsu 頓悟漸修 K.; *tongo zenshū* J. Sudden enlightenment/gradual cultivation.

tripiṭaka S.; *sanzō* 三蔵 J. Lit. three baskets or storehouses; the three sections of the Buddhist Canon: *sūtra*, *vinaya*, and *śāstra*.

triratna S.; *sanbō* 三宝 J. The Three Jewels: Buddha, Dharma, and Saṅgha.

tso-ch'an 坐禪 C.; *zazen* J. Sitting in meditation.

tsung 宗 C.; *shū* J. Lineage of teachings; school; sect.

upāya, upāya-kauśalya S.; *fang-pien* 方便 C.; *hōben* J. Skillful means used by the Buddha and by bodhisattvas to help oneself and others realize enlightenment.

vajrayāna S.; *chin-kang-ch'eng* 金剛乗 C.; *kongōjō* J. Diamond Vehicle; tantric Buddhism.

vāsanā S. Karmic residues, good or bad, that permeate the mind; latent, habitual tendencies.

vihāra S., P. Monastery.

vinaya S.; *ritsu* 律 J. Precepts, the second basket of the Tripiṭika. The Ritsu school was one of the six Nara schools.

vipassanā P.; *vipaśyanā* S.; *kuan* 觀 C.; *kan* J. Insight, contemplation.

wu 無 C. *mu*; J. Nothingness. "No!" in answer to the question: "Has the dog Buddha-nature?" in the first kōan of the *Mumonkan* (Gateless barrier) collection.

wu-shan 五山 C.; *gozan* J. "Five Mountains"; system of ranking temples, introduced into Japan from China.

yakṣa S.; *yasha* 夜叉 J. In India, an indigenous tree-spirit that could bring either blessings or calamity; sometimes regarded as protector of Buddhism.

yamabushi 山伏 J. Mountain ascetics of the *shugendō* (q.v.) movement, associated with Shingon or Tendai Buddhism.

yeh-shih C. Fundamental activating consciousness that creates the bifurcation between subject and object.

Yogācāra S. The consciousness-only (*cittamātra, vijñaptimātra* S.; *wei-shih* 唯識 C.; *yuishiki* J.) school of Buddhism, founded by Asaṅga and Vasubandhu.

yongji 靈知 K. Mysterious power of insight.

yu-lu 語録 C.; *goroku* J. Recorded sayings (of Zen masters).

zazen. See *tso-ch'an*.

Zen. See *dhyāna*.

zettai mu 絶対無 J. Absolute nothingness, in Kyoto school philosophy.

Contributors

ALFRED BLOOM is Professor Emeritus, University of Hawaii. He received his Ph.D. from Harvard University, taught world religions and Buddhism at the University of Oregon, University of Hawai'i, and the Institute of Buddhist Studies. His works include *Shinran's Gospel of Pure Grace, Shoshinge, Strategies for Modern Living: A Commentary with Text of the Tannisho,* and *The Life of Shinran Shonin.*

ROBERT E. BUSWELL, JR. is Professor and Chair of the Department of East Asian Languages and Cultures at the University of California, Los Angeles, where he also serves as Director of the Center for Korean Studies. A specialist in the Korean Buddhist tradition, his books include *The Zen Monastic Experience: Buddhist Practice in Contemporary Korea, Tracing Back the Radiance: Chinul's Korean Way of Zen,* and *The Formation of Ch'an Ideology in China and Korea.*

JULIA CHING is Professor at the University of Toronto, where she holds the R. C. and E. Y. Lee Chair, and is a fellow of the Royal Society of Canada. Her fifteen books include a recent literary memoir, *The Butterfly Heals: A Life between East and West.*

EGIL FRONSDAL received his Ph.D. in Buddhist Studies from Stanford University in 1998 and is currently teaching at the Sati Center for Buddhist Studies in Palo Alto, California. His studies focus on early Indian Mahāyāna, Buddhist ethics, and Buddhism in the modern West.

DAVID LION GARDINER is Assistant Professor in the Department of Religion at Colorado College. He specializes in early Japanese Buddhism and has published articles and translations related to the early Shingon school. He is currently working on a monograph on Kūkai.

HANAYAMA SHINSHŌ 花山信勝 (1898–1995) studied Indian Philosophy and Buddhism at Tokyo Imperial University, after which he taught at several universities before returning to his Alma Mater in 1946. He was granted the Imperial Academy Award for his study of Prince Shōtoku's commentary on the *Saddharmapuṇḍarika-sūtra.* After his retirement in 1959, he was active for many years in the United States as the Bishop of the Buddhist Churches of America.

HANAYAMA SHŌYŪ 花山勝友 (1931–1995) completed his Ph.D. in Indian Philosophy and Buddhism at Tokyo University and later taught at the State University of New York and at Seton Hall University. Until his recent death, he was Professor at Musashino Women's College in Tokyo and was in charge of the research office of the Bukkyō Dendō Kyōkai. His works include *Understanding Buddhism* and *The Heart of the Heart Sūtra,* both in Japanese.

JAMES W. HEISIG is Director of the Nanzan Institute for Religion and Culture in Nagoya, Japan. He is general editor of a nineteen-volume series of books that includes twelve titles directly related to the thought of the Kyoto School of philosophy, and is also coeditor of the recently published *Rude Awakenings: Zen, the Kyoto School, and the Question of Nationalism.*

GILBERT JOHNSTON is Professor Emeritus of Eckerd College in St. Petersburg, Florida. He received his Ph.D. at Harvard University in East Asian religions, specializing in the thought of Kiyozawa Manshi and the attempt of Meiji-Era Buddhism to understand itself in terms consonant with nineteenth-century Western philosophy.

THOMAS P. KASULIS is Professor of Comparative Studies at The Ohio State University. He specializes in comparative philosophy and religion, a field in which he has authored or co-edited six books, including *Zen Action/Zen Person*. His current research is on the development of Japanese philosophy from ancient times through the modern period.

FUJIMOTO KIYOHIKO 藤本浄彦 is Professor of Pure Land Buddhist Thought at Bukkyō University, Kyoto. His works include *A Study of Existential Theories of Religion, The Pure Land Theory of Hōnen* (both in Japanese); and in Western languages *A Study of Hōnen's Doctrine of Akunin-shoki, The Modernization Movement and the Traditional Education of the Pure Land Sect,* and *Begründer des japanischen Amida-Buddhismus, Heileger Hōnen*.

SALLIE KING is Professor in the Department of Philosophy and Religion at James Madison University. She served as president of the Society for Buddhist-Christian Studies from 1995–1997. Her publications include *Passionate Journey: The Spiritual Autobiography of Satomi Myodo* and *Buddha Nature*, as well as a coedited volume, *Engaged Buddhism: Buddhist Liberation Movements in Asia*.

FRANZ AUBREY METCALF received his Ph.D. from the University of Chicago Divinity School in 1997. He continues to study psychological development and American Zen Buddhism. He is currently working with the Forge Institute and teaching at California State University, Los Angeles.

MICHEL MOHR is Professor at the International Research Institute for Zen Buddhism in Hanazono University, Kyoto. His publications include the recent work *Traité sur l'Inépuisable Lampe du Zen: Tōrei et sa vision de l'éveil*.

SUNG BAE PARK is Professor of East Asian Philosophy and Religions in the State University of New York at Stony Brook. His works include *Buddhist Faith and Sudden Enlightenment, Wonhyo's Commentary on the "Treatise on Awakening of Mahāyāna Faith,"* and *The Four-Seven Debate: An Annotated Translation of the Most Famous Controversy in Korean Neo-Confucian Thought*.

LAUREL RASPLICA RODD is Professor of Japanese at the University of Colorado, Boulder. She specializes in Japanese classical literature. Her publications include *Nichiren: Selected Writings* and *Kokinshu: A Collection of Poems Ancient and Modern*.

MINAMOTO RYŌEN 源 了圓 is Professor Emeritus of Japanese intellectual history, Tōhoku University, and the author of some eighteen books and over one hundred articles in Japanese, including *Form, Studies in the Idea of Practical Learning in the Early Modern Period*, and *Buddhism and Confucianism*.

HENG-CHING SHIH 釋恆清 is Professor in the Department of Philosophy and founder of the Center for Buddhist Studies at National Taiwan University. Her publications include *Syncretism of Ch'an and Pure Land Buddhism and the Theory of Buddha-Nature*.

SHIMAZONO SUSUMU 島薗 進 is Professor of religious studies at the University of Tokyo. His recent works include *New Spirituality Movements in the Global Society* and *The Potential of Religion Today: Aum Shinrikyō and Violence*, both in Japanese.

HENRIK H. SØRENSEN did doctoral studies in East Asian Cultures and Languages, specializing in Buddhist culture in China and Korea, as well as esoteric Buddhism in general. He is currently a Senior Researcher at the National Museum of Copenhagen. He is also co-founder of the Seminar for Buddhist Studies and principal editor of its journal, *Studies in Central and East Asian Religions*.

TAMARU NORIYOSHI 田丸徳喜 is Professor Emeritus of the University of Tokyo. He served as past president of the Japanese Association of Religious Studies and is an honorary lifetime member of the International Association for the History of Religions. He is the author of *History and Problems of the Study of Religion* (in Japanese) and coeditor of *Religion in Japanese Culture*.

TSUCHIDA TOMOAKI 土田友章 completed his M.A. work at Tokyo University with a thesis on Dōgen, after which he moved to Harvard University, where he wrote a doctoral thesis on Buddhist-Confucian interaction in China. He currently teaches Japanese thought and religion at Nanzan University in Nagoya, Japan, and pursues a side interest in ethics.

ROYALL TYLER is on the faculty of The Australian National University in Canberra. His research has concerned premodern Japanese literature as well as Japanese mountain cults and Buddhist-Shinto syncretism. In the latter area his major publication is *The Miracles of the Kasuga Deity*.

UMEHARA TAKESHI 梅原 猛, a popular historian of Japanese culture and ideas, is former director of the International Research Center for Japanese Studies. His works on Buddhism include *Saichō Meditation, Lotus and Other Tales of Medieval Japan,* and a two-volume work entitled *Shōtoku Taishi*.

WAKIMOTO TSUNEYA 脇本平也 is Professor Emeritus of the University of Tokyo and Chair of the Board of Directors of the International Institute for the Study of Religions in Japan. His Japanese writings include *A Critical Biography of Kiyozawa Manshi, A Comparative Religions Study of Death,* and *Introduction to the Science of Religion*.

PAUL B. WATT is Professor and Director of Asian Studies and Chair of Religious Studies at DePauw University; he has also taught at Grinnell College and Columbia University. A specialist in Japanese intellectual and religious history, he is the author of numerous essays on Buddhism and on the interaction between religion and Japanese culture.

DALE S. WRIGHT is Professor of Religious Studies and Asian Studies at Occidental College in Los Angeles. In addition to numerous articles on Buddhism in scholarly journals, he is author of *Philosophical Meditations on Zen Buddhism* and coeditor of *The Koan: Texts and Contexts in Zen Buddhism*.

PHILIP YAMPOLSKY (1920–1996) was Professor of Japanese at Columbia University, as well as librarian of Columbia's East Asian Library. A scholar of Chinese and Japanese religions and a specialist in Zen studies, his numerous translations and publications include *The Platform Sutra of the Sixth Patriarch, The Zen Master Hakuin: Selected Writings*, and *Selected Writings of Nichiren*.

MIMI HALL YIENGPRUKSAWAN is Professor of Japanese Art at Yale University. She specializes in Buddhist art and culture of the medieval era, with emphasis on the social and material dimensions of icon production. She is author of *Hiraizumi: Buddhist Art and Regional Politics in Twelfth-Century Japan*.

Photographic Credits

The editors and publisher wish to thank the varied museums, religious institutions, and individuals for providing photographs and granting permission to reproduce the illustrations in this volume.

1, 5. Tokyo National Museum and Yōtoku-in, Kyoto.

2, 3, 4, 6, 7. Institute for Zen Studies, Kyoto.

8, 17, 18, 20, 22, 32. Tokyo National Museum.

9, 10, 11, 13, 14, 15, 16. Henrik H. Sørensen, private collection.

12, 19, 21, 25. Kyoto National Museum.

23. Ian Reader, private collection.

24. Kōsei Publishing Co., Tokyo.

26. Nara National Museum.

27. Kuon-ji, Yamanashi Prefecture.

28. Hōkyō-ji, Fukui Prefecture.

29. Nisōdō, Nagoya, Japan.

30. Shōun-ji, Osaka, and Osaka Metropolitan Museum of Art.

31. Kōrin-ji, Tokyo.

33. Ōtani University, Kyoto and Jōkoku-ji, Niigata Prefecture.

34. Ueda Shizuteru, private collection.

35. Takeuchi Yoshinori, private collection.

36. Kurasawa Yukihiro, private collection.

37. Heng-Ching Shih, private collection.

38. Sōka Gakkai, Tokyo.

39, 40. Sulak Sivaraksa, private collection.

41. The Eastern Buddhist Society, Ōtani University, Kyoto.

Index of Names

Abe Chōichi, 22
Abe Masao, 290, 386
Abe Ryūichi, 200
Acalanātha, 407, 410, 412, 511, 513
Addiss, Stephen, 325, 327
Aitken, Robert, 32, 481, 501, 503, 506, 509–10
Akamatsu Toshihide, 272
Ākāśagarbha, 240
Akiyama Kanji, 309, 324, 326
Akizuki Ryōmin, 318, 324–26, 386
Akṣobhya, 397, 407, 411, 511
Akubyō, 259
Almond, Philip C., 495
Amaterasu, 145, 244–45, 251
Ambedkar, B. R., 472, 481
Amida Buddha, xix, 31, 149, 161–62, 189, 194, 201–5, 207–10, 212–18, 220, 223, 225–33, 236–37, 240, 244–45, 249, 279, 282–83, 330, 408, 451, 511, 513–15, 517–20; A.-dera, 351–53; A.-faith, 279. See also Amita, Amitābha, Amitāyus, A-mi-t'o
Amita, 511
Amitābha, 45, 113, 115, 161, 229, 341, 395, 397, 407–8, 411–12, 511, 519
Amitāyus, 229, 511
A-mi-t'o, 31
Amogasiddhi, 411
Amoghapāśa, 161, 412
Amoghavajra, 176
An Lu-shan, 9, 15
An Pyŏng-jik, 131–32
Anan, 411
Ānanda, 130, 411
Ananda Metteya, 485
Anderson, Reb, 509
Andira, 411

Andrews, Allan A., 211
Anesaki, Masaharu, 254
Annen. See Saichō
Anteira, 411
Ariga Toshitaka, 416
Aris, Michael, 481
Aristotle, 369, 382, 386
Ariyaratne, A. T., 471, 481
Arnold, Sir Edwin, 483
Arntzen, Sonja, 306
Āryāvalokiteśvara, 412
Asai Endō, 453
Asaṅga, 130, 391–92, 396, 521
Ashikaga Tadayoshi, 267–68
Ashikaga Takauji, 267
Ashikaga Takayoshi, 268
Ashikaga Yoshimitsu, 268, 271
Ashikaga Yoshimochi, 267
Ashuku, 411, 511
Aston, W. G., 143
Aśvaghoṣa, 68, 70, 78, 200
A-tao, 77
Atō Ōtari, 174
Augustine, Morris J., 211–12
Avalokiteśvara, 117, 161, 222, 401, 407, 411–12, 465, 512

Baker, Richard, 509
Bankei Yōtaku, xx, 291, 295–303, 305–6, 321, 343–44, 346
Barnes, Nancy J., 480
Barry, Brian, 132
Batō Kannon, 407
Batchelor, Philip C., 495
Bazara, 411
Beal, Samuel, 414
Bellah, Robert, 345–46
Benchō. See Shōkōbō Benchō

Benkyō. *See* Shiio Benkyō
Bennet, Alan, 485
Benzaiten, 410
Bergson, Henri, 382, 386
Berling, Judith, 335
Berrigan, Daniel, 479, 481
Berry, Mary Elizabeth, 324, 328
Bhaiṣajyaguru, 397, 408, 411, 512
Bibashi, 161
Bielefeldt, Carl, 200
Birushana, 146, 408
Bishamonten, 410
Blavatsky, Elena Petrovna, 484
Blofeld, John, 35, 43
Bloom, Alfred, xix, 237–38
Bodhidharma, xiv–xv, 3, 5–8, 11–13,
    24–25, 32, 37, 116, 258, 289–90,
    292, 320, 500, 508
Bodiford, William M., 273, 508–10
Boehme, Jacob, 382
Bonten, 410
Boucher, Sandy, 495
Brahmā, 67, 410
Brocchieri, Paula Beonio, 346
Buddhadasa, 481
Buddhalocanī, 408, 415
Buswell, Robert E., Jr., xvii, 22, 107, 130–32
Butchō-son, 408
Butsugen Butsumo, 408, 415

Cabezón, José Ignacio, 415
Calvin, John, 169
Candraprabha, 411
Cannon, Sir Alexander, 128
Carlson, Kyogen, 509
Carus, Paul, 485
Cash, Johnny, 413
Cayce, Edgar, 128
Chah, 490
Chan-chia, 432
Chan-jan, 167
Chang Chung-yuan, 43, 53
Chang Man-t'ao, 434
Chang Shang-ying, 18
Chang-weng. *See* T'ien-t'ung Ju-ching
Chao-chou Ts'ung-shen, 29, 46, 95–96, 98
Ch'en, Kenneth, 254
Cheng Ch'eng-kung, 417
Cheng Yen, 428–31
Ch'eng Yi, 50, 53

Ch'eng-kuan, 15, 66
Chia-hsiang Chi-tsang, 427
Chiang T'san-t'eng, 434
Chien-chen, 169
Chigi, 444–45. *See also* Chih-i
Chih Kuang, 420
Chih-hsien, 4, 11
Chih-i, xiii, 167, 170, 187, 190–91, 200,
    204, 251, 254, 277, 444, 520
Chih-p'an, 47
Chih-yen, 10, 67
Chikō, 201
Chin Chuang, 418
Ching Chia-yi. *See* Ching, Julia
Ching, Julia, xvi, 53
Chin'gak Hyesim, 80, 97, 102
Ch'ing-yüan Hsing-ssu, 4, 12
Chinkai, 204
Chinmyu, King, 77
Chinul, xvii, 73, 79–84, 86–90, 94–97,
    99–100, 102–3, 107–8, 112–14, 126
Chi-tsang. *See* Chia-hsiang Chi-tsang
Chi-yüan, 262
Cho Myŏng-gi, 63
Chŏng Hogyŏng, 132
Chŏngjo, 115
Chou Hsuan-te, 422, 424
Chou Tun-yi, 50
Choŭi Ŭisun, 116
Chu Ch'i-ch'ang, 434
Chu Hsi, 49–50, 53, 331–34, 344, 348
Ch'u Ying-kuang, 432
Chuang-tzu, xv, xxiii, 311
Chueh Li, 419
Chu-hung Yun-ch'i, 22
Chun Shin-yong, 143
Chung-feng Ming-pen, 22
Cleary, Thomas, 39, 42–43, 290
Coates, Harper Havelock, 211–12
Collcutt, Martin, 273
Confucius, xv, 48, 77, 137, 333–35, 340, 349
Cooey, Paula M., 480
Covell, Jon Carter, 306
Cozin, Mark, 132
Cusanus, 213, 370

Dahlke, Paul, 486
Daiga, 329
Daiitoku, 407
Daikashō, 411

Daikyū Ebō, 319
Dainichi, xviii, 161, 240, 242, 245, 408, 516. See also Mahāvairocana
Dainichi Nōnin, 256–60
Daiō. See Nanpo Jōmyō
Daishū Zenjo, 318
Daitō, 23, 185, 269–71, 308, 323, 328, 357, 414
Dalai Lama, 432, 464–66, 470, 474, 478, 480–81
De Bary, William Theodore, 143, 172, 185, 200, 340, 345, 415
Den Sutejo, 297
Dengyō, 164, 200, 232
Dennison, Ruth, 490
Descartes, René, 382
Deshimaru Taisen, 501
Dharmākara, 217, 229, 380, 511
Dharmapāla, 150, 513
Dharmapāla, Anagārika, 482, 484, 488–89
Dhiravamsa, 487
Diderot, Denis, 157
Diem Dinh Ngo, 461
Dilworth, David, 387
Dīpaṃkara Buddha, 35
Dix, Griffin, 131–32
Dobbins, James, 238
Dōgen, xv, xix–xx, 172, 186, 192, 194, 199–200, 206, 210, 254, 256, 259–63, 272, 274–90, 321, 330, 382, 386, 450, 519, 524
Dōji, 152
Dōju Sōkaku, 312
Dōkō Ryōe, 219, 324, 327
Dōkyō Etan, 53, 147, 152, 166, 310–12, 324
Dōni. See Nakazawa Dōni
Douglas, Gordon, 485
Dumoulin, Heinrich, 22, 32, 53, 132, 306
Dunne, John D., 391, 413
Durand, Gilbert, 413
Durt, Hubert, 143

Eakin, William R., 480
Eckel, Malcolm David, 391–92, 396–98, 413–15
Eckhart, 382
Edmonds, Philip, 480
Egen. See Kanzan Egen
Eisai, xx, 172, 256–60, 274, 279, 289

Ejō. See Koun Ejō
Ekachai, Sanitsuda, 480
Ekadāśamukha, 412
Ekākṣaroṣṇīṣa-cakra, 408
Ekan, 259–61
Ekkei Shuken, 318
Eliade, Mircea, 413
En no Gyōja, 158
Enchin, 172, 241
Enji Tōrei, 309, 326
Enni Ben'en, 260, 265–66, 315, 324
Ennin, 172, 201, 222, 241
Epictetus, 362, 364–65
Eppsteiner, Fred, 481
Erasmus, 106
Eshin-ni, 223, 225

Fages, Martine, 132
Fa-hsien, 392, 394, 397
Fa-ju, 6
Fa-jung, 10, 26
Fa-tsang, 66–68, 190
Faure, Bernard, 510
Fa-yen Wen-i, 17, 19, 22, 53, 315
Feldman, Christina, 495
Feniger, Siegmund, 486
Fenollosa, E. F., 360
Fields, Rick, 495
Foard, James, 199, 253–54
Fo-chao Te-kuang, 49, 258
Fo-jih Ch'i-sung, 19
Foucault, Michel, 391, 400, 413
Foucher, Alfred, 394, 414
Foulk, Griffith, 323, 328
Foster, Nelson, 32
Fox, Richard, xx
Franck, Frederick, 387
Fronsdal, Egil, xxi
Fudō-myōō, 412, 511, 513
Fugen, 409, 518
Fujii Nichidatsu, 466
Fujimoto Kiyohiko, xix
Fujiwara Chikayasu, 246
Fujiwara clan, 206, 222, 259–60
Fujiwara Michinaga, 202
Fujiwara Yorimichi, 202
Fukuda Gyōkai, 357
Fukūkenjaku, 161, 412
Fukushima Masato, 452
Funaoka Makoto, 323, 326

Fung Yu-lan, 53
Funnuō, 410
Furuta Shōkin, 272, 346
Fuse Shōō, 344–45

Gakkō, 411
Galilei Galileo, 382
Gandhi, Mahatma, 457, 460, 466, 479
Gaṇeśa, 410
Ganjin, 169
Ganjō, Shami, 330
Gardiner, David Lion, xix
Gasan Jitō, 319
Gautama, 393–94, 397–98, 413
Gazan Jōseki, 262
Gedatsu Shōnin, 162
Genkū, 204, 279. *See also* Hōnen
Genshin, 172, 201, 204, 209, 211, 226
Gessen Zenne, 314, 319
Geuth, Anton, 485
Ghosananda, 460, 465, 474, 480
Gien, 260, 262
Gijun, 260
Gimello, Robert M., 22
Gira, Dennis, 238
Glassman, Bernie, 478, 506, 510
Godaigo, Emperor, 265, 267, 270
Goenka, Satya Narayan, 490
Gokomatsu, Emperor, 270
Goldstein, Joseph, 489, 494
Gombrich, Richard, 494
Gómez, Luis O., 211–12, 237
Go-mizunoo, 291
Gomyō, 152, 158, 169
Gotō Kōson, 309, 326
Grapard, Alan C., 200
Gregory, Peter N., 22, 53, 107, 414–15
Griffiths, Paul, 391, 395–97, 413–14
Grimm, Georg, 486
Groner, Paul, 172, 199–200, 414
Gross, Rita M., 480, 509–10
Guṇabhadra, 6
Gudō Tōshoku, 313–14
Gumoku Shinshō, 351
Gunānanda, 484
Gyōki, 157, 169, 288
Gyōkū, 211

Habito, Ruben, 200
Hachiman, 160, 251

Hakamaya Noriaki, 200, 413
Hakeda Yoshito, 78, 184–85, 200
Hakuin Ekaku, xx, 307–28, 334, 343, 524
Hakuyūshi, 310–11, 323–24, 326
Hallisey, Charles, 414
Han Kidu, 131–32
Han Tung, 432
Han Yŏngun, 119–22, 124, 129, 131
Han Yü, 48
Hanayama Shinshō and Shōyu, xviii, 143
Hanazono, Emperor, 269–71
Han'guk Sasang Yŏn'guhoe, 77
Hanh, 456, 462, 464, 471, 474, 478–81,
    501, 506
Han-shan, 310, 382
Hase Hoshū, 358
Haskel, Peter, 306, 346
Hatano clan, 262
Hatano Yoshishige, 260, 275
Hattō, 263
Hattori Shōon, 221
Hayagriva, 407, 412
Hayashi Yukimitsu, 327
Hegel, G. W. F., 360, 363, 371, 376–77,
    380, 382
Heidegger, Martin, xx, 380
Heisig, James W., xx, 388
Heizei, Emperor, 167, 177
Hewavitarne, Don David, 484
Higuma Takenori, 453
Hino clan, 222
Hirakawa Akira, 395, 414
Hirota, Dennis, 211, 238
Hŏ Hŭngsik, 107
Hōchibō Shōshin, 187–90, 192–94,
    197–200, 293
Hōjō clan, 266–67, 270
Hōjō Shigetoki, 247
Hōjō Tokimune, 265, 270
Hōjō Tokiyori, 247, 276
Hölderlin, Friedrich, xiv
Hōnen, xix, 157, 170, 172, 186, 189, 192,
    194, 203–24, 226–27, 231, 235, 259,
    274–75, 279, 450–51
Hōnenbō Genkū, 204
Hoover, Thomas, 32
Hori Ichirō, 211
Hori, Victor Sōgen, 325, 328
Horigome Nichijun, 453
Horner, I. B., 107

Hōsen Daibai, 350
Hŏung Pou, 110–12, 114, 130
Hōzō, 511
Hsiao Yun, 431
Hsien T'ien, 418
Hsing Yun, 491
Hsing-man, 167
Hsuan Hua, 501, 506, 509
Hsü-an Huai-ch'ang, 257
Hsuan-tsung, Emperor, 9, 16
Hsueh-feng I-ts'un, 17
Hsüeh-tou Ch'ung-hsien, 20
Hsü-t'ang Chih-yü, 269
Hu Shih, 23
Huang Ti, 311, 324
Huang-po Hsi-yüan, xvi, 16, 29–30, 35–43
Hu-ch'iu Shao-lung, 266
Hui-chi, 16
Hui-k'o, 3, 6, 24, 289
Hui-kuo, 176–77, 180
Hui-neng, 3–4, 6–13, 15, 28, 44, 69, 93, 280
Hui-yüan, 66, 71
Humphreys, Christmas, 494
Hung-chih Cheng-chüeh, 21, 30, 46, 49
Hung-jen, 3, 6, 8
Huntington, Susan L., 394, 414
Hurvitz, Leon, 199, 253–54
Hyŏbŏng, 127
Hyŏnjong, King, 103

Ichiji-kinrin, 408
Ichikawa Hakugen, 292–95, 306, 322, 326
I-ching, 351
Iemitsu, 291
I-fu, 7
I-hsing, 176
Iida Tōin, 323, 326
Ike no Taiga, 325
Ikeda Daisaku, 452, 454
Ikeda Eishun, 357
Ikkyū Sōjun, 270–71, 306
Imaeda Aishin, 272
Imagawa clan, 264
Imai Seiichi, 326
Imakita Kōsen, 326, 333, 335–36
I-ming, 177
Indra, 150, 410
Innis, R. 413
Inoue Nobutaka, 452–53

Inzan Ien, 319
Ippen, 210, 450
Ishida Baigan, xx, 303, 337–38, 340, 345–47, 519
Ishii Kyōdō, 212
Ishii Shinpo, 221
Ishii Shūdō, 272
Ishikawa Jishun, 310
Ishikawa Jōzan, 310
Ishikawa Ken, 346
Itō Jinsai, 349
Itō Kazuo, 326
Ittō Shōteki, 291
Iyo, Prince, 174
Izuyama Kakudō, 325–26, 346

Jacinto Zavala, Agustín, 386–88
Jackman, Robert, 490
Jackson, David and Denise, 415
Jakuen, 262
James, William, 369
Jaspers, Karl, 367, 386
Jen Ying-ch'iu, 324
Jesus Christ, 385, 387
Jien, 222
Jigenbō Eikū, 204
Jihōbō Genkō, 204
Jinpa, Geshe Thupten, 481
Jippan, 204
Jiun Sonja, xx, 348–58
Jizō, 162, 407, 514
Jōfugyō, 248, 517
Jōgyō, 239, 251–52, 443, 514
Johnston, Gilbert, xx, 366
Jōkakubō Kōsai, 211, 218, 514
Jōkei, 162–63, 279
Joko Beck, 477, 506–7
Jones, Charles B., 434
Jones, Ken, 481
Jōyō Daishi, 276
Ju-ching. See T'ien-t'ung Ju-ching
Jūichimen Kannon, 412
Junna, Emperor, 179

Kabat-zinn, Jon, 493–95
Kabilsingh, Chatsumarn, 481
Kabutogi Shōkō, 254
Kahin, George McT., 480
Kajitani Sōnin, 318, 326
Kakuan, 259–60

Kakumyōbō Chōsai, 210
Kakunyo, 225, 235
Kakushin-ni, 225, 235
Kalland, Arne, 132
Kalton, M. C., 336
Kamata Shigeo, 53, 326
Kameyama Takurō, 325
Kamstra, J. H., 143
Kan'ami, 288
Kanezane Kujō, 206, 222
Kanmu, Emperor, 147, 166–68, 174
Kannon, 149, 159, 161–62, 215, 222–23,
    225, 245, 263, 401, 407, 411–12,
    512, 518
Kant, Immanuel, 172, 360, 375–76,
    379–80
Kanzan Egen, 269, 271, 313, 324, 326-27
Kapleau, Philip, 501, 503, 505, 507
Kasan Genku, 318
Kashiwabara Yūsen, 335, 345–46
Kashō, 515
Kasō Sōdon, 270
Kasuga clan, 162–63
Kasulis, Thomas P., xvi, xviii, 32
Kāśyapa, 515
Katō Bunnō, 254
Katō Shōshun, 309, 323, 326–27
Katsumata Shunkyō, 200
Kawakami Kozan, 318–19, 325–26
Keel, Hee-sung, 107
Keenan, John P., 413
Keiga, 204
Keirin Sūshin, 314
Keizan Jōkin, 262, 287
Kendall, Laurel, 131–32
Kengan Zen'etsu, 314
Kerouac, Jack, 500
Khemma, Ayya, 491, 495
Khitan Liao, 103, 105
Khodharāja, 410
Khumbīra, 411
Kichijōten, 410
Kierkegaard, Søren, 380, 382
Kikumura Norihiko, 238
Kim Chigyŏn, 107
Kim Uchang, 130–33
Kim Young-tae (Yŏngt'ae), 78, 130, 133
Kimnara, 411
Kinami Takuichi, 346, 358
King, Sallie B., ix, xxi, 455, 480–81, 523

King, Winston L., 212, 221, 306, 346
Kinmei, Emperor, 137
Kinō Kazuyoshi, 254
Kirk, James, 254
Kisala, Robert, 454
Kitagawa, Joseph, 185
Kiuchi Gyōō, 172
Kiyota Minoru, 254
Kiyozawa Genshō, 361
Kiyozawa Manshi, xx, 359–66
Kōben. See Myōe
Kōbō Daishi, 164, 174, 181, 184–85, 200,
    282
Kōen, 204
Koga Hidehiko, 326
Kōgaku Sōen, 323
Kogetsu Zenzai, 314, 319, 324
Kōgon, Emperor, 267
Kohō Useki, 307
Kōin, 259
Kōken, Empress, 147, 152, 166
Kondō Tesshō, 211
Kongō-misshaku, 517
Kornfield, Jack, 480, 489, 492, 494–95
Kōsai. See Jōkakubō Kōsai
Kōsaka Masaaki, 386, 388
Kōshō. See Kūya
Kōson Isan, 309, 326
Koun Ejō, 260–61, 275
Kōya. See Kūya
Kōzuki Yasunori, 348–49
Kraft, Kenneth, 323, 328, 481, 510
Kṣitigarbha, 407, 409, 411, 514
Kuan-yin, 417, 424, 512
Kubota Shōbun, 254
Kuga Michichika, 274
Kujō Motofusa, 274
Kūkai, xviii–xix, xxii, 153, 155–56, 160,
    164–65, 167–68, 170, 172, 174–85,
    189–92, 196, 198–200, 240, 244–45,
    254, 282, 399–400, 415, 518–19
Kumārajīva, xiv
Kundalī, 407, 409
Kuroda Toshio, 197–98, 200
Kusan Sunim, 125–26, 128, 132
Kusumoto Bun'yū, 53
Kūya, 202–3, 210
Kyŏnghŏ, 117–20, 131–32
Kyōraimon'in, 352

LaFleur, William, 290
Lai, Whalen, 23, 418
Lancaster, Lewis R., 23, 78, 107
Lan-hsi Tao-lung, 265, 269
Laube, Johannes, 388
Ledermann, Ilse, 491
Ledi Sayadaw, 488, 494
Lee Ki-Baik, 78, 424
Lee, Peter H., 78, 107
Lee Ping-nan, 413, 424
Lee Young Ho, 132
Legge, James, 392, 394, 397
Leibniz, G. W., 171
Li Kung-tso, 323
Li T'ung, 50
Li T'ung-hsüan, 66, 84, 87, 89, 94, 107
Lin Chao-en, 332, 335
Lin-chi I-hsüan, xvi, 16–17, 20–21, 27,
    29–30, 32, 36, 38, 41, 43, 46–47, 49,
    94–95, 99, 101–2, 115–17, 126,
    130–31, 260, 279, 282, 289, 351,
    417, 518
Ling-lu, 35
Lingwood, Dennis P. E., 481
Ling-yu, 16–17
Lokakṣema, 414
Loori, Daido, 506
Lopez, Donald S., 107
Lotze, Rudolf Hermann, 360
Lu Chiu-yüan, 49
Lu I, 9
Lung Hua, 418
Luther, Martin, 169, 221

Machida Zuihō, 309, 325–26
Macy, Joanna, 471, 480–81
Maezumi Taizan, 500–1, 503, 506, 509–10
Maha Ghosananda, 460, 465, 474, 480
Mahākāśyapa, xiv, 24, 31, 411, 515
Mahākassapa, 515
Mahāsi Sayadaw, 488–89, 494
Mahāsthāmaprāpta, 215, 411, 518
Mahāvairocana, xviii, 161, 165, 175–77,
    180, 182–83, 398–400, 407–9,
    411–12, 415, 516. See also Dainichi
Mahoney, Jane Sharada, 480
Maitreya, 59, 127, 162, 174, 201, 232,
    413, 422, 516
Maitri AIDS Hospice, 477
Makakashō, 515

Makiguchi Tsunesaburō, 436–37, 442,
    451–54
Mandell, Jacqueline, 489
Mangong, 120
Mañjuśrī, 117, 163, 168, 407, 409, 411,
    507, 516
Māra, 412
Maraldo, John, 132, 388
Marananta, 77
Masutani Fumio, 254
Ma-tsu Tao-i, xvi, 10, 12–16, 29–30,
    33–36, 39, 41–43, 286
Matsudaira Tadatomo, 312
Matsumoto Shirō, 200
Matsunaga Daigan and Alicia, 173, 212,
    254
Matthiessen, Peter, 509–10
McDaniel, Jay B., 480
McMullen, James, 336
McRae, John R., 23
Meihō Sotetsu, 262
Meiji, Emperor, 276
Mekira, 411
Mencius, 48, 331, 334, 340–41, 344, 349,
    513
Merzel Genpo, 506
Metcalf, Franz Aubrey, xxi
Metteya, Ananda, 485
Miao Kuo, 421
Mihira, 411
Minamoto clan, 206
Minamoto Ryōen, xx, 306, 335
Minamoto Yoriie, 257
Minamoto Yoritomo, 193, 277
Ming-chiao Chi-sung, 48
Mingun Jetawun Sayadaw, 488
Miroku, 151, 162–63, 516
Mitsu-no-obito clan, 165
Miura Isshū, 32, 328
Miura Yasuhiro, 357, 357–58
Miyasaka Yūshō, 184–85
Miyata Kōichi, 453
Miyazaki Eichū, 254
Mochizuki Kankō, 254, 453
Mochizuki Shinkyo, 416
Mohr, Michel, xx, 325, 327–28
Mok Jeong-bae, 132
Monju, 162, 409, 516
Mononobe clan, 138
Monsai Tōnin, 291

Moore, Osbert, 486
Mori, Daikyō, 326
Morinaga Sōkō, 32, 335
Morrell, Robert E., 199
Motoori Norinaga, 321
Mugaku Sogen, 265
Mujaku Dōchū, 314
Muneyama Yoshifumi, 323, 327
Munindra, Anagārika, 489–90
Muniśri, 177
Munjŏng, Queen, 110
Munō, 219
Murakami Shigeyoshi, 453
Musō Soseki, 266–70, 272
Myōan Yōsai. See Eisai
Myōdō Taiju, 356
Myōe, 279
Myōzen, 260, 274–75, 279

Nagao Gadjin, 351, 414
Nāgārjuna, 165, 218, 226, 515, 518
Nakamaki Hirochika, 452–53
Nakamoto Tominaga, 355–57
Nakamura Hajime, 143, 453
Nakamura Hiroji, 312, 324, 327
Nakatomi clan, 137
Nakazawa Dōni, 342–46
Nan. See Sutasilo
Nan Huai-Chin, 32
Nan T'ing, 420
Ñāṇamoli, 486
Nan-ch'uan, 29
Nanpo Jōmyō, 269, 271, 315, 324
Nantenbō, 323
Nan-yüeh Huai-jang, 4, 12, 34–35, 280
Naoki Kimihiko, 325, 327
Naong Hyegŭn, 102
Narada Mahathera, 491
Naraen-kongō, 517
Nattier, Jan, 211, 497, 510
Neumann, Karl Eugen, 485
Nhat Hanh, 456, 462, 464, 471, 474,
    478–81, 501, 506
Nhu, 461
Nichiō, 330–31
Nichiren, xix, xxi, 140, 157, 163, 172, 186,
    192, 195, 206, 239–55, 259, 330,
    341, 343–44, 435–54, 466, 474, 480,
    508, 512, 514, 516
Nichizō, 161

Nietzsche, Friedrich, 380, 382
Nikkan, 442
Nikkō, 411, 442
Ninchō, 219
Ninkō Teiki, 349, 351
Nippō Sōshun, 271
Nishida Kitarō, 299, 368–79, 381–83,
    385–88
Nishimura Eshin, 323, 325, 327
Nishino Tatsukichi, 453
Nishitani Keiji, 368, 372, 374–76, 378,
    381–88
Nishiyama Shigeru, 442, 454
Niu-t'ou Fa-jung, 26
Nōnin. See Dainichi Nōnin
Nosco, Peter, 358
Nukariya Kaiten, 130, 132
Numrich, Paul, 508
Nyanaponika, 486
Nyanatiloka, 485–86, 491

Oguri Ryōun, 338–39
Ogyū Sorai, 333
Ōhashi Jijō, 453–54
Ōhashi Ryōsuke, 387
Ōhashi Shunnō, 211
Ohisu Jundō, 272
Okamura Keishin, 357–58
Oldenberg, Hermann, 483
O'Leary, Joseph S. 173
Ōno Yasuyuki, 452, 454
Ōryū Genrō, 322, 327
Osbert Moore, 486
Ōta Koboku, 415
Ōtsuki Mikio, 327
Ōuchi clan, 271
Ōuchi Seiran, 357
Ou-i Chih-hsu, 22

Packer, Toni, 477, 505, 507
Paekp'a Kungsŏn, 115–17
Pai Sheng, 420, 432
Pak Chŏngbin, 122
Park Chong-hong, 63, 77
Park, Sung Bae, xvii, 63, 77–78, 107–8
P'ei Hsiu, 15–16
Peirce, C. E., 413
Petzold, Bernard, 173
Pine, Red, 32
Plotinus, 382

P'o-an Tsu-hsien, 266
Powell, William F., 32
Prabhūtaratna, 240, 251, 517
Prajñā, 177
Prajñātāra, 13
Prasenajit, King, 394
Prebish, Charles, 510
Preston, David, 509–10
P'u-chi, 6–9
Pulgyohak T'ongin Hoe, 77
Pyŏksong Chiŏm, 130

Quang Duc, 461
Queen, Christopher L., 481

Rāgarāja, 407
Rahula, Walpola, 481
Rankei Dōryū, 265
Ratnasambhava, 411
Reader, Ian, 510
Reigen Etō, 319
Renchū, 258
Rennyo, 235–38, 329–30, 335, 364, 517
Reynolds, Frank E., 414
Rhi Ki-yong, 75, 78
Rhys Davids, T. W., 483, 485
Rikugawa Taiun, 323, 327
Risetsu, 312
Robert, Jean-Nöel, 173
Rodd, Laurel Rasplica, xix, 254
Rogers, Ann T. and Minor L., 238, 335
Roshana, 146
Roth, Gustav, 396, 414–15
Rowell, Galen, 480
Rubira, 411
Ryōchū, 218–19
Ryōe Dōkō, 219
Ryōgen, 201
Ryōnin, 202–4
Ryūkan, 210, 218, 514

Sadāparibhūta, 248, 517
Saeki Tagimi, 174
Saga, Emperor, 167, 177
Sahasrabhūja, 411–12
Saichō (Hirono), xviii, xxii, 139, 155–56, 158, 160, 164–72, 176–78, 184, 187, 189–91, 198–200, 232, 241–42, 251, 519, 524

Saigin, 330
Śākyamuni, xiv, 24, 31, 127, 130, 137, 139–40, 160–63, 172, 195, 212, 226, 229, 242–44, 251–52, 276, 282–83, 289, 349, 351, 380, 391, 393–94, 397, 399–401, 408, 411, 414–15, 438–39, 442–44, 456, 507–8, 517–18
Sakuramachi, Emperor, 352
Salzburg, Sharon, 495
Samantabhadra, 67, 117, 409, 411–12, 518
Sanada Nobuyuki, 312
Sanford, James H., 306
Santi Asoke, 435
Sarasvatī, 410
Sargent, E., 53
Śāriputra, 411, 428
Sasaki, Ruth Fuller, 32, 36, 38, 43, 325, 328
Satō Kokyū, 307
Saunders, Dale, 415
Sawa Ryūken, 401, 407, 415
Sawada Anderson, Janine, 309, 328, 346
Schelling, F. W. J., 380, 382
Schopen, Gregory, 414
Schopenhauer, Arthur, 485–86
Schumacher, E. F., 480
Seidenstuecker, Karl, 485
Seisetsu Shūcho, 314
Seishi, 411, 518
Sekida Katsuki, 32
Seng-ts'an, 3, 6, 24
Senju Kannon, 411
Seung Sahn, 500–1, 509
Shacklock, Floyd, 366
Shaka, 162, 205, 401. See also Śākyamuni
Shakku, 223. See Shinran
Shaku Sōen, 307, 327, 499
Shami Ganjō, 330
Shan Hui, 419
Shaner, David Edward, 253–54
Shan-tao, 204–5, 207–8, 213, 215, 222, 226, 233
Sharf, Robert H., 322, 328
Sharihotsu, 411
Shattock, E. H., 494
Shen Shu, 432
Sheng-yen, 32
Shen-hsiu, 4, 6–8, 10, 28, 33
Shen-hui, 6–9, 11, 15, 21, 28, 33
Shibata Kyūō, 344

Shibata Minoru, 341, 344–47
Shibayama Zenkei, 32, 324, 327
Shidō Munan, 291, 303–6, 313, 325
Shigeno Nobunao, 262
Shih Heng-Ching, xxi,
Shih-shuang Ch'u-yüan, 17
Shih-te, 382
Shih-t'ou Hsi-ch'ien, 12, 14–15
Shiio Benkyō, 220–21
Shijōkō Butchō, 408
Shikyō Eryō, 318
Shim Jae-ryong, 132
Shimano Eidō, 328
Shimazaki Bennei, 221
Shimazono Susumu, xxi, 452, 454
Shin Pŏpin, 130, 132
Shinki Dokumyō, 310, 326. See also Hakuin
  Ekaku
Shinohara Hisao, 23
Shinran, xix, 157, 172, 186, 189, 192, 194,
  211, 218, 221–38, 254, 275, 279,
  282, 329, 359, 361, 364, 380, 450–51
Shinshi Kakushin, 263, 265
Shiō Zenhō, 288
Shiramizu Hiroko, 454
Shitennō, 410
Shōben, 258
Shoemaker, Jack, 32
Shōgei, 219
Shōitsu, 260
Shōju Rōnin, 310, 324, 326–27
Shōkōbō Benchō, 209, 218–19
Shōmu, Emperor, 146–47, 157
Shōshin. See Hōchibō Shōshin
Shōtoku Taishi, xviii, 138–41, 143, 169,
  171, 201, 222
Shūhō Myōchō, 269–71, 323
Shunjō, 203
Shun'oku Myōha, 268
Shun-tao, 77
Siddhartha, 458
Sivaraksa, Sulak, 473–74, 481, 525
So T'aesan, 122–24
Sobin, 487
Soen Sa Nim. See Seung Sahn
Sōhan Genpō, 310
Sŏngch'ol, 126, 128, 132
Sŏngch'ŏng, 115
Sŏng-myŏng, King, 137
Sørensen, Henrik H., xvii, 130–32

Sōsan Taesa, 112
Sosurim, King, 77
Spencer, Herbert, 360
Spinoza, Baruch, 360, 363
Sponberg, Alan, 397, 415
Śrī, 410
Śrīmālā, Queen, 139
Stone, Jacqueline, 200
Su Tung-p'o, 18
Śubhākarasiṃha, 400
Sudāna, 413
Sugi, 105–6
Sugiyama Juhō, 321
Sugiyama Yōsen, 321
Suh Kikun, 107
Suiko, Empress, 138, 140
Suiō Genro, 318
Sumedho, 490–91, 495
Sung-yüan Ch'ung-yüeh, 266
Sutasilo, Nan, 457–58, 480
Suu Kyi, Aung San, 473–74, 481
Suzuki, D. T., 299, 307, 321, 324, 336,
  373, 382, 486, 499–501
Suzuki Ichijō, 254
Suzuki Shōsan, 306, 343, 346
Suzuki Shunryu, 509–10
Suzuki Taizan, 272
Swanson, Paul L., 173, 200, 413
Swearer, Donald, 481
Syngman Rhee, 110

Tachibana Hayanari, 176
T'aego Pou, 102
Tahō, 517
Ta-hui Tsung-kao, 20–21, 30, 46–47,
  49–50, 53, 94–99, 102, 107, 126,
  258, 261, 266, 316, 515
Taigen Shigen, 325
Taihan, 168
Taikan Bunshu, 309, 326
Taira clan, 206, 259
Taira no Kagekiyo, 259
Tairei Shōkan, 319
Taiun Sogaku, 322
Tajima Kunji, 366
Takagami Kakushō, 185
Takagi Yutaka, 254–55
Takahashi Tōru, 130, 133
Takahatake, Takamichi, 238
Takashina Tōnari, 177

Takenuki Genshō, 327
Takeuchi Naoji, 325, 327
Takeuchi Yoshio, 53
Takizawa Katsumi, 386
Takuan, xx, 291–95, 303, 305–6, 331–33
Takujū Kosen, 319
Tamaki Kōshirō, 290, 335
Tamamura Takeji, 272
Tamura Enchō, 143
Tamura Yoshirō, 173, 199–200, 254–55, 450–51, 453–54
Tanabe Hajime, 368, 372, 374–83, 386–88
Tanabe Shigeharu, 452
Tanabe, Willa Jane, 172
Tanahashi Kazuaki, 327
Tanaka Kōichi, 325, 327
Tanaka Ryōshō, 23
T'an-luan, 226
T'an-yen, 71
Tao An, 420
Tao-ch'ien, 50
Tao-ch'o, 207, 226
Tao-hsin, 3, 6, 10, 25–26
Tao-hsüan, 152
Tao-yüan, 47
Teikan, 297
Teiki, 349–51
Tejima Tōan, 303, 306, 342
Tendō Nyōjō, 260
Tetsugen Glassman, 506
Tettō Gikō, 270
Tettsū Gikai, 260–62, 275, 287
Thammakai, 435
Tien-an, 501, 506
T'ien-t'ung Ju-ching, xv, 260–62, 274–75, 282, 519
Tipton, Steven, 509–10
Toda Jōsei, 436–40, 442, 446, 448–49, 451–54, 518
Tōgai, 349
Togashi Iehisa, 262
Tokimori, 252
Tokimune, 251, 265–66
Tokisuke, 251
Tokiwa Daijo, 53
Tokiwa Gishin, 309, 327
Tokoro Shigemoto, 255
Tokuhon, 219
Tokuitsu, 191
Tokunaga Eisoku, 359–60, 364

Tōrei Enji, 323, 309, 326
Tōrin Soshō, 312
Trailokyavijaya, 400, 409–10
Ts'ao-shan Pen-chi, 17, 29
Tsomo, Karma Lekshe, 481
Tsuchida Tomoaki, xx
Tsuchima Michihito, 454
Tsujii Hirohisa, 327
Tung-shan Liang-chieh, 17, 29, 32, 513
Tweed, Thomas, 495
Tworkov, Helen, 509–10
Tyler, Royall, xviii, 346
Tz'u Hang, 421

U Ba Khin, 489–90
U Chŏngsang, 130
U Nārada, 488
U Sobhana. See Mahāsi Sayadaw
Ueda Yoshifumi, 238
Uefuji Kazuyuki, 454
Ugai Tetsujō, 220
Ui Hakuju, 77, 173
Ŭich'ŏn, 79–80, 82–83, 104–5
Uisang, 60
Umehara Takeshi, xviii, 185, 254
Ungo Kiyō, 313
Unno Taitetsu, 388
Unpō Zenjō, 295
Unshō, 357
Uruma Tokikuni, 203
Uṣṇīṣa, 408

Vairocana, 88, 117, 146, 397–98, 408
Vaiśravaṇa, 410
Vajra, 183, 411
Van Bragt, Jan, 221
Van der Wetering, Janwillem, 509–10
Vasubandhu, 148, 165, 226, 241, 521
Veith, Ilza, 324
Vidyārāja, 409, 516
Vikirnoṣṇīṣa, 408
Vimalakīrti, xv, 139–41, 351, 419, 424, 428
Viśiṣṭacaritra, 239, 514
Visser, M. V de., 143
Vivekananda, 485
Voltaire, F. M. A., 157

Waddell, Norman, 297, 299, 306, 309, 323, 328, 346

Wagner, Edward W., 78
Wakimoto Tsuneya, xx, 221, 366
Wang An-shih, 18
Wang Kŏn, xvii
Wang Yang-ming, 51, 333
Wan-sung Hsing-hsiu, 21
Wargo, Robert, 306
Watanabe Shōkō, 184–85
Watson, Burston, xxiii
Watt, Paul B., xviii, xx, 358
Watts, Alan, 500
Wei Chueh, 424, 432
Wei-man Hsueh-hui, 424
Weinstein, Stanley, 173
Weitsman, Mel, 509
Wesley, Charles, xx
Wilson, William Scott, 306
Windelband, W., 172
Wŏn'gwang, 58
Won-tek, 132
Wŏnyho, 63, 79–80, 82–83, 104–5
Woodward, F. L., 488
Wright, Dale, xvi
Wu, Empress, 7, 10–11, 28
Wu, John C., 32
Wu-hsüeh Tsu-yüan, 265
Wu-men Hui-k'ai, 21, 265
Wu-tsung, Emperor, 15

Yagi Seiichi, 386
Yakṣa, 411, 521
Yakushi, 149, 162, 168, 408, 512
Yamada Kōdō, 326
Yamamoto Shichihei, 347
Yamāntaka, 407, 409–10, 412
Yamauchi Chōzō, 325, 327
Yamazaki Bennei, 220–21
Yamazaki Masakazu, 386
Yampolsky, Philip, xvi, xx, 23, 78, 272, 309, 323, 325, 328

Yanagida Seizan, 10, 23, 33, 273, 309, 325, 327
Yanagisawa Yasumitsu, 352
Yang-ch'i Fang-hui, 18
Yao, 332–33, 339
Yasha, 521
Yasutani, 502
Yen P'ei, 420
Yen Yuan, 335
Yi Chongik, 108
Yi Kyu-bo, 105, 107
Yi Nŭnghwa, 119
Yi T'oegye, 331, 336
Yi Yŏngcha, 130
Yiengpruksawan, Mimi Hall, xxiii
Yin-yüan Lung-ch'i, 313
Yōkan, 204
Yokoi Yūhō, 290
Yōmei, Emperor, 138
Yōsō Sōi, 270
Yu Chai-shin, 78, 107
Yü Ch'ing-fang, 418
Yu Dong-shik, 78
Yüan-piao, 77
Yüan-wu K'o-ch'in, 20, 94
Yün-chü Tao-ying, 17
Yung-ming Yen-shou, 22, 45, 53
Yün-men Wen-yen, 17, 19, 48, 282
Yün-yen T'an-sheng, 17
Yusa Michiko, 386

Zeami Motokiyo, 288, 369, 386
Zeami Motomasa, 288
Zenju, 158
Zennebō Shōku, 210, 218
Zenran, 225
Zenshin, 223. See Shinran
Zeuxis, 413
Zōshun, 204

Index of Subjects

Abhidharma-kośa, 148, 515

Affirmation-in-negation, 372, 377, 519

Āgamas, 364, 427

Agonkyō, 511

Ahiṃsā, 459–60, 511

Ālaya-vijñāna, 25, 511

Analects, 48, 107, 333–35, 341, 344

Anātman, 511, 516

Anattā, 486, 511

Androcentrism, 407, 503

Animals, 12, 171, 409–12, 440–41, 445, 470–71, 477, 512, 517

Aniyata Rāśi, 74, 76

Anjin Hōmon, 291, 293, 332

Ankoku-ji, 267

Anthropomorphic, 394–96, 407

Apocrypha, xiii, 11, 15, 22, 68

Appanā samādhi, 488

Apsarās, 411

Architecture, 58, 145, 154, 157, 174, 262, 418, 497

Arhat, 195, 411, 428, 511, 515–16

Armies, arms, 103, 297, 383, 396, 401, 407, 409, 411–13, 461–62, 468

Ascetics, asceticism, xiii–xiv, xviii, 12, 51, 121, 124, 152, 154–55, 158, 164–65, 168, 175, 260, 263, 277, 279, 297, 513, 519, 521

Ashikaga period, 263, 265–71

Ashura, asura, 171, 440, 511–12, 517

Atheism, 485

Avataṃsaka sūtra, 60, 78, 83–85, 117, 130, 150, 175, 395, 398, 413, 512

Bakufu, 193, 251, 268, 270, 272, 309, 313

Bhikkhunī(s), 421, 428, 431, 491, 501

Bhikkhu(s), 421, 428, 481, 498, 500–1, 508–9

Bodaishin, 512

Bodhi, 93, 137, 200, 248, 277, 280–82, 284, 287, 289–90, 485, 512

Bodhicitta, 94

Bodhisattva(s), xviii–xix, xxi–xxiii, 25, 67, 75, 92, 121, 124, 140–42, 149, 160–62, 168, 171, 180, 182, 184, 190–91, 202, 215, 217, 222, 225, 229, 232–33, 239–41, 243–46, 248, 251–53, 258, 284, 334, 380, 395–97, 399, 401, 407, 409–12, 424, 440, 443, 445, 465–66, 502, 507, 509, 511–12, 514–18, 520

Bodhisattva-yāna, 513

Bodhi-tree, 300

Bonnō, 450–51, 512

Bosatsu, 151, 409, 443, 512. *See also* Bodhisattva

Brahmanism, xiv

Buddha(s), *passim;* B.-being(s), 396, 398–400, 411; B.-body, 182, 194; B.-embryo, 25; B.-field(s), 395–98, 408, 512; B.-land, 250; B.-mind, 194, 286, 343, 502, 512; B.-nature, xiii–xiv, 13, 26, 36, 41, 47, 52, 64–66, 80, 87, 89, 95–97, 111, 119, 127, 129, 141, 172, 189, 191, 194, 196, 220, 229–30, 241, 277, 284–85, 292, 294–95, 334, 354, 467, 512, 517, 521; B.-realm, 192; B.-way, 275–76, 279–85, 287, 289–90

Buddhadhātu, 80, 512

Buddhagotra, 512

Buddhahood, xviii–xix, 31, 34–35, 40, 84, 86–87, 89, 91, 93–94, 101, 141–42, 175, 183, 187–90, 195–96, 198, 207, 229, 232, 241, 243–44, 246, 250, 276, 280, 282, 285, 287, 354,

364, 399, 409, 413, 437, 440–41,
  443–44, 446–47, 450–51, 512,
  515–16, 519–20
Buddhakṣetra, 395, 512
Buddhasasana Samagama, 485
Buddhatā, 284, 512, 520
Buddhavacana, 103
Buddhist Peace Fellowship, 477, 479–81
Bunsei period, 323
Buppō, 236, 517
Bushidō, 290
Busshō, 272, 354, 454, 512. *See also*
  Buddha-nature
Butsudo, 512. *See also* Buddha-field
Butsudō, 290. *See also* Buddha-way
Byōdō-in, 202

Celibacy, 12–23, 418, 477, 484, 502, 509
Ch'an chiao yi-chih, 45
Ch'an-men kuei-shih, 14
Ch'an-kuan ts'e-chin, 22, 323
Ch'an-yüan chu-ch'üan chi-tu hsü, 45
Ch'an-yüan ch'ing-kuei, 14, 257
Ch'ao Feng Monastery, 417
Ching-te-ssu, 275, 279
Che Punhwangsa Hyosong Mun, 62
Ch'en Hsi Buddhist Society, 422
Ch'eng-chu school, 340
Chin Chuang, 418
Chin-kang san-mei ching, 11
Ch'ing-te ch'uan-teng lu, 19, 47
Ching-te-ssu, 275, 279
Chion-in, 219, 221
Chiu pa yen k'ou e kuei t' o lo ni ching, 130
Ch'iu T'ang-shu, 15
Chōei-ji, 350
Chōfuku-ji, 352
Chogye school, 102–3, 110, 124
Chosa sŏn, 112
Chosŏn dynasty, xvii, 80, 109–12, 114–17,
  120, 125–26, 130–33
Chosŏn Pulgyo yusin non, 120, 131
Christian(ity), xiii, 52–53, 120, 123–24,
  170, 220, 372, 377, 379–80, 382,
  385, 387, 448, 479, 482–84
Ch'uan fa chieh, 11, 512
Ch'uan fa-pao chi, 6
Ch'uan-fa cheng-tsung chi, 47
Ch'uan-hsin fa-yao, 35, 41
Ch'uan-teng lu, 19, 47, 50, 53

Chung-hua Institute of Buddhist Studies, 425
Chungtai Monastery, 432–33
Chung-tao Society, 422
Compassion, xviii–xix, xxi, 59, 142,
  194–95, 220, 222–23, 225, 228–29,
  233–37, 338, 385, 393, 396, 409,
  412, 429, 431, 441, 455–58, 461,
  466, 468, 470–71, 473, 477–79, 481,
  492, 512, 516
Confucianism, xiv, xvi, xx, 4, 7, 19, 29, 44,
  48, 51–53, 57–59, 77, 80, 109, 122,
  125, 145–46, 151, 179, 183, 265,
  300, 305–6, 322, 329–37, 340–41,
  343–44, 348–49, 351, 355–56, 358,
  418, 424, 448
Consciousness-only school, 279, 427, 521
Cosmology, xiv, 52, 401, 471, 516
Counter-illumination, 87

Daian-ji, 178
Daibutsu-ji, 261, 275
Daijō-ji, 262, 287
Daimoku, 195, 249, 252, 437–39, 441–47,
  512
Daimyō, 264, 271
Dainichikyō, 165, 175, 185, 191, 398
Daitō shiyūki, 414
Daitoku-ji, 264, 266, 268–71, 291, 306,
  310, 313
Darani, 512. See also *Dhāraṇī*
Daruma-shū, Daruma school, 257–60, 262
Defilement, 65, 88, 91, 93–96, 100–1, 145,
  218, 228, 512
Deities, 31, 137, 157–58, 160–62, 190,
  197, 240, 245, 251, 263, 512, 516–17
Demon(s), 248, 410; D.-possession, 59
Denkōroku, 263
Deva(s), 25, 171, 410, 512
Dhāraṇī, 112, 130, 153, 175, 180, 182,
  184, 398, 409, 416, 512
Dhamma. *See* Dharma
Dhammapada, 460
Dhamma Yietra, 460–61
Dharma, xiv, xvi, xix, xxi, 14, 29, 32, 47,
  60, 64, 67–69, 72, 74–76, 80–82, 94,
  100–1, 112, 127, 130, 138, 148,
  150–51, 174, 180, 199, 203, 207,
  232, 234, 236–37, 244, 246, 252–54,
  262, 276, 281–82, 284, 286, 289,
  294, 312–13, 318–19, 341, 344,

348–53, 355–57, 391, 396–97, 408,
411, 417, 419–20, 422, 424–25, 428,
442–44, 446–47, 460, 480–81, 484,
492, 500, 502–3, 506–8, 512–13,
515–16, 519–20; D.-assemblies, 424;
D.-body, 192, 200, 515; D.-buddha,
446; D.-combat, 127; *D.-dhātu*, 80,
86–88, 101, 117, 513; D.-field, 67;
D.-gate, 67; D.-heirs, 282; D.-lecture,
128; D.-master, 66, 419–21, 423–24,
426, 428, 431; D.-names, 418; *D.
rājā*, 138; D.-teaching, 417; D.-treas-
ure, 6, 11; D.-wheel, 286; D.-world,
73
Dharmakāya, 71, 90, 112, 141, 180, 182,
241–42, 245, 298, 300–1, 317, 396,
513, 516, 520
Dhyāna, 24, 27, 30, 397, 500, 512–13, 521
Diamond Sūtra, 8, 26, 28, 293, 332, 353,
419, 519
Dō, 286, 288, 290, 516
Dōbō dōgyō, 225
Dragon(s), 263, 321, 351
Dream(s), 90, 111, 161, 213, 222–25, 240,
249, 323
Duḥkha, 511

Edo period, 219, 288, 329, 336
Ego, 84, 98, 183, 227, 304, 384, 467–69
Egocentric, 25, 29, 150, 234
Egoism, 227, 234
Egoity, 385
Eihei kōroku, 261, 276, 285
Eihei-ji, 261–64, 275–76, 287
Ekayāna, 139–42, 171, 513. *See also* One-
vehicle Buddhism
Ekō, 229, 513
Ekphrasis, 399, 413
Emptiness, xiii–xvi, 19, 27–28, 31, 62, 71,
116, 126, 150, 171, 258, 294–95,
298, 300–1, 345, 354, 383–85, 392,
395, 413, 427, 456, 508, 510, 513,
515; E.-in-fullness, 385. See also *Kū,
Śūnyatā*
Engaku-ji, 266–67, 307, 314
Enlightenment, *passim*; cultivation-E., 51;
gradual E., 28, 242; sudden E., 28,
46, 49, 73, 78, 91–93, 108, 113–14,
231, 520; Sudden-gradual E., 126;
Sudden-sudden E., 126

Enpuku-ji, 318
Enryaku-ji, 168, 190, 204, 274–75, 277
Eschatology, 385
Esoteric(ism), 60, 84, 111, 113–14, 153,
155, 160, 167, 172–73, 175–80,
183–85, 187, 189–92, 196–99, 209,
240–42, 244, 256–57, 259–60,
262–65, 269–70, 399–400, 432, 435,
438–40, 442, 477, 484, 515–16,
518–19
Esoteric-exoteric, 160
Ethics, xxi, 19, 50, 52, 58–59, 120,
122–23, 126–27, 169, 189, 191, 234,
236, 330, 340, 344–45, 353–54,
356–57, 363, 374, 385, 429, 459–60,
463, 470, 474, 479, 481, 485, 492,
495, 506, 509–10, 514
Ethnic(ity), 289, 379, 464, 467, 482, 487,
497–98, 506
Exoteric(ism), 160, 178, 180, 182–83, 197,
240–41, 515
Exoteric-esoteric, 158, 160, 197
Ex-stasis, 385

Fa Kuang Institute of Buddhist Studies, 425
Fa Yun Institute of Buddhist Studies, 419
Fa Yun Monastery, 417, 419
Feminism, 475–77, 479–80, 493, 495, 509
Fo Kuang Shan, 476
Fo-tsu t'ung-chi, 47
Foundation for the Preservation of the
Mahāyāna Tradition of the Gelugpa,
432
Four Beginnings, 331
Fudōchi shinmyō roku, 332
Fugan-ji, 288
Fukanzazengi, 275–76, 285
Fushō fumetsu, 297, 513

Garbha, 520
Garbhadhātu, 399
Gedatsu, 162, 439, 513
Gedō, 234, 513; *G. shinga*, 332
Gender, 234, 396, 407, 410, 412, 415, 503
Genjōkōan, 386
Genju-ha, 22
Genkō era, 267
Genkō shakusho, 256
Genpei war, 187
Gensō, 228, 517

God(s), xviii, 52, 58, 116, 184, 200, 213, 241, 244–47, 251, 290, 372–73, 382, 385–86, 401, 407, 410, 412, 448–49, 512, 519. *See also* Deities
Goddess, 244, 428
God-talk, 373
Gohonzon, 438–39, 442, 444, 446–47, 449, 451
Goi kenketsu, 263
Gozan, 261–72, 291, 313, 513–14, 519, 521

Haein Monastery, 105
Haibutsu kishaku, 220, 513
Hai-dong shu, 68
Hajaku-ji, 259–60
Hakuin oshō nenpu, 309, 326
Hakusan Tendai, 260, 263
Heaven(s), 51–52, 114, 144, 149, 183, 201, 215, 245, 247, 252, 303, 318, 332, 334–35, 339–40, 344–45, 373, 382, 394, 396, 410–11, 440, 445, 512, 517
Heian period, xviii–xx, xxii, 142, 147, 153, 155–56, 160, 164–203, 222
Heiraku-ji, 212, 238, 254, 272–73, 453–54
Hekiganroku, 32, 263
Hell(s), 16, 114, 171, 182, 202, 302, 304, 440, 445, 460, 512, 517; H.-beings, 514
Hermit(s), 25–26, 248, 310–11
Hieizan. *See* Mount Hiei
Higashi Hongan-ji, xxii, 360–62
Hijiri, 202, 204–5, 211, 279, 513
Hinayāna, 14, 75, 82, 141, 148, 168, 170, 183, 195, 284, 364, 440, 516, 519
Hinduism, 183, 472
Hisosan-ji, 152
Hōben, 243, 520. *See also* Skillful means, *Upāya*
Hokkai, 294–95, 513
Hokke gengi shiki, 187, 200
Hokkegisho, 140, 143
Hokkekyō, 140, 254, 452–54
Hōkyō zanmai, 263
Hongaku, xix, 187–90, 192, 194–95, 197–200, 241–42, 249, 445, 450–51, 514
Hongan-ji, xxii, 235–37, 360–62
Honji-suijaku, 161, 245, 248, 514
Honmon butsuryūkō, 448
Honmon-ji, 442

Hōraku-ji, 349–50
Hōrin-ji, 275, 309, 326
Hōryū-ji, 139
Hosshin, 182, 513; *H. seppō*, 192; *H. kōan*, 317
Hossō, 147–52, 158, 160, 191, 210, 231, 513–14
Hossō-shū, 279
Ho-tse school, 7, 9, 15, 30, 90
Ho-tse temple, 7, 9
Hōyōki, 285
Hsi Lai Temple, 418
Hsien T'ien, 418
Hsi-ming-ssu, 176, 185
Hsin hua-yen lun, 66
Hsin-yu Buddhist Cultural Center, 424
Hua Fan College, 431
Huan Gan University, 431
Huang-lung school, 18, 257
Hua-yen, xiii, xvii–xviii, 15, 22, 29–30, 45, 50, 60, 66–67, 80, 82, 89–90, 107, 149–50, 182–83, 196, 512, 519. *See also* Hwaŏm, Kegon
Hua-yen ching su, 66
Hua-yen t'an hsüan chi, 66
Hu-ch'iu school, 266
Hwaŏm, 60, 63, 66–68, 71, 73, 80, 84, 86–87, 99, 101–2, 111, 130, 512. *See also* Hua-yen, Kegon
Hwarangdo, 58–59
Hyakurenshō, 258
Hyakurokkosōjō, 442

Ibullansa Temple, 77
I Ching, 29
Ikuei school, 360
Illumination, 21, 30, 46, 52, 97, 243, 339–42, 400, 513
Insight Meditation Society, 489, 492
International Buddhist Society, 485
Interpenetration, 57, 60, 63, 66–68, 77, 84, 86, 88, 151, 341, 519–20
Invocation of the name, 249. See *Nenbutsu*
Inzō, 401, 516
Ise, 245, 437
Ita maṇḍala, 442

Japanization, 131, 156–58, 160, 162, 324, 418
Jigyō no ichinen sanzen, 439
Jiji-muge, 151, 519

Jingo-ji, 177
Jishō-ji, 318
Jōbutsugi, 244
Jōchi-ji, 267
Jōdo sect, xxii, 201, 203, 206, 211,
    221–22, 226–27, 237–38, 282,
    329–30, 359–60, 366, 447, 508, 514.
    See also Jōdoshū
Jōdo Shinshū, xxii, 206, 222, 226–27,
    237–38, 329–30, 359–60, 366, 508,
    514. *See also* Shin Buddhism
Jōdoshū, xxii, 209, 211, 218–21, 224, 329.
    See also Jōdo sect
Jōgan-in, 310
Jōgyō-zammai, 201, 222, 514
Jōjū-ji, 262
Jufuku-ji, 257, 267
Jūji yujutsubon, 443
Jūjū shinron, 179, 183, 185, 191, 200
Jūnyoze, 440, 445, 514

Kaimeimon'in, 352
K'ai Yuan Monastery, 419
Kalyānamitras, 119
Kamakura period, xix, 157, 159, 174,
    186–87, 189, 203, 206, 208, 239,
    251, 253, 256, 266–68, 277, 308, 357
Kami, 137–38, 145, 152–53, 157–58,
    160–63, 244–45, 248, 514; *K.*-body,
    158; *K.*-buddha, 162; *K.*-realm, 158.
    See also Deities, Gods
Kanahōgo, 308
K'an-hua, 21, 46, 515–16
Kanhwa Sŏn, 101–2
Kanjin honzonshō, 440, 444–45, 450
Kanjinron, 444
Kanmuryōjukyō, 415
Kao-seng Fa-hsian chuan, 413
Kan-ting chi, 66
Karma, 16, 65, 114–15, 127, 183, 302,
    305, 330, 438, 459, 462–63, 481, 520
Karunā, 461, 516
Kāya, 393, 414
Kāya-vijñāna, 519
Kegon, 147, 149–52, 167, 170, 204, 231,
    279, 363, 512. *See also* Hua-yen,
    Hwaŏm
Keirin-ji, 350–51
Keisō dokuzui, 308, 318
Keitoku dentō roku, 263

Kenbutsu, 282
Kenchō-ji, 265–67, 270
Kenmitsu, 160, 162, 197, 200, 515; *K.*
    bukkyō, 160, 162; *K. taisei,* 197
Kennin-ji, 257, 259–60, 265, 267, 274–75
Kenshō, 94, 232, 258, 297, 317, 321–22,
    502, 515
Kenshō jōbutsu ron, 258
Kenyaku seikaron, 340
Khanika samādhi, 488
Khmer Rouge, 460
Kichijō-ji, 261
Kisillon so, 68, 72, 75, 78
Kiyosumi-dera, 240
Kleśa, 512
Kōan, xv–xvi, 19–22, 30, 32, 46–47, 49,
    52, 95, 259, 264, 269–70, 272, 286,
    301, 306, 312, 315–19, 321–22,
    324–26, 328, 334–35, 346, 498–99,
    502, 513–16, 521
Kōfuku-ji, 160, 162, 204, 206, 259, 279
Kojiki, 144, 153, 356
Kōjiki kitei, 352
Kokūzō gumonji no hō, 175
Kōki-ji, 352–53
Kōkoku-ji, 263
Kōmeitō, 453, 474
Kongan, 95, 97, 113, 116, 126, 131, 515
Kongōchōkyō, 176, 398
Konpon sōsei, 350, 352
Koreanization, 59
Koryŏ dynasty, xvii, 63, 76, 79–109, 126
Koryŏ-kuk sinjo taejang kyojŏng pyŏllok, 106–7
Kosāmbi, 414
Kōshō Hōrin-ji. *See* Hōrin-ji
Kōshō-ji, 259–60, 280
Kōyasan, 185, 358. *See also* Mount Kōya
Kū, 148–49, 298, 515. *See also* Emptiness,
    Śūnyatā
Kuomintang, 420
Kuon-ji, 252, 254
Kuse chūwi, 120
Kushu shotoku, 188
Kyōge betsuden, 257
Kyōgyōshinshō, 225–26, 231, 237–38, 380
Kyonsŏng, 94, 515
Kyoto school, xx, 367–88, 521–22

Laity, xvii, 13, 20, 36, 110, 119, 122, 124,
    129, 141–42, 146, 169, 226, 247,

252, 316, 323, 419, 423–24, 452,
   455–57, 459, 462, 474, 476, 488,
   492–93, 498, 500–3
Laṅkāvatāra Sūtra, 6, 8, 24–26, 28
Lay-sister(s), 122–24. *See also* Nun(s)
Leng-ch'ieh shih-tzu chi 6
Liberation, xiii, xxi, xxiii, 82, 91, 93, 110,
   115, 121, 189, 205, 220, 232, 253,
   301, 439, 443–44, 476, 480–81
Life-force, 436–42, 446–49, 451–53
Life-in-death, 380
Lin-chi school, 17, 20, 46, 101–2, 417. *See*
   also Rinzai Zen
Ling Ch'uan monastery, 417, 419, 424
Ling Yun monastery, 417, 419
Li-tai fa-pao chi, 11
Liturgy, 112, 114, 124, 147, 190, 197, 401
Liu-tsu t'an-ching, 10
Lotus Sūtra, xviii–xix, 140–41, 147, 160–61,
   165–67, 171–72, 187–88, 195, 200,
   229, 239–54, 277, 282, 312, 330,
   344, 395, 419, 435, 438–39, 442–44,
   446, 452–53, 466, 512–18, 520
Loving-kindness, 488, 492, 495
Lung Hua, 418

Mādhyamika, xxii, 60, 63, 148–49, 183,
   201, 414, 427, 515, 518
Mādhyamika-kārikā, 427
Madhyamaka, 515
Magic, 24, 58, 138, 146, 152, 156, 175,
   184, 202, 232, 234, 241, 397–98,
   409, 411–12
Maha Bodhi Society, 485
Mahāparinirvāṇa, 64, 394, 517
Mahāsi Center, 489, 494
Mahāvagga, xxiii
Mahāyāna, xiii–xiv, 14, 44–45, 59, 64,
   68–75, 77–78, 126, 139–42, 148–50,
   168–71, 175, 180, 183, 189–90, 195–
   96, 199, 226, 228, 242, 251, 284,
   298, 301, 331–32, 345, 349, 354,
   395–401, 409–14, 427, 432, 435,
   486, 492, 502–3, 511–13, 516–17
Maitri, 516
Makashikan, 444
Makumōzō, 345
Maṇḍala, 175, 177, 182–84, 190, 201,
   240–41, 251, 283, 356, 398–401,
   407, 415, 439, 442, 514, 516, 520

Mantra, 112–14, 127, 175, 180, 182, 184,
   190, 197, 241, 249, 283, 356, 398,
   401, 443, 512, 516, 519
Mappō, 192–93, 203, 227, 232, 244,
   247–49, 251, 438, 441–44, 446, 516,
   519
Marxism, 379, 383, 471
Meiji period, xx, 121, 143, 163, 197,
   219–20, 276, 308, 319, 324–25, 327,
   335–36, 357, 359–60, 365, 375, 381,
   513
Meiji restoration, 121, 143, 335–36
Metanoetics, 380, 387
Metaphysic(s), xvi, 19, 45, 52, 60, 149–51,
   199, 249, 288, 363, 369, 372–73, 380
Metsudo, 516
Mettā sutta, 460
Miao-fa lien-hua ching, 516
Michi, 288–90, 292, 357, 516
Mikkyō, 153, 155, 160, 184–85, 357,
   515–16
Mind; M.-cultivation, 28; M.-dharma, 112;
   M.-essence, 438; Mindfulness, 322,
   468, 477, 486–90, 492–94, 511, 518;
   M.-nature, 87, 92; M.-only, 64, 112,
   286, 427; M.-stuff, 112; M.-to-mind,
   84, 502; M.-transmission, 84
Ming dynasty, 22, 31, 313, 417
Missionary (activity), xviii, xx, 77, 109–10,
   130, 132, 482, 485–86, 499
Mizuyakushi-ji, 352
Mo ho chih kuan, 444
Mōanjō, 343
Modernity, modernization, xx, xvii, 119–21,
   129, 219–21, 335, 357, 420, 479,
   483, 486
Mondō, 516
Monjō no honmon, 444
Montei no honmon, 444
Morality, xxii, 50, 92, 122, 145, 183,
   230–31, 329, 331, 352–53, 355, 371,
   376
Mount Hiei, xviii–xix, 155, 160, 164–66,
   168–69, 172, 184, 186–90, 197,
   201–2, 204–6, 210–11, 222–23,
   226–27, 231, 256–60, 263, 274
Mount Kōya, xviii, 160, 164, 178–79, 184,
   189, 202
Mount Ta Kang, 417
Mount Wu-ku Kuan-yin, 417

Mount Yueh Mei, 417
Muditā, 516
Mudrā, 175, 182, 190, 241, 356, 398–99, 401, 415, 516
Muga, 332, 341, 511, 516
Mumonkan, 32, 47, 265, 325, 521
Muromachi period, 142, 262–64, 266–68, 271–72, 313, 329
Muryōgi-kyō, 437
Music, 58, 145, 154, 215
Musō, 266–70, 272
Myōhō-ji, 466
Myōhōrengekyō, 241, 251
Myōkōnin-den, 330
Myōō, 409, 511, 516
Myōshin-ji, 264, 266, 268–69, 271, 297, 308, 312–14, 318, 326
Mystic(ism), 44, 46, 51–52, 283, 287, 385, 401, 409, 438, 488, 500
Myth(ology), xiv, 25, 146, 151, 153, 198, 229, 289, 313, 380, 385

Name-recitation, 503. See also *Nenbutsu*
Namu-amida-butsu, 237, 282
Nan-hai-chi-kuei-nei-fa ch'uan, 351
Nan-k'e T'ai-shou chuan, 323
Nan-tsung school, 7
Nanzen-ji, 267
Nara period, 144–45, 147, 150–53, 155, 160, 197–98, 201
Naropa Institute, 478, 480
Nationalism, 197, 249, 307, 322, 328, 388, 420, 448
Nehangyō, 517
Nehan myōshin, 516
Nenbutsu, 172, 189, 194–95, 197, 202, 204–23, 226–28, 231, 233–34, 237–38, 249, 258, 314, 341, 517. See also Recitation of the name
Nenbutsu-shōshinge, 226
Neo-Confucianism, xvii, 19, 22, 48–52, 244, 266, 313, 331, 335, 338, 340–42, 344–46, 349, 381, 512–13, 515
Neo-Kantianism, 371, 375
Nibbāna, 489
Nichiren honbutsuron, 442
Nichiren Shōshū, 435–36, 440, 442–48, 450–54, 508
Nichirenshū, 329–30, 442, 453–54; N.

Fujihɑ̄ 442
Nieh-p'an ching, 517
Nien-fo, 22, 45, 517
Nihilism, xx, 381, 383–85, 387
Nihongi, 143–44, 357
Nihonshoki, 137, 144
Nihonzan Myōhō-ji sect, 466
Nirvāṇa, xiii, 44, 64–65, 67–68, 74, 78, 81, 93, 127, 129–30, 149, 170, 232–33, 240–41, 243, 247, 284, 286, 294, 331, 391, 447, 473, 493, 513–14, 516–17
Nishi Hongan-ji, xxii
Nisōshijū, 231
Niu-t'ou school, 10, 26, 28
Niyata rāśi, 74, 76
Noh, 288, 369
No-mind, 28, 291, 293, 303, 306, 333, 516
Non-backsliding, 74, 76
Non-becoming, 141
Non-being, 141
Non-dharma, 67
Non-differentiation, 385, 445
Non-discrimination, 66, 69, 72, 299, 303
Non-dual(ity), 69, 76, 86, 90, 93, 112, 117, 141, 183, 200, 303, 322, 503
Non-existence, 97, 294–95, 456
Non-nothingness, 294
Non-retrogression, 74, 232
Non-returner, 511
Non-seeking, 35
Non-self. *See* No-self
Non-sentient, 290, 445
Non-substantial(ity), 112, 140, 395, 398, 412
Non sŭngnyŏ chi kyoyuk, 120
Nonviolence, 456, 459, 462, 468, 470, 474–75, 481, 485
No-self, xv, 40, 292, 332, 486, 511. See also *Anātman, Muga*, Selflessness
Nothingness, 294–95, 299–301, 311, 368, 370–74, 376–77, 379–81, 385, 387, 510, 521; N.-in-love, 380
No-thought, 90, 92, 95–96
Noumenal, noumenon, 50, 84, 86, 88, 92, 331, 399, 515
Nun(s), 15, 119–20, 123, 141, 281, 284, 297, 418–25, 428, 431, 455–56, 461–62, 464, 473–76, 480, 490–91, 498, 501–3, 509

Nung-so, 69, 517
Nunneries, 124, 352, 425, 491
Nyŏmbul, 113–14, 517

Ō, 231
Ōbaku school, xxii, 517
Ogikuden, 442
Ōjō, 451, 517
Omosu honmon-ji, 442
Once-returner, 511
Oneness, 88, 237, 282, 332, 363
One-vehicle Buddhism, 139, 171, 195. *See also* Ekayāna
Onjō-ji, 259
Orategama, 316, 323, 326–27
Orientalism, 374
Ōryō, 257
Ōsō, 228, 517
Other-Power, 45, 189, 195, 204, 227–33, 236–37, 329, 359, 361, 364–65, 380, 519–20
Ōtōkan school, 266, 269, 308
Otokuni-dera, 178
Oxhead school, 10, 28. *See also* Niu-t'ou school

Paekche dynasty, 57–58, 60, 77, 137
Pai-chang yu-lu, 38–39, 42–43
Pāli Canon, 483–86, 517
P'an-chiao, 66–67, 517
Pao-ching san-mei, 17
Pao-lin chuan, 11, 13
Paramārtha, 66
Paramārthasatya, 64, 517
Parinirvāṇa, 103
Passions, 24–25, 51, 204, 216, 237, 258, 450
Penis, 393
Pi-kuan, 24
Pilgrim(age), 102, 157, 162, 392, 414, 423
Pi-yen lu, 20–21, 47
P'o-an school, 266
Po-jo, 517
Pŏp, 123
Prajñā, 67, 69, 92–95, 112, 150, 177, 517–18
Prajñāpāramitā, 26, 395, 415
Pratibhāsa, 413
Pratibimba, 413
Pratītyasamutpāda, 427

Pratyekabuddha, 171, 195, 517; *P.-yāna,* 513
Praxis, xiv, xxi, 59, 77, 89–90, 92, 94, 199, 371–72, 374, 376, 380–81, 399–400, 435
Prayer, 20, 105, 142, 232, 240, 272, 401
Precept(s), 148, 204, 342, 471, 475, 478; P.-platform, 515; P.-transmission, 421. *See also Vinaya*
Preta, 171, 512, 517
Priestess, 146
Prophecy, 211, 248, 249–52
Proselytization, xxiii, 244, 253
Protestantism, 170
Proto-Shintō, 145–46, 151, 153
Psychoanalysis, 494
Pulsŏng, 111, 127
P'yŏngdŭng chuwi, 120

Recitation of the name, 215, 227, 230, 233. *See also Nenbutsu*
Reincarnation, 128
Reiyūkai, 435, 448
Rengekyō, 344, 437, 440–44, 446, 466, 516. *See also Lotus Sūtra*
Ri, 116, 188, 199, 354, 515
Richi, 183, 315–16
Richi funi, 183
Riji-muge, 151
Riki sabetsuron, 292, 332
Rinzai Zen, 16, 22, 29, 32, 47, 97, 112, 256–64, 266–67, 269, 272–73, 279, 289, 291, 295, 297, 307–10, 313–15, 318–19, 323, 325, 328, 333, 343, 499, 502–3, 509, 513, 515
Risenkufū, 304
Risshō Kōseikai, 467, 480
Rites, ritual, xiv, 33, 48, 59, 111–12, 120, 130–33, 137, 142, 145–46, 148, 153–54, 161, 177–79, 184, 190, 198, 200, 202, 209, 219, 252, 281, 316, 330, 335, 371, 375, 394, 399–401, 411–12, 415, 489–90, 498, 505, 507, 511–12, 516; Ritualism, 283, 398, 516
Ritsu, 147–48, 152, 187, 250, 267, 521. *See also* Precepts, *Vinaya*
Rōhatsu, 264, 322
Rokudō, 512, 514, 517
Rokuon-in, 268
Rokuon-sōroku, 268

Rokurōsō, 442
Ropparamitsu-ji, 275
Rūpakāya, 396
Ryūmon-ji, 297
Ryūtaku-ji, 319, 323

Sach'al yŏng, 110
Sadan. See Four Beginnings
Saddharmapuṇḍarika Sutrā, 130, 239
Sage(s), xx, xiv, 49–50, 131, 139, 179, 248,
    258, 311, 333–34, 336, 440; S.-king,
    25
Saihō shinan shō, 213, 221
Saihō-ji, 361
Saint(hood), 82, 193, 195, 210–11, 219,
    239, 251, 284, 488, 493, 511, 519
Sakyadhitā International Association of
    Buddhist Women, 475
Salvation, xvi, xix, 31, 81, 115, 120,
    171–72, 193–95, 204–5, 217–19,
    233, 239, 246–50, 253, 370, 397–98,
    435–36, 442, 448–54, 518
Samādhi, 11, 69, 92–95, 201, 213, 215–16,
    311, 322, 397, 488, 514, 518. See also
    Zanmai
Śamatha-vipaśyanā, 519
Sambhogakāya, 71, 180, 396, 518
Saṃgha, 419, 421, 424, 428, 431. *See also*
    Saṅgha
Samnak vipassanā, 488
Samnon (school), 60. *See also* San-lun, Sanron
Saṃsāra, xiii, xxi, 44, 65, 67–68, 93, 115,
    128, 188–89, 391, 409, 518
Samurai, 193, 291, 295, 330, 337, 342–43,
    348, 360; S.-zen, 306, 346
Samvṛti, 66
Samvṛtisatya, 64, 517
San-chü, 115, 518
Sandai sōron, 262
Sandhinirmocana sūtra, 67
Sangakuroku, 178
Sangan tennyū, 230
Saṅgha, 75–76, 79, 109–10, 119–21,
    124–26, 433, 474, 490, 493, 498–99,
    501–4, 506, 520. *See also* Saṃgha
San-hsüan, 115, 518
San'ikun, 329
San-lun (school), xiii, 60, 427, 518. *See also*
    Samnon, Sanron
Sanmai, 209, 213–14, 518. See also *Zanmai*

Sanmai Hottokuki, 209, 214
Sanmaya-kai, 191, 518
Sanmitsu, 182, 190, 518
Sanmon, 240
Sanron (school), 147–50, 152, 201, 204,
    518. *See also* Samnon, San-lun
Sanzen, 249–50, 264, 438–40, 444–45,
    514, 518
Sarvāstivāda, xiii, 148, 395, 518
Sarvodaya Shramadana, 457–58, 471,
    480–81
Sasa muae, 84, 99, 519
Śatasāhasrikā-prajñāpāramitā, 393
Satipaṭṭhāna sutta, 486–88
Satori, 46, 284, 289, 298, 303, 515
Satyasiddhi, 148
Sectarian(ism), xxii, 60, 64, 67, 76, 82, 87,
    110, 121, 186, 193, 197–98, 261,
    344, 348, 350, 355, 357, 395, 427,
    475, 502; Suprasectarian, 348,
    351–52, 356
Secularization, xvii, 120–22, 291, 329, 432
Seishinshugi, 359, 362, 366
Seizan-ha, 210
Self-awakening, xxiii, 368, 372, 376, 379,
    381, 385, 420
Self-awareness, 301, 370, 376–77, 379–80
Self-centered(ness), 40, 304, 343
Self-consciousness, 292, 299, 304
Self-cultivation, 52, 114, 124, 332
Selfhood, 292, 373
Selfless(ness), 288, 338, 343, 456, 459–60,
    463, 479. *See also* No-self
Self-nature, 66, 86, 93–94, 292, 294, 306
Self-power, 359, 364, 519–20
Senchaku, 206, 518
Senchakushū, 205–6, 209–11, 213–15,
    217–18, 223
Sengoku period, 263–64, 271
Sennan gūkyo roku, 331
Sesshin, 264, 502, 518
Sex(uality), 225, 284, 408, 415, 418, 431,
    459, 476, 502–4, 509, 518, 520
Sexism, 457
Shakubuku, 330, 436, 441, 444, 454, 518
Shakumon, 241–42, 439, 443, 518
Shana-gō, 519
Shana-gyō, 191, 519
Shao-lin temple, 24
Shido kegyō, 349

Shih-men cheng-t'ung, 47
Shikan taza, 194, 502, 506, 519
Shin Buddhism, 223, 235–36, 238, 335, 366. *See also* Jōdo Shinshū
Shingon, xviii, 153, 155–56, 160, 167, 170, 172, 174–76, 178–79, 182–85, 189–91, 196–97, 200, 231, 233, 236, 240, 242, 244, 254, 257, 264, 267, 272, 282–83, 341, 346, 349–50, 353, 356–58, 400, 511, 516–22; S. Risshū, 349
Shingonshū shogaku Kyūritsuron mokuroku, 178
Shinnyoen, 435
Shintō, xviii, 137–38, 142, 146, 158, 161, 163, 197, 290, 330, 448, 517, 519; S.-buddhist, 160, 163
Shitennō-ji, 139
Shō, 170, 185, 213, 221, 253, 284, 289, 295, 514
Shōbōgenzō, 261, 263, 275–77, 280–86, 288–90, 516
Shōdō, 206
Shōdōmon, 193, 519
Shōgun, 252, 257, 265, 267, 291
Shōin-ji, 312, 318
Shōji Jissō gi, 178
Shōju-an, 311–12
Shōkoku-ji, 268, 325
Shōrin-ji, 319
Shōsōrin ryaku shingi, 314
Shōtō shōkaku ron, 258
Shou-leng-yen-ching, 283
Shōwa era, 220
Shugeishuchi-in, 179
Shugendō, xviii, 152, 172, 263, 519, 521
Shūmon Mujintō ron, 317
Shūseisha, 342
Śīla, 92, 518
Silla dynasty, xvii, 57–61, 63, 65–67, 69, 71, 73, 75–80, 83, 103, 137, 143
Sinp'yŏn chejong kyojang ch'ongnok, 104, 107
Skillful means, 321, 468, 513, 520. See also *Hōben*, *Upāya*
Sōgen-ji, 325
Sōji-ji, 262
Sōka Gakkai, xxi, 435–54, 467, 474, 480, 508
Soku-hi, 373, 519
Sokushin jōbutsu, 178, 180, 192, 233, 241–42, 356, 445–46, 519

Sokushin jōbutsu gi, 178
Sōmoku jōbutsu, 198
Sŏngch'ŏng, 115
Songgwang Temple, 114
Songmunsa Temple, 77
Sŏnmun sabyon mano, 116–17
Sŏnmun sugyŏng, 115
Sōtō Zen, xix, 17, 29, 47, 194, 256, 259, 261–64, 268, 272–73, 275–76, 281–82, 287–88, 306–7, 314, 321, 323, 350, 357, 418–19, 499, 502–3, 507, 509–10, 519. *See also* Ts'ao-tung Zen
Soul, 363–64, 372, 377, 382, 384, 465, 486
Spiritualism, 359, 361, 363, 365
Śrāvaka, 140, 171, 440, 445, 514, 519
Śrāvaka-yāna, 513
Śrīmālādevī, 139, 141, 171
Śrīmāladevī-siṃhanāda, 428
Ssangye Temple, 114
Ssu-chu cheng-i k'ao, 331
Stūpa, 130, 251, 393–96, 519
Suchness, 65, 73, 75–76, 100, 112, 115, 180, 438, 440, 520
Sukhāvatī, 113, 397, 519
Sukhāvativyūha, 201, 207, 395
Sung-yüan school, 266
Śūnyatā, 19, 27, 71, 140, 385, 427, 515. See also Emptiness, *Kū*
Susŏn sa, 114
Sutta-nipāta, 107
Suwŏl toryang konghwa pulsa yŏhwan binju mongchung mundap, 111
Szechwan school, 11–12, 15

Ta-ch'eng ch'i-hsin lun, 72
T'aego school, 125
Ta hsien Monastery, 421
T'ai-chi, 52
Taichung Pure Land Buddhist Society, 424
Taimitsu, 189
Taiseki-ji, 442
Taishō period, 106, 220, 307, 322, 326, 415, 426
Takada-ha, 235
Takaosan-ji, 167, 177–80, 183
Ta-li, 426, 520
T'ang dynasty, 4, 7, 9–10, 15, 17–20, 22, 33, 36, 45, 130, 154, 167, 190, 256, 323, 434, 501

Taṇhā, 456
Tannishō, 364
Tantra, 60, 520
Tantric, xviii, xxii, 167–68, 175, 184, 516, 519–520
Tantric-style, 158
Tantrism, xviii, 172, 185, 398
Tao, Taoism, xiv–xvi, 4, 7, 15, 24–26, 47–51, 53, 57–60, 80, 153, 175, 179, 183, 269, 290, 292, 311, 330, 334, 341, 418, 420, 516
Ta-t'ang hsi-yü chi, 414
Tathāgata, xxiii, 62, 84, 116–17, 230, 232, 242, 244, 247, 299, 359–60, 394, 401, 438, 443, 520; T. Sŏn, 116–17
Tathāgatagarbha, 25, 82, 89, 427, 520
Tathāgatakāya, 393
Tathatā, 520
Tattvasaṃgraha, 176
Ta-yün Temple, 7
Tenjukoku mandara, 201
Tenmangu Shrine, 295
Tenrei banshō myōgi, 179
Tenryū-ji, 267, 319
Tenzo kyōkun, 276, 280
Tetsu Senchakusha, 218
Thaumaturgy, 146–47, 149, 151–55, 197
Theology, theologians, 52, 82, 88, 146, 373, 377, 381–82
Theosophy, 484–86
Theravāda, xxi, 44, 142, 414, 424, 458, 470, 475, 482–87, 489–94, 511
Theravādin, 508–9
Therīgāthā, 428
Thien, 506, 508, 513
T'ien-t'ai, xiii, xviii-xix, xxii, 3, 13, 29, 45, 47–48, 53, 79, 167, 182–83, 187, 191, 196, 200, 204, 256, 277, 322, 520
T'ien-t'ung Temple, 260, 274–75, 279
Tōdai-ji, 146, 148, 157, 160, 166, 168, 178, 191, 269
Tōfuku-ji, 260, 265, 267
Tō-ji, 178–79
Tōkai-ji, 291, 333
Tokugawa period, xx, 147, 198, 219, 261, 264, 272, 305, 307–9, 313, 319, 329–31, 333, 335–37, 339, 341–43, 345–53, 355, 357–58, 360, 515
Tōmyōki, 232

T'ong pulgyo, 57, 60, 68, 76–77, 79, 520
Tonŏ chŏmsu, 113, 520
Tōru hosshin, 182
Tōshōdai-ji, 169
Transcendence, 31, 52, 151, 277, 281, 283, 285–86, 289, 329, 373, 391
Trāyastriṃśa, 394
Trikāya, 71, 180, 518
Tripiṭaka, xiii, xvii, 4, 11, 13, 18–19, 103–6, 204–5, 275, 422, 484, 520; T.-master, 426
Tripiṭika, 18, 518, 520–21
Triyāna, 513
Truth-body, 71, 513
Ts'ao-tung Zen, 17, 21, 29–30, 46–47, 49, 97, 275, 417–418. *See also* Sōtō Zen.
Tso-ch'an, 46, 520–521
Tsung-ching lu, 22, 45, 257
Ts'ung-jung lu, 21
Tsu-t'ang chi, 18
Tsurezuregusa, 341
Tz'u chi kung-te hui, 428

Upāya, 230, 468, 513, 520. See also *Hōben*, *Skillful means*
Upāya-kauśalya, 520
Upekkhā, 516

Vajrayāna, 398–400, 409, 411, 415, 520
Vāsanā, 65, 520
Vihāra, 486–87, 520
Vijñānavāda, 279
Vijñapti, 413
Vijñaptimātra, 16, 521
Vinaya, 115, 126, 147–48, 172, 209, 264, 349–52, 355, 357–58, 475, 490, 520–21. *See also* Precepts
Vipassanā, 487–95, 521
Vipaśyanā, 93, 521
Vipaśyin, 161
Visuddhimagga, 486, 488

Wei-man Hsueh-hui, 424
Westernization, 456, 458, 482
Wisdom-king, 411
Wŏn Buddhism, xvii, 122–24, 131–32, 476
Wŏnhyo taesa chonjip, 63
World-affirmation, 451
World Parliament of Religions, 483, 485, 499

World-renunciation, 449, 493
Wu-chia cheng-tsung tsan, 325
Wu-men-kuan, 325

Yachū-ji, 349
Yakushi-ji, 168
Yamabushi, xviii, 152, 521
Yasenkanna, 311, 324, 326–27
Yŏlban chong'yo, 64, 78
Yogācāra, xiii, xxii, 16, 25, 45, 60, 63, 82, 112, 149–50, 160, 183, 302, 391, 396, 414, 427, 511, 513, 521
Yoga, xiv
Yōgana, 144
Yōgi, 257, 260

Yōhō-ji, 442
Yōjōryū school, 257
Yōkō-ji, 262–63
Yoraesŏn, 116
Yüan-chüeh ching, 15
Yüan dynasty, 14, 17, 21–22, 53, 102, 126
Yü-ch'üan Temple, 6–7

Zanmai, 213, 263, 518. See also *Samādhi*
Zazen, 46, 194, 257, 264, 275, 283, 295, 303, 314–15, 377, 444, 498–99, 502–3, 515, 520–21
Zen'on shingi, 257
Zenrin-ruiju, 263
Zōjō-ji, 219